P9-EMB-764

Handbook of Formative Assessment

Formative assessment has recently become a focus of renewed research as state and federal policy makers realize that summative assessments have reached a point of diminishing returns as a tool for increasing student achievement. Consequently, supporters of large-scale testing programs are now beginning to consider the potential of formative assessments to improve student achievement. The mission of this *Handbook of Formative Assessment* is to comprehensively profile this burgeoning but loosely coupled field of study. Written by leading international scholars and practitioners, each chapter includes a discussion of key issues that dominate formative assessment policy and practice today, as well as those that are likely to affect research and practice in the coming years. Key features include:

Comprehensive – 19 chapters cover all aspects of formative assessment including classroom assessment, large-scale applications, technological applications, applications for special needs students, K-12 applications, psychometric considerations, case studies, and discussion of alternative assessment formats such as portfolios and performance assessments.

Integrative – Thoughtful attention is given to the possibilities for integrating large-scale and classroom assessments.

Practical – Provides practical guidance on how to conduct formative assessments that generate credible information to guide instruction.

Global – Provides perspectives from leading international scholars and practitioners whose expertise spans diverse settings, student populations, and educational systems.

Accessible Style – Although grounded in the latest research, the book's style and tone has been carefully crafted to make it accessible to both the textbook and professional markets. It will also be a critical reference book for policy makers and researchers in teacher preparation, assessment, curriculum, educational administration, and educational policy studies.

Heidi L. Andrade (EdD Harvard) is Assistant Professor of Educational Psychology and Methodology at the University of Albany, State University of New York where she teaches courses on classroom assessment, educational psychology, and self-regulated learning.

Gregory J. Cizek (PhD Michigan State University) is Professor of Educational Measurement and Evaluation at the University of North Carolina where he teaches courses in applied testing, statistics, and research methods.

Handbook of Formative Assessment

Edited by
Heidi L. Andrade
and
Gregory J. Cizek

Routledge
Taylor & Francis Group
NEW YORK AND LONDON

First published 2010
by Routledge
270 Madison Ave, New York, NY 10016

Simultaneously published in the UK
by Routledge
2 Park Square, Milton Park, Abingdon, Oxon OX14 4RN

Routledge is an imprint of the Taylor & Francis Group, an informa business

© 2010 Taylor & Francis

Typeset in Minion by EvS Communication Networx, Inc.
Printed and bound in the United Kingdom on acid-free paper by TJ International Ltd, Padstow, Cornwall

All rights reserved. No part of this book may be reprinted or reproduced or utilised in any form or by any electronic, mechanical, or other means, now known or hereafter invented, including photocopying and recording, or in any information storage or retrieval system, without permission in writing from the publishers.

Trademark Notice: Product or corporate names may be trademarks or registered trademarks, and are used only for identification and explanation without intent to infringe.

Library of Congress Cataloging-in-Publication Data
Handbook of formative assessment / edited by Heidi L. Andrade and Gregory J. Cizek.
p. cm.
Includes bibliographical references and index.
1. Educational evaluation—Handbooks, manuals, etc. 2. Educational tests and measurements—Handbooks, manuals, etc. 3. Academic achievement—Testing—Handbooks, manuals, etc. I. Andrade, Heidi L. II. Cizek, Gregory J.
LB2822.75.H355 2010
371.26—dc22
2009015611

ISBN 10: 0-415-99319-9 (hbk)
ISBN 10: 0-415-99320-2 (pbk)
ISBN 10: 0-203-87485-4 (ebk)

ISBN 13: 978-0-415-99319-7 (hbk)
ISBN 13: 978-0-415-99320-3 (pbk)
ISBN 13: 978-0-203-87485-1 (ebk)

CONTENTS

PREFACE

Educational reforms involving assessment have become a regular feature of attempts to improve achievement in American schools. Minimum competency testing, teacher competency testing, high school graduation tests, end-of-course tests, and many other manifestations of the same impulse have come and (mostly) gone. The same goals—improving teacher quality and student achievement—can be seen in current reform ideas embodied in the statewide, standardized, every-pupil testing mandated by the No Child Left Behind Act (2001).

Although some positive effects of these reforms are evident, the overall effects of assessment-based reforms are often contested, and negative consequences of large-scale tests used for accountability clearly exist. Whether the benefits outweigh the negative effects is a matter of enduring debate, but there is perhaps a consensus that gains in achievement prompted by large-scale assessment reform initiatives have been modest and likely reached a point of diminishing returns.

In recent years, many assessment specialists, curriculum planners, classroom teachers, and educational leaders have begun to consider and promote an alternative—or at least supplementary—mechanism for stimulating achievement gains in schools. That strategy is formative assessment, and it represents a unique, powerful, and plausible avenue for future policy development, reform initiatives, and, most of all, classroom-based approaches that promote greater learning.

The concept and practice of formative assessment will be explored in depth in the chapters of this *Handbook of Formative Assessment*, so for now a streamlined definition will suffice. In brief, formative assessment is the collection of information about student learning, gathered in the course of some unit of instruction, for one or more of the following primary purposes: (1) identifying a student's strengths and weaknesses; (2) assisting educators in the planning of instruction; (3) aiding students in guiding their own learning, revising their work, and gaining self-assessment skills; and (4) fostering increased autonomy and responsibility for learning on the part of the student. Formative assessment is not evaluative, but directive in nature.

As a topic of research over approximately the last 20 years, and having been practiced in classrooms for decades, the methods and benefits of formative assessment are well-documented. There is broad agreement among both researchers and educators that formative assessment should be on the front burner of education reform efforts because its potential is so great. We believe that the topic of formative assessment is timely, the research base on formative assessment has reached a point of relative maturity, and a compilation of evidence and guidance regarding formative assessment will help educators and policy makers to rigorously implement and further examine this important strategy.

This *Handbook of Formative Assessment* represents research-based, practical information that will be of interest to a broad array of educators, researchers, and policy makers. We conceptualized the volume as one that provides a research-based, practical collection of current knowledge and practice in formative assessment, and will serve as an up-to-date, forward-looking, comprehensive in scope, broadly applicable, and highly accessible resource. We have attempted to ensure a consistent style and approach in each chapter that will appeal to a wide audience and facilitate broad utility. For example, we believe that this *Handbook* will appeal to those who work in the field of assessment or whose work is affected by assessment, including researchers and assessment developers in testing companies, state departments of education, or school districts, as well as front-line educational personnel in schools: teachers, principals, school board members, and others whose professional lives are centered on the same target as the focus of this book—improving student achievement. We also expect the book to be a resource for policymakers, including those at district, state, and national levels, as deliberations continue about the potential role of formative assessment in educational reforms. Finally, this *Handbook of Formative Assessment* is intended to provide information about cutting edge research and applications for graduate students wrestling with current challenges in curriculum, assessment, educational psychology, and educational policy. Of course, ultimately, we hope that this work serves students, for whom the systems we call schools are organized to engage and benefit.

The present volume covers all aspects of formative assessment, including classroom assessment, large-scale applications, technological advances, case studies, K-12 contexts, psychometric considerations, applications for students with special needs, and the diversity of formative assessment formats. Importantly, as is evident from even a cursory look at the Table of Contents, this volume is the result of contributions from many leading international scholars and practitioners who bring expertise and perspectives spanning diverse settings, student populations, and educational systems. Each chapter author is a highly respected and prominent contributor to the field of formative assessment.

This *Handbook of Formative Assessment* is comprised of three major sections. The first of the three subdivisions, "Foundations of Formative Assessment," provides a conceptual overview of the topic. The chapters in this section provide the groundwork for the rest of the volume. The first chapter, by Gregory Cizek, provides an overview of formative assessment, traces its roots, and suggests some of the challenges that lie ahead. In chapter 2, Dylan Wiliam reviews the research on formative assessment, and examines the different definitions that have been proposed. He proposes a new definition for formative assessment based on the extent to which assessment improves instructional decisions made by teachers and the learners themselves, and explores some of the consequences of this definition for theory and practice. In the final chapter of the opening section, James McMillan provides a framework to examine how different educational objectives and classroom contextual factors affect the nature and effectiveness of formative assessment.

The second section, "Formative Assessment Methods and Practice," provides concrete information regarding the latest advances in formative assessment techniques and technologies. The chapters in this section summarize current research and offer practical insights to help readers understand the strengths, limitations, potential applications, and cautions when formative assessment is applied in classroom settings. The first chapter in this section, by Keith Topping, considers peers as a source of formative assessment and gives guidelines for implementation. Chapter 5, by Jill Davidson and Jay Feldman, discusses the opportunities for formative assessment that exist at schools using performance based assessments such as exhibitions as high-stakes measures of achievement, and describes the ways that preparation for and completion of such demonstrations of mastery exemplifies a continuum of assessment from formative to summative. In chapter 6, Heidi Andrade synthesizes recent scholarship on formative assessment, student self-assessment, and self-regulated learning, and makes recommendations for capitalizing on the potential for students to be their own best source of feedback about learning and academic performance. In chapter 7, Thomas Guskey reviews the work of Benjamin S. Bloom, who introduced the phrase *formative assessment* in the early 1970s and described how such assessments could be used by teachers to provide more favorable learning conditions for many students through instructional strategies labeled "mastery learning."

Michael Russell, the author of chapter 8, explores several challenges to formative assessment which computer-based tools can help teachers overcome, and provides a detailed description of four tools that address one or more of these challenges. Chapter 9, by Maria Araceli Ruiz-Primo, Erin Marie Furtak, Carlos Ayala, Yue Yin, and Richard J. Shavelson, describes a focused study of formative assessment in a K-12 science context. In their chapter, Ruiz-Primo and her colleagues present the results of a study on the influence of embedded assessments on student learning and motivation. The chapter presents the methodological, logistical, and practical choices made during the study, and reflects on what failed, what worked, and conditions that led to the study's unexpected outcomes.

Three chapters in Part II focus on the applications of formative assessment with diverse populations. Adapting formative assessments for students with special needs is the topic of chapter 10, by Stephen Elliott, Ryan Kettler, Peter Beddow, and Alexander Kurz. This chapter focuses on methods for meaningfully including students identified with disabilities in formative assessment programs through the use of testing accommodations and test development innovations based on item development research, universal design principles, and cognitive load theory. In chapter 11, Jamal Abedi summarizes the research on the assessment of English Language Learners (ELLs), focusing on the factors that interfere with their understanding of instructional and assessment materials. He also provides recommendations for ways in which formative assessments can be used to improve the quality of education for ELL students. In chapter 12, Carla Meskill introduces the reader to the daily formative assessment practices of English to Speakers of Other Languages (ESOL) professionals. The promise of formative assessment for improving the performance of at-risk students is the focus of chapter 13, by Gerunda Hughes. Hughes provides a discussion of how students' personal characteristics often interact with learning environments in ways that place them at risk of academic failure. She builds on the existing literature to outline formative assessment practices that can maximize learning and reduce or eliminate students' risk of academic failure.

In chapter 14, Rick Stiggins describes the specific classroom assessment competencies that teachers need to master in order to use formative assessment productively, as well as the assessment competencies that school leaders need to master in order to design and implement balanced assessment systems. Chapter 15, by Christina Schneider and Bruce Randel, provides a strong complement to the preceding chapter. Schneider and Randel analyze the research literature on professional development in formative classroom assessment, synthesize the characteristics of professional development programs that are likely to promote change in teachers and students, discuss the significant challenges to conducting experimental research in this area, and highlight where more research is warranted.

Part III of the *Handbook*, "Challenges and Future Directions for Formative Assessment" assembles information and advice on lingering and potential future challenges in formative assessment. In the first chapter in this section, chapter 16, Susan Brookhart addresses the question of how formative and summative classroom achievement information mix in practice, first describing the ways in which scholars have suggested they should or should not mix, then documenting ways that both students and teachers do mix formative and summative information, and finally suggesting research that investigates what teachers and students can do with assessment information in order to facilitate learning. In chapter 17, Denny Way, Robert Dolan, and Paul Nichols describe some of the psychometric challenges to implementing formative assessment in the most technically sound manner, using Web- and computer-based assessments as illustrative examples. A look at strategies and policies for incorporating formative assessment at levels larger than individual classrooms is the focus of chapter 18, by Doug Rindone and Duncan MacQuarrie. In that chapter, Rindone and MacQuarrie describe the current status of formative assessment in the United States by summarizing survey data from state assessment directors, as well as the work of state collaborative projects sponsored by the Council of Chief State School Officers.

A case study of one such large-scale implementation in Nebraska is provided by Chris Gallagher in chapter 19. Gallagher examines the prospects for designing state policy frameworks that take full advantage of both formative and summative assessments. He explores the lessons provided by the unique assessment work of Nebraska, which first designed a statewide system of local assessments that combined formative and summative assessments and then, in the wake of a new state testing law, designed a larger accountability framework to preserve and enhance its districts' integrative assessment systems. In the final chapter of the *Handbook*, Chapter 20, Heidi Andrade provides an overarching synthesis of the volume, addressing both common themes and future directions for research into and the practice of formative assessment.

As the contents of each section suggest, this *Handbook* reflects, by design, a best guess as to the key aspects that dominate formative assessment policy and practice today, and those that are likely to affect research and practice in the coming years. Overall, we think that the coverage, scope, and rigor represented in these chapters provide not only a snapshot of the current status of formative assessment but also help clarify the road ahead for both researchers and practitioners.

In producing this *Handbook of Formative Assessment*, we note that our work on this book has been aided significantly by many people. First, the *Handbook* would obviously not have been possible without the broad participation and generous contributions of the most exceptionally qualified authorities in the field. Each chapter author has successfully tackled the challenging task of describing a key aspect of formative assessment in a way that is rigorous, up-to-date, and useful to readers with diverse backgrounds and interests. Their collective willingness to labor in the interest of disseminating knowledge, extending research, and promoting improved formative assessment practice is one of the highest forms of public service. We are doubly indebted to the authors who served as "Critical Friends" to other authors in this volume: Their generous and constructive feedback on each chapter made this a better book.

Collectively, we are both indebted to the reviewers of the prospectus for this book, who provided support and sound advice. We are also grateful to our editor at Routledge/ Taylor & Francis, Lane Akers, for his expert guidance.

Individually, the authors of this book would like to acknowledge many others. I (HLA) thank Greg Cizek for the opportunity to work with him on this book. I initially agreed to the collaboration because I knew that Greg and I came to the topic from different but complementary perspectives—I am an educational psychologist, he is a psychometrician—and I appreciated the fact that he was keen on exploring the commonalities and tensions inherent in those perspectives. I have since come to prize his extraordinary combination of wisdom and open mindedness: His mind can engage any idea, consider the options, reasons, or evidence, and return a sensible conclusion in 3 seconds or less. Given another second or two he can provide comic relief which, of course, made the work pleasant as well as intellectually rewarding. I am privileged to call him a colleague and friend.

I am also grateful to my husband, Albert, and our son Sam, who provide daily doses of inspiration to do good work in education, and then come home again.

I (GJC) consider myself to be extremely fortunate to have been able to collaborate with Heidi Andrade on this project. She is one of the most thoughtful, analytic, and rigorous colleagues one could encounter. It was our first time working together on a project; I learned a great deal from the collaboration and I hope we have many more such opportunities. Her high level of commitment to the project, her depth of knowledge in the area of formative assessment, her keen editorial skills, and her thoughtful insights cutting across topics and chapters served not only to challenge me to meet the high standards she set, but improved the entire volume immensely. Equally if not more important, I have appreciated Heidi's friendship and collegial—and genial—working style.

I also appreciate the support for this work provided by the School of Education at the University of North Carolina at Chapel Hill and the encouragement of Dean Bill McDiarmid to complete this work. I am particularly grateful for the support provided by the Kenan research leave program which was critical in the early stages of this work when the *Handbook* was conceptualized. I am indebted to the publisher of this book

Routledge/Taylor & Francis, which has a long and successful history of publishing important works in the social sciences. I want particularly to recognize Lane Akers, Senior Editor at Routledge, who has for several years across many different projects been a source of encouragement and become a good friend.

Finally, I am grateful for the continuing support of my wife, Rita, and our children, A. J., Caroline, David, and Stephen, and little Elaina who I join in thanking God for showering his abundance on the American educational system and in pleading his continuing favor.

HLA/GJC

I

Foundations of Formative Assessment

I

Foundations of Formative Assessment

1

AN INTRODUCTION TO FORMATIVE ASSESSMENT
History, Characteristics, and Challenges

GREGORY J. CIZEK

Formative assessment offers great promise as the next best hope for stimulating gains in student achievement. In this chapter, the roots and nature of the concept are explored, and a definition and key characteristics of formative assessment are provided with contrasts to its high-profile cousin, summative assessment. Finally, several challenges that threaten successful implementation of formative assessment are noted, with challenges described separately for classroom and—if demonstrated to be feasible—large scale contexts.

ASSESSMENT IN EDUCATION

In K-12 education contexts, large-scale achievement tests consistently attract the most attention in terms of policy maker initiatives, student and educator focus, and public awareness. Since at least the 1970s, when states such as Florida implemented consequential pupil competency tests, they have been a centerpiece of reform efforts, accountability systems, instructional emphasis, and in some instances, an understandable source of anxiety for those affected by the results. Such competency tests are designed to measure accumulated learning over an extended time (often, a school year).

These tests are categorized as *summative* assessments. In brief, any test or other system of information gathering is a summative assessment if it meets the following two criteria: (1) it is administered at the end of some unit of instruction (e.g., unit, semester, school year); and (2) its purpose is primarily to categorize the performance of a student or system. That is, its main purpose is obtain a measurement of achievement to be used in decision making; assigning grades; awarding or denying a diploma, license, or credential; making promotion/retention decisions; or classifying test takers according to defined performance categories such as the now-familiar *Basic, Proficient*, and *Advanced*. Because this primary purpose requires high quality information about *overall* test performance, summative assessments are typically designed to yield highly reliable and valid total scores. A less flattering way of characterizing this characteristic is to note that summative assessments are usually course-grained. As such, they are typically not intended—and are thus less well-suited—to provide individual diagnostic information about students, to yield effective remediation recommendations, to identify specific areas for individualizing instruction, and so on.

Because of their relative maturity and (often) important stakes attached to performance on them, summative assessments are the most visible, consequential, and (sometimes) controversial tests encountered in education today. It is understandable why this is so. For one, the sizeable allocation of financial resources in support of summative, every-pupil accountability tests administered across the United States in compliance with the No Child Left Behind Act (2002) warrants greater attention to ensure that the investment is well-placed. Second, as indicated previously, the stakes for students, educators, and levels of educational organization (e.g., schools, districts, etc.) are often very high. Finally, because of their level of visibility and familiarity even to those outside of educational contexts, discussions about the role and results of summative assessments can be joined by a broad spectrum of the interested public.

In contrast to summative assessment stands what has been called *formative* assessment. In subsequent sections of this chapter—indeed in all of the chapters in this volume—the concept will be explored in considerable depth and detail, but a brief introduction will be provided here. A test or other system of information gathering would be considered a formative assessment if it meets two criteria. First, a formative assessment is administered midstream, in the course of some unit of instruction. In addition, the primary purpose of formative assessment is one or more of the following: to identify the student's strengths and weaknesses; to assist educators in the planning of subsequent instruction; to aid students in guiding their own learning, revising their work, and gaining self-evaluation skills; and to foster increased autonomy and responsibility for learning on the part of the student.

Whereas summative testing has dominated the assessment landscape in terms of large-scale educational policy and prominence, formative assessment is beginning to attract increased interest. There are a number of reasons why this is the case. For one, summative large scale assessments initially accomplished an explicit intended objective of their implementation; namely, focusing attention on and raising educational achievement. There is compelling evidence that summative testing has had beneficial effects (Phelps, 2005a) on student achievement. However, although it is also true that the public continues to strongly support such testing (Phelps, 2005b) there is increasing opposition to additional mandated summative testing (Wang, Beckett, & Brown, 2006), and U.S. education is likely witnessing a point of diminishing returns for this strategy (Cizek, 2001).

Enter formative assessment. In juxtaposition to concerns about additional summative assessment, there appears to be an enthusiasm for a closer look at and increased use of formative assessment. There are sound reasons for the enthusiasm. Among educators, researchers, and policy makers, there appears to be a heightened awareness that formative assessment—the long neglected bridesmaid in the testing party—has the potential to provide missing linkages between classroom practice and large-scale assessments and, perhaps most importantly, represent the next best hope for promoting greater achievement gains for students.

A growing body of research on formative assessment exists. A number of applications of formative assessment have been documented, and a few *planned assessment systems* (Cizek, 1995; Cizek & Rachor, 1994) are being designed or implemented to investigate the extent to which formative assessment can be integrated into, alongside, or in conjunction with extant summative programs. In short, formative assessment is promising; a look at formative assessment is timely; and investment into formative assessment has the potential to yield substantial dividends. These characteristics have motivated the production of this *Handbook of Formative Assessment* and they suffuse the chapters in this volume. In the remaining portions of this introduction, we will first take a closer look at the roots of formative assessment, evolution of the concept, and the current conceptualizations.

ROOTS AND HISTORY OF FORMATIVE ASSESSMENT

The roots of formative assessment can be traced to a monograph of the American Educational Research Association (AERA) in which Scriven (1967) first coined the term *formative evaluation*. The publication in which Scriven's use of the term appeared was a volume of the AERA's Monograph Series on Curriculum Evaluation. The term was clearly grounded in the practice of program evaluation, and the context in which Scriven introduced the concept was one in which the effectiveness of school programs and curricula was the object of inquiry. In Scriven's and other early works, the broader conceptualization of assessment had not yet been developed to the extent it is today, and the focus of information-gathering related to student achievement was squarely on the evaluative aspect of that activity.

The concept of formative evaluation attained broader recognition when it was popularized in association with the influential volume by Benjamin Bloom and his associates entitled the *Handbook of Formative and Summative Evaluation of Student Learning* (Bloom, Hastings, & Madaus, 1971). Although that volume is perhaps most well-known for its elaboration of taxonomies of educational objectives introduced previously by Bloom (1956), its explication of the distinction between two concepts—formative and summative evaluation—is considered foundational. Bloom et al. first described what they meant by *summative evaluation*:

> We have chosen the term "summative evaluation" to indicate the type of evaluation used at the end of a term, course, or program for purposes of grading, certification, evaluation of progress, or research on the effectiveness of a curriculum, course of study, or educational plan.... Perhaps the essential characteristic of summative evaluation is that a judgment is made about the student, teacher, or curriculum with regard to the effectiveness of learning or instruction *after* [emphasis added] the learning or instruction has taken place. It is this act of judgment which produces so much anxiety and defensiveness in students, teachers, and curriculum makers. We do not believe it is possible to escape from the use of summative evaluation, nor would we wish to do so. (1971, p. 117)

It is clear from their definition that Bloom and his colleagues (1971) were extending the term *summative evaluation* beyond the usage that Scriven (1967) had in mind. As the preceding definition implies, summative evaluation was not confined to a program evaluation context, but was also seen as relevant to the assessment of learning and to individual students. Bloom et al. then contrasted summative evaluations—arguably the most prominent assessments at that time—with evaluations that served a different purpose. According to Bloom et al.:

> Formative evaluation is for us the use of systematic evaluation *in the process of* [emphasis added] curriculum construction, teaching and learning for the purpose of improving any of these three processes.... This means that in formative evaluation one must strive to develop the kinds of evidence that will be most useful in the process, seek the most useful method of reporting the evidence, and search for ways of reducing the negative effect associated with evaluation—perhaps by reducing the judgmental aspects of evaluation or, at least, by having the users of the formative evaluation (teachers, students, curriculum makers) make the judgments. (1971, p. 118)

Here, too, we can see in the use of the term *formative evaluation* that a connection to the area of program evaluation was still apparent. However, although the seminal ideas of Bloom and his colleagues (1971) are recognized for their influence on the practice of program evaluation, the implications of those ideas have surely had a profound impact on the field of assessment as well. For example, Bloom's expanded definition clearly foreshadowed the linkages and uses of the formative approach he outlined for the assessment of individual students and toward the aim of improving teaching and learning.

Finally, Bloom's work suggested important distinctions between *evaluation* and *assessment* that are now widely accepted. In brief, in the context of education, evaluation refers to the act of ascribing worth or merit to the results of an information-gathering procedure (such as assigning grades on a test). Assessment is much broader; it refers to a planned process for gathering and synthesizing information relevant to the purposes of discovering and documenting students' strengths and weaknesses, planning and enhancing instruction that is appropriate given the student's learning needs, or making recommendations related to educational goals for a student (Cizek, 1997).

CURRENT CONCEPTIONS OF FORMATIVE ASSESSMENT

Since the introduction of the concept, formative assessment has evolved in its meaning and it has spawned substantial interest and research. From one perspective, formative assessment can be defined in terms of what it is not: Typically, formative assessment has been characterized—as foreshadowed by Bloom in the preceding paragraph—by the absence of an evaluation aspect; that is, by avoiding the assignment of penalties, grades, or other accountability-related consequences for the person(s) participating in the assessments.

But formative assessment is much more than this. Broadly conceived, formative assessment refers to the collaborative processes engaged in by educators and students for the purpose of understanding the students' learning and conceptual organization, identification of strengths, diagnosis of weaknesses, areas for improvement, and as a source of information that teachers can use in instructional planning and students can use in deepening their understandings and improving their achievement. The possible formats of formative assessments are correspondingly broad. Formative assessment information can be gleaned from information-gathering activities such as traditional classroom tests, but also from observations, oral questioning, class discussions, projects, portfolios, homework, performance assessments, group work with peer feedback, student self-assessment, and other sources. Regardless of format, however, the distinguishing characteristic of formative assessments is that their design and primary goal is the gathering of information for the purpose of adapting teaching and learning to the current functioning and future needs of students (Black & Wiliam, 1998a).

As this definition implies, the locus of formative assessment activities is typically at the classroom level and the concept of formative assessment is one that resonates strongly with classroom teachers. However, although a primary focus of formative assessment is that of information gathering in support of educators' instructional planning activities, current usage of the term equally, if not to a greater extent, highlights the notions of student engagement and responsibility for learning, student self-assessment, and self-direction. The oft-cited and highly influential research synthesis conducted by Black and Wiliam concluded that well-designed and implemented formative assessment can have profound effects on student achievement, with effect sizes for formative assessment practices compared to control conditions ranging from .4 to .7. Moreover, they hypothesized that formative assessment may be differentially effective, with greater gains evident for low-achieving students and students with special needs, such as those identified with learning disabilities (1998b).

Another commonly encountered aspect of current conceptions of formative assessment is that they should be student-centered (Stiggins, 2005). From this perspective, the key consumer and user of the information yielded by formative assessments is the student. Accordingly, it is important that the feedback be seen by the student as helpful to him or her for enhancing desired skills, refining learning of valuable objectives, and fostering intrinsic motivation by eschewing a connection to evaluations such as grades, which are often viewed by students as external rewards or punishments.

One of the most comprehensive descriptions of formative assessment has been produced by Shepard (2006) in her chapter on classroom assessment prepared for the fourth edition of *Educational Measurement* (Brennan, 2006). Drawing on the work of Black and Wiliam (1998b), Sadler (1989), and Atkin, Black, and Coffey (2001), Shepard's description presents a model of formative assessment as a tool for helping to guide student learning as well as to provide information that teachers can use to improve their own instructional practice. A distillation of the key elements of the model proposed by Shepard and an elaboration of that model that draws upon other recent work in the area by Andrade (2000; Andrade, Du, & Wang, 2008), Brookhart (2003), McManus (2008), and Shute (2008) is shown in Table 1.1. The table lists a constellation of key characteristics of formative assessment. While not all of the characteristics must be present for an assessment to be considered formative, each characteristic has been identified for its potential to maximize the achievement, development, and instructional benefits of this type of assessment.

Although not all of the elements listed in Table 1.1 have to be combined in any

Table 1.1 Ten Characteristics of Formative Assessment

1. Requires students to take responsibility for their own learning.
2. Communicates clear, specific learning goals.
3. Focuses on goals that represent valuable educational outcomes with applicability beyond the learning context.
4. Identifies the student's current knowledge/skills and the necessary steps for reaching the desired goals.
5. Requires development of plans for attaining the desired goals.
6. Encourages students to self-monitor progress toward the learning goals.
7. Provides examples of learning goals including, when relevant, the specific grading criteria or rubrics that will be used to evaluate the student's work.
8. Provides frequent assessment, including peer and student self-assessment and assessment embedded within learning activities.
9. Includes feedback that is non-evaluative, specific, timely, related to the learning goals, and provides opportunities for the student to revise and improve work products and deepen understandings.
10. Promotes metacognition and reflection by students on their work.

particular application of formative assessment, subsets of the characteristics have been implemented in various configurations. In subsequent chapters in this volume, examples of these configurations are described and effects on student achievement are summarized. Implementations of formative assessment are not without challenges, however. The following section provides an overview of some of the significant challenges and suggests research and development efforts for the future.

FORMATIVE ASSESSMENT CHALLENGES

Although formative assessment represents one of the current best hopes for further increases in student learning, many challenges face this form of assessment, and the eventual efficacy of formative assessment initiatives is not certain. Challenges loom on two levels: classroom and state. Many of these challenges are investigated in greater depth in subsequent chapters in this *Handbook*, so the following sections of this chapter will present only an introduction to some of the most important issues. We first turn to the challenges facing formative assessment in the classroom.

Formative Assessment: Classroom Challenges

At the classroom level, seven noteworthy challenges exist. Each of these challenges is enumerated and briefly described in the list below.

Purpose The biggest challenge ahead for implementing formative assessment in the classroom is identification of and adherence to a clear, focused purpose for the assessments. As research has indicated and as subsequent chapters in this volume will address, the power of formative assessments lies in their nonevaluative nature, their focus on providing timely, specific, corrective feedback, and on actively engaging the learner in valuable educational experiences. The efficacy of formative assessments will be compromised if they devolve into mere quizzes or assignments.

Resources Development of relevant and rich formative assessments requires a substantial investment in teacher time for development, administration, and feedback on the assessments. Depending on the activity, the implementation of a formative assessment may require additional costs for supplies, space, or other tangible items. Thus, a second challenge facing formative assessment at the classroom level involves the commitment of resources to support professional development, time for planning, administration and feedback, and support for additional materials as needed to implement an effective assessment program.

Preparation It has been well documented that training in assessment is woefully lacking for teachers, principals, and nearly all educators who use assessments or rely on assessment information (Hills, 1991; O'Sullivan & Chalnick, 1991; Popham, 2009). Much of that research has been conducted largely with respect to training in traditional psychometric concepts and summative assessment practices. Although contemporary textbooks have evolved to focus less on statistical foundations and more on relevant classroom information gathering practices (see, for example, Airasian & Russell, 2008), a documented lack of preparation in formative assessment still exists (Stiggins, 1999). For formative assessment to be successfully implemented in classrooms, a significant challenge must be addressed: Preservice and in-service training for educators must evolve to provide two different competencies: the concepts necessary to administer and interpret traditional summative assessments, and the skills required for developing and interpreting classroom-based formative assessments.

Validity Validity refers to the degree to which evidence supports the interpretations or inferences that are intended to be drawn from assessment information (Cizek, 2009). Many sources of invalidity threaten the confidence that can be placed in an intended inference. One threat to validity seems particularly powerful and underresearched in the classroom assessment context. Bias (or differential functioning of items or tasks) has been thoroughly researched in large-scale summative testing programs (Camilli, 2006), but the area has received little attention in any formative assessment contexts. For example, optical scanners used in large-scale assessments make the scoring of bubble sheets highly objective, but the influences of human preferences, prejudices, and personalities are unavoidable in more subjective classroom contexts.

Textbooks in educational measurement geared primarily toward preservice and in-service teachers are noticeably devoid of information on classroom assessment bias. According to one text:

> Classroom teachers need to know that assessment bias exists. Assessment bias in [large-scale] educational tests is probably less prevalent than it was a decade or two ago.... However, for the kinds of teacher-developed assessment procedures seen in typical classrooms, systematic attention to bias eradication is much less common. (Popham, 2008, p. 81)

Debunking the notion that educators' classroom assessment practices—particularly those that are less formal and formative in nature—are inherently untainted by threats to validity such as observer- and scoring bias is a significant first challenge toward ensuring the validity of formative assessment information. For formative assessment to achieve its potential for providing accurate, actionable information, field-based techniques that educators can use to detect and reduce the extent of bias in formative classroom assessments must be developed, disseminated, and incorporated into the preservice training and professional development of educators.

Accommodations   In traditional summative assessment contexts, an assessment accommodation is a deviation from standard test administration conditions that does not threaten or alter the characteristic being measured or the accuracy of the intended inference. The goal of providing any accommodation is to enable all test takers, including students with special needs, to demonstrate their true levels of knowledge, skill, and abilities. In formative assessment contexts, the requirement for standardized administration conditions is far less important, although the goal of obtaining accurate information about students remains paramount. Thus, for example, prompting or other teacher interactions that may be proscribed in large-scale summative contexts may be deemed entirely appropriate in a formative assessment context.

A good deal of work has been done to specify appropriate accommodations and to investigate the effects of accommodations on student achievement in large-scale applications. For example, Thurlow and Thompson (2004) have provided a framework and examples of accommodations that include changes in assessment setting, timing, scheduling, test presentation, response format, and permissible tools. Abedi and his colleagues (see, for example, Abedi, Hofstetter, & Lord, 2004) have also investigated language-related assessment accommodations such as linguistic simplification to reduce potential construct-irrelevant variation in test performance when language skill is not an intended object of the measurement process.

However, variations in assessment format and procedures also have the potential to reduce the validity of information yielded and to threaten the accuracy of intended inferences. Such changes are typically referred to as assessment modifications. Whereas there now exists a growing body of research on both accommodations and modifications in the context of large-scale summative assessments, little work has been done to extend the existing work to formative assessment contexts. Arguably, the instructional decisions made based on formative assessment information may be as consequential as those made based on information from summative testing. Thus, an important challenge for the future of formative assessment will be to begin consideration of the role of accommodations in that context or, as a first step, to ascertain the extent to which concern about accommodations even translates to the formative arena.

Compliance   In an increasingly litigious world, educators have become more sensitive to their responsibilities to adhere to formal guidelines and regulations affecting schools. Along with the more recent No Child Left Behind (NCLB, 2002) legislation, the Family Educational Rights and Privacy Act (FERPA, 1974), the Individuals with Disabilities Education Act (IDEA, 2004) and numerous other federal and state laws exist to guide even seemingly small details of classroom life. Whereas much of the existing legislation related to assessment has been enacted primarily with summative testing as a frame of reference, the relevance of law, policy, and administrative rules to emerging formative assessment should be considered. For example, should formative assessments be considered when crafting a student's Individualized Education Plan

(IEP)? Should important formative assessment information be documented? Does formative assessment information constitute protected educational records? Answering these and numerous other questions that have been considered almost exclusively in a summative context represents a looming challenge for implementing formative assessments in a more systematic way.

Time A key to successful implementation of formative assessment will be the development of high-quality assessment events, the purposeful integration of formative assessment into classroom activities, and the iterative use of formative assessment results to inform the next instructional steps for teachers and refinement of learning goals for students. Each of these requires a considerable investment in time to plan and conduct the activity—time that is currently allocated to different purposes in many classrooms. Assuming a constant school day, a major challenge for implementing and sustaining formative assessment will be the reallocation of time and effort to support instructional planning, modified instructional practices, and individualization of instruction on the part of teachers and students. Given the organizational structures and time constraints of current educational systems, it is possible only to speculate about the extent of reallocation that is necessary or practical. Indeed, of all the impediments to successful implementation of formative classroom assessment, reconfiguring daily classroom life and reorganizing the instructional day to provide the time necessary for effective formative assessments may represent the biggest challenge of all. Research and development projects that help operationalize the possibilities for such reconfigurations will provide much needed guidance.

Formative Assessment: Large-Scale Challenges

Accompanying the increasing interest in formative assessment for classroom-based applications is increasing attention to formative assessment from more macroperspectives. At state and national levels, policy makers have begun to realize that a point of diminishing returns has been reached with respect to the use of annual, every-pupil, summative assessments for promoting increased student achievement. Advocates of large-scale summative testing are now examining the potential for formative assessments to support that goal as new educational reforms are contemplated. In many states, formative assessment has become a centerpiece of research, development, and policy initiatives aimed at forming more coherent and comprehensive assessment systems and stimulating greater gains in student learning.

Examples of this macrolevel attention being garnered by formative assessment can be seen in the formative assessment initiatives underway in several states and large urban districts such as Nebraska and New York City. In addition, the national association of heads of state education agencies, the Council of Chief State School Officers (CCSSO), has initiated two projects focused on formative assessment: the Formative Assessments in a Comprehensive Assessment System (FACAS) study group and the Formative Assessment for Students and Teachers (FAST) project, described in a subsequent chapter (Rindone & MacQuarrie, this volume). The FACAS group was formed to address "the challenges facing states as they attempt to incorporate or assist districts in incorporating formative assessments into a standards-based comprehensive assessment system" (Council of Chief State School Officers [CCSSO], 2008a, p. 1). The FAST project was initiated because:

> There has been substantial interest in formative assessment among U.S. educators during recent years. Increasing numbers of educators regard formative assessment as a way not only to improve student learning, but also to increase student scores on significant achievement examinations. (CCSSO, 2008b, p. 1)

Interest and enthusiasm alone, however, will not suffice to enable formative assessment to realize the expectations that are accompanying large-scale implementations of the concept. As with classroom-level implementations, several challenges exist for large-scale application of formative assessment. The following paragraphs identify three such challenges, the first two of which bear the same label as similar challenges already described at the classroom level but reflect key differences in application between the two levels.

Purpose   The potential for large-scale application of formative assessment is controversial and the primary concern relates to the intended purpose. As described previously in this chapter, the nature of effective formative assessment includes nonevaluative feedback, tailored to the specific strengths and weaknesses of individual students, with major responsibility for learning vested in students themselves. By their nature, large-scale assessments have neglected or necessarily eschewed these characteristics. For example, large-scale assessments are typically evaluative, with rewards and sanctions often attached for students, educators, and systems. By design, typical large-scale assessments are inadequate for providing diagnostic information about individual students (see Cizek, 2007), and are not intended to foster their sense of personal responsibility for learning.

Nonetheless, legislators, policy makers, and commercial interests appear eager to capitalize on the promise of formative assessment to promote increased academic achievement. According to a report published in *Education Week*, the formative assessment market is one of the fastest-growing segments of test publishing (Olson, 2005). The report documented the entry of the dominant testing company, Educational Testing Service (ETS), into K-12 formative assessment via the creation of online item banks that educators can use to produce classroom assessments aligned with their state's content standards. The report indicated that:

> The ETS Formative Assessment Item Bank includes more than 11,000 standards-based mathematics and language arts questions that teachers can use to craft classroom tests and quizzes to track student performance throughout the year and modify instruction when necessary. Districts also can use the item bank to design benchmark, or interim, assessments aligned with their states' end-of-year tests. (p. 7)

According to the ETS (2008) description, its Formative Assessment Item Bank contains items that measure mathematics, reading, and writing for grades K-12 and science for grades 3–12. While the majority of the items are multiple-choice format, the item bank also contains short and extended constructed-response items. Educational Testing Service claims that items in the bank have been aligned to content standards of several states including states with large and diverse populations such as California, New York, Florida, New Jersey, Texas, Ohio, and Virginia.

Despite the potential usefulness of vast, teacher-accessible item pools, attempts to extend formative assessment on a large scale will require much additional research to ensure that necessary modifications and compromises will not corrupt it, as occurred when attempts were made to extend portfolio assessments to high-stakes, large-scale applications (see Herman & Winters, 1994). Smaller, more frequent, teacher-created summative assessments are not necessarily formative at all, regardless of item formats or the depth or alignment of the item pools from which they are drawn. Further, it is not clear how well such item banks will support accurate identification of individual strengths and weaknesses.

Some assessment experts have expressed concern that the very concept of formative assessment is being hijacked by those who seek to implement it for large-scale uses that are inconsistent with its fundamental nature and aims (see Shepard, 2000), and that state- or national-level implementations could undercut its efficacy. In addition, whereas the dominant force on the assessment landscape—summative testing programs—has been criticized for the potential to drive teaching and learning in undesirable ways, the concern exists that the same phenomenon, and possibly other unintended consequences, might accompany large-scale implementations of formative assessment. To paraphrase the words of the song, "Won't Get Fooled Again," the concern is that the new boss will be the same as the old boss.

There remains, of course, a useful distinction between assessment as an integrated aspect of instruction and assessment as dissociated from instruction for purposes of evaluation. In the former case, assessments can be embedded in instructional events or instructional in themselves. Such embedding lends itself well to formative assessment and the instructional value of the assessment experience is inextricably linked to formative information that is acquired by the student and teacher. However, it is also true that assessments designed primarily for evaluation need not—and often do not—provide incidental instructional value, such as when the assessment is conducted to arrive at an instructional or placement decision that must be made. It will be important to keep these essential differences in purpose squarely at the forefront when contemplating any assessment reforms.

In the end, whether formative assessment will find any systematic application at levels above the classroom remains to be seen and even pursuing that goal is, to some extent, controversial. The answer will lie in the extent to which those applications manage to achieve reasonable fidelity to the nature of formative assessment and to maintain a crisp focus on the purposes that formative assessments best accomplish.

Resources   It is often mistakenly believed that an inordinate amount of time and financial resources are expended on state testing programs. In fact, the extent and cost of large-scale summative testing have been well documented (see, for example, Phelps, 2000) and the amount of time and money that states allocate to typical large-scale summative testing is actually surprising modest. An analysis by Hoxby (2002) of state spending on assessments used to gather accountability-related information revealed no state spent as much as 1% of its elementary and secondary budget on these assessments. Goodman and Hambleton (2005) estimated that only one-third of 1% of the state of Massachusetts' entire education budget was earmarked for testing.

If spending on summative testing is modest, the amount of resources devoted to formative assessment is miniscule. Although no dependable figures exist, it is safe to say that resources allocated to optional formative assessments pale in comparison to the allocations flowing to assessments mandated by federal requirements such as NCLB and by state accountability systems.

For formative assessment to become thoroughly infused into either local or larger contexts, a sizable investment will be needed. In addition to funding the preservice training and professional development needs already noted, states will need to allocate resources to develop and disseminate model formative assessment activities, demonstrate alignment of formative assessment activities to state content standards, and develop evidence-based recommendations for follow-up activities and instructional options that educators can employ following administration of formative assessments. Most importantly, states that seek to expand formative assessment beyond the classroom will need to investigate possible strategies for doing so (such as so-called "tiered" assessment systems) and to ensure that such systems maintain fidelity to the characteristics that produce formative assessment's desirable benefits.

Technical Quality   If any formative assessment systems prove workable on a large-scale—and it is not yet clear that this will be possible or desirable—there will almost certainly be an interest in aggregating and analyzing the information yielded by those assessments for informing instructional decisions, curriculum development, or other uses. For the aggregated data to effectively inform decision making, it must meet certain quality criteria.

Traditionally, the criteria of reliability and validity have been applied to large-scale summative assessment data collection, and the imperative for alignment between content standards, instructional practices, and assessments has been brought to the forefront in recent years as part of the reviews that the U.S. Department of Education conducts of state assessment programs. However, the nature of formative assessment changes the ways in which the traditional criteria are conceptualized at the classroom level (Cizek, 2009) and these criteria may need further reconceptualization in large-scale formative applications. Little work has been done in this area to date and formulating standards for large-scale formative assessments represents a significant challenge that will require collaborative work on the part of policy makers, instructional specialists, and psychometricians.

CONCLUSION

Assessment has, for at least the last 50 years, been a centerpiece of many educational improvement efforts and reform proposals. Commonly, the initiatives have invoked summative assessments for gathering valid and dependable, but fairly coarse-grained information about student achievement, with the assessment information typically collected on an annual basis and used for evaluation, accountability, or other consequential purposes such as student promotion or graduation. To be sure, some unanticipated negative side effects of these initiatives have occurred, but the results of this focus on educational outcomes have generally been positive and have produced improvements in student achievement.

With the emphasis on summative, accountability testing likely having reached its peak, interest in other potentially efficacious alternatives has increased and research on formative assessment suggests that it may represent a timely, effective, and powerful reform. The contrast between summative and formative assessment has its roots in the distinction between summative and formative evaluation as those concepts evolved in the 1960s and early 1970s.

Whereas the focus of summative assessments is on coarse-grained information for evaluation purposes with little direct application to instructional interventions for individual students, the focus of formative assessment is nearly opposite. Although both types of assessment would ideally be linked to accepted content standards, the focus of formative assessment is on obtaining fine-grained information about student strengths and weaknesses in a nonevaluative context in which both the teacher and student see the information as valuable and useful for determining the subsequent activities that would be most beneficial for reaching predetermined educational goals.

A modest but compelling research base now supports the use of formative assessment procedures at the classroom level, but controversy and uncertainty surround the potential for extending formative assessment to higher levels such as state testing programs. If it is determined that formative assessment's benefits can only be fully realized if limited to classroom-level applications, at least seven challenges will need to be addressed, including preservice educator training in the use of formative assessment and changes to in-service educator scheduling to allow the time required for planning, conducting, and following up on formative assessment. In addition, if it is determined that formative assessment can also be incorporated into a comprehensive or tiered system that comprises levels above the individual classroom, at least three other challenges will need to be addressed. Two of these challenges—fidelity to purpose and allocation of adequate resources—are challenges also present at the classroom level, but with somewhat different dimensions when the issue is considered at the policy level.

In the end, however, addressing the challenges and embracing the potential power of formative assessment offers substantial promise for stimulating greater gains in students' achievement and responsibility for their learning. While large-scale summative achievement testing has played a prominent role in reform efforts, yielded increases in student achievement, and will likely remain a key component of future testing and accountability systems, the methods and benefits of formative assessment are also well documented, and there is broad interest among educators, policy makers, and researchers in implementing formative assessment as the next best hope for realizing even greater increases in student achievement. The chapters in this volume provide a comprehensive and important foundation for this goal by describing the key characteristics of effective formative assessment, analyzing implementation success across contexts and content areas, and critiquing current practice with an emphasis on providing practical, research-based suggestions for current practice and future research and development.

Of course, the success of any reform depends on the professionalism of those who implement the innovation and the fidelity of the implementation to the characteristics that account for its efficacy. To that end, the promise of formative assessment must ultimately be situated in broad, fresh, and innovative examination of educator preparation, in-service support, effective personnel evaluation and mentoring, the ability to collect and analyze high-quality information about student achievement and the structure of schools themselves—an ambitious agenda to be sure, but one that must be pursued to ensure that all students are provided with the tools they need to engage successfully in the careers of their choosing and to sustain the promise of a democratic republic.

REFERENCES

Abedi, J., Hofstetter, C. H., & Lord, C. (2004). Assessment accommodations for English language learners: Implications for policy-based empirical research. *Review of Educational Research, 74*, 1–28.

Airasian, P. W., & Russell, M. (2008). *Classroom assessment* (6th ed). New York: McGraw-Hill.

Andrade, H. L. (2000). Using rubrics to promote thinking and learning. *Educational Leadership, 57*(5), 13–18.

Andrade, H. L., Du, Y., & Wang, X. (2008). Putting rubrics to the test: The effect of a model, criteria generation, and rubric-referenced self-assessment on elementary school students' writing. *Educational Measurement: Issues and Practice, 27*(2), 3–13.

Atkin, J. M., Black, P., & Coffey, J. (2001). *Classroom assessment and the national science education standards.* Washington, DC: National Academy Press.

Black, P., & Wiliam, D. (1998a). Inside the black box: Raising standards through classroom assessment. *Phi Delta Kappan, 80*(2), 139–148.

Black, P., & Wiliam, D. (1998b). Assessment and classroom learning. *Assessment in Education, 5*(1), 7–74.

Bloom, B. S. (Ed.). (1956). *Taxonomy of educational objectives: The classification of educational goals.* New York: McKay.

Bloom, B. S., Hastings, J. T., & Madaus, G. F. (Eds.). (1971). *Handbook of formative and summative evaluation of student learning.* New York: McGraw-Hill.

Brennan, R. L. (Ed.). (2006). *Educational measurement, fourth edition.* Westport, CT: Praeger.

Brookhart, S. M. (2003). Developing measurement theory for classroom assessment purposes and uses. *Educational Measurement: Issues and Practice, 22*(4), 5–12.

Camilli, G. (2006). Test fairness. In R. L. Brennan (Ed.), *Educational measurement* (4th ed., pp. 221–256). Westport, CT: Praeger.

Cizek, G. J. (1995). The big picture in assessment and who ought to have it. *Phi Delta Kappan, 77*(3), 246–249.

Cizek, G. J. (1997). Learning, achievement, and assessment: Constructs at a crossroads. In G. D. Phye (Ed.), *Handbook of classroom assessment* (pp. 1–32). San Diego, CA: Academic.

Cizek, G. J. (2001). More unintended consequences of high-stakes testing. *Educational Measurement: Issues and Practice, 20*(4), 19–27.

Cizek, G. J. (2007). Formative classroom assessment and large-scale assessment: Implications for future research and development. In J. A. McMillan (Ed.), *Formative classroom assessment* (pp. 99–115). New York: Teachers College Press.

Cizek, G. J. (2009). Reliability and validity of information about student achievement: Comparing the contexts of large-scale and classroom testing. *Theory into Practice, 48*(1), 63–71.

Cizek, G. J., & Rachor, R. E. (1994). The real testing bias: The role of values in educational assessment. *NASSP Bulletin, 78*(560), 83–93.

Council of Chief State School Officers. (2008a). *Formative assessments in a comprehensive assessment system study group.* Washington, DC: Author. http://www.ccsso.org/Projects/scass/projects/comprehensive_assessment_systems_for_esea_title_i/study_groups/1960.cfm

Council of Chief State School Officers. (2008b). *Formative assessments for students and teachers.* Washington, DC: Author. http://www.ccsso.org/content/PDFs/ FAST%20history%20and%20mission%2008-09.pdf

Educational Testing Service. (2008). *ETS formative assessment item bank.* Retrieved July 21, 2008, from http://www.ets.org/portal/site/ets/menuitem.1488512ecfd5b8849a77b13bc3921509/?vgnextoid=f55aaf5e 44df4010VgnVCM10000022f95190RCRD&vgnextchannel=c1f1253b164f4010VgnVCM10000022f95190 RCRD

Family Educational Rights and Privacy Act. 20 U.S.C.1232. (1974).

Goodman, D., & Hambleton, R. K. (2005). Some misconceptions about large-scale educational testing. In R. P. Phelps (Ed.), *Defending standardized testing* (pp. 91–110). Mahwah, NJ: Erlbaum.

Herman, J. L., & Winters, L. (1994). Portfolio research: A slim collection. *Educational Leadership, 52*(2), 48–55.

Hills, J. R. (1991). Apathy concerning grading and testing. *Phi Delta Kappan, 72*, 540–545.

Hoxby, C. M. (2002). The cost of accountability. In W. M. Evers & H. J. Walberg (Eds.), *School accountability* (pp. 47–73). Stanford, CA: Hoover Institution.

Individuals with Disabilities Education Act, 20 U.S.C. 1400. (2004).

McManus, S. (2008). *Attributes of effective formative assessment.* Washington, DC: Council of Chief State School Officers. http://www.ccsso.org/publications/ details.cfm?Publication ID=362]

No Child Left Behind Act, 20 U.S.C. 6301. (2002).

Olson, L. (2005, March 2). ETS to enter formative-assessment market at K-12 Level. *Education Week*, p. 7.

O'Sullivan, R. G., & Chalnick, M. K. (1991). Measurement-related course work requirements for teacher certification and recertification. *Educational Measurement: Issues and Practice, 10*(1), 17–19, 23.

Phelps, R. P. (2000). Estimating the cost of standardized student testing in the United States. *Journal of Education Finance, 25*, 343–380.

Phelps, R. P. (2005a). The rich, robust research literature on testing's achievement benefits. In R. P. Phelps (Ed.), *Defending standardized testing* (pp. 55–90). Mahwah, NJ: Erlbaum.

Phelps, R. P. (2005b). Persistently positive: Forty years of public opinion on standardized testing. In R. P. Phelps (Ed.), *Defending standardized testing* (pp. 1–22). Mahwah, NJ: Erlbaum.

Popham, W. J. (2008). *Classroom assessment: What teachers need to know* (5th ed.). Boston: Prentice Hall.

Popham, W. J. (2009). Assessment literacy for teachers: Faddish or fundamental? *Theory Into Practice, 48*(1), 4–11.

Sadler, D. R. (1989). Formative assessment and the design of instructional assessments. *Instructional Science, 18*, 119–144.

Scriven, M. (1967). The methodology of evaluation. In R. W. Tyler, R. M. Gagne, & M. Scriven (Eds.), *Perspectives on curriculum evaluation* (pp. 39–83). Chicago: Rand McNally.

Shepard, L. A. (2000). The role of assessment in a learning culture. *Educational Researcher, 29*(7), 4–14.

Shepard, L. A. (2006). Classroom assessment. In R. Brennan (Ed.), *Educational measurement* (4th ed., pp. 624–646). Westport, CT: Praeger.

Shute, V. J. (2008). Focus on formative feedback. *Review of Educational Research, 78*, 153–189.

Stiggins, R. J. (1999). Evaluating classroom assessment training in teacher education programs. *Educational Measurement: Issues and Practice, 18*(1), 23–27.

Stiggins, R. J. (2005). *Student-involved assessment for learning.* Upper Saddle River, NJ: Prentice Hall.

Thurlow, M. L., & Thompson, S. J. (2004). Inclusion of students with disabilities in state and district assessments. In G. Walz (Ed.), *Measuring up: Assessment issues for teachers, counselors, and administrators* (pp. 161–176). Austin, TX: Pro-Ed.

Wang, L., Beckett, G., & Brown, L. (2006). Controversies of standardized assessment in school accountability reform: A critical synthesis of multidisciplinary research evidence. *Applied Measurement in Education, 19*, 305–328.

2

AN INTEGRATIVE SUMMARY OF THE RESEARCH LITERATURE AND IMPLICATIONS FOR A NEW THEORY OF FORMATIVE ASSESSMENT

DYLAN WILIAM

If what students learned as a result of a particular sequence of instruction was predictable, there would be no need for assessment. Educators could just compile an inventory of what they had taught and use this inventory as a catalogue of what students had learned. This was, in effect, the underlying assumption of the educational model in the medieval English universities of Oxford and Cambridge, where a bachelor's degree was conferred after the completion of a certain period of residence. Of course, as research studies (e.g., Denvir & Brown, 1986a, 1986b)—and the experience of educators—attest, what students learn from a particular sequence of instruction can be very different from what the teacher intended to teach them. That is why assessment is a central and perhaps even a defining feature of effective instruction: Assessment is the only way that we can know whether what has been taught has been learned. In a very real sense, therefore, assessment is the bridge between learning and teaching.

Assessment is what makes the routine coming together of teachers and students for the purpose of creating learning different from, for example, that of a teacher speaking into a video camera that is then transmitted to students in another room: Together, teachers and students can ensure that information about student achievement, gained through assessment, can be used to adjust the instruction in order to better meet student learning needs. This is the essence of formative assessment: the idea that evidence of student achievement is elicited, is interpreted, and leads to action that results in better learning than would have been the case in the absence of such evidence (Wiliam & Black, 1996).

The origins of the term *formative assessment* have been detailed elsewhere (see Cizek, this volume; Guskey, this volume; Wiliam, 2007a). The aim of this chapter is to build on the basic idea of formative assessment to try to provide a clear theoretical basis for the ways in which assessment can support learning, to show how the various formulations of the notion of formative assessment that have been proposed over the last 40 years can be encompassed within a broader overarching framework, and to indicate briefly how that framework connects to research in related areas.

REVIEWS OF RESEARCH ON FEEDBACK AND FORMATIVE ASSESSMENT

One of the powerful metaphors that underlie the theory of action of formative assessment is the idea of *feedback*, developed originally in the field of systems engineering (see Wiener, 1948). As Ramaprasad (1983) noted, the defining feature of feedback is that the information generated within the system must have some effect on the system. Information that does not have the capability to change the performance of the system is not feedback. Ramaprasad said: "Feedback is information about the gap between the actual level and the reference level of a system parameter which is used to alter the gap in some way" (p. 4). Commenting on this, Sadler (1989) noted:

> An important feature of Ramaprasad's definition is that information about the gap between actual and reference levels is considered as feedback only when it is used to alter the gap. If the information is simply recorded, passed to a third party who lacks either the knowledge or the power to change the outcome, or is too deeply coded (for example, as a summary grade given by the teacher) to lead to appropriate action, the control loop cannot be closed, and "dangling data" substituted for effective feedback. (p. 121)

In this view, feedback cannot be separated from its instructional consequences. It is therefore not surprising that over the last quarter century, a number of substantial reviews have appeared concerning the impact of assessment practices on students and their learning in the context of the classroom (Allal & Lopez, 2005; Bangert-Drowns, Kulik, Kulik, & Morgan, 1991; Black & Wiliam, 1998a, 1998b; Brookhart, 2004, 2007; Crooks, 1988; Dempster, 1991, 1992; Elshout-Mohr, 1994; Fuchs & Fuchs, 1986; Hattie & Timperley, 2007; Kluger & DeNisi, 1996; Köller, 2005; Natriello, 1987; Nyquist, 2003; Shute, 2008; Wiliam, 2007a).

The reviews resist any easy synthesis due to differences in their starting assumptions, their theoretical bases, and their remits, and besides, a detailed summary of each of these reviews is beyond the scope of this chapter (Brookhart, 2004). Nevertheless, some significant themes emerge.

The first theme is that the outcomes of assessment are used in a multiplicity of ways, with different uses that are often in conflict (Black & Wiliam, 1998a; Crooks, 1988; Natriello, 1987). In particular, the use of assessments for summative purposes (such as determining a grade on a course) appears to reduce the extent to which they can serve to support learning.

The second common theme is that different kinds of feedback may be differentially effective for different kinds of learning. For example, the kinds of feedback that are most effective in developing lower-level skills and content knowledge may not be the most effective for higher-order skills (Dempster, 1991, 1992; Elshout-Mohr, 1994), and in particular, that immediate feedback appears to be more effective for procedural learning, while delayed feedback may be more effective for higher-order outcomes (Shute, 2008).

The third, and perhaps most important, theme is that the most effective feedback focuses attention prospectively rather than retrospectively. The important question is not, "What did I get right and what did I get wrong?" but, "What next?" (Bangert-Drowns et al., 1991; Fuchs & Fuchs, 1986; Hattie & Timperley, 2007; Nyquist, 2003). Short-term studies can be particularly misleading in this respect, because while certain kinds of feedback interventions—defined by Kluger & DeNisi (1996, p. 255) as "actions taken by (an) external agent(s) to provide information regarding some aspect(s) of one's task performance"—can increase performance, they may do so by changing the kind of motivation. For example, a feedback intervention may show positive effects by increasing task motivation, but then future learning would require continuous feedback. Even where the emphasis is on task-learning processes, feedback interventions may encourage shallow learning, thus making higher-order goals more difficult to achieve (Kluger & DeNisi, 1996; Shute, 2008).

EFFECT SIZES IN REVIEWS OF RESEARCH ON FORMATIVE ASSESSMENT AND THEIR LIMITATIONS

The reviews of research cited above produce a range of estimates of the size of the effect that the use of formative feedback might be expected to have on learning. Bangert-Drowns et al. (1991), found an average effect of around one-fourth of a standard deviation for feedback in testlike events, while Kluger and DeNisi (1996) and Nyquist (2003) found that feedback produced larger effect sizes—around 0.4 standard deviations—although both noted that the variability across different studies was extremely high. Black and Wiliam (1998a) and Shute (2008) suggested that typical effect sizes were in the range 0.4 to 0.7 and 0.4 to 0.8 respectively while a review of 74 meta-analyses of the effects of feedback by Hattie and Timperley (2007) found an average effect size of 0.95 standard deviations across 4,157 studies.

The use of standardized effect sizes to compare and synthesize studies is understandable, because few of the studies included in the various reviews published sufficient details to allow more sophisticated forms of synthesis to be undertaken, but relying on standardized effect sizes in educational studies creates substantial difficulties of interpretation, for two reasons.

First, as Black and Wiliam (1998a) noted, effect size is influenced by the range of achievement in the population. An increase of 5 points on a test where the population standard deviation is 10 points would result in an effect size of 0.5 standard deviations. However, the same intervention when administered only to the upper half of the same population, provided that it was equally effective for all students, would result in an effect size of over 0.8 standard deviations, due to the reduced variance of the subsample. An often-observed finding in the literature—that formative assessment interventions are more successful for students with special educational needs (for example in Fuchs & Fuchs, 1986)—is difficult to interpret without some attempt to control for the restriction of range, and may simply be a statistical artifact.

The second and more important limitation of the meta-analytic reviews is that they fail to take into account the fact that different outcome measures are not equally sensitive to instruction (Popham, 2007). Much of the methodology of meta-analysis used in education and psychology has been borrowed uncritically from the medical and health sciences, where the different studies being combined in meta-analyses either use the same outcome measures (e.g., 1-year survival rates) or outcome measures that are reasonably consistent across different settings (e.g., time to discharge from hospital care). In education, to aggregate outcomes from different studies it is necessary to assume that the outcome measures are equally sensitive to instruction.

It has long been known that teacher-constructed measures have tended to show greater effect sizes for experimental interventions than obtained with standardized tests, and this has sometimes been regarded as evidence of the invalidity of teacher-constructed measures. However, as has become clear in recent years, assessments vary greatly in their sensitivity to instruction—the extent to which they measure the things that educational processes change (Wiliam, 2007b). In particular, the way that standardized tests are constructed reduces their sensitivity to instruction. The reliability of a test can be increased by replacing items that do not discriminate between candidates with items that do, so items that all students answer correctly, or that all students answer incorrectly, are generally omitted. However, such systematic deletion of items can alter the construct being measured by the test, because items related to aspects of learning that are effectively taught by teachers are less likely to be included than items that are taught ineffectively.

For example, an item that is answered incorrectly by all students in the seventh grade and answered correctly by all students in the eighth grade is almost certainly assessing something that is changed by instruction, but is unlikely to be retained in a test for seventh graders (because it is too hard), nor in one for eighth graders (because it is too easy). This is an extreme example, but it does highlight how the sensitivity of a test to the effects of instruction can be significantly affected by the normal processes of test development (Wiliam, 2008).

The effects of sensitivity to instruction are far from negligible. Bloom (1984) famously observed that one-to-one tutorial instruction was more effective than average group-based instruction by two standard deviations. Such a claim is credible in the context of many assessments, but for standardized tests such as those used in the National Assessment of Educational Progress (NAEP), one year's progress for an average student is equivalent to one-fourth of a standard deviation (NAEP, 2006), so for Bloom's claim to be true, one year's individual tuition would produce the same effect as 9 years of average group-based instruction, which seems unlikely. The important point here is that the outcome measures used in different studies are likely to differ significantly in their sensitivity to instruction, and the most significant element in determining an assessment's sensitivity to instruction appears to be its distance from the curriculum it is intended to assess.

Ruiz-Primo, Shavelson, Hamilton, and Klein (2002) proposed a five-fold classification for the distance of an assessment from the enactment of curriculum, with examples of each:

1. *Immediate*, such as science journals, notebooks, and classroom tests;
2. *Close*, or formal embedded assessments (for example, if an immediate assessment asked about number of pendulum swings in 15 seconds, a close assessment would ask about the time taken for 10 swings);
3. *Proximal*, including a different assessment of the same concept, requiring some transfer (for example, if an immediate assessment asked students to construct

boats out of paper cups, the proximal assessment would ask for an explanation of what makes bottles float or sink);

4. *Distal*, for example a large-scale assessment from a state assessment framework, in which the assessment task was sampled from a different domain, such as physical science, and where the problem, procedures, materials and measurement methods differed from those used in the original activities; and

5. *Remote*, such as standardized national achievement tests.

As might be expected, Ruiz-Primo et al. (2002) found that the closer the assessment was to the enactment of the curriculum, the greater was the sensitivity of the assessment to the effects of instruction, and that the impact was considerable. For example, one of their interventions showed an average effect size of 0.26 when measured with a proximal assessment, but an effect size of 1.26 when measured with a close assessment.

In none of the meta-analyses discussed above was there any attempt to control for the effects of differences in the sensitivity to instruction of the different outcome measures. By itself, it does not invalidate the claims that formative assessment is likely to be effective in improving student outcomes. Indeed, in all likelihood, attempts to improve the quality of teachers' formative assessment practices are likely to be considerably more cost-effective than many, if not most, other interventions (Wiliam & Thomson, 2007). However, failure to control for the impact of this factor means that considerable care should be taken in quoting particular effect sizes as being likely to be achieved in practice, and other measures of the impact, such as increases in the rate of learning, may be more appropriate (Wiliam, 2007c). More importantly, attention may need to be shifted away from the size of the effects and toward the role that effective feedback can play in the design of effective learning environments (Wiliam, 2007a). In concluding their review of over 3,000 studies of the effects of feedback interventions in schools, colleges and workplaces, Kluger and DeNisi observed that:

> considerations of utility and alternative interventions suggest that even an FI [feedback intervention] with demonstrated positive effects should not be administered wherever possible. Rather additional development of FIT [feedback intervention theory] is needed to establish the circumstance under which positive FI effects on performance are also lasting and efficient and when these effects are transient and have questionable utility. This research must focus on the processes induced by FIs and not on the general question of whether FIs improve performance— look how little progress 90 years of attempts to answer the latter question have yielded. (1996, p. 278)

The remainder of this chapter reviews a number of recent definitions of formative assessment and proposes a definition of formative assessment in terms of the function that assessment evidence fulfills; specifically, the extent to which assessment supports and improves instructional decisions. The consequences of this definition are then examined, focusing in particular on how formative assessment may be operationalized, and the chapter concludes by sketching out briefly some links to other related areas of research and some priorities for future research.

DEFINITIONS OF FORMATIVE ASSESSMENT

A variety of definitions of the term *formative assessment* have been proposed over the years. In their review, Black and Wiliam (1998a) defined formative assessment "as encompassing all those activities undertaken by teachers, and/or by their students, which provide information to be used as feedback to modify the teaching and learning activities in which they are engaged" (p. 7). In a subsequent publication, addressed to policymakers and practitioners, Black and Wiliam adopted the following definition:

> We use the general term *assessment* to refer to all those activities undertaken by teachers—and by their students in assessing themselves—that provide information to be used as feedback to modify teaching and learning activities. Such assessment becomes *formative assessment* when the evidence is actually used to adapt the teaching to meet student needs. (1998b, p. 140)

Cowie and Bell (1999) adopted a slightly more restrictive definition by limiting the term to assessment conducted and acted upon while learning was taking place. They defined formative assessment as "the process used by teachers and students to recognize and respond to student learning in order to enhance that learning, during the learning" (p. 32). The requirement that the assessment be conducted during learning was also embraced by Shepard, Hammerness, Darling-Hammond, and Rust (2005) in their definition of formative assessment as "assessment carried out during the instructional process for the purpose of improving teaching or learning" (p. 275). In their review of formative assessment practices across eight national and provincial systems, the Organization for Economic Cooperation and Development (OECD) also emphasized the principle that the assessment should take place during instruction: "Formative assessment refers to frequent, interactive assessments of students' progress and understanding to identify learning needs and adjust teaching appropriately" (Looney, 2005, p. 21). In a similar vein, Kahl (2005) wrote: "A formative assessment is a tool that teachers use to measure student grasp of specific topics and skills they are teaching. It's a 'midstream' tool to identify specific student misconceptions and mistakes while the material is being taught" (p. 11).

Broadfoot et al. (1999) argued that improving learning through assessment depended on five key factors: (1) the provision of effective feedback to pupils; (2) the active involvement of pupils in their own learning; (3) adjusting teaching to take account of the results of assessment; (4) a recognition of the profound influence assessment has on the motivation and self-esteem of pupils, both of which are crucial influences on learning; and (5) the need for pupils to be able to assess themselves and understand how to improve.

Broadfoot et al. (1999) suggested that the term *formative assessment* was unhelpful to describe such uses of assessment because "the term 'formative' itself is open to a variety of interpretations and often means no more than that assessment is carried out frequently and is planned at the same time as teaching" (p. 7). Instead they suggested instead the use of the term *assessment for learning*.

The first use of the term assessment for learning appears to be in a paper given at the annual conference of the Association for Supervision and Curriculum Development

(James, 1992); the same year a book entitled Testing for Learning was published (Mitchell, 1992). Assessment for Learning was used as the title of a book three years later (Sutton, 1995), but the first use of the term assessment for learning as a counterpoint to assessment of learning appears to be by Gipps and Stobart (1997). The use of the term was popularized in the United Kingdom by Broadfoot et al. (1999) and in the United States by Stiggins (2002). The definition given by the Assessment Reform Group (Broadfoot et al., 2002) is: "Assessment for learning is the process of seeking and interpreting evidence for use by learners and their teachers to decide where the learners are in their learning, where they need to go and how best to get there" (pp. 2–3).

Whereas many authors have used the terms *formative assessment* and *assessment for learning* interchangeably, or as different labels for the same idea, Black, Harrison, Lee, Marshall, and Wiliam (2004) distinguished between the terms as follows:

> Assessment for learning is any assessment for which the first priority in its design and practice is to serve the purpose of promoting students' learning. It thus differs from assessment designed primarily to serve the purposes of accountability, or of ranking, or of certifying competence. An assessment activity can help learning if it provides information that teachers and their students can use as feedback in assessing themselves and one another and in modifying the teaching and learning activities in which they are engaged. Such assessment becomes "formative assessment" when the evidence is actually used to adapt the teaching work to meet learning needs. (p. 10)

Perhaps the most important point here is the distinction between formative and summative in terms of the function the assessment serves, rather than the assessment itself. Wiliam and Black (1996) argued that attempting to use the words *formative* and *summative* to describe assessments leads to contradiction, since the same assessment instrument, and even the same assessment outcomes, could be used both formatively and summatively. While locating the distinction in terms of the purpose of the assessment overcomes some difficulties, it still leaves open the possibility that assessment evidence might be collected with the intention of supporting learning, but might never actually do so.

A NEW THEORY OF FORMATIVE ASSESSMENT: PRECISION IN DEFINITION

In order to provide a comprehensive definition of formative assessment, Black and Wiliam (2009) proposed that assessment is formative:

> to the extent that evidence about student achievement is elicited, interpreted, and used by teachers, learners, or their peers, to make decisions about the next steps in instruction that are likely to be better, or better founded, than the decisions they would have taken in the absence of the evidence that was elicited. (p. 6)

In explicating this definition, Black and Wiliam (2009) elaborated on five key points. First, *anyone can be the agent in formative assessment*. Although in many cases the decisions will be made by the teacher, the definition also includes those situations in which the decisions are made by the learners themselves, or their peers.

Second, *the focus of the definition is on decisions*. Black and Wiliam (2009) noted that the focus of the definition could be on the intentions of those involved in instruction in collecting the evidence, but then data collection activities that did not impact learning in any way would be potentially formative, which would be contrary to common sense (and indeed to the literal meaning of the term formative). Such a definition would, in that sense, be too open. On the other hand, the definition of Black and Wiliam (1998b) focused on the outcome. It required that the assessment did in fact lead to better learning, which would appear to be a rather stringent criterion, because there could be many situations in which actions that might be expected to increase learning might not do so, given to the unpredictable nature of learning (and students). The focus on decisions is also consistent with Alexander's definition of pedagogy as:

> the act of teaching together with its attendant discourse of educational theories, values, evidence and justifications. It is what one needs to know, and the skills one needs to command, in order to make and justify the many different kinds of decision of which teaching is constituted. (2008, p. 47)

Third, *the definition focuses on next steps in instruction*. The term *instruction* is used to describe any planful activity intended to create learning, which is here defined as an increase, brought about by experience, in the capacities of an organism to act, or react in response to stimuli, in valued ways. The term *instruction* thus subsumes the roles of both the teacher and the learner. This use of the term will be unfamiliar to some readers since the term *instruction* is used in some contexts to denote a transmissionist approach to teaching, but such a connotation is quite definitely not intended here. In this context it is worth noting that there are languages where the same word is used for both teaching and learning (Welsh: *dysgu*; Maori: *ako*). It is this inclusive sense of the word *instruction*, which denotes both teaching and learning that is intended here.

Fourth, *the definition is probabilistic*. Locating the burden of definition of the term *formative* in the resulting action creates the difficulty that proof of effect is impossible to establish, requiring the verification of a counterfactual claim: that what occurred was different (and better than) what would have happened in the absence of the assessment (but did not do so). Requiring that the decisions are likely to be better reflects the fact that even the best designed interventions will not always result in better learning for all students.

Finally, *the assessment need not change the planned instruction*. The definition requires that decisions are either better or better founded, than decisions made without the evidence elicited as part of the assessment process. The second possibility is included to include those cases where the assessment indicates to the teacher that the best course of action is in fact that which the teacher had intended prior to the elicitation of evidence. In this case, formative assessment would not change the course of action, but it would mean that it was better grounded in evidence. (On this point, thanks are due to Jim Popham, who, through relentless probing, forced a clarification of this aspect of the definition.)

From this definition, Black and Wiliam proposed that formative assessment is, in essence, concerned with "the creation of, and capitalization upon, 'moments of contingency' in instruction for the purpose of the regulation of learning processes" (2009, p. 6). A theory of formative assessment is therefore much narrower than an overall theory of teaching and learning, although it links in significant ways to other aspects of teaching and learning, since how teachers, learners, and their peers create and capitalize on these moments of contingency entails considerations of instructional design, curriculum, pedagogy, psychology, and epistemology.

Moments of contingency can be synchronous or asynchronous. Examples of synchronous moments include teachers' real-time adjustments during one-on-one teaching or whole class discussion. Asynchronous examples include teachers' feedback, the use of evidence derived from homework, or students' summaries made at the end of a lesson, each used to plan a subsequent lesson. Furthermore, these asynchronous moments might be used to modify the instruction of those from whom the evidence was collected, or the teacher may collect evidence about difficulties experienced by one group, and use this to modify instruction for another group of students at some point in the future.

Teachers' responses to information about student learning can be one-to-one or group-based. Responses to a student's written work are usually one-on-one, but in classroom discussions the feedback will be in relation to the needs of the subject-classroom as a whole, and may be an immediate intervention in the flow of classroom discussion, or a decision about how to begin the next lesson.

A NEW THEORY OF FORMATIVE ASSESSMENT: DEFINITIONAL CONSEQUENCES

In this section, two particular consequences of the definition of formative assessment just described are explored: the kinds of decisions that formative assessments can support, and the immediacy of the instructional adjustments that are informed by the assessments.

What Kinds of Assessment Are Formative?

It follows from the proposed definition for formative assessment that any assessment that provides evidence that has the potential to improve instructional decision making can be formative, whether these decisions are taken by teachers, peers, or the learners themselves. The assessment might simply monitor the achievement of students, indicating that for some students, the instruction was unsuccessful. If the teacher then organizes additional instruction for those students, even if it is to go over the material again but more slowly, then this is potentially formative. If the assessment provides additional information that locates the precise nature of the students' difficulties, then it is diagnostic. The most useful assessments, however, are those that yield insights that are instructionally tractable. In other words, not only do they identify which students are having difficulties (the monitoring assessment) or locate the specific difficulties (the diagnostic assessment): They also yield insights into the kinds of next steps in instruction (including possibly steps to be taken by learners) that are likely to be most effective.

To give a concrete example, suppose a class has taken a test that assesses the ability to find the largest or smallest fraction in a given set. Knowing the scores of the students on this test would provide a monitoring assessment. It would identify those students who had mastered this skill sufficiently well to move on, and those who need more help. If the teacher organized additional instruction for these latter students, either by holding an additional class at the end of the day, or through the provision of targeted learning materials, the test would be formative (or more precisely, would function formatively), because the availability of the test scores allowed the teacher to make a better instructional decision than he or she would have been able to make in the absence of the information about the test scores.

If her test had been carefully constructed, there might also be *diagnostic* information in the students' responses. For example, the teacher might notice that most of the students who got low scores on the test had far greater success with items that included a number of unitary fractions (fractions with 1 as the numerator) than those without unitary fractions. Although this would be useful information, this insight does more to locate the learning difficulty than to indicate what should be done to overcome it— the teacher could focus instructional intervention on nonunitary fractions, which is likely to be more appropriate than reteaching the whole topic. However, if the teacher can see from the responses that many of the students are operating with a naïve strategy that the smallest fraction is the one with the largest denominator, and the largest fraction is the one with the smallest denominator—a strategy that is successful with unitary fractions (Vinner, 1997)—then this provides information for the teacher that is instructionally tractable. Such assessments not only signal the problem (monitoring) and locate it (diagnosing). They situate the problem within a theory of action that can suggest measures that could be taken to improve learning. The best formative assessment therefore identifies recipes for future action.

Note that in the three scenarios about the fraction item, in each case the assessment functioned formatively, because information was used to make instructional decisions that were likely to be better than those that would have been taken in the absence of the evidence. However, the fact that in all three cases the assessment functioned formatively did not mean that all three ways of using the evidence were likely to be equally effective. By definition, assessments that yield diagnostic insights are likely to lead to better instructional decisions than those that simply monitor student achievement, and those that yield insights that are instructionally tractable would be better still.

One of the differences between assessments that monitor, those that diagnose and those that yield insights that are instructionally tractable is a matter of the specificity of the information yielded—to be instructionally tractable, the assessment needs to yield more information than simply whether learning is taking place, or, if it is not, what specifically, is not being learned. But for an assessment outcome to be instructionally tractable, it must also entail theories of curriculum and theories of learning.

Instructional tractability entails a theory of curriculum because the focus is on answering the question: "What next?" This implies that there is a clear notion of a learning progression; that is, a description of the "knowledge, skills, understandings, attitudes or values that students develop in an area of learning, in the order in which they typically develop them" (Forster & Masters, 2004, p. 65). Instructional tractability also entails a theory of learning, because before a decision can be made about what evidence to elicit, it is necessary to know not just what comes next in learning, but what kinds of difficulties learners have in making those next steps. The links between formative assessment and theories of learning are spelled out in more detail in Black and Wiliam (2005), Brookhart (2007), Wiliam (2007a), and Black and Wiliam (2009) and are summarized briefly in a subsequent section of this chapter, "A New Theory of Formative Assessment: Key Instructional Processes."

CYCLE LENGTHS FOR FORMATIVE ASSESSMENT

In the example of the fractions test discussed above, the action taken by the teacher follows quickly from the elicitation of the evidence about student achievement. In general, however, formative assessment allows for cycles of elicitation, interpretation, and action of any length, provided the information is used to inform instructional decisions. Consider the following six scenarios.

Scenario 1. In spring 2008, a science supervisor in a school district needed to plan the summer workshops that would be offered to eighth-grade science teachers in the district. She analyzed the scores obtained by the districts' eighth-grade students on the 2007 tests and noted that, whereas the average scores on science tests were comparable to the state average, performance on earth science items was much lower than the state average. The teacher decided to make earth sciences the focus of the professional development activities offered in summer 2008. The workshops were well attended by the district's eighth-grade science teachers. Teachers returned to school in fall 2008, and implemented revised instructional methods based on their learning over the summer. As a result, the achievement of eighth-grade students on earth sciences items improved in the tests taken in spring 2009.

Scenario 2. Each year, a group of high school teachers of Algebra I reviewed students' performance on a state-wide Algebra I test. They looked at the difficulty level (proportion correct) for each item on the test. Where item difficulties were lower than expected, they looked at how instruction on that aspect of the curriculum was planned and delivered, and at ways in which the instruction could be strengthened in the following year.

Scenario 3. A school district used a series of interim tests that were keyed to the curriculum and administered at intervals of 6 to 10 weeks to check on student progress. Students whose scores were below the threshold determined to be necessary to have an 80% chance of passing the state test were required to attend additional instruction on Saturdays.

Scenario 4. In elementary and middle school mathematics and science teaching in Japan, a teaching unit is typically allocated 13 or 14 lessons (Lewis, 2002). The content usually occupies only 10 or 11 of the lessons, allowing time for a short test to be given in the 11th or 12th lesson, and for the teacher to use the remaining lessons to reteach aspects of the unit that were not well understood.

Scenario 5. During the last 3 minutes of a lesson, a history teacher who had been teaching about problems of bias in historical sources asked the students to answer, on a 3-inch by 5-inch index card, the question "Why are historians concerned about bias in historical sources?" The students turned in these "exit passes" as they left the class. The teacher read through the students' responses and then discarded the exit passes, having decided that the students' answers indicated a good enough understanding for the teacher to move on to a new chapter in the next lesson.

Scenario 6. A middle school science teacher had been teaching students to distinguish between different kinds of levers. After explaining that the key principle of the classification of levers concerns the relative arrangement of the load, the effort, and the fulcrum, she illustrated the principle with three examples: a see-saw (type 1), a wheel-barrow (type 2), and a deep sea fishing rod (type 3). To check on the students' understanding, she asked the class how a pair of tweezers would be classified, asking each student to hold up one, two, or three fingers to indicate their response. She was surprised that most of the students indicated that they thought the tweezers were a type 2 lever. When she asked them why, the students indicated that this was because there are two arms to the tweezers. She realized that it was necessary to introduce more examples, such as a pair of scissors and a nutcracker, because the students needed to understand that it is the relative distribution of the effort, load, and fulcrum that is important, not the number of components.

Now, let us recall the definition of formative assessment proposed by Black and Wiliam (2009):

> Practice in a classroom is formative to the extent that evidence about student achievement is elicited, interpreted, and used by teachers, learners, or their peers, to make decisions about the next steps in instruction that are likely to be better, or better founded, than the decisions they would have taken in the absence of the evidence that was elicited. (p. 6)

According to this definition, in each of the six scenarios, the assessment functioned formatively because evidence from the assessment was interpreted and used to make decisions that were likely to be better (or in the case of example 5, better founded) than the decisions that would have been made in the absence of that evidence. The length of the formative assessment cycle was also attuned to the capacity of the system to respond to the evidence generated—for example, there is little point in generating information on a daily basis if the decisions that the evidence is to inform are only taken on a monthly basis (Wiliam & Thompson, 2007).

However, many of these six scenarios would fail to be formative under some of the definitions discussed above. In particular, Shepard (2007) and Kahl (2005) might resist the idea that the use of assessment in examples 1, 2, and 3 were formative. They would likely point out that many test vendors have uncritically adopted the label *formative* and often have simply applied the label to tests originally designed to serve a summative function (see also Popham, 2006). Shepard (2007) argues that "what makes formative assessment *formative* is that it is immediately used to make adjustments so as *to form* new learning" (p. 281). Yet, in each of the six examples above, assessment evidence

Table 2.1 Cycle Lengths for Formative Assessment

Type	Focus	Length
Long-cycle	Across marking periods, quarters, semesters, years	4 weeks to 1 year
Medium-cycle	Within and between instructional units	1 to 4 weeks
Short-cycle	Within and between lessons	Day by day: 24 to 48 hours Minute by minute: 5 seconds to 2 hours

was used to make adjustments so as to form new learning. Examples 1, 2, and 3 fail to meet the requirement for immediacy imposed by Cowie and Bell (1999), Looney (2005), and Shepard (2007), but arguably, so also does example 4, depending on one's definition of immediacy.

The research literature supports the contention that the kinds of formative assessment illustrated in examples 4, 5, and 6 are more likely to increase learning, and by a greater amount, than the uses in examples 1, 2, and 3. Indeed, as Shepard (2007) argues, there is relatively little evidence that interventions such as examples 1, 2, and 3, are likely to have much impact at all. However, it seems odd to say that these examples are not formative in order to be able to reserve the term *formative* for those kinds of assessments that do make a significant difference to student outcomes. Rather, it would seem to make more sense—and to do less violence to the vernacular use of the word—to decide that where the assessment forms the direction of future learning, it can be described as formative, but to acknowledge that there are different kinds of cycle-length in formative assessment, as proposed by Wiliam and Thompson (2007), and shown in Table 2.1.

It is also, arguably, good *realpolitik* in that it seems unlikely that test publishers would agree to forgo the additional sales of their tests that they can expect from branding their tests as formative (and thus lay claim to a body of research about efficacy in practice) simply because they are asked to do so by researchers. The important question is therefore not, "Is this assessment formative?" but, "How does the use of this assessment improve learning?" and, echoing the conclusions of Kluger and DeNisi (1996), "How sustainably does this assessment improve learning?"

To answer this last question, and to understand what kinds of formative assessments are likely to be most effective, it is necessary to go beyond the functional definition of formative assessment, and look in more detail at the underlying processes.

A NEW THEORY OF FORMATIVE ASSESSMENT: KEY INSTRUCTIONAL PROCESSES

The systems approach to formative assessment proposed by Ramaprasad (1983), and which provides the basis for the definition of assessment for learning adopted by the Assessment Reform Group (Broadfoot et al., 2002), draws attention to three key instructional processes: (1) establishing where the learners are in their learning; (2) establishing where they are going; and (3) establishing what needs to be done to get them there.

The definition of formative assessment adopted here is based on a crossing of the process dimension (where learners are in their learning, where they are going, how to get there) with that of the agent of the instructional process (teacher, peer, learner). The resulting nine cells can be collapsed into the five key strategies of formative assessment as shown in Figure 2.1 (Wiliam & Thompson, 2007). The focus of Figure 2.1 is the subject classroom. As Black and Wiliam (2005) observe, the activities that take place when students are learning mathematics are very different from those that take place when students are learning English language arts. The role of the students and the teacher, and the nature of their interactions with each other and with the discipline are likely to be different too. Furthermore, the subject classroom is, of course, nested within a school, which in turn is located in a community, and so on. Although it is beyond the scope of this chapter, any adequate account of formative assessment will have to acknowledge these multiple contexts. The stance taken in this chapter is that, ultimately, assessment must feed into actions in the subject classroom in order to affect learning; this simplification seems reasonable, at least as a first order approximation (see Black and Wiliam (2005) and Pryor and Crossouard (2005) for examples of sociocultural approaches to the implementation of formative assessment.

The framework represented by Figure 2.1 suggests that assessment for learning can be conceptualized as consisting of five key strategies (Wiliam & Thompson, 2007):

1. clarifying, sharing, and understanding learning intentions and criteria for success;
2. engineering effective classroom discussions, questions, and tasks that elicit evidence of learning;
3. providing feedback that moves learners forward;
4. activating students as instructional resources for one another; and
5. activating students as the owners of their own learning.

A detailed account of each of these five key strategies can be found in Wiliam (2007a). In the remainder of this chapter, each of the strategies is summarized briefly, and the

	Where the learner is going	Where the learner is right now	How to get there
Teacher	Clarifying learning intentions and sharing and criteria for success (1)	Engineering effective classroom discussions. activities and tasks that elicit evidence of learning (2)	Providing feedback that moves learners forward (3)
Peer	Understanding and sharing learning intentions and criteria for success (1)	Activating students as instructional resources for one another (4)	
Learner	Understanding learning intentions and criteria for success (1)	Activating students as the owners of their own learning (5)	

Note: Numbers in parentheses indicate to which of the five key strategies an aspect relates

Figure 2.1 Aspects of formative assessment.

chapter concludes with some thoughts about future directions for research, theory, and practice.

Clarifying, Sharing, and Understanding Learning Intentions and Criteria for Success

The first strategy involves clarifying, communicating, and understanding learning intentions and criteria for success with students. At times it will be possible to specify the learning intentions in terms of clear goals, with narrowly drawn criteria for success; for example, when the teacher is trying to help students learn how to balance a chemical equation. At other times, particularly in creative work, such precision would be neither possible nor desirable, as when students are engaged in exploring the possibilities of painting with acrylics. In such situations, the teacher might be operating with a broad "horizon" (Black et al., 2003, p. 68) of possible, and acceptable, goals; different students can pursue different avenues. However, it is important to note that it is not the case that "anything goes." Although there may be a broad range of different directions in which learners might usefully go, there will be some that the teacher regards as unlikely to lead to useful learning, at which point the teacher would probably intervene to redirect the learner's activities.

An important consequence of this view of formative assessment is that, whereas it is necessary for there to be clarity about what is to be learned, what the learners are to learn is completely independent of formative assessment (Wiliam, 2007a). In other words, a commitment to formative assessment does not entail any particular view of what the learning intentions should be, nor does it entail a commitment to any particular view of what happens when learning takes place. This is important because, in many formulations of formative assessment, there is an implication that a commitment to formative assessment entails a commitment to certain kinds of learning goals; for example, to deep learning. While deep learning may indeed be desirable, it does not necessarily take place by a commitment to formative assessment, which can be used to help students reach instrumental or more shallow goals just as well as ultimate or deeper goals.

Even if learning intentions and criteria for success with students are clarified, communicated, and understood, it also makes no prescription about who determines the learning goal. While the youngest learners may have relatively little choice over what they are to learn, as they get older they will assume greater responsibility. However, even within further and higher education, where the student chooses courses of study, there will generally be an established curriculum, so that the actual learning intentions, and the associated success criteria, are likely to be a matter for negotiation between learner and teacher.

Engineering Effective Classroom Discussions, Activities, and Tasks that Elicit Evidence of Learning

The second strategy listed in Figure 2.1 focuses on the elicitation of evidence of achievement. While this elicitation will frequently take the form of questioning, it is important to note that any actions that elicit evidence that can be used to inform instruction are also included. For example, for teachers of students with multiple and profound learning difficulties, it may be that evidence of learning is elicited by touch rather than through anything recognizable as a question.

The important point here is that not all elicited evidence is equally useful. Some kinds of evidence will support only a monitoring or a diagnostic function. As noted above, for the evidence elicited to be instructionally tractable, the evidence that is elicited and the way in which it is elicited will need to be driven by both a clear understanding of the learning intentions (whether defined narrowly or broadly) an understanding of progressions in learning (Heritage, 2008), and of the difficulties that learners experience.

However, it would be a mistake to assume that diagnostic assessments are always to be preferred to monitoring assessments, and those that yield instructionally tractable insights into learning are always to be preferred to diagnostic assessments because the range of available decisions might be limited. If the only available decision is whether to require the student to repeat the grade or not, then a simple assessment of the proportion of the intended learning that has been learned will be sufficient. A more diagnostic assessment would be required if the decision is "Which parts of this chapter do I need to review with the class before the end-of-chapter test?"

Nevertheless, in general, to be most effective, instruction needs to be tailored to the specific needs of individual learners, and so a greater range of instructional alternatives than simply repeating sequences of instruction will be required. For formative assessment to be instructionally tractable, the teacher must first be clear about the range of alternative instructional moves that are possible, should then decide what kinds of evidence would be useful in choosing among the relevant alternatives, and only then elicit the evidence needed to make the decision. In other words, the choice of what kind of evidence to elicit is driven by a theory of learning and almost all the intellectual heavy lifting is done before the teacher actually elicits the evidence of achievement.

Providing Feedback that Moves Learners Forward

The requirement for feedback that moves learning forward—the third strategy in Figure 2.1—emphasizes the fact that effective formative assessment is prospective, rather than retrospective. It is the view through the windshield rather than the rear-view mirror or, as Douglas Reeves has memorably suggested, it is the difference between a medical examination and a postmortem (personal communication, October 31, 2008). This encapsulates the two key findings of Kluger and DeNisi (1996) and Hattie and Timperley (2007) discussed above: (1) that it is more productive to think about the processes that are triggered by the feedback intervention, and (2) that feedback interventions are likely to be more effective if they cue attention to the task, how the learner works on the task, and the processes of self-regulation in which the learner engages rather than cue attention to the self. Perhaps even more simply, feedback is likely to be more effective when it causes a cognitive rather than an affective reaction. Of course, whether this happens depends not only on the quality of the feedback, but also on the learner, and the learning milieu in which the feedback is given and received (Black & Wiliam, 2005, 2009)

The other aspect of feedback that moves learning forward is related to instructional adjustments. Instead of providing feedback to the learner, the assessment outcomes may instead provide feedback for the teacher so that he or she can modify the instruction in order to be more effective (whether for the students on whom the data were collected or some other students being taught at some point in the future). In other words, the assessment might be more formative for the teacher than the student.

Activating Students as Owners of Their Own Learning

The last two of the key strategies listed in Figure 2.1 are related to the role of learners in the formative assessment process, including the extent to which students are owners of their own learning and active as learning resources for each other and, for convenience, are here discussed in the reverse order of their appearance in Figure 2.1. For students to become owners of their own learning they need both to own the curricular objectives, and to be active in guiding their own learning—in other words, they must become self-regulated learners. The notion of self-regulated learning is a rich focus of inquiry, with a vast literature of its own, most of which is highly relevant to the notion of formative assessment. Below, a brief summary of some of the most important points is presented so that the interested reader can pursue them in more detail.

Winne (1996) defined self-regulated learning as a "metacognitively governed behavior wherein learners adaptively regulate their use of cognitive tactics and strategies in tasks" (p. 327). Others have pointed out that learners often possess, but do not deploy, the necessary self-regulation skills, and that the problem may be a lack of motivation or volition (Corno, 2001). Still others have argued for the need to look at issues of self-regulation with broader theoretical frames including sociocultural (Hickey & Mc-Caslin, 2001; McCaslin & Hickey, 2001) or social constructivist (Op't Eynde, DeCorte, & Verschaffel, 2001) perspectives.

One of the most general definitions of self-regulation is provided by Boekaerts (2006), who defines the concept as "a multilevel, multicomponent process that targets affect, cognitions, and actions, as well as features of the environment for modulation in the service of one's goals" (p. 347). According to Boekaerts, distinguishing between cognitive and motivational aspects of self-regulated learning is difficult because self-regulated learning is both metacognitively governed *and* affectively charged.

A number of ways of bringing together the motivational and cognitive perspectives on self-regulation have been proposed; summaries of some of these can be found in Wiliam (2007a). For the purpose of this chapter, and in particular in terms of the strategy of activating students as owners of their own learning, a model that is particularly relevant is the *dual processing theory* developed by Boekaerts (1993). According to Boekaerts:

> It is assumed that students who are invited to participate in a learning activity use three sources of information to form a mental representation of the task-in-context and to appraise it: (1) current perceptions of the task and the physical, social, and instructional context within which it is embedded; (2) activated domain-specific knowledge and (meta)cognitive strategies related to the task; and (3) motivational beliefs, including domain-specific capacity, interest and effort beliefs. (2006, p. 349)

When the task appraisal is positive, energy is activated along the growth pathway where the goal is to increase competence. Boekaerts describes this sort of self-regulation as *top-down* because the flow of energy is directed by the student. Attention shifts toward the well-being pathway, where the goal is to prevent threat, harm, or loss when the task appraisal is negative. This form of self-regulation is termed *bottom-up* by Boekaerts because it is triggered by cues in the environment, rather than by learning goals. Where such bottom-up regulation is the norm, then learning is obviously compromised. However, in certain cases it can be positive because, by temporarily attending to well-being, the student may find a way to shift energy and attention back to the growth pathway.

Of course, the relationship between top-down and bottom-up pathways of regulation is dynamic, rather than being a stable feature of an individual learner. Boekaerts (2001) found no direct link between domain-specific motivational beliefs and learning intention in any of the mathematics classrooms under study; students' decisions about whether to invest effort in a mathematics assignment depended primarily on their appraisal of the specific task in front of them, although Ross, Rolheiser, and Hogaboam-Gray (2002) found that students' decisions about whether to invest effort were also influenced by friends and parents.

One of the major strengths of the dual-processing model is that it supports the integration of a variety of different perspectives on the broad idea of activating students as owners of their own learning, including the relationship between motivation and interest, the way that learners attribute their successes and failures in learning, and the way they develop ideas about their self-efficacy.

For example, when students are interested in a task, they are likely to engage in activity along the growth pathway (Hidi & Harackiewicz, 2000). When students are not personally interested in a task, interest may be sparked by something in the task situation, thus also triggering activity along the growth pathway. Where interest is not the main driver of attention, considerations of task value versus cost will become important (Eccles et al., 1983). In terms of the theories of motivation proposed by Deci and Ryan (1994), activity along the growth pathway is associated with motivation stemming from values within the individual while activity along the well-being pathway is associated with values originating outside the individual. In terms of achievement goal theory (Dweck & Leggett, 1986), students displaying mastery orientation are likely to be activating the growth pathway, while those displaying performance orientation are likely to be activating the well-being pathway.

Self-efficacy beliefs (Bandura, 1977) can drive progress along either pathway. Along the growth pathway, self-efficacy drives adaptive cognitive and metacognitive strategy use, whereas along the well-being pathway, self-efficacy beliefs are likely to steer the learner away from performance-avoidance goals and toward performance-approach goals. Similarly views of ability as incremental (Dweck, 2000) help the learner stay on the growth pathway, whereas entity views of ability direct activity toward the well-being pathway, where details of the task-in-context, appraised in the light of views of personal capability, will influence decisions about whether to engage in the task.

Activating Students as Learning Resources for One Another

The final strategy listed in Figure 2.1 is to activate students as learning resources for one another. In some ways this strategy provides a focus for the other four strategies, because it combines aspects of each of them. In order for students to assess the work of others, they have to internalize the learning intentions or the success criteria, and these understandings then become available to the students for use in their own productions (Black et al., 2003). Furthermore, because assessing someone else's work is less emotionally charged than attempting to assess one's own, peer-assessment provides a useful stepping-stone to effective self-assessment, and thus to improved self-regulation in learning (Black et al., 2003, p. 62). In peer tutoring and in other forms of collaborative learning, the peer is frequently cast in the role of teacher, so eliciting evidence and providing feedback are foremost. Indeed, the boundaries between the strategies frequently become blurred. When teachers ask students to review their learning by constructing test items (with correct answers) as studied by Foos, Mora, and Tkacz (1994) students need to think carefully about the learning intentions of the work they have been studying, and about what makes a good way of eliciting evidence. When such items are administered to other learners (Fontana & Fernandes, 1994), students are active as learning resources for one another, and are therefore also improving their own skills of self-regulation.

SUMMARY AND SUGGESTIONS FOR FUTURE WORK

This chapter has provided a brief history of the idea of formative assessment, together with a review of the research that supports its efficacy in educational settings. While there are inevitable methodological problems in synthesizing the results from studies that use different instruments to measure outcomes and are conducted in different traditions, there can be little doubt that increased use of formative assessment is one of the most educationally effective and most cost effective ways of increasing student achievement. Moreover, the effects appear to be generalizable across learning of different types, in a range of contexts, and for learners of all ages.

As the idea of formative assessment has developed, the definition of the term *formative* has ranged from a description of the timing of an assessment (any assessment before "the big one") to a description of a kind of instrument. However, since the evidence from an assessment instrument can be used in a range of ways, this chapter has proposed a definition of formative assessment in terms of the extent to which evidence of learner achievement is used to inform decisions about teaching and learning. In particular, formative assessment is concerned with the creation of, and capitalization upon, moments of contingency in instruction (including both teaching and learning) with a view to regulating learning processes more effectively.

Although somewhat abstract in its formulation, this definition supports immediate application to educational settings in terms of five key strategies:

1. clarifying, sharing and understanding learning intentions and criteria for success;
2. engineering effective classroom discussions, questions, and tasks that elicit evidence of learning;
3. providing feedback that moves learners forward;
4. activating students as the owners of their own learning; and
5. activating students as instructional resources for one another.

The five strategies are, of course, not the only important processes in instruction, but they do appear to be powerful lenses for thinking about practice, and thus for supporting teachers in engaging with wider issues of psychology, pedagogy, and curriculum.

As Kluger and DeNisi (1996) have suggested, further studies designed to identify more precisely the size of impact on student learning that can be achieved with formative assessment are unlikely to be helpful. What is likely to be helpful are studies that relate the kinds of feedback interventions to the learning processes they engender. Such studies, conducted over extended periods of time (at least a year) would also show whether high quality instruction is compatible with increased success on standardized tests, which will be important in developing an understanding of how to improve instruction in settings that make extensive use of tests that are used to hold students and teachers accountable. Without such evidence, attempts at reform are likely to be met with the reactions such as: "I'd love to teach for deep understanding, but I have to raise my test scores."

However, such studies are likely to be ultimately far less important than studies of how to support teachers in making greater use of formative assessment in their own practice. Certainly, everything about what makes for the most effective uses of formative assessment has not yet been discovered; however, enough is known to build a substantial consensus around the kinds of classrooms that are most effective. Far less is known about how to get more such classrooms. As Black and Wiliam (1998a) pointed out:

> It is hard to see how any innovation in formative assessment can be treated as a marginal change in classroom work. All such work involves some degree of feedback between those taught and the teacher, and this is entailed in the quality of their interactions which is at the heart of pedagogy. (p. 16)

There are some success stories here (e.g., Wiliam, Lee, Harrison, & Black, 2004), but very little is known about the factors that support the implementation of educational innovations at scale (Coburn, 2003; Thompson & Wiliam, 2008). In order to secure the improvements in educational outcomes that the existing research on formative assessment has shown is possible, designing ways of supporting teachers to develop their practice of formative assessment at scale must be the main priority.

REFERENCES

Alexander, R. (2008). *Essays on pedagogy*. York, UK: Dialogos.

Allal, L., & Lopez, L. M. (2005). Formative assessment of learning: A review of publications in French. In J. Looney (Ed.), *Formative assessment: Improving learning in secondary classrooms* (pp. 241–264). Paris: Organization for Economic Cooperation and Development.

Bandura, A. (1977). Self-efficacy: Towards a unifying theory of behavioral change. *Psychological Review, 84*(2), 191–215.

Bangert-Drowns, R. L., Kulik, C.-L. C., Kulik, J. A., & Morgan, M. T. (1991). The instructional effect of feedback in test-like events. *Review of Educational Research, 61*(2), 213–238.

Black, P., Harrison, C., Lee, C., Marshall, B., & Wiliam, D. (2003). *Assessment for learning: Putting it into practice*. Buckingham, UK: Open University Press.

Black, P., Harrison, C., Lee, C., Marshall, B., & Wiliam, D. (2004). Working inside the black box: Assessment for learning in the classroom. *Phi Delta Kappan, 86*(1), 8–21.

Black, P. J., & Wiliam, D. (1998a). Assessment and classroom learning. *Assessment in Education: Principles, Policy, and Practice, 5*(1), 7–73.

Black, P. J., & Wiliam, D. (1998b). Inside the black box: Raising standards through classroom assessment. *Phi Delta Kappan, 80*(2), 139–148.

Black, P., & Wiliam, D. (2005). Developing a theory of formative assessment. In J. Gardner (Ed.), *Assessment and learning* (pp. 81–100). London: Sage.

Black, P. J., & Wiliam, D. (2009). Developing the theory of formative assessment. *Educational Assessment, Evaluation, and Accountability, 21*(1), 5–31.

Bloom, B. S. (1984). The search for methods of instruction as effective as one-to-one tutoring. *Educational Leadership, 41*(8), 4–17.

Boekaerts, M. (1993). Being concerned with well being and with learning. *Educational Psychologist, 28*(2), 149–167.

Boekaerts, M. (2001). Context sensitivity: Activated motivational beliefs, current concerns and emotional arousal. In S. Volet & S. Järvelä (Eds.), *Motivation in learning contexts: Theoretical advances and methodological implications* (pp. 17–31). Oxford, England: Pergamon.

Boekaerts, M. (2006). Self-regulation and effort investment. In K. A. Renninger & I. E. Sigel (Eds.), *Handbook of child psychology: Vol. 4. Child psychology in practice* (6th ed., pp. 345–377). New York: Wiley.

Broadfoot, P. M., Daugherty, R., Gardner, J., Gipps, C. V., Harlen, W., James, M., et al. (1999). *Assessment for learning: Beyond the black box*. Cambridge, UK: University of Cambridge School of Education.

Broadfoot, P. M., Daugherty, R., Gardner, J., Harlen, W., James, M., & Stobart, G. (2002). *Assessment for learning: 10 principles*. Cambridge, UK: University of Cambridge School of Education.

Brookhart, S. M. (2004). Classroom assessment: Tensions and intersections in theory and practice. *Teachers College Record, 106*(3), 429–458.

Brookhart, S. M. (2007). Expanding views about formative classroom assessment: A review of the literature. In J. H. McMillan (Ed.), *Formative classroom assessment: Theory into practice* (pp. 43–62). New York: Teachers College Press.

Coburn, C. (2003). Rethinking scale: moving beyond numbers to deep and lasting change. *Educational Researcher, 32*(6), 3–12.

Corno, L. (2001). Volitional aspects of self-regulated learning. In B. J. Zimmerman & D. H. Schunk (Eds.), *Self-regulated leaning and academic achievement: Theoretical perspectives* (2nd ed., pp. 191–225). Hillsdale, NJ: Erlbaum.

Cowie, B., & Bell, B. (1999). A model of formative assessment in science education. *Assessment in Education: Principles, Policy, and Practice, 6*(1), 32–42.

Crooks, T. J. (1988). The impact of classroom evaluation practices on students. *Review of Educational Research, 58*(4), 438–481.

Deci, E. L., & Ryan, R. M. (1994). Promoting self-determined education. *Scandinavian Journal of Educational Research, 38*(1), 3–14.

Dempster, F. N. (1991). Synthesis of research on reviews and tests. *Educational Leadership, 48*(7), 71–76.

Dempster, F. N. (1992). Using tests to promote learning: A neglected classroom resource. *Journal of Research and Development in Education, 25*(4), 213–217.

Denvir, B., & Brown, M. L. (1986a). Understanding of number concepts in low-attaining 7-9 year olds: Part 1. Development of descriptive framework and diagnostic instrument. *Educational Studies in Mathematics, 17*(1), 15–36.

Denvir, B., & Brown, M. L. (1986b). Understanding of number concepts in low-attaining 7–9 year olds: Part II. The teaching studies. *Educational Studies in Mathematics, 17*(2), 143–164.

Dweck, C. S. (2000). *Self-theories: Their role in motivation, personality and development*. Philadelphia: Psychology Press.

Dweck, C. S., & Leggett, E. L. (1986). Motivational processes affecting learning. *American Psychologist, 41*(10), 1040–1048.

Eccles, J. S., Adler, T. F., Futterman, R., Goff, S. B., Kaczala, C. M., Meece, J. L., et al. (1983). Expectancies, values, and academic behaviors. In J. T. Spence (Ed.), *Achievement and achievement motivation* (pp. 75–146). San Francisco: W. H. Freeman.

Elshout-Mohr, M. (1994). Feedback in self-instruction. *European Education, 26*(2), 58–73.

Fontana, D., & Fernandes, M. (1994). Improvements in mathematics performance as a consequence of self-assessment in Portugese primary school pupils. *British Journal of Educational Psychology, 64*(4), 407–417.

Foos, P. W., Mora, J., & Tkacz, S. (1994). Student study techniques and the generation effect. *Journal of Educational Psychology, 86*(4), 567–576.

Forster, M., & Masters, G. N. (2004). Bridging the conceptual gap between classroom assessment and accountability. In M. Wilson (Ed.), *Towards coherence between classroom assessment and system accountability:*

103rd Yearbook of the National Society for the Study of Education (Part II, pp. 51–73). Chicago: University of Chicago Press.

Fuchs, L. S., & Fuchs, D. (1986). Effects of systematic formative evaluation: A meta-analysis. *Exceptional Children, 53*(3), 199–208.

Gipps, C. V., & Stobart, G. (1997). *Assessment: A teacher's guide to the issues* (3rd ed.). London: Hodder and Stoughton.

Hattie, J., & Timperley, H. (2007). The power of feedback. *Review of Educational Research, 77*(1), 81–112.

Heritage, M. (2008). *Learning progressions: Supporting instruction and formative assessment.* Washington, DC: Council of Chief State School Officers.

Hickey, D. T., & McCaslin, M. (2001). A comparative, sociocultural analysis of context and motivation. In S. Volet & S. Järvelä (Eds.), *Motivation in learning contexts* (pp. 33–55). Oxford, UK: Pergamon.

Hidi, S., & Harackiewicz, J. M. (2000). Motivating the academically unmotivated: A critical issue for the 21st century. *Review of Educational Research, 70*(2), 151–179.

James, M. (1992, April). *Assessment for learning.* Assembly session at the annual conference of the Association for Supervision and Curriculum Development, New Orleans, LA.

Kahl, S. (2005, September 21). Where in the world are formative tests? Right under your nose! *Education Week, 25*(4), 11.

Kluger, A. N., & DeNisi, A. (1996). The effects of feedback interventions on performance: A historical review, a meta-analysis, and a preliminary feedback intervention theory. *Psychological Bulletin, 119*(2), 254–284.

Köller, O. (2005). Formative assessment in classrooms: A review of the empirical German literature. In J. Looney (Ed.), *Formative assessment: Improving learning in secondary classrooms* (pp. 265–279). Paris: Organization for Economic Cooperation and Development.

Lewis, C. C. (2002). *Lesson study: A handbook of teacher-led instructional change.* Philadelphia: Research for Better Schools.

Looney, J. (Ed.). (2005). *Formative assessment: Improving learning in secondary classrooms.* Paris: Organisation for Economic Cooperation and Development.

McCaslin, M., & Hickey, D. T. (2001). Educational psychology, social constructivism, and educational practice: A case of emergent identity. *Educational Psychologist, 36*(2), 133–140.

Mitchell, R. (1992). *Testing for learning.* New York: Free Press.

National Assessment of Educational Progress. (2006). *The Nation's Report Card: Mathematics 2005* (Vol. NCES 2006-453). Washington, DC: Institute of Education Sciences.

Natriello, G. (1987). The impact of evaluation processes on students. *Educational Psychologist, 22*(2), 155–175.

Nyquist, J. B. (2003). *The benefits of reconstruing feedback as a larger system of formative assessment: A meta-analysis.* Unpublished master's thesis. Nashville, TN, Vanderbilt University.

Op't Eynde, P., DeCorte, E., & Verschaffel, L. (2001). "What to learn from what we feel?" The role of students' emotions in the mathematics classroom. In S. Volet & S. Järvelä (Eds.), *Motivation in learning contexts: Theoretical advances and methodological implications* (pp. 149–167). Oxford, UK: Pergamon.

Popham, W. J. (2006). Phony formative assessments: Buyer beware! *Educational Leadership, 64*(3), 86–87.

Popham, W. J. (2007, April). *Determining the instructional sensitivity of accountability tests.* Paper presented at the annual meeting of the American Educational Research Association, Chicago.

Pryor, J., & Crossouard, B. (2005, September). *A sociocultural theorization of formative assessment.* Paper presented at Sociocultural Theory in Educational Research and Practice Conference, Brighton, UK.

Ramaprasad, A. (1983). On the definition of feedback. *Behavioural Science, 28*(1), 4–13.

Ross, J. A., Rolheiser, C., & Hogaboam-Gray, A. (2002). Influences on student cognitions about evaluation. *Assessment in Education: Principles, Policy, and Practice, 9*(1), 81–95.

Ruiz-Primo, M. A., Shavelson, R. J., Hamilton, L., & Klein, S. (2002). On the evaluation of systemic science education reform: Searching for instructional sensitivity. *Journal of Research in Science Teaching, 39*(5), 369–393.

Sadler, D. R. (1989). Formative assessment and the design of instructional systems. *Instructional Science, 18*, 119–144.

Shepard, L. A. (2007). Formative assessment: Caveat emptor. In C. A. Dwyer (Ed.), *The future of assessment: Shaping teaching and learning* (pp. 279–303). Mahwah, NJ: Erlbaum.

Shepard, L. A., Hammerness, K., Darling-Hammond, L., Rust, F., Snowden, J. B., Gordon, E., et al. (2005). Assessment. In L. Darling-Hammond & J. Bransford (Eds.), *Preparing teachers for a changing world: What teachers should learn and be able to do* (pp. 275–326). San Francisco, CA: Jossey-Bass.

Shute, V. J. (2008). Focus on formative feedback. *Review of Educational Research, 78*(1), 153–189.

Stiggins, R. J. (2002). Assessment crisis: The absence of assessment for learning. *Phi Delta Kappan, 83*(10), 758–765.

Sutton, R. (1995). *Assessment for learning.* Salford,UK: RS Publications.

Thompson, M., & Wiliam, D. (2008). Tight but loose: A conceptual framework for scaling up school reforms. In E. C. Wylie (Ed.), *Tight but loose: Scaling up teacher professional development in diverse contexts* (RR-08-29, pp. 1–44). Princeton, NJ: Educational Testing Service.

Vinner, S. (1997). From intuition to inhibition: Mathematics, education and other endangered species. In E. Pehkonen (Ed.), *Proceedings of the 21st conference of the International Group for the Psychology of Mathematics Education* (Vol. 1, pp. 63–78). Lahti, Finland: University of Helsinki Lahti Research and Training Centre.

Wiener, N. (1948). *Cybernetics, or the control and communication in the animal and the machine.* New York: Wiley.

Wiliam, D. (2007a). Keeping learning on track: Classroom assessment and the regulation of learning. In F. K. Lester Jr. (Ed.), *Second handbook of mathematics teaching and learning* (pp. 1053–1098). Greenwich, CT: Information Age.

Wiliam, D. (2007b, April). *An index of sensitivity to instruction.* Paper presented at the annual meeting of the American Educational Research Association, Chicago, IL.

Wiliam, D. (2007c). Content *then* process: Teacher learning communities in the service of formative assessment. In D. B. Reeves (Ed.), *Ahead of the curve: The power of assessment to transform teaching and learning* (pp. 183–204). Bloomington, IN: Solution Tree.

Wiliam, D. (2008). International comparisons and sensitivity to instruction. *Assessment in Education: Principles, Policy, and Practice, 15*(3), 253–257.

Wiliam, D., & Black, P. J. (1996). Meanings and consequences: A basis for distinguishing formative and summative functions of assessment? *British Educational Research Journal, 22*(5), 537–548.

Wiliam, D., Lee, C., Harrison, C., & Black, P. J. (2004). Teachers developing assessment for learning: impact on student achievement. *Assessment in Education: Principles Policy and Practice, 11*(1), 49–65.

Wiliam, D., & Thompson, M. (2007). Integrating assessment with instruction: What will it take to make it work? In C. A. Dwyer (Ed.), *The future of assessment: Shaping teaching and learning* (pp. 53–82). Mahwah, NJ: Erlbaum.

Winne, P. H. (1996). A metacognitive view of individual differences in self-regulated learning. *Learning and Individual Differences, 8*, 327–353.

3

THE PRACTICAL IMPLICATIONS OF EDUCATIONAL AIMS AND CONTEXTS FOR FORMATIVE ASSESSMENT

JAMES H. MCMILLAN

Formative assessment in educational practice and research is ubiquitous. The importance of formative assessment is well established, as illustrated by extensive empirical research, chapters in measurement texts, and programs touted by testing companies that purport to facilitate the gathering of formative data to influence instruction. It is helpful to think about formative assessment as primarily a part of an ongoing instructional process. This puts the emphasis on how instructional adjustments will be made as learning occurs and is consistent with the need to demonstrate validity in assessing performance as indicated by how the data are used. We know from years of research that effective instruction depends on many factors, including the style of teaching, objectives, characteristics of students, and the context for learning. There should be strong emphasis, then, on what teachers do with assessment data and how instructional variables may influence the effectiveness of applying different variations of the entire process of formative assessment.

Two such factors are explored in this chapter—educational aims (standards and objectives), and the context of instruction as influenced by sociocultural influences, classroom environment, student ability and achievement, subject matter, and grade level. While there is little empirical research that directly addresses the influence of these factors on student learning as part of formative assessment, there is much research and theory that can be used to provide a foundation for building a research agenda that takes these important factors into consideration. For example, Narciss and Huth (2004) developed a conceptual framework in which instructional objectives and learner characteristics are important to the effectiveness of formative feedback. Also, there is significant broader literature about giving students feedback, and some of that research bears directly on the role feedback plays in formative assessment (Hattie & Timperley, 2007).

Figure 3.1 shows how educational aims and contextual differences can influence various aspects or components of formative assessment. These possible influences will be explored in greater detail, with supporting research and some conjecture about how certain factors influence different aspects of formative assessment.

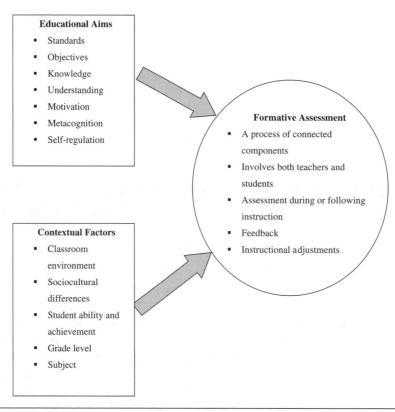

Figure 3.1 The impact of educational aims and contextual factors on formative assessment.

First, it is helpful to describe formative assessment as having different degrees of key characteristics. This way of conceptualizing formative assessment will be useful in examining the influence of educational aims and learning contexts.

FORMATIVE ASSESSMENT AS A CONTINUUM OF CHARACTERISTICS

In 1998, Paul Black and Dylan Wiliam published their seminal article, "Assessment and Classroom Learning." In this article they point out that "the term formative assessment does not have a tightly defined and widely accepted meaning" (p. 7). Since this article was published, much has been written about what formative assessment is, but there are important variations of essential characteristics that are influenced by aims and contexts. Based on the work of Black and Wiliam and others (e.g., Popham, 2008; Sadler, 1989) formative assessment is generally characterized by five features: (1) It is a *process* of several components, not simply a specific test or other assessment; (2) it is used by *both teachers and students;* (3) it takes place *during instruction;* (4) it provides *feedback* to students; and (5) it provides *instructional adjustments* or correctives.

It is helpful to think about these characteristics in terms of a continuum, much like the role of the qualitative researcher is described. That is, a qualitative study can differ with respect to the role of the researcher, from being an unknown observer, to conducting interviews, to becoming a participant in the setting. It helps us to understand the importance of aims and context if we recognize the range of possible variations on how formative assessment is conducted.

There are essentially different versions of formative assessment. Some versions may have feedback provided after an instructional unit, while others will occur on a minute by minute basis as instruction progresses. As pointed out by Wiliam and Leahy (2007), some may think of quarterly benchmark tests as formative. These kinds of tests, however, are not very formative. At best, such assessments can serve as early warning summative assessments, and perhaps predict end-of-year results. However, in a study of Mid-Atlantic school districts in the United States, little relationship was found between benchmark testing results during the school year and scores on end-of-year state accountability tests (Brown & Coughlin, 2007).

Table 3.1 presents an overview of essential formative assessment characteristics. What is called formative assessment can differ with respect to which characteristics are included. Some definitions might only include evidence of student learning and

Table 3.1 Variations of Formative Assessment Characteristics

Characteristic	Low-level Formative	Moderate-level Formative	High-level Formative
Evidence of student learning	Mostly objective, standardized	Some standardized and some anecdotal	Varied assessment, including objective, constructed response, and anecdotal
Structure	Mostly formal, planned, anticipated	Informal, spontaneous, "at the moment"	Both formal and informal
Participants involved	Teachers	Students	Teachers and students
Feedback	Mostly delayed (e.g., give a quiz and give students feedback the next day) and general	Some delayed and some immediate and specific	Immediate and specific for low achieving students, delayed for high achieving students
When done	Mostly after instruction and assessment (e.g., after a unit)	Some after and during instruction	Mostly during instruction
Instructional adjustments	Mostly prescriptive, planned (e.g., pacing according to an instructional plan)	Some prescriptive, some flexible, unplanned	Mostly flexible, unplanned
Choice of task	Mostly teacher determined	Some student determined	Teacher and student determined
Teacher-student interaction	Most interactions based primarily on formal roles	Some interactions based on formal roles	Extensive, informal, trusting, and honest interactions
Role of student self-evaluation	None	Tangential	Integral
Motivation	Extrinsic (e.g., passing a competency test)	Both intrinsic and extrinsic	Mostly intrinsic
Attributions for success	External factors (teacher; luck)	Internal stable factors (e.g., ability)	Internal, unstable factors (e.g., moderate student effort)

feedback, while others contain all 11 characteristics. For example, commercial test publishers claim to provide formative assessment, although the feedback is given to the teacher, not students, with little or no emphasis on instructional adjustments. Teachers may be adept at providing meaningful feedback with little emphasis on student self-evaluation.

Additionally, the nature of formative assessment can vary according to how each characteristic is defined and put into practice. The terms *Low-level*, *Moderate-level*, and *High-level* in Table 3.1 are used as a rubric to highlight these differences. At one end of this continuum, *low-level* formative is rudimentary or primitive formative assessment, which resembles summative assessment. Here the process could be as simple as having students take a test and giving feedback. There would be some intent to improve student performance with feedback, but without some instructional adjustments, labeling this as formative is misleading.

High-level formative involves a complete package that fully integrates ongoing as well as end of unit assessment with instruction. The roles of teachers and students, within a supportive and trusting environment, are such that both are invested in improved student achievement. There is an emphasis on developing student dispositions, such as self-assessment, intrinsic motivation, mastery goal orientation, and independent learning, as well as cognitive outcomes. In between these ends of the continuum, it is possible to have some but not all desired characteristics. These differences will be important in showing how educational aims and context play a role in how formative assessment is implemented in schools

EDUCATIONAL AIMS: STANDARDS AND LEARNING OBJECTIVES

Educational aims can refer to general goals or more specific objectives for student learning. There are cognitive, as well as affective aims and goals that are directly related to content, such as for students to become good citizens. In this chapter the discussion of aims is limited to the level of student cognition that is required, with subsequent consideration of how formative assessment could be operationalized for these different types of thinking.

The standards-based education movement, along with tests-based accountability policy, has had a profound impact on teaching, learning, and formative assessment. One effect on formative assessment in the classroom is that all or most of instruction is focused on the content standards covered by the tests, on passing these tests themselves, and the level of learning that is tested is aligned to the content standards. The level of knowledge that is emphasized will be translated into formative assessment at the same level.

Knowledge and Deep Understanding

Consider the difference between "knowledge" or "simple knowledge" and "deep understanding" (McMillan, 2007; Wiggins & McTighe, 2005). This difference is highlighted by standards-based testing and the lack of teacher skills to assess deep understanding and other higher order forms of cognition. Many standards-based test items focus on what are generally thought to be "lower level" knowledge and skills, despite specifications that call for higher order levels of thinking (Webb, 1999). Webb (2002) reported that more than half of the standards studied required a higher level of cognition than what was measured in test items. Since the strength of multiple-choice items is the ability to measure knowledge and basic skills, these items tend to be at that level of cognition (Lane, 2004).

Furthermore, these tests typically cover an entire year. There is a need to cover much material and to do so with efficiency. The emphasis is on right and wrong, and teachers are required to pace their instruction to cover all the material. In addition, teachers tend to write test items at the simple knowledge level, even though they claim to be testing application, analysis, or synthesis (Crooks, 1988), and they tend to ask recall-type questions in class (Stiggins, Griswold, & Wikelund, 1989).

At issue here is how the cognitive level of test items influences the nature of formative assessment that teachers use. An emphasis on simple knowledge results in teaching and assessment that focuses on what is remembered, something students can reproduce when asked. Perkins (1993) refers to this kind of knowledge as "fragile," resulting in recall or remembering simple explanations, and ritualized skills and applications. Key verbs for this kind of learning include *identifies, retrieves, selects, names, recognizes, reproduces,* and *defines.*

When the emphasis is on deep understanding, instruction and assessment are quite different. Deep understanding involves thinking about one's knowledge and using knowledge for problem-solving, critical thinking, and reflection. It is a matter of applying knowledge to novel problems and tasks. Thinking and reasoning become the focus of teaching, as contrasted with dispensing knowledge. It includes students' ability to explain, justify, compare, and contrast and think flexibly with knowledge. With deep understanding students learn about something in depth—the idea is to develop depth of understanding rather than breadth of knowledge. Students learn how to connect new knowledge with what they already understand and to make connections between existing cognitive frameworks and new information.

What are the implications of simple knowledge and deep understanding objectives for formative assessment? How is formative assessment operationalized for teachers stressing knowledge, and how is this different when teachers want to develop deep understanding? Table 3.2 provides a summary of these differences based on the five essential features of formative assessment noted earlier. There are two rather different types of formative assessment: Formative assessment for knowledge focuses on teachers providing feedback that tells students if their recall or recognition, or other type of remembering, is correct. This is done as teachers first instruct, then test, then verify response accuracy (Kulhavy & Stock, 1989). It is essentially knowledge of results. There may be some instructional adjustments, usually for groups of students or an entire class, but often there is no time provided in pacing guides for much additional teaching.

It has been argued that without such instructional correctives the assessment is not formative (Wiliam & Leahy, 2007). That is, there is a need to show students the discrepancies between their current performance and learning goals, with an emphasis on how to close this gap

In contrast, developing deep understanding by students requires a far different type

Table 3.2 Formative Assessment for Teachers Stressing Knowledge and Deep Understanding Objectives

Formative Feature	Knowledge Emphasis	Deep Understanding Emphasis
A *process* of several components, not simply a specific test or other assessment	Tends to include few components, stressing that students show they know and telling them if they are right or wrong.	Tends to include many components in which teachers continuously cycle assessments, feedback, and instruction.
Used by *both teachers and students*	Used primarily by teachers, with little student input such as correcting answers themselves.	Used by both teachers and students, with an emphasis on student reflection, self-assessment, and self-monitoring.
Takes place *during instruction*	Takes place as a series of small "tests" of knowledge, checking briefly during lessons.	Instruction, assessment, and feedback are seamlessly integrated and continuously looped.
Provides *feedback* to students	Feedback is primarily an indication of "right" or "wrong," and tends to be general for all students. Tends to be judgmental.	Feedback focuses on challenges, questions, probes, focusing on specific, individualized communication. Tends to be informational.
Provides *instructional adjustments* or correctives	Instructional adjustments are minor; students are told to "relearn," or "try again."	Students and teachers determine new ways to learn; leads to differentiated instruction.

of formative assessment, one that is rich with opportunities for frequent teacher–student interaction, which is an essential component of formative assessment that emphasizes the social role that is important in the development of understanding (Driver & Scott, 1995). Students are just as involved in formative assessment as teachers.

When deep understanding is the goal, there is an emphasis on student formative self-assessment. Students judge their performance or progress and determine what further learning is needed. Self-assessment assumes that students have the capacity for recognizing gaps in learning and know how to carry out instructional correctives (Black & Wiliam, 1998). There is a climate of learning that includes continuous cycling of assessment, feedback, and instruction, which occur as students learn.

Perhaps the most significant difference between knowledge-oriented formative assessment and deep understanding formative assessment is in the feedback that is provided to students. With deep understanding, feedback is focused less on right or wrong and more on what students can do to deepen their understanding. Such feedback may include questions, challenges to students, and probes that connect current learning with what students already know and understand. There is an emphasis on situated cognition in deep understanding, so teachers may urge students to apply their understanding to new contexts. In addition, feedback is more specific and individualized.

Not surprisingly, feedback for deep understanding is most consistent with constructivist learning theory and research on the effectiveness of formative feedback. When feedback is individualized, the information can readily be incorporated by the student. Formative feedback as scaffolding enables students to engage in high-level cognitive functions, such as problem solving and facilitation of explanation-centered learning (Shute, 2008). Kluger and DeNisi (1996) have conducted studies that show how feedback can influence metacognitive processes that are central to constructivist theories of learning and motivation. The meta-analysis by Bangert-Drowns, Kulick, Kulick, and Morgan (1991) found support for feedback that helps students monitor and change cognitive operations, adapting these operations so that new information is better incorporated with existing understandings. Other studies have shown how initial cognitive structures form the basis for needed adjustments that result in greater learning (Narciss & Huth, 2004).

Although there are many factors that should be taken into consideration, including student ability level and whether feedback should be immediate or delayed, research shows that specific messages to students that are not too complex nor simple verification are most effective (Brookhart, 2008; Shute, 2008). Feedback for deep understanding supports a mastery orientation to motivation, in which students receive information about the task at hand in an effort to improve understanding, rather than a performance orientation in which feedback is focused on getting a certain grade or passing a test.

It should be noted that targeted student knowledge is essential and that knowledge is the foundation for understanding. The emphasis here is intended to show how deep understanding is best facilitated by formative assessment and that much assessment of simple knowledge is *low-level* formative, as indicated in Table 3.1.

Metacognition and Self-Regulation

Two important skills are supported when using formative assessment for deep understanding: metacognition and self-reflection. Metacognition refers to the students' monitoring, reflecting on, and directing their thinking (Pellegrino, Chudowsky, & Glaser, 2001). It involves monitoring of understanding, being aware of strategies that are used for learning, and recognizing when specific learning goals have been met or need to be revised or improved. A strong case can be made that all students need metacognitive skills for effective problem solving and thinking, but if the emphasis is on knowledge that is remembered, metacognition is unlikely to be a needed skill.

Metacognition is similar to self-regulation, in which students are self-directive. Self-regulation is proactive, in the sense that students set goals, select learning strategies, and processes, and monitor progress toward learning (Zimmerman, 2008). Self-reflective students are actively involved in their own learning and apply metacognitive skills. They use thinking skills such as rehearsal, elaboration, and organization, manage time during learning, keep notes, and seek help when needed. Self-regulating students make decisions about what and how they will learn. They actively devise learning strategies to improve performance. Self-regulation is a broader construct that includes metacognition, self-evaluation, self-reaction, and self-assessment. An emphasis on self-regulation helps students realize that they are responsible for their learning, and that they have the skills they need to take an active role in monitoring and evaluating their performance. These skills allow students to enhance deep understanding (Hattie & Timperley, 2007). Deep understanding is fostered in the sense that learning is connected with current knowledge and understandings.

From the standpoint of formative assessment of deep understanding, metacognition focuses on the process of learning more than the product or outcome. It encourages students to develop self-appraisal and self-management skills that enhance self-directed learning. Students learn how and when to request feedback. They become adept at error detection and correction skills.

THE IMPORTANCE OF CONTEXTUAL FACTORS FOR FORMATIVE ASSESSMENT

Research and practice in education have demonstrated that effective education is not a "one way fits all" enterprise, nor is formative assessment (Kusimo et al., 2000; Tierney & Charland, 2007). There are many contextual factors, such as being in rural or urban environments, students' background characteristics (e.g., socioeconomic status, race, ethnicity, cognitive style, learning modalities), resources, grade level, subject matter, teacher experience, and classroom climate, all of which could affect best practices and their impact on students. There has been very little research that focuses on formative assessment and specific contextual factors, and not all aspects of the school context can be reviewed here. This chapter emphasizes literature that shows how five specific contextual factors may influence formative assessment. These five factors represent some major contextual differences that may need to be taken into account in implementing formative assessment.

The five factors include: (1) classroom environment, (2) sociocultural differences, (3) student ability and achievement, (4) grade level, and (5) subject. Each class is unique with respect to these characteristics. This reality suggests that effective formative assessment is something that is *adapted*, rather than *adopted* (Keeley, 2008). The most important lesson, perhaps, is for teachers to attend carefully to characteristics of their students. These characteristics must be taken into account along with other contextual variables that may influence how well formative assessment can be implemented.

Figure 3.2 illustrates possible interactions between three critical formative assessment components and contextual factors. Each cell represents the possibility of an interaction. For instance, the nature of feedback may differ for elementary as compared to secondary grades, or the manner in which the teacher determines current understanding may differ by subject.

Classroom Environment

Successful high-level formative assessment requires a classroom climate or environment that is conducive to informal questioning and observation, sharing of ideas, safety in taking risks, a norm for giving and receiving feedback, and a clear message by teachers that learning, rather than test performance, is the most important purpose of being in school (Turner et al., 2002). The environment must be supportive of student efforts to receive and act on feedback, and to be willing to fail without negative consequences (Sadler, 1989). Both confirmation and disconfirmation of performance are welcomed.

High-level formative assessment requires that students feel comfortable debating and defending their viewpoints and answers, incorporating the feedback of others, and sharing ideas openly with one another. Classroom norms need to promote social interaction and collaboration, as well as respect, trust, honest communication, and an appreciation and acceptance of student differences (Keeley, 2008). There needs to be

	Contextual Factors				
Formative Assessment Component	Classroom Environment	Sociocultural Differences	Student Ability	Subject Matter	Grade Level
Assessing student understanding during instruction ("at the moment")	Some teachers are better than others in cultivating an informal climate, with trusting communication.	Some students more comfortable than others with an informal climate.	Easier for elementary grades.	Easier for assessing mathematics.	More during instruction in elementary than secondary.
Feedback	Older students need more mastery goal orientations.	Some students respond better than others to oral feedback.	More immediate for low-achieving students.	More spontaneous in English than in mathematics.	More immediate in elementary than secondary.
Instructional adjustments	Older students can have a greater role in self-assessment.	Some students more comfortable with self-assessment.	High achieving students more receptive to different instruction.	Easier to proscribe in mathematics than English.	Immediate for elementary students.

Figure 3.2 Possible interactions between three formative assessment components and contextual factors.

transparency, in which the criteria used to evaluate student work are public and examples are available for all students. The environment must be student-centered, one in which students value and engage actively in applying evaluative criteria in reviewing and improving their work (Stiggins, 2008). Teachers and students engaged in *high-level* formative assessment are partners in learning.

The classroom environment can also differ with respect to the goal structure that is set by the teacher. Goal orientations provide expectations for students' interpretations and reactions to achievement tasks and demands. These orientations are either mastery or performance, though it is common to see both functioning in a classroom (Dweck, 1996; Linnenbrink, 2005). If the goal structure is primarily performance in orientation, with students competing with others and striving for achievement, performance is the primary motivation, as defined by doing well on summative assessments and using social comparisons or normative standards. In contrast, mastery goals focus on developing competence, not just showing competence, and improvement in learning based on self-referenced standards (Pintrich, Conley, & Kempler, 2003).

Formative assessment is most effective in classrooms that emphasize mastery goal orientation. This kind of environment encourages students to seek help (Butler, 1998), to work harder (Farrell & Dweck, 1985), and to have a willingness to accept and use feedback to promote learning. The teacher is more willing to provide helpful feedback and suggest additional activities for further learning, and the student accepts this feedback not as a criticism but as needed information to direct improving competence. As students become more competent, teachers may transfer responsibility of learning to students, resulting in more peer assessment and feedback, self-assessment, and self-reflection (Turner et al., 2002). In contrast, self-assessment, intrinsic motivation, and more autonomy in learning replace teacher-directed student activities, extrinsic motivation, and a performance-oriented environment (Deci & Ryan, 1985).

Popham (2008) emphasizes the need for a shift from a traditional classroom climate to one that is assessment-informed. This change leads to high learning expectations for all students, student responsibility for their learning, and informal assessments that provide data for instructional adjustments. Popham suggests five steps for establishing a classroom climate more friendly to formative assessment: (1) informing students of what is expected (the ground rules); (2) constantly seeking and nurturing trust that a new way of thinking about assessment and learning is needed; (3) modeling and reinforcing appropriate behavior; (4) soliciting student feedback about classroom climate; and (5) assessing the affective status of students.

Sociocultural Differences

The second contextual factor listed in Figure 3.2 is the nature of sociocultural differences in a group of students. The classroom context is heavily influenced by social and cultural mores. In the United States, society is becoming increasingly culturally diverse. The social relationships, cultural norms, and behavioral expectations, all set within larger school and community norms, provide important differences in the manner in which formative assessment is effectively provided (Pryor & Crossouard, 2008). While it is relatively easy to encourage teachers to "take into account students' cultures" when implementing formative assessment, there are no clear guidelines that can be used as rules for taking sociocultural differences into consideration. As each classroom and teacher is different, so too will be the implementation of formative assessment. Research does, however, tell us something about what to be aware of and what to look for.

One way to avoid cultural bias is to simplify the language, sentence structure, vocabulary, and syntax of formative assessments (Abedi, this volume; Wiggins, 1993). It is also helpful for teachers to introduce and explain language that may not be familiar or may have different meanings, depending on student ethnicity, dominant native language, or socioeconomic status. This reduces student dependency on language used by the dominant culture, and can be very helpful in framing feedback. Another action teachers can take is to ask students if they would like clarification or further information. Here the observational skills of the teacher are important. Teachers need to be able to notice and act upon nonverbal cues (McMillan, 2007).

Since much of formative assessment relies on an interaction between the teacher and student, and language is a crucial part of that interaction, it is incumbent on teachers to make a special effort to understand student communication, to show respect for and never denigrate a student's language, and to work at drawing out student responses that may otherwise be masked by a student's reluctance based on cultural background. The best indicators of students' understanding may be what they show within their social group (Shepard, 2006). Whether the teacher should or should not force students from different backgrounds to accommodate to the dominant culture is debatable, but initially, until a norm in the classroom is developed, teachers are most effective when they can reach and communicate with students in the students' native language.

The nature of the teacher–student relationship is crucial to formative assessment. This includes development of a sense of belonging in the group and acceptance by other students and the teacher. If students believe that they are accepted, regardless of their differences with other students, they will be more likely to participate in class and to not conform or disengage to protect their identity (Osterman, 2000). When an authentic, trusting, and caring relationship develops, interactions will be more honest and useful (Bell & Cowie, 2001). Students accept feedback from teachers when they believe teachers have the students' best interests in mind. Furthermore, students are more likely to be honest and to initiate contact through questions.

Cultural differences may be important in initial teacher assessments of students. As pointed out by Shepard (2006), student responses may be based on inherent cultural norms that make it difficult for the teacher to make accurate judgments about prior knowledge. For example, some cultures may not use decontextualized questions, such as "What shape is this?" The divergence from their culturally normative discourse could make it difficult for some students to answer this kind of question in class.

Other student sociocultural factors that may impact specific aspects of formative assessment include cognitive style and thinking orientation (McMillan, 2007; Trumbull & Pacheco, 2005). Some students may have a more field dependent (global) rather than field independent (analytical) cognitive style. Some may be more holistic than analytical in their thinking. Some students are stronger with oral rather than written instruction. While these trends may be specific to a given culture, it is important for teachers to view culturally different students as individuals who may or may not exhibit characteristics of dominant mores (Bell & Cowie, 2001). Formative assessment that is *low level* may ignore these cultural differences, while formative assessment that is *high level* varies in questions asked, interpretation of student responses, and what is needed to create the most positive classroom environment based on students' cultural characteristics.

Student Ability and Achievement

The third contextual factor that influences the effectiveness of formative assessment is student ability and achievement. There is some evidence that low-achieving students may need more immediate feedback, while higher-achieving students may benefit more from delayed feedback, especially with complex tasks (Mason & Bruning, 2001). There is also evidence that low-ability students benefit from receiving the correct response, rather than feedback such as "try again," and self-referenced attributions to effort and ability that helps students understand that progress is due to their efforts and capability (Shute, 2008). It could be that higher achieving students are affected more by challenge and questioning and that lower ability students need more verification and confirmation of being on track.

It has been shown that, for low achieving students, immediate specific feedback is needed, while for high achieving students, effective feedback is contingent on the level of the task. For high achieving students, immediate feedback is needed on lower level tasks, but delayed feedback is best on higher level tasks (Mason & Bruning, 2001). Higher achieving students may need less specific feedback than low achieving students.

When prior knowledge is low, there should be an emphasis on response contingency (correct or incorrect), while with high prior knowledge there should be more emphasis on reviewing relevant information to enable students to determine their errors in thinking. In general, the more extensive the prior knowledge base, the more elaborative the feedback can be to facilitate learning. This is because students have a larger base of information to which new ideas can be related and applied (Mason & Bruning, 2001). It allows for more student-generated thinking and behavior to seek what is needed to reach the learning target.

Within these general rules are exceptions. Academically successful students are receptive to feedback, and they are aware that they need this information to improve their knowledge, understanding, and skills. They tend to be engaged and motivated, with a sense of self-determination that, in one sense, requires minimum feedback, or something general such as "great work" or "excellent." However, high achieving students need much more than verification that they are correct; these students need specific feedback that challenges them to learn more and is focused on the subsequent learning that would be worthwhile (Brookhart, 1997, 2008). It is best to include feedback about the process of their learning as well as the content of their responses.

It is not in the best interest of low-achieving students to only give immediate feedback. Otherwise, an undesirable self-fulfilling prophesy may be reinforced. With struggling students, feedback is more effective if it is based on what they did correctly and how their efforts are specifically related to attainment of the learning targets. This kind of task-specific feedback is helpful because it stresses the importance of learning, rather than the ability or status of the student. Comparisons should not be made with the performance of other students, only to the criteria. Complex tasks should be broken into smaller, more manageable steps. Often only one or two points can be made to help students focus on a part of what is learned, rather than the whole.

It is also helpful to check with struggling students, just as it is with all students, to make sure they understand the feedback. If students are completely inattentive to feedback, these negative behaviors need to be addressed. Feedback must be honest, but there is a need to avoid a self-fulfilling prophesy in which poor work is expected, produced, and then criticized (Brookhart, 2008).

The nature of feedback provided to students with different levels of ability and achievement illustrates the difference between *low-level* and *high-level* formative assessment summarized in Table 3.1. While a claim could be made that assessment is formative if most any kind of feedback is provided, feedback that differs based on ability and achievement represents a more sophisticated understanding and application.

Grade Level

The fourth contextual factor that affects formative assessment is grade level. At the elementary level, teachers depend heavily on observations of students to inform their evaluation of student progress (Gipps, McCallum, & Hargreaves, 2000). This means that it is essential for teachers to attend to and accurately interpret student behavior, whether verbal or nonverbal. Facial expressions and body language are indicators of understanding and engagement (McMillan, 2007). Oral and written brief feedback is necessary for younger students, in which a small number of indications of success are used: improvement suggestions, reminder prompts, scaffolded prompts, and example prompts (Clarke, 2003). In a recent study by Andrade, Du, and Wang (2008), third and fourth grade students were able to generate criteria from exemplars and use self-assessment, and students using these skills showed stronger writing scores. This suggests that it is possible for elementary students to understand and apply evaluative criteria and engage in self-assessment.

Because of the structure of elementary school, in which teachers are primarily responsible for one class, it is much easier to adjust time and assignments to determine student understanding, give individual specific feedback, and accommodate learning inadequacies. At this level, teachers can spend sufficient time with students, either individually or in small groups and engage in formative assessment that occurs "on the fly" or "at the moment" or "at a teachable moment." This also allows students time to immediately think about and evaluate their learning. Middle and high school teachers typically do not have that time. Consequently, feedback is often delayed and more planned than spontaneous.

With older students, techniques can depend more on student initiative. One simple method, for example, is the traffic light approach. With this technique students are taught how to use green, red, and yellow self-adhesive spots as "traffic lights" when they hand in their work. The colors reflect their evaluation of their understanding of what is being learned. A green spot indicates that they are confident that they understand the material, a red spot that they do not understand it, and a yellow spot that they are unsure (Harlen, 2007). Secondary students can use other methods to communicate with teachers, including the use of computer prompts while engaged in learning, to give the teacher feedback in terms of their self-evaluations.

These types of techniques are needed for formative assessment to occur during teaching. More typically, secondary students take quizzes or tests or hand in papers that are then graded and returned, with suggestions for further learning. Some may refer to this process as formative assessment, but its nature and impact are not the same as when assessment, evaluation, feedback, and instructional suggestions are made concurrently with instruction.

It would also be more appropriate for older students to make decisions about what further instruction is needed to help them with a complete understanding of what is taught. Teachers can provide choices ahead of time so that it is relatively easy for students to indicate how they would like to proceed, for example, relearning with a new way of taking notes, meeting with the teacher or other students, using the computer to find additional ways of learning, or reading and studying other teacher-provided materials.

Older students are more capable of constructing and using scoring rubrics, and reflecting on their performance. This activity is helpful in internalizing evaluative criteria and studying examples of previously submitted work. Andrade et al. (2008) summarize the results of several studies of middle and high school students that show how student use of rubrics can influence student achievement and understanding of evaluative criteria.

Rubrics can also be used for student self-assessment. Self-assessment and self-evaluation are excellent techniques for older students, and increasingly are seen as effective skills for formative assessment (McMillan & Hearn, 2008). It has been demonstrated that self-assessment is a very valuable skill to enhance the effective use of feedback (Andrade, this volume; Black & Wiliam, 1998; Sadler, 1989; Sadler & Good, 2006). Furthermore, self-evaluation with appropriate teacher feedback focused more on the process of applying evaluative criteria than on the correct answer can enhance student motivation by reinforcing internal attributions and promoting self-efficacy. Students are more able to see that understanding is under their control and will have positive expectations about further learning. If students are unable to relate feedback to the reasons for poor performance, self-efficacy may be diminished (Hattie & Timperley, 2007).

In summary, elementary teachers have the time and opportunity to observe learning, evaluate student understanding, give feedback, and apply instructional correctives. These approaches are more teacher- than student-directed, though older elementary students are capable of self-evaluation. At the secondary level, students have the cognitive skills they need to self-assess, self-evaluate, and pick instructional correctives when needed, but there is less teacher attention toward individual students and often an emphasis on simple knowledge. At the secondary level, teachers need systems to monitor learning, provide feedback, and identify subsequent instruction.

Subject Matter

The fifth and final contextual factor is the subject matter. For the most part, the literature does not specifically compare subject matters in terms of what formative assessment consists of or how it is operationalized. There is no paucity, however, of literature applying formative assessment to subject matters individually (e.g., Bell & Cowie, 2001; Black & Harrison, 2001; Harlen, 2007; Marshall, 2007). Virtually all subject matters have integrated formative assessment to some extent, and have identified resources that help teachers implement formative assessment in their classrooms.

Much of the research on formative assessment has been done with math and science (Tierney & Charland, 2007), in which there is a relatively clear path of progression of targeted outcomes (Marshall, 2007). In these subjects, especially mathematics, there is often a predetermined sequence of what is learned and how it is taught. This affects formative assessment because feedback and instructional correctives are relatively easy to conduct for most students. Often teachers fill-in or elaborate on what is presented in books or online to identify learning gaps and specify what next steps are needed for closing the gaps. There is a predictive nature to the assessment, almost as if it could all be computerized with appropriate links based on errors. The formative assessment tends to be planned and structured.

In English and the humanities, however, teaching and progression becomes "a more meandering, organic affair" (Marshall, 2007, p. 137). English, in particular, emphasizes ideas, imagination, and creativity. Humanities teachers tend to use questioning and feedback in a dynamic way to enhance students' thinking and deep understanding. They are initiated based on student contributions and questions, which are often impromptu, varied, and unpredictable. Much student assessment, then, is done "at the moment," without preplanned feedback and responses. These outcomes are more challenging to assess than science and mathematics outcomes, whether summative or formative.

This is not to say that science and mathematics classrooms cannot share these characteristics. Stemhagen and Smith (2008) assert that viewing mathematics as unique contributes to the lack of social interaction needed for student self-assessment and self-directed learning, as well as the social construction of mathematical knowledge. Philosophical assumptions about teaching mathematics in the current standards-based world of education are particularly entrenched, and, by extension, math influences the sciences.

It is easier to focus on content, simple understanding, and a highly prescribed sequence of learning. Curriculum and assessments tend to be well aligned, promoting planned formative and summative assessment. This is what occurs with benchmark or quarterly testing. The tests are administered, using the same format as high-stakes accountability tests (usually multiple-choice), graded, and returned to teachers for planning subsequent instruction. This sequential set of steps encourages an emphasis on simple understanding.

When mathematics and science teachers emphasize inquiry, thinking skills, and problem solving, there is greater emphasis on "at the moment" formative assessment. For example, as students are engaged in projects, teachers continuously monitor progress, give feedback, and make suggestions. There is a greater likelihood of developing an appropriate climate and student self-assessment, self-reflection, and metacognitive skills, though many mathematics and science projects are structured and predictable.

Most important, perhaps, is that formative assessment in different subjects is more the same than different. Teaching in all subjects can be guided by the same principles of constructivist learning theory and the need for students to develop thinking skills and deep understanding associated with what they are learning. This means that instruction and formative assessment needs to focus on meaningful patterns, connections, and application, rather than on isolated facts and concepts. If teaching is highly regulated, paced, content driven, tightly defined and prescribed, the opportunities for formative assessment are limited, no matter what subject is being taught. These characteristics drive formative assessment more than content does.

SUMMARY

The purpose of this chapter was to introduce ways that formative assessment can vary, depending on educational aims and contextual factors. The idea that there could be important differences in the degree of formative assessment (*low-level, moderate-level* or *high-level*) or in the number of characteristics employed (e.g., assessment and feedback without instructional correctives) was used to illustrate how aims and context need to be considered. That is, the nature of effective formative assessment will vary, based on the cognitive level the outcomes and on contextual factors. Educational aims that stress deep understanding, reasoning, metacognition, and self-regulation are better suited to *high-level* formative assessment than are targets that emphasize simple knowledge. A classroom climate that is characterized by trust, respect, tolerance for differences, open and honest communication, collaboration, and a mastery orientation is more likely to support effective formative assessment. Students need to be encouraged to take risks and self-monitor. Specific practices that result in effective *high-level* formative assessment depend on previous student achievement, sociocultural traits, age, and subject matter.

Formative assessment is not a "one size fits all" practice. Rather, it is differentiated, depending on student characteristics, learning objectives, and situational factors. There are many variables to consider in effectively developing and implementing different levels of formative assessment. While several of these factors have been considered here, further research will provide a better understanding of the impact of these factors on implementing effective formative assessment in different contexts.

NOTE

The author is grateful for helpful and constructive comments on earlier drafts of this chapter from Lisa Abrams and Jason Smith of Virginia Commonwealth University, Rick Stiggins, and the book editors.

REFERENCES

Andrade, H. L., Du, Y., & Wang, X. (2008). Putting rubrics to the test: The effect of a model, criteria generation, and rubric-referenced self-assessment on elementary school students' writing. *Educational Measurement: Issues and Practice, 27*(2), 3–13.

Bangert-Drowns, R. L., Kulik, C. C., Kulik, J. A., & Morgan, M. T. (1991). The instructional effect of feedback in test-like events. *Review of Educational Research, 61*, 213–238.

Bell, B., & Cowie, B. (2001). *Formative assessment and science education.* London: Kluwer.

Black, P., & Harrison, C. (2001). Feedback in questioning and marking: The science teacher's role in formative assessment. *School Science Review, 82*, 55–61.

Black, P., & Wiliam, D. (1998). Assessment and classroom learning. *Assessment in Education: Principles, Policy and Practice, 5*(1), 7–73.

Brookhart, S. M. (1997). A theoretical framework for the role of classroom assessment in motivating student effort and achievement. *Applied Measurement in Education, 10*, 161–180.

Brookhart, S. M. (2008). *How to give effective feedback to your students.* Alexandria, VA: Association of Supervision and Curriculum Development.

Brown, R. S., & Coughlin, E. (2007). *The predictive validity of selected benchmark assessments used in the Mid-Atlantic Region* (Issues & Answers Report, REL 2007-N. 017). Washington, DC: U.S. Department of Education, Institute of Educational Sciences, National Center for Education Evaluation and Regional Assistance, Regional Educational Laboratory Mid-Atlantic.

Butler, R. (1998). Determinants of help seeking: Relations between perceived reasons for classroom help-avoidance and help-seeking behaviors in an experimental context. *Journal of Educational Psychology, 87*, 630–643.

Clarke, S. (2003). *Enriching feedback in the primary classroom: Oral and written feedback from teachers and children.* London: Hodder & Stoughton.

Crooks, T. J. (1988). The impact of classroom evaluation practices on students. *Review of Educational Research, 58*(4), 438–481.

Deci, E. L., & Ryan, R. M. (1985). *Intrinsic motivation and self-determination in human behavior.* New York: Plenum.

Driver, R., & Scott, P. (1995). Mind in communication: A response to Erick Smith. *Educational Researcher, 23*(7), 27–28.

Dweck, C. (1996). Social motivation: Goals and social-cognitive processes. In J. Juvonen & K. R. Wentzel (Eds.), *Social motivation* (pp. 181–198). New York: Cambridge University Press.

Farrell, E., & Dweck, C. S. (1985). *The role of motivation processes in transfer of learning.* Unpublished manuscript.

Gipps, R., McCallum, B., & Hargreaves, E. (2000). *What makes a good primary school teacher? Expert classroom strategies.* London: Routledge Falmer.

Guskey, T. R. (2007). Formative classroom assessment and Benjamin S. Bloom: Theory, research, and practice. In J. H. McMillan (Ed.), *Formative classroom assessment: Theory into practice* (pp. 63–68). New York: Teachers College Press.

Harlen, W. (2007). Formative classroom assessment in science and mathematics. In J. H. McMillan (Ed.), *Formative classroom assessment: From theory into practice* (pp. 136–152). New York: Teachers College Press.

Hattie, J., & Timperley, H. (2007). The power of feedback. *Review of Educational Research, 77*(1), 81–112.

Keeley, P. (2008). *Science formative assessment.* Thousand Oaks, CA: Corwin.

Kluger, A. N., & DeNisi, A. (1996). The effects of feedback interventions on performance: A historical review, a meta-analysis, and a preliminary feedback intervention theory. *Psychological Bulletin, 119*(2), 254–284.

Kulhavy, R. W., & Stock, W. (1989). Feedback in written instruction: The place of response certitude. *Educational Psychology Review, 1*(4), 279–308.

Kusimo, P., Ritter, M. G., Busick, K., Ferguson, C., Trumbull, E., & Solano-Flores, G. (2000). *Making assessment work for everyone: How to build on student strengths.* San Francisco: WestEd.

Lane, S. (2004). Validity of high-stakes assessment: Are students engaged in complex thinking? *Educational Measurement: Issues and Practice, 43*(3), 6–14.

Linnenbrink, E.A. (2005). The dilemma of performance-approach goals: The use of multiple goal contexts to promote students' motivation and learning. *Journal of Educational Psychology, 97*(2), 197–213.

Marshall, B. (2007). Formative classroom assessment in English, the humanities, and social sciences. In J. H. McMillan (Ed.), *Formative classroom assessment: From theory into practice* (pp. 136-152). New York: Teachers College Press.

Mason, V. J., & Bruning, R. (2001). *Providing feedback in computer-based instruction: What the research tells us.* Lincoln, NB: Center for Instructional Innovation, University of Nebraska-Lincoln. Retrieved July 9, 2008, from http://dwb.unl.edu/Edit/MB/MasonBruning.html

McMillan, J. H. (2007). *Classroom assessment: Principles and practice for effective standards-based education* (4th ed.). Boston: Allyn & Bacon.

McMillan, J. H., & Hearn, J. (2008). Student self-assessment: The key to stronger student motivation and higher achievement. *Educational Horizons, 87*(1), 40–49.

Narciss, S., & Huth, K. (2004). How to design informative tutoring feedback for multi-media learning. In H. M. Niegemann, D. Leuther, & R. Brunken (Eds.), *Instructional design for multimedia learning* (pp. 181-196). Munster, NY: Waxmann.

Osterman, K. E. (2000). Students' need for belonging in the school community. *Review of Educational Research, 70*(3), 323–367.

Pellegrino, J. W., Chudowsky, N., & Glaser, R. (2001). *Knowing what students know: The science and design of educational assessment.* Washington, DC: National Academy Press.

Perkins, D. (1993). *Smart schools.* New York: Simon and Schuster.

Pintrich, P. R., Conley, A. M., & Kempler, T. M. (2003). Current issues in achievement goal theory research. *International Journal of Educational Research, 39*, 319–337.

Popham, W. J. (2008). *Transformative assessment.* Alexandria VA: Association for Supervision and Curriculum Development.

Pryor, J., & Crossouard, B. (2008). A socio-cultural theorization of formative assessment. *Oxford Review of Education, 34*(1), 1–20.

Sadler, D. R. (1989). Formative assessment and the design of instructional systems. *Instructional Science, 18*(2), 119–144.

Sadler, D. R., & Good, E. (2006). The impact of self- and peer-grading on student learning. *Educational Assessment, 11*(1), 1–31.

Stemhagen, D., & Smith, J. W. (2008). Dewey, democracy, and mathematics education: Reconceptualizing the last bastion of curricular certainty. *Education and Culture: The Journal of the John Dewey Society, 24*(2), 25–40.

Shepard, L. A. (2006). Classroom assessment. In R. L. Brennan (Ed.). *Educational measurement* (4th ed., pp. 623–646). Westport, CT: Praeger.

Shute, V. J. (2008). Focus on formative feedback. *Review of Educational Research, 78*(1), 153–189.

Stiggins, R. J. (2008). *Introduction to student-involved assessment for learning* (5th ed.). Upper Saddle River, NJ: Merrill/Prentice Hall.

Stiggins, R. J., Griswold, M. M., & Wikelund, K. R. (1989). Measuring thinking skills through classroom assessment. *Journal of Educational Measurement, 26*, 233–246.

Tierney, R. D., & Charland, J. (2007, April). *Stocks and prospects: Research on formative assessment in secondary classrooms.* Paper presented at the annual meeting of the American Educational Research Association, Chicago.

Trumbull, E., & Pacheco, M. (2005). *Leading with diversity: Cultural competencies for teacher preparation and professional development, Part II: Culture.* Providence, RI: The Education Alliance.

Turner, J. C., Midgley, C., Meyer, D. K., Gheen, M., Anderman, E. M., & Kang, Y. (2002). The environment and students' reports of avoidance strategies in mathematics: A multimethod study. *Journal of Educational Psychology, 94*(1), 88–106.

Webb, N. L. (1999). *Alignment of science and mathematics standards and assessments in four states* (NISE Research Monograph N. 18). Madison, WI: University of Wisconsin-Madison, National Institute for Science Education.

Webb, N. L. (2002, April). *An analysis of the alignment between mathematics standards and assessments for three states.* Paper presented at the annual meeting of the American Educational Research Association, New Orleans, LA.

Wiggins, G. (1993). *Assessing student performance: Exploring the purpose and limits of testing.* San Francisco: Jossey-Bass.

Wiggins, G., & McTighe, J. (2005). *Understanding by design.* Alexandria, VA: Association for Supervision and Curriculum Development.

Wiliam, D., & Leahy, S. (2007). A theoretical foundation for formative assessment. In J. H. McMillan (Ed.). *Formative classroom assessment: Theory into practice.* New York: Teachers College Press.

Zimmerman, B. J. (2008). Investigating self-regulation and motivation: Historical background, methodological developments, and future prospects. *American Educational Research Journal, 45*(1), 166–183.

II

Formative Assessment Methods and Practice

4

PEERS AS A SOURCE OF FORMATIVE ASSESSMENT

KEITH J. TOPPING

Formative feedback has been promoted as essential in skill development and motivation, and has been studied endlessly, with somewhat mixed results (Shute, 2008). These equivocal results partly stem from the great variety in forms of feedback, contexts for feedback, learner characteristics, and outcomes measured. Feedback can have negative consequences, so it is important to ask what we can learn about *effective* formative feedback. Critical or controlling feedback, grades with a low level of specificity, and interruptive or distracting feedback can have a negative effect. Task-level feedback tends to be more specific and timely than general feedback. Black and Wiliam (1998) also distinguish directive and facilitative feedback, the first telling the student what needs to be revised, the second providing comments and suggestions to encourage students in their own revision. It is likely that both are necessary—the first to provide short term development of the work, and the second to enhance transfer to new tasks.

Formative feedback can thus be both positive and negative in content, and is tricky even for teachers. Positive feedback enables students to be assured what aspects of their work are satisfactory, and to focus their limited processing capacities on aspects needing improvement. The effectiveness of feedback depends upon the receptivity or "mindfulness" of the recipient (Bangert-Drowns, Kulik, Kulik, & Morgan, 1991). Feedback can be norm-referenced or self-referenced, and there is evidence that self-referenced feedback is more effective, especially for students of lower ability (Shute, 2008). Negative feedback indicates a gap between what is and what should be—the art of the assessor to feed back only sufficient negative information to avoid dispiriting the student and encourage the making of modest improvements. Feedback which either lacks specificity or is too directive could be damaging. Feedback which is too long will be ignored. Narciss and Huth (2004) argue that feedback can vary in content, function, and presentation, and each of these requires consideration.

It seems that there is a lot for the assessor to handle. How certain can we be that a teacher is considering all these variables in giving formative feedback? And in relation to peer assessment, how could a peer assessor develop all these competences? There are many more students than teachers in most classrooms. Consequently, feedback from peers can be more immediate, timely, and individualized than teacher feedback. True, it may take peers some time to develop the appropriate skills, and they will certainly need training, but their availability is overwhelming.

Peer assessment also promotes reflection. The assessed student might not accept any of the peer feedback but has to pause and reflect when confronted with it, perhaps leading to alternative changes to the work. Students react differently to feedback from adults and peers. The former is perceived as authoritative (however wrongly) but poorly explained, while the latter gives richer feedback that is open to negotiation (e.g., Cole, 1991).

Thus peer assessment is an effective but underutilized type of formative assessment. It helps gather information for adapting teaching and learning to the current functioning and future needs of students (Topping, 2009). It can be summative or formative or both; a formative view is presented here.

DEFINITION

Assessment is the determination of the amount, level, value, or worth of something. Peer assessment is an arrangement for learners to consider and specify the level, value, or quality of a product or performance of other equal-status learners (Topping & Ehly, 1998). "Equal status" can be interpreted exactly or with flexibility; in the latter case, a peer can be anyone within a few years in the education system. It is classroom-based, frequent, and relatively brief. It may operate through classroom tests, discussions, projects, or homework. The work to be assessed can include writing, oral presentations, portfolios, test performance, or other skilled behaviors. This may be coupled with oral questioning in small groups or dyads. In formative peer assessment, learners give elaborated, qualitative, formative feedback about the relative worth of each other's work. Peer assessment can be done one-to-one or mutually in small groups. The latter yields greater aggregate reliability but involves more time. It can be done face-to-face or remotely. Feedback from peers can be given anonymously, if required.

Thus formative peer assessment capitalizes on its richness as a form of feedback. The intention is to help learners help each other plan their learning, identify their strengths and weaknesses, target areas for remedial action, and develop a better product or performance. The practicalities dictate that peer assessment usually needs to be conducted in dyads or small groups, since to do it more widely would involve all learners in too much assessment. Although learning gains for both the assessee and assessor are expected, an excess of assessment would be difficult to justify.

TYPOLOGY

Many different kinds of peer assessment exist. Ways in which peer assessment can vary are identified below, and the following discussion is not exhaustive. Peer assessment can operate in different curriculum areas or subjects. It can occur in or out of class. Consequently, involvement in peer assessment can develop transferable skills for life, since all of us may expect to be peer assessor and peer assessee at different times and in different contexts.

A wide variety of products or outputs can be peer assessed, including writing, port-folios, oral presentations, test performance, or other skilled behaviors. The participant constellation can vary: The assessors and the assessed may be individuals or pairs or groups. Directionality can vary as well. Peer assessment can be one-way, reciprocal, or mutual. Assessors and assessed may come from the same or different year of study, and be of the same or different ability. Finally, the objectives of peer assessment may vary: The teacher may target cognitive or metacognitive gains, time saving, or other goals.

Obviously, performance as a peer assessor is likely to improve with practice. Along the way, both assessors and assessed should develop their social, communicative, meta-cognitive and other personal and professional skills. A peer assessor with less skill at assessment but more time in which to do it can produce an assessment of equal reli-ability and validity to a teacher. Peer feedback is available in greater volume and with greater immediacy than teacher feedback. However, implementation is not without cost in teacher time, particularly at the outset.

THEORETICAL UNDERPINNINGS

A deep understanding of how peer assessment obtains its positive effects should enable both researchers and practitioners to design ever more adaptive and effective forms of peer assessment. However, for many years peer assessment was undertheorized, sup-ported simply by old sayings such as "to teach is to learn twice." In the last 25 years, a number of researchers have conducted work that has strong implications for building a theory of peer learning (e.g., Chi, Siler, Jeong, Yamauchi & Hausmann, 2001; King, 1998; Sluijsmans & Prins, 2006). But because a plethora of theories does not help the hard-pressed practitioner, synthesis into a single theoretical model has been sought.

The model in Figure 4.1 (Topping, 2005) initially assigns some of the main subpro-cesses of peer assessment into five categories. The first of these includes organizational or structural features of the learning interaction, such as the need and press inherent in peer assessment toward increased time on task and actually engaged with task; the need for both helper and helped to elaborate goals and plans; the individualization of learning; the immediacy of feedback possible within the small-group or one-on-one situation; and the variety of a novel kind of learning interaction.

The cognitive conflict category encompasses the Piagetian school of thought. This concerns the need to loosen cognitive blockages formed from old myths and false beliefs by presenting conflict and challenge via one or more peers. By contrast, Vygotskian theory incorporates support and scaffolding from a more competent other, necessitat-ing management of activities to be within the Zone of Proximal Development of both parties in order to avoid any damaging excess of challenge (Vygotsky, 1978). The helper seeks to manage and modulate the demands upon the learner made by information processing to maximize the rate of progress—neither too much nor too little. The helper also provides a cognitive model of competent performance. The cognitive demands upon the helper are great in terms of monitoring learner performance and detecting, diagnosing, correcting, and otherwise managing misconceptions and errors; herein lies much of the cognitive exercise and benefit for the helper.

Peer assessment also makes heavy demands upon the communication skills of both helper and helped, and in so doing develops those skills. All participants might never

Groups of Processes Influencing Effectiveness:

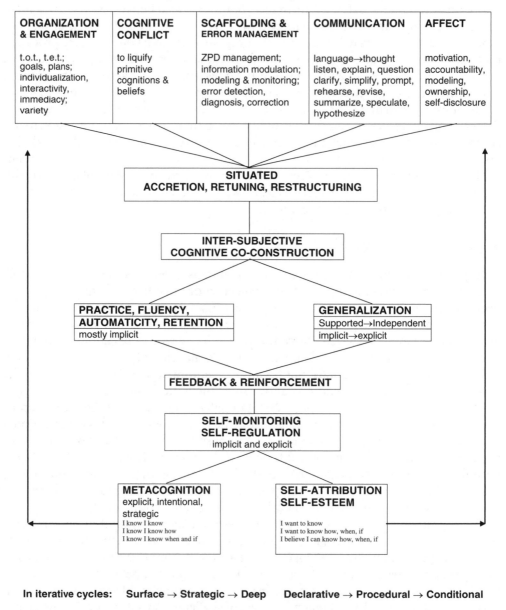

Figure 4.1 Peer assisted learning: Groups of factors influencing effectiveness.

have truly grasped a concept until they had to explain it to another, embodying and crystallizing thought into language—another Vygotskian idea, of course. Listening, explaining, questioning, summarizing, speculating, and hypothesizing are all valuable skills of effective peer assessment which should be transferable to other contexts.

The affective component of peer assessment is also very powerful. A trusting relationship with a peer who holds no position of authority might facilitate self-disclosure of ignorance and misconception, enabling subsequent diagnosis and correction that could not occur otherwise. Modeling of enthusiasm and competence, and belief in the possibility of success by the helper can influence the self-confidence of the helped, while a sense of loyalty and accountability to each other can help to keep the pair motivated and on task.

These five categories or subprocesses of level 1 feed into a larger onward process in level 2 of extending each other's declarative knowledge, procedural skill, and conditional and selective application of knowledge and skills. This occurs by adding to and extending current capabilities (accretion), modifying current capabilities (retuning), and, in areas of completely new learning or cases of gross misconception or error, building new understanding (restructuring). These are somewhat similar to Piagetian concepts of assimilation and accommodation. This leads in level 3 to the joint construction of a shared understanding between helper and helped, which is adapted to the idiosyncrasies of their perceptions (i.e., is intersubjective), is firmly situated within the current authentic context of application, and forms a foundation for further progress.

As a result of the processes in the first three levels of Figure 4.1, peer assessment enables and facilitates a greater volume of engaged and successful practice, leading to consolidation, fluency, and automaticity of thinking, and social, communicative, and other core skills (level 4). Much of this might occur implicitly; that is, without the helper or helped being fully aware of what is happening with them. Simultaneously or subsequently, peer assessment can lead to generalization from the specific example in which a concept is learned, extending the ability to apply that concept to an ever widening range of alternative and varied contexts.

Both helper and helped give feedback to each other, implicitly or explicitly (level 5). Indeed, implicit feedback is likely to have already occurred spontaneously in the earlier stages. Peer assessment causes a very substantial increase in the quantity and immediacy of feedback to the learner. Explicit reinforcement might stem from within the partnership or beyond it, by way of verbal or nonverbal praise, social acknowledgment and status, official accreditation, or even more tangible reward. However, reinforcement should not be indiscriminate or predominantly focused on effort.

As the learning relationship develops, both helper and helped should become more consciously aware of what is happening in their learning interaction, and more able to monitor and regulate the effectiveness of their own learning strategies in different contexts (level 6). Development into fully conscious explicit and strategic metacognition (level 7) not only promotes more effective onward learning, it should make helper and helped more confident that they can achieve even more, and that their success is the result of their own efforts. In other words, they attribute success to themselves, not to external factors, and their self-esteem is heightened.

As the peer assessment relationship develops, the model continues to apply as the learning moves from the shallow, instrumental surface level to the strategic level, and on to the deep level, as the students pursue their own goals rather than merely those set for them. Similarly, learning proceeds from the declarative (statements of existing fact) into the procedural (indicating how a situation developed and came to be) and conditional (suggesting what other alternatives might have been possible) (level 8). These affective and cognitive outcomes feed back into the originating five subprocesses—a continuous, iterative process.

Of course, it is unlikely that peer assessment in practice will neatly follow these levels or stages. Many may be missing. Sometimes one level will occur before another which appears to follow it in the model. Most likely a number of events will occur which seem to be combinations of items in a level or across levels. Even where students work through to level 8, they may begin again at the outset, usually but not always in relation to a new or varied task.

Both assessor and assessee can operate and benefit from more elaborate and cognitively demanding forms of peer assessment aimed to utilize all options at all levels. This might be enhanced and assured by role reciprocation. The greater the differential in ability or experience between helper and helped, the less cognitive conflict and the more scaffolding might be expected. Too great a differential might result in minimal cognitive engagement (let alone conflict) for the helper and unthinking but encapsulated acceptance (with no retuning or coconstruction) by the helped. Of course, if the helper is older, more experienced, and therefore more credible but actually has no greater knowledge or ability than the helped, then a mismatch and faulty learning might occur in a different way.

Teachers need to consider and seek to respond to the challenges evident in the lower and later levels of the figure, including the development of generalization, self-regulation, metacognition, and enhanced self-esteem and motivation (levels 4, 6, and 7), as well as the progressions from implicit to explicit (levels 4 and 6–8), and from dependency on support to increasing independence (throughout). Teachers should also carefully scaffold the shift from simple thinking to higher order and more abstract thinking (level 8), and the completion of the loop or joining of the circle with continuing acceleration for both helper and helped.

RELIABILITY AND VALIDITY

The reliability and validity of peer assessment must be considered in relation to the reliability and validity of assessment by teachers. The findings suggest that there is not much difference between teachers and peers in terms of the quality of their feedback (e.g., Topping, 1998, 2003). However, the more elaborated the formative feedback is, the more opportunity there is for it to vary between assessors (both peer-peer and teacher-peer). Students could receive parallel elaborated feedback which contains contradictions, and have to make sense of the various views or contradictions themselves.

The degree of correspondence between peer and teacher assessments might be termed "accuracy" of peer assessment, if one assumed that expert assessments were themselves highly reliable and valid. However, this latter is a doubtful assumption. Consequently, many purported studies of "reliability" could be considered studies of "validity," since they compare peer assessments with assessments made by professionals, rather than with those of other peers or the same peers over time.

Some studies compare marks, scores, and grades awarded by peers and staff (e.g., Magin & Helmore, 2001). This raises concerns about the uncertain psychometric properties of such scoring scales, such as their sensitivity to small changes and the extent to which they have similar properties across an entire scale, as well as the alignment of the mode of assessment with teaching and learning outcomes. More open-ended, formative feedback avoids these problems.

Research findings on the reliability and validity of peer assessment mostly emanate from studies in higher education (e.g., Falchikov, 2001). In a wide variety of subject areas and years of study, the products and performances assessed have included essays, hypermedia creations, oral presentations, multiple choice test questions, practical reports, and individual contributions to a group project. Over 70% of the studies find reliability and validity adequate, while a minority of studies find them variable (Falchikov & Goldfinch, 2000; Topping, 1998).

A tendency for peer marks to bunch around the median is sometimes noted. Student belief in the reliability of peer assessment varies from high to low, quite independently of actual reliability. Weaker reliability findings can be explained in part by differences in contexts, the level of the course, the product or performance being evaluated, the contingencies associated with those outcomes, clarity of judgment criteria, and the training and support provided. Reliability tends to be higher in advanced courses, and lower for the assessment of behavioral skills in practice settings than for academic products such as writing or presentations. Discussion, negotiation, and joint construction of assessment criteria with learners is likely to deepen understanding, give a greater sense of ownership, and increase reliability (Karegianes, Pascarella, & Pflaum, 1980; MacArthur, Schwartz, & Graham, 1991). Peer assessments are generally more reliable when supported by training, checklists, demonstrations of practice, teacher assistance, and monitoring.

In summary, peer assessment offers triangulation and thus seems likely to improve the overall reliability and validity of a class's assessments. A peer assessor with less skill at assessment but more time in which to do it can produce an equally reliable and valid assessment as a member of staff. Peer feedback should be available in greater volume and with greater immediacy than teacher feedback, which compensates for any quality disadvantage.

ADVANTAGES AND DISADVANTAGES OF PEER FEEDBACK

It has been suggested that peer assessment is not costly in terms of teachers' time. However, some authors (e.g., Falchikov, 2001) caution that there might be no saving of time in the short to medium term, since establishing good quality peer assessment requires time for organization, training and monitoring. Of course, time might be saved in the longer term. If peer assessment continues to be supplementary to teacher feedback rather than a substitution for it, then no time saving is likely. However, peer assessment can lead teachers to scrutinize and clarify assessment objectives and purposes, criteria, and grading scales. Additionally, there are likely to be metacognitive benefits for teachers as well as learners.

Any group can suffer from negative social processes, such as social loafing (failing to participate), free rider effects (having the work of others accepted as one's own), diffusion of responsibility, and interaction disabilities (Salomon & Globerson, 1989). Social processes can influence and contaminate the reliability and validity of peer assessments.

Peer assessments can be partly determined by friendship bonds, enmity, other power processes, group popularity of individuals, perception of criticism as socially uncomfortable or rejecting and inviting reciprocation, or collusion to submit average scores leading to lack of differentiation. Social influences could be particularly strong with high stakes assessment, for which peer assessments could drift toward leniency.

Both assessors and assessees can experience initial anxiety about the peer assessment process. Giving positive feedback first will reduce assessee anxiety and improve subsequent acceptance of negative feedback. In addition, students should be told that peer assessment involves students directly in learning, and should promote a sense of ownership, personal responsibility, and motivation. Teachers can also point out that peer assessment can increase variety and interest, activity and interactivity, identification and bonding, self-confidence, and empathy with others for assessors, assessees, or both.

EVIDENCE OF EFFECTIVENESS

Considering the evidence of effectiveness in the literature, it is clear that peer assessment is most researched in higher education (Topping, 1998). However, it is also researched in elementary and high schools, where there is substantial work on peer assessment of social competence (Topping, 2003). It is also researched in workplace settings, most often in relation to medical practitioners, where peer assessment of professional skills might be trickier than that of school performance (e.g., Evans, Elwyn, & Edwards, 2004).

Peer assessment has been successfully deployed with very young students and those with special educational needs or learning disabilities (e.g., Scruggs & Mastropieri, 1998). Students as young as grade 4 (9 years old) have been successfully involved. Importantly, there are gains from functioning as either assessor or assessee.

The evidence on the effectiveness of peer assessment in writing is substantial, particularly in the context of peer editing (O'Donnell & Topping, 1998; Yang, Ko, & Chung, 2005). Peer assessment can focus on the whole written product, or components of the writing process, such as planning, drafting, or editing. It is also used with classes studying English as a second or additional language (ESL, EAL) and foreign languages (Saito, 2008).

Though teachers often value the feedback provided by peer writing response groups, students sometimes need to be educated about its benefits. Weaver (1995) surveyed over 500 teachers. Regardless of the stage in the writing process (early vs. late), these teachers generally found peer responses to be more effective than their own. In contrast, students stated they found the teacher's responses to be more helpful in all stages of writing. There are implications here for how students are introduced to peer assessment. With more resistant students, introduction should be gradual and include much concrete activity before any labeling of the process.

HOW TO ORGANIZE PEER ASSESSMENT

Many teachers successfully involve learners in collaborative learning and thereby relinquish some direct control of classroom content and management. However, some teachers could be anxious about going so far as to include peer assessments as part of summative assessment, where consequences follow from terminal judgments of accomplishments. This is a reasonable concern. By contrast, the conception of peer assessment presented here is formative. The feedback is given while the learning is actually happening, helping students plan their own learning, identify their own strengths and weaknesses, target areas for remedial action, and develop metacognitive and other personal and professional skills. It does not involve students in assigning final grades.

Social factors also require consideration by the teacher. When peer assessment is carefully organized, potentially negative social issues can be ameliorated and students can develop social and communication skills, negotiation and diplomacy, and teamwork skills. Learning how to give and accept criticism, justify one's own position, and reject suggestions are all useful transferable social skills.

Providing effective feedback or assessment is a cognitively complex task requiring understanding of the goals of the task and the criteria for success, and the ability to make judgments about the relationship of the product or performance to these goals. Webb and Farivar (1994) identified the conditions for effective helping: (1) relevance to the goals and beliefs of the learner; (2) relevance to the particular misunderstandings of the learner; (3) an appropriate level of elaboration; (4) timeliness; (5) comprehension by the help-seeker; (6) an opportunity to act on help given; (7) motivation to act; and (8) constructive activity which involves reciprocal cognitive demands for a purpose meaningful to the participants.

Good organization is perhaps the most important quality of implementation integrity, leading to consistent and productive outcomes. Important planning issues evident in the literature are outlined below (see Topping, 2003).

1. Seek to work with colleagues rather than developing the initiative alone.
2. Clarify purpose, rationale, expectations, and acceptability with all stakeholders. Is the aim cognitive, attitudinal, social, or emotional gain? Specify the nature of the products of learning to be assessed. Broach the idea with the students very early, and over time seek their advice on and approval of the scheme.
3. Involve participants in developing and clarifying assessment criteria. Students need to be involved in developing the criteria for assessment in order to feel a sense of ownership and decrease any anxiety, even if they come out with something similar to what the teacher would have given them anyway. Small group discussion of teacher-proposed draft criteria should lead to a modest amount of suggested change.
4. Match participants and arrange contact. Generally aim for same-ability peer matching. If the peer partners are from the same class, roughly list them in order of ability in the subject of assessment, and pair the first two, the second two, and so on down the list (or the first three, or four, if you are developing peer response groups). Pairs or groups of students at the bottom of the list may be operating at the lowest level, but with some teacher support they may gain more than expected, as they will be involved in the same processes but at a simpler level.
5. Provide quality training, examples, and practice. Quality training will make a great deal of difference. Talk to the pairs about what is expected of them; for example the roles and behaviors expected of assessor and assessee. Then show them how

to do it, using a role play between two adults. Then immediately have the pairs practice peer assessment on a very short task selected for the purpose. While they practice, circulate to monitor their performance. Give feedback and coaching where needed.

6. Provide guidelines, checklists, or other tangible scaffolding, such as a simple sheet with not more than eight reminders in note form of what to remember. Some kind of written or pictorial reminders or clues to the process to be followed will help. Give this to individual pairs and also post in the classroom.

7. Specify activities and timescale. Make clear what needs to be done, within what time scale, and what records (if any) need to be kept. What of those who finish early—should extra peer assessment work be available or can they switch to some other kind of work? What of those who finish late—how can they be given time scales and reminders to keep them up to speed? How will the sequence of activities unfold over time? Pupils may get further apart in the tasks, but should they take some responsibility for managing this themselves?

8. Monitor the process, and coach. Whenever the students are involved in peer assessment, be the "guide on the side" not the "sage on the stage." Keep a low profile and circulate among the pairs, giving feedback, coaching, and sequencing activities as necessary.

9. Examine the quality of peer feedback. Particularly in the early days, check at least a portion of the peer assessments against your own assessments of the work. Choose a high, middle, and low ability student for this. Do not be surprised if the feedback is different from your own. The more elaborated feedback there is, the greater the chance it will be diverse. If it is very different, discuss this with the partners involved.

10. Moderate reliability and validity of feedback. Over time, keep consistent checks on the match between peer assessments (if more than one peer assesses the same piece of work), and on the relationship between peer and teacher assessments: Do not assume the teachers' assessments are any more reliable than those of the peers! You might want to match yours against the average of several peer assessments.

11. Evaluate and give feedback. Give the students information about your observations of their performance as peer assessors and also your check on the reliability of their assessments. Unless they have this information, their ability to provide useful feedback will not change for the better.

FUTURE OPPORTUNITIES

Consideration must be given to the sustainability of peer assessment, which has moved from a method in which a few students most like the teachers were recruited as assessors, to one where a great many students are recruited as assessors and work with a wide range of assessees. This tendency is likely to develop further. Some educational establishments have already developed whole-school approaches to the deployment of various forms of peer assessment. However, greater critical mass does not ensure sustainability. Where the main driver or organizer is one person, his or her departure can lead to the collapse of the initiative. It is important that several colleagues are engaged in a peer learning program, and that embedding the program across the learning organization and succession planning is carefully considered well in advance. Research should explore the contextual effectiveness of a variety of systems.

There is no better apprenticeship for being a helper than being helped. Schools with whole-school models of peer assessment capitalize on this, so a tutee in a lower grade knows from the outset that this is preparation for being a tutor later. Ambivalence about receiving help decreases as students are helped in preparation for becoming helpers (Robinson, Schofield, & Steers-Wentzell, 2005). The asymmetry between helper and helped is reduced, and any stigma associated with receiving help disappears. All students have the opportunity to help, which makes them all feel equally valuable and worthwhile. Sometimes students who are assessed in one subject are simultaneously assessors to students in a lower grade in the same subject. Those who are assessed in one subject might be assessors to their own age peers in another subject. Even the most able student in any grade can be presented with problems that require the help of an even more capable student from a higher grade, and thereby learn that no one is as smart as all of us. Research should explore the social and emotional aspects of involvement in this kind of continuous arrangement over time, as well as added value in attainment.

Over time a critical mass of teachers who support peer assessment can develop in a school. Peer assessment builds on students' strengths and mobilizes them as active participants in the learning process: This is true for teachers as well as students. Not only do helpers learn the subject better and more deeply, but they also learn transferable skills in helping and cooperation, listening and communication. Peer assessment encourages personal and social development. All of this influences the school ethos, developing a cultural norm of helping and caring. Peer assessment can contribute to a sense of cohesive community. Teachers need to be aware of these possibilities and push peer assessment to achieve these goals as substantially as possible. Research should explore the extent of development in transferable skills for both students and teachers.

In recent years, information technology has begun to permeate peer learning in various ways (Roberts, 2006). Peer assessment at a distance in online communities has been extensively explored (e.g., Prins, Sluijsmans, Kirschner, & Strijbos, 2005). Davies (2006), Wen and Tsai (2008) and Sitthiworachart and Joy (2008) have researched computerizing peer assessment. Yang et al. (2005) and Sung, Chang, Chiou, and Hou (2005) have explored computerized peer assessment in school classes. Software has been developed to help manage peer learning, providing a management information system for the coordinator or facilitator of a program (e.g., Bull & McCalla, 2002; Cho, Schunn, & Wilson, 2006; Gehringer, Ehresman, Conger & Wagle, 2007; Liu, 2005). Careful management is particularly necessary in cross-age or cross-institution peer assessment in complex distributed environments.

Formative computer-aided assessment has been linked to tutoring systems, so that both helpers and helped receive regular, frequent, and timely feedback on the effectiveness of their learning together (e.g., Topping, Samuels, & Paul, 2008). Systems have been devised for tutoring aided by artificial intelligence (e.g., Graesser et al., 2008), which are likely to progress in the future. Research should continue to explore the effectiveness of communicative and management tools relevant to peer assessment.

Finally, there is the matter of the cost-effectiveness of peer assessment. Savings of time are unlikely in the short run, when the teacher will have much to do to set up the peer assessment and manage its operation. However, once it is running, some saving of teacher time might be expected. What of the students? They will spend more time involved in assessment, as either helper or helped. If this has gains for both in the cognitive, attitudinal, and social areas, it will certainly be justified. Research should carefully consider the obvious and the hidden costs of peer assessment, in order to develop systematic cost-effectiveness comparisons, both within types of peer assessment and between types of peer assessment and competing procedures.

CONCLUSION

This chapter encourages teachers to take a balanced and evidence-based view of peer assessment as a type of formative assessment, and incorporate it thoughtfully in their practice. Peer assessment tends to be at least as high, and often higher in terms of reliability and validity in comparison to teacher assessment, which tends not to be high. Reliability of peer assessment tends to be highest in relation to: the degree of advancement in the course; the nature of the product or performance assessed; the extent to which criteria have been discussed and negotiated; the nature of assessment instrumentation; the extent to which an aggregate judgment rather than detailed components are compared; the amount of scaffolding, practice, feedback, and monitoring provided; and the contingencies associated with the assessment outcome. Irrespective of relatively high reliability, student acceptance is variable. Computer assisted peer assessment shows considerable promise.

Peer assessment needs training and practice, arguably on neutral products or performances before full implementation, which should feature monitoring and moderation. Teachers will be able to draw guidance on how best to implement peer assessment from the section of this chapter entitled "How to Organize Peer Assessment." Of course, some of the variables in their situations will be beyond their control. Other variables somewhat within their control will be subject to time constraints. Nonetheless, a developmental process may be started which leads toward more sophisticated peer assessment in at least some areas of the curriculum.

REFERENCES

Bangert-Drowns, R. L., Kulik, C. C., Kulik, J. A., & Morgan, M. T. (1991). The instructional effect of feedback in test-like events. *Review of Educational Research, 61*, 213–238.

Black, P., & Wiliam, D. (1998). Assessment and classroom learning. *Assessment in Education, 5*(1), 7–74.

Bull, S., & McCalla, G. (2002). Modeling cognitive style in a peer help network. *Instructional Science, 30*, 497–528.

Chi, M. T. H., Siler, S. A, Jeong, H., Yamauchi, T., & Hausmann, R. G. (2001). Learning from human tutoring. *Cognitive Science, 25*, 471–533.

Cho, K., Schunn, C. D., & Wilson, R. W. (2006). Validity and reliability of scaffolded peer assessment of writing from instructor and student perspectives. *Journal of Educational Psychology, 98*, 891–901.

Cole, D. A. (1991). Change in self-perceived competence as a function of peer and teacher evaluation. *Developmental Psychology, 27*, 682–688.

Davies, P. (2006). Peer assessment: Judging the quality of students' work by comments rather than marks. *Innovations in Education and Teaching International, 43*(1), 69–82.

Evans, R., Elwyn, G., & Edwards, A. (2004). Review of instruments for peer assessment of physicians. *British Medical Journal, 328*, 1240–1243.

Falchikov, N. (2001). *Learning together: Peer tutoring in higher education.* London & New York: Routledge Falmer.

Falchikov, N., & Goldfinch, J. (2000). Student peer assessment in higher education: A meta-analysis comparing peer and teacher marks. *Review of Educational Research, 70,* 287–322.

Gehringer, E., Ehresman, L., Conger, S. G., & Wagle, P. (2007). Reusable learning objects through peer review: The Expertiza approach. *Innovate, 3*(5). Retrieved June 28, 2007, from http://www.innovateonline.info/index.php?view=article&id=365

Graesser, A. C., D'Mello, S. K., Craig, S. D., Witherspoon, A., Sullins, J., McDaniel, B., et al. (2008). The relationship between affect states and dialogue patterns during interactions with AutoTutor. *Journal of Interactive Learning Research, 19,* 293–312.

Karegianes, M. L., Pascarella, E. T. & Pflaum, S. W. (1980). The effects of peer editing on the writing proficiency of low-achieving tenth grade students. *Journal of Educational Research, 73,* 203–207.

King, A. (1998). Transactive peer tutoring: Distributing cognition and metacognition. *Educational Psychology Review, 10*(1), 57–74.

MacArthur, C. A., Schwartz, S. S., & Graham, S. (1991). Effects of a reciprocal peer revision strategy in special education classrooms. *Learning Disabilities Research and Practice, 6,* 201–210.

Magin, D., & Helmore, P. (2001). Peer and teacher assessments of oral presentation skills: How reliable are they? *Studies in Higher Education, 26,* 287–298.

Narciss, S., & Huth, K. (2004). How to design informative tutoring feedback for multimedia learning. In H. M. Neigemann, D. Leutner, & R. Brunken (Eds.), *Instructional design for multimedia learning* (pp. 181–195). Munster, NY: Waxmann.

Liu, E. Z. F. (2005). To propose a reviewer dispatching algorithm for networked peer assessment system. *International Journal of Instructional Media, 32*(1), 85–95.

O'Donnell, A. M., & Topping, K. J. (1998). Peers assessing peers: Possibilities and problems. In K. J. Topping & S. Ehly (Eds.), *Peer-assisted learning* (pp. 255–278). Mahwah, NJ: Erlbaum.

Prins, F., Sluijsmans, D., Kirschner, P.A., & Strijbos, J.W. (2005). Formative peer assessment in a CSCL environment: A case study. *Assessment & Evaluation in Higher Education, 30,* 417–444.

Roberts, T. S. (Ed.) (2006). *Self, peer and group assessment in e-learning.* Hershey, PA: IGI Global.

Robinson, D. R., Schofield, J. W., & Steers-Wentzell, K. L. (2005). Peer and cross-age tutoring in math: Outcomes and their design implications. *Educational Psychology Review, 17,* 327–362.

Saito, H. (2008). EFL classroom peer assessment: Training effects on rating and commenting. *Language Testing, 25,* 553–581.

Salomon, G., & Globerson, T. (1989). When teams do not function the way they ought to. *International Journal of Educational Research, 13,* 89–99.

Scruggs, T. E., & Mastropieri, M. A. (1998). Tutoring and students with special needs. In K. J. Topping & S. Ehly (Eds.), *Peer-assisted learning* (pp. 165–182). Mahwah, NJ: Erlbaum.

Shute, V. J. (2008). Focus on formative feedback. *Review of Educational Research, 78*(1), 153–189.

Sitthiworachart, J., & Joy, M. (2008). Computer support of effective peer assessment in an undergraduate programming class. *Journal of Computer Assisted Learning, 24,* 217–231.

Sluijsmans, D., & Prins, F. (2006). A conceptual framework for integrating peer assessment in teacher education. *Studies in Educational Evaluation, 32,* 6–22.

Sung, Y. T., Chang, K. E., Chiou, S. K., & Hou, H. T. (2005). The design and application of a web-based self- and peer-assessment system. *Computers and Education, 45,* 187–202.

Topping, K. J. (1998). Peer assessment between students in college and university. *Review of Educational Research, 68,* 249–276.

Topping, K. J. (2003). Self and peer assessment in school and university: Reliability, validity and utility. In: M. S. R. Segers, F. J. R. C. Dochy, & E. C. Cascallar (Eds.), *Optimizing new modes of assessment: In search of qualities and standards* (pp. 55–87). Dordrecht: Kluwer Academic.

Topping, K. J. (2005). Trends in peer learning. In K. Wheldall (Ed.), *Developments in educational psychology: How far have we come in 25 years?* (pp. 59–73). London: Routledge Falmer.

Topping, K. J. (2009). Peer assessment. *Theory into Practice, 48*(1), 20–27.

Topping, K. J., & Ehly, S. (Eds.). (1998). *Peer-assisted learning.* Mahwah, NJ: Erlbaum.

Topping, K. J., Samuels, J., & Paul, T. (2008). Independent reading: The relationship of challenge, non-fiction and gender to achievement. *British Educational Research Journal, 34,* 505–524.

Vygotsky, L. S. (1978). *Mind in society: The development of higher psychological processes* (Eds., M. Cole, V. John-Steiner, S. Scribner, & E. Souberman). Cambridge, MA: MIT Press.

Weaver, M. E. (1995). Using peer response in the classroom: Students' perspectives. *Research and Teaching in Developmental Education, 12*, 31–37.

Webb, N. M., & Farivar, S. (1994). Promoting helping behavior in cooperative small groups in middle school mathematics. *American Educational Research Journal, 31*, 369–395.

Wen, M. L., & Tsai, C. C. (2008). Online peer assessment in an inservice science and mathematics teacher education course. *Teaching in Higher Education, 13*(1), 55–67.

Yang, J. C., Ko, H. W., & Chung, I. L. (2005). Web-based interactive writing environment: Development and evaluation. *Educational Technology and Society, 8*(2), 214–229.

5

FORMATIVE ASSESSMENT APPLICATIONS
OF CULMINATING DEMONSTRATIONS OF MASTERY

JILL DAVIDSON AND JAY FELDMAN

Effective assessments enhance rather than interrupt student learning. Whereas there are many reasons to assess student understanding—to determine the progress of students' learning, to identify areas of strength and problematic areas where students need more support, to determine pedagogical and curricular effectiveness, and to determine whether students have mastered the full range of skills and essential content points—the assessment itself can and should allow students to show and build upon that learning in new and innovative ways. This chapter focuses on summative, high-stakes demonstrations of mastery to illustrate a continuum between formative and summative assessments, and demonstrates the ways that such assessments are an integral component of school design and ongoing improvement aimed at intellectual quality. Prior to demonstrating the ways that high-stakes, summative demonstrations of mastery create encouraging conditions for formative assessment, this section defines the key terms upon which understanding of this chapter's argument depends: formative assessment, performance-based assessment system, and exhibitions.

FORMATIVE ASSESSMENT

Formative assessment is an aspect of the instructional process; it provides the information needed to adjust teaching and learning as they are taking place by informing teachers and students about student understanding and teacher effectiveness at a point when timely adjustments can be made (Boston, 2002; Davis, 2007). In this way, formative assessment enhances learning (Stiggins, 2007).

PERFORMANCE-BASED ASSESSMENT SYSTEMS

Performance-based assessment (often termed performance assessment) requires students to demonstrate that they have mastered specific skills and competencies by performing task or producing work (Sweet, 1993). Performance-based assessment is designed to demonstrate what a student knows and can do at any point along the continuum that runs between formative and summative assessment. At the end points of the continuum, performance-based assessments can be strictly formative, designed to provide feedback about learning and instruction. Performance-based assessments also can be summative demonstrations of student mastery at the end of a course, unit, grade, or phase of schooling as the final step in an ongoing system of performance-based formative assessment. Along the continuum, projects, in-class work, and assignments in which students are engaged form the basis for high-stakes exhibitions. Work of this sort is focused on results rather than rewards, and is designed so that with proper support and scaffolding, all students can succeed, a key to effective formative assessment (Black & Wiliam, 1998).

Demonstrations of mastery based on school-wide outcomes and high-level competencies can be assessed through a performance-based assessment system—an integrated approach to education that requires that assessment must be continually incorporated into the day-to-day learning activities of every student. A performance-based assessment system requires students to engage in time-intensive, in-depth research projects, papers, and other rigorous performance tasks that require students to think like historians, solve problems like mathematicians, conduct experiments as scientists do, critically interpret works of literature, and speak and write clearly and expressively.

The connection of daily classroom work that emphasizes formative assessment to final exhibitions ensures that students and educators experience exhibitions as the culmination of a system of performance-based assessment that is scaffolded from year to year, is consistent across classrooms, is designed equitably for all students to succeed, and is at the center of the school's instructional design and practice. In these ways, exhibitions assure continuity between classroom assessment methods and high-stakes final assessments. Performance-based assessments can be thought of as performance only, as the summation of students' learning, and as the main goal of teachers and students. In reality, the process of preparing for high stakes performance-based assessments such as exhibitions is an intensely formative learning experience. In fact, a key component of an exhibition is that scaffolding is explicit in supporting students to reach school-wide student outcomes over the course of their career. As Fuchs (1996) has written, "A major impetus for the performance assessment movement has been the need to reconnect large-scale and classroom assessment to learning so that assessment affects learning positively, enhancing instruction."

EXHIBITIONS

Public, culminating demonstrations of mastery, often termed exhibitions, mark the high-stakes, summative end of the assessment continuum and performance-based system. They occur at culminating moments such as at the conclusion of a unit of study, the transition from one level of schooling to the next, and graduation; student progress depends in large part on their successful completion. Although the preparation for, presentation, and content of exhibitions vary from student to student and school to school, exhibitions can generally be described as student presentations of their own work through verbal, written, visual, and other means. Exhibitions typically assess significant episodes of learning and growth, and demonstrate interdisciplinary mastery of content and skills. They are then evaluated by teachers, judges from outside the immediate school community, and peers. The use of the term *exhibitions* to describe public, high-stakes, culminating demonstrations of mastery employed was proposed by Theodore R. Sizer in 1984 as a high-leverage school reform strategy. Sizer conceived of exhibitions as a paradigm shift from evaluating academic achievement primarily by Carnegie units and other measures of "seat time" to methods that ensure accountability through public demonstrations of academic achievement that are engaging, relevant, challenging, and aligned to established standards of achievement. The practice of exhibitions was refined and documented by the early work of the Coalition of Essential Schools (Cushman, 1990; McDonald, Smith, Turner, Finney, & Barton, 1993; Sizer, 1992), a national school reform and restructuring organization committed to advancing performance assessment as the preferred method for student evaluation in all schools nationwide. The use of exhibitions has been further developed through the subsequent decades by many schools. According to Lyne (2007):

> An exhibition is a demonstration of mastery on many levels. When students prepare and present…their own work to a public audience, they are demonstrating mastery of more than the traditional academic skills. The process that culminates in the exhibition teaches students to present themselves articulately and powerfully and to work independently to a high standard.

HOW PERFORMANCE-BASED ASSESSMENT SUPPORTS STUDENT LEARNING

Characterized by a close association between assessment and instruction, exhibitions are examples of embedded assessment (Chudowsky & Pellegrino, 2003). Schools that use exhibitions employ embedded formative assessment practices in classroom settings to rehearse, emphasize, and otherwise reinforce progress toward successful final outcomes. Exhibitions have also been described as authentic assessment because they simulate the kinds of open-ended challenges faced by people working in a field of study (Darling-Hammond, Ancess, & Falk, 1995; Newmann & Associates, 1996; Wiggins, 1993). Exhibitions and other high-stakes, performance-based assessments are frequently cited as effective forms of formative assessment because students receive frequent feedback on the quality of their work and multiple opportunities to revise and improve before they formally present it for summative evaluation (Darling-Hammond, Ancess, & Falk, 1995; Gallagher, 2007; Newmann & Associates, 1996; Nichols & Berliner, 2007; Stiggins, 2005; Wiggins, 2006).

Newman and Associates (1996) define clear advantages of exhibitions in schools and school systems committed to authentic intellectual achievement for all students, describing alignment between assessment and instruction and demonstrating the benefits for all learners that result. Within the first decade of their use, the potential of exhibitions to move schools to adopt and refine structures that support high-quality intellectual achievement was apparent (Darling-Hammond et al., 1995; McDonald et al., 1993). In addition, schools that place a central focus on exhibitions and other forms of performance-based assessment at both classroom and culminating levels demonstrate lower high school drop-out rates, higher college-going rates, and improved college performance and persistence (Coalition of Essential Schools, 2006; Foote, 2007).

Finally, formative assessment that leads to culminating demonstrations of mastery is an essential strategy to increase equity and the opportunity for all students to succeed. According to Guskey, "Teachers who use classroom assessments as part of the instructional process help all of their students do exactly what the most successful students have learned to do for themselves" (2007, p. 26). Stiggins has written that "assessment practices that permitted (and even encouraged) some pupils to give up on learning must be replaced by practices that engender hope and sustained effort for all pupils" (2007, p. 13), and he argues that formative assessment represents that sort of practice. Guskey's and Stiggins's statements apply with equal validity to exhibitions.

CONDITIONS REQUIRED FOR PERFORMANCE-BASED ASSESSMENTS TO ALIGN WITH FORMATIVE ASSESSMENTS

The New York Performance Standards Consortium (NYPSC) provides information about the conditions required to implement formative assessment practices in schools that use summative, culminating public demonstrations of mastery (New York Performance Standards Consortium, 2003). The NYPSC led an effort by concerned educators, family members, and students that successfully advocated for legislation exempting its 28 member schools from most of New York's state-mandated high-stakes standardized Regents tests, thus creating the conditions in the schools for a strong focus on the demonstration of mastery through portfolio and exhibition. The NYPSC has created an interschool system for performance assessment using exhibitions, creating rubrics, gathering educators to look at student work, and assembling a performance review board of educators, academics, and other authorities to review student work and the processes by which it is evaluated (Cook & Tashlik, 2005), thus establishing standards and reliability across schools.

A complete list of the seven essential components that schools need to implement performance-based assessment systems has been developed by the NYPSE and is provided in appendix A. Three of these components incorporate elements of formative assessment, and are the lenses through which the role formative assessments play is analyzed in the case study that follows. The first formative assessment element is the use of embedded assessment in the form of cross-grade level rubrics for tasks and assignments that scaffold work as students move through the curriculum. The second element is a set of strategies designed to increase student self-reflection geared toward improving understanding, such as rehearsal opportunities to practice elements of an exhibition in the classroom through questioning, conversation, and informal presentations. The third element is commitment to the endeavor to guide students toward becoming independent and self-regulated learners as they prepare for demonstrations.

THE ROLE OF FORMATIVE ASSESSMENT IN CULMINATING DEMONSTRATIONS OF MASTERY: A CASE STUDY

Amy Biehl High School (ABHS) is a charter school in Albuquerque, New Mexico with a year-round schedule serving 200 9th through 12th grade students. Amy Biehl High

School uses exhibitions, which the school terms "demonstrations," to assess student learning and teacher effectiveness in all of its subject areas. The key ways in which formative assessment is used to support summative, high-stakes performance-based assessments in the form of exhibitions are the use of embedded assessment to scaffold work, the incorporation of opportunities for rehearsal in the process of preparing for exhibitions, and the effort throughout that process to shape students to become independent and self-regulated learners. Amy Biehl educators accomplish this through the identification of areas of strength and challenge guided by a cycle of inquiry that is generated and maintained by both educators and students.

Amy Biehl student John Salazar's final science demonstration illustrates the dynamics of a summative demonstration of mastery. When John, a junior at ABHS, gave a 20-minute demonstration on the emotion of music in front of his teachers, peers, and outside experts, he presented much more than the product of his independent research study. His presentation was a culmination of an extensive body of work that includes similar work over his 3 years at the school that scaffolded his ability to appear before an audience of peers, teachers, and outside experts to defend his ideas, process, data analysis, and conclusions. That audience evaluated his performance using rubrics with which John and other students were closely familiar. During each of his 3 years at ABHS, John completed a science exhibition based upon an independent research project at each grade level and provided feedback on the presentations of higher level students using the same rubrics. For his final demonstration of mastery, John completed a 9-month independent study, wrote and received feedback on three drafts of his written paper, identified and interacted with experts outside of the school, and continually evaluated his own performance according to ABHS's rubrics and school-wide expectations.

In fact, all ABHS science students—within the scope of ABHS's 3-year science curriculum, these are generally 9th, 10th, and 11th graders—complete independent study projects (ISP) that feature independent research and play a part in determining students' progress toward more advanced course material, concurrent college enrollment, and graduation. Amy Biehl's science curriculum is integrated, with students studying biology, chemistry, and physics all 3 years. In 11th grade students present their ISPs—the culmination of their science work at ABHS—in front of teachers, peers, and outside community members who may include professionals from Sandia National Lab, professors from the University of New Mexico and New Mexico Technical Institute, and engineers from a local utility company. The role of these outside experts is crucial; as ABHS science teacher Rob Shauger explains, "It is really important to get the kids to comprehend what the end product needs to be. We have to up the stakes for the kids, and with outside people, kids rise to the occasion" (R. Shauger, personal communication, September 26, 2008).

The Use of Embedded Assessments that Scaffold Work

As noted previously, exhibitions are examples of embedded assessment (Chudowsky & Pellegrino, 2003). All of the activities and assessments in the course reinforce the skills and knowledge that students are required to demonstrate in their exhibitions. An example of this can be seen in the activities listed in the ABHS "9th Grade Science Outcomes:

Chemistry Unit" reproduced in appendix B. The key to this consistency is that ABHS students use the same rubric for all three science grade levels; the five-level rubric creates scaffolding by evaluating students at 100% when they score a 3 in 9th grade, a 4 in 10th grade, and a 5 in 11th grade. This rubric for culminating demonstrations is aligned to the rubrics used to convey expectations for lab reports and other classroom work products, thereby corresponding to students' daily classroom work, and providing students with ample opportunities to practice using the rubric. The rubric is also aligned with "Habits of Mind and Heart," which is the school's articulation of the intellectual and emotional dispositions that students are expected to demonstrate (see appendix C). The rubric is also aligned with "Profile of an Amy Biehl High School Science Graduate"—a description of what students need to know and be able to do to graduate from ABHS prepared to successfully access both postsecondary education and career pathways (see appendix D). The Habits of Mind and Heart and graduate profile description are ABHS's cornerstone statements about expectations for students. They are the basis for every class, every planned element of school culture, and every learning activity in which students engage. In science classes, teacher assessment of students' demonstration of the Habits of Mind and Heart account for 15% of the overall outcomes-based grade.

Students obtain additional scaffolding through familiarity with assessment expectations gleaned as a result of their routine evaluation of other students' demonstrations. Ninth graders evaluate 10th graders' demonstrations, and 10th graders evaluate 11th graders' demonstrations. These peer assessments contribute to the summative statements about the ways that students' performances demonstrated what they know and what they can do. As well, students also use the rubric to assess their peers' in-class work, securing the experience of assessing at least five projects each year, including those that align with what they will do the next year.

The Role of Formative Assessment in Rehearsal and Revision

Effective performance-based assessment systems use strategies for corrective action: feedback on written work, in-class informal evaluations, feedback provided by students to other students during group work sessions, narrative reports, conferences among students, parents, and teachers, after-school homework labs, and peer tutoring. All ABHS students at each grade level write at least four in-depth lab reports prior to their ISP demonstrations. Teachers meet individually with students preparing ISPs at least twice per year outside class to discuss students' progress. The time commitment to support this by teachers is considerable, but they consider it essential to provide students with the experience of working intensively on a paper and making it as excellent as possible through multiple revisions

As well, students revise the written components of their projects multiple times in writers' workshops geared toward scientific papers, and submit three draft submissions to the teachers with feedback from the teacher according to the rubric. "The key is making sure kids are on the right track," reports Shauger (personal communication, September 26, 2008). Peers provide formative feedback as well, and students engage in self-evaluations. In addition to the support for scaffolding that this peer evaluation provides, as discussed in the section above, peer feedback serves as a source of feedback that "enhances in students a sense of self-control over learning" (Nicol & Macfarlane-Dick, 2006, p. 11).

Independent Self-Regulated Learning

Stiggins (2007) points out that in order for instruction to be successful, students need to believe in themselves and their power to achieve, and that effective formative assessment practices are a key strategy to building student confidence and engagement. A performance-based assessment system requires formative and summative documentation that demonstrates students' effort and growth over time. Such evidence includes student work samples; attendance data; rate and quality of assignment completion; quizzes and tests; student self-evaluations; parent–teacher conferences; and review of student work patterns and work products by staff members. This evidence, when considered at regular intervals provided by multiple opportunities of rehearsal and revision, provides the basis for a cycle of inquiry that students can use to assess their own progress, and that educators can use to assess their effectiveness.

Amy Biehl High School focuses on utilizing community resources such as teacher and upper-level student expertise to model the understanding that science is not a solitary endeavor and to push students to take the lead in directing their learning. As ABHS science teacher Rob Shauger observes, "No one knows everything, so why not have an expert be your mentor? One of the beautiful things about small schools is the ability to use the community. A student will ask me about their geology project, and I will direct them to the staff member with expertise in that area" (personal communication, September 26, 2008). Students then set up meeting times with teachers/expert sources outside of the regular school day. Shauger says, "This helps students to understand what to do to move the work forward when they don't know the answer. It's all about getting them to understand that they don't have all the answers, but they need to know how to find and utilize the answers" (personal communication, September 26, 2008).

Stiggins (2007, pp. 17–18) supports the idea that formative assessment can help students "watch themselves grow," thus supplying evidence to students that with they can reach learning targets. This encourages students to engage and push themselves toward success, is supported when formative assessment is done with a clear, public, well-known set of standards and rubrics such as the ABHS science outcomes and the aligned rubrics used both in formative and high-stakes summative assessments of work.

EXHIBITIONS AS A LEVER FOR SCHOOL IMPROVEMENT

Exhibitions—students' demonstrations of mastery of what a school wants them to know and be able to do—form the backbone of a school's work. Because exhibitions are central to the daily work of schools that their use affects almost all other school practices, implementing a performance-based assessment system is a challenging and complex practice to implement effectively in schools without a sustained commitment to significant restructuring. Therefore, exhibitions have great potential to be a lever that can galvanize thoughtful school design or redesign for to increase equity, personalization, student engagement, and the maintenance of high academic standards for all students. Amy Biehl, for example, was designed with the explicit aim of supporting a performance-based assessment system that utilizes exhibitions to demonstrate student achievement and teacher and school effectiveness, and that incorporates the three conditions that foster the use of formative assessment practices that build toward culminating demonstrations of mastery. A reexamination of those three conditions illuminates the ways that such assessment can be the goal from which a school can plan for increased student achievement.

The first, embedded assessment through the use of rubrics provides a specific example of how planning backwards from exhibitions is related to other school-wide practices. Rubrics that are aligned with public and prominent school-wide outcomes communicate expectations from the first day of the freshman year. The rubrics describe a progressive scaffold for students, identifying not only the standards of work needed to pass their senior year exhibitions, but also the expected benchmarks of a student developing toward these standards across the years.

The second, the use of a set of strategies designed to increase student self-reflection geared toward improving understanding through repetition, rehearsal, and the completion of work related to the end goal, serves another purpose. Such opportunities for practice and revision provide educators the data they need to recalibrate what they are asking students to know and do in order to improve their practice and effectiveness. Both exhibitions and the work that students to as they progress toward them provide feedback to teachers on their teaching and information for the school's cycle of continuous improvement. This cycle of inquiry—characterized by adults engaging in the collaborative practice of looking at student work, analyzing data to determine the effectiveness of their pedagogy and curriculum, and choosing courses of action to produce improved student results—depends on formative assessments for generation of data, check-ins to determine the effectiveness of curricular and pedagogical changes, and other collaborative practices. A well-functioning professional learning community, with sufficient time and support, is a necessary component to a cycle of inquiry that can use data produced by assessments along the formative–summative continuum.

The third practice suggested by the ABHS case study is to guide students toward becoming independent and self-regulated learners as they prepare for demonstrations; but this is not something that can happen in isolated classes or within one department. Clearly, this effort to scaffold learning to bring out students' skills in independent thinking and critical skills necessary for their lives beyond secondary school as 21st century learners and citizens, needs to be a coordinated, school-wide effort. Statements of expectation and outcomes such as the Habits of Mind and Heart, used across all grades, disciplines, and structures within the school, help ensure this coordination. Such statements result when school community members come together to plan backward from their goals for students to determine the pedagogical, curricular, and assessment practices that must result.

CHALLENGES FACED BY SCHOOLS COMMITTED TO USING EXHIBITIONS AS HIGH-STAKES ASSESSMENTS

Although schools can gain tremendous advantages when they align formative assessments to culminating high-stakes demonstrations of mastery, many struggle to secure the sort of appropriate conditions for such work as described by the NYPSC (2003). Three main challenges contribute to difficulty implementing performance assessment systems: (1) lack of alignment between school structures and designs and performance-based assessment; (2) lack of support for teacher workload, training, and professional learning community; and (3) lack of policies that support the use of exhibitions.

Schools that seek to begin assessing students effectively and meaningfully via exhibitions and other forms of performance assessment require significant restructuring. Exhibitions are not stand-alone exercises sprung on students in their senior year; they are connected to every intentional action in a school community. Exhibitions require a systemic commitment that starts with a school's mission and then plans backward to support and rethink curriculum, structures, support systems, tools, and day-to-day decisions. For example, exhibitions require a school-wide emphasis on professional development for advisors and teachers to develop, execute, and refine a program in which performance assessment is valued and prioritized (Peters, 2007). This includes planning days focused on authentic assessment, developing the regular practice of looking at adult and student work, and communication and calibration across grade levels. Whereas schools that have made this commitment to a performance-based system report powerful results for students (Coalition of Essential Schools, 2006), such restructuring is clearly an undertaking not all schools are prepared to carry out.

The work required from individual teachers can be an obstacle to creating a performance assessment system that aligns formative and summative assessment. According to Reeves: "[S]ome school systems talk a good game about improved achievement for students, [but] they are willing to purse that goal only as long as the process does not cause discomfort for the adults" (2007, p. 9). Performance assessment may well fall into that category of discomfort; it demands considerable time and effort from teachers, as is evident from the ABHS case study. According to ABHS teacher Rob Shauger:

> We meet with each student one-on-one throughout the year at least twice outside class in writer workshops on scientific papers. It takes a lot of effort and time to evaluate 60 to 80 scientific research papers that need to follow a set format. It is not something that you can do on a whim, but it is valuable and worth it to spend that time out of class giving that feedback. The kids need to have the experience of taking a paper and making it as good as it can get through multiple revisions. That's something that isn't emphasized in science, that scientists need to be good writers. (personal communication, September 26, 2008)

In a school that is not structured to support a performance assessment system, it is not possible to assume this level of teacher commitment not just from exceptionally dedicated educators, but from every teacher. In addition to the time spent evaluating the work as Shauger described, this sort of assessment requires professional development and common planning time to calibrate standards for work, communication time with students, family members, and teachers outside of the department to communicate those standards. This intense, focused work cannot happen in schools that do not establish clear expectations for educators, do not allocate enough time, do not provide appropriate training and professional development, and do not establish a professional learning community.

A third challenge is the lack of widespread policies that support high-stakes performance-based assessments as valid and reliable measures. A recent impediment to the widespread use of exhibitions as classroom assessments and high-stakes culminating demonstrations of mastery has been the prevailing national policy climate, which frequently leads schools to focus on preparing students for large scale, externally imposed, high-stakes, standardized tests that provide little opportunity for performance-based assessment (Nichols & Berliner, 2007). Competing demands and priorities prevent exhibitions from being a regular feature of classroom instruction and assessment, and in schools that do attempt to maintain a performance-based assessment system, the power of students' culminating exhibitions is diluted because they have not been a consistent part of the learning experience (Davidson, 2009).

CONCLUSION

Examples of schools that have addressed the first two challenges outlined previously in this chapter by creating structures and teacher preparation that support and sustain a performance assessment system are available among many schools that are affiliated with the Coalition of Essential Schools (Benitez, Davidson, & Flaxman, 2009). As for the third challenge, some states are currently working toward including locally-created, high-stakes, performance-based assessments as a part of their high school graduation requirements (Hirsch, 2007). The Rhode Island Diploma System, for example, requires exhibitions or portfolios as a component of high school graduation requirements (Rhode Island Diploma System Local Assessment Toolkit, 2004). Until recently, Nebraska's state assessment system used locally controlled, performance-based demonstrations of mastery that align with exhibitions (see Gallagher, this volume). Such statewide efforts create conditions for exhibitions to guide assessment and instruction not only on the school level, but also on the district and state levels, developing alignment and capacity throughout school systems and the state departments of education that support them.

The New York Performance Standards Consortium (NYPSC) is a strong example of Black and Wiliam's (1998) recommendations for improving teachers' use of formative assessment by working with local groups of educators committed to formative assessment in their schools, disseminating their work, reducing policy and other obstacles, and researching the effectiveness of formative assessment. The work of NYPSC serves to link formative classroom assessment to exhibitions by creating the conditions for sustained daily focus on the knowledge and skills to be evaluated by exhibitions and by ensuring the standards by which student work is evaluated, not just within a school but among a group of schools.

High-stakes demonstrations of mastery align with and make the daily work of formative classroom assessment more meaningful and effective. Correspondingly, formative assessments are necessary elements of culminating demonstrations of mastery. Comprehensive assessment systems include multiple assessment types that are matched with the needs of teachers and learners, and effective assessment systems are characterized by a continuum that moves between formative and summative assessments in ways that always maintain assessment as a vehicle for student learning and educator improvement.

Aligning demonstrations of mastery of school-wide outcomes and high-level competencies with daily, classroom based formative assessment creates that continuum, and makes teaching and learning more meaningful and effective.

REFERENCES

Amy Biehl High School. (2008a). *Ninth grade science outcomes: Chemistry unit*. http://www.abhs.k12.nm.us/classes/Science/documents/OUTCOMESMAP.xls

Amy Biehl High School. (2008b). *Habits of mind and heart*. http://www.abhs.k12.nm.us/classes/Science/documents/HabitsofMindandHeart-handout.doc

Amy Biehl High School. (2008c). *Profile of an ABHS science graduate*. http://abhs.k12.nm.us/classes/Science/Mitch/documents/ABHSmath-sciGradProf2004.doc

Benitez, M., Davidson, J., & Flaxman, L. (2009). *Small schools, big ideas: The essential guide to successful school transformation*. San Francisco: Jossey-Bass.

Boston, C. (2002). The concept of formative assessment. *Practical Assessment, Research & Evaluation, 8*(9). Retrieved September 9, 2008, from http://PAREonline.net/getvn.asp?v=8&n=9

Black, P., & Wiliam, D. (1998). Inside the black box: Raising standards through classroom assessment. *Phi Delta Kappan, 80*(2), 139–148.

Chudowsky, N., & Pellegrino, J. (2003). Large-scale assessments that support learning: What will it take? *Theory into Practice, 42*, 75–83.

Coalition of Essential Schools (2006). *Measuring up: Demonstrating the effectiveness of the Coalition of Essential Schools*. Oakland, CA: Author.

Cook, A., & Tashlik, P. (2005). Making the pendulum swing: challenging bad education policy in New York State. *Horace 21*(4). Retrieved February 25, 2009, from http://www.essentialschools.org/cs/resources/view/ces_res/380

Cushman, K. (1990). Performance and exhibitions: The demonstration of mastery. *Horace 6*(3). Retrieved November 19, 2008, from http://www.essentialschools.org/cs/resources/view/ces_res/138

Darling-Hammond, L., Ancess, J., & Falk, B. (1995). *Authentic assessment in action: Studies of schools and students at work*. New York: Teachers College Press.

Davidson, J. (2009). Exhibitions: Connecting classroom assessment with culminating demonstrations of mastery. *Theory Into Practice, 4*(1), 36–43.

Davis, A. (2007). Involving students in the classroom assessment process. In D. Reeves (Ed.), *Ahead of the curve: The power of assessment to transform teaching and learning* (pp. 31–57). Bloomington, IN: Solution Tree.

Foote, M. (2007). Keeping accountability systems accountable. *Phi Delta Kappan, 88*(5), 359–363.

Fuchs, L. (1996). Connecting performance assessment to instruction: A comparison of behavioral assessment, mastery learning, curriculum-based measurement, and performance assessment. Retrieved August 8, 2008, from, http://www.ericdigests.org/1996-1/based.htm

Gallagher, C. (2007). *Reclaiming assessment: A better alternative to the accountability agenda*. Portsmouth, NH: Heinemann.

Guskey, T. (2007). Using assessments to improve teaching and learning. In D. Reeves (Ed.), *Ahead of the curve: The power of assessment to transform teaching and learning* (pp. 15–29). Bloomington, IN: Solution Tree.

Hirsch, L. (2007). The deep irony of No Child Left Behind: Lisa Hirsch interviews Linda Darling-Hammond. *Horace 23*(1). Retrieved December 14, 2008, from http://www.essentialschools.org/cs/resources/view/ces_res/406

Lyne, H. (2007). Presenting themselves with power and passion. *Horace 23*(1), Retrieved December 12, 2008, from http://www.essentialschools.org/cs/resources/view/ces_res/408

McDonald, J., Smith, S., Turner, D., Finney, M., & Barton, I. (1993). *Graduation by exhibition: Assessing genuine achievement*. Alexandria, VA: Association for Supervision and Curriculum Development.

New York Performance Standards Consortium. (2003). Schools need seven components to implement the performance-based assessment system. New York: Author. Retrieved August 8, 2008, from http://performanceassessment.org/performance/pcomponents.html

Newmann, F., & Associates. (1996). *Authentic achievement: Restructuring schools for intellectual quality*. San Francisco: Jossey-Bass.

Nicol, D. J., & Macfarlane-Dick, D. (2006). Formative assessment and self-regulated learning: A model and seven principles of good feedback practice. *Studies in Higher Education, 31*(2), 199–218.

Nichols, S., & Berliner, D. (2007). *Collateral damage: How high-stakes testing corrupts America's schools.* Cambridge, MA: Harvard Education Press.

Peters, G. (2007). Structural and curricular design: What changes when an essential school commits to exhibitions. *Horace 23*(1). Retrieved December 11, 2008, from http://www.essentialschools.org/cs/resources/view/ces_res/411

Reeves, D. (2007). From the bell curve to the mountain: A new vision for achievement, assessment, and equity. In D. Reeves (Ed.), *Ahead of the curve: The power of assessment to transform teaching and learning* (pp. 1–12). Bloomington, IN: Solution Tree.

Rhode Island Department of Education (2004). Rhode Island diploma system local assessment toolkit. Providence, RI: Author. Retrieved November 29, 2008, from http://www.ridoe.net/highschoolreform/dslat/

Sizer, T. (1984). *Horace's compromise: The dilemma of the American high school.* Boston: Houghton Mifflin.

Sizer, T. (1992). *Horace's school: Redesigning the American high school.* Boston: Houghton Mifflin.

Stiggins, R. (2005). From formative assessment to assessment for learning: A path to success in standards-based schools. *Phi Delta Kappan, 87*(4), 324–328.

Stiggins, R. (2007). Conquering the formative assessment frontier. In J. H. McMillan (Ed.), *Formative classroom assessment: Theory into Practice* (pp. 8–28). New York: Teachers College Press.

Sweet, D. (1993). *Performance Assessment.* United States Department of Education, Office of Research, Office of Educational Research and Improvement. Retrieved December 12, 2008, from http://www.ed.gov/pubs/OR/ConsumerGuides/perfasse.html

Wiggins, G. (2006). *Healthier testing made easy.* Retrieved January 3, 2008, from http://www.edutopia.org/node/1498

Appendix A New York Performance Standards Consortium's Required Components to Implement Performance-Based Assessment

Active learning
- Discussion-based classrooms
- Project-based assignments
- Original research and experiment design
- Student choice embedded in course work

Formative and summative documentation
- Transcripts of previous school history including attendance and grades
- An intake process that includes interview and writing samples
- Cumulative documentation: attendance, course performance, tests
- Student reports
- Parent–teacher conferences
- Staff review of work patterns and work products

Strategies for corrective action
- Feedback on written work
- Narrative reports
- Student–teacher conferences
- Parent–teacher conferences
- After-school homework labs
- Peer tutoring

Multiple ways for students to express and exhibit learning
- Writing: literary essays, research papers, playwriting, poetry, lyrics
- Oral presentations: discussions, debate, poetry reading, dramatic presentation, external presentations
- Artistic renderings: sculpture, painting, drawing, photography

Graduation level performance-based tasks aligned with learning standards
- Analytic literary essay
- Social studies research paper
- Original science experiment
- Application of higher level mathematics

External evaluators of student work
- Experts in various disciplines (such as writers, scientists, historians)

- Other interested evaluators (such as teachers from other schools)
- PAR Board members [Oversight of the performance assessment system is carried out by an external board, The Performance Assessment Review Board, which reviews both student work and the process by which is it graded.]

A focus on professional development
- School-based and center-based workshops which strengthen inquiry-based teaching
- Sessions reviewing student work and teacher assignments
- Opportunities to critique student presentations and scoring procedures
- Mentoring of less experienced teachers by master teachers
- Refining rubrics and reviewing performance assessment processes
- Support for school-based research

From: New York Performance Standards Consortium (2003).

Appendix B 9th Grade Science Outcomes: Chemistry Unit

OUTCOME	PROFICIENT LEVEL	HIGHLY PROFICIENT LEVEL	Assessments	Activities
Understand how atomic interactions give way to bulk properties	1. Explain the differences between the four types of chemical bonds. 2. Explain how the types of bonds affect how substances interact. 3. Demonstrate how molecular formulas give way to molecular shape.	1. Describe how subatomic particles determine the type of bonds within a molecule.		A2 4 types of reactions A3 Lab report q2
Identify and classify properties of matter using trends in the periodic table.	1. Determine electron configuration from the periodic table. 2. Determine atomic structure and properties from information in the periodic table. 3. Explain the electronegativity trend in the periodic table and how it influences properties of matter.	1. Explain how energy is absorbed and released resulting in photons. 2. Predict the type of reaction that would occur based on the atomic properties of its reactants.		BHP1 4 types of reactions BHP2 Lab Report q2, Environmental Problem

(continued)

Appendix B Continued

OUTCOME	PROFICIENT LEVEL	HIGHLY PROFICIENT LEVEL	Assessments	Activities
Understand and be able to use properties of matter to classify substances.	1. Use density, reactivity, melting point, and boiling point to identify substances. 2. Explain how the structure of a compound influences its reactivity.	1. Explain why understanding reactivity is important and where it can be used. 2. Explain how reactivity changes among isomers.		C1 Powders Lab CHP1 Under the Sink Lab, Environmental Problem C2 Lab Report q2, Environmental Problem
Understand the basic structure of an atom.	1. Identify location, relative size and charge of protons, neutrons and electrons in an atom. 2. Describe how electrons are arranged in various elements. 3. Describe how strong and weak nuclear force keep an atom together.	1. Explain how quarks are arranged to create protons and neutrons. 2. Describe how the electron energy levels influence bonding types and the release of photons.		D1 Bohr Model diagrams, Lewis Structure worksheets D2 Periodic table color coding, interpretation work DHP2 4 types of reactions
Understand how the structure and energy of compounds drives chemical reactions.	1. Balance chemical equations. 2. Identify reactants, products, and catalysts in a reaction. 3. Describe endothermic and exothermic reactions.	1. Predict the products of a reaction given the reactants and environment. 2. Predict whether a reaction is exothermic or endothermic.		E1, E2, E3 Balance reactions in 4 types labs E1, E2, E3 Lab Report q2
Understand the chemistry of everyday compounds.	1. Identify key components of acids and bases. 2. Explain how to sort components of a mixture. 3. Explain how chemistry and its advancements have shaped society.	1. Infer uses of a compound based on the pH. 2. Mathematically represent pH		F2, F3 Under the Sink Lab F1, F2, F3, FHP1, FHP2 Environmental Problem

From: Amy Biehl High School (2008b). Reprinted with permission.

Appendix C Amy Biehl High School "Habits of Mind and Heart"

The Habit of Perspective: The ability to address questions from multiple viewpoints and to use a variety of ways to solve problems.

The Habit of Evidence: The ability to bring together relevant information, to judge the credibility of sources, to find out for oneself.

The Habit of Connection: The ability to look for patterns and ways that things fit together in order to utilize diverse material to form new solutions.

The Habit of Convention: The ability to acknowledge accepted standards in any area in order to be understood and to understand others.

The Habit of Service to the Common Good: The ability to recognize the effects of one's actions upon others, coupled with the desire to make the community a better place for all.

The Habit of Collaboration: The ability to work effectively with others, accepting and giving appropriate assistance.

The Habit of Ethical Behavior: The ability to understand how personal values influence behavior and to live one's life according to ethical principles.

From: Amy Biehl High School (2008b).

Appendix D Profile of an Amy Biehl High School Science Graduate

---

The intent of math and science curricula is as follows: Science is essentially an attempt to better understand the phenomena of the world and Math is a tool by which to describe/define the discovered patterns of examined phenomena.

In general terms, an ABHS Graduate can do the following in the context of Science:

1. Problem solving
2. Critical & creative thinking (analysis/synthesis/informed & respectful application curiosity)
3. Relationship to community/broadened scope of humanity
4. Presentation of/responsibility for self
5. Explanation of work's impact on self and/or others in the community.

Attempting to further delineate what the above 4 parts mean, by the time an ABHS learner graduates she or he will have demonstrated the following:

1. Take any topic and become more informed through research of materials, both traditional and from the Internet.
2. Provide evidence of research through proficient use of conventions of citation.
3. Critically analyze any topic. Critically analyze = follow the Scientific Method—hypothesize/predict outcomes with reason; provide background of topic; report details of work (materials & methods); report results/outcomes of experiments/projects; describe/explain the results in explicit detail using math; make recommendations for future work based on current experiments/prior findings; think reflectively on the work/project and provide insight on how to proceed/alter the current work.
4. Demonstrate the use of the tools of mathematics/statistics to analyze/interpret results or to make recommendations.
5. Show proficiency in number sense in describing outcomes of work/project and the relationships present therein; e.g., "the trees grow twice as fast as the grasses" or "the speed of decline is directly proportional to the rate of the depth," or "30% of all students refuse to study math."
6. Create and develop visuals, specifically graphs and tables, to facilitate explanations and assertions.

From: Amy Biehl High School (2008c).

6

STUDENTS AS THE DEFINITIVE SOURCE
OF FORMATIVE ASSESSMENT

Academic Self-Assessment and the Self-Regulation of Learning

HEIDI L. ANDRADE

> If formative assessment is exclusively in the hands of teachers, then it is difficult
> to see how students can become empowered and develop the self-regulation skills
> needed to prepare them for learning outside university and throughout life. (Nicol
> & Macfarlane-Dick, 2006, p. 200)

> Where am I going? How am I [d]oing? and Where to next? An ideal learning en-
> vironment or experience occurs when both teachers and students seek answers to
> each of these questions. Too often, teachers limit students' opportunities to receive
> information about their performances in relation to any of these questions by assum-
> ing that responsibility for the students.... Students, too often, view feedback as the
> responsibility of someone else, usually teachers, whose job it is to provide feedback
> information by deciding for the students how well they are [d]oing, what the goals
> are, and what to do next. (Hattie & Timperley, 2007, pp. 88, 101)

Nearly every author in this volume has identified the primary goal of formative assessment as providing feedback to students and teachers about the targets for learning, where
students are in relation to those targets, and what can be done to fill in the gaps. In this
chapter, it is argued that students themselves can be thought of as the definitive source
of such feedback, given their constant and instant access to their own thoughts, actions,
and works. To researchers in the area of self-regulated learning, such a position is not
new: It has long been known that effective learners tend to monitor and regulate their
own learning and, as a result, learn more and have greater academic success in school
(Pintrich, 2000; Zimmerman & Schunk, 2001). However, the assertion that students
themselves are the definitive source of feedback is a relatively new way of thinking
about the role of the student in assessment. This chapter makes the case for students
as key producers and consumers of formative assessment information, drawing on

the research on self-assessment and self-regulated learning. The primary goal of the chapter is to offer an expanded conception of the role that students can play in their own learning, as well as to propose practical approaches to scaffolding self-regulation and assessment.

Self-regulated learning is the process whereby learners set goals for their learning and then attempt to monitor, regulate, and control their cognition, motivation, and behavior in order to reach their goals (Pintrich, 2000). Self-assessment is a process of formative assessment during which students reflect on the quality of their work, judge the degree to which it reflects explicitly stated goals or criteria, and revise their work accordingly (Andrade & Boulay, 2003). To oversimplify a bit, studies of self-regulated learning have concentrated on how students manage learning *processes*, including, for example, understanding a text, sticking to a study schedule, or maintaining the motivation to achieve, while studies of self-assessment have focused on students' judgments of the *products* of their learning, such as written papers, oral presentations, or solutions to mathematical problems. A central purpose of both self-assessment and self-regulation is to provide learners with feedback that they can use to deepen their understandings and improve their performances.

Hattie and Timperley's (2007) review of the research on feedback suggests that it can have very powerful effects on achievement, with a whopping average effect size of 0.79. They put this effect size into perspective by comparing it to other influences on achievement, including direct instruction (0.93), reciprocal teaching (0.86), and students' prior cognitive ability (0.71). They also note that, compared to over 100 factors known to affect achievement, feedback is in the top 5 to 10 in terms of effect size. They conclude that "feedback is among the most critical influences on student learning" (p. 102).

Research has indicated that feedback tends to promote learning and achievement (Bangert-Drowns, Kulik, Kulik, & Morgan, 1991; Brinko, 1993; Butler & Winne, 1995; Crooks, 1988; Hattie & Timperley, 2007; Kluger & DeNisi, 1996) if delivered correctly (Shute, 2008); however, most students get little informative feedback on their work (Black & Wiliam, 1998). This scarcity is due in part to the fact that few teachers have sufficient time in the typical school day to regularly and promptly respond to each student's work. Fortunately, research also shows that students themselves can be useful sources of task feedback via self-assessment (Andrade, Du, & Wang, 2008; Ross, Rolheiser, & Hogaboam-Gray, 1999), and effective producers of process and regulation feedback via self-regulation (Boekaerts, Pintrich, & Zeidner, 2000; Nicol & Macfarlane-Dick, 2006; Zimmerman & Schunk, 2001). Because self-assessment and self-regulation involve students in thinking about the quality of their own products and processes rather than relying on their teacher as the sole source of evaluative judgments (or getting no feedback at all), they are key elements of formative assessment.

To date, however, only self-assessment has been included in theory and practice related to formative assessment. With few exceptions (e.g., Nicol & Macfarlane-Dick, 2006), self-regulation has received little consideration in the literature on formative assessment. A central argument of this chapter is that self-regulation and self-assessment are complementary processes that can lead to marked improvements in academic achievement and autonomy.

SELF-ASSESSMENT

As indicated previously, self-assessment is a process of formative assessment during which students reflect on the quality of their work, judge the degree to which it reflects explicitly stated goals or criteria, and revise accordingly. The emphasis here is on the word *formative*: Self-assessment is done on drafts of works in progress in order to inform revision and improvement. The primary purpose of engaging students in careful self-assessment is to boost learning and achievement. It does so by serving as a readily available source of feedback about the students' own understandings and performances.

According to the above definition, self-assessment is task-specific. This distinguishes it from other forms of self-assessment such as judging strong or weak abilities (e.g., reading, interpersonal skills, leadership, language). Such a process, which can be called self-reflection, is intended to promote self-discovery and awareness (Harrington, 1995) rather than to improve performance on a specific task.

Self-assessment is also not a matter of determining one's own grade. That is self-evaluation, which involves students in grading their work, perhaps as part of their final grade for an assignment or a class (e.g., Sadler & Good, 2006). Given what we know about human nature, as well as findings from research regarding students' tendency to inflate self-evaluations when they will count toward formal grades (Boud & Falchikov, 1989), this chapter subscribes to a purely formative type of student self-assessment.

Features of Self-Assessment

There are number of ways to engage students in effective self-assessment. In general, the process involves three steps. The first step is *articulating expectations*. The expectations for the task or performance are clearly articulated, either by the teacher, by the students, or both together, perhaps by reviewing model assignments or cocreating a rubric.

The second step involves *critique of work in terms of expectations*. Students create rough or first drafts of their assignment, be it an essay, word problem, lab report, volleyball serve, or speech. They monitor their progress on the assignment by comparing their performances-in-progress to the expectations. An example from writing (Andrade, Du, & Wang, 2008) involves students in seeking evidence of success in their drafts. Using colored pencils, students underline key phrases in a rubric with one color (e.g., they underline "clearly states an opinion" in blue on their persuasive essay rubric), then underline or circle in their drafts the evidence of having met the standard articulated by the phrase (they underline their opinions in blue in their persuasive essay drafts). If they find they have not met the standard, they write themselves a reminder to make improvements when they write their final drafts. This process is followed for each criterion on the rubric, with pencils of various colors.

The third, and final, step is *revising*. In this step, students use the feedback from their self-assessments to guide revision. This last step—revision—is crucial. Students are savvy, and will not self-assess thoughtfully unless they know that their efforts can lead to opportunities to actually make improvements.

Table 6.1 Necessary Elements for Effective Student Self-Assessment

1. Awareness of the value of self-assessment
2. Access to clear criteria on which to base the assessment
3. A specific task or performance to assess
4. Models of self-assessment
5. Direct instruction in and assistance with self-assessment, including feedback
6. Practice
7. Cues regarding when it is appropriate to self-assess
8. Opportunities to revise and improve the task or performance

Adapted from Goodrich (1996)

Conditions for Self-Assessment

Although even young students typically are able to think about the quality of their own work, they do not always do so. Often this is because one or more necessary conditions are not present. Goodrich (1996), notes that in order for effective self-assessment to occur, students need each of the elements shown in Table 6.1.

The list of conditions shown in Table 6.1 might seem prohibitive but student self-assessment is feasible and is occurring in many schools around the world (Deakin-Crick, Sebba, Harlen, Guoxing, & Lawson, 2005). Several of the key conditions listed above, which include modeling, cueing, direct instruction, and practice, are commonly employed classroom practices. The second condition—access to clear criteria on which to base self-assessment—can be met by reviewing models or introducing a rubric (Andrade, 2000).

Research on Self-Assessment

Actively involving students in self-assessing their work has been associated with noticeable improvements in performance. Research on the effects of student self-assessment covers a wide range of content areas including social studies (Lewbel & Hibbard, 2001), science (Duffrin, Dawes, Hanson, Miyazaki, & Wolfskill, 1998; White & Frederiksen, 1998), and external examinations (MacDonald & Boud, 2003). In each case, students were either engaged in written forms of self-assessment using journals, checklists and questionnaires, or oral forms of self-assessment, such as interviews and student–teacher conferences.

Much of the research on self-assessment has focused on writing and mathematics. Studies of writing have found a positive relationship between self-assessment and quality of writing (Andrade & Boulay, 2003; Andrade, Du, & Wang, 2008; Ross, Rolheiser, & Hogaboam-Gray, 1999). The improvements in students' writing include more effective handling of sophisticated qualities such as ideas and content, organization, and voice—not just mechanics. In mathematics, self-assessment has been associated with increased autonomy and mathematical vocabulary (Stallings &Tascione, 1996), and dramatically higher performances on word problem solutions (Ross, Hogaboam-Gray, & Rolheiser, 2002). Black, Harrison, Lee, Marshall, and Wiliam's (2004) study of formative assessment practices in math and science classes for 11- to 15-year-olds also revealed a strong relationship between formative assessment, including self-assessment, and achievement.

These authors concluded that "the development of self-assessment by the student might have to be an important feature of any programme of formative assessment" (p. 14).

Another possible benefit of self-assessment is that it could be helpful to students who do not seek help or engage in learning because of perceived threats to self-esteem or social embarrassment (Hattie & Timperley, 2007). By self-assessing, students engage in the important processes of reorienting to the goals of an assignment and determining how to make improvements, without the threat of negative feedback or perceived insults from a peer. The ego-protective feature of self-assessment may be especially important for some students. This might explain, in part, why students typically report that they value it (Andrade & Du, 2007) as long as it does not become self-evaluation by counting toward a grade (Ross, Rolheiser, & Hogaboam-Gray, 1998).

Although the research on self-assessment has illuminated a powerful way in which students can serve as both the producers and consumers of feedback, it has been limited by a focus on concrete products, assignments, and tasks. Hattie and Timperley's (2007) review of feedback placed a strong emphasis on the need for feedback on processes and regulation as well as on tasks. The field of self-regulated learning represents a rich source of information about how students generate and respond to feedback about *how* they work.

SELF-REGULATED LEARNING

Being a self-regulated learner means exercising executive control over one's own learning or, to use the lingo of young students, "being the boss of yourself." More formally, self-regulated learning is a dynamic process of striving to meet learning goals by generating, monitoring, and modifying one's own thoughts, feelings, actions, and, to some degree, context. Self-regulated learners use a wide variety of strategies and tactics to promote learning, such as task interpretation, goal setting, planning, selecting and adapting learning strategies, seeking help and feedback, managing affect and motivation, administering rewards, arranging study spaces and schedules, and monitoring and evaluating progress toward their goals. Self-regulation is situated within a complex context, including but not limited to the classroom. As a result, it influences and is influenced by a multitude of factors, including personal characteristics (e.g., temperament, self-efficacy, motivation), social circumstances (e.g., family and cultural values, peer pressure, teacher expectations), and physical conditions (e.g., noisy or quiet, online or face to face), each of which reciprocally influences the others (Boekaerts et al., 2000; Butler & Cartier, 2004; Pintrich, 2000; Winne, 2001; Zimmerman & Schunk, 2004).

Features of Self-Regulated Learning

There are many elements of self-regulation, and several competing models (e.g., Butler & Cartier, 2004; Pintrich, 2000; Winne, 2001; Zimmerman, 2000), each of which make important contributions to our emerging understanding of this complex phenomenon. One of the most commonly accepted models was proposed by Zimmerman (2000); the model includes three main phases that function cyclically. The three phases include: *forethought*, which precedes efforts to learn and involves consideration of the goals, expectancies, and standards for the task at hand, as well as strategic planning and self-efficacy judgments; *performance* or *volitional control*, which occurs during learning and involves self-monitoring and the use of learning management strategies; and *self-reflection*, a phase that follows learning efforts and involves the self-evaluation of mastery, causal attributions, and reactions to the task and performance; it leads back to the forethought phase that precedes the next learning efforts. Each of the three phases of Zimmerman's (2000) model has multiple components. For example, the forethought phase involves analyzing a task, setting goals for performance, selecting strategies, making plans, managing one's motivational beliefs and expectations, and so on.

This chapter focuses on the aspects of self-regulation most closely associated with self-assessment. Zimmerman's model includes two subphases that involve explicit self-assessment: self-observation and self-judgment. Self-observation means tracking specific aspects of one's own performance, the conditions that surround it, and the effects that it produces as one engages in a task. In other words, self-observation means paying attention to what you are doing, why you are doing it, and how it helps you (Schoenfeld, 1987). Self-judgment involves judging one's performance against criteria or standards. It also entails making causal attributions by determining, for example, whether poor performance is due to ineffective learning strategies, insufficient effort, inadequate instruction, or something else.

Research on Self-Regulated Learning

Several decades of study of self-regulated learning have produced a rich and elaborate body of knowledge. Briefly, the research suggests that self-regulation and academic achievement are closely related: Students who set goals, make flexible plans to meet them, and monitor their progress tend to learn more and do better in school than students who do not. Less effective learners, in contrast, have minimal self-regulation strategies and depend much more on external factors such as the teacher, peers, or the task for guidance and feedback (Hattie & Timperley, 2007; Pintrich, 2000; Zimmerman & Schunk, 2004). Fortunately, self-regulation is learnable. Studies have shown that all kinds of students, including those with mild to moderate cognitive impairments (Brown & Palincsar, 1982), can learn to monitor and regulate their own learning more effectively.

A SYNTHESIS

In addition to having much in common with each other, theories of self-assessment and self-regulation have many commonalities with recent scholarship on formative assessment. The simple model in Figure 6.1 represents formative assessment and self-assessment as two aspects of self-regulation. The figure draws on the three phase model of self-regulation proposed by Zimmerman (2000) and includes: *Forethought*, which is when learners set goals and make plans for reaching them; *Performance and Control*, which occurs during learning and involves self-monitoring and the use of learning management strategies; and *Reflection*, during which learners evaluate and reflect on their work.

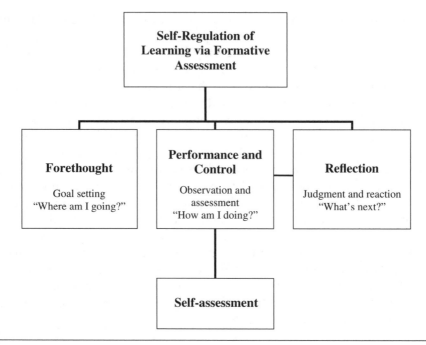

Figure 6.1 Self-regulated learning and formative assessment.

The model also incorporates the conception of feedback in learning proposed by Hattie and Timperley (2007), in which they identify the main purpose of feedback as reducing discrepancies between one's goal and one's current understandings and performance. According to Hattie and Timperley, feedback that effectively closes the gap between current states and the target must address three questions: "Where am I going? (What are the goals?), How am I going [or doing]? (What progress is being made toward the goals), and Where to next? (What activities need to be undertaken to make better progress?)" (p. 82). As indicated in Figure 6.1, self-regulation theory posits that effective learners ask similar questions, and engage in regular self-assessments of their work.

Figure 6.1 represents a synthesis of Zimmerman's taxonomy and the three questions posed by Hattie and Timperley (2007): Forethought involves learners in asking "Where am I going?" and "What are the goals?" The performance and self-reflection phases include, among other things, self-assessment by asking oneself, "How am I doing? What progress is being made toward the goals?" as well as "Where to next? What activities need to be undertaken to make better progress?" The link between the performance and control phase and the reflection phase indicate how effective learners will respond to perceived deficiencies in their work or approaches to it by revisiting and revising it.

Oneself as a Source of Formative Assessment

"Where am I going?" "How am I doing?" "Where to next?" These questions can refer to the quality of one's work or one's learning processes, depending on how they are asked and answered..Hattie and Timperley (2007) noted that feedback that aims at improving students' strategies and processes as well as making improvements in the task at hand are most powerful. The key challenge for educators, of course, is in figuring out how to scaffold self-assessment and regulation while at the same time teaching important content and skills. This section describes several such efforts. It does not discuss stand-alone courses that teach self-regulation skills (e.g., Dembo & Seli, 2008).

Some scholars have capitalized on the similarities between self-regulation and self-assessment and designed instructional techniques that promote both. Paris, for example, created a portfolio assessment process that scaffolds self-regulation (Paris & Ayres, 1994), and has written about the role of self-assessment in providing students with opportunities to monitor and understand their own learning (Paris & Paris, 2001). Perry, VandeKamp, Mercer, and Nordby (2002) emphasize how even young learners in third grade can effectively self-regulate their behaviors after analyzing the results of a nonthreatening assessment. These and other approaches described below combine the goals of student self-regulation and self-assessment in practical classroom applications, often emphasizing one or the other. In each case, recommendations are made for enhancing the regulatory or assessment aspects of the instructional design.

Strategic Content Learning

Butler (2002) designed an instructional model called Strategic Content Learning (SCL) in order to promote self-regulated learning in secondary and postsecondary students with learning disabilities. Her approach emphasizes the value of coconstructing learning strategies with students rather than teaching predefined strategies. Butler recommends, among other things, having students submit a list of performance criteria and personalized learning strategies as part of an assignment, and helping students self-assess their work prior to submission. She also recommends promoting strategy development by facilitating discussions about strategies that might meet task demands, having students try them out, and articulating strategies they plan to use in the future.

For instance, one English teacher in Butler's (2002) study created a strategy form that students revised and turned in across a sequence of writing assignments:

> In a first column students described each assignment in turn (e.g., writing a first narrative paragraph). In a second column students outlined the strategies they planned to use to complete that row's assignment. In a third column, students interpreted teacher feedback on each assignment in light of specific task criteria (generated in a class discussion before starting the project). In a final column, students recorded ideas they had about how to improve their performance for the upcoming assignment. (p. 90)

The process described by the English teacher includes a minor element of self-assessment—cocreating task-specific criteria for an assignment—as well as major components of self-regulation. In order to more comprehensively include self-assessment, a column or separate form could be added that asks students to assess their work according to the cocreated task criteria before receiving and interpreting their teacher's feedback. A hypothetical example of such a form is shown in Table 6.2. The form reveals that the

Table 6.2 Strategy form (Based on Butler, 2002)

Assignment	Strategies	Self-Assessment	Teacher's Feedback	Next Time
1. Persuasive essay	1a. Brainstorm reasons, pro and con. 1b. Outline. 1c. First draft. 1d. Self-assess, revise. 1e. Get feedback from teacher. 1f. Write final draft.	My first draft has strong reasons for my opinion but doesn't consider other points of view. My sentences are correct but the tone is boring and spelling is a mess.	Your second draft has clear, relevant reasons in support of your claim, and touches on the opposite point of view. You could elaborate on why your opinion is better. I recommend finding words and phrases that make it sound like you care about this topic, and using the computer to spell check.	Pick a topic that I care about.
2. Auto-biography	2a. Read an autobiography to see how it is written. 2b. Look at photos of my life to get ideas for a theme.			

student using it is working on two assignments: a persuasive essay and an autobiography. The student has completed the persuasive essay assignment, and the strategies used by the student, the student's self-assessment, the teacher's feedback, and ideas for making improvements to future writing projects are shown.

Project-Based Portfolio Assessment

Alonso-Tapia (2002) studied a project-based portfolio assessment for 14- to 16-year-old students that includes both process-oriented self-regulation and task-specific self-assessment. As part of the portfolio process, students produce and reflect on written work. They write responses to questions referring to the writing process, such as: What strategies have I used to decide what to say? Does my portfolio include drafts, schemes, or products deriving from brainstorms? What questions have I asked myself to organize the text? Have I considered the purpose of my essay and the readers' needs? Have I considered potential arguments against my point of view and addressed them (as far as possible)? Have I revised the written text? Students also respond to questions referring to the content of their writing: Have I articulated my point of view well enough? Why do I think so? What kinds of comment have I received from my classmates about my point of view? Do I agree with them or not? Why?

Portfolios like those described by Alonso-Tapia (2002) are especially good vehicles for reflection on process and product; in fact, reflection is one of the primary purposes of portfolio-based assessment (Danielson & Abrutyn, 1997; Seidel et al., 1997; Wolf, 1989). In order to enhance the self-assessment aspect of this portfolio project, students could be engaged in generating a list of qualities of excellent pieces of work, and in a process of judging their own work in relation to those qualities. This process would be followed by opportunities to revise.

King's Medway Oxford Formative Assessment Project (KMOFAP)

A final example of a classroom practice that combines self-regulation and self-assessment comes from work done by Black et al. on formative assessment practices in classrooms (2004), which emphasizes the importance of student self-assessment. Some of the approaches they describe represent a blurring of the distinction between self-assessment and self-regulation because they require students to assess their understanding of a topic or lesson—a metacognitive act.

A tool they called "traffic lights" serves as a powerful example of the integration of self-assessment and self-regulated learning. Students in the math and science classes they studied used red, amber, and green icons to indicate their perceptions of the extent to which they understood the content being studied. They did so in a variety of ways, such as labeling their work with a color, or placing a red, amber, or green cup on their desks during a lecture or demonstration (Wiliam, 2008). The teachers could immediately respond to the students' confidence in their understanding by, for example, pairing up the greens and ambers to clarify areas of confusion between them, while the teacher helps the red students as a group. According to Black et al. (2004), the traffic lights allowed for

> instant differentiation but the recognition of the learning needs has been done by the students, allowing the teacher to focus on steering the remedial action. Because the response to their needs is immediate, students begin to realize that revealing their problems is worthwhile, as the focus of the teaching is to improve learning. (p. 52)

Strategic Content Learning, portfolio-based assessment, and traffic lights represent a small sample of the many ways in which students can be their own and their teachers' best source of formative assessment information. Students have instant, ongoing access to their own thoughts, actions, and works, and there is ample evidence that they can accurately self-assess and self-regulate under the right conditions (Paris & Paris, 2001). The challenge is in creating the right conditions.

GENERAL PRINCIPLES FOR SUPPORTING SELF-ASSESSMENT AND SELF-REGULATION

Lacking supportive conditions, students across the K-16+ educational span often do not have well-developed skills in self-assessment and self-regulation. Self-evaluation strategies were found by Zimmerman and Martinez-Pons (1988) to be one of the least used self-regulation strategies by American students. Writing about their work with 11- to 15-year-olds in the United Kingdom, Black et al. (2004) state that one of their most difficult tasks was helping students to think of their work in terms of learning goals. This section presents a list of general principles for classroom practices that cue, scaffold, and even push students to self-regulate and self-assess.

Creating a Culture of Critique

It is easy to blame students for failing to think about their own work or thinking, but the extant assessment and evaluation ethos can inhibit self-assessment and regulation

(Ames, 1992). Hattie and Timperley (2007) note that "the climate of the classroom is critical, particularly if disconfirmation and corrective feedback at any level is to be welcomed and used by the students (and teachers). Errors and disconfirmation are most powerful in climates in which they are seen as leading to future learning" (p. 100). As with many other school-related topics, self-assessment and self-regulation are likely to work only when students perceive them to be valued and valuable, and to the extent that teachers' messages about the relationships between effort, understanding, and grades are influential.

Where Am I Going? Setting Learning Goals

Research on the effectiveness of feedback has shown that "goals without clarity as to when and how a student (and teacher) would know they were successful are often too vague to serve the purpose of enhancing learning" (Hattie & Timperley, 2007, p. 88). Effective goal setting involves articulating clear, reasonably challenging goals regarding the type or level of performance expected of students. Students should set goals for nearly everything, more or less—assignments, the processes they are using to complete them, and the regulatory mechanisms they employ.

One popular way to set task-specific goals is to distribute a rubric to students or, better, to cocreate one with them. Checklists, scoring guidelines, and detailed assignment briefs can serve the same purpose, particularly when they are discussed or generated with students (Andrade, 2000; Butler, 2002). Genuine interaction between teacher and students enhances the process of goal setting because "goals are more effective when students share a commitment to attaining them" (Hattie & Timperley, 2007, p. 89).

Because "a great deal of student behavior that we see in the context of the classroom should be labeled as 'compliance', 'self-control' or 'self-management' rather than self-regulation" (Boekaerts, 2001, p. 598), Boekaerts highlights the need to distinguish between students' personal goals and teachers' imposed goals. Students' personal goals are often related to valued future goals. Brickman and Miller (2000) have illustrated the ways in which goals that students believe are instrumental to future goal attainment, such as attending college or beginning a career, provide the foundation for meaningful self-regulation. In light of this and related research, teachers should engage students in setting goals that are meaningful to them.

How Am I Doing? Aiding Students in Generating Feedback for Themselves

Previous portions of this chapter have presented research-based evidence that students can provide feedback for themselves under the right conditions. The right conditions include at least the following:

1. guidance in articulating the criteria by which they assess their learning processes and products;
2. learning how to apply the criteria by assessing their work and approaches to it;
3. getting feedback on their self-assessments of both process and product;
4. being offered help in using self-assessment data to improve;

5. providing sufficient time for revision of assignments and adjustments to strate-gies;
6. making some self-assessments private, since students might say or write what they think their teachers want to read; and
7. *not* turning self-assessment into self-evaluation by counting it toward a grade (Andrade & Valtcheva, 2009; Butler, 2002; Macguire, Evans, & Dyas, 2001; Ross, 2006; Thompson, Pilgrim, & Oliver, 2005).

In addition, the self-assessment done by students should be near-term. Zimmerman (2000) notes that the "temporal proximity of one's self-observations is a critical variable. Self-feedback that is delayed precludes a person from taking corrective action in a timely fashion" (p. 20).

Finally, a caveat: Feedback has its limitations. According to Hattie and Timperley (2007), feedback is

> not "the answer"; rather, it is but one powerful answer. With inefficient learners, it is better for a teacher to provide elaborations through instruction than to provide feedback on poorly understood concepts.... Feedback can only build on something; it is of little use when there is no initial learning or surface information. (p. 104)

This general caveat might also apply to self-generated feedback in particular: In a review of student self-ratings, Boud and Falchikov (1989) concluded that high achieving students tended to underrate their performance, while lower achieving students tended to overrate it. This finding has been replicated in more recent research (e.g., Dochy, Segers, Sluijsmans, 1999), and suggests that students who struggle with school work need extra help understanding their tasks, the criteria for them, and the self-assessment process.

Where to Next? Providing Time and Assistance with Revision or Revisiting

Closing the gap between where students are and where they are headed is what makes formative assessment and feedback powerful (Sadler, 1989). Students are unlikely to thoughtfully self-assess or self-regulate unless they know these acts will lead to better grades, deeper understanding, and more well-developed skill sets. Thus, revision and revisiting are essential components of self-regulation and assessment.

In addition to the obvious need to allow and encourage students to revise their work and rethink their approaches to it, there is the less obvious need to explicitly revisit causal attributions, or students' beliefs about the internal and external causes of their success or failure (Weiner, 1986). Given what is known about the influence of causal attributions on strategy choices, persistence, and achievement, it is essential to teach students to make accurate attributions.

The question "Where to next?" can also be extended to other contexts and assignments. Butler (2002) cites the literature that argues for mindful approaches to transfer (e.g., Perkins & Salomon, 1989), and notes the need to help students construct self-regulatory skills that can transfer to subsequent learning. She argues that this can be done by promoting self-regulation in the context of meaningful work, supporting students in articulating strategies in their own words, and having students discuss when and why certain strategies promote success.

RECOMMENDATIONS FOR FUTURE RESEARCH AND DEVELOPMENT

Although much is known about the relationships between self-regulated learning, self-assessment, and achievement, compelling questions and puzzles remain. For instance, much of the research on feedback has been done using traditional tests and selected-response item formats that utilize one correct or best response (see Bangert-Drowns, et al., 1991; Crooks, 1988; Hattie & Timperley, 2007), perhaps because they are more readily subjected to experimental control (Shute, 2008). Limitations regarding generalizations to performance assessment apply. More research is needed on the qualities of and conditions for self-generated feedback on open-ended tasks and process-related strategies.

Similarly, much of the research on feedback involves feedback generated by external sources. Whereas the premise of this chapter rests on the assumption that self-generated feedback behaves much like feedback from tests, teachers, and technology, some research suggests that students respond differently to feedback from different sources (Andrade, Wang, Du, & Akawi, 2009; Bronfenbrenner, 1967, 1970; Dweck, Davidson, Nelson, & Enna, 1978). Students' responses to self-generated feedback should be investigated via new research that compares the effects of feedback provided by students themselves, their peers, their teachers, and technology (e.g., Graesser, McNamara, & VanLehn, 2005). Such research should include questions related to the relationships between self-assessment and self-regulation: Is regular self-assessment of tasks associated in meaningful ways with self-regulated learning?

Finally, cross-cultural research on students' responses to self-assessment is also needed. Research on feedback suggests that students from collectivist cultures such as South Korea prefer indirect, group-focused feedback, compared to students from individualist cultures such as the United States, who preferred direct, individual feedback (de Luque & Sommer, 2000). It is not yet known whether or not this pattern of responsivity to feedback extends to self-assessment.

CONCLUDING REMARKS

This chapter has made a case for students as a valuable source of formative assessment information by reviewing and synthesizing the literatures on self-assessment and self-regulated learning, and proposing some general principles for creating the conditions under which self-assessment and self-regulation can thrive. Although students can be expected to complain at first that self-assessment and self-regulation are "a big pain" (Andrade & Du, 2007, p. 164), they are likely to value both as they gain experience and expertise. Teachers might have a similar reaction when scaffolding self-assessment and self-regulation in their classrooms. It can seem like a big pain at first but it accrues benefits that cannot be won in any other way. Students have exclusive access to their own thoughts and actions, and can and should be considered the definitive source of formative assessment information.

REFERENCES

Alonso-Tapia, J. (2002). Knowledge assessment and conceptual understanding. In M. Limón & L. Mason (Eds.), *Reframing the processes of conceptual change* (pp. 389–413). Dordrecht, the Netherlands: Kluwer.

Ames, C. (1992). Achievement goals and the classroom motivational climate. In D. H. Schunk & J. L. Meece (Eds.), *Students' perceptions in the classroom* (pp. 327–348). New York: Erlbaum.

Andrade, H. (2000). Using rubrics to promote thinking and learning. *Educational Leadership, 57*(5), 13–18.

Andrade, H., & Boulay, B. (2003). Gender and the role of rubric-referenced self-assessment in learning to write. *Journal of Educational Research, 97*(1), 21–34.

Andrade, H., & Du, Y. (2007). Student responses to criteria-referenced self-assessment. *Assessment and Evaluation in Higher Education, 32*(2), 159–181.

Andrade, H., Du, Y., & Wang, X. (2008). Putting rubrics to the test: The effect of a model, criteria generation, and rubric-referenced self-assessment on elementary school students' writing. *Educational Measurement: Issues and Practices, 27*(2), 3–13.

Andrade, H., & Valtcheva, A. (2009). Promoting learning and achievement through self-assessment. *Theory into Practice, 48*(1), 12–19.

Andrade, H., Wang, X., Du, Y., & Akawi, R. (2009). Rubric-referenced assessment and self-efficacy for writing. *The Journal of Educational Research, 102*(6), 287–302.

Bangert-Drowns, R. L., Kulik, C. C., Kulik, J. A., & Morgan, M. T. (1991). The instructional effect of feedback in test-like events. *Review of Educational Research, 61*(2), 213–238.

Black, P., Harrison, C., Lee, C., Marshall, B. & Wiliam, D. (2004). *Assessment for learning: Putting it into practice.* Maidenhead, England: Open University Press.

Black, P., & Wiliam, D. (1998). Inside the black box: Raising standards through classroom assessment. *Phi Delta Kappan, 80*(2), 139–148.

Boekaerts, M. (2001, August). *Bringing about change in the classroom: Strengths and weaknesses of the self-regulated learning approach.* Presidential Address presented at the 9th European Conference of the Association of Learning and Instruction. Fribourg, Switzerland.

Boekaerts, M., Pintrich, P., & Zeidner, M. (Eds.). (2000). *Handbook of self-regulation.* San Diego, CA: Academic.

Boud, D., & Falchikov, N. (1989). Quantitative studies of student self-assessment in higher education: A critical analysis of findings. *Higher Education, 18*, 529–549.

Brickman, S., & Miller, R. (2000). The impact of sociocultural context on future goals and self-regulation. In D. McInerney & S. Van Etten (Eds.), *Research on sociocultural influences on motivation and learning* (Vol. 1, pp. 119–138). Greenwich, CT: Information Age.

Brinko, L. T. (1993). The practice of giving feedback to improve teaching. *Journal of Higher Education, 64*(5), 574–593.

Bronfenbrenner, U. (1967). Response to pressure from peers versus adults among Soviet and American school children. *International Journal of Psychology, 2*(3), 199–207.

Bronfenbrenner, U. (1970). Reactions to social pressure from adults versus peers among Soviet day school and boarding school pupils in the perspective of an American sample. *Journal of Personality and Social Psychology, 15*, 179–189.

Brown, A. L., & Palincsar, A. S. (1982). Inducing strategic learning from texts by means of informed, self-control training. *Topics in Learning and Learning Disabilities, 2*(1), 1–17.

Butler, D. (2002). Individualizing instruction in self-regulated learning. *Theory into Practice, 41*(2), 81–92.

Butler, D., & Cartier, S. (2004). Promoting effective task interpretation as an important work habit: A key to successful teaching and learning. *Teachers College Record, 106*(9), 1729–1758.

Butler, D., & Winne, P. (1995). Feedback and self-regulated learning: A theoretical synthesis. *Review of Educational Research, 65*(3), 245–281.

Crooks, T. (1988). The impact of classroom evaluation practices on students. *Review of Educational Research, 58*(4), 438–481.

Danielson, C., & Abrutyn, L. (1997). *An introduction to using portfolios in the classroom.* Alexandria, VA: Association for Supervision and Curriculum Development.

Deakin-Crick, R., Sebba, J., Harlen, W., Guoxing, Y., & Lawson, H. (2005). *Systematic review of research evidence of the impact on students of self- and peer-assessment: Protocol.* London: EPPI-Centre, Social Science Research Unit, Institute of Education, University of London.

de Luque, M., & Sommer, S. (2000). The impact of culture on feed-back-seeking behavior: An integrated model and propositions. *Academy of Management Review, 25*(4), 829–849.

Dembo, M., & Seli, H. (2008). *Motivation and learning strategies for college success: A self-management approach* (3rd ed.). New York: Erlbaum.

Dochy, F., Segers, M., & Sluijsmans, D. (1999). The use of self-, peer and co-assessment in higher education: A review. *Studies in Higher Education, 24*(3), 331–350.

Duffrin, N., Dawes, W., Hanson, D., Miyazaki, J., & Wolfskill, T. (1998). Transforming large introductory classes into active learning environments. *Journal of Educational Technology Systems, 27*(2), 169–178.

Dweck, C., Davidson, W., Nelson, S., & Enna, B. (1978). Sex differences in learned helplessness: II. Contingencies of evaluative feedback in the classroom and III. An experimental analysis. *Developmental Psychology, 14*(3), 268–276.

Goodrich, H. (1996). *Student self-assessment: At the intersection of metacognition and authentic assessment.* Unpublished doctoral dissertation, Harvard University, Cambridge, MA.

Graesser, A., McNamara, D., & VanLehn, K. (2005). Scaffolding deep comprehension strategies through Point&Query, AutoTutor, and iSTART. *Educational Psychologist, 40*(4), 225–234.

Harrington, T. (1995). *Assessment of abilities.* Greensboro, NC: ERIC Clearinghouse on Counseling and Student Services.

Hattie, J., & Timperley, H. (2007). The power of feedback. *Review of Educational Research, 77*(1), 81–112.

Kluger, A., & DeNisi, A. (1996). The effects of feedback interventions on performance: A historical review, a meta-analysis, and a preliminary feedback intervention theory. *Psychological Bulletin, 119*(2), 254–284.

Lewbel, S. R., & Hibbard, K. M. (2001). Are standards and true learning compatible? *Principal Leadership, 1*(5), 16–20.

MacDonald, B., & Boud, D. (2003). The impact of self-assessment on achievement: The effects of self-assessment training on performance in external examinations. *Assessment in Education, 10*(2), 209–220.

Maguire, S., Evans, S., & Dyas, L. (2001). Approaches to learning: A study of first year geography undergraduates. *Journal of Geography in Higher Education, 25*(1), 95–107.

Nicol, D., & Macfarlane-Dick, D. (2006). Formative assessment and self-regulated learning: a model and seven principles of good feedback practice. *Studies in Higher Education, 31*(2), 199–218.

Paris, S., & Ayres, L. (1994). *Becoming reflective students and teachers with portfolios and authentic assessment.* Washington, DC: American Psychological Association.

Paris, S. G., & Paris, A. H. (2001). Classroom applications of research on self-regulated learning. *Educational Psychologist, 36*(2), 89–101.

Perkins, D., & Salomon, G. (1989). Are cognitive skills context-bound? *Educational Researcher, 18*(1), 16–25.

Perry, N., VandeKamp, K., Mercer, L., & Nordby, C. (2002). Investigating teacher–student interactions that foster self-regulated learning. *Educational Psychologist, 37*(1), 5–15.

Pintrich, P. (2000). The role of goal orientation in self-regulated learning. In M. Boekaerts, P. Pintrich, & M. Zeidner (Eds.), *Handbook of self-regulation* (pp. 452–502). San Diego, CA: Academic.

Ross, J. (2006). The reliability, validity, and utility of self-assessment. *Practical Assessment, Research, and Evaluation, 11*(10). Retrieved January 11, 2007, from http://pareonline.net/getvn.asp?v=11&n=10

Ross, J. A., Hogaboam-Gray, A., & Rolheiser, C. (2002). Student self-evaluation in grade 5–6 mathematics effects on problem-solving achievement. *Educational Assessment, 8*(1), 43–59.

Ross, J. A., Rolheiser, C., & Hogaboam-Gray, A. (1998). Skills-training versus action research in-service: Impact on student attitudes to self-evaluation. *Teaching and Teacher Education, 14*(5), 463–477.

Ross, J. A., Rolheiser, C., & Hogaboam-Gray, A. (1999). Effects of self-evaluation training on narrative writing. *Assessing Writing, 6*(1), 107–132.

Sadler, D. R. (1989). Formative assessment and the design of instructional systems. *Instructional Science, 18*, 119–144.

Sadler, P., & Good, E. (2006). The impact of self- and peer-grading on student learning. *Educational Assessment, 11*(1), 1–31.

Schoenfeld, A. H. (1987). What's all the fuss about metacognition? In A. Schoenfeld (Ed.), *Cognitive science and mathematics education* (pp. 189–215). Hillsdale, NJ: Erlbaum.

Seidel, S., Walters, J., Kirby, E., Olff, N., Powell, K., & Veenema, S. (1997). *Portfolio practices: Thinking through the assessment of children's work.* Washington, DC: NEA Publishing Library.

Shute, V. (2008). Focus on formative feedback. *Review of Educational Research, 78*(1), 153–189.

Stallings, V. & Tascione, C. (1996). Student self-assessment and self-evaluation. *Mathematics Teacher, 89*(7), 548–555.

Thompson, G., Pilgrim, A., & Oliver, K. (2005). Self-assessment and reflective learning for first-year university geography students: A simple guide or simply misguided? *Journal of Geography in Higher Education, 29*(3), 403–430.

Weiner, B. (1986). *An attributional theory of motivation and emotion.* New York: Springer-Verlag.

White, B. Y., & Frederiksen, J. R. (1998). Inquiry, modeling, and metacognition: Making science accessible to all students. *Cognition and Instruction, 16*(1), 3–118.

Wiliam, D. (2008, March). *Changing classroom practice.* Presentation at the annual meeting of the American Educational Research Association, Classroom Assessment Special Interest Group, New York.

Winne, P. (2001). Information processing models of self-regulated learning. In B. Zimmerman & D. Schunk (Eds.), *Self-regulated learning and academic achievement: Theory, research, and practice* (pp. 153–189). New York: Longman.

Wolf, D. (1989). Portfolio assessment: Sampling student work. *Educational Leadership, 46*(7), 35–39.

Zimmerman, B. (2000). Attaining self-regulation: A social cognitive perspective. In M. Boekaerts, P. Pintrich, & M. Zeidner (Eds.), *Handbook of self-regulation* (pp. 13–41). New York: Academic.

Zimmerman, B., & Martinez-Pons, M. (1988). Construct validation of a strategy model of student self-regulated learning. *Journal of Educational Psychology, 80*(3), 284–290.

Zimmerman, B., & Schunk, D. (2001). *Self-regulated learning and academic achievement: Theoretical perspectives* (2nd ed.). Mahwah, NJ: Erlbaum.

Zimmerman, B., & Schunk, D. (2004). Self-regulating intellectual processes and outcomes: A social cognitive perspective. In D. Dai & R. Sternberg (Eds.), *Motivation, emotion, and cognition: Integrative perspectives on intellectual functioning and development* (pp. 323–349). Mahwah, NJ: Erlbaum.

7

FORMATIVE ASSESSMENT
The Contributions of Benjamin S. Bloom

THOMAS R. GUSKEY

> If I have seen a little further, it is by standing on the shoulders of giants. (Sir Isaac Newton, February 5, 1676)

In the 17th century, Sir Isaac Newton stressed that great advances in science come not from reinventing or renaming established principles. Rather, they come from building on the principles developed by others to create new knowledge and extend scientific understanding. The ideas he developed built upon the work of those who came before him, and he readily acknowledged the importance of those scientists' contributions. He knew that he stood on the shoulders of giants.

The most significant advances in education today similarly are built on principles established in the past. Researchers today also stand on the shoulders of giants. Too often, however, the contributions of those who came before and established the foundation on which current work is built are not acknowledged. Instead, established principles are simply renamed or reinvented and credit for developing them is not appropriately attributed. This seems to be particularly the case in the use of classroom formative assessments.

Educators at all levels today are beginning to recognize the importance of classroom formative assessments. They are coming to see how assessments *for* learning can be used to improve a wide variety of student learning outcomes. Many also believe that using assessments as learning tools, rather than simply as evaluation devices that mark the end of instruction, is a new idea. Some have even been told that the powerful effects of classroom formative assessments on student learning have been recognized for only about a decade, dating back to the work of Black and Wiliam (1998).

The truth of the matter is that the importance of using classroom assessments formatively, to guide improvements in teaching and learning, has a long and rich history in education. In fact, value of formative assessments was identified nearly four decades ago. In their influential book, *Handbook on Formative and Summative Evaluation of Student*

Learning, Benjamin Bloom, Thomas Hastings, and George Madaus (1971) described the benefits of offering students regular feedback on their learning progress through classroom formative assessments. Bloom then went on to outline specific strategies teachers could use to implement formative assessments as part of regular classroom routines, both to improve student learning and to reduce gaps in the achievement of different subgroups of students (Bloom, 1971a). It was Bloom who initiated the phrase *formative assessments* and who provided practical guidance for the use of formative assessments in modern classrooms (see Guskey, 2007a).

This chapter focuses on Benjamin Bloom's work on classroom formative assessments through the instructional strategies he labeled *mastery learning.* Specific applications of Bloom's theory are reviewed, the essential elements involved in implementing mastery learning and classroom formative assessments are considered, and common misinterpretations of Bloom's ideas are described. Finally, research on the effectiveness of mastery learning and classroom formative assessments is reviewed and discussed.

THE CONTRIBUTIONS OF BENJAMIN S. BLOOM

In the 1960s, Bloom and his graduate students at the University of Chicago were engaged in a series of studies on individual differences in school learning. Although their evidence showed that many factors outside of school affect how well students learn (Bloom, 1964), Bloom was convinced that teachers have potentially a strong influence as well.

While observing classrooms, Bloom noted that teachers displayed little variation in their instructional practices. Most teachers taught all of their students in much the same way and provided all students with the same amount of time to learn. Students for whom these instructional methods and time were ideal learned excellently. The majority of students found these methods and time only moderately appropriate and learned somewhat less. Students for whom the instruction and time were inappropriate due to differences in their backgrounds or learning styles tended to learn very little. In other words, little variation in the teaching resulted in great variation in student learning. Under these conditions, the pattern of student achievement often resulted in a normal distribution of performance, as shown in Figure 7.1.

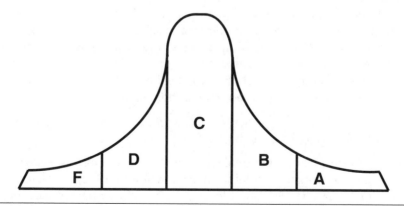

Figure 7.1 Distribution of achievement (grades) in traditional classrooms.

To attain better results and reduce variation in student achievement, Bloom reasoned that teachers would have to increase variation in their teaching. Because students vary in their learning styles and aptitudes, Bloom suggested that educators at all levels must differentiate instruction to better meet students' individual learning needs. The challenge was to find practical ways to do this within group-based classrooms so that all students learn well.

In searching for such a strategy, Bloom considered two different sources of evidence. First, he explored research on the ideal teaching and learning situation in which an excellent tutor is paired with each student. Particularly impressive to Bloom was the work of early pioneers in individualized instruction, especially Washburne (1922) and his Winnetka Plan, and Morrison (1926) and his University of Chicago Laboratory School experiments. In examining this evidence, Bloom tried to determine what critical elements in one-to-one tutoring and individualized instruction could be transferred to group-based classroom settings.

Second, Bloom looked at studies of the learning strategies of academically successful students, particularly the work of Dollard and Miller (1950). From this research he tried to identify the activities of high-achieving students in group-based classrooms that distinguish them from their less successful classmates.

Bloom saw value in teachers' traditional practice of organizing the concepts and skills to be learned into instructional units. He believed that approach offered students a valuable framework for organizing their learning. He also thought it vital for teachers to assess student learning at the end of each instructional unit. But to Bloom, most teachers' classroom assessments did little more than verify for whom their initial instruction was and was not appropriate.

A far better approach, according to Bloom, would be for teachers to use their classroom assessments as learning tools, both to provide students with feedback on their learning progress and to guide the correction of learning errors. In other words, instead of using assessments only as evaluation devices that mark the end of a unit, Bloom recommended that they be used as an integral part of the instructional process to identify individual learning difficulties and to prescribe remediation procedures.

This is precisely what takes place when an excellent tutor works with an individual student. If the student makes an error, the tutor first points out the error (feedback) and then follows up with further explanation and clarification (correctives) to ensure the student's understanding. Many academically successful students engage in these activities without the assistance of a tutor in the traditional sense, typically following up the mistakes they make on quizzes and assessments. They ask the teacher about the items they missed, look up the answer in the textbook or other resources, or rework the problem or task so that they do not repeat those errors.

Bloom's Mastery Learning

Bloom outlined a specific instructional strategy to make use of this feedback and corrective procedure, labeling it learning for mastery (Bloom, 1968), and later shortening the name to simply mastery learning (Bloom, 1971a). To use mastery learning, teachers first organize the concepts and skills they want students to learn into instructional units that typically involve approximately a week or two of instructional time. Following initial instruction on the unit, teachers administer a brief formative assessment based on the unit's learning goals. Bloom borrowed the term *formative* from Scriven (1967), who used it to describe program evaluation activities performed during the implementation of a program in order to inform developers of potential problems. Similarly in classrooms, rather than signifying the end of the unit, a formative assessment is designed to give students information, or feedback, on their learning. It helps students identify what they have learned well to that point and what they need to learn better (Bloom, Hastings, & Madaus, 1971; Bloom, Madaus, & Hastings, 1981). Careful inspection of the items missed or the criteria not met on a carefully constructed formative assessment shows students precisely where they need to focus their attention in order to meet the learning goals set for the unit and achieve success.

Teachers then pair with each formative assessment specific corrective activities for use in addressing learning difficulties. The correctives are typically matched to each item or set of prompts within the assessment so that students need work on only those concepts or skills not yet mastered. In other words, the correctives are individualized. They may point out sources of information on a particular concept, such as page numbers in the textbook or workbook where that concept is discussed. They may identify alternative learning resources such as different textbooks, learning kits, alternative materials, DVDs, videos, or computerized instructional lessons. Or, they may simply suggest sources of additional practice, such as study guides, independent or guided practice activities, or collaborative group activities (Guskey, 2008).

With the feedback and corrective information gained from a formative assessment, each student has a detailed prescription of what more needs to be done to master the concepts or skills from the unit. This just-in-time correction prevents minor learning difficulties from accumulating and becoming major learning problems. It also gives teachers a practical means to vary and differentiate their instruction in order to better meet students' individual learning needs. As a result, more students learn well, master the important learning goals in each unit, and gain the necessary prerequisites for success in subsequent units.

When students complete their corrective work after a class period or two, Bloom recommended they take a second formative assessment. This second, parallel assessment covers the same concepts and skills as the first, but includes different problems, questions, or prompts. As such, it serves two important purposes. First, it verifies whether or not the correctives truly helped students overcome their individual learning difficulties. Second, it offers students a second chance at success and, hence, has powerful motivational value.

Bloom also recognized that some students are likely to perform well on the first assessment, demonstrating their mastery of the unit concepts and skills. For these students, the teacher's initial instruction was appropriate, and they have no need for corrective work. To ensure their continued learning progress, Bloom recommended that teachers provide these students with special enrichment or extension activities to broaden their learning experiences. Enrichment activities often are self-selected by students and might involve special projects or reports, academic games, or a variety of complex but engaging problem-solving tasks. Figure 7.2 illustrates this instructional sequence.

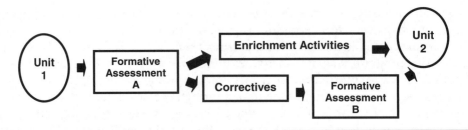

Figure 7.2 The mastery learning instructional process.

Through this process of regular classroom formative assessments, combined with the correction of individual learning errors, Bloom believed all students could be provided with a more appropriate quality of instruction than is possible under more traditional approaches to teaching. As a result, nearly all students might be expected to learn well and truly master the unit concepts or learning goals (Bloom, 1976, 1981). This, in turn, would drastically reduce the variation in students' achievement levels, narrow or eliminate achievement gaps, and yield a distribution of achievement more like that shown in Figure 7.3.

In all of his descriptions of mastery learning, however, Bloom emphasized that reducing variation in students' achievement does not imply making all students the same. Even under these more favorable learning conditions, some students undoubtedly will learn more than others, especially those involved in enrichment activities. But by recognizing relevant, individual differences among students and then adapting instruction to better meet these diverse learning needs, Bloom believed the variation among students in how well they learn specific concepts or master a set of well-articulated learning

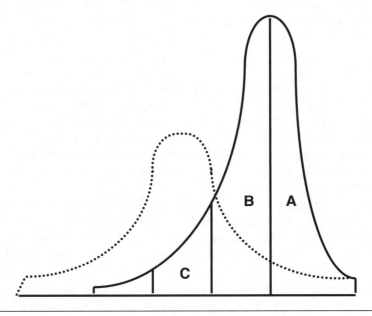

Figure 7.3 Distribution of achievement (grades) in mastery learning classrooms.

goals could eventually reach a "vanishing point" (Bloom, 1971b, title). In other words, all students would be helped to learn well the knowledge and skills prescribed in the curriculum. As a result, gaps in the achievement of different groups of students would be closed (see Guskey, 2007b).

Essential Elements of Mastery Learning

After Bloom described his ideas, numerous programs based on mastery learning principles sprung up in schools throughout the United States and around the world (see Block, 1971, 1974; Block & Anderson, 1975; Hymel & Dyke, 1993; Reezigt & Weide, 1990, 1992; Wu, 1994; Yildiran, 2006). Although differing from setting to setting, the programs true to Bloom's ideas included two essential elements: (1) the feedback, corrective, and enrichment process; and (2) instructional alignment (Guskey, 1997).

Feedback, Correctives, and Enrichment   Teachers who use mastery learning provide students with frequent and specific feedback on their learning progress through regular, classroom formative assessments. This feedback is both diagnostic and prescriptive (Hattie & Timperley, 2007). It reinforces precisely what students were expected to learn, identifies what they learned well, and describes what needs to be learned better (Guskey, 2003). By reviewing the questions they answered incorrectly or the criteria they did not meet, students gain individualized information about their learning progress. In other words, the feedback they receive is item-, task-, or criterion-specific. Two students might attain exactly the same score on the formative assessment and yet receive very different feedback depending on the items or criteria missed. As a result, the steps they take to remedy those problems might differ as well.

Likewise, by analyzing the items most frequently answered incorrectly or the criteria most frequently missed, teachers gain highly specific information about the effectiveness of their original instruction. They know precisely what skills or concepts were taught well and which ones might require a different approach. In this way, classroom formative assessments not only help students improve their learning, they also help teachers improve the quality of their instructional strategies. The National Council of Teachers of Mathematics (NCTM) emphasizes this same element in its latest iteration of the standards for school mathematics. To overcome inequities in mathematics instruction, the NCTM stresses the use of assessments that support learning and provide useful information to both teachers and students (NCTM, 2000). Ainsworth and Viegut (2006), Marzano, Pickering, and Polluck (2001), Smith, Smith, and DeLisi (2001), and Stiggins (2008) similarly emphasize the vital nature of feedback from assessments *for* learning.

By itself, however, the feedback offered through regular classroom formative assessments does little to improve student learning. In other words, formative assessments alone yield little if any improvement. Regardless of their form, structure, or quality, formative assessments simply measure student learning, they do not improve it. Measuring something more often and more accurately does nothing to make it better. If that were the case, then all that would be required in a successful weight-loss program would be more frequent weighings on a better scale. Clearly, that is not enough. Just as being weighed more often and more accurately does not help a person lose weight, the use of regular classroom formative assessment alone does not improve student learning. It is what happens after the formative assessment that makes the difference.

Significant improvement requires the feedback gained from a formative assessment to be paired with correctives—activities that offer guidance and direction to students on how to remedy their learning problems (see Guskey, 2008). Because of individual differences among students, no single method of instruction works best for all. To help every student learn well, therefore, teachers must differentiate their instruction, both in the initial teaching and especially through the corrective activities (Bloom, 1976). In other words, to decrease variation in results, teachers must increase variation in their teaching.

Effective corrective activities possess three essential characteristics (see Guskey, 1997). First, they present the concepts differently. For example, if a language arts unit initially taught the use of metaphors in poetry with a deductive approach (presenting the general concept and then giving specific examples), the corrective activity might use an inductive approach (presenting a variety of specific examples and building an understanding of the general concept from these examples). The most effective corrective activities involve a change in format, organization, or method of presentation.

Second, effective corrective activities engage students differently in learning. They consider different learning styles or modalities (Given, 2000; Lawrence, 1997; Sternberg, 1994) or different forms of intelligence (Armstrong, 2000; Gardner, 2006; Silver, Strong, & Perini, 2000). If science students initially learned about cell structure through a group activity, for example, a good corrective might involve an individual activity, such as reviewing an informative Web site and then using the computer to write and illustrate a report. If students originally learned the events of the American Revolutionary War in social studies by reading passages in their textbook and studying wall maps and charts (verbal and visual intelligences), a useful corrective might employ a group discussion of the events (auditory learning style and interpersonal intelligence). To make a corrective strategy effective, students' engagement in learning must be qualitatively different from what took place during the initial instruction.

Finally, effective corrective activities provide students with successful learning experiences. If an activity does not help students overcome their learning difficulties and experience success, the teacher should abandon it for another option. Corrective experiences should make students better prepared, more confident, and more motivated for future learning tasks.

The best ideas for effective corrective activities generally come from fellow teachers. Teaching colleagues often can offer new ways of presenting concepts, different examples, and alternative materials. Professional development opportunities that provide teachers with time for such sharing reduce the workload of individual teachers and typically yield higher quality activities (Guskey, 1998, 2000, 2001). Faculty meetings devoted to examining classroom formative assessment results and developing corrective strategies also work well. Such meetings might involve district level personnel or content experts from local colleges and universities.

On any given classroom formative assessment, some students will demonstrate their mastery of unit concepts and skills on the first try and will have no need for corrective activities. These students need opportunities to extend their learning through enrichment or extension activities, rather than sitting around and biding their time while other students engage in corrective work. Effective enrichment activities provide students with valuable, challenging, and rewarding learning experiences. As described earlier, enrichment activities offer students opportunities to broaden and expand their learning. They reward students for their learning success and challenge them to go further. If students see enrichment as busy work or as simply more and harder tasks, however, they will have no incentive to perform well on formative assessments. So rather than being narrowly restricted to the content of specific instructional units, enrichment activities should be broadly construed to cover a wide range of related topics.

Students should have some degree of choice in selecting enrichments. For example, if a particular student has special interest in some aspect of the subject, using enrichment time to prepare a report on that topic not only provides a unique learning opportunity but also enhances this student's motivation to do well in subsequent formative assessments so that he or she can return to working on the report. Other examples of enrichment activities include advanced learning activities designed for creative expression, challenging academic games and exercises, various multimedia projects, and serving as a peer tutor for a classmate.

Some creative teachers find it easy to develop different types of enrichment activities for their students. Others struggle to create such learning experiences. Besides consulting with colleagues, many teachers turn to materials designed for gifted and talented students as their primary resource for enrichment. Certain publishers focus specifically on activities that genuinely extend students' learning by involving them in higher-order skills (e.g., Critical Thinking Press & Software, Pacific Grove, CA; Dale Seymour Publications, Palo Alto, CA; and Thinking Works, St. Augustine, FL). Further, the gamelike nature of many of these activities motivates students to want to take part. Most teachers use class time in early instructional units to engage all students in enrichment activities, both to encourage participation and to enhance students' motivation on future formative assessments.

Teachers implement the feedback, corrective, and enrichment process in a variety of ways. Many use short, paper-and-pencil quizzes as formative assessments to give students feedback on their learning progress. But formative assessments also can take the form of essays, compositions, projects, reports, performance tasks, skill demonstrations, oral presentations, or any device used to gain information about students' learning progress. In essence, teachers adapt the format of their formative assessments to match their instructional goals.

Following a formative assessment, some teachers divide the class into separate corrective and enrichment groups. While the teacher directs corrective activities, guaranteeing that all students who need the extra time and assistance take part, the other students work on self-selected, independent enrichment activities. Other teachers pair with colleagues and use a team-teaching approach: One teacher oversees corrective activities while the other teacher monitors enrichments. Still other teachers use cooperative learning activities in which students work together in teams to ensure all reach the mastery level. Because students have their own personal scores on the formative assessment, individual accountability is assured. Offering the entire team special recognition or credit if all students attain mastery on the second formative assessment encourages group responsibility (Johnson, Johnson, & Holubec, 1994).

Feedback, corrective, and enrichment procedures are crucial to mastery learning, for it is through these procedures that mastery learning differentiates and individualizes instruction. In every instructional unit, students who need extended time and opportunity to remedy learning problems receive these through the correctives. Students who learn quickly and find the initial instruction highly appropriate have opportunities to extend their learning through enrichment. As a result, all students experience more favorable learning conditions and more appropriate, higher quality instruction (Bloom, 1977). Similar elements provide the foundation for more recently developing instructional approaches including differentiated instruction (Tomilson, 2003) and understanding by design (Wiggins & McTighe, 2005).

Formative, Interim, and Summative Assessments   The primary purpose of formative assessments is to provide feedback to both students and teachers in order to guide corrective activities when needed. From Bloom's perspective, classroom formative assessments most closely resemble the performance checks or unit quizzes that teachers typically administer after a week or two of instruction. This is different from some current interpretations of formative assessments as in-the-moment checks, such as having students write answers on small whiteboards and hold them up so the teacher can determine students' current level of understanding, or clickers that gather instant electronic data on questions posed to the class by the teacher (Black & Wiliam, 1998; Leahy, Lyon, Thompson, & Wiliam, 2005). These in-the-moment checks allow teachers to adapt their instruction during lessons to determine which concepts are understood and which need further explanation. While these quick checks can be powerful instructional tools, Bloom envisioned formative assessments to be more formal checks on the learning goals of an instructional unit. More than a single question or prompt, formative assessments in their various forms provide evidence on broader understandings and higher level skills.

Bloom also saw formative assessments as differing from interim or benchmark assessments that teachers might administer every 4 to 9 weeks (Marshall, 2008; Popham, 2006). While these assessments are useful in tapping broader course goals and more complex skills, waiting 4 to 9 weeks to check on the learning progress of students seemed much too long. Students who fell behind early would have too difficult a time catching up. For this reason, Bloom stressed that a formative assessment should focus on the learning goals for an instructional unit and would occur perhaps after only a week or two of instructional time.

At the same time, Bloom also recognized the need for teachers to gather cumulative evidence on student learning for grading and evaluation purposes. This he believed could be accomplished through summative assessments. These larger-scale summative assessments are similar to the major examinations, compositions, or projects that teachers use as primary sources of evidence in assigning students' grades and determining proficiency. They differ from formative assessments in three important ways. First, summative assessments offer a much more cumulative evaluation of learning. Whereas formative assessments focus on a limited number of learning goals so that students who fall behind at the beginning will not have difficulty catching up, summative assessments measure the degree to which larger goals or objectives have been attained. In addition, summative assessments typically cover skills or concepts from three or four instructional units and may require an entire class period for students to complete.

Second, summative assessments differ from formative assessments in their level of generalization. Because of limited assessment time, all of the important elements from each learning unit cannot be included in a single summative assessment. Therefore, summative assessments are usually designed to focus on broad abilities and larger course outcomes rather than on the specific details of each learning unit. The level of generalization in a summative assessment will depend, of course, upon the subject area, grade level, and desired learning goals. Nonetheless, in most cases, summative assessments are more general in focus than are individual formative assessments.

Third, summative assessments have a different purpose from formative assessments. In most cases, summative assessments are designed to gather cumulative information on students' learning so proficiency on particular skills or tasks can be determined and grades or marks assigned. While formative assessments are used primarily to check students' learning progress and to pinpoint any learning difficulties they may be experiencing, summative assessments are used primarily for grading and evaluation purposes.

Despite their differences in scope and purpose, summative assessments always address the same concepts or skills addressed on the formative assessments. In other words, they do not include anything new or unfamiliar to students. While a summative assessment may not include items or prompts about every concept or skill from every instructional unit, they never include elements that students have not seen before. Instead, summative assessments offer cumulative evidence on the learning goals from several units over which students have already been offered feedback on their learning and opportunities to correct any learning errors.

Managing Feedback, Correctives, and Enrichment   Some teachers fear that taking time for corrective and enrichment activities after a formative assessment will lessen the amount of material that they will be able to cover. In other words, they believe that they will have to sacrifice coverage to allow a higher level of learning, and as a result, some students may learn better, but all will learn less.

Corrective and enrichment activities initially do add time to instructional units. Especially in early units, these activities must be done in class, under the teacher's direction, and typically require a class period or two. Teachers who ask students to complete correctives outside of class as a homework assignment or during special study sessions held before or after school rarely experience success. Instead, they quickly discover that those students who could benefit most from the corrective process are the least likely to take part. Teachers who engage students in corrective activities in class, under their direction, however, help students gain direct evidence of the personal benefits the process offers. As a result, students develop increased confidence in learning situations and are more likely to undertake corrective activities on their own.

After students become accustomed to the corrective process and realize its advantages, teachers can begin reducing the class time they allocate to correctives. They use more student-initiated activities and ask students to complete more of their corrective work outside of class, often as homework. As students remedy their learning problems in early units, they perform better on formative assessments in subsequent units. This leads to more students becoming involved in enrichment activities and fewer engaged in correctives. The amount of corrective work students need in order to reach the proficiency standard also diminishes (Whiting, Van Burgh, & Render, 1995).

Modest changes in instructional format further lessen the extra time needed. Many teachers, for example, eliminate review sessions prior to formative assessments. Instead, they shift that time to the corrective and enrichment process. With the results from the formative assessment, teachers become more efficient in their reviews. Rather than reviewing everything, they can concentrate on only those concepts and skills that pose problems for students. In addition, by allowing fast learners to demonstrate their proficiency and move on to enrichment activities, teachers can spend their time working with a smaller group of students who most need their assistance. With more students reaching the proficiency standard in each succeeding unit, most teachers also find that their instructional pace in later units can be more rapid.

In general, teachers do not need to sacrifice content coverage to implement corrective and enrichment activities, but they must be flexible in pacing their instruction. The time used for correctives and enrichments in early units yields powerful benefits that will make things easier later on. This extra time can then be made up in later units by spending less time on reviews and increasing the instructional pace. Teachers at all levels must keep in mind what needs to be accomplished by the end of any learning sequence, but they also must see students' pathways to that end in more flexible and accommodating terms.

Instructional Alignment   Besides feedback, correctives, and enrichment, one additional element is essential to mastery learning. Bloom stressed that reducing variation in student learning and closing achievement gaps further requires consistency among all instructional components. He labeled this "instructional alignment" (Bloom, 1971a, p. 52).

Bloom believed three major components composed the teaching and learning process. To begin, there must be specific ideas about what students are expected to learn and be able to do; that is, learning goals or standards. Next comes instruction that, ideally, results in proficient learners—students who have learned well and whose proficiency can be assessed through some form of assessment or evaluation. Mastery learning adds a feedback and corrective component through the use of classroom formative assessments, allowing teachers to determine for whom their initial instruction was appropriate and for whom an alternative approach may be needed.

Although essentially neutral with regard to what is taught, how it is taught, and how learning is assessed or evaluated, mastery learning requires consistency or alignment among these instructional components, as shown in Figure 7.4. For example, if students are expected to learn higher level skills such as those involved in making applications, solving complex problems, or developing thoughtful analyses, mastery learning stipulates that instructional activities must be planned to give students opportunities to practice and actively engage in those skills. It also requires that students be given

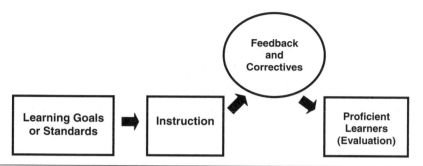

Figure 7.4 Major components in the teaching and learning process.

specific feedback on how well they have learned those skills through the formative assessment process, coupled with directions on how to correct any learning errors. Finally, procedures for assessing or evaluating students' learning should reflect those higher level skills as well.

To ensure alignment among instructional components, teachers must make a number of crucial decisions. First, they need to decide what concepts or skills are most important for students to learn and most central to students' understanding. Teachers must determine, for example, if they want students to learn only basic skills, or if they want students to develop higher level skills and more complex cognitive processes. Second, teachers need to decide what evidence best reflects students' mastery of those basic or higher level skills. Critics sometimes challenge teachers' abilities to make these crucial decisions. But, in essence, teachers at all levels make these decisions in conducting regular classroom activities. Every time they administer an assessment, grade a paper, or evaluate students' learning, teachers communicate to students what is most important to learn. Using mastery learning simply compels teachers to use more thought, intention, and purpose when making these decisions.

MISINTERPRETATIONS OF MASTERY LEARNING

Some early attempts to implement mastery learning were based on narrow and inaccurate interpretations of Bloom's ideas. These programs focused on only low-level skills; attempted to break learning down into small, patchy segments; employed narrow, one-dimensional formative assessments; and insisted that students master each segment before being permitted to move on. Teachers in these programs were regarded as little more than managers of materials and record-keepers of student progress.

Nowhere in Bloom's writing, however, can this kind of narrowness and rigidity be found. In fact, Bloom emphasized quite the opposite. He considered thoughtful and reflective teachers vital to the successful implementation of mastery learning and continually stressed flexibility in its application, especially in the design and implementation of formative assessments. In his earliest description of the process Bloom wrote:

> There are many alternative strategies for mastery learning. Each strategy must find some way of dealing with individual differences in learners through some means

of relating instruction to the needs and characteristics of the learners.... Guiding students with respect to courses they should or should not take, providing different streams for different groups of students, the non-graded school, and alternative high school schedules are all attempts to provide an organizational structure that permits and encourages mastery learning. (1968, pp. 7–8)

Bloom further emphasized his belief that instruction in mastery learning classrooms, along with the included classroom formative assessments, should focus on higher level learning goals, not simply basic skills. He noted:

I find great emphasis on problem solving, applications of principles, analytical skills, and creativity. Such higher mental processes are emphasized because this type of learning enables the individual to relate his or her learning to the many problems he or she encounters in day-to-day living. These abilities are stressed because they are retained and utilized long after the individual has forgotten the detailed specifics of the subject matter taught in the schools. These abilities are regarded as one set of essential characteristics needed to continue learning and to cope with a rapidly changing world. (1978, p. 578)

Modern research studies have shown mastery learning to be particularly effective when applied to instruction focusing on higher level learning goals such as problem solving, drawing inferences, deductive reasoning, and creative expression (Arredondo & Block, 1990; Blakemore, 1992; Clark, Guskey, & Benninga, 1983; Kozlovsky, 1990; Mevarech & Werner, 1985). When well implemented, the mastery learning process helps teachers close achievement gaps in a broad range of learning goals from basic skills to highly complex cognitive processes.

Other misinterpretations come from secondary teachers who believe that the constraint of limited class time will inhibit their efforts to implement mastery learning (Guskey, 1997). They assume that introducing classroom formative assessments, together with accompanying corrective and enrichment procedures, will reduce the amount of material they would be able to cover. In other words, they would have to sacrifice curriculum coverage for the sake of mastery. But as discussed earlier, minor alterations in instructional pacing typically resolve this concern.

Early mastery learning units usually require more time. Teachers who provide class time for students to complete corrective activities often find themselves behind other teachers who teach in more traditional ways after the first two or three units. But once students become familiar with the process, mastery learning teachers generally pick up their pace. Because students in mastery learning classes spend a larger portion of their time actively engaged in learning, they make more rapid progress than students in more traditionally taught classes (Arlin, 1973; Fitzpatrick, 1985).

As students catch on, they also do better on initial formative assessments. With fewer students involved in correctives and less corrective work needed, teachers reduce the class time allocated to corrective activities. And because mastery learning students learn the concepts and skills from early units well, they are better prepared for later, more advanced units. Instruction in later units can therefore be more rapid and include fewer review activities. Most teachers discover that with slight adjustments in the pacing of their instruction—slightly more time spent in early units but less time in later ones—they can cover just as much material using mastery learning, and in some cases more, because they were able to use more traditional approaches to instruction (Block, 1983; Guskey, 1983, 1987).

RESEARCH RESULTS ON MASTERY LEARNING

Teachers generally find that implementing mastery learning with regular classroom formative assessments requires relatively modest changes in their instructional procedures. Excellent teachers use many aspects of mastery learning in their classes already, and others have discovered that the process blends well with their current teaching strategies (Guskey, 1989).

Despite the modest nature of these alterations, however, extensive research evidence shows that using mastery learning can have exceptionally positive effects on student learning. A study by Whiting et al. (1995) investigated the cognitive and affective student learning outcomes over 36 semesters in high school distributive education classes using mastery learning. Data gathered from more than 7,000 students showed that implementing mastery learning had a statistically significant positive influence on students' test scores and grade point averages as well as on measures of their attitudes toward school and learning.

Another field experiment conducted in elementary and middle school classrooms in Michigan used students as their own controls to evaluate the results of implementing mastery learning (Anderson et al., 1992). Six classrooms were included in the sample involving grades 3 through 6, plus a fifth/sixth split grade, and a special education resource room class, for a total of six teachers and 94 students. A series of six, one-hour professional development sessions were held to acquaint teachers with mastery learning. All six teachers chose mathematics as the content area for implementation. Test results compared the unit test scores in the fall of 1991 with the test results after the implementation of two mastery learning units in the spring of 1992. Students were also assessed for any change in their feelings of self-efficacy using the Self-Concept of Academic Ability Scale (Brookover, Thomas, & Paterson, 1964). Statistically significant gains in both achievement and self-efficacy were found for the mastery learning taught classes.

Even more impressive results came from a comprehensive, meta-analysis of mastery learning research that considered the results from 108 controlled evaluations of student performance in upper elementary grade, high school, and college level classes (Kulik, Kulik, & Bangert-Drowns, 1990). The authors concluded:

> We recently reviewed meta-analyses in nearly 40 different areas of educational research (J. Kulik & Kulik, 1989). Few educational treatments of any sort were consistently associated with achievement effects as large as those produced by mastery learning.... In evaluation after evaluation, mastery programs have produced impressive gains. (Kulik, Kulik, & Bangert-Drowns, 1990, p. 292)

Developing procedures for feedback through formative assessments, correctives, and enrichments, along with ensuring instructional alignment, takes relatively little time and effort, especially if tasks are shared collaboratively among teaching colleagues.

Studies consistently show, however, that deliberate implementation of these elements helps many more students learn well, significantly reduces variation in student learning outcomes, and closes gaps in the achievement of different groups of students at any level of education (Walberg, 1986). Some researchers have even suggested that the superiority of Japanese students in international comparisons of achievement in mathematics operations and problem solving may be due largely to the widespread use in Japan of instructional practices similar to mastery learning (Nakajima, 2006; Waddington, 1995).

Research evidence also shows that the positive effects of mastery learning are not limited to cognitive or achievement outcomes. The process also yields improvements in students' confidence in learning situations, school attendance rates, involvement in class sessions, attitudes toward learning, and a variety of other affective measures (Block & Burns, 1976; Guskey & Pigott, 1988; Whiting & Render, 1987). This multidimensional impact has been referred to as mastery learning's multiplier effect, and makes it an especially powerful tool in school improvement efforts.

CONCLUSION

Classroom formative assessments offer educators a valuable tool to improve student learning. The regular use of formative assessments helps students identify their individual learning errors so that specific steps can be taken to remedy those difficulties before they accumulate and become major learning problems. Such assessments also help teachers improve the quality of their instruction by identifying the particular concepts and skills their original instruction helped most students attain and those that may need to be revisited and revised. But what must always be kept in mind is that simply gathering accurate information on student learning through well-designed classroom formative assessments is not enough. What students and teachers do with that information is what counts the most.

To realize the true benefits of formative classroom assessments, teachers at all levels need to focus attention on how best to use assessment results to close achievement gaps and help all students learn well. Specifically, they must provide students with alternative pathways to learning success through thoughtfully constructed and carefully managed corrective activities. Engaging students in diverse corrective activities or exciting and challenging enrichment activities, depending on their performance on well-designed classroom formative assessments, offers the practical means to do just that. Formative assessments provide teachers with an exceptionally valuable tool in their efforts to help all students learn well.

FUTURE RESEARCH, THEORY, AND PRACTICE

Numerous factors influence student learning, many lying beyond classroom walls and outside of control of educators. An Educational Testing Service report, for example, identified a wide range of environmental factors that may contribute to achievement gaps, the majority of which are external to schools (Barton, 2003). Denying the role of these outside influences will not endow teachers and schools with the capacity to reduce achievement gaps, and efforts to address these home and community-based challenges must continue (Rothstein, 2004).

Nevertheless, the impediments to learning in students' environments outside of school should never become a basis for lowering expectations about what can be done to help them learn well in school. The feedback through formative assessments, correctives and enrichments, and instructional alignment elements of mastery learning represent powerful tools that teachers can use to capitalize on the influence they have. They are not, of course, the only factors of importance. In his later writing, Bloom described exciting work on other ideas designed to attain results even more positive than those typically achieved with classroom formative assessments and mastery learning (Bloom, 1984a, 1984b, 1988).

Anania (1981, 1983), and Burke (1983), who were Bloom's doctoral students, compared student learning under three different instructional conditions. The first was *conventional instruction* in which students were taught in group-based classes that included about 30 students and where periodic assessments were given mainly for the purposes of grading. The second was *mastery learning*, where students again were taught in group-based classes of about 30 students but were administered regular formative assessments for feedback, followed by individualized corrective instruction and parallel second assessments to determine the extent to which they mastered specific learning goals. The third was *tutoring*, where a good tutor was paired with each student. Under tutoring, students were also administered regular formative assessments, along with corrective procedures and parallel second assessments, although the need for corrective work under tutoring was usually quite small.

The differences in students' final achievement under these three conditions were striking. Using the standard deviation (sigma) of the control (conventional) class as the measure of difference, Bloom's students discovered that:

> The average student under tutoring was about two standard deviations above the average of the control class (the average tutored students was above 98% of the students in the control class). The average student under mastery learning was about one standard deviation above the average of the control class (the average mastery learning student was above 84% of the students in the control class).... Thus under the best learning conditions we can devise (tutoring), the average student is 2 sigma above the average control student taught under conventional group methods of instruction. (Bloom, 1984a, p. 4)

Bloom referred to this as the "2 Sigma Problem":

> The tutoring process demonstrates that *most* students do have the potential to reach this high level of learning. I believe an important task of research and instruction is to seek ways of accomplishing this under more practical and realistic conditions than the one-to-one tutoring, which is too costly for most societies to bear on a large scale. This is the "2 Sigma" problem. Can researchers and teachers devise teaching-learning conditions that will enable the majority of students under *group instruction* to attain levels of achievement that can at present be reached only under tutoring conditions? (Bloom, 1984a, pp. 4–5)

Bloom believed that attaining this high level of achievement would probably require more than just improvements in the quality of group instruction. Researchers and teachers might also need to find ways to improve home environmental support of students' school learning, students' learning processes, the curriculum and instructional materials, and a focus on higher level thinking skills. Efforts to encourage parent involvement in preschool programs show particular promise (Arnold, Zeljo, Doctoroff, & Ortiz, 2008). Nevertheless, careful attention to these elements of mastery learning, especially the classroom formative assessment and corrective process, allows educators at all levels to make great strides in their efforts to reduce variation in student achievement and close achievement gaps. These elements offer educators the tools needed to help students of different racial, ethnic, and socioeconomic backgrounds all learn excellently, succeed in school, and gain the many positive benefits of that success.

REFERENCES

Ainsworth, L., & Viegut, D. (2006). *Common formative assessments: How to connect standards-based instruction and assessment.* Thousand Oaks, CA: Corwin.

Anania, J. (1981). *The effects of quality of instruction on the cognitive and affective learning of students.* Unpublished doctoral dissertation, University of Chicago.

Anania, J. (1983). The influence of instructional conditions on student learning and achievement. *Evaluation in Education: An International Review Series, 7*(1), 1–92.

Anderson, S., Barrett, C., Huston, M., Lay, L., Myr, G., Sexton, D., et al. (1992). *A mastery learning experiment* (Technical Report). Yale, MI: Yale Public Schools.

Arlin, M. N. (1973). *Rate and rate variance trends under mastery learning.* Unpublished doctoral dissertation, University of Chicago, Chicago.

Armstrong, T. (2000). *Multiple intelligences in the classroom* (2nd ed.). Alexandria, VA: Association for Supervision and Curriculum Development.

Arnold, D. H., Zeljo, A., Doctoroff, G. L., & Ortiz, C. (2008). Parent involvement in preschool: Predictors and the relation of involvement to preliteracy development. *School Psychology Review, 37*(1), 74–90.

Arredondo, D. E., & Block, J. H. (1990). Recognizing the connections between thinking skills and mastery learning. *Educational Leadership, 47*(5), 4–10.

Barton, P. E. (2003). *Parsing the achievement gap: Baselines for tracking progress* (Policy information report). Princeton, NJ: Educational Testing Service.

Black, P., & Wiliam, D. (1998). Inside the black box: Raising standards through classroom assessment. *Phi Delta Kappan, 80*(2), 139–144.

Blakemore, C. L. (1992). Comparison of students taught basketball skills using mastery and nonmastery learning methods. *Journal of Teaching in Physical Education, 11*(3), 235–247.

Block, J. H. (Ed.). (1971). *Mastery learning: Theory and practice.* New York: Holt, Rinehart & Winston.

Block, J. H. (Ed.) (1974). *Schools, society and mastery learning.* New York: Holt, Rinehart & Winston.

Block, J. H. (1983). Learning rates and mastery learning. *Outcomes, 2*(3), 18–23.

Block, J. H., & Anderson, L. W. (1975). *Mastery learning in classroom instruction.* New York: Macmillan.

Block, J. H., & Burns, R. B. (1976). Mastery learning. In L. S. Shulman (Ed.), *Review of research in education* (Vol. 4, pp. 3–49). Itasca, IL: Peacock.

Bloom, B. S. (1964). *Stability and change in human characteristics.* New York: Wiley.

Bloom, B. S. (1968). Learning for mastery. *Evaluation Comment* (UCLA-CSIEP), *1*(2), 1–12.

Bloom, B. S. (1971a). Mastery learning. In J. H. Block (Ed.), *Mastery learning: Theory and practice* (pp. 47–63). New York: Holt, Rinehart & Winston.

Bloom, B. S. (1971b). *Individual differences in school achievement: A vanishing point?* Bloomington, IN: Phi Delta Kappan International.

Bloom, B. S. (1976). *Human characteristics and school learning.* New York: McGraw-Hill.

Bloom, B. S. (1977). Favorable learning conditions for all. *Teacher, 95*(3), 22–28.

Bloom, B. S. (1978). New views of the learner: Implications for instruction and curriculum. *Educational Leadership, 35*(7), 563–576.

Bloom, B. S. (1981). *All our children learning: A primer for parents, teachers, and other educators.* New York: McGraw-Hill.

Bloom, B. S. (1984a). The 2 sigma problem: The search for methods of group instruction as effective as one-to-one tutoring. *Educational Researcher, 13*(6), 4–16.

Bloom, B. S. (1984b). The search for methods of group instruction as effective as one-to-one tutoring. *Educational Leadership, 41*(8), 4–17.

Bloom, B. S. (1988). Helping all children learn in elementary school and beyond. *Principal, 67*(4), 12–17.

Bloom, B. S., Hastings, J. T., & Madaus, G. (1971). *Handbook on formative and summative evaluation of student learning.* New York: McGraw-Hill.

Bloom, B. S., Madaus, G. F., & Hastings, J. T. (1981). *Evaluation to improve learning.* New York: McGraw-Hill.

Brookover, W., Thomas, S., & Paterson, A. (1964). Self-concept of ability and school achievement. *Sociology of Education, 37,* 271–278.

Burke, A. J. (1983). *Students' potential for learning contrasted under tutorial and group approaches to instruction.* Unpublished doctoral dissertation, University of Chicago.

Clark, C. R., Guskey, T. R., & Benninga, J. S. (1983). The effectiveness of mastery learning strategies in undergraduate education courses. *Journal of Educational Research, 76*(4), 210–214.

Dollard, J., & Miller, N. E. (1950). *Personality and psychotherapy.* New York: McGraw-Hill.

Fitzpatrick, K. A. (1985, April). *Group-based mastery learning: A Robin Hood approach to instruction?* Paper presented at the annual meeting of the American Educational Research Association, Chicago, IL.

Gardner, H. (2006). *Multiple intelligences: New horizons.* New York: Basic Books.

Given, B. K. (2000). *Learning styles* (rev. ed.). Oceanside, CA: Learning Forum.

Guskey, T. R. (1983). Clarifying time related issues. *Outcomes, 3*(1), 5–7.

Guskey, T. R. (1987b). Rethinking mastery learning reconsidered. *Review of Educational Research, 57*(2), 225–229.

Guskey, T. R. (1989). Every teacher can be the best. *Vocational Education Journal, 64*(1), 20–22.

Guskey, T. R. (1997). *Implementing mastery learning* (2nd ed.). Belmont, CA: Wadsworth.

Guskey, T. R. (1998). Making time to train your staff. *The School Administrator, 55*(7), 35–37.

Guskey, T. R. (2000). *Evaluating professional development.* Thousand Oaks, CA: Corwin.

Guskey, T. R. (2001). Mastery learning. In N. J. Smelser & P. B. Baltes (Eds.), *International Encyclopedia of Social and Behavioral Sciences* (pp. 9372–9377). Oxford, England: Elsevier Science.

Guskey, T. R. (2003). How classroom assessments improve learning. *Educational Leadership, 60*(5) 6–11.

Guskey, T. R. (Ed.). (2006). *Benjamin S. Bloom: Portraits of an educator.* Lanham, MD: Rowman & Littlefield Education.

Guskey, T. R. (2007a). Formative classroom assessment and Benjamin S. Bloom: Theory, research, and practice. In J. H. McMillan (Ed.), *Formative classroom assessment: Theory into practice* (pp. 63–78). New York: Teachers College Press.

Guskey, T. R. (2007b). Closing achievement gaps: Revisiting Benjamin S. Bloom's "Learning for Mastery." *Journal of Advanced Academics, 19*(1), 8–31.

Guskey, T. R. (2008). The rest of the story. *Educational Leadership, 65*(4), 28–35.

Guskey, T. R., & Pigott, T. D. (1988). Research on group-based mastery learning programs: A meta-analysis. *Journal of Educational Research, 81*(4), 197–216.

Hattie, J., & Timperley, H. (2007). The power of feedback. *Review of Educational Research, 77*(1), 81–112.

Hymel, G. M., & Dyke, W. E. (1993, April). *The internationalization of Bloom's learning for mastery: A 25-year retrospective-prospective view.* Paper presented at the annual meeting of the American Educational Research Association, Atlanta, GA.

Johnson, D. W., Johnson, R. T., & Holubec, E. J. (1994). *The nuts & bolts of cooperative learning.* Edina, MN: Interaction.

Kozlovsky, J. D. (1990). Integrating thinking skills and mastery learning in Baltimore County. *Educational Leadership, 47*(5), 6.

Kulik, C. C., Kulik, J. A., & Bangert-Drowns, R. L. (1990). Effectiveness of mastery learning programs: A meta-analysis. *Review of Educational Research, 60*(2), 265–299.

Kulik, J. A., & Kulik, C. C. (1989). Meta-analysis in education. *International Journal of Educational Research, 13*(2), 221–340.

Lawrence, G. D. (1997). *Looking at type and learning styles.* Gainesville, FL: Center for Applications of Psychological Type.

Leahy, S., Lyon, C., Thompson, M., & Wiliam, D. (2005). Minute-by-minute and day-by-day. *Educational Leadership, 63*(3), 18–24.

Marshall, K. (2008). Interim assessments: A user's guide. *Phi Delta Kappan, 90*(1), 64–68.

Marzano, R. J., Pickering, D. J., & Polluck, J. E. (2001). *Classroom instruction that works.* Alexandria, VA: Association for Supervision and Curriculum Development.

Mevarech, Z. R., & Werner, S. (1985). Are mastery learning strategies beneficial for developing problem solving skills? *Higher Education, 14*(4), 425–432.

Morrison, H. C. (1926). *The practice of teaching in the secondary school.* Chicago: University of Chicago Press.

Nakajima, A. (2006). A powerful influence on Japanese education. In T. R. Guskey (Ed.), *Benjamin S. Bloom: Portraits of an educator* (pp. 109–111). Lanham, MD: Rowman & Littlefield Education.

National Council of Teachers of Mathematics. (2000). *Principles and standards for school mathematics.* Reston, VA: Author. Available: http://standards.nctm.org/document/index.htm

Popham, W. J. (2006). Phony formative assessments: Buyer beware. *Educational Leadership, 64*(3), 86–87.

Reezigt, B. J., & Weide, M. G. (1990, April). *The effects of group-based mastery learning on language and arithmetic achievement and attitudes in primary education in the Netherlands.* Paper presented at the annual meeting of the American Educational Research Association, Boston, MA.

Reezigt, G. J., & Weide, M. G. (1992, April). *Mastery learning and instructional effectiveness.* Paper presented at the annual meeting of the American Educational Research Association, San Francisco.

Rothstein, R. (2004). A wider lens on the black-white achievement gap. *Phi Delta Kappan, 86* (2), 104–110.

Scriven, M. S. (1967). The methodology of evaluation. In R. W. Tyler, R. M. Gagne, & M. Scriven (Eds.), *Perspectives of curriculum evaluation* (AERA Monograph Series on Curriculum Evaluation, No. 1; pp. 39–83). Chicago: Rand McNally.

Silver, H. F., Strong, R. W., & Perini, M. J. (2000). *So each may learn: Integrating learning styles and multiple intelligences.* Alexandria, VA: Association for Supervision and Curriculum Development.

Smith, J. K., Smith, L. F., & DeLisi, R. (2001). *Natural classroom assessment: Designing seamless instruction & assessment.* Thousand Oaks, CA: Corwin.

Sternberg, R. J. (1994). Allowing for thinking styles. *Educational Leadership, 52*(3), 36–40.

Stiggins, R. (2008). *An introduction to student-involved assessment for learning* (5th ed.). Upper Saddle River, NJ: Merrill, Prentice Hall.

Tomilson, C. (2003). *Fulfilling the promise of the differentiated classroom: Strategies and tools for responsive teaching.* Alexandria, VA: Association for Supervision and Curriculum Development.

Waddington, T. (1995, April). *Why mastery matters.* Paper presented at the annual meeting of the American Educational Research Association, San Francisco.

Walberg, H. J. (1986). Syntheses of research on teaching. In M. C. Wittrock (Ed.), *Handbook of research on teaching* (3rd ed., pp. 214–229). New York: Macmillan.

Washburne, C. W. (1922). Educational measurements as a key to individualizing instruction and promotions. *Journal of Educational Research, 5,* 195–206.

Whiting, B., & Render, G. F. (1987). Cognitive and affective outcomes of mastery learning: A review of sixteen semesters. *The Clearing House, 60*(6), 276–280.

Whiting, B., Van Burgh, J. W., & Render, G. F. (1995, April). *Mastery learning in the classroom.* Paper presented at the annual meeting of the American Educational Research Association, San Francisco.

Wiggins, G., & McTighe, J. (2005). *Understanding by design* (2nd ed.). Alexandria, VA: Association for Supervision and Curriculum Development.

Wu, W. Y. (1994, April). *Mastery learning in Hong Kong: Challenges and prospects.* Paper presented at the annual meeting of the American Educational Research Association, New Orleans, LA.

Yildiran, G. (2006). *Multicultural applications of mastery learning.* Istanbul, Turkey: Faculty of Education, Bogazici University.

8

TECHNOLOGY-AIDED FORMATIVE ASSESSMENT OF LEARNING
New Developments and Applications

MICHAEL K. RUSSELL

Over the past decades, access to computers has increased sharply and led to more frequent use by teachers and students, particularly for writing, research, and communication via e-mail (Becker, 1999; Russell, O'Brien, Bebell, & O'Dwyer, 2002). To date, the vast majority of research on educational uses of computers has focused on factors that influence teachers' use of technology to develop student understanding of concepts and skills. In the field of educational testing, research has focused on the use of computer-based technologies to deliver summative assessments. These studies generally focus on the effect that mode of assessment (e.g., paper versus computer) has on student performance, or on ways that computers can be used to more efficiently estimate student achievement (e.g., adaptive testing). Recently, however, a small but growing body of research has begun investigating the use of computers for formative assessment.

Formative assessment is the process of collecting and analyzing information about student's knowledge and understanding prior to or during instruction for the purpose of informing instruction or assisting students in improving their work. To effectively inform instruction, proximity and alignment of formative assessments with instructional goals is paramount (Black & Wiliam, 1998). Today, there are many computer-based tools that can be used to collect information about student learning. However, unless that information is closely aligned with and collected in proximity to learning goals (i.e., for the current or next lesson), it does not meet the definition of formative assessment. Periodic tests given to monitor progress toward broad learning objectives also do not fall within this definition of formative assessment. Instead, these periodic assessments are considered interim assessments. Similarly, while the results from summative assessments can be used to identify topics and skills that students appear to have mastered or that need further development, the gap between the receipt of summative information and the next opportunity to develop further specific knowledge and skills precludes this use of summative tests as a form of formative assessment.

In the context of this chapter, a computer-based technology is defined as any device that relies on computer-based algorithms to record, process, and present information, and includes such tools as desktop and laptop computers, handheld computers (e.g., PalmPilots), student response devices, Web-based applications, or cell phones that enable Web-based communications (e.g., iPhones). While there are many ways in which computer-based technologies can be used to support formative assessment, this chapter limits its focus to four promising uses. These uses include: (1) systematically monitoring student progress to inform instructional decisions; (2) identifying misconceptions that may interfere with student learning; (3) providing rapid feedback on student writing; and (4) collecting information about student learning needs during instruction.

The first tool to be discussed here is mCLASS, a software tool designed to help teachers efficiently collect and analyze information about each student's development of reading skills. Next, the Diagnostic Algebra Assessment (DAA) system and DIAGNOSER are examined. These tools are designed to help teachers identify misconceptions that students hold which interfere with their development of algebraic and physics understanding. The DAA system also links teachers and students to learning activities that are designed to correct a given misconception. The use of automated essay scoring tools to provide students with rapid preliminary feedback on their writing is then examined. Finally, classroom response systems are explored. These response systems enable students to provide responses to critical questions posed during instruction and then efficiently categorize student responses so that teachers can quickly assess student understanding and make appropriate modifications during instruction.

MONITORING STUDENT PROGRESS TO INFORM INSTRUCTION: MCLASS READING

Great emphasis has recently been placed on data-based decision making in education (Kowalski & Lasley, 2008). Within the confines of the classroom, teachers often collect a substantial amount of data about student learning but struggle to make good use of that data. For example, in many early elementary classrooms, teachers use running records to monitor students' progress in developing reading skills (Shea, 2000). Running records require teachers to observe an individual student as the student reads a passage aloud. Traditionally, the teacher has a paper-based copy of the same passage and marks portions of a word that are mispronounced, skipped, repeated, corrected, or otherwise present the student with a challenge. Once the student finishes reading, the teacher typically tallies categories of errors and records the tallies in a notebook. Over a period of time, these records provide evidence that the teacher can use to assess the development of a student's reading skills.

Although reading records are used in thousands of elementary classrooms, the process of documenting, tracking, and reporting progress using paper-based records is cumbersome and limiting. Too often, the wealth of data provided by reading records sits in a file cabinet and it is used only to make gross assessments of reading progress. Because of their detailed nature, however, reading records have the potential to provide fine-grained assessments of specific challenges students encounter when reading.

To enhance the efficiency and utility of reading records, Wireless Generation developed mCLASS:Reading, a palm-based application that allows teachers to capture information about students' reading skills electronically. The application allows teachers to create profiles for each student in their classroom. It displays an electronic copy of the text that a student reads aloud. As the student reads, the teacher records errors directly on a PalmPilot. Upon completion of the passage, mCLASS automatically tallies the number of marks recorded for each error type. The teacher then uploads the student's new record to a database on her computer.

Once uploaded, the teacher may examine the student's record using a variety of visual displays. One visual allows the teacher to view the frequency with which a specific type of error occurs over a period of observations. Another display allows the teacher to examine the change in a student's reading level over a period of time. A different display allows the teacher to compare a given student to his or her peers in order to identify peers who are having similar challenges or are at a similar reading level. Using these visuals, a teacher is able to make more informed decisions about small-group instruction or reading partners. The software also allows teachers to identify books that are aligned with a student's current reading level and challenges.

By collecting data electronically, uploading that data to a central database, and providing several tools for exploring the results of reading records, mCLASS:Reading can enable formative assessment. It does so by simplifying the assessment of student reading skills in three ways. First, it has a large number of commonly read texts built into its database. When a student selects a text to read for his reading record, the teacher does not need to access a paper copy of the text. Instead, the teacher can access the text and record all errors directly on a PalmPilot. This reduces the preparation required prior to conducting a reading record.

Second, rather than tabulating the number and type of reading errors on paper and then transferring this record to a database, mCLASS:Reading performs these tasks automatically. Automatic tabulation saves time and assures the data are available in a timely manner to make informed decisions about instructional practices. Finally, the data is presented using numerical and graphical displays. Reports summarizing a single running record, multiple running records for a specific student, or a synthesis of all students in the class are generated. These reports simplify the process of analyzing data collected across multiple observations and from several students to make informed decisions about classroom instruction. In comparison to traditional paper-based records, computer-based tools like mCLASS:Reading can streamline the assessment process and provide rich data in an easy to interpret format.

Recognizing the potential for electronic data collection and analysis to improve the efficiency and utility of formative assessment, Wireless Generation has developed several companion tools to assist with formative assessment in language arts and mathematics. mCLASS:DIBELS allows teachers to assess a wide array of literacy development skills, and mCLASS:Math assists teachers as they collect and analyze data that focuses on the development of specific mathematics skills.

Although the research base on the effects of hand-held tools designed to assist in the collection and analysis of classroom-based data is relatively limited, those studies that do exist suggest that these tools are effective for helping teachers to improve student learning. Specifically, research provides evidence that teachers review and analyze data collected using handheld data collection tools, and that this increased use results in improvements in students reading skills (Hupert & Heinze, 2006; Hupert, Heinze, Kanaya, & Perez, 2004; Sharp & Risko, 2003).

These positive effects result in part from teachers having easy access to data they can use to have longer, more detailed discussions with students and their parents about students' strengths, weaknesses, and needs. These discussions then lead to more nuanced decisions about how to support a student's learning needs (Hupert & Hinze, 2006).

Analyses that examine the relationship between the frequency with which mCLASS is used to assess the development of reading skills and changes in reading proficiency provides evidence that frequent use of mCLASS is associated with improvements in student reading skills (Hupert & Hinze, 2006). Researchers examined the use of mCLASS handheld reading assessment tools in several school districts in New Mexico that adopted mCLASS as part of a reading first initiative. They reported that teachers made more frequent use of data collected using the handheld devices than they did when data was collected on paper, and that the use of this data helped improve student reading skills at a faster rate (Hupert & Hinze, 2006). A separate analysis of the use of handheld progress monitoring tools that focused on data collected by approximately 10,000 teachers across 31 states for approximately 200,000 students in pre-K through sixth grade also indicated that more frequent use of progress monitoring data was associated with larger effects on student reading skills (Hupert, Heinze, Gunn, & Stewart, 2007). While running records are commonly used for students reading below grade level, this analysis indicated that frequent use of mCLASS was effective for low, middle, and high-level readers.

Researchers attribute the positive effects of mCLASS to at least three factors: (1) teachers paying close attention to student reading skills; (2) students participating in the assessment process by having immediate access to the outcome of assessment; and (3) teachers having access to clear and appropriate goals for the students (Hupert, Heinze, Gunn, Stewart, & Honey, 2007). A separate study (Hupert & Heinze, 2006) also suggests that the ease with which data can be collected and analyzed using tools like mCLASS improves the relevance of data for classroom instructional decisions. Increased relevance results from the outcomes of assessment being detailed enough to identify specific student needs, immediate enough to allow teachers to make timely and informed decisions, and sensitive enough for teachers to detect changes in student learning (Hupert & Heinze, 2006).

Research conducted to date provides a preliminary body of evidence that the use of handheld progress monitoring tools helps teachers with two critical elements for formative assessment. First, by making a large collection of reading material readily available to teachers and making it easy for teachers to record observations as a student reads a given text, handheld progress monitoring tools help teachers collect information about students' reading skills in an efficient manner. Second, once data are collected, computer-based software allows teachers to view student information in a variety of ways, such as close inspection of a single record, a comparison of multiple records collected over time for a single student, or records collected for multiple students. These multiple views help teachers interpret student data and facilitate decision making about how to help improve student skills.

DIAGNOSING STUDENT MISCONCEPTIONS: THE DIAGNOSTIC ALGEBRA ASSESSMENT SYSTEM

Achievement tests are used regularly by classroom teachers and by state testing programs to measure knowledge and understanding. Several studies, however, indicate that teachers can predict the performance of their students on achievement tests with a high degree of accuracy (Cullen & Shaw, 2000; Demaray & Elliott, 1998; Hoge & Coladarci, 1989; Mulholland & Berliner, 1992). This suggests that most achievement tests do not provide teachers with new information that can inform their classroom instruction. Although they are not ordinarily developed to do so, it is nonetheless true that typical large-scale achievement tests do not provide meaningful information about *why* students perform as they do.

The dearth of new and useful information provided to teachers by typical large-scale achievement tests stems from several characteristics of those tests. Foremost among these characteristics is that such tests, by design, focus on placing students on a single scale that represents ability within a given domain, and a focus on whether or not students respond correctly to a given item without considering the thought processes applied to reach a given response. Despite efforts to incorporate open-ended items into some tests, most test items result in dichotomous information about a student—whether the student answered the item correctly or incorrectly.

In rare cases, some items ask students to describe their reasoning but these items are dependent upon students' descriptions of their processes, which are often incomplete or inaccurate reflections of the actual process of answering questions. As a result, these items provide indirect and crude insight into students' cognitive processes. Other items require students to show their work but the criteria used to score these items do not consider the strategies used to answer the item. Instead, the scoring criteria focus on which of the procedures required to solve the problem were applied accurately.

As a National Research Council report on student assessment states, "Advances in the cognitive and measurement sciences make this an opportune time to rethink the fundamental scientific principles and philosophical assumptions serving as the foundations for current approaches to assessment" (Pellegrino, Chudowsky, & Glaser, 2001, p. 1). Among the several conclusions reached by the NRC Committee on the Foundations of Assessment were:

> Assessments should focus on identifying the specific strategies children are using for problem solving....
>
> ...assessments, especially those conducted in the context of classroom instruction, should focus on making students' thinking visible to both their teachers and themselves so that instructional strategies can be selected to support an appropriate course for future learning.
>
> One of the most important roles for assessment is the provision of timely and informative feedback to students during instruction and learning so that their practice of a skill and its subsequent acquisition will be effective and efficient. (Pellegrino et al., 2001, pp. 4–5)

Although the recommendations by the National Research Council were made in 2001,

8 years later no large-scale testing program has embraced them. There have, however, been a few small-scale efforts to enhance the instructional value of testing by combining computer-based testing and advances in the cognitive sciences. As one example, in 2004, the Technology and Assessment Study Collaborative launched an effort to develop a multistaged, multilevel diagnostic assessment system (Russell, O'Dwyer, & Miranda, 2009).

Known as the Diagnostic Algebra Assessment system (DAA), the initiative set out to develop a comprehensive online assessment and instruction system that contains three key features. First, the system provides teachers with access to a series of online tests, each of which focuses on a specific algebraic concept. For each test, items are designed to measure student understanding of the concept. For students who perform poorly, each test is also designed to examine whether the student holds a known misconception that is specific to the measured concept. Thus, each test provides a measure of student understanding of a given concept and, for low performing students, an estimate of the probability that a student holds a specific misconception that is interfering with his or her understanding.

A second feature of the system is the provision of immediate feedback to teachers. An initial report sorts students into three categories. The first category includes students who performed well on the test and appear to have a solid understanding of the tested concept. The second category contains students who did not perform well and who appear to hold a specific misconception related to the tested concept. The third category contains students who also did not perform well but who do not appear to hold an associated misconception. By classifying students into three categories, teachers develop a better understanding of how well their students are performing and why some students are struggling with a given concept.

A third feature of the system is that it links teachers to lessons and activities designed to help students correct a given misconception. Students identified as having a given misconception are also connected to the relevant learning activities.

The DAA is still in development but preliminary research provides evidence that this approach to diagnostic assessment is effective for improving student learning (Russell, O'Dwyer, & Miranda, 2009). Examining the use of the DAA by 44 teachers working with more than 900 students, Russell et al. found that the combination of diagnostic assessments that focus on specific algebraic concepts and misconceptions, provide immediate feedback to teachers about the performance of each individual student, and present links to instructional activities that target specific misconceptions were associated with larger decreases in misconceptions and larger increases in algebraic understanding.

These findings parallel those of Minstrell and his colleagues (Thissen-Roe, Hunt, & Minstrell, 2004) who have developed and examined the use of diagnostic assessments in physics. Like the DAA, Minstrell's DIAGNOSER provides teachers with access to a set of short tests, each of which focuses on a specific physics concept. The tests provide teachers with an estimate of the degree to which the students understand the concept and the extent to which a misconception specific to that concept may be interfering with understanding of the concept.

Research on DIAGNOSER suggests that the assessments built into it provide teachers with valuable information about student understanding and the presence of specific misconceptions (Thissen-Roe et al., 2004). Specifically, data indicated that the diagnostic information helped teachers recognize that some misconceptions believed to occur commonly were held by only a few students, while other misconceptions that were thought to be rare were in fact relatively common among students. Data also indicated that students whose teachers used DIAGNOSER performed approximately 14 percentile points higher than their peers whose teachers did not employ it.

While efforts to develop embedded diagnostic tests that are designed to help inform instruction remain in their infancy, research suggests that these systems hold promise for providing teachers and students with immediate access to information designed to inform instructional practices. To date, however, these systems have not been made widely available. While efforts are underway to develop similar assessment tools for geometry, these diagnostic systems are also currently limited to a few concepts in algebra, physics, and chemistry. Nonetheless, the DAA and DIAGNOSER provide sound examples of how teachers can capitalize on the widespread availability of computers in schools to develop and deliver tests that provide valuable diagnostic information that can be used to help improve student learning.

PROVIDING RAPID FEEDBACK ON STUDENT WRITING: AUTOMATED ESSAY SCORING

Scoring students' writing is time consuming. In some cases, the time required to score essays results in substantial delays in providing feedback to students about their work. By the time feedback is provided, its value is often decreased because students have moved on to other assignments. To decrease the time required to score written responses and increase the reliability of scores for written responses, methods of using computers to analyze written responses have been developed (see Shermis & Burstein, 2003 for an overview).

Work on computer-based scoring of writing dates back to the work of Ellis Page during the late 1960s. Since Page's (1966, 1968) pioneering efforts, four approaches to computer-based scoring have evolved. These approaches include Project Essay Grading (PEG), Latent Semantic Analysis (LSA), e-Rater, and Bayesian Essay Test Scoring (BETSY). The techniques used by these approaches range from simple frequency counts of words, punctuation, and errors to advanced probabilistic Bayesian models (for a more detailed description of these methods, see Dikli, 2006).

Despite the differences in the specific methods employed, each approach follows the same four steps in developing and applying a scoring model. First, a small number of human readers are trained and then score a relatively small set of essays. Second, a computer-based scoring model is developed. To develop a scoring model, a sample of essays along with the scores awarded by human readers is analyzed. This analysis quantifies several features of the essays including the frequency of words, word combinations, phrases, grammar errors, spelling errors, and other semantic characteristics. These frequencies are used to create a model that predicts the human score. In reality, the computer algorithm does not actually award a score to an essay, but instead predicts the score that a human reader is likely to award the essay given the presence of the identified features.

Third, to check the accuracy of the scoring model, a second set of essays scored by human readers is entered into the system. The scoring model calculates a score for each essay, and the scores awarded by the human readers and the scoring model are compared. In many cases, the level of agreement between the human reader and the model exceeds 95% (Dikli, 2006). This level of agreement is often the same or higher than the scores awarded when two human readers are used to score the same set of essays.

Fourth, when high levels of agreement result, the scoring model is applied to the full set of essays. If agreement is unacceptable, the model is adjusted until a satisfactory level of agreement is reach. Once reached, scores for thousands of students are produced in a matter of hours instead of weeks, allowing students to get feedback on their work almost instantaneously while reducing the cost of scoring student work dramatically.

Although many people may bristle at the idea of having a computer score something as personal and qualitative as writing, all four of these systems have been shown to provide reliable scores for various types of student writing (Foltz, Gilliam, & Kendall, 2000; Page, 1995; Rudner & Liang, 2002). In addition, methods have been developed to detect essays that contain unexpected responses or employ unusual writing styles. Such essays are then identified during the scoring process and can be submitted to a human for scoring.

At least three states and several other large-scale testing programs are exploring the use of these approaches to score essays. But these systems are also proving valuable in classrooms. As Page (1995) and McCollum (1998) explore more fully, computer analysis of writing can be useful in two contexts. First, when working with younger writers, systems like PEG can provide frequent, instant feedback about mechanical aspects of a student's writing. After working on an essay for a given period of time, a student can submit his or her essay for a score. Depending on the algorithm used, the student then receives several scores; for example, one focusing on English conventions, another on content, and another on structural elements such as the way in which ideas or arguments are grouped or presented. Based on this information, the student has the opportunity to reflect on his or her writing, make revisions, and submit it for another score. While the final score is typically awarded by the student's teacher, allowing students to submit drafts, receive immediate feedback and then revise their writing reinforces the writing and revision process and allows students to receive more frequent and timely feedback on their writing.

Another way in which essay scoring technologies are useful in the classroom is related to subject specific courses, like U.S. history, where writing assignments typically focus on understanding of a given event or series of events. The focus of these essays tends to be on demonstrating knowledge and understanding, rather than on developing persuasive or creative writing skills. For content-based writing assignments, latent semantic analysis (LSA) essay scoring systems that base scores on how words are combined to form ideas can provide students with valuable preliminary feedback. Since LSA techniques focus on word combinations, these algorithms can be used to provide feedback on important topics, issues, or arguments that appear to be missing from a student's essay. By receiving instant, content-based feedback during the writing process, students can be provided with frequent opportunities to rethink their work, search for additional information, and revise their papers.

While a substantial body of research has examined the psychometric properties of scores awarded by these systems, very little research has focused on the efficacy of its use in the classroom setting. One study by Scharber, Dexter, and Riedel (2008) focused on the use of automated essay scoring in a university-level course and revealed several interesting findings. Among them were the need for students to trust the scores produced by the system and the need for the system to provide feedback that is aligned with the criteria ultimately used by the teacher when scoring the essay. When these two critical factors are in place, evidence suggests that automated essay scoring can help students develop higher-scoring essays.

A separate pair of studies that examined the effects of the use of automated essay scoring software for 11,000 essays produced by approximately 2,000 students in upper elementary, middle, and high school also found that it had positive effects on the quality of student writing. These effects include producing longer essays, producing fewer mechanical errors (spelling/grammar), and receiving higher scores (Shermis, Garvin, & Diao, in press). This research also found that feedback provided to students had the largest effects for eighth graders as compared to those students in upper elementary or high school. It is unclear why the effects were larger for eighth grade students, but the fact that the use of automated essay scoring had positive effects across all four grade levels holds promise for the use of such systems to provide preliminary feedback on student writing.

Clearly, automated essay scoring has potential to save time and provide students with more immediate feedback. Nonetheless, in its current form, there are a few notable shortcomings. First, because it requires teachers to train the system by first scoring a number of essays and submit them for analysis by the system, computer scoring may only be practical for assignments that are given to large numbers of students or are repeated each year. Second, while the feedback provided to students is highly reliable, it is also limited to specific aspects of a students' writing and in no way approximates the thoughtful and thorough comments that a teacher can provide. Third, computer scoring of writing requires that written passages be submitted in an electronic format; this requirement may pose a barrier to the use of automated scoring in schools that lack adequate technological resources. Despite these limitations, advances in the algorithms and methods used to develop scoring models hold promise to expand the type of feedback and improve the quality of preliminary feedback provided to students.

COLLECTING INFORMATION ABOUT STUDENT LEARNING DURING INSTRUCTION: STUDENT RESPONSE SYSTEMS

Collecting information about student knowledge, understanding, and interest is critical during instruction. While well-constructed questions can help teachers collect information about student thinking, questions posed to an entire classroom typically produce evidence from only a small number of students (Airasian & Russell, 2007). Many teachers attempt to supplement information from a limited sample of students by examining students' body language. This supplemental information, however, provides crude and often inaccurate information about students' cognitive processes and affective attitudes.

Instead of relying on evidence from a few students or interpreting students' body language, student response systems allow teachers to quickly collect information directly from all students within a classroom. Student response systems consist of a set of hand-held devices that students use to record responses to a question posed by the teacher. The hand-held devices take the form of PalmPilots or wireless clickers that are similar to a television remote control. The devices communicate wirelessly with software running on the teacher's computer. Typically, the teacher poses a question and presents students with multiple-choice answer options. All students in the classroom are then given an opportunity to respond using their handheld device. The software automatically tabulates responses and summarizes the data for the teacher in a visual/graphical display or a table. The teacher can use using an LCD projector connected to the computer to show students a summary of their responses.

As an example, a teacher who is helping students develop an understanding of how to calculate a statistical mean might present students with a table of numbers, ask the students to find the mean, and then present them with four answer options. One option might represent the actual mean, a second the mode, a third the median, and a fourth a common arithmetic error made while calculating the mean. Similarly, a teacher helping students develop their ability to conjugate verbs in Spanish might present a verb, ask students to conjugate it in the past tense, and then present a list of options. One option would represent the correct conjugation while the others might represent conjugations for different tenses or for different pronouns. For both examples, students would work on the problem and then use their response pads to record their solution.

As students record their answer, the system tallies responses and displays the percentage of students selecting each answer option on the teacher's computer. This summary provides teachers with a clear sense of how many students were able to correctly solve the problem posed and whether additional instruction is required. As an example, if a substantial percentage of students select the median instead of the mean, the teacher may decide to spend more time differentiating a mean and median. However, if the majority of students selected either the mean or the response that represents a common arithmetic error made while calculating a mean, the teacher may opt to proceed with the lesson, but note that some students may need opportunities to improve their arithmetic skills.

In addition to making group level decisions, student response systems allow responses to be linked to each individual. While it may not be practical to examine individual responses during instruction, teachers can examine responses by each student to identify patterns in their responses, to assess their level of understanding, or to inform instructional modifications for each student.

In addition to allowing teachers to take a quick measure of cognitive skills and knowledge, student response systems can also be useful for assessing students' affective attitudes and beliefs. While body language and facial expressions can reveal what students feel, they can also be misleading. Similarly, while broad questions can provide insight into how a few students feel, they rarely lead to a solid understanding of the class as a whole. By asking students to use a response system to respond to questions about whether or not they are confused, whether they would like another example, or whether they are ready to move on to a new topic or issue, teachers can obtain input from a broader sample of students and allow students to share their feelings in a way that is anonymous to their peers.

Despite the growing use of student response systems in K-12 and higher education classroom, the body of research focusing on their use and effect is small. Yet, the research conducted to date suggests that the response systems have a positive effect on learning and the classroom learning environment (Horowitz, n.d.). These effects are reported to occur, in part, due to increases in student engagement during instruction (Burnstein & Lederman, 2001; Guthrie & Carling, 2004). This research also shows that teachers believe students are more responsive to questions posed during instruction. Teachers also report a strong desire to continue using the systems after becoming accustomed to them, while their students report wanting to participate in future classes that also employ response systems (Horowitz, n.d.).

Despite these benefits, the value of classroom response systems is dependent on the quality of questions posed and the response options offered by teachers. While these systems can provide diagnostic information about students' current state of understanding, response options must be carefully crafted to assure they represent a given misconception, misunderstanding, or common error. In addition, the use of response systems requires a moderate investment by schools and requires that all students have access to a responder. Finally, while most systems provide easy-to-use graphic displays that summarize data, teachers must become accustomed to quickly interpreting this information in order to make valid and effective decisions during instruction.

Despite these limitations, however, student response systems allow teachers to improve the accuracy and generalizability of information collected and used by teachers to inform instruction. As the technology evolves, student responses systems will likely develop the capacity for teachers to pose open-ended questions that require students to produce their own responses or to show their work, increasing the diagnostic value of information collected by students during instruction.

LOOKING TO THE FUTURE

A large body of research provides evidence that formative assessment is an effective tool for improving student learning (Black & Wiliam, 1998). Effective format assessment requires teachers to collect accurate information about their students' current state of knowledge and understanding in a timely manner, and for that information to be closely aligned with the current focus of instruction. In addition, this information must be analyzed efficiently and either used by teachers to modify instruction to meet a student's current instructional need or used by students to improve their understanding or the quality of their work (Black & Wiliam, 1998). Given the speed with which computer-based technologies can collect, analyze, and report information, computer-based tools have great potential to increase the efficiency and the individualization of formative assessment.

The examples presented in this chapter represent a small sample of the many ways in which computer-based technologies are currently being used to assist with formative assessment. These examples, however, demonstrate the several benefits technology can bring to teachers and their students. As seen in each example, technology can greatly increase the speed with which information is collected and summarized. As seen with mCLASS:Reading and student response systems, technology provides teachers with flexibility to collect, explore, and view data about student understanding and affective feelings in a variety of ways. Technology-based tools also allow teachers to collect a broader sample of information from their students. This benefit is evident in the larger number of students from which teachers can collect information using classroom response systems.

The level of detail and the ease with which teachers are connected to resources aligned with student's needs is also facilitated by technology. The DAA system and DIAGOSER provide examples of tools that provide detailed information about each student's conceptual understanding and connect students to learning activities aligned with their current needs.

Finally, technology provides opportunities to improve the timeliness with which information is provided to teachers and their students. As seen with the automated essay scoring systems, students can receive near instant feedback on their writing as they produce drafts of essays. Similarly, student response systems allow teachers to access information from students while instruction is still in progress.

Although each of these benefits holds promise to enhance formative assessment practices, each requires investments in technology by schools and their teachers. More importantly, these tools require teachers to apply judgment when making instructional decisions based on data produced by these systems. And, although it is tempting to allow technology to prescribe solutions and actions, the use of technology for formative assessment should be limited to providing teachers with more timely and rich information that they can use to make informed decisions about instructional practices and the current needs of their students.

As summarized in this chapter, a small body of research provides preliminary evidence that the use of the computer-based tools described here can be used to improve student knowledge, understanding, and skills. As these, and other technology-based tools are improved, it is important that the body of research also improves. Many of the studies summarized here have focused on small samples of classrooms and have been conducted by researchers who are closely linked with the development of the tools. As the tools become available in larger numbers of classrooms, it will be important for the size and scope of future research to expand. Where possible, it will also be important that future research be conducted by researchers who do not have vested interests in the outcome of the studies. Finally, given the cost of purchasing and training teachers to use technology-based formative assessment tools, it will be valuable, where feasible and ethical, to employ research methods that allow stronger comparisons between current methods of formative assessment and computer-based solutions.

Despite the many ways in which the research base can be improved and expanded, preliminary evidence suggests that many computer-based tools can aid formative assessment. Tools like the DAA and DIAGNOSER can help teachers identify misconceptions and misunderstandings that may interfere with the development of a student's conceptual understanding during the initial stages of instruction. Other tools, like the mCLASS:Reading can help teachers identify recurrent patterns or challenges a student encounters. And, tools like classroom responses systems and automated essay scoring software can greatly increase the speed with which information is collected from or returned to students, allowing understanding and skills to improve before a lesson or body of work is completed. In each of these ways, computer-based tools can help teachers implement formative assessment practices in a manner that is timely, aligned with current instruction, and, in many cases, individualized to meet each student's current learning needs.

REFERENCES

Airasian, P. W., & Russell, M. (2007). *Classroom assessment: Concepts and applications* (6th ed.). Boston: McGraw-Hill.

Becker, H. (1999). *Internet use by teachers: Conditions of professional use and teacher-directed student use.* Irvine, CA: Center for Research on Information Technology and Organizations.

Black, P., & Wiliam, D. (1998). Assessment and classroom learning. *Assessment in Education, 5*(1), 7–74.

Burnstein, R. A., & Lederman, L. M. (2001). Using wireless keypads in lecture classes. *The Physics Teacher, 39,* 8–11.

Cullen, J., & Shaw, S. (2000). *The accuracy of teacher prediction of student test performance for students referred to special education.* Danbury, CT: Department of Education and Educational Psychology, Western Connecticut State University.

Demaray, M. K., & Elliott, S. N. (1998). Teachers' judgments of students' academic functioning: A comparison of actual and predicted performances. *School Psychology Quarterly, 13*(1), 8–24.

Dikli, S. (2006). An overview of automated scoring of essays. *Journal of Technology, Learning, and Assessment, 5*(1). Retrieved January 12, 2009, from http://escholarship.bc.edu/jtla/vol5/1/

Foltz, P., Gilliam, S., & Kendall, S. (2000). Supporting content-based feedback in online writing evaluation with LSA. *Interactive Learning Environment, 8*(2), 111–129.

Guthrie, R. W., & Carlin, A. (2004, August). Waking the dead: Using interactive technology to engage passive learners. *Proceedings of the Tenth Americas Conference on Information Systems,* New York.

Hoge, R. D., & Coladarci, T. (1989). Teacher-based judgments of academic achievement: A review of the literature. *Review of Educational Research, 59,* 297–313.

Horowitz, H. M. (n.d.). Student response systems: Interactivity in the classroom. Retrieved July 15, 2008, from https://sharepoint.cisat.jmu.edu/tsec/jim/CRS/Pedagogical%20Studies.htm

Hupert, N., & Heinze, C. (2006) Results in the palms of their hands: Using handheld computers for data-driven decision making in the classroom. In M. van't Hooft & K. Swan (Eds.), *Ubiquitous computing in education: Invisible technology, visible impact* (pp. 211–229). Mahwah, NJ: Erlbaum.

Hupert, N., Heinze, J., Gunn, G., & Stewart, J. (2007). Using technology-assisted progress monitoring to drive improved student outcomes. In E. Mandinach & M. Honey (Eds.), *Linking data and learning* (pp. 130–150). New York: Teachers College Press.

Hupert, N., Heinze, J., Gunn, G., Stewart, J., & Honey, M. (2007). An analysis of technology-assisted progress monitoring to drive improved student outcomes. *Wireless Generation.* Retrieved January 12, 2009, from http://www.wirelessgeneration.com/resources/research.html#01

Hupert, N., Martin, W., Heinze, C., Kanaya, T., & Perez, H. (2004, June). *Trends in the use of handheld technology to support student reading assessment.* Paper presented at the National Educational Computing Conference, New Orleans, LA..

Kowalski, T., & Lasley, T. J. (2008). *Handbook of data-based decision making in education.* London: Taylor & Francis.

McCollum, K. (1998). How a computer program learns to grade essays. *The Chronicle of Higher Education.* Retrieved January 12, 2009, from http://chronicle.com/free/v45/i02/02a03701.htm

Mulholland, L. A., & Berliner, D. C. (1992, April). *Teacher experience and estimation of student achievement.* Paper presented at the Annual Meeting of the American Educational Research Association, San Francisco, CA.

Page, E. (1966). The imminence of grading essays by computer. *Phi Delta Kappan, 47,* 238–243.

Page, E. (1968). The use of computers in analyzing student essays. *International Review of Education, 14*(2), 210–221.

Page, E. (1995, August). *Computer grading of essays: A different kind of testing?* Paper presented at a meeting of the American Psychological Association, New York.

Pellegrino, J. W., Chudowsky, N., & Glaser, R. (Eds.). (2001). *Knowing what students know: The science and design of educational assessment.* Washington, DC: National Academy Press.

Rudner, L., & Liang, T. (2002, April). *Automated essay scoring using Bayes' theorem.* Paper presented at the meeting of the National Council on Measurement in Education, New Orleans, LA.

Russell, M., O'Brien, E., Bebell, D., & O'Dwyer, L. (2003). *Students' beliefs, access, and use of computers in school and at home.* Boston, MA: Boston College, Technology and Assessment Study Collaborative. Retrieved January 12, 2009, from http://www.intasc.org/PDF/useit_r2.pdf

Russell, M., O'Dwyer, L, & Miranda, H. (2009). Diagnosing students' misconceptions in algebra: Results from an experimental pilot study. *Behavior Research Methods, 41*(2), 414–424.

Scharber, C., Dexter, S., & Riedel, E. (2008). Students' experiences with an automated essay scorer. *Journal of Technology, Learning, and Assessment, 7*(1). Retrieved January 12, 2009, from http://www.jtla.org

Sharp, D., & Risko, V. (2003). *All in the palm of your hand: Lessons from one school's first steps with handheld technology for literacy assessments.* Report to the Information Infrastructure Project, Network on Teaching and Learning for the John D. and Catherine T. MacArthur Foundation. Chicago: Center for School Improvement, University of Chicago. Retrieved August 10, 2004, from cs/tech.uchicago.edu.800/iis/pubs

Shea, M. (2000). *Taking running records.* New York: Scholastic.

Shermis, M. D., & Burstein, J. (Eds.). (2003). *Automated essay scoring: A cross-disciplinary perspective.* Mahwah, NJ: Erlbaum.

Shermis, M. D., Garvin, G., & Diao, Y. (in press). The impact of automated essay scoring on writing outcome. *Journal of Technology, Learning, and Assessment.*

Thissen-Roe, A., Hunt, E., & Minstrell, J. (2004). The DIAGNOSER project: combining assessment and learning. *Behavior Research Methods, Instruments, and Computers, 36*(2), 234–240.

9

FORMATIVE ASSESSMENT, MOTIVATION, AND SCIENCE LEARNING

MARIA ARACELI RUIZ-PRIMO, ERIN MARIE FURTAK, CARLOS AYALA, YUE YIN, AND RICHARD J. SHAVELSON

Other chapters in this volume have highlighted the great potential of formative assessments to aid in student learning. However, in order to live up to this potential, teachers must be prepared to enact formative assessments in a manner consistent with their design. In the absence of adequate preparation, there is no guarantee that formative assessments alone will benefit student achievement. This chapter describes the results of a study designed to test Black and Wiliam's (1998) finding that feedback closely connected to instruction and focus on improving performance should produce a large, positive effect on students' learning and motivation. The chapter presents the methodological, logistical, and practical choices made during the study and reflects on what failed, what worked, and what conditions led to the study's unexpected outcome.

A MODEL OF FORMATIVE ASSESSMENT

Classroom assessment includes all actions taken by the teacher to gather information about student learning. It becomes formative in nature when assessment information is used to adjust instruction to help students achieve learning goals. Formative assessment makes student thinking transparent to teachers and helps students come to know the criteria by which their performance will be evaluated (Black & Wiliam, 1998; Duschl, 2003; Sadler, 1989).

The implementation of formative assessment is often described as consisting of multiple steps or processes, summarized by Ramaprasad (1983) as three questions: Where are we going? Where are we now? and How will we get there? The "Where are we going?" step involves the teacher setting and clarifying learning goals and the information that will be considered as evidence of achieving those learning goals. The "Where are we now?" step refers to the specific practices in which teachers seek to understand students' current and prior knowledge, as well as their conceptual frameworks as they relate to the learning goals. Finally, the "How will we get there?" step includes teacher design or modification of instruction to meet students' needs. Bell and Cowie (2001) similarly describe formative assessment practices as a cycle of three distinct activities: gathering information about student learning, analyzing/interpreting this information, and acting-on/using this information with the intention of improving student learning.

Central to each of these three steps suggested by Ramaprasad (1983) or Bell and Cowie (2001) is the role of the teacher. To make the teacher's role more explicit, an expansion of the formative assessment models just described is proposed here. The expansion includes six assessment pedagogies necessary for effective enactment of formative assessments (Ayala & Brandon, 2008).

First, teachers need to understand the content, from both a disciplinary and a pedagogical perspective (e.g., learning goals, student misconceptions, and how students develop competence in that domain). Second, teachers must understand the variety of assessment tools available to them to assess student knowledge through both formal and informal methods, and understand how these different tools give us different information. Third, teachers need to know when and how to use formative assessments, which includes understanding the timing and method to implement these assessments, as well as using student discussion and administration of formal formative assessment tasks. Fourth, teachers need to be able to analyze the information collected, which includes collecting, managing, and interpreting the information collected from the tools. Fifth, once the information is analyzed, teachers need to know how to take action with both feedback and additional instructional activities if necessary. Finally, teachers need to understand the value of formative assessment practices. Each of these pedagogies will be described in more detail in the following sections.

UNDERSTANDING THE CONTENT

Understanding the content for formative assessment entails not only knowing the science of it, but also the places where students typically struggle, their misconceptions, and how best to address these challenges. The new tools of learning progressions are beginning to map the content and misconceptions relevant to formative assessment and, therefore, show promise to scaffold teachers' knowledge (see Kennedy & Wilson, 2007). In-depth knowledge of the content allows teachers to set clear learning goals, which are the starting point for effective formative assessment. Only with clear learning goals can teachers determine the gap between where students are and where they should be, and then think about appropriate strategies to reduce the gap.

UNDERSTANDING THE TOOLS

Understanding the tools involves not only knowing the diverse assessment prompts that can be used to elicit students' emerging understandings, but selecting the right one to tap the right knowledge at the right time. An assessment prompt is the question, task, or situation used to elicit student responses that will help to make their thinking explicit, and span a continuum depending on four factors: the amount or type of planning involved, the formality of the assessment, the nature and quality of the data sought, and the nature of the feedback (Furtak & Ruiz-Primo, 2008).

Whether this prompt is directed to an individual student or the whole class is a choice that teachers need to make according to the formality of the information gathering. A teacher can gather information about student learning at any level of interaction, be it one-on-one or speaking with the whole class. For example, a teacher may follow up on a student's question by asking another question (informal and unplanned), or the teacher might prepare and pose to the whole class a question designed to challenge their thinking and make it more explicit (more formal and planned). Furthermore, a teacher might administer a written assessment prompt to the entire class to systematically collect information about what students know (formal and planned).

Formative assessment, then, can be conceived as falling on a continuum from informal and unplanned to formal and planned, with three benchmark points: (1) on-the-fly formative assessment occurs when teachable moments unexpectedly arise in the classroom; (2) planned-for-interaction formative assessment is also used during instruction but deliberately prepared before class; and (3) formal formative assessment involves the administration of assessments embedded in a curriculum unit to ensure that students have achieved important instructional goals before moving to the next unit. These benchmark points are illustrated in Figure 9.1. In any of these forms of formative assessment, if a teacher notices a learning gap, he or she may timely modify and adjust his or her teaching, such as reviewing or reteaching difficult concepts, to help students close the learning gap (Furtak & Ruiz-Primo, 2008; Shavelson, Yin, Furtak, Ruiz-Primo, & Ayala 2008a; Shavelson, Young et al., 2008b).

Information that is gathered informally, either through questions or high quality discussions, can present a challenge because it requires teachers to have confidence and in-depth subject-matter knowledge (Atkin, Coffey, Moothy, Sato, & Thibeault, 2005; Furtak & Ruiz-Primo, 2008; Ruiz-Primo & Furtak, 2006, 2007). In contrast, formal, written assessment activities—often called embedded assessments—are generally considered a more concrete way to gather information from students and elicit their ideas so that teachers can make educated decisions based on formal evidence.

Furthermore, teachers also need to understand that different types of assessment prompts tap different types of knowledge. For formative assessment purposes, assessment prompts that focus on memorizing information do not help. Formative assessment prompts should tap more than just the simple, factual knowledge so common in science classrooms. Prompts should go beyond this declarative knowledge (knowing that) and procedural knowledge (knowing how) and extend to schematic knowledge (knowing why).

Figure 9.1 Formative assessment continuum. From Shavelson, R. J., Young, D. B., and Ayala, C. C., et al. (2008). On the impact of curriculum-embedded formative assessment on learning: A collaboration between curriculum and assessment developers. *Applied Measurement in Education, 21,* 295–314. Used with permission.

KNOWING WHEN AND HOW TO IMPLEMENT FORMATIVE ASSESSMENTS

A critical component in the use of formative assessment is to understand when and how the assessment should be implemented. Informally, teachers should be able to capitalize on all opportunities that the classroom work and interactions provide for gathering information about what students know. More formally, teachers should identify the critical junctures or waypoints where they should check in with students to see that they are progressing as expected in their knowledge, skills, or ability before moving on to new concepts. At these critical junctures, teachers might develop or select assessment tools that they will use to assess students' knowledge.

Diverse instructional approaches should also be considered when implementing formative assessments (e.g., discussions at tables, think-pair-shares, taking votes, and having students argue ideas). Teachers need to understand when to use particular approaches. For example, if a teacher is interested in facilitating a discussion about the range of student responses to questions posed, capturing anonymous student responses facilitates potential student discussion about the results because of the reduced stigma of not having problematic responses linked to a particular student.

KNOWING HOW TO ANALYZE THE INFORMATION

Once teachers have successfully gathered information (e.g., by implementing formal embedded assessments), it becomes important to interpret what students know (or do not know) and are able to do (or not able to do) and to understand where students stand in relation to the overall learning goals. Teachers should be able to make an on-the-fly judgment about what a student's response is reflecting; for example, a common misunderstanding (Ruiz-Primo & Furtak, 2006, 2007). Analyzing one student response is not the same as analyzing all students' responses; such analysis should be more systematic. For example, teachers can organize students' responses on the board according to different levels of understanding or different mental models, or review students' responses to determine the exact percentage of students with each mental model. Through these analyses, teachers can identify which students may need more individual help and which may know enough to help their peers. This sets us up for the next step.

KNOWING HOW TO TAKE ACTION

Just as collecting information about what students know can vary along the continuum from on-the-fly to planned, the teacher's analysis of the information and the responses to that information can take on the form of feedback and design of the next instructional activity. This step is critical for formative assessment to be successful. It includes teachers' feedback to students, and the design of or adjustment to instruction to meet students' needs or move forward. If teachers elicit and analyze information but do not use it to design strategies to close the gap and move students forward in their learning, the main purpose of formative assessment is lost. Both informal and formal formative assessments require completing the loop. This is often the most challenging step for any teacher (Furtak, Ruiz-Primo et al., 2008; Ruiz-Primo & Furtak, 2006, 2007).

The feedback provided by the teacher can also come in different forms, from verbal responses given in class, to thoughtful, written feedback on students' work. Teachers can provide feedback directly in dialogue, as written comments, or arrange for students to get feedback from each other. The teacher can also provide feedback indirectly by encouraging students to discuss their ideas and the evidence that supports them, so that students can realize the discrepancies between their ideas and evidence, and possibly change their ideas. When necessary, teachers may review or reteach a topic to ensure that students close the learning gap.

Several researchers are currently engaged in efforts to make providing feedback a less difficult skill for teachers. Kennedy and Wilson (2007) propose progress variables, which allow teachers to categorize students according to levels of understanding that suggest the next steps for student learning. Similarly, Minstrell's DIAGNOSER system utilizes prescriptive activities to help guide teacher and student toward next steps once formative assessment information has been collected (Minstrell & vanZee, 2003).

UNDERSTANDING THE VALUE OF FORMATIVE ASSESSMENT

This last component, more than being the last step in the set of pedagogies, should be consider similar to a belief that permeates the other pedagogies. Teachers must not only be able to enact formative assessments through the pedagogies described above, but must also understand of the value of formative assessment in helping students learn. At first glance, formative assessment appears time-consuming, and requires rich teaching experience and good teaching skills. Developing an understanding of the benefits of formative assessment can help teachers to overcome these impressions and move toward realizing new, more effective practices in their classrooms.

In the next section, a study conducted by the authors of this chapter is described. The study examined the impact of a formal formative assessment—the kind of formative assessment at the right-hand side of Figure 9.1. In particular, it explored the impact of formal formative assessments embedded in a curriculum on student learning and motivation.

FORMAL FORMATIVE ASSESSMENT, MOTIVATION, AND STUDENT LEARNING

A small, randomized study was conducted to test Black and Wiliam's (1998a) contention that feedback based on formative assessment would produce a large positive effect on students' learning. The description provided in this chapter is general and emphasizes those aspects that might be useful for other researchers who are interested in conducting this type of study, as well as for teachers who are interested in exploring some of the ideas in their own classrooms. More information about the study can be found the special issue of *Applied Measurement in Education* (2008) and in other sources (e.g., Furtak & Ruiz-Primo, 2008; Ruiz-Primo & Furtak, 2006, 2007; Shavelson et al., 2008a; Yin, 2005).

The project tested a "big idea" related to formative assessment; namely, that "for a relatively small investment—embedding conceptually coherent formative assessments in a nationally used science curriculum—a big learning payoff would be realized" (Shavelson et al., 2008b, p. 293). With this big idea in mind, the Stanford Education Assessment Laboratory (SEAL) partnered with the Curriculum Research and Development Group (CRDG) at the University of Hawaii to examine the impact of embedded formative assessment on student learning and motivation during the 2003–2004 school year. The study was guided by two research questions: Can embedded formative assessments improve students' achievement? And, can embedded formative assessments improve students' motivational beliefs?

The study involved embedding assessments in the "Foundational Approaches in Science Teaching" (FAST) program, a multidisciplinary, inquiry-based middle-school science program (Pottenger & Young, 1992) developed by the Curriculum Research and Development Group (CRDG) and aligned with the National Science Education Standards (Rogg & Kahle, 1997). The study focused on the first 12 investigations of the physical science strand of FAST 1, The Local Environment, in which students investigate concepts such as mass, volume, and density to develop an explanation for sinking and floating based on relative density. The assessments that were developed for this study focused on density and relative density of the object, and the medium in which the object sinks or floats.

The Intervention: Formative Embedded Assessment Prompts

The intervention was a set of formal formative assessments embedded into the FAST curriculum. The formative assessments were developed by researchers in a five-phase process: (1) mapping and experiencing the curricular unit in which the formative assessments were to be embedded; (2) determining the unit goal to be assessed; (3) determining the critical points where the assessments should be embedded; (4) defining the assessment development guidelines; and (5) developing the assessments (Ayala et al., 2008).

Mapping and Experiencing the Investigations   This phase focused on distilling the FAST curriculum to its essence. To do so, the researchers identified the critical concepts, procedures, or explanations that students construct within each of the investigations, the types of knowledge being tapped, the knowledge necessary in later investigations, and the characteristics of student activities.

Researchers also rolled up their sleeves and experienced the activities the same way that students would, in order to help them come to understand the rationale underlying a particular sequence of investigations, why the activities were structured the way they were, and what opportunities they provided students to develop and construct understanding.

After experiencing the FAST investigations, researchers created storyboards that mapped the critical aspects addressed in each investigation, including the critical concepts, procedures, and explanations. Mapping the FAST investigations revealed that the curriculum relied on declarative and procedural knowledge, but failed to emphasize schematic knowledge. To make up for this weakness, the embedded assessments were developed to support students' construction of schematic knowledge (e.g., explaining why things sink or float).

Determining the Learning Goals   Mapping and experiencing the unit in which the assessments were to be embedded facilitated the researchers' understanding of the overarching learning goal, which is critical in the development of embedded assessments. The learning goal would be the one assessed at the end of the unit and, therefore, should guide the focus of the embedded assessments along the way.

In this study, attention was focused on the critical idea of "Why things sink or float" rather than defining the goal in the form of an objective (e.g., "students would understand relative density"). The assessment development team considered the development of this schematic knowledge to be fundamental to teaching relative density. Ultimately, the goal around which the embedded assessments were designed and developed was "understanding why things sink or float."

Determining the Critical Junctures of the Curricular Units   Given the goal of the project to embed assessments in the FAST curriculum, a critical question in designing the formal formative assessments was, "What should the assessments be and where should we embed them?" In the process of mapping and experiencing the unit, the points (natural joints) were identified in the instructional sequence in which the formative assessments were to be embedded. These natural joints in the curriculum have three qualities; they are points at which: (1) a subgoal of the overarching unit goal should have been achieved, meaning that there is a body of knowledge and skills sufficiently comprehensive to be assessed; (2) teachers need to know about student understanding before they can proceed with further instruction; and (3) feedback to students is critical to improving and refining their understanding of the material already taught (Ayala et al., 2008; Shavelson, SEAL & CRDG, 2005).

Five natural joints were identified as locations for embedded assessments in the 12 investigation sequences (see Figure 9.2). Once the joints and the concepts, procedures, and explanations that were the focus of the unit were identified, the assessments were developed, piloted, and revised. Piloting the embedded assessments was a critical step, not only to refine the assessment but also to learn the issues involved in their implementation and use. During piloting, assessment tasks were found to be too long and too many, and the term *assessment* tended to make teachers use formative assessment in a summative manner.

First 12 Investigations of the FAST1 Physical Science Unit by Section																	
Section A: Mass					Section B: Volume						Section C: Density						
1	2	3	4	Joint 1	5	6	Joint 2	7	Joint 3	8	9	10	Joint 4	11	Joint 5	12

Figure 9.2 Identified joints in the sequence of the 12 FAST investigations.

Based on the feedback from the pilot study, the assessment prompts were changed and improved. The number of assessments was reduced and the name of our formative assessments was changed from "embedded assessments" to "reflective lessons" to avoid the usual summative teaching script that the word *assessment* evoked for the teachers who participated in the pilot (Lucks, 2003). The reflective lessons were designed to elicit and make public student conceptions of sinking-and-floating, to encourage communication and argumentation based on evidence from the investigations (reflective lessons), to challenge students' conceptions of why things sink and float, and to help students track and reflect on their conceptions of sinking and floating (e.g., Duschl, 2003).

The reflective lessons were composed of a carefully designed sequence of assessment prompts that were similar to the investigations students conducted. They enabled teachers to step back to check student understanding at the critical joints and to reflect on the next steps for moving forward in developing scientific explanations. In this way, the reflective lessons evolved from assessment activities to learning activities intended to provide instructional information to both the student and the teacher.

Two types of embedded formal assessment tasks were developed. The first type of assessment focused on procedural and schematic knowledge by employing four tasks: (1) interpreting a graph; (2) engaging in a predict-observe-explain (POE) assessment; (3) constructing a response to the question, "Why do things sink and float?"; and (4) responding to a predict-observe question designed to prompt students to move to a higher conceptual level. Figure 9.3 shows an example of one of the POE assessments. The second type of assessment task, a concept map, focused on the students' connected declarative knowledge (Ruiz-Primo & Shavelson, 1996). The formative assessments were grouped together into sets or "suites" and distributed through the unit at important conceptual junctures as shown in Figure 9.4.

The first type—the procedural and schematic knowledge formative assessments— were intended to be enacted across a period of days and to be interspersed with discussions in a sequence, as shown in the left-hand portion of Figure 9.5. The second type—the declarative knowledge formative assessment— was implemented in one day; this type is shown in the right-hand portion of Figure 9.5.]

Analyzing the students' responses to the pilot assessments and looking again at the FAST investigations led to a critical development in the study: the FAST Relative Development Trajectory, shown in Figure 9.6. The figure shows a trajectory in the development of students' conceptual understanding of buoyancy. It corresponds to the FAST 1 through 12 investigations, focusing first on mass, then volume, then mass and volume, then density, and finally, relative density. The trajectory was intended to be a guide for teachers so that they might better understand and identify the typical progression of student understanding through the course of the unit. It was expected that the trajectory would help teachers decide what to do next with the students, such as what questions to ask or what activities to do to help the students move forward.

The relative developmental trajectory shown in Figure 9.6 illustrates a progression of student understandings across the 12 investigations, starting at the lower left corner with alternative conceptions and moving toward the top right to density of objects and density of medium. During the unit, students are expected to use increasingly more sophisticated concepts to explain sinking and floating, and students' understanding and their ability to articulate their understanding is predicted to increase.

You have six blocks. Blocks 1, 2, and 3 are made of one material, while blocks 4, 5 and 6 are made of another material.

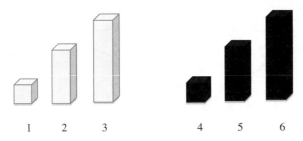

The density of blocks 1, 2, and 3 is 0.91 g/cm³, while the density of blocks 4, 5, and 6 is 1.2 g/cm³.

For each block, predict whether it will sink, float, or subsurface float in water. Give your reasons for your predictions.		
Block	Circle prediction	Reasons for your predictions
1	Sink Float Subsurface Float	
2	Sink Float Subsurface Float	
3	Sink Float Subsurface Float	
4	Sink Float Subsurface Float	
5	Sink Float Subsurface Float	
6	Sink Float Subsurface Float	

For each block, record whether it sank or floated.			
Block	Block sank, floated, or subsurface floated?	Your prediction correct? (circle)	Explain what you observed and why it happened.
1	Sink Float Subsurface Float	Yes or No	
2	Sink Float Subsurface Float	Yes or No	
3	Sink Float Subsurface Float	Yes or No	
4	Sink Float Subsurface Float	Yes or No	
5	Sink Float Subsurface Float	Yes or No	
6	Sink Float Subsurface Float	Yes or No	

Figure 9.3 Reflective lesson POE assessment at investigation 10. From Furtak, E. M., and Ruiz-Primo, M. A. (2008). Making students' thinking explicit in writing and discussion: An analysis of formative assessment prompts. *Science Education, 92*(5), 799-824. Used with permission.

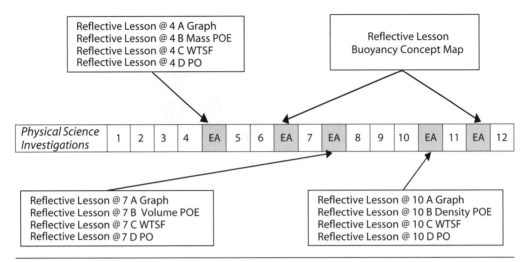

Figure 9.4 Placement of formative assessments within FAST unit. From Ayala, C., C., Shavelson, R. J., Ruiz-Primo, M.A., et al. (2008). Formal embedded assessments to reflective lessons: The development of formative assessment studies. *Applied Measurement in Education, 21,* 315–334. Used with permission.

The Participants

Twelve FAST teachers, trained by the CDRG group in the implementation of FAST as part of the adoption of the curriculum, were matched in pairs in a prepost comparison group experimental design according to school demographics. One teacher from each pair was then randomly assigned to either the experimental or comparison group. To examine the impact of embedded formative assessments on student achievement and motivation, students in both groups were given achievement tests and a motivation questionnaire before and after the sinking and floating unit.

Neither the comparison nor the experimental teachers were informed about the design of the study when they were recruited. Experimental teachers were told that the

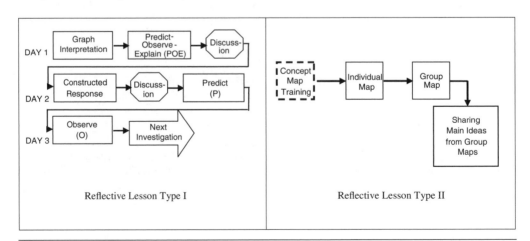

Figure 9.5 Sequence of formative assessments in two types of reflective lessons.

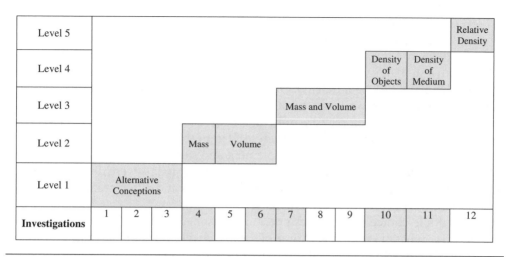

Figure 9.6 FAST bouyancy learning trajectory.

study was to assist curriculum designers to improve the curriculum and were asked to implement the embedded formative assessments designed by the researchers as if they were other FAST investigations. The comparison teachers were told that researchers were studying experienced teachers' enactment of the FAST curriculum, and thus to keep their regular teaching practice.

Comparison and experimental teachers were trained separately prior to the beginning of the school year. Training for both groups included an orientation to the study, the exchange of ideas about how they taught the FAST physical science investigations, instructions on how to use the study reporting tools (e.g., teacher logs), and how to set up video cameras in their classrooms. In addition, the experimental group teachers were trained in the use of formative assessments (see Ayala et al., 2008 for details). The additional training involved an iterative cycle for each assessment suite (the carefully designed sequence of embedded assessment prompt) with the following four steps: (1) experiencing the assessment suite as students when the project staff modeled the implementation of the suite; (2) discussing it as practitioners, noting the procedural skills needed as well as the role of eliciting students' conceptions and using those conceptions to build an empirically justifiable knowledge claim; (3) implementing the assessment suite with students at a lab school (CRDG's summer school program); and (4) reflecting on the experience in terms of improving their administration of and teaching with reflective lessons.

Measuring Student Outcomes

Two different kinds of student outcomes were measured: achievement and motivation. Student achievement was measured using four different measures; student motivation was measured using a questionnaire developed to test the link between formative assessment, motivation, and learning. Each of these measures is described in the following sections.

Achievement Assessments   To assess the impact of intervention (that is, embedded formative assessments) on student achievement, four summative assessments tapping different types of knowledge were developed: a multiple-choice test, a performance assessment, a short-answer assessment, and a predict-observe-explain assessment (see Yin, 2005; Yin et al., 2008 for details). Only the multiple-choice test was administered as the pretest for two reasons. First, the other three assessments were heavily curriculum content loaded and, therefore, were difficult for students to correctly respond to before instruction. Second, the cost-benefit trade-off led to the decision not to use these assessments, as they were expensive to implement and students would have no idea how to respond to them at the pretest. The summative assessments were developed by the researchers to measure the FAST instructional objectives and different knowledge types (i.e., declarative, procedural, and schematic).

The multiple-choice test was designed to be aligned with instructional objectives and the three types of knowledge. Some of the items were very similar to what students experienced in the FAST investigations (developed based on the content of the investigations) while others were selected from well-established external sources such as Trends in International Mathematics and Science Study (TIMSS) and National Assessment of Educational Progress (NAEP; see Ruiz-Primo, Shavelson, Hamilton, & Klein, 2002).

The performance assessment was designed mainly to tap into students' procedural knowledge, such as planning and conducting an experiment, making observations, drawing conclusions, and recording procedures. Each student was provided with equipment, such as four blocks with different densities, water, graduated cylinders, rulers, overflow cans, and other necessary supplies. Then they were asked to find the density of a block with a given mass and the density range of a mystery liquid. To solve the first problem, students needed to measure the volume of the block using either a ruler or an overflow container, and then students needed to apply the density formula to calculate density. To solve the second problem students needed to apply the idea that if an object's density is larger than that of a liquid, it sinks; if it is smaller, it floats.

The constructed response question, "Why do things sink or float?" measured students' schematic knowledge. This open-ended question was expected to provide substantial information about students' conceptual understanding.

The predict-observe-explain assessment was also designed to assess students' schematic knowledge. The test administrator showed students that a bar of soap sank in water. Students were asked to predict what would happen if the soap was cut into two unequal pieces (1/4 and 3/4) and put in water and explain their predictions. After students turned in their predictions and explanations, the test administrator put the two pieces of soap in water and asked students to record their observations and to reconcile their predictions. The predict-observe-explain posttest was intended to examine whether students understood two main points: that density is a property of a material and will not change with size, and that an object sinks or floats depending on its density (relative to the medium's density) instead of its volume or mass.

Analytical scoring systems were developed to score students' responses to the performance assessment, the short-answer question, and the POE assessment. The reliability and validity of all the assessments were evaluated. The internal consistency of the multiple-choice test was above .80 and interrater agreement between scorers of the short answer and POE assessments was always above 80%. Because the achievement tests were designed to measure students' knowledge in the same domain with different emphases, moderately high correlations among them were found. Correlations between different assessments ranged from .39 to .69, providing evidence for construct validity.

Motivation Questionnaire   A 46-item motivation questionnaire was developed to test the link between formative assessment, motivation, and learning. The 5-point Likert-type scales, ranging from 1 (strongly disagree) to 5 (strongly agree), measured different motivational beliefs that were hypothesized to be related to formative assessment. Some beliefs were expected to be positively associated with learning, such as task goal orientation (e.g., "I like science work that I will learn from, even if it is hard to learn at first"), perceived task-goal orientation context (e.g., "Our teacher gives us time to really explore and understand new ideas"), self-efficacy in science (e.g., "I can do almost all the work in science class if I do not give up"), and interest in science (e.g., "I enjoy the activities in my science class"). Other scales measured beliefs that may prevent learning, including ego approach orientation (e.g., "I want to do better than other students in my science class"), ego avoidance orientation ("One reason that I might not participate in science class is to avoid looking stupid"), perceived performance-goal orientation context (e.g., "Our teacher calls on smart students more than other students"), and fixed ability (e.g., "How well I do in science depends on how smart I was when I was born").

All motivational belief constructs reached an acceptable reliability level (alpha greater than .70) except for fixed ability (alpha = .44 based on three items). Confirmatory factor analyses provided support for the theoretical relationship between the motivation subscales and their corresponding items. The motivation questionnaire was administered to students in both groups at pre- and posttest.

Impact of Formative Assessment on Student Outcomes

Given the nested nature of the study design—students nested in teachers and teachers nested in treatment groups—hierarchical linear modeling (HLM) was applied to examine the effects of formative assessment on students' achievement and motivation (Yin et al., 2008). Hierarchical linear modeling was used in an exploratory fashion because the small number of teachers in each group provided little statistical power.

Surprisingly, results of the study did not support hypotheses about the effect of formative assessment on student achievement and motivation: the experimental group did not significantly outperform the comparison group on the achievement tests or the motivation measures. In fact, the students in the comparison group, on average, scored slightly higher than the experimental group on the multiple-choice test, performance assessment, and total achievement score, although the difference was not statistically significant (Yin, et al., 2008).

However, students in the experimental group had significantly lower score variance than the comparison group on the POE assessment, $F = 4.09$, $p < .05$. That is, the achievement gap between higher achievers and lower achievers in the experimental group was not as wide as that in the comparison group.

The results from the HLM analyses showed that students' motivation and achievement scores significantly varied among students and across teachers. Unfortunately, the embedded formative assessment treatment did not explain the variation among teachers. On average, the experimental group students did not benefit from the embedded formative assessment they received.

Why did the formative assessments used in the study fail to improve learning and motivation? The classroom videos collected over the course of the study helped to provide an explanation.

Evaluating the Fidelity of Implementation of the Intervention: Teachers' Implementation of the Embedded Assessments

Given the unexpected outcome of the study, exploration of the fidelity of implementation between the design of the treatment and what actually happened in the classrooms became an integral part of the project postmortem. It was reasoned that this information would help determine whether the results observed in the project could be attributed to an absence of a formative assessment treatment effect, a poor conceptualization of formative assessments in this study, or to an implementation that not only varied between teachers, but also strayed considerably from what had been intended by the assessment designers (Ruiz-Primo, 2003, 2005). The form and extent of the intervention teachers actually delivered were compared to the observed learning gains of their students (Furtak, Ruiz-Primo, Shemwell et al., 2008).

The implementation study (Ruiz-Primo, 2003) examined the fidelity of the enactment of the FAST investigations and the embedded assessments. The implementation study became a set of research projects conducted to understand the link between the treatment (i.e., the intended curriculum) and the measured student learning (i.e., the achieved curriculum). The basic premise of these studies was to help explain the results of the experiment as well as to discern differential effectiveness within the experimental group.

The primary source of data for the implementation study was videotapes made each day of the unit by the teachers themselves. These videotapes were supplemented by site visits over a two or three-day period during the course of the implementation of the FAST investigations.

To measure the fidelity of implementation by the experimental teachers in the study, the intended curriculum included in the *Teacher Guide* (SEAL, 2003) to the formative assessments was first mapped. Next, the videotaped lessons were coded according to the intended curriculum as a measure of the extent to which teachers enacted the formative assessments as intended in the study. This enactment was divided into two subcategories. The first subcategory was *treatment structure*, or the extent to which all of the assessments were implemented, the sequence in which they were implemented, the extent to which they incorporated discussions, and timing within and between assessments. The subcategory was *quality of delivery* of the formative assessments, which included eliciting student conceptions, tracking and clustering student conceptions, asking students to provide reasons for their explanations, and having students argue ideas and evidence. Finally, the performance of students on the prepost achievement test was compared to determine the learned curriculum.

Results of the implementation study indicated that adherence to the treatment structure varied by type of embedded assessment. Higher levels of adherence to the structure were observed in the reflective lesson suites (graph interpretation, POE, open-response, and performance assessment) than in the concept maps, leading us to conclude that the former has been emphasized but the latter has not in the *Teacher Guide* and the teacher training. Teachers devoted much more time to the discussion of the reflective lesson suite than the information gathered from the concepts maps.

Although the extent to which teachers implemented, sequenced and timed the formative assessments differed from our expectations, the quality with which teachers delivered them departed even more from the envisioned implementation Some aspects of formative assessment were implemented across teachers (e.g., whole class discussions), while some others (e.g., clustering students' conceptions or asking for students' explanations) were almost completely absent from most of the teachers' lessons. For example, in a typical reflective lesson, one of the teachers in the experimental group (who will be referred to as "Robert"—a fictitious name) kept eliciting students' responses, many of which were based upon misconceptions. However, after collecting different ideas from students, Robert did not address any misconceptions.

Whole classroom conversations and collecting information from students, alone, do not constitute high-fidelity implementation. Taking action upon students' ideas by clustering students' conceptions and asking for explanations, elaborations, and supporting evidence were the most fundamental characteristics and intentions of the embedded assessments, and were not enacted by the teachers in the experimental group.

Each teacher's congruence with the treatment processes was translated into a ranking for the quality of delivery, meaning that the higher the percentage of time those processes were implemented, the higher the teacher's ranking. These results and average teacher rankings are plotted alongside the pretest/posttest change scores in Figure 9.7.

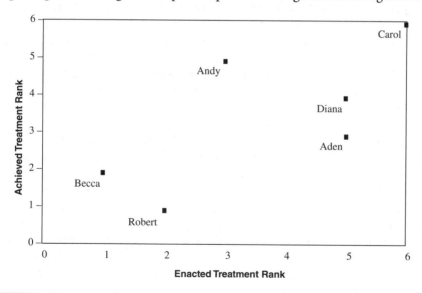

Figure 9.7 Correlation between ranks of teacher's enacted treatment (quality of delivery) and achieved treatment (pre-posttest gain score). From Ayala, C., C., Shavelson, R. J., Ruiz-Primo, M.A., et al. (2008). Formal embedded assessments to reflective lessons: The development of formative assessment studies. *Applied Measurement in Education, 21,* 315–334. Used with permission.

This result supports the contention that simply giving students the embedded assessments in sequence may not be enough to help students learn; the quality of delivery of the critical teaching strategies is an essential element in helping students learn.

While conclusions cannot be drawn that the variation among the teachers' implementations of the treatment led to the differences in student learning found in the study, the results at least suggest a correlation between the consistency of treatment enactment with the project's intention and student learning. The discrepancy between some experimental teachers' enacted treatment and what was intended helps explain why the experimental group overall did not outperform the comparison group.

LESSONS LEARNED: THE GAP BETWEEN THE FORMATIVE ASSESSMENT PREMISES AND THE REALITY

Researchers gain ample experience in the course of designing and conducting an investigation, yet rarely do they focus on the issues that shaped research design decisions or the reasoning that lead to inappropriate decisions. There is no single, right way to design a study (Cronbach et al., 1980), and experience should always inform how things could be improved for follow-up research efforts. This section focuses on the lessons learned in the study with the intention of informing those who would like to adventure in conducting a similar study what should take into consideration.

The Incomplete Formative Assessment Cycle

Black and Wiliam (1998) found that feedback—the "How we will get there?" part of the formative assessment cycle—was the intervention that had an impact on student learning. Furthermore, Hattie and Timperley (2007) found that the quality of feedback impacts the extent to which that feedback helps students improve their performance. It should come as no surprise, then, that the teachers who more consistently closed the formative assessment cycle had students with higher learning gains in the study. We found that using the information gathered to adjust instruction and determining how to reduce the gap, or "How we will get there?" were insufficiently implemented by many experimental teachers. Although variations were observed across teachers in quantity and quality, we know, based on the evidence collected in the implementation study, that, overall, teachers could get students to share their ideas, but did not take action on that information to adjust their instruction. Clearly, adjusting instruction or taking action is easier to recommend than to do.

What decisions in the study design lead teachers to these findings? As mentioned previously, teachers in the experimental group were never informed that the study was about the impact of formative assessment practices on students' learning and motivation, and the formative assessment cycle was never formally presented to them as such. Focus was mainly on designing formal formative embedded assessments, the Reflective Lessons, that could allow teachers to elicit students' conceptions, encourage communication of ideas, encourage argumentation (comparing and contrasting students' alternative conceptions), and reflect with students about their conceptions. Therefore, these four components were the core of the *FAST Teachers' Guide to the*

Reflective Lessons (Stanford Education Assessment Laboratory, 2003). In retrospect, focus was mainly on the strategies that were considered critical for making students' thinking explicit, but insufficiently on how teachers would use the information gained. Although the FAST Developmental Trajectory was intended to provide teachers with a tool to determine the level of students' understanding and provide suggestions for instructional activities to help them move forward, the study revealed that teachers were in need of specific strategies for how to address students' conceptions and move students toward learning goals.

In Retrospect, the Researchers' Failure to Inform the Teachers about the Impact of Formative Assessment on Student Learning   If the teachers understood the value of these assessments then letting students struggle with the material would be viewed as more a part of the process because then both the teacher and student would know what the learning goals would be (e.g., knowing how to predict whether the soap will sink or float and why). Teachers also need tools to help them manage and work with the information that they collect. For example, one teacher developed a method of sorting student papers into different levels of the developmental trajectory by placing them between his fingers—one space for each level.

Related to this issue is the fact that experimental teachers were provided with the formative embedded assessments but they were not involved in the exercise of defining and discussing the learning goals behind the 12 FAST investigations—the "Where we are going?" part of the loop. Whether involving teachers more actively in defining the learning goal would make a difference is questionable. Researchers have found that teachers do not necessarily have clarity about the unit learning goals or can explain why a particular sequence of instructional activities is relevant to achieve the goal (Ruiz-Primo & Li, 2002; Shavelson, 1995). Some teachers find it difficult to articulate what they are pursuing and why. It is a must to involve teachers in reflecting about what and why they are teaching certain activities, especially in the context of formative assessment. In the end, not having clarity about the learning goals makes it difficult for teachers to determine where students are in relation to the learning goals and how they can get there.

BEYOND THE QUALITY OF FORMATIVE EMBEDDED ASSESSMENTS

Given that formative assessment is in vogue as a tool for educational reform, it is not difficult to find companies that propose to develop assessments to be embedded in curricula, curriculum developers that include embedded assessments in their materials, or school districts that develop embedded assessments to administer on demand across schools. All these strategies are based on the premise that implementing formal formative embedded assessments will lead to increased student learning. However, as found in the study, the administration of formative embedded assessments by themselves is unlikely to have an impact. Without high quality professional development, the mere administration of the assessments in terms of gathering information and even the analysis of the information gathered will not guarantee a change in teaching practices. When embedded assessments are administered, it only informs teacher of where their students are in relation to the goals. Teachers must also know where they want students to be at the end of a unit, and how to design and adjust instruction that can get them there.

Knowing exactly how to reduce the gap between where students are and where they need to be is yet another, related challenge. In the study, researchers maintained weekly phone conversations with the teachers, especially the experimental teachers, to find out what problems and issues they were dealing with in the implementation of the reflective lessons. On one occasion, an experimental teacher told the researchers that she found out through the embedded assessments that several students still believed air was the reason that objects sink or float. She asked the researchers how to address this misconception. The research group brainstormed a set of activities for the teacher to use. This experience made it clear to the research group that coming up with diverse teaching activities and strategies was not an easy task for us and we wondered how difficult it could be for teachers in the solitude of their classrooms to come up with ideas and strategies.

Another finding that should be considered is that high quality embedded assessments are not enough. Assessment developers, school districts, or curriculum developers need to provide teachers not only with learning trajectories that can help teachers identify where students are in their level of understanding based on the information gathered through the embedded assessments, but they also need to help them to come up with activities and strategies that they can use with students at different levels of the trajectories.

It can be argued that the developmental trajectory produced for the study can be a learning progression because it describes successively more sophisticated ways of thinking about the topic of sinking and floating (Duschl, Schweingruber, & Shouse, 2007). Although it has been proposed that learning progressions should expand over a broad span of time (e.g., 6 to 8 years), it is likely that shorter span learning progressions can be developed (e.g., for modules, set of units, a series of investigation) with the idea of guiding teachers on how students can build students' understanding (see Kennedy & Wilson, 2007).

Critical levels of understanding from learning progressions can be used to define activities and strategies to help teachers use the information collected or gathered, but learning progressions in themselves are not enough; learning progressions need to be accompanied by what Davis and Krajcik (2005) called *educative curriculum materials* that will help teachers learn the rationale underlying the progression, and have concrete tools to help students move along that progression.

In summary, continuing work on formative assessment implementation must consider the six assessment pedagogies involved in formative assessment described by Ayala and Brandon (2008): (1) understanding the content—understanding the content from the pedagogical perspective, such as learning progressions and student misconceptions; (2) understanding the tools—a variety of ways to find out what students know, using both formal and informal methods; (3) knowing when and how to carry out these activities, using assessment conversations and administration of formal formative assessment tasks; (4) knowing how to interpret information; (5) knowing how to take action—understanding what next base to provide for the information with both feedback and additional instructional activities if necessary; and (6) understanding the value of formative assessment. Although the first four of these assessment pedagogies were emphasized in the study described in this chapter, additional research and development on all six of the pedagogies will be necessary to fully realize the potential of formative assessment.

REFERENCES

Atkin, J. M., Coffey, J. E., Moorthy, S., Sato, M., & Thibeault, M. (2005). *Designing everyday assessment in the science classroom.* New York: Teachers College Press.

Ayala, C. C., & Brandon, P. R. (2008). Building evaluation recommendations for improvement: Insights from student formative assessments. In N. L. Smith & P. R. Brandon (Eds.), *Fundamental issues in evaluation* (pp. 159–166). New York: Guilford.

Ayala, C., Shavelson, R. J., Ruiz-Primo, M. A., Brandon, P. R., Yin, Y., Furtak, E. M., et al. (2008). From formal embedded assessments to reflective lessons: The development of formative assessment studies. *Applied Measurement in Education, 21*(4), 315–334.

Bell, B., & Cowie, B. (2001). *Formative assessment and science education.* Dordrecht, the Netherlands: Kluwer.

Black, P., & Wiliam, D. (1998). Assessment and classroom learning. *Assessment in Education, 5*(1), 7–74.

Cronbach, L. J., Robinson Ambron, S., Dornbush, S. M., Hess, R. D., Hornik, R. D., Phillips, D. C., et al. (1980). *Toward reform of program evaluation.* San Francisco: Jossey-Bass.

Davis, E. A., & Krajcik, J. (2005). Designing educative curriculum materials to support teacher learning. *Educational Researcher, 34*(3), 4–14.

Duschl, R. A. (2003). Assessment of inquiry. In J. M. Atkin & J. E. Coffey (Eds.), *Everyday assessment in the science classroom* (pp. 41–59). Washington, DC: National Science Teachers Association.

Duschl, R. D., Schweingruber, H. A., & Shouse, A. W. (Eds.). (2007). *Taking science to school. Learning and teaching science in grades K-8.* Washington, DC: The National Academies Press.

Furtak, E., & Ruiz-Primo, M. A. (2008). Making students' thinking explicit in writing and discussion: An analysis of formative assessment prompts. *Science Education, 92*(5), 799–824.

Furtak, E., Ruiz-Primo, M. A, Shemwell, J. T., Ayala, C., Brandon, P. R., Shavelson, R. J., & Yin, Y. (2008), On the fidelity of implementing embedded formative assessments and its relation to student learning. *Applied Measurement in Education, 21*(4), 360–389.

Hattie, J., & Timperley, H. (2007). The power of feedback. *Review of Educational Research, 77*(1), 81–112.

Kennedy, C. A., & Wilson, M. (2007). *Using progress variables to interpret student achievement and progress* (BEAR Report Series, 2006-12-01). University of California, Berkeley.

Lucks, M. (2003). *How do we get there from here? Formative assessment and feedback practices in two middle school science classrooms.* Unpublished master's thesis, Stanford University, Stanford, CA.

Minstrell, J., & van Zee, E. (2003). Using questions to assess and foster student thinking. In M. Atkin & J. Coffey (Eds.), *Everyday assessment in the science classroom* (pp. 61–73). Arlington, VA: National Science Teachers Association.

Pottenger, F. M., & Young, D. B. (1992). *The local environment: FAST 1. Foundational approaches to science teaching* (2nd ed.). Honolulu, HI: Curriculum Research and Development Group.

Ramaprasad, A. (1983). On the definition of feedback. *Behavioral Science, 28*(1), 4–13.

Rogg, S., & Kahle, J. B. (1997). *Middle level standards-based inventory.* Oxford, OH: Miami University.

Ruiz-Primo, M. A. (2003). *On implementation and opportunity to learn.* Stanford, CA: Stanford Education Assessment Laboratory. Unpublished manuscript.

Ruiz-Primo, M. A. (2005). *A multi-method and multi-source approach for studying fidelity of implementation* (CSE: Technical Report 677). Los Angeles: University of California, Los Angeles, Center for Research on Evaluation, Standards, and Student Testing.

Ruiz-Primo, M. A., & Furtak, E. M. (2006). Informal formative assessment and scientific inquiry: Exploring teachers' practices and student learning. *Educational Assessment, 11*(3–4), 205–235.

Ruiz-Primo, M. A., & Furtak, E. M. (2007). Exploring teachers' informal formative assessment practices and students' understanding in the context of scientific inquiry. *Journal of Research in Science Teaching, 44*(1), 57–84.

Ruiz-Primo, M. A., & Li, M. (2002, April). *Vignettes as an alternative teacher evaluation instrument: A pilot study*. Paper presented at the meeting of the American Education Research Association, New Orleans, LA.

Ruiz-Primo, M. A., & Shavelson, R. J. (1996). Problems and issues in the use of concept maps in science assessment. *Journal of Research in Science Teaching, 33*(6), 569–600.

Ruiz-Primo, M. A., Shavelson, R. J., Hamilton, L., & Klein, S. (2002). On the evaluation of systemic education reform: Searching for instructional sensitivity. *Journal of Research in Science Teaching, 39*(5), 369–393.

Sadler, D. R. (1989). Formative assessment and the design of instructional systems. *Instructional Science, 18*, 119–144.

Shavelson, R. J. (1995). On the romance of science curriculum and assessment reform in the United States. In D. K. Sharpes & A-L. Leino (Eds.), *The dynamic concept of curriculum: Invited papers to honour the memory of Paul Hellgren* (Research Bulletin 90, pp. 57–76). Finland: University of Helsinki, Department of Education.

Shavelson, R., Stanford Educational Assessment Laboratory (SEAL), and Curriculum Research & Development Group (CRDG). (2005). *Embedding assessments in the FAST curriculum: The romance between curriculum and assessment*. Stanford, CA: Authors.

Shavelson, R. J., Yin, Y., Furtak, E. M., Ruiz-Primo, M. A., & Ayala, C. (2008a). On the role and impact of formative assessment on science inquiry teaching and learning. In J. Coffey, R. Douglas, & C. Stearns (Eds.), *Assessing science learning. Perspectives from research and practice* (pp. 21–36). Arlington, VA: National Science Teachers Association.

Shavelson, R. J., Young, D., Ayala, C., Brandon, P., Furtak, E., Ruiz-Primo., M. A., et al. (2008b). On the impact of curriculum-embedded formative assessment on learning: A collaboration between curriculum and assessment developers. *Applied Measurement in Education, 21*(4), 295–314.

Stanford Education Assessment Laboratory [SEAL]. (2003). *Teacher's guide to the reflective lessons*. Stanford, CA: Stanford Education Assessment Laboratory. Unpublished manuscript.

Yin, Y. (2005). *The influence of formative assessments on student motivation, achievement, and conceptual change*. Unpublished doctoral dissertation, Stanford University, Stanford, CA..

Yin, Y., Shavelson, R. J., Ayala, C.C., Ruiz-Primo., M. A., Brandon, P. R., Furtak, E. M., et al. (2008). On the impact of formative assessment on student motivation, achievement, and conceptual change. *Applied Measurement in Education, 21*(4), 335–359.

10

RESEARCH AND STRATEGIES FOR ADAPTING FORMATIVE ASSESSMENTS FOR STUDENTS WITH SPECIAL NEEDS

STEPHEN N. ELLIOTT, RYAN J. KETTLER, PETER A. BEDDOW, AND ALEXANDER KURZ

Over six million students identified with disabilities attend public schools in the United States today. The vast majority of these students receive their instruction in general education classrooms and are part of schools' assessment and accountability programs. Federal laws such as the Individuals with Disabilities Education Act (IDEA; 1997, 2004) and No Child Left Behind Act (NCLB; 2002), equity principles, and sound instruction practices are all intended to ensure the meaningful inclusion of students with special needs in all phases of the instruction–assessment–instruction cycle, whether it is for large-scale accountability purposes or simply one school's approach to effective education.

Students identified with disabilities learn and behave much like their peers without disabilities, yet some of their characteristics make it more difficult at times for them to learn. These students, regardless of their identified disabilities, often take longer to learn the same material as their peers, require more instructional supports to interact with and respond to instructional tasks, and benefit from less complex tasks to enhance attention and reduce working memory load.

The accurate measurement of the knowledge and skills of these students often is challenging, but can be done well with the use of inclusive assessment methods (Elliott, Braden, & White, 2001). Such methods include testing accommodations, item and test modification principles, and repeated measurements with feedback. These methods have a growing research base with summative assessments, particularly those used for NCLB accountability purposes. There is not, however, a similar research base for these inclusive methods with formative assessments. This is somewhat surprising, given the increasing use of formative assessments for progress monitoring, school accountability programs, and preparation for statewide accountability programs required under NCLB.

As we examine inclusive assessment methods for formative assessments in this chapter, it is important to understand that we are applying what is known about these methods from summative assessments and experimental research programs on testing accommodations. In addition, our perspectives on inclusive assessment recently have expanded with the application of universal design principles (Center for Universal Design, 1997) and cognitive load theory (Clark, Nguyen, & Sweller, 2006; Sweller, 1994) to our research on item modifications for alternate assessments based on modified achievement standards (Elliott, Kettler, & Roach, 2008; Elliott et al., 2008; Kettler et al., 2008).

The central goals for the use of all the inclusive methods that we discuss and support are (1) to increase accessibility and (2) to improve the technical soundness of testing results. These are eminently achievable and measurable goals for all assessments where the results are used to make important decisions about student achievement.

PURPOSE AND DEFINITION OF TESTING ACCOMMODATIONS

One of the most common methods for increasing the accessibility and meaningful participation of students with disabilities in assessments is the prescription of specific changes to testing procedures. Such changes are commonly referred to as *testing accommodations*. Testing accommodations *are changes in the way a test is administered or responded to by a student*. Testing accommodations are intended to offset distortions in test scores caused by a disability, without *invalidating* or changing what the test measures or changing the intended interpretation associated with a given test performance (McDonnell, McLauglin, & Morrison, 1997). When appropriate testing accommodations are used, the resulting test scores are considered to be more valid indicators of a student's knowledge and skills.

Federal laws (i.e., IDEA, NCLB) require the participation of students with special needs in statewide assessments, but do not define what constitutes an appropriate accommodation. To ameliorate this definitional dilemma, Hollenbeck, Rozek-Tedesco, and Finzel (2000) recommended that appropriate accommodations yield (1) alterations that do not change the construct(s) measured by the test; (2) alterations that are prescribed and administered based on individual need; (3) resulting scores that reflect an interaction paradigm whereby increases in students' scores are greater for students for whom the alterations were intended; and (4) inferences from resulting scores that are similar across nonaccommodated and accommodated conditions. To the degree that these four attributes are present, a particular test alteration is more likely to qualify as an accommodation and less likely to be a modification.

When referring to testing, the term *modification* historically has been used to describe a change in the construct being measured by the assessment (e.g., Hollenbeck et al., 2000). Based on this definition, modifications have been assumed to undermine the comparability of test scores between students taking the test under standard and modified conditions. Moreover, modifications to tests, test conditions, or test items may be made at large for a group of test takers and thus do not represent changes based on individual need. Modifications, like accommodations, require validation research to determine whether they have altered the construct being measured. New research and theory on test and item modification supports the use of some modifications as a tool to increase the validity of test score inferences. More will be said about these kinds of modifications in the next section.

It is important to note that not all students identified with disabilities need accommodations to meaningfully participate in testing, and to provide a valid or accurate account of their abilities. More importantly, for a small number of students with more severe disabilities, testing accommodations actually are not enough. These students' educational goals and daily learning experiences can involve content that differs significantly from that contained in state or district standards. Although many of the individualized education plan (IEP) goals of these students should be aligned with the state's academic content standards, a student's current performance may differ significantly from the performance standards expected based on grade level. Consequently, students in this situation usually participate in an alternate assessment to meaningfully measure their abilities and provide valid results.

Many different testing accommodations are allowable as long as they do not change the meaning of the content being assessed (i.e., reduce the validity of the test scores). Accommodations are commonly grouped into four categories, based on the aspect of testing that is altered: (1) timing, (2) assessment environment, (3) presentation format, or (4) recording or response format (Elliott, Kratochwill, & Gilbertson-Schulte, 1999). The IDEA Act has entrusted IEP teams with the responsibility to determine the appropriate testing accommodations for individual students with disabilities for large scale assessments, and it is likely that the same determinations are typically used for formative assessments. Most state departments of education have detailed rules or guidance about testing accommodations that are highly consistent with recommendations made by test companies. Examples of this include the *Guidelines for Inclusive Test Administration* (CTB/McGraw-Hill, 2005) and *State Participation and Accommodation Policies for Students with Disabilities* (Thurlow, House, Boys, Scott, & Ysseldyke, 2000).

Accommodations are intended to maintain and facilitate the measurement goals of an assessment, rather than to modify the questions or content of the tests. Accommodations often involve changes to the testing environment (e.g., Braille or large print materials, the amount of time a student has to respond, the quietness of the testing room, assistance in reading instructions) or the method by which a student responds to questions (e.g., orally with a scribe, pointing to correct answers). Testing accommodations should not involve changes in the content of test items. Accommodations generally result in some minor changes in the procedures for administration or response upon which a test was standardized. Consequently, because many educators have been taught to follow standardization procedures exactly, there may be some reluctance to use accommodations.

The keys to the selection and appropriate use of testing accommodations are fivefold. First, accommodations must be determined on a case-by-case basis for each student by his or her IEP team. Second, knowledge of the instructional accommodations that a student currently receives should guide considerations of testing accommodations. This point is particularly critical in the case of formative assessments, in which the cycle between instruction and assessment is likely to be tight. Third, accommodations are intended to make the test a more accurate measure of what a student knows or can do. That is, IEP teams must select accommodations that are likely to facilitate a student's participation in a testing program, but not likely to change or invalidate the intended meaning of a test score. Fourth, the accommodations must be implemented as planned. This is not always easy, given the testing demands on many educators to accommodate multiple students during the same test or because of a lack of receptivity on the part of some students, especially adolescents (Feldman, Kim, & Elliott, 2008; Lang, Elliott, Bolt, & Kratochwill, 2008). Fifth, it is critical that educators document which accommodations seem to effectively facilitate access and responding for students.

RESEARCH ON TESTING ACCOMMODATIONS AND TEST PERFORMANCE OF STUDENTS WITH SPECIAL NEEDS: KEY FINDINGS

A key theoretical determinant regarding whether an accommodation is appropriate for a student is the presence of an interaction paradigm or differential boost (Phillips, 1994), whereby the accommodation is only considered valid if it benefits students for whom it is intended more than it benefits students for whom it is not intended. Elliott and colleagues conducted and published a number of studies intended to measure this interaction effect by having students with disabilities and students without disabilities complete tests both with accommodations and without accommodations. Measuring the impact of testing accommodations on a performance assessment featuring a series of constructed response tasks, Elliott, Kratochwill, and McKevitt (2001) found an effect size for students with disabilities (.88) that was double the effect size for students without disabilities (.44). Schulte, Elliott, and Kratochwill (2001) used the same design with a research version of TerraNova's standardized math test, finding evidence of an interaction paradigm on multiple-choice questions, but not on constructed-response questions.

McKevitt and Elliott (2003) found that teacher-recommended accommodations did not help students regardless of disability status, and that a read-aloud accommodation combined with teacher accommodations boosted the scores of both students with disabilities and students without disabilities, when the outcome measure was a research version of TerraNova's standardized reading test. Kettler et al. (2005) also found strong evidence of an interaction paradigm in a sample of fourth grade students on a research version of the TerraNova reading test. The effect size for students with disabilities was .42, compared to .13 for students without disabilities. The same interaction was not significant in an eighth grade sample, likely due to reluctance on the part of the students to use the accommodations. Feldman et al. (2008) determined that, when provided accommodations, students with disabilities benefit from an interaction paradigm in self-efficacy and motivation, and that this paradigm corresponds with increases in test scores.

Fuchs, Fuchs, and colleagues (Fuchs & Fuchs, 2001; Fuchs, Fuchs, & Capizzi, 2006; Tindal & Fuchs, 2000) have done a number of research studies on testing accommodations, and have developed an instrument to help teachers determine whether an accommodation works for an individual student by testing the student both with and without the accommodation. In the spirit of the interaction paradigm, the Dynamic Assessment of Testing Accommodations (Fuchs & Fuchs, 2001) is designed to measure the effects of individual accommodations for individual students in reading and mathematics. In a meta-analytic study, Tindal and Fuchs (2000) found that the most effective accommodations were reading problems aloud for students with disabilities in math, and providing large print or Braille for the visually impaired.

Based on studies of individual accommodations, Fuchs et al. (2006) concluded that extended time does not provide a differential boost (Fuchs, Fuchs, Eaton, Hamlett, Binkley, et al., 2000; Fuchs, Fuchs, Eaton, Hamlett, & Karns, 2000; Tindal & Fuchs, 2000), but that reading a test orally does provide a differential boost (Fuchs, Fuchs, Eaton, Hamlett, & Karns, 2000). The researchers also found that it is unlikely that one accommodation or set of accommodations would be appropriate for the entire population of students with disabilities (Fuchs, Fuchs, Eaton, Hamlett, Binkley, et al., 2000), that teachers may be influenced by students' demographic characteristics when selecting accommodations (Fuchs & Fuchs, 2001), and that students with severe reading deficits may benefit from reading a test aloud (Fuchs & Fuchs, 2001). Lastly, Fuchs et al. (2006) indicated that testing accommodations decisions must be individualized, that the meaningfulness of test scores is the most important consideration, and that this area of research remains critical because of the mandate that students with disabilities be included in large-scale assessments of achievement.

Sireci and Pitoniak (2007) published a review of testing accommodations research. The researchers found that, across studies, testing accommodations often help students with disabilities, but that they also sometimes help students without disabilities, and therefore must be selected on an individual basis. Sireci and Pitoniak also emphasized the necessity of identifying the construct that a test is designed to measure, in order to evaluate whether a specific accommodation is appropriate. They commended research in which students take tests in both accommodated and nonaccommodated conditions, in order to directly evaluate the interaction paradigm. Finally, Sireci and Pitoniak indicated that extra time is an appropriate accommodation when speed of response is not being measured, and that having a test read aloud to a student is an appropriate accommodation when reading is not being measured.

In the aforementioned studies, researchers have rarely if ever been specific about whether their studies were intended for summative or formative assessments. The administration of the test is typically the last step in data collection, with any theoretical differences between summative and formative assessments left to be considered by the reader. We believe that it is reasonable to generalize the findings from these studies on standardized multiple-choice tests or short research forms to formative assessments.

PURPOSE AND DEFINITION OF ITEM AND TEST MODIFICATIONS

Recent changes in federal legislation (U.S. Department of Education, 2007) allow states and districts to use a modified version of the general education achievement test for up to 2% of all students counted as proficient. This alternate assessment must be based on modified academic achievement standards (AA-MAS) and it is only appropriate for students with disabilities whose IEPs refer to grade-level content goals, whose inability to reach proficiency is the result of their disability, and who are considered highly unlikely to attain proficiency on the regular assessment. Acceptable modifications to the standard test can be made with the intent of providing universal access and reducing cognitive load, so that scores on an AA-MAS validly reflect the same constructs measured by the general education test.

It is important to note that, in the case of an AA-MAS, a new test is being created only for eligible students with disabilities. At this time, the effect of this new policy on formative assessments is unclear, because states are not legally required to develop and administer alternate assessments based on modified achievement standards. In the *2007 Survey of States* (Altman et al., 2008), it was reported that 33 states were considering the development of AA-MAS by changing their existing grade-level tests. The procedures for designing an AA-MAS, however, hold significant potential for influencing the design of more accessible tests; using them to improve formative assessment is promising for a much larger sample of students, many of whom have not been identified with a special need.

According to the new policy guidelines regarding AA-MAS, *modifications* are changes to a test that may decrease its difficulty, while still measuring the same construct(s). Much like testing accommodations, modifications are intended to facilitate access to the assessment for students who are eligible so that their scores can be meaningfully compared with the scores of students who take the general education test. Unlike testing accommodations, modifications change aspects of the test and its constituent items that may make the overall test easier without changing the grade level of the content or the constructs the items are intended to measure.

Modifications used to refine or enhance tests for eligible students should increase the students' access to the tests, which are intended to reflect the general curriculum content that students had the opportunity to learn. A study by Kettler et al. (2008) applied principles of universal design, cognitive load theory, and test item research to the modification of multiple-choice items for an eighth-grade formative assessment program developed by Discovery Education Assessment. They found that for many items they could successful accomplish the goal of increasing accessibility for students with special needs without changing the grade-level construct being measured. The researchers also found that their enhancements did not change the depth of knowledge or significantly alter the readability of the items.

The Center for Universal Design recommends the consideration of seven principles for the universal design of environments, products, and services "to be usable by all people, to the greatest extent possible, without the need for adaptation or specialized design" (2008, p. 1). Table 10.1 includes a list of these principles, along with definitions and guidelines that correspond to each. Although not intended specifically for testing, these principles should be considered when developing any formative assessment or summative test. They serve as an appropriate starting point for developing items that are maximally accessible for students with disabilities who consistently achieve below proficiency.

The principle of simplicity and intuitiveness, for example, proposes that the environment, product, or service should be easy to understand, and one of the principle's guidelines suggests the elimination of unnecessary complexity. This may be accomplished by reducing the length or complexity of sentences, converting unfamiliar notation on a mathematics problem, or removing unnecessary graphics. While these modifications could be helpful for any student, they likely would be especially helpful for a student identified with a disability and a history of poor test performance.

Table 10.1 Universal Design Principles, Definitions, and Example Guidelines

Universal Design Principle	Definition	Example Guideline
Equitable Use	Useful and marketable to people with diverse abilities.	Provide the same means of use for all users: identical whenever possible; equivalent when not.
Flexibility in Use	Accommodates a wide range of individual preferences and abilities.	Facilitate the user's accuracy and precision.
Simple and Intuitive Use	Easy to understand, regardless of the user's experience, knowledge, language skills, or current concentration level.	Eliminate unnecessary complexity.
Perceptible Information	Communicates necessary information effectively to the user, regardless of ambient conditions or the user's sensory abilities.	Maximize legibility of essential information.
Tolerance for Error	Minimizes hazards and the adverse consequences of accidental or unintended actions.	Discourage unconscious action in tasks that require vigilance.
Low Physical Effort	Can be used efficiently and comfortably and with a minimum of fatigue.	Minimize repetitive actions.
Size and Space for Approach and Use	Appropriate size and space is provided for approach, reach, manipulation, and use regardless of user's body size, posture, or mobility.	Accommodate variations in hand and grip size.

Modifications to regular assessments that are designed to help students who consistently fail to meet proficiency can also be guided by cognitive load theory. Conceptualized by Sweller (1994) and based on Miller's (1956) classic 7 +/− 2 article on the limitations of working memory, cognitive load theory thus far has been applied mostly to classroom instruction to improve efficiency and student learning; however, we believe it has clear implications for test construction. The theory posits that there are three types of short term memory loads for learning tasks: intrinsic load, germane load, and extraneous load.

Intrinsic load is characterized by the complexity of a task and is heavily influenced by the associated goals. Germane load is characterized by the additional work that is relevant to the associated goal. Including germane load in learning tasks, although not necessary for meeting the primary goals of instruction, is thought to increase the generalizability of the learning outcomes. Extraneous load is memory load unrelated to the task, and results in a waste of mental resources that could otherwise be allocated to the intrinsic and germane load. Learning typically is made more efficient by decreasing the extraneous load of a task without affecting the intrinsic load or the germane load.

Cognitive load theory has clear applicability to test item development. For example, consider the item shown in Figure 10.1. If the stated goal of the item is to assess the application of geometric formulas to the calculation of total area, then the intrinsic load can be represented by finding the areas of each of the constituent figures and their combined sum (i.e., 300 + 150 = 450). In the original form of the item, examples of extraneous load may include the demand that students turn to the back of the test booklet to find

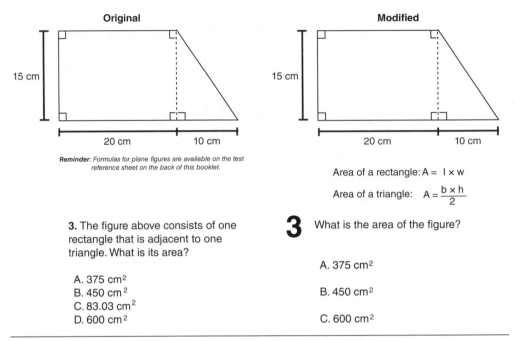

Original

15 cm

20 cm   10 cm

Reminder: Formulas for plane figures are available on the test reference sheet on the back of this booklet.

3. The figure above consists of one rectangle that is adjacent to one triangle. What is its area?

A. 375 cm²
B. 450 cm²
C. 83.03 cm²
D. 600 cm²

Modified

15 cm

20 cm   10 cm

Area of a rectangle: A = l × w

Area of a triangle: $A = \dfrac{b \times h}{2}$

3 What is the area of the figure?

A. 375 cm²

B. 450 cm²

C. 600 cm²

Figure 10.1 Grade seven mathematics item in original and modified forms.

the relevant formulas and subsequently carry them (either in working memory or on scratch paper) to the item page, and the complex verbiage in the item stem (e.g., the words *consists* and *adjacent)*. The listing of the answer choices in a random, rather than a sequential order also may increase the extraneous load for some test-takers.

As illustrated in the modified version of the figure, cognitive load theory can be applied to test items by removing or reducing their extraneous load without affecting the intrinsic load or grade level of the item, thus increasing the validity of the inferences that can be made from the results. Key cognitive load theory guidelines identified by Clark et al. (2006) include using cues to focus attention on content and eliminating nonessential text, visuals, and audio. We revisit this item later in this chapter and provide a data framework to support these modifications.

Research on item development also offers guidance regarding the modification of formative assessments. For example, there is strong empirical evidence that supports reducing the number of response options for multiple-choice items. A reduction in the number of response options not only reduces the reading load and complexity of decisions required of the test-taker, but it may decrease the difficulty of the task as well. Rodriguez's (2005) meta-analysis of 27 studies addressed the question, "What is the optimal number of response options for a multiple-choice test?" Using the psychometric criteria of item difficulty, item discrimination, and test score reliability, Rodriguez concluded that:

> Three options are optimal for [multiple-choice] items in most settings. Moving from 5-option items to 4-option items reduces item difficulty by .02, reduces item discrimination by .04, and reduces reliability by .035 on average. Moving from 5- to

3-option items reduces item difficulty by .07, does not affect item discrimination, and does not affect reliability on average.... Moving from 4- to 3-option items reduces item difficulty by .04, increases item discrimination by .03, and increases reliability slightly by .02. (p. 10)

While a number of states are using this item modification strategy for alternate assessments designed for students with disabilities, Rodriguez's (2005) findings suggest that reducing the number of distractors reduces the reading load of the entire test while slightly enhancing the psychometric properties of the test, even for the general population. This type of modification is consistent with the goal of making items more accessible to students with special needs and has real potential for use with multiple-choice items on formative assessments.

Following from the principles of universal design and cognitive load theory, as well as best practice research for item development, a number of specific strategies have become common practice for developing tests. Based on a survey of the most common modifications used across six states, Lazarus, Thurlow, Christenson, and Cormier (2007) of the National Center on Educational Outcomes reported that removing a distractor from a multiple-choice item, reducing the number of items on the test, and simplifying language were the most common modifications, followed closely by reducing the number and length of reading passages. Additionally, the authors identified a separate set of modifications that typically have been considered testing accommodations. These included increasing font size and reducing the number of items per page.

ITEM MODIFICATIONS AND THE TEST PERFORMANCES OF STUDENTS WITH SPECIAL NEEDS: INITIAL RESEARCH FINDINGS

As noted early in this chapter, federal policy concerning students with disabilities and testing, especially the 2007 policy on alternate assessments based on modified achievement standards, has highlighted the importance of research on item and test modifications. These federal policies have also highlighted the paucity of such research and suggested that, for a significant portion of students with disabilities, more than testing accommodations are needed to facilitate inclusive and valid measurement.

Cognitive labs or think aloud protocols are one starting point for researchers and test developers who have begun to study the effects of item modifications on student performances (Johnstone, Liu, Altman, & Thurlow, 2007). These cognitively focused labs are experiments during which students take tests and provide feedback by talking aloud about their thoughts and their strategies. Students are trained to verbalize their thoughts, and are only prompted when they have not spoken for several seconds.

Johnstone et al. used a design that featured each student completing half of the items in their original form, and half in a form that was modified to be more accessible. All of the items were in reading. The researchers found that reducing nonconstruct related vocabulary and the number of negative prefixes, in both the question stem and answer choices, were the most effective modifications. Students in the study reported preferring that important words be printed in bold, but this modification did not make a difference in performance. The small sample size ($n = 8$) in the study limited the generalizability of its results.

Roach, Beddow, Kurz, Kettler, and Elliott (in press) used a cognitive lab to study the reaction to item modifications by students with disabilities and students without disabilities. All students ($N = 8$) in the study completed eight reading items and eight mathematics items, half of which were in their original form and half of which were in a modified form. Findings from this study indicated that the use of visuals with items was sometimes helpful and sometimes distracting, as students with disabilities were more likely to appreciate the visuals in reading, while students without disabilities were more likely to endorse visuals in mathematics. Students from all groups endorsed the use of explicit instructions and bold type. Elimination of one incorrect answer choice was reported as a helpful modification by students without disabilities in both reading and mathematics, as well as by students with disabilities when referring to mathematics. Roach et al. concluded that (1) the modifications were too conservative and were unlikely to help students who employed incorrect strategies; (2) readability was an issue on both original and modified items for students with disabilities; and (3) all students spent less time, required less prompts, and guessed more often on modified items.

Kettler et al. (2008) examined whether tests composed of modified items would have the same level of reliability, and whether the modification process would help reduce the item difficulty between students who would be eligible for an AA-MAS and students who would not be eligible. Three groups of students ($N = 755$) defined by eligibility and disability status took original and modified versions of reading and mathematics tests. The students were provided limited reading support in a third experimental condition. The interaction between condition and group status was minimal, indicating that reliability was maintained through the modification process. Mean item difficulties decreased more for students who would be eligible for the AA-MAS than for noneligible groups, indicating an interaction paradigm that supports the validity of the modification process. Exploratory analyses showed that shortening the question stem may be a highly effective modification, and that adding graphics to reading items is a questionable modification.

The scores of all three groups of students in the aforementioned study were significantly improved by item modifications (Kettler et al., 2008). In both reading and mathematics, the effect of modification for students with disabilities who would be eligible for an AA-MAS (reading = .40 SD, mathematics = .26 SD) was higher than the same effect for students without disabilities (reading = .37 SD, mathematics = .15 SD) or for students with disabilities who would not have been eligible (reading = .38 SD, mathematics = .21 SD). These effects were not significantly different across groups, and did not provide additional evidence of an interaction.

The scores from the Kettler et al. study (2008), however, were obtainable within a framework of conservative modifications made by education experts and representatives from six state departments of education. This point is important because the final regulations of NCLB indicate that modifications may make a test easier, as long as they do not render the test below grade level. The boundary on how much easier an item can become is therefore not dictated by the performance of students without disabilities, who in practice would never take a modified test, but rather by the item's grade-level determination after modification.

Clearly, more research on item modifications is needed and is expected as more states and their test development partners design large-scale alternate achievement tests for students with persistent academic difficulties. Individuals interested in designing more inclusive formative assessments stand to benefit from this research; however, it is likely to be another 4 or 5 years before a substantial body of evidence exists about these modifications and their effects on the technical soundness of resulting scores. Meanwhile, based on strong theory and the initial research we have completed and have underway with item modifications, we can put forth some conservative guidance.

GUIDELINES FOR ADAPTING FORMATIVE ASSESSMENTS FOR STUDENTS WITH SPECIAL NEEDS

The development of formative assessments for use with students with special needs requires a systematic review of test features with a focus on accessibility. Beddow, Kettler, and Elliott (2008) have defined accessibility as "the extent to which an environment, product, or service eliminates barriers and permits equal access to all components and services for all individuals" (p. 1). To the extent that the accessibility of an assessment is improved for the population for whom it is designed, the resulting scores will be more precise, more accurate, and more meaningful across the range of that population. Thus, if the accessibility of a test is enhanced, the inferences that are made from the results of the test will be more valid, and better information will be available to shape instruction and to meet students' individual needs.

The process of developing accessible assessments, whether for formative or summative purposes, must be grounded in theory and research. Specifically, guidelines must represent a synthesis of principles of universal design and accessibility (e.g., Johnstone, Thurlow, Moore, & Altman, 2006), cognitive load theory (e.g., Clark et al., 2006), and fairness (e.g., Educational Testing Service, 2008) as well as research on item writing and test development (e.g., Haladyna, Downing, & Rodriguez, 2002). Accordingly, Beddow et al. (2008) developed the *Test Accessibility and Modification Inventory* (TAMI™), a decision-making tool for designing and adapting assessments with the goal of making them more accessible for students with special needs. The TAMI has been used successfully by educators and test design specialists from several states to modify existing multiple-choice items and to guide the writing of original items.

The TAMI inventory consists of 86 accessibility descriptors across two primary sections: Item Analysis (51 descriptors) and Computer-Based Test Analysis (35 descriptors). Examples of individual categorical descriptors are listed in Table 10.2. The primary organization of the Item Analysis section is based on the five key elements of a test item: Passage/Item Stimulus, Item Stem, Visuals, Answer Choices, and Page & Layout. The Item Analysis section also contains a Fairness category which consists of considerations for analyzing items with respect to fairness to individuals and groups. The second section of the TAMI is divided into four categories based on key dimensions of computer-based assessments: Test Delivery System (i.e., login, user selection, test selection, navigation, response selection, etc.), Test Layout, Training, and Audio. Each category contains a set of descriptors to facilitate the development of accessible computer-based or online tests.

The TAMI utilizes Accessibility Worksheets that correspond to each section of the

Table 10.2 Organization of the Test Accessibility and Modification Inventory

Item Analysis	Example Descriptors
1. Passage/Item Stimulus (10 descriptors)	1.5 Sentence structure is as simple as possible given the construct being measured. 1.7 Essential words or vocabulary items use bold font to facilitate identification. 1.8 Passage or stimulus does not require construct-irrelevant knowledge and skills for item response. 1.9 Passage and/or stimulus is viewable on the same page as visuals, item stem, and answer choices.
2. Item Stem (10 descriptors)	2.1 Text includes only words essential for responding. 2.9 Item stem is positively worded (i.e., avoiding not questions.)
3. Visuals (11 descriptors)	3.2 Visuals are relevant to essential item content. 3.11 When visuals are self-explanatory, words are not added.
4. Answer Choices (6 descriptors)	4.3 All distractors are plausible ("attractors"). 4.4 All answer choices are necessary. 4.6 The order and construction of the answer choices are logical and deliberate.
5. Page/Item Layout (9 descriptors)	5.6 The entire item (stimulus, visuals, stem, and answer choices) is visible on the same page/screen. 5.7 Page includes ample white space to prevent the item from appearing cluttered. 5.9 Visuals are integrated into the item stimulus and item stem, rather than placed off to the side.
6. Fairness (5 descriptors)	6.3 Item avoids material that may unnecessarily evoke emotion or controversy. 6.4 Item uses appropriate terminology to describe individuals and groups.
Computer-Based Test Analysis	
1. Test-Delivery System (20 descriptors)	1.1 Test delivery system (login, user selection, test selection, test navigation, response selection) is intuitive and user-friendly. 1.2 Test delivery system requires no extraneous input. 1.6 Alternative input methods are available for test-takers with special needs (e.g., speech recognition or a touch screen for test-takers who are not able to operate a mouse). 1.14 Pop-up translations and definitions of key words or phrases are available. 1.17 Navigation system includes the ability to return to any item within the test at any time.
2. Test Layout (5 descriptors)	2.2 Pages are designed to draw attention toward on-screen elements necessary to complete items. 2.5 When all item elements cannot fit on the same page, each element can be viewed with one click.
3. Training (2 descriptors)	3.1 System includes a training module to familiarize test-takers with essential test elements.
4. Audio (9 descriptors)	4.3 Whenever possible, audio supplements item text and/or visual content, rather than duplicating it. 4.4 Test-takers may point-and-click on individual words to be read aloud at any time during item completion to facilitate access to item content.

inventory. These worksheets provide a team of users with a consistent framework for documenting their analyses of items and recommended revisions. To analyze items, raters use the Item Accessibility Worksheets to record an accessibility rating for each category on a 4-point scale (0 = not accessible; 1 = minimally accessible; 2 = moderately accessible; 3 = maximally accessible). The ratings are then summed to yield a Total Accessibility Score which can be used to facilitate comparison across a large item pool. Additionally, the worksheet can be used to record recommended item modifications and to document final changes to items. Similarly, to analyze computer-based tests, raters use the Computer-Based Test Accessibility Worksheets to record their categorical ratings, recommend modifications, and document final changes. An examination of several salient item-level and computer-test level attributes from the TAMI follow.

Item-Level Analysis

Revising an existing multiple-choice item with the aim of improving its accessibility typically involves the analysis of five key elements: the item passage or stimulus, the item stem, visuals or graphics, answer choices, and the overall layout of the item on the page or screen. Collectively, these elements may be considered the anatomy of an item. Accordingly, the process of analyzing and modifying items to increase their accessibility for students with special needs can follow this structure. After recording the construct(s) or skill(s) the target item is designed to measure, as well as the intended depth of knowledge of the item, the primary goal of the process should be to reduce extraneous information, unnecessary complexity, and the length of any text across the item stimulus, stem, and answer choices.

Follow-up readability analyses can be used to ensure any modifications have not reduced the grade level of the item. It is often possible to completely rewrite wordy passages to eliminate unnecessary complexity and simplify language without affecting the readability or grade level of the original text. It is also important to clarify that the reading level of an item and the grade level of its content, although on similar scales, represent two distinct constructs. We have found the readability of an item, task, or performance may be substantially higher or lower than the grade-level content that it is written to reflect.

As previously mentioned, based on a meta-analysis of over 80 years of item-writing research, Rodriguez (2005) concluded that the optimal number of answer choices for a multiple-choice item usually is three. Before undertaking the task of reducing the number of distractors across a multiple-choice test, item writers should standardize their procedures for selecting distractors for removal. To preserve the psychometric properties of the item, Rodriguez advised eliminating the least-selected distractor, unless doing so would leave another implausible or unintentionally misleading distractor. Documenting these and other procedures is important to retain the integrity of the process and thus the validity of the test following modification.

Other recommended changes include rewording an item or passage to use the active voice, eliminating idioms, using bold font for essential vocabulary terms, line-numbering passages and poems if specific lines are referenced in stems, embedding referenced lines from passages in the stimulus, increasing white space to reduce the appearance of clutter, and adjusting the page layout so that all elements appear on one page.

The decision to add visuals to items or passages should be made with caution. Specifically, a visual should be added only when it contains information that is essential for responding. Visuals should not be added for the sole purpose of increasing student interest or motivation; adding these types of visuals actually may increase cognitive load and decrease accessibility. Further, visuals should be integrated into the body of an item or passage whenever possible, rather than being placed off to the side. When visuals are integrated properly, respondents should be able to read the entire item or passage as a whole, without the need to glance back and forth between the visual and other text to retrieve requisite information for responding. Finally, visuals should clearly represent intended images, and embedded text should not repeat text that is contained in other parts of the item or passage. Extraneous text may increase the reading load of the item or passage, and even increase its difficulty (Clark et al., 2006).

Recall the original and modified versions of a grade seven mathematics item contained in Figure 10.1. Enhancements to the original item included increasing white space, increasing the font size of the item number, simplifying the language in the item stem, eliminating a distractor, and reordering the answer choices. Additionally, formulas requisite for responding to the item were moved from the back of the test booklet and placed beneath the figure.

Figure 10.2 contains a sample grade 6 reading item in original and modified forms. Enhancements include increasing the font size, removing nonessential text, eliminating the least-selected distractor, adding bold font for the vocabulary word in the passage, and removing the visual. It should be noted that, while it may be argued the visual included in the original version of the item is relevant to the item, it contains no information essential for responding. Further, the image of a man using a hammer may cue the test-taker to select option A, "building."

Original

No Swimming Today

My Uncle Reginald approached me with a strange smile on his face. He had arrived in his pickup truck. It was old and rusty. His truck reminded me of the one my father and I used to haul wood from the mill on Old Post Road.

Uncle Reginald had returned from the army where he had spent two years in a country I had never heard of before. I could listen to Uncle Reginald tell stories all day long. He rarely discussed his experiences in battle or the hardships of life in the barracks, but he loved to talk about the funny things that happened on the weekends.

"Hi Uncle Reggie!" I called out as I ran from the front porch. I had been shucking some corn for Mama. "Are we going to Saunter Creek today to *catch* crawdads?"

He shook his head and motioned to the side of the barn. He had unloaded a very tall stack of wooden posts, two shovels, a sledgehammer, There was also a huge roll of wire. I bet that wire could wrap around all the fields in Barro County, I thought to myself.

"We're finally going to build that new corral," he said.

I knew I was in for an arduous day.

7. Based on the passage, what would be the most precise definition of the word *arduous*?

   A. building
   B. relaxing
   C. tiring
   D. easy

Modified

No Swimming Today

Uncle Reggie approached me, smiling. He had arrived in his pickup truck.

"Hi Uncle Reggie!" I called out. "Are we going swimming today?"

"No," he said, pointing to the side of the barn. I turned and saw a stack of wooden posts and boards, two shovels, and a large hammer.

"You are going to help me build a fence," he said.

I took a deep breath. It was going to be an **arduous** day.

7 What is the definition of **arduous**?

   A. building

   B. tiring

   C. relaxing

Figure 10.2 Sample grade six reading item in original and modified forms.

Table 10.3 Item statistics for sample items

	Original Item			Modified Item			Change		
	p	ME	R	p	ME	R	Δp	ΔME	ΔR
Reading Item #7 (Grade 6)	0.24	−1.45	6.8	0.76	0.67	5.7	+0.52	+2.12	-1.1
Math Item #3 (Grade 7)	0.36	−1.81	8.2	0.57	0.45	5.6	+0.21	+.26	-2.6

Response Frequencies							
	Original Item				Mathematics Item		
	A	B	C	D	A	B	C
Reading Item #7	45%	18%	**24%**	13%	10%	**76%**	14%
Math Item #3	21%	**36%**	3%	40%	18%	**57%**	25%

Note. p = proportion correct; ME = mental ease z-score; R = readability index; **bold** = answer key.

Hypothetical field-test data for the sample items, based on our cognitive lab research, are presented in Table 10.3. For each item, we present the proportion of students who responded correctly to each item (item difficulty), mean mental ease (i.e., test-taker self-reported perception of the cognitive demand of the item, reported as intraindividual z-scores), and the grade-level readability for the item. For both items, as expected, the proportion of students who responded correctly and the mental ease were higher for the modified version of the item compared to the original version. Readability, while reduced for the modified versions of both items, was most significantly reduced for the mathematics item.

Figure 10.3 contains a visual representation of these data to demonstrate the putative effect of these types of item enhancements. The cognitive efficiency of an item may be represented by plotting mental ease (the reciprocal of cognitive load) on the abcissa and difficulty (proportion correct) on the ordinate (Paas, Tuovinen, Tabbers, & Van Gerven, 2003). High-efficiency items, or items for which the demand for cognitive resources is low and the proportion of students who respond correctly is high, are plotted in the first quadrant. Low-efficiency items, or items with high cognitive load and a small proportion of students who respond correctly, are plotted in the third quadrant. The cognitive efficiency plot of the sample reading and mathematics items indicates the original versions of reading item 7 and mathematics item 3 are located in the low-efficiency quadrant. The enhanced versions of both items are located in the high-efficiency quadrant. As per our stated modification goals, these data indicate that the enhancements increased the cognitive efficiency of the items.

Computer-Based Test Analysis

Support for the conversion from paper-and-pencil tests to computer-based assessments has increased across the international marketplace of assessment technology and the research literature in recent years, and the shift to using computers for the majority of assessments is widely perceived as inevitable (Bennett, 2001; Kerrey & Isakson, 2000). Indeed, research supports the use of computer-based assessments to facilitate efficient

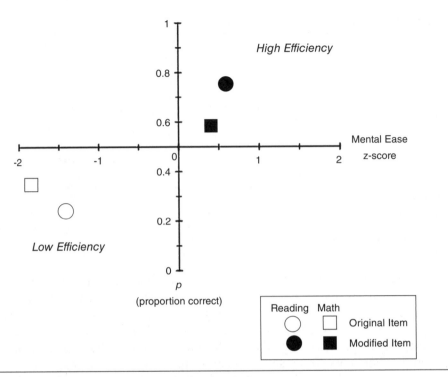

Figure 10.3 Cognitive efficiency plot for sample reading and mathematics items.

measurement and feedback across the range of tested constructs and student abilities. Given that many formative assessments are designed to provide rapid and detailed feedback, computerized assessments are important. If used appropriately, computer-based tests can be a cost-effective way to simplify the test-taking process, reduce barriers, and increase the reliability of scores and the validity of resulting inferences.

It is essential, however, that developers of computer-based formative assessments attend closely to test features that may increase or decrease their accessibility. To the extent that the results of a test for students with special needs contain error because of barriers due to poor implementation of computer technology, the inferences made from results may be invalid, instructional adjustments based on these inferences may be incorrect, and ultimately, student needs may be unmet. Guidelines that should be considered before developing a computer-based formative assessment for students with special needs follow. Many of these guidelines are based on recommendations for accessible computer assessments by the National Center on Educational Outcomes (e.g., Johnstone et al., 2006) and are concurrent with Web resources from the Web Accessibility Initiative (Web Accessibility Initiative, 2008), which has proposed a set of guidelines to ensure Web content is accessible to all users, including those with disabilities. The Web Content Accessibility Guidelines (WCAG) were approved in December of 2008.

First, the test delivery system should be designed to be accessible by all computer users with a range of abilities. This includes ensuring the accessibility of procedures for login, user selection, test selection, test navigation, and response selection. Further, the test delivery system should contain a training module to familiarize test-takers with all test procedures, and students should be trained to use the system prior to the actual test event.

The test delivery system should be intuitive and simple, with as little input demand as possible (Burgstahler, 2008). The system should require only a mouse or a touch screen to access every feature, and all icons should be sufficiently large to reduce the need for fine motor dexterity. Icons should be clearly labeled and feedback should be given for all successful input. For timed tests, an on-screen clock should be available, if not visible at all times. Likewise, the system should include an on-screen indicator of test progress (e.g., "Question 10 out of 35") and user progress should be saved after each item in case the student needs a break or a malfunction occurs. The test-taker should be permitted to navigate to any item during the test. To the extent that students are permitted to make persistent marks (e.g., take notes) in the test booklets for paper-based equivalent tests, computer-based test systems should include similar features.

Screen elements should be arranged such that the item stimulus or passage, item stem, visuals, and answer choices are visible simultaneously for all items (Clark et al., 2006). In cases where passages do not fit on the same screen as respective items, referenced passages should be available with minimal input. Nonessential items (e.g., on-screen clocks) should be able to be toggled on or off. The screen should be uncluttered and designed to draw attention toward item elements that are necessary for responding.

If test developers determine that audio should be included as part of a computer-based assessment, they should consider five points. First, audio should only be used to facilitate access to text or visual content that is required for responding. Using audio to reiterate content that is already available actually may increase the cognitive load of items (Clark et al., 2006). Second, audio should only be used when it does not alter the target construct(s) of the test (e.g., audio should not be used to narrate a homophone-identification item). Third, if audio is used to reduce the reading load of an item, test-takers should be permitted to point-and-click on individual words, rather than being required to hear all of the recorded text. Fourth, audio should support text and visuals and should not be used alone for content that may need to be referenced during item completion. Fifth, headphones with adjustable volume should be available to facilitate hearing and focus (for the individual test-taker as well as for others in the testing location). Finally, whether or not audio is added to a test to enhance its accessibility, all extraneous computer audio (i.e., beeps, system sounds) should be eliminated (Johnstone et al., 2007).

Nimble Assessment Systems has developed an online software application called NimbleTools that integrates many of the recommendations contained in the TAMI. NimbleTools uses a flexible interface that adapts to individual student needs by embedding accessibility and accommodation tools such as read-aloud options, tab/enter/switch navigation, presentation of signed text, magnification, item masking, user-generated passage highlighting, auditory calming, talking calculator and formula sheets, and extended time. A tracking function ensures accurate reporting of accommodations used.

Results of several validity studies of NimbleTools suggest students: (1) performed significantly better when computer-based accommodations were provided than when accommodations were provided by a human proctor; and (2) preferred the computer-based accommodations over those provided by a human proctor (Hoffmann, 2007; Russell, Johnstone, Higgins, & Hoffmann, 2008). NimbleTools has undergone numerous iterative revisions based on feedback from several states following usability studies, and has been used with samples ranging from 40 to 10,000 students with and without special needs.

FORMATIVE FEEDBACK AND ITS USE WITH STUDENTS WITH SPECIAL NEEDS

The shift to computer-based testing as the primary mode of student assessment provides the opportunity to use feedback to enhance performance, a technique that has strong empirical support, but has not necessarily been practical on an individual basis. Feedback is information provided to persons about their responses to tasks (Narciss & Huth, 2006). Unlike positive reinforcement, feedback is not provided to increase responses but to increase students' knowledge about their own learning. Feedback is an important consideration within formative assessment because it provides the opportunity to immediately assess student response to individualized instruction.

Kulik and Kulik (1988) performed a meta-analysis of 53 studies of the relationship between the timing of feedback and its effectiveness. The reviewers coded the studies into three categories: (1) applied studies that featured classroom materials; (2) experimental studies on the acquisition of test content; and (3) list learning studies. In most studies, immediate feedback occurred right after the item, while delayed feedback occurred at least a day later. In 9 of 11 applied studies included in the meta-analysis, immediate feedback was superior to delayed feedback (mean effect size = .28). Immediate feedback was also superior in list studies (effect size = .34). The trend for experimental studies was the opposite, with delayed feedback being superior to immediate feedback in 13 out of 14 studies (mean effect size = –.36). The researchers concluded that classroom teachers should develop or seek programs that provide immediate feedback, because it appeared to be the more effective choice in applied settings.

More recent studies have also supported the use of feedback in educational assessment, and have helped elaborate on what types of feedback are optimal. Butler, Karpicke, and Roediger (2007) examined the effect of answer-until-correct (AUC) feedback with the effect of standard feedback (simply presenting students with the correct answer). The researchers found that students who received feedback did much better than students who did not (68–74% correct versus 51% correct), but differences based on type of feedback and timing of feedback were nonsignificant.

In a study involving the impact of bug-related tutoring (BRT) on subtraction performance, Narciss and Huth (2006) found that method to be superior to feedback that indicates only whether a student's answer is correct, or indicates only the correct answer to the question. The BRT group outperformed the standard condition group in terms of number of task types learned (effect size = .28), errors corrected from pretest to posttest (effect size = .28), posttest performance level (effect size = .20), and motivation (effect size = .12). The researchers attributed the positive relationship between BRT and learning to (1) matching the feedback systematically to task requirements; (2) providing feedback in steps without the correct response available; (3) starting with only students who had relatively high error rates; and (4) controlling the rate of the learning process based on mastery of previous tasks.

Yeh (2006) published an applied evaluation of a rapid assessment procedure embedded within the curriculum of one Texas school district for all students, K-12. Students completed the STAR Reading test to learn their level, then selected and read appropriate books, and afterward completed a computer-based comprehension quiz. Quantitative evaluations of the reading assessment have shown effect sizes of about .2 standard deviations on the state proficiency tests for fifth-grade students, with students across the elementary grade range showing improvement.

Researchers indicate that feedback has a positive effect on learning, that this effect is greatest in applied settings when it is immediate, and that feedback is most effective when it includes corrective instruction. These conclusions are evident whether the outcome measure of interest is student performance or motivation. These findings are relevant to formative assessment because corrective feedback on an individual basis can be a useful testing support for students with special needs who will be retested periodically.

CONCLUSION

Formative assessments are intended to provide an accurate measurement of students' knowledge and skills that can guide and inform instructional decision making and student learning. Accommodated testing procedures and test modifications hold the potential to allow students with special needs greater access to a test's measured constructs, and thus can improve the validity of test score inferences and the test's overall technical soundness. While the inclusion of students with special needs in formative assessments is clearly desirable, it holds some of the same challenges regarding the validity of test results as does their inclusion in summative assessments. Research on testing accommodations for summative assessments suggests that appropriate changes in testing procedures related to presentation, response, timing, and setting should be guided by individual need and instructional accommodations, the goal of providing greater access to measured constructs rather than a change thereof, and accurate implementation of prescribed accommodations. Research has provided evidence that appropriate testing accommodations can yield improved score validity, increased test scores for many students, and higher self-efficacy and motivation.

Research has further afforded developers and users of formative assessments an array of test modification strategies for adapting formative assessments to students with special needs. Methods based on universal design principles and cognitive load theory include strategies such as removing a weak or poor performing distractor from a multiple-choice item, simplifying language, shortening question stems, highlighting or bolding critical information, adding white space, and removing extraneous information. Developers of formative assessments can further guide their item and test modification development efforts with research-based decision-making tools such as the TAMI.

The research on feedback offers a meaningful extension that is specific to formative assessment's unique purpose, namely to direct teaching and learning over the course of instruction. By providing students with immediate and corrective feedback, formative assessments can positively impact student performance and motivation.

Ultimately, all the practices discussed in this chapter involving testing accommodations, item and test modifications, and feedback extensions for formative assessment are concerned with the same hallmark of good educational measurement: accurate assessment of student knowledge and abilities in order to increase student learning. The basis for these research-based practices has been established with summative assessments and provides the foundation for improving more inclusive formative assessments. Much more research is needed to guide the development and use of on-demand assessments of students with special needs.

REFERENCES

Altman, J. R., Lazarus, S. L., Thurlow, M. L., Quenemoen, R. F., Cuthbert, M., & Cormier, D. C. (2008). *2007 survey of states: Activities, changes, and challenges for special education.* Minneapolis, MN: University of Minnesota, National Center on Educational Outcomes.

Beddow, P. A., Kettler, R. J., & Elliott, S. N. (2008). *Test accessibility and modification inventory.* Nashville, TN: Vanderbilt University. http://www.peabody.vanderbilt.edu/tami.xml

Bennett, R. E. (2001). *How the internet will help large-scale assessment reinvent itself.* Retrieved January 1, 2009, from http://epaa.asu.edu/epaa/v9n5.html

Burgstahler, S. (2008). *Designing software that is accessible to students with disabilities.* Retrieved August 21, 2008, from http://www.washington.edu/doit/Brochures/PDF/design_software.pdf

Butler, A. C., Karpicke, J. D., & Roediger, H. L. (2007). The effect of type and timing of feedback on learning from multiple-choice tests. *Journal of Experimental Psychology, 13*(4), 273–281.

Center for Universal Design. (2008). *About UD.* Retrieved August 21, 2008, from http://www.design.ncsu.edu/cud/about_ud/about_ud.htm

Clark, R. C., Nguyen, F., & Sweller, J. (2006). *Efficiency in learning: Evidence-based guidelines to manage cognitive load.* San Francisco: Pfeiffer.

CTB/McGraw-Hill. (2005). *Guidelines for inclusive test administration.* Retrieved January 29, 2009, from http://www.ctb.com/media/articles/pdfs/general/guidelines_inclusive.pdf

Educational Testing Service. (2008). *ETS fairness and review guidelines.* Retrieved August 21, 2008, from http://www.ets.org/Media/About_ETS/pdf/overview.pdf

Elliott, S. N., Braden, J. P., & White, J. (2001). *Assessing one and all: Educational accountability for students with disabilities.* Arlington, VA: Council for Exceptional Children.

Elliott, S. N., Kettler, R. J., Beddow, P. A., Kurz, A., Compton, E., McGrath, D., et al. (2008). *Using modified items to test students with and without persistent academic difficulties: Effects on groups and individual students.* Nashville, TN: Peabody College of Vanderbilt University.

Elliott, S. N., Kettler, R. J., & Roach, A. T. (2008). Alternate assessments of modified achievement standards: More accessible and less difficult tests to advance assessment practices? *Journal of Disability Policy Studies, 19*(3), 140–152.

Elliott, S. N., Kratochwill, T. R., & Gilbertson-Schulte, A. (1999). *Assessment accommodations checklist/guide.* Monterey, CA: CTB/McGraw-Hill.

Elliott, S. N., Kratochwill, T. R., & McKevitt, B. C. (2001). Experimental analysis of the effects of testing accommodations on the scores of students with and without disabilities. *Journal of School Psychology, 39*(1), 3–24.

Feldman, E. S., Kim, J. S., & Elliott, S. N. (2008). *Attitudes and reactions to large-scale assessments: An experimental investigation of the effects of accommodations on adolescents' self-efficacy and test performance.* Madison, WI: University of Wisconsin.

Fuchs, L. S., & Fuchs, D. (2001). Helping teachers formulate sound test accommodation decisions for students with learning disabilities. *Learning Disabilities Research and Practice, 16,* 174–181.

Fuchs, L. S., Fuchs, D., & Capizzi, A. M. (2006). Identifying appropriate test accommodations for students with learning disabilities. *Focus on Exceptional Children, 37*(6), 1–8.

Fuchs, L. S., Fuchs, D., Eaton, S. B., Hamlett, C., Binkley, E., & Crouch, R. (2000). Using objective data sources to enhance teacher judgments about test accommodations. *Exceptional Children, 67*(2), 67–81.

Fuchs, L. S., Fuchs, D., Eaton, S. B., Hamlett, C., & Karns, K. (2000). Supplementing teacher judgments of mathematics test accommodations with objective data sources. *School Psychology Review, 29,* 65–85.

Haladyna, T. M., Downing, S. M., & Rodriguez, M. C. (2002). A review of multiple-choice item-writing guidelines for classroom assessment. *Applied Measurement in Education, 15*(3), 309–334.

Hoffmann, T. (2007). *Final report for universal assessment system phase in research*. Wellesley, MA: Nimble Assessment Systems.

Hollenbeck, K., Rozek-Tedesco, M., & Finzel, A. (2000, April). *Defining valid accommodations as a function of setting, task, and response*. Presentation at the meeting of the Council for Exceptional Children, Vancouver, BC, Canada.

Individuals with Disabilities Education Act, 20 U. S. C. §1400 et seq. (1997).

Individuals with Disabilities Education Improvement Act of 2004. (2004). Pub. L. No. 108-446, § 118 Stat. 2647.

Johnstone, C., Liu, K., Altman, J., & Thurlow, M. (2007). *Students think aloud reflections on comprehensible and readable assessment items: Perspectives on what does and does not make an item readable* (Technical Report 48). Minneapolis, MN: University of Minnesota, National Center on Educational Outcomes.

Johnstone, C., Thurlow, M., Moore, M., & Altman, J. (2006). *Using systematic item selection methods to improve universal design of assessments* (Policy Directions 18). Minneapolis, MN: University of Minnesota, National Center on Educational Outcomes.

Kerrey, B., & Isakson, J. (2000, December). *The power of internet learning: Moving from promise to practice* (Report of the Web-based Education Commission). Retrieved August 21, 2008, from http://www.ed.gov/offices/AC/WBEC/FinalReport/WBECReport.pdf

Kettler, R. J., Niebling, B. C., Mroch, A. A., Feldman, E. S., Newell, M. L., Elliott, S. N., et al. (2005). Effects of testing accommodations on math and reading scores: An experimental analysis of the performance of students with and without disabilities. *Assessment for Effective Intervention, 31*(1), 37–48.

Kettler, R. J., Rodriguez, M. R., Bolt, D. M., Elliott, S. E., Beddow, P. A., & Kurz, A. (2008). *Modified multiple-choice items for alternate assessments: Reliability, difficulty, and the interaction paradigm*. Nashville, TN: Peabody College of Vanderbilt University.

Kulik, J. A., & Kulik, C. C. (1988). Timing of feedback and verbal learning. *Review of Educational Research, 58*(1), 79–97.

Lang, S. C., Elliott, S. N., Bolt, D. M., & Kratochwill, T. R. (2008). The effects of testing accommodations on students' performances and reactions to testing. *School Psychology Quarterly, 23*(1), 107–124.

Lazarus, S. S., Thurlow, M. L., Christensen, L. L., & Cormier, D. (2007). *States' alternate assessments based on modified achievement standards (AA-MAS) in 2007* (Synthesis Report 67). Minneapolis, MN: University of Minnesota, National Center on Educational Outcomes.

McDonnell, L. M., McLaughlin, M. J., & Morrison, P. (Eds.). (1997). *Educating one and all: Students with disabilities and standards-based reform*. Washington, DC: National Academy.

McKevitt, B. C., & Elliott, S. N. (2003). Effects and perceived consequences of using read-aloud and teacher-recommended testing accommodations on a reading achievement test. *School Psychology Review, 32*(4), 583–600.

Miller, G. A. (1956). The magical number seven, plus or minus two: Some limits on our capacity for processing information. *Psychological Review, 62*, 81–97.

Narciss, S., & Huth, K. (2006). Fostering achievement and motivation with bug-related tutoring feedback in a computer-based training for written subtraction. *Learning and Instruction, 16*, 310–322.

No Child Left Behind Act, (2001). 20 U. S. C. § 16301 et seq.

Paas, F., Tuovinen, J. E., Tabbers, H., & Van Gerven, P. W. M. (2003). Cognitive load measurement as a means to advance cognitive load theory. *Educational Psychologist, 38*(1), 63–71.

Phillips, S. E. (1994). High-stakes testing accommodations: Validity versus disabled rights. *Applied Measurement in Education, 7*(2), 93–120.

Roach, A. T., Beddow, P. A., Kurz, A., Kettler, R. J., & Elliott, S. N. (in press). Using student responses and perceptions to inform item development for an alternate assessment based on modified achievement standards. *Exceptional Children.*

Rodriguez, M. C. (2005). Three options are optimal for multiple-choice items: A meta-analysis of 80 years of research. *Educational Measurement: Issues and Practice, 24*(2), 3–13.

Russell, M., Johnstone, C., Higgins, J., & Hoffmann, T. (2008). *FCAT computer accommodations pilot study report.* Tallahassee, FL: Department of Education.

Schulte, A. G., Elliott, S. N., & Kratochwill, T. R. (2001). Effects of testing accommodations on standardized mathematics test scores: An experimental analysis of the performances of students with and without disabilities. *School Psychology Review, 30*(4), 527–547.

Sireci, S. G., & Pitoniak, M. J. (2007). Assessment accommodations: What have we learned from research? In C. C. Laitusis & L. L. Cook (Eds.), *Large scale assessment and accommodations: What works?* (pp. 53–65). Arlington, VA: Council for Exceptional Children.

Sweller, J. (1994). Cognitive load theory, learning difficulty and instructional design. *Learning and Instruction, 4*, 295–312.

Thurlow, M. L., House, A., Boys, C., Scott, D., & Ysseldyke, J. (2000*). State participation and accommodations policies for students with disabilities: 1999 update* (Synthesis Report 29). Minneapolis, MN: University of Minnesota, National Center on Educational Outcomes.

Tindal, G., & Fuchs, L. S. (2000). *A summary of research on test changes: An empirical basis for defining accommodations*. Lexington, KY: Mid-South Regional Resource Center Interdisciplinary Human Development Institute.

U.S. Department of Education. (2007). *Title I: Improving the academic achievement of the disadvantaged; Individuals with disabilities act (IDEA); Final rule* (Federal Register 72, no. 67). Washington, DC: U.S. Government Printing Office.

Web Accessibility Initiative. (2008). Web content accessibility guidelines (WCAG) Version 2.0. Available from http://www.w3.org/

Yeh, S. S. (2006). High-stakes testing: Can rapid assessment reduce the pressure? *Teachers College Record, 108*(4), 621–661.

11

RESEARCH AND RECOMMENDATIONS FOR FORMATIVE ASSESSMENT WITH ENGLISH LANGUAGE LEARNERS

JAMAL ABEDI

Research on the instruction and assessment of English Language Learners (ELL) suggests that these students are faced with dual challenges: learning a new language and learning academic content in a language that they are trying to learn. For ELL students, the outcomes of formative assessment could contribute greatly to their academic success both in learning a new language and mastering academic content knowledge. For example, research has clearly demonstrated that ELL students are in a difficult position when they are presented with instructional and assessment materials that are linguistically complex and culturally biased. The outcomes of formative assessments could help explain how these factors affect their learning and how such sources of bias can be identified and controlled.

The purpose of this chapter is twofold. First, to provide a summary of research on the assessment of ELL students focusing on the factors that interfere with their understanding of instructional and assessment materials, and second, to present a discussion of how formative assessments can be used to improve the quality of education for ELL students. Recommendations for developing more reliable and valid formative assessments for ELLs are offered at the end of the chapter.

SUMMATIVE VERSUS FORMATIVE ASSESSMENTS FOR ENGLISH LANGUAGE LEARNERS

The main purpose of summative assessment is to provide information on what students have learned in a given period within a content area. Since these assessments are typically conducted at the end of formal classroom instruction, the results may not provide constructive feedback to teachers for improving the instruction for those students. As indicated by Herman and Baker (2005), educators "wisely recognize that information from annual state tests is often too little, too late" (p. 1). On the other hand, formative assessments are typically referred to as classroom assessments, or assessment *for* learning

(Stiggins & Chappuis, 2006). Formative assessments are ongoing and enable teachers to monitor student progress in order to improve instruction before it is too late for that instruction to have an impact on overall learning. Formative assessments can provide valuable information to help teachers understand students' instructional needs as they are conducted during the instructional term (Heritage, Kim & Vendlinski, 2008; Herman, Osmundson, Ayala, Schneider, & Timms, 2006).

Therefore, the two assessments have different goals and objectives. Shepard (2000) argues that formative assessment should be used to improve learning, and calls for a change in culture in order for this to effectively happen. Shepard also indicates that the social meaning of evaluation should be revised to allow for more interaction between instruction and assessment, considering that the current perception that a single, annual, summative test can adequately identify unique student needs.

In this chapter we will elaborate on how knowledge about the content, technical aspects (reliability, validity, item characteristics) and linguistic structure of summative assessment could help in the development of formative assessments that may be useful tools in informing curriculum and instruction for ELL students. Information from formative assessment is critical for teachers of English language learners in developing an effective instructional program from which these students can benefit.

BENEFITS OF FORMATIVE ASSESSMENT

In a comprehensive review of formative assessment literature spanning kindergarten to college and across all content areas in education, Black and Wiliam (1998a) presented substantial evidence that formative assessment can increase learning outcomes and achievement. They defined formative assessment as "encompassing all those activities undertaken by teachers, and/or by their students, which provide information to be used as feedback to modify the teaching and learning activities in which they are engaged" (p. 2). In their follow-up paper, Black and Wiliam (1998b) presented strong evidence that improving formative assessment practices raises standards. Notably, many of the studies indicated that improving formative assessment practices particularly helped low achievers. Similarly, Stiggins (2002) argues that improving classroom assessment is pivotal to advancing student achievement.

Feedback from teachers to students is an important component of formative assessment. The literature calls for specific, descriptive feedback that allows students to learn from their work in order to advance further (Black & Wiliam, 1998b; Sadler, 1989; Stiggins, 2002). Herman and Choi (2008) examined the relationship of students' learning to teachers' judgment of students' understanding. The outcome of this study showed a consistent positive relationship between teachers' judgment and student learning. The study stressed the power of assessment in improving student learning using information for formative assessment.

Formative assessment can also increase students' motivation and self-esteem. In an exploratory study of 370 students, Miller and Lavin (2007) studied whether or not formative assessment helped increase the self-esteem of students aged 10 to 12. The data suggested that students' overall self-perception improved, and that these benefits increased over time. When exposed to formative assessment practices, students demonstrated a greater degree of self-competence and became more aware of the learning process and how to achieve their academic goals.

The literature summarized above suggests that formative assessment provides useful information for teachers in improving the quality of instruction for all students. The underlying question in this chapter is whether or not the outcome of formative assessment can improve the academic performance of ELL students given the technical issues in the assessment of these students, including the impact of language factors on the validity of their assessments.

ASSESSMENT CONSIDERATIONS FOR ENGLISH LANGUAGE LEARNERS

Many different linguistic features have been identified that negatively affect ELL students' performance. These features include those that slow down the reader, make misinterpretation more likely, and add to the reader's cognitive load, thus interfering with concurrent tasks. Examples of these features include unfamiliar vocabulary, complicated grammatical structures, and styles of discourse that include extra material, abstractions, and passive voice (Abedi, 2006b; Abedi, Lord, & Plummer, 1997). While these linguistic features may impact the academic performance of all students, including native speakers of English, the level of impact on ELL student performance is more profound.

Research findings also show that ELL students have less opportunity to learn when they are compared with their non-ELL peers (Herman & Abedi, 2004). The reduced opportunity to learn for ELL students has been linked with the linguistic complexity of instructional materials (Abedi & Herman, in press). That is, the higher the level of linguistic complexity of instructional materials, the lower the level of opportunity to learn as reported by ELL students.

The substantial performance gap between ELL and non-ELL students in many content areas may be due to factors such as the complex linguistic structure of the assessments (Maihoff, 2002; Solano-Flores & Trumbull, 2003), and the impact of cultural factors (Gándara & Rumberger, in press). Malmberg and Sumra (2001) indicated the sociocultural factors such as socioeconomic status (SES) of the family, parent education, and school-level SES may impact student performance. Spinelli (2008) suggests that cultural and linguistic factors may impact the classification of students and may cause misclassification of ELL students in a learning disability category. She states that assessment measures (such as formative assessments) that fairly and accurately identify individual strengths and areas of need may result in a more accurate classification, and reduce the likelihood of misclassification of ELL students as learning disabled.

Formative assessment can be an effective and efficient tool in the hands of teachers, school officials, and curriculum planners to help identify the most influential factors contributing to their ELL students' learning and inform the design of a curriculum that addresses many of these factors. To provide useful information, formative assessment should be free of linguistic and cultural biases. Therefore, it is imperative to understand the role of language and cultural factors in assessment in general and in formative assessment in particular.

Assessments with complex linguistic structure may provide results that are unreliable, invalid, and therefore, misleading. If formative assessments are to be useful in assisting teachers and others involved in the academic career of ELL students, then these assessments should also be free of any linguistic and cultural biases. "Cultural bias" refers to any cultural factors that may differentially impact the performance of ELL students. Solano-Flores and Nelson-Barber (2001) introduced the concept of "cultural validity" as a form of test validity that links many linguistic and cultural factors to ELL students' assessment outcomes.

The Need for Formative Assessments of English Language Learners

Compared to their native, English-speaking peers, ELL students are faced with a more challenging academic career. They have to learn a new language and they have to learn content knowledge in an unfamiliar language. As elaborated by Meskill (this volume), "there are considerable differences between learning a language in formal settings for limited use outside of the target culture ('foreign language learning') and mastering the language of the culture in which one lives and studies" (p. 199). Because of the greater challenges faced by ELL students, proper assessment and appropriate instruction are critical to ensure they are not to be left behind.

The key element in providing appropriate instruction for these students is to understand their academic needs. There are many questions that can be posed with respect to ELL students' academic careers. For example, what are their linguistic needs? What is their current level of proficiency in English? In what content areas do they have difficulty? How do the linguistic factors interact with their understanding of content materials? Are they at the level of proficiency in English where they can meaningfully participate in the statewide summative assessment and benefit from instruction in English? A well-designed battery of formative assessments can address these issues and can provide valuable information for teachers and curriculum designers for these students.

Formative Assessments Inform Instruction for ELL Students

English language learner students are assessed in two different, yet related, areas: (1) their level of English language proficiency (ELP) and (2) their level of content knowledge. Thus, formative assessment covers two major areas for ELL students: assessing their level of ELP and assessing their knowledge in content areas such as mathematics, science, language arts, and social sciences. In both of these areas, the results of formative assessment can be of great value to teachers and curriculum planners in designing instructional materials that best fit their needs.

Formative Assessment of English Proficiency   Students' level of English proficiency plays a very important role in their understanding of instruction in content areas (Abedi, 2007). Students who are not at the level of English proficiency necessary to understand academic instruction in English may become frustrated and may lose interest and attention. They may also be misclassified as students with learning disabilities (Abedi, 2006a; Artiles, Rueda, Salazar, & Higareda, 2005). Therefore, assessment of students' ELP level is the most important first step in providing effective and appropriate instruction to these students. They must have sufficient proficiency in academic English in all four domains (reading, writing, speaking, and listening) to be able to make academic progress. Results of ELP tests are often not available to teachers at the time when they may be utilized to guide instructional planning. Information on ELL students' level of ELP is needed before instruction begins and during the instruction so that teachers can design and adjust instruction based on the students' linguistic needs.

A comprehensive ELP formative assessment can help teachers of ELL students to determine if they are proficient enough in academic English to benefit from instruction in English. English language proficiency assessment information that is obtained through formative assessment would be the most useful as it provides a timely update of students' levels of proficiency in areas that are essential in understanding instruction. For example, a low level proficiency in reading may result in low test score in math for ELL students not necessarily due to a lack of student knowledge in math, but because of students' poor English reading skills. The outcome of formative assessment in reading will help teachers understand the situation and remedy the problem.

Formative Assessment of Content Knowledge Results of studies on the opportunity to learn have shown that lack of proficiency in English may be a major obstacle in ELL students learning content knowledge (Abedi & Herman, in press; Herman & Abedi, 2004). Formative assessment can identify areas where students have difficulty in instructional and assessment materials. Teachers can then carefully examine the linguistic structure of those sections of the materials that ELL students performed poorly. If complex linguistic structures are identified, then reducing those complexities can help improve student learning.

ELL students may have the content knowledge but may be unable to express and demonstrate such knowledge due to linguistic barriers. It might be necessary to provide formative assessments that demonstrate other ways of knowing such as drawing a diagram of a life cycle to demonstrate scientific knowledge or providing hands-on-performance materials to give them a better opportunity to express their knowledge (Shavelson, Baxter, & Pine, 1991; Solano-Flores & Shavelson, 1997).

CHARACTERISTICS OF HIGH QUALITY FORMATIVE ASSESSMENTS

Traditionally, formative assessment is conducted at the classroom level where there is a direct impact on instruction. It may also be conducted at the district, state, or even national level. There are similarities and differences between formative assessments at each level. At the classroom level, formative assessments can be more focused on the content of materials taught by the teacher, and can take many different forms, such as paper and pencil format, observation of student performance, judging students' performance based on information that teachers collect during the instructional period, and in a computer format. State and national formative assessments, on the other hand, may focus on the overall state and national content standards.

At whatever level formative assessments are conducted and used, there are some basic requirements that they should meet in order to provide accurate information. Herman and Baker (2005) discussed six criteria that determine the validity and efficiency of formative assessments. These criteria include: (1) alignment, (2) diagnostic value, (3) fairness, (4) technical quality, (5) utility, and (6) feasibility. We will present our discussion of the characteristics of high quality formative assessment within this framework suggested by Herman and Baker, as it fits well with the focus on formative assessment for ELL students (see also, Linn, Baker, & Dunbar, 1991).

Alignment to Standards

The first requirement for obtaining accurate information from formative assessments is that they must be aligned to content standards. State content standards define the knowledge, concepts, and skills that students should learn at each grade level. Both summative and formative assessments should represent state content standards, otherwise "their results tell us little about whether students are making adequate progress toward achieving the standard and performing well on the assessment" (Herman & Baker, 2005, p. 2). For ELL students, formative assessment should focus on two different areas: (1) students' level of English proficiency (ELP), which should be aligned with the state ELP standards, and (2) students' level of proficiency in content areas such as mathematics and science, which should be aligned with the state content standards.

Provision of Diagnostic Information   The second requirement for accurate performance assessment outcomes is that the assessment is *capable of providing diagnostic information*. One of the major goals of formative assessment is to provide diagnostic information on students' academic performance. "A test with high diagnostic value will tell us not only whether students are performing well but also why students are performing at certain levels and what to do about it" (Herman & Baker, 2005, p. 5). The diagnostic aspect of performance assessment is of paramount importance for ELL students, since their level of proficiency in English determines their success in content based learning. Such information can help teachers to: (1) facilitate student learning in the English language, and (2) reduce unnecessary linguistic complexity of the instructional materials with which students have difficulty. Similarly teachers can help ELL students in the area of writing, where they may have more difficulty (e.g., extended constructed response items where students have to explain their responses).

Fairness   The third requirement for accurate performance assessment outcome is *fairness*. As Herman and Baker (2005) indicated, a fair formative test provides accurate information for all students from different cultural and linguistic backgrounds. However, variables such as unnecessary linguistic complexity and cultural factors may introduce bias into the formative assessment outcomes. Such biases may have a more profound impact on ELL students than any other subgroup of students. To provide a fair assessment for all students, including ELL students, all sources of biases should be identified and controlled.

Technical Quality of Formative Assessments

The fourth requirement for accurate performance assessment outcome is technical quality. Assessments that are reliable and valid provide accurate information about what students know and are able to do. There are many different factors that could negatively impact the reliability and validity of assessments for all students (e.g., Allen & Yen, 1979; Thorndike, 2005). Assessments for ELL students may have additional sources of threat to reliability and validity, such as the unnecessary linguistic complexity of the assessment.

Results of studies on the assessment of ELL students have demonstrated that the unnecessary linguistic complexity of content-based assessments is a likely source of measurement error, having more impact on the reliability of assessment for the ELL subgroup. The linguistic complexity of test items as a source of construct-irrelevant variance may also influence the validity of assessment for these students (Abedi, 2006b). Results of analyses of existing data show a substantial gap in reliability (internal consistency) and validity (concurrent validity) between ELL and non-ELL students on test items that are linguistically complex (Abedi, 2006b,). A more detailed discussion of reliability and validity of formative assessments and suggestions on how to improve the technical quality of such assessments for ELL students may be helpful to highlight these important characteristics.

Reliability and Validity   Reliability problems arise when responses are not consistent across repeated testing (American Educational Research Association, American Psychological Association, & National Council on Measurement in Education, 1999; Thorndike, 2005). For example, when students do not understand the language of test items, their responses may vary on different occasions of taking the same test (Abedi, 2006b). Results of analyses of data from multiple locations across the United States indicate a large gap in the reliability coefficients obtained from samples of ELL and non-ELL students. This is mainly due to the multidimensional nature of assessment outcomes for ELL students, as these assessments are influenced by language factors.

The gap in reliability decreases as the level of language demand of the assessment decreases. For example, the internal consistency coefficients (alpha) for native speakers of English students ranged from .898 for math to .805 for science and social science. For ELL students, however, alpha coefficients differed considerably across the content areas. In math, where language factors might not have as much influence on performance, the alpha coefficient for ELL (.802) was slightly lower than the alpha for English-only students (.898). For English language arts, science, and social science; however, where there is more language involved, the gap of the alpha coefficient between English-only and ELL students was substantially larger. Averaging over English language arts, science, and social science, the alpha coefficient for English-only students was .808 as compared to an average alpha of .603 for ELL students.

To improve the reliability of formative assessments for ELL students, all sources of measurement error, including biases due to linguistic and cultural factors, should be identified and controlled. Abedi (2006b) provides information about how to conduct linguistic modification of test items to reduce the level of unnecessary linguistic complexity of the test and increase the reliability of assessments for these students.

The main validity issue is "whether the test measures what we want to measure, all of what we want to measure, and nothing but what we want to measure" (Thorndike, 2005, p. 145). Therefore, if the test measures anything other than the focal construct(s), then the validity of the interpretations of scores on the test is diminished. For example, if test items on a mathematics test have a complex linguistic structure, then the test measures not only the construct relevant to the purpose of the test (mathematics), it also measures a construct that is irrelevant to the purpose of the test (language). Thus, linguistic factors may seriously affect the validity of inferences drawn using this assessment. Results of analyses of existing state and national data show that the higher the level of language demand in the test, the higher the performance gap between ELL and non-ELL students due to the impact of construct-irrelevant factors (Solano-Flores, 2008).

Utility and Feasibility

The fifth criterion for formative assessment is utility. That is, formative assessments should provide useful information for teachers, students, and parents. For ELL students, high utility formative assessments provide diagnostic information on English proficiency as a prelude to learning academic content. High utility formative assessments also provide useful feedback on student learning in content areas. Due to the immediacy of formative assessments, such feedback will help teachers to revise instructional and assessment materials to address ELL students' academic needs.

The sixth criterion for efficient formative assessments is *feasibility*. National, state, district, and classroom assessments take a substantial amount of students' time in schools. Teachers complain that too much testing takes time away from instruction. Therefore, assessments should be worth the extra time and resources that are needed for conducting them. High quality formative assessments inform instruction, offer ongoing feedback to students throughout the learning process, and provide useful information for teachers and curriculum planners necessary to the design of effective instruction. Because of their highly challenging academic careers, this feature is especially important for ELL students.

RESEARCH ON THE ASSESSMENT OF ELL STUDENTS

Due to the importance of formative assessment in shaping and improving instruction for all students, substantial attention has been paid to research in this area for the general student population. However, research on formative assessments for ELL students is scarce. There has been a great deal of attention given to summative assessments for ELL students due to their importance in state and national assessment and accountability requirements (e.g., Abedi, 2004; NCLB, 2002). The findings from research on summative assessment could, to some degree, be applied to formative assessment for ELL students. Therefore, in the absence of any major systematic effort to address issues concerning formative assessments specifically for ELL students, a summary of some of the studies focused on assessment in general of ELL students is provided in this section. Findings from summative assessments of ELL students can then be applied in developing reliable and valid formative assessments for these students.

Language factors greatly influence assessment outcomes for ELL students. The two case scenarios below illustrate this point. These scenarios are based on findings from research on the assessment of ELL students (see, for example, Abedi, 2002, 2006b).

Case One. Maria is a fourth grade student who recently transferred from a high-ranking public school in Mexico. She passed grade 4 math for the first semester with a high score (at the above-proficient level) in Mexico. By the end of the third week in a U.S. school, she was tested again on her math content knowledge. She got a very low score (below proficient). Her U.S. teacher is not sure whether Maria's low score is due to lack of math content knowledge or lack of understanding of the math test items.

Case Two. Jose is another fourth grade student who transferred to the same U.S. school that Maria attends. His math score at the school from his native country was quite low (below proficient). He obtained a similar score in the U.S. school. The teacher, who does not know enough about Jose's academic background, has difficulty explaining his performance.

As evident from the two case scenarios presented above, it is extremely difficult to interpret assessment outcomes (whether formative or summative) when they are confounded with linguistic and cultural factors. Language factors affect performance outcomes, especially for English language learners. Students' content knowledge in areas such as mathematics, science, or social studies may not be truly assessed if students cannot understand the language of the test (Abedi, 2006b; Kiplinger, Haug, & Abedi, 2000; Maihoff, 2002; Solano-Flores & Trumbull, 2003). Research shows that even minor changes in the wording of content-related test items can change ELL student performance (Abedi & Lord, 2001; Abedi, Lord, Hofstetter, & Baker, 2000; Abedi, Lord, & Plummer, 1997; Cummins, Kintsch, Reusser, & Weimer, 1988; De Corte, Verschaffel, & DeWin, 1985; Hudson, 1983; Riley, Greeno, & Heller, 1983).

Linguistic Complexity

Some studies have focused on the effects of the linguistic complexity of assessment on the performance of ELL students. For example, results of analyses of the National Assessment of Educational Progress (NAEP) data (Abedi, Lord, & Plummer, 1997) show that ELL students had difficulty with the test items that were longer and were more linguistically complex. The study also found that ELL students exhibited a substantially higher number of omitted/not-reached test items since it took them much longer to read and understand assessment questions.

In analyzing test data from four different U.S. locations, Abedi (2002) compared the performance of ELL and non-ELL students in several different content areas. Among these content areas, reading has the highest level of language demand since language is central to the construct being measured. However, in the science and math tests, understanding of the science and math content—not the language—is the focus of assessment. At one of the data sites, ELL students in grade 10 had a mean reading score of 24.0 ($SD = 16.4$) as compared with a mean reading score of 38.0 ($SD = 16.0$) for non-ELL students, a difference of 14 score points. The difference between ELL and non-ELL mean NCE scores for science was 9.7, substantially less than the 14 score points difference in reading. For math, the difference in average scores between ELL and non-ELL students was 2.8. For 11th grade students, the ELL/non-ELL performance difference was 15.9 for reading, 11.2 for science, and close to 0 for math computation. These results were consistent with the results of analyses from the other data sites in the study.

To reduce the level of impact of unnecessary linguistic complexity on the assessment of ELL students, a linguistic modification approach to the content-based assessment was proposed (Abedi, Lord, & Plummer, 1997). In this approach, guidelines are provided on how to revise assessment questions to be more accessible in terms of linguistic structure, without affecting the construct being measured. The researchers developed a linguistically modified version of the assessment based on the proposed framework and compared student performance taking this modified assessment with the performance of another group taking the original form of the assessment. The original and modified versions were randomly assigned to students. In general, the results suggested that the linguistic modification approach makes assessments (both summative and formative) more accessible to ELL students.

In one study, the impact of linguistic complexity of assessment was tested on a sample of 1,031 eighth grade students in Southern California (Abedi & Lord, 2001). The math items for eighth grade students were modified to reduce the complexity of sentence structures and to replace potentially unfamiliar vocabulary with more familiar words without changing the content-related terminologies (i.e., mathematical terms were not changed). The results showed significant improvement in the scores of ELL students and also non-ELLs in low and average level mathematics classes, but the changes did not affect the scores of higher performing non-ELL students, since those students understand complex math problems without needing much language context.

The outcome of this study cross-validated another study in which the impact of language factors on the mathematics performance of English learners was examined (Abedi, Lord, Hofstetter, & Baker, 2000). This study was conducted on a sample of 1,394 eighth graders in schools with a high enrollment of Spanish speakers. Results showed that modification of the language contributed to improved performance on 49% of the items; the ELL students generally scored higher on shorter/less linguistically complex problem statements. The results of this study also suggest that lower performing native speakers of English benefited from the linguistic modification of the assessment as well.

Other studies were conducted to obtain cross-validation evidence on the impact of language factors on the assessment of ELL students. These studies examined the impact of language factors by focusing on the effectiveness of the language modification approach in reducing the performance gap between ELL and non-ELL students. In one of these studies, which included 1,594 eighth grade students, test items from the NAEP and the Third International Math and Science Study (TIMSS) were used (Abedi, Courtney, & Leon, 2003). The results indicated that the linguistically modified version of the test improved the ELL students' scores without affecting the non-ELL students' scores. Other studies have had similar results (e.g., Maihoff, 2002), including those that involved students in grades 4 and 8 (Kiplinger, Haug, & Abedi, 2000; Rivera & Stansfield, 2001).

In summary, the research evidence shows that linguistic complexity is a major source of measurement error in assessment outcomes for ELL students. Research findings also suggest that reducing the level of unnecessary linguistic complexity of assessments (linguistic modification) may help improve assessment validity and reliability for these students. Some people argue that reducing the complexity of academic content may change the construct being taught and assessed. However, in the language modification approach, the language factors that are related to the content of assessment and instruction are distinguished from the unnecessary linguistic complexity of the text in both assessment and instruction, and modifications are focused only on the language that is unrelated to the content being measured. Decisions about what was language-related and what was language-unrelated was made by a team of content and linguistic experts.

Research findings presented in this section showed substantial performance gaps between English language learners and their native English speaking peers. Because there is no evidence to suggest any difference between ELL and non-ELL students in their ability to learn, these gaps are alarming. The evidence suggests that the lower performance of ELL students is mainly due to the impact of language factors on instruction and assessment. While the research on the impact of language on assessment has been conducted mainly in the area of summative assessments, the findings of these studies can be generalized to formative assessments as well.

GUIDELINES FOR CREATING RELIABLE, VALID, AND EFFECTIVE FORMATIVE ASSESSMENTS FOR ELLS

For formative assessments to provide useful information, they must be reliable, valid, and comprehensive in content. There are many factors that may impact the reliability and validity of formative assessments that should be considered (e.g., Allen & Yen, 1979; Thorndike, 2005). Among the most important factors to consider in the development of formative assessments for ELL students is controlling for sources of construct-irrelevant variance. Linguistic and cultural biases could impact both the reliability and validity of inferences from assessments of ELL students. The outcomes of formative assessments which are highly confounded with such sources of bias may not be useful.

General Recommendations for Creating Formative Assessments for ELLs

Some general recommendations should be noted at the outset. First, formative assessments should be based on state content standards, to the extent possible. Formative assessments based on state content standards provide objective and comprehensive information about student levels of achievement on a broader scale. Second, the technical characteristics of formative assessments should be clearly examined. Among these characteristics, data on validity, reliability, and item bias through differential item functioning analysis (DIF) should be provided (e.g., Abedi, Leon, & Kao, 2008; Martiniello, 2008). Information on the items that function differently across ELL/non-ELL categories could be of great value to teachers because such information could help identify possible sources of bias in instructional materials.

A third general recommendation is that the assessment should follow a standard test administration protocol to the extent possible, so that the outcome of these assessments can be comparable across different conditions. Finally, formative assessments for ELL students should include items that address linguistic issues. An English language proficiency (ELP) assessment should include the four major domains (reading, writing, listening, and speaking) and content-based assessments should include questions to address academic language proficiency (Bailey, Butler, & Sato, 2007).

Creating Reliable and Valid Formative Assessments

Although it may be difficult to replicate formal research-based testing methods in classroom settings, the following recommendations are suggested when possible. For more informal and frequent formative assessments, some of these suggestions may be impractical, but for more formal and less frequent grade level, school- or district-wide formative assessments, these steps are strongly recommended.

Use a Reasonable Number of Questions   Determine the maximum number of questions that can be included in terms of class time period. Remember that an assessment with too many questions may take too much time out of instruction, and assessments with too few test items may not be reliable or have sufficient content coverage to provide accurate information. As a rule of thumb to create a reliable test, we recommend a minimum of 20 test items.

Determine the Format of the Test   The format may not need to follow the state summative assessment. It should have different types of items such as multiple-choice and written response items. The written response (open-ended) items should include short essays (extended constructive response) as these items provide an opportunity for teachers to evaluate students' writing ability on content assessments. The test may also include other types of assessment, such as portfolios and performance assessments.

Establish Content and Construct Validity   Ensure that the content of the formative assessment corresponds to the state content standards in the relevant subject areas. Such information is usually available through state department of education websites.

Write All Questions Clearly and Concisely   Avoid language that is complex and culturally biased. Table 11.1 provides descriptions of low, moderate, and high linguistic complexity. There are at least five guidelines that can help in reducing the linguistic complexity of assessments. These include: (1) avoid words that are unfamiliar or rarely used; (2) avoid test items that are very long or have complex sentence construction; (3) use concrete terms, since items that are presented in abstract forms are more difficult for ELL students to understand; (4) do not use difficult subordinate, conditional, or adverbial clauses; and (5) use the active voice and concrete presentations of sentences to the extent possible, since ELL students have difficulty with passive voice and abstract or impersonal presentations.

Get Feedback From Students   Whenever possible, discuss the assessment with two or three students in another class studying the same content, at the same grade level, who are not likely to take the test. Ask them individually about areas that they have difficulty understanding, due either to language or cultural issues.

Table 11.1 Continuum of Linguistic Complexity and Item Characteristics

1	Items with no linguistic complexity:
	✓ Familiar or frequently used words; word length generally shorter
	✓ Short sentences and limited prepositional phrases
	✓ Concrete item(s) and a narrative structure
	✓ No complex conditional or adverbial clauses
	✓ No passive voice or abstract or impersonal presentations
2	Items with a minimal level of linguistic complexity:
	✓ Familiar or frequently used words; short to moderate word length
	✓ Moderate sentence length with a few prepositional phrases
	✓ Concrete item(s)
	✓ No subordinate, conditional, or adverbial clauses
	✓ No passive voice or abstract or impersonal presentations
3	Items with a moderate level of linguistic complexity:
	✓ Unfamiliar or seldom used words
	✓ Long sentence(s)
	✓ Abstract concept(s)
	✓ Complex sentence/conditional tense/adverbial clause(s)
	✓ A few passive voice or abstract or impersonal presentations
4	Items with a high level of linguistic complexity:
	✓ Relatively unfamiliar or seldom used words
	✓ Long or complex sentence(s)
	✓ Abstract item(s)
	✓ Difficult subordinate, conditional, or adverbial clause(s)
	✓ Passive voice/abstract or impersonal presentations
5	Items with a maximum level of linguistic complexity:
	✓ Highly unfamiliar or seldom used words
	✓ Very long or complex sentence(s)
	✓ Abstract item(s)
	✓ Very difficult subordinate, conditional, or adverbial clause(s)
	✓ Many passive voice and abstract or impersonal presentations

Get Feedback From Colleagues   Whenever possible, ask a colleague with a linguistic background to review a test using the information provided in Table 11.1 to identify items that are linguistically complex. Reduce the level of linguistic complexity of items based on the feedback from the colleague and students in step 5.

Check Reliability   Whenever possible, estimate the reliability of newly developed formative assessments by giving the test to students in a class taught by a colleague, and give it again to the same students after a week or so. Compare responses given by the same students on the first and second administration of the test and look for consistency between the two administrations. As a rule of thumb, items with 80% (or higher) consistency over time can be considered reliable.

Providing Feedback Based on the Outcome of Formative Assessments

When providing feedback to ELL students based on the results of formative assessments, the following four guidelines can ensure that the feedback is useful to students: (1) Be as specific as possible and avoid general terms such as *good*, *poor*, or *not adequate*; (2) Think of providing feedback as consisting of the same steps taken in teaching a lesson, such as identification of a goal, direct instruction, guided practice, independent practice, and assessment. Provide a clear goal for a task, explain the expectations for the task, provide instruction and guided support for achieving the goal, including interacting with the student to check for understanding and whether or not he or she has the prerequisite skills and strategies, and finally, let the student work independently before reassessing progress toward the goal. (3) Present evidence from formative assessment about how the lack of language proficiency could lead to a lack of understanding of the content. For example, show how unfamiliar vocabulary resulted in a lack of understanding of content. (4) When providing ELP feedback, be sure to include the student's areas of need in each of the four domains—reading, writing, speaking, and listening.

SUMMARY AND SUGGESTIONS

The No Child Left Behind (2002) Act, which is the most recent reauthorization of the Elementary and Secondary Education Act (ESEA) of 1965, mandates the inclusion of all students in statewide accountability to promote higher achievement for every student, including English language learners. However, there are major issues concerning the instruction and assessment of ELL students. As discussed in this chapter, research on the assessment of ELL students shows a substantial performance gap between ELL and non-ELL students. While the inclusion mandate highlights the need for attention to the academic careers of ELL students, it should be considered only the first step. Including ELL students into mainstream instruction and assessment without proper attention to their academic needs could have grave consequences for their academic futures.

English language learner students constitute a heterogeneous group. They are from different countries with different language backgrounds, and different levels of proficiency in English and their native language. Therefore, the same curriculum may not serve all ELL students. Formative assessments can be the best source of information for teachers and others who are involved in their academic careers in recognizing the individual needs of these students and helping them reach the level of academic achievement that every student deserves.

English language learner students face very challenging academic careers because they must learn a new language and learn new content knowledge in that new language. Summative assessment outcomes may provide useful information on the academic progress of ELL students. However, information about the outcomes of these assessments may be too little too late. These outcomes come to light when instruction has officially ended and teachers may no longer be able to use assessment results in addressing ELL needs through instruction.

In addition, the assessment and accountability system for ELL students is more complex than for many other student subgroups. Because ELL students must first learn the English language in order to be able to learn content knowledge in English, the main issue is whether they have reached the level of proficiency in English that is needed to benefit from instruction and assessment in an English-only environment. Formative assessments can shed light on the issues in two areas. First, formative assessment can assess students' levels of proficiency in different English language proficiency domains (reading, writing, speaking, and listening) to determine their readiness to participate in mainstream instruction and assessment. Formative assessment can then examine students' performance in content-based areas to determine if the linguistic complexity of instructional materials (teacher lectures, textbooks, etc.) affects students' understanding of instruction.

Formative assessments are typically constructed and used at the classroom level by teachers. While this provides a more direct representation of what the teacher has taught, it may not have the technical quality that such an important assessment should have. Teachers often may not have the technical background that is needed to develop a sound formative assessment system and may not have resources for pilot and field testing these assessments. Furthermore, the teacher-made formative assessments may not cover state content standards that should guide instruction and assessment for all students. On the other hand, formative assessments developed by test publishers or states may not be at the level of specificity that teachers would desire. It is therefore imperative to pay careful attention to both the content and technical characteristics of formative assessments that are used for students.

Test developers and textbook writers must also be prepared to develop formative assessments for ELL students based on findings from research on assessments for these students. Such research points specifically to the impact of unnecessary linguistic complexity of instruction and assessment. It is important for the developers of formative assessments for ELL students to have a good understanding of the impact of linguistic and cultural factors on their assessments and to incorporate suggestions recommended by research in this area into the assessment. Assessments (whether formative or summative) that are free from unnecessary linguistic complexity will be more accessible to all students.

ACKNOWLEDGMENTS

The author acknowledges the contributions of Rita Pope, who contributed substantially with editorial comments and assisted in structuring and revising the paper, as well as Shannon Cannon, who provided valuable comments and suggestions during the revision process.

REFERENCES

Abedi, J. (2002). Standardized achievement tests and English language learners: Psychometrics issues. *Educational Assessment, 8*(3), 231–257.

Abedi, J. (2004). The No Child Left Behind Act and English language learners: Assessment and accountability issues. *Educational Researcher, 33*(1), 4–14.

Abedi, J. (2006a). Psychometric issues in the ELL assessment and special education eligibility. *Teacher's College Record, 108*(11), 2282–2303.

Abedi, J. (2006b). Language issues in item-development. In S. M. Downing & T. M. Haladyna (Eds.), *Handbook of test development* (pp. 377–398). Mahwah, NJ: Erlbaum.

Abedi, J. (2007). (Ed.). *English language proficiency assessment in the nation: Current status and future practice.* Davis, University of California.

Abedi, J., Courtney, M., & Leon, S. (2003). *Effectiveness and validity of accommodations for English language learners in large-scale assessments* (CSE Tech. Rep. No. 608). Los Angeles: University of California, National Center for Research on Evaluation, Standards, and Student Testing.

Abedi, J., & Herman, J. (in press). Assessing English language learners' opportunity to learn mathematics: Issues and limitations. *Teachers College Record.*

Abedi, J., Leon, S., & Kao, J. (2008). *Examining differential item functioning in reading assessments for students with disabilities.* Los Angeles: University of California, Center for the Study of Evaluation/National Center for Research on Evaluation, Standards, and Student Testing.

Abedi, J., & Lord, C. (2001). The language factor in mathematics tests. *Applied Measurement in Education, 14*(3), 219–234.

Abedi, J., Lord, C., Hofstetter, C., & Baker, E. (2000). Impact of accommodation strategies on English language learners' test performance. *Educational Measurement: Issues and Practice, 19*(3), 16–26.

Abedi, J., Lord, C., & Plummer, J. (1997). *Language background as a variable in NAEP mathematics performance* (CSE Tech. Rep. No. 429). Los Angeles: University of California, National Center for Research on Evaluation, Standards, and Student Testing.

Allen, M. J., & Yen, W. M. (1979). *Introduction to measurement theory.* Monterey, CA: Brooks-Cole.

American Educational Research Association, American Psychological Association, & National Council on Measurement in Education. (1999). *Standards for educational and psychological testing.* Washington, DC: American Educational Research Association.

Artiles, A. J., Rueda, R., Salazar, J., & Higareda, I. (2005). Within-group diversity in minority disproportionate representation: English language learners in urban school districts. *Exceptional Children, 71*, 283–300.

Bailey, A., Butler, F., & Sato, E. (2007). Standards-to-standards linkage under Title III: Exploring common language demands in ELD and science standards. *Applied Measurement in Education, 20*(1), 53–78.

Black, P., & Wiliam, D. (1998a). Assessment and classroom learning. *Assessment in Education: Principles, Policy & Practice, 5*(1), 7–74.

Black, P., & Wiliam, D. (1998b). Inside the black box: Raising standards through classroom assessment. *Phi Delta Kappan, 80*(2), 139-148.

Cummins, D. D., Kintsch, W., Reusser, K., & Weimer, R. (1988). The role of understanding in solving word problems. *Cognitive Psychology, 20*, 405–438.

De Corte, E., Verschaffel, L., & DeWin, L. (1985). Influence of rewording verbal problems on children's problem representations and solutions. *Journal of Educational Psychology, 77*(4), 460–470.

Gándara, P., & Rumberger, R. (in press). Immigration, language, and education: How does language policy structure opportunity? In J. Holdaway & R. Alba (Eds.), *Education of immigrant youth: The role of institutions and agency.* New York: Social Science Research Council.

Heritage, M., Kim, J., & Vendlinski, T. (2008, March). *From evidence to action: A seamless process in formative assessment?* Paper presented at the American Educational Research Association Annual Meeting, New York.

Herman, J. L., & Abedi, J. (2004). *Issues in assessing English language learners' opportunity to learn mathematics* (CSE Tech. Rep. No. 633). Los Angeles: University of California, National Center for Research on Evaluation, Standards, and Student Testing.

Herman, J. L., & Baker, E. L. (2005). Making Benchmark Testing Work. *Educational Leadership, 63*(3), 48–54.

Herman, J. L., & Choi, K. (2008). *Formative assessment and the improvement of middle school science learning: From assessment to evidence.* Los Angeles: University of California, National Center for Research on Evaluation, Standards, and Student Testing.

Herman, J. L., Osmundson, E., Ayala, C., Schneider, S., & Timms, M. (2006). *The nature and impact of teachers' formative assessment practices* (CSE Technical Report 703). Los Angeles: University of California, National Center for Research on Evaluation, Standards, and Student Testing.

Hudson, T. (1983). Correspondences and numerical differences between disjoint sets. *Child Development, 54*, 84–90.

Kiplinger, V. L., Haug, C. A., & Abedi, J. (2000, April). *Measuring math—not reading—on a math assessment: A language accommodations study of English language learners and other special populations.* Presented at the annual meeting of the American Educational Research Association, New Orleans, LA.

Linn, R., Baker, E. L., Dunbar, S. (1991). Complex, performance-based assessment: Expectations and validation criteria. *Educational Researcher, 20,* 15–21.

Maihoff, N. A. (2002, June). *Using Delaware data in making decisions regarding the education of LEP students.* Paper presented at the Council of Chief State School Officers 32nd Annual National Conference on Large-Scale Assessment, Palm Desert, CA.

Malmberg, L., E., Sumra, S. (2001) Socio-cultural factors and Tanzanian primary school students' achievement and school experience [Special issue]. *Journal: Utafiti,* n.s. 4, 207–219.

Martiniello, M. (2008). Language and the performance of English-language learners in math word problems. *Har-*

vard Educational Review, 78(2). Retrieved August 26, 2008, from http://www.edreview.org/harvard08/2008/su08/s08marti.htm

Miller, D., & Lavin, F. (2007). But now I feel I want to give it a try: Formative assessment, self-esteem and a sense of competence. *The Curriculum Journal, 18*(1), 3–25.

No Child Left Behind Act of 2001, Pub. L. No. 107-110, 115 Stat. 1425 (2002).

Riley, M. S., Greeno, J. G., & Heller, J. I. (1983). Development of children's problem-solving ability in arithmetic. In H. P. Ginsburg (Ed.), *The development of mathematical thinking.* New York: Academic Press.

Rivera, C., & Standsfield, C. W., (2001, April). *The effects of linguistic simplification of science test items on performance of limited English proficient and monolingual English-speaking students.* Paper presented at the Annual Meeting of the American Educational Research Association, Seattle, WA.

Sadler, D. R. (1989). Formative assessment and the design of instructional systems. *Instructional Science, 18,* 119–144.

Shavelson, R. J., Baxter, G. P., & Pine, J. (1991). Performance assessment in science. *Applied Measurement in Education, 4*(4), 347–362. Retrieved August 26, 2008, from http://www.informaworld.com/10.1207/s15324818ame0404_7

Shepard, L. A. (2000). The role of assessment in a learning culture. *Educational Researcher, 29*(7), 4–14.

Solano-Flores, G. (2008). Who is given tests in what language, by whom, when, and where? The need for probabilistic views of language in the testing of English language learners. *Educational Researcher, 37*(4), 189–199.

Solano-Flores, W., & Nelson-Barber, S. (2000, April). *Cultural validity of assessments and assessment development procedures.* Paper presented at the annual meeting of the American Educational Research Association, New Orleans, LA.

Solano-Flores, G., & Shavelson, R.J. (1997). Development of performance assessments in science: Conceptual, practical, and logistical issues. *Educational Measurement: Issues and Practice, 16*(3), 16–24.

Solano-Flores, G., & Trumbull, E. (2003). Examining language in context: The need for new research and practice paradigms in the testing of English-language learners. *Educational Researcher, 32*(2), 3–13.

Spinelli, C. G. (2008). Addressing the issue of cultural and linguistic diversity and assessment: Informal evaluation measures for English language learners. *Reading & Writing Quarterly, 24*(1), 101–118.

Stiggins, R. (2002). Assessment crisis: The absence of assessment for learning. *Phi Delta Kappan, 83*(10), 758–765.

Stiggins, R., & Chappuis, J. (2006). What a difference a word makes. *Journal of Staff Development 27*(1), 10–14.

Thorndike, R. M. (2005). *Measurement and Evaluation in Psychology and Education.* Upper Saddle River, NJ: Pearson, Merrill.

12

MOMENT-BY-MOMENT FORMATIVE ASSESSMENT OF SECOND LANGUAGE DEVELOPMENT

ESOL Professionals at Work

CARLA MESKILL

It is a complex, highly idiosyncratic undertaking to learn another language, and learning another language while simultaneously mastering academic content knowledge *in* that language is doubly challenging. Compounding these challenges is the fact that children from a variety of linguistic, cultural, educational, and familial backgrounds each brings an individual target language development trajectory that is shaped by such factors. Consequently, in U.S. classrooms, teachers of English to Speakers of Other Languages (ESOL) must conduct continuous, ongoing formative assessments of the linguistic development of each of their English language learners (ELLs). Such ongoing assessments of individual development are the basis upon which continuous instructional decisions are subsequently made.

This chapter focuses on the formative assessment practices of professional ELL educators. The chapter outlines formative assessment as it is commonly conceptualized in the field of language education and used in instructional processes. Examples from a longitudinal study of two K-8 ESOL classrooms then illustrate the complex calculus employed by ESOL professionals as they undertake ongoing, individual assessment of learner development and, in turn, respond in instructionally meaningful ways that push learner development. In order to adequately capture this aspect of the work of ESOL professionals, particularly the forms of on-going, formative assessment that they typically utilize in this work, first a series of important definitions and distinctions regarding the learning of a new language are presented. The role of formative assessment in supporting and advancing English language learners through this process is then taken up; first as constructs in the field, second as actual illustrations of this formative assessment activity and, finally, as a model of the calculus employed by experienced educators when undertaking these formative assessments.

FORMATIVE ASSESSMENT IN ESOL INSTRUCTION

More and more frequently, children whose mother tongue is not English are entering U.S. schools. Their backgrounds, needs, and assets are as diverse as the planet's population. Accurately assessing the language, literacy, and conceptual development of bilingual children in U.S. schools is, consequently, a highly complex undertaking, and it is one that does not lend itself well to one-size-fits-all approaches. Indeed, any static assessment of the dynamic, multifaceted developmental process of bilingual, biliterate, and bicultural growth is inherently inadequate. So dynamic is this development that Vygotsky boldly observed about all children that "to establish child development by the level reached on the present day means to refrain from understanding child development" (Vygotsky, 1933, as quoted in Lantolf & Poehner, 2008, p. 15). When a new language and new culture are the case, the situation is considerably more complex. In short, the multiple and ever-changing linguistic and conceptual forms of growth in development for a bilingual child are extremely difficult to capture as a static reality (Solano-Flores, 2008). Formative assessment is thus an integral and indispensable tool for all ESOL professionals.

LEARNING A SECOND LANGUAGE

In considering the development of bilingual children who experience schooling in a language other than their mother tongue, preliminary, critical distinctions must be made. First, there are considerable differences between learning a language in formal settings for limited use outside of the target culture (i.e., foreign language learning) and mastering the language of the culture in which one lives and studies. In the former, language is taught as subject matter, not as a tool on which daily survival and academic success depend. Indeed, in contrast to foreign language learning where actual productive use of the foreign language is often rare, learning in a second language environment means mastering contextually appropriate ways of knowing, understanding, and communicating in one's immediate daily context. These ways of knowing, understanding, and communicating are most often substantially different from the ways of the home and of the home culture (Au & Kawahami, 1994).

Another marked difference between foreign and second language learning is that adolescent and adult learners of foreign languages employ mature learning strategies to what is ostensibly subject matter: grammar, vocabulary, pronunciation, and select aspects of the target culture. Young ELLs, by contrast, are acquiring both their mother tongue and a second language naturalistically by interacting with the target language environment and speakers within that environment. In this way, they quickly and easily pick up ways of everyday comprehending and producing the new language. This kind of experiential acquisition is typically limited to what Cummins (1979) terms *basic interpersonal communication* (BICs). For English language learners in U.S. schools, however, in order to achieve academic success, the more onerous undertaking of mastering what Cummins terms *cognitive academic language proficiency* (CALP), is the imperative.

In one important respect there is similarity between foreign and second language learning: It is widely accepted that language development thrives on, and indeed requires meaningful and purposeful interaction with other users of the language, particularly users who are willing to pursue joint meaning making (Atkinson, 2002; Ellis, Tanaka, & Yamazaki, 1994). This social view of learning with human interaction at its core recognizes that classrooms are jointly created environments whereby activity is orchestrated around the immediate needs of diverse learners (Freeman, 2007). Indeed, ESOL classrooms are most often safe havens where meaning making is given precedence over correct form and where linguistic errors and repairs are treated simultaneously as normal features of conversational discourse and as opportunities for formative appraisals; appraisals that become, as will be illustrated, a language professional's chief fodder for teachable moments (Firth & Wagner, 1997).

The centrality of productive meaning making with others is directly reflected in the rationale for and the anatomy of the formative assessment strategies commonly used in ESOL practices. The following section describes the work of the ESOL professional, the knowledge and epistemologies that guide her complex and demanding praxis, and the central role formative assessment plays in her instructional practices.

ESOL PRACTICES: ATTENDING TO EACH CHILD'S PROGRESS

A central, integral component of ESOL professionals' work is to sufficiently understand each child's individual learning trajectory as regards both acquisition of the second language and mastery of academic content. This continuous appraisal of individual learner development is formative assessment. It is the ongoing judgments of education professionals that shape and guide subsequent instructional responses that guarantee movement along each child's second language and academic learning trajectory, in addition to steering larger decisions about grouping and placements. Such ongoing assessments are guided by teachers' knowledge bases regarding second language acquisition, cross-cultural understanding, and the language and literacy requirements of U.S. schools. This knowledge base frames teachers' understandings of each ELL student's needs and shapes each of the academic language trajectories on which she keeps continuous tabs as development proceeds.

What and How Do ESOL Professionals Assess?

According to Edelsky (2006), the goals of any assessment are to reflect complex events, value the diversity of all learners, respect teachers' professional judgments and their accrued knowledge about each learner, and promote deep, meaningful learning. Assessing ELLs' progress in academic English is no exception. Learner progress is assessed in terms of an individual's moment-by-moment comprehension and production of the target academic language. The degrees to which learners successfully comprehend the language around them and make their intended meanings known in the target language are the fundamental yardsticks by which progress is measured.

Because accuracy of comprehension and production are context and task dependent, ESOL professionals construct and guide activity that stimulates and invites the forms of comprehension and production they wish to assess. A typical moment in an ELL's day entails reading, writing, comprehending, and speaking English. Experienced ESOL professionals seek out formative information as children undertake these activities. They seek out clues to lexical, syntactic, morphological, and pragmatic comprehension and production that they use in calculating optimal instructional responses, their goal being to exercise and develop the academic language needed to participate and succeed in school.

Academic Language   While there is some debate over the anatomy and terminology associated with academic versus informal language, there is general agreement that the former is more complex and more challenging than the latter (Bailey & Heritage, 2008). There is no question that academic language is linguistically distinct from what is used in informal, nonschool contexts, and that its acquisition is critical for the academic success of all students (Cazden & Beck, 2003; Schleppergrell, 2004). However, whereas academic language was once statically labeled as abstract or low context, new techniques that fall under the umbrella of "Sheltered English" purposely render language and concepts that are otherwise abstract into being immediate and concrete (Echevarria, Vogt, & Short, 2008). In short, Sheltered English makes academic, discipline-specific language and concepts accessible and comprehensible. English language learners thus learn English with and through academic content.

The underlying premises for the teaching of language via academic content are (1) language is best learned through meaningful use in a variety of contexts with school curricula as ideal resources for language focus; (2) teaching language through academic content keeps learners on age-appropriate conceptual and developmental tracks; and (3) language and curricula are mutually supportive; language is thought and thought is language.

In keeping with these principles, formative assessment procedures in high context instructional venues for low context academic concepts are proving more successful than traditional teaching in the academic content areas (Snow, Porche, Tabors, & Harris, 2007). For example, Meskill, Mossop, and Bates (1999) and Rea-Dickins and Gardner (2000) found that ESOL teachers, while teaching language via academic content, report systematically utilizing performance data and their developmental locations in continuous curricular decision making and teaching events. A skilled language educator can elicit information that reveals individual learner development through a myriad of instructional conversational strategies (Dalton & Sison, 1995; Meskill & Anthony, 2005, 2007).

FORMATIVE ASSESSMENT IN LANGUAGE EDUCATION: THEORY AND RESEARCH

Since the 1970s, theory and practice in the field of language education have been chiefly steered by the tenets of communicative language teaching (Ellis, 2003; Savignon, 1997). In response to the fundamental question of what it means to know a language, Hymes's (1972) definition—saying the right thing, in the right way, with the desired effect—has resonated in the language education community since its inception. At the same time, it is widely recognized that such a definition of communicative competence excludes determining competence via traditional means of assessment. Indeed, testing outcomes can only be meaningful in language education if the assessment provides directly relevant information on a student's ability to use language effectively in an authentic task and context (Canale, 1988). Language learning assessments, then, should be genuine communication with all the complexities that communication implies: context, production, process, subjectivity, interactivity, and adaptivity. It has even been suggested that standardized test constructors use language classroom processes and the instructional expertise inherent therein as guides in developing more authentic language assessments (Canale, 1987).

Subsequent proposals and initiatives for assessing language development communicatively can be subsumed under the umbrella term *performance assessment* whereby authentic, contextualized, meaning-centered language comprehension and production are seen as the means through which a learner's current level of proficiency in an additional language can truly be determined. Application of observations, checklists, portfolios, interactive journals, peer and self reviews, and anticipation guides represent some of the tools ESOL professionals employ to undertake ongoing performance assessments (Genesee, Lindholm-Leary, & Saunders, 2004; Genesee & Upshur, 1996).

In the past 3 decades the field has also seen the line between assessment and instruction fade, with fresh emphasis on integrated instruction and assessment practices (Hargreaves, 2005; Lapp, Fisher, Flood, & Cabello, 2001). Assessment has become a tool of and is therefore inseparable from instruction, whereby a teacher's instructional moves are calculated to be responsive to learner comprehension or production of the target language. Using the resulting moment-by-moment assessments in determining next steps in teaching means "turning assessment into a learning event" (Hargreaves, 2005, p. 213).

Part and parcel of language teacher orchestration of such instructional events is the teacher's and the learner's focus on a particular syntactic form, a phonetic or morphological challenge, or the correct use of a lexical item. Orchestration of heightened attention to particular elements in student comprehension and production is achieved through the design of the task or activity of the moment and the teacher-run instructional conversation. Known generally as communicative form focused instruction (Ellis, 2003; Lightblown & Spada, 2006), this approach to language instruction employs informed incidental assessment by narrowing the range of what both learner and instructor attend to, thereby encouraging the learner to self-monitor and self-correct. For the instructor, focusing on specific forms during communication also facilitates formative assessment and informs the subsequent instructional moves she will make to push the individual student's learning.

In recent decades it has been widely accepted within the ESOL professional community that content learning and target language acquisition by ELLs are best accomplished through ongoing, collaborative, and productive interactions that support their gradual appropriation of relevant discourses (Donato, 2000; Meskill, Mossop, & Bates, 1999). Well trained teachers interact with ELLs and mediate their discourse development toward the discipline-specific discourses of the school content areas (Gibbons, 2003). In order to successfully mediate, they must calculate each student's current English language level, the student's conceptual status regarding the content, and the target disciplinary discourse at the moment, with the outcome of this calculation resulting in mediations, or what Gibbons terms *bridges*, that push student learning in the appropriate direction on a "mode continuum" (Gibbons, 2003, p. 251). Considering that these complex calculations also include consideration of what all teachers continually compute regarding time, scheduling, and shifting physical and psychological contexts, the set of factors that figure into quality instruction for ELLs is large.

Dynamic Assessment

Recent work in ongoing language learner assessment that is grounded in Vygotskian developmental views of learning is known as dynamic assessment (Lantolf & Poehner, 2008; Lantolf & Thorne, 2006). The approach is predicated on the view of language appropriation as the appropriation of tools for thought. When dynamic assessment is applied in language learning assessment, two interrelated child performances are observed: (1) independent performance; and (2) performance that is mediated by a more capable peer. As such, meaningful assessments are only possible if those assessments are accompanied by instruction; a more capable peer using the evaluative information gleaned from independent performance to instruct and facilitate the next level of linguistic and conceptual complexity.

Proponents argue that dynamic assessment has consequential validity in that it assists instructors in making more informed decisions about a learner's future instruction. Another key difference between traditional notions of feedback and dynamic assessment's mediation lies in the content and purpose of teacher–learner interactions, with dynamic assessment leading, indeed pushing learners along the Vygotskian zone of proximal development.

According to Lantolf and Poehner (2004), "dynamic assessment integrates assessment and instruction into a seamless, unified activity aimed at promoting learner development through appropriate forms of mediation that are sensitive to the individual's (or in some cases a group's) current abilities" (p. 50). It is mediation whose aim is the potential development of the learner by pushing her in the direction of development chiefly through speech. It is focused on "future-in-the-making" (p. 53) rather than on performance of abilities in the present. As such, dynamic assessment should not be confused with scaffolding (assisted performance), as the scaffolding metaphor implies that a more knowledgeable peer's aim in assistance is to simply move the learner along toward successful completion of an utterance or a task (Valsiner & van der Veer, 1993) whereas dynamic assessment is more concerned with a learner's developing abilities. Scaffolding is merely a leg up, where dynamic assessment attempts to directly develop a learner's abilities as they unfold and includes assisted transference of the mediation to a novel task. Dynamic assessment "provides insights into learners' abilities not generally afforded by other assessments while simultaneously helping learners move to higher levels of functioning" (Poehner, 2008, p. 89).

These contemporary views of formative assessment in language education share the basic notion of teachers seeing, responding to, and learning about students' learning in order to glean developmental information upon which they can base their subsequent instructional strategies in the short and long term. In summary, contemporary views of formative assessment in ELL instruction can be characterized as having five major characteristics: (1) ongoing; (2) individual; (3) additive; (4) informative in steering subsequent design of instruction; and (5) a primary source of evaluative input. Just how ongoing formative assessment practices unfold in ESOL contexts is illustrated in the following section.

Assessing Academic Language and Content through Instructional Conversation

In this section of the chapter, two examples will be provided. The first example illustrates a TESOL professional using formative assessment as she teaches and reinforces specific lexical items and their pronunciation. The second example illustrates the use of identity texts in teaching the language of school.

In the first example, fifth and sixth grade ELLs are working with their ESOL teacher at computers in the back of the classroom. In this classroom, planning for instructional objectives is largely based on the content and concepts children are encountering in their mainstream content classes, in tandem with moment-by-moment language and content assessments that gauge each child's current state of development. This teacher utilizes her understanding of each child's ability level as it is cumulatively evidenced through what the children say, understand, write, and read. The assessments in these examples are facilitated by what the children and teacher see and do on the computer screen.

The language/content objective of their activity is the language of problem solving and U.S. history, a topic replete with new language and concepts for ELLs. Prior to the following scenario, the group has been reviewing the readings in their social studies texts. The software they use, Where in the U.S.A. is Carmen San Diego? is an engaging game commonly used to complement social studies, and is familiar to this group. During this computer-based session, the ESOL teacher orchestrates productive conversations around what the children see and interact with on the computer screen. The teacher continuously assesses her students' learning and responds to the teachable moments the activity affords by: (1) employing her knowledge of each child's developmental trajectory; (2) estimating comprehension of what she says and what appears on the screen; and (3) judging competence via students' speech and the choices they make. The students work in pairs at the computers as the teacher circulates to assess and capitalize on teachable moments, which are highlighted in bold.

Boy 1: (reading from the screen) The agencia
Teacher: **Agency?**
Boy 1: The agency is counting on you to complete this mission. Is programmed for a jump to 1-8-7-6
Teacher: **Eighteen seventy-six?**
Boy 1: Yeah. Eighteen seventy-six. Like Thomas Edison in New Jersey…
Teacher: **Thomas Edison?**
Boy 1: Incan..incan..descant light bulb designed in 1-8, Eighteen seventy-nine.
Teacher: **Who is that person? (pointing to the picture on the screen)**
Boy 2: Thomas Edison.
Teacher: **Thomas Edison. He invented all those things (pointing at the screen). The incandescent light bulb. What kind of light bulb?**

Boy 1 and Boy 2: Incandescent.

Boy 2: (reading from the screen) He is off in eighteen thirty-one to vote for John Quincy Adams for Congress in the state named after William Penn.

Teacher: **There are three clues there, right?**

Boy 1: He's gonna um vote for Quincy in a state named after William Penn.

Teacher: **Does anybody know what state that is?**

Boy 2: Pennsylvania.

Teacher: Right. **When?**

Boy 1 & 2: (in unison) Eighteen thirty-one.

During a video talk-back session of this language learning event, the ESOL teacher reported that these boys had been having difficulty with pronouncing and using language particular to U.S. history (dates, place names, proper names); her goal for this session was to review and promote conceptual and phonetic fluency as well as reinforce the people, places, and events they had been studying in their regular classes. As the three converse around comprehension and the informed problem solving and decision making that is needed to be successful in Carmen, we can see the teacher's formative assessment calculus in play. Indeed, she later shared the rationale behind her pairing of these two particular boys, one stronger in reading, the other in speaking, as a strategy to boost complementary skills by modeling and verbal interaction. This segment exemplifies the moment-by-moment work of ESOL professionals as they simultaneously assess individual learner growth in English and content knowledge while pushing the instructional conversation toward improved comprehension and production. Later in this teaching and learning event, a number of dates, place and proper names are worked through while activity remained centered on the intrinsic pull of being immersed in the game.

In addition to using instructional conversations like these as a means of formative assessment and the teaching strategies it generates, ESOL teachers use a variety of methods to document individual student learning in such a way that growth and development are made visible. Linguistic and conceptual development over time can be documented via observation notes, check lists, running records, teacher summaries, and child self- or peer assessments. Such portfolio items can serve to provide cumulative evidence of progress as well as a dynamic yardstick upon which instructional activity can be designed, undertaken, and incorporated in further documentation. Ongoing documentation is critical for instructional planning, informing mainstream teachers and school administrators. It is also a valuable tool to share with students and their parents. Evidence of a learner's successes in comprehension and production from a wide a variety of academic contexts and activities whose substance is repeated at advancing levels over time serves as excellent, documentable measures of learner progress.

Assessing Academic Language and Content through Identity Texts

The previous example illustrated moment-by-moment meaning making with special emphasis on the productive use of language common to social studies. In that brief example, the teacher employed formative assessment strategies to steer learners toward comprehension and production of the target language and academic concepts. Similar purposes are achieved in this second example through the use of identity texts.

Identity texts are student products created in supportive ESOL environments that value formative assessment as an integral, critical component of instructional processes. They are identity texts "insofar as students invest their identities in these texts (written, spoken, visual, musical, or combinations multimodal form) that then hold a mirror up to students in which their identities are reflected back in positive light" (Cummins, Brown & Sayers, 2007, p. 219). In describing these identity texts, Cummins (2008) emphasizes their crucial roles in both formative assessment and ELL children's developing sense of self as a bilingual person. With the popularity of multimodal productivity tools, these kinds of identity texts are becoming prevalent in classrooms of all kinds, but have a special role in ongoing, formative assessment for language and academic growth.

In the following example, the ESOL teacher is committed to informing her individual learners as well as the larger community about each child's strengths and abilities. She is also committed to ongoing assessment, making productive use of learning milestones and student products as evidence and reinforcement of their progress and achievements. Part of the identity text activity is making clear to learners what learning will be evidenced in their products through assessment rubrics, in order to enable student self-assessment along the way.

The following illustration is from a combined pull-out class of K-2 ELLs. The ESOL instructor has the children complete open-ended sentences about themselves with her and their peers' support. The activity resulted in the production of a short biography which included a digital photo taken of the children as they typed the story on the computer. As they worked, the older children assisted the younger ones with these tasks. The ESOL teacher reported, "As I had anticipated, there was a great deal of interaction as they talked and shared with one another. I listened and responded when I saw opportunities for language learning to get pushed. After each narrative was printed, the children took these back to their [mainstream] classroom to share with their [mainstream] classmates before taking it home for their parents to keep." Here is a sample from the session:

> My name is DEBORAH. I am EIGHT years old. I am the DAUGHTER of JEFF and KYOMI and the SISTER of ALICE. My favorite color is ROBIN'S EGG BLUE. My favorite food is RICE. I like to GO SWIMMING. I speak ENGLISH and JAPANESE.

While the child was composing her identity text, the ESOL teacher used the opportunity to both assess her linguistic development and respond to her meaning-focused activity in instructionally productive ways. When Deborah was searching for an English word for her favorite color, the instructor led her to one of many colorful pictures on the classroom walls and motioned for her to indicate the color, urging, "Do you see your color?" Having studied the array of blues, Deborah pointed definitively to a robin's egg on a poster of North American birds. "This," she said proudly. "Ah, blue, right?" responded the teacher. "Yes, blue." "We call this bird (pointing) a robin." "Robin," repeated Deborah (also pointing). At this point the teacher led the child back to the computer and dictated the word *Robin*. When Deborah has successfully typed the word, she looks up at the teacher and gestures the shape of an egg with her thumb and index finger. "Egg. Robin's egg blue. Let's write it." With direct assistance with the

English possessive apostrophe, Deborah succeeds in producing her identity text, one that accurately expresses her preference for robin's egg blue.

This text will become part of Deborah's interactive ESOL portfolio, whereby her ESOL teacher attaches to each submission a sheet of paper, sometimes more than one, on which she and Deborah will communicate throughout the school year. Here the focus is on communicating about the learning as expressed in each portfolio item:

Nice to meet you, Deborah! You can speak TWO languages. That's wonderful. Can you fill in these sentences too?

My nickname is _____.

My favorite subject is _____.

In this context, the ESOL instructor uses each child's portfolio to (1) document for her instructional planning; (2) document for others; and (3) communicate directly through speech and writing with the individual child about her learning progress while responding to teachable moments. It is through simultaneous response to the form and content of such texts that ESOL educators and others can provide supportive, assessment-based feedback to children, their parents and the larger school community.

This interactive use of portfolios has been alternatively labeled *fluency journal* or *fluency portfolio* in language education, a practice whereby the emphasis on student writing and teacher responding lies in written fluency over formal composition. "If teachers respond to their meaning in writing, students are often motivated to rely on their conceptual thinking to write on a deeper level" (Mahn, 2008, p. 131).

USING FORMATIVE ASSESSMENTS AS LEARNING EVENTS

A model of moment-by-moment ELL assessment begins with the premise that action on the part of both participants (teacher and learner) is essential. This action, like the vast majority of human communication, is fast and rarely neat and tidy. Indeed, assessment of dynamic language development is "done more or less on the hoof…you sort of snatch opportunities and you amend in your head and in your ongoing practice, against the summative in which you've actually got particular targets in mind, and you know what you're aiming for, and you either achieve them or partially achieve them" (Focal Teacher, cited in Rea-Dickins & Gardner, 2000, p. 232).

In its being "on the hoof" or "on the fly," formative assessment is an imperfect form of evaluation. Much of the real time opportunity for assessment can be missed by even the most experienced and attentive teaching professionals. Just as there are errors in formal assessments, error is inherent in the kinds of on the fly human judgments and responses reported here. The difference with formative assessment, however, is that the consequences of such errors are most often fleeting and amenable to further learning interactions. This kind of fast paced discourse analysis can be likened to the work of an ethnographer who continually attends and thereby builds knowledge through analysis (García, 1992; Tinajero & Hurley, 2001). It is this genre of formative assessment that is the essential component in the craft of ESOL instruction.

Integral to the work is the ESOL professional's internal syllabi; one for the group as a whole and one for each learner. Learner syllabi map out a learner's trajectory, or a literacy continuum (Lapp et al., 2001). Such syllabi, continua, or trajectories exist in the minds of skilled ESOL educators for each and every English language learner (Meskill et al., 1999). In moment-by-moment decision making, this assessment of learner growth and progress determines subsequent instructional/conversational moves. It is wholly conversational in that it is an authentic negotiation of meaning with others for a productive purpose. It is wholly instructional in that it pushes individual learners along their given trajectories toward linguistic and academic competence; ESOL professionals elicit linguistic output from which subsequent instructional conversation plans will derive. They also make active use of learner output and actions in their instructional decision making. This is a central aspect of academic language learning: moment-by-moment formative assessment via the instructional conversation. The first step is eliciting comprehension and production moves on the part of learners. The knowledge mechanics involved in eliciting and responding to productive student language are complex (Gibbons, 2003; Swain, 1985). Figure 12.1 visually represents the interplay of such elements.

Moment-by-moment formative assessment of learner output, recognition of a teachable moment, and a responsive, targeted piece of instructional conversation are common events in ESOL environments. The real time calculus that ESOL professionals employ reflects a complex knowledge base that includes deep and ongoing understanding of individual children's linguistic and conceptual development in the context of U.S. school culture, as well as an understanding of the English language and how it is acquired (Andrews, 2003; Goldenberg & Patthey-Chavez, 1994). The calculus in turn generates appropriate instructional moves within meaning-focused instructional tasks and the accompanying linguistically and conceptually productive conversations. Teachers of English to speakers of other languages link the knowledge gained from their ongoing formative assessments to their knowledge of the curricular demands of the institution and the individual child.

The direct linkages ESOL professionals make between ESOL class activity and the

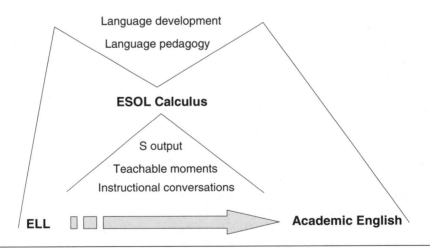

Figure 12.1 Moment-by-moment formative assessment in ELL instruction.

goals and processes of their students' mainstream classes demonstrate the power of enrichment. In the enrichment model, teachers work in tandem with the children's subject matter teachers to ensure their students are skilled in the language and concepts they need to achieve in the mainstream. They likewise work with mainstream teachers to exchange information that both need to better understand and accommodate ELL children in their classes. Armed with this knowledge, mainstream and ESOL teachers can make adjustments accordingly (Echevarria et al., 2008). Although knowledge banks about individual students are difficult to pass on from one educator to another (Rea-Dickins & Gardner, 2000), there are essential accommodations that regular classroom teachers can make (e.g., Goldenberg, 2008) and content knowledge to be shared with the ESOL professional.

CONCLUSION

Although all teachers of ELLs cannot be expected to possess the background, skills, and experience needed to effectively undertake ongoing formative assessments, much headway is currently being made in this direction. Where 10 years ago U.S. teachers never dreamed of having ELLs in their mainstream classrooms, chances are now quite good that they will have linguistic minority children to teach during their careers. Fortunately, along with this increase in ELLs has come multiple efforts to provide non-ELL teachers with background, techniques, and new understandings about newcomers and their linguistic and cultural needs and challenges (Meskill, 2005; Snow et al., 2007; Walqui, 2006).

The goal for English language learners in U.S. schools is that they become full participants in the academic mainstream discourses. Principally, they need to be able to read, write, and understand English sufficiently well to master the content of regular classes and, like their native speaker counterparts, succeed on formal assessments. By conducting and responding productively to ongoing formative assessments of individual progress, ESOL professionals support student progress toward this goal.

In the future, as digital recording technologies become more accessible to educators, the process of ongoing formative assessment for language education will no doubt be further refined and facilitated. Changes to a learner's language trajectory can be documented in real time, serve as rich, flexible data, and can be put to even better, more productive uses in formative assessment practices. Running records of individual children's linguistic and academic development can be used as instructional resources for learner self-assessments, teacher and learner review, instructional planning, as well as for instruction per se. Indeed, in language teacher education, recorded video sequences provide optimal models of powerful instructional conversations, as well as material for analysis in the teacher calculus that factors into the enactment of the verbal, nonverbal and written instructional moves.

REFERENCES

Andrews, S. (2003). Teacher language awareness and the professional knowledge base of the L2 teacher. *Language Awareness*, *12*(2) 81–95.

Atkinson, D. (2002). Toward a sociocognitive approach to second language acquisition. *The Modern Language Journal*, *86*(4), 525–545.

Au, K., & Kawahami, A. (1994). Cultural congruence in instruction. In E. Hollins, J. King, & W. Hayman (Eds.), *Teaching diverse populations: Formulating a knowledge base* (pp. 5–23). Albany, NY: State University of New York Press.

Bailey, A. L., & Heritage, H. M. (2008). *Formative assessment for literacy learning: Developing reading and academic language proficiency together, Grades K-6.* Thousand Oaks, CA: Corwin.

Canale, M. (1987). Language assessment: The method is the message. In D. Tannen & J. Alatis (Eds.), *The interdependence theory, data, and application* (pp. 249–262). Washington, DC: Georgetown University Press.

Canale, M. (1988). The measurement of communicative competence. *Annual Review of Applied Linguistics, 8,* 67–84.

Cazden, C. & Beck, S. (2003). Classroom discourse. In A. Graesser, M. Gernsbacher, & S. Goldman (Eds.), *Handbook of discourse processes* (pp. 165–197). Mahwah, NJ: Erlbaum.

Cummins, J. (1979). Cognitive/academic language proficiency, linguistic interdependence, the optimum age question and some other matters. *Working Papers on Bilingualism, 19,* 121–129.

Cummins, J. (2008). Technology, literacy and young second language learners. In L. Parker (Ed.), *Technology-mediated learning environments for young English learners* (pp. 61–98). Mahwah, NJ: Erlbaum.

Cummins, J., Brown, K., & Sayers, D. (2007). *Literacy, technology and diversity.* Boston: Allyn & Bacon.

Dalton, S., & Sison, J. (1995). *Enacting instructional conversation with Spanish-speaking students in middle school mathematics* (Research Report 12). Washington, DC: Center for Applied Linguistics/National Center for Research on Cultural Diversity and Second Language Learning.

Donato, R. (2000). Sociocultural contributions to understanding the foreign and second language classroom. In J. Lantolf (Ed.), *Sociocultural theory and second language learning* (pp. 27–50). New York: Oxford University Press.

Echevarria, J., Vogt, M. E., & Short, D. (2008). *Making content comprehensible to English learners: The SIOP model* (3rd ed.). Boston: Pearson Allyn & Bacon.

Edelsky, C. (2006). *With literacy and justice for all: Rethinking the social in language education.* Mahwah, NJ: Erlbaum.

Ellis, R. (2003). *Task-based language learning and teaching.* New York: Oxford University Press.

Ellis, R., Tanaka, Y., & Yamazaki, A. (1994). Classroom interaction, comprehension, and the acquisition of L2 word meanings. *Language Learning, 44,* 449–491.

Firth, A., & Wagner, J. (1997). On discourse, communication, and (some) fundamental concepts in SLA research. *Modern Language Journal, 81,* 285–300.

Freeman, D. (2007). Research "fitting" practice: Firth and Wagner, classroom language teaching, and language teacher education. *The Modern Language Journal, 91*(5), 893–906.

García, E. (1992). Effective instruction for language minority students: The teacher. *Journal of Education, 173*(2), 130–141

Genesee, F., Lindholm-Leary, K., Saunders, W., & Christian, D. (2004). *Educating English language learners: A synthesis of research evidence.* Santa Cruz, CA: Center for Research on Education, Diversity & Excellence.

Genesee, F., & Upshur, J. (1996). *Classroom-based evaluation in second language education.* New York: Cambridge University Press.

Gibbons, P. (2003). Mediating language learning: Teacher interactions with ESL students in a content-based classroom. *TESOL Quarterly, 37*(2), 247–273.

Goldenberg, C. (2008). Teaching English language learners: What the research does and does not say. *American Educator,* 8–23.

Goldenberg, C., & Patthey-Chavez, G. (1994). *Discourse processes in instructional conversations: Interactions between teachers and transition readers.* Santa Cruz, CA: National Center for Research in Cultural Diversity and Second Language Learning, University of California, Santa Cruz.

Hargreaves, E. (2005). Assessment for learning? Thinking outside the (black) box. *Cambridge Journal of Education, 35*(2), 213–224.

Hymes, D. (1972). *Towards communicative competence.* Philadelphia: University of Pennsylvania Press.

Lantolf, J., & Poehner, M. (2004). Dynamic assessment of L2 development; bringing the past into the future. *Journal of Applied Linguistics, 1*(1), 49–72.

Lantolf, J., & Poehner, M. (2008). Introduction: Sociocultural theory and the teaching of second languages. In J. Lantolf & M. Poehner (Eds.), *Sociocultural theory and the teaching of second languages* (pp. 1–32). London: Equinox.

Lantolf, J., & Thorne, S. (2006). *The sociogenesis of second language development.* New York: Oxford University Press.

Lapp, D., Fisher, D., Flood, J., & Cabello, A. (2001). An integrated approach to the teaching and assessment of language arts. In S. Hurley & J. Tinjero (Eds.), *Literacy assessment of second language learners* (pp. 1-26). Boston: Allyn & Bacon.

Lightblown, P., & Spada, N. (2006). *How languages are learned.* New York: Oxford University Press.

Mahn, H. (2008). A dialogic approach to teaching L2 writing. In J. Lantolf & M. Poehner (Eds.), *Sociocultural theory and the teaching of second languages* (pp. 115–138). London: Equinox.

Meskill, C. (2005). Infusing English language learner issues throughout professional educator curricula: The Training All Teachers Project. *Teachers College Record, 107*(4), 739–756.

Meskill, C., & Anthony, N. (2005). Foreign language learning with CMC: Forms of online instructional discourse in a hybrid Russian class. *System, 33*(1), 89–105.

Meskill, C., & Anthony, N. (2007). Learning to orchestrate online instructional conversations: A case of faculty development for foreign language educators. *Journal of Computer Assisted Language Learning, 20*(1), 5–19

Meskill, C., Mossop, J., & Bates, R. (1999). *Electronic texts and English as a second language environments.* Albany, NY: National Research Center on English Learning and Achievement. Retrieved April 14, 2008, from http://cela.albany.edu/reports/meskill/meskillelectronic12012.pdf

Poehner, M. (2008). *Dynamic assessment: A Vygotskian approach to understanding and promoting L2 development.* Berlin: Springer Science and Business Media.

Rea-Dickins, P. (2001). Mirror, mirror on the wall: Identifying processes of classroom assessment. *Language Testing, 14*(4), 429–462.

Rea-Dickins, P., & Gardner, S. (2000). Snares and silver bullets: Disentangling the construct of formative assessment. *Language Testing, 17*(2), 215–243.

Savignon, S. (1997). *Communicative competence.* New York: McGraw-Hill.

Schleppergrell, M. (2004). *The language of schooling.* Mahwah, NJ: Erlbaum.

Snow, C. E., Porche, M. V., Tabors, P. O., & Harris, S. R. (2007). *Is literacy enough? Pathways to academic success for adolescents.* Baltimore, MD: Brookes.

Solano-Flores, G. (2008). Who is given tests in what language by whom, when and where? The need for probabilistic views of language in the testing of English language learners. *Educational Researcher, 37*(4), 189–199.

Swain, M. (1985). Communicative competence: Some roles of comprehensible input and comprehensible output in development. In S. Gass & C. Madden (Eds.), *Input in second language acquisition* (pp. 235–253). Rowley, MA: Newbury House.

Tinajero. J., & Hurley, S. (2001). Assessing progress in second-language acquisition. In S. Hurley & J. Tinjero (Eds.), *Literacy assessment of second language learners* (pp. 27–42). Boston: Allyn & Bacon.

Valsiner, J., & van der Veer, R. (1993). The encoding of distance: The concept of the zone of proximal development and its interpretations. In R. Cocking & K. Renninger (Eds.), *The development and meaning of psychological distance* (pp. 35–62). Hillsdale, NJ: Erlbaum.

Walqui, A. (2006). Scaffolding instruction for English language learners: A conceptual framework. *The International Journal of Bilingual Education and Bilingualism, 9*(2), 159–180.

13

FORMATIVE ASSESSMENT PRACTICES
THAT MAXIMIZE LEARNING FOR STUDENTS AT RISK

GERUNDA B. HUGHES

Maximizing the learning for all students should be a realistic, attainable goal for any educational system that truly values the development of all of its human capital. Yet, as the title of this chapter suggests, there are special populations of students that require specific strategies or practices to maximize their learning. Employing business-as-usual practices in the learning environment with so-called at-risk students may not be sufficient in helping them maximize their learning. This chapter will focus on the formative assessment strategies that maximize learning for students who are at risk. But what makes these students at risk, and what is the nature of the formative assessment practices that will maximize their learning? Consideration of these questions begins with what it means to be "at risk."

WHAT DOES IT MEAN TO BE "AT RISK"?

When the term *at risk* is used to describe a population, it begs the question: At risk of what? Individuals can be at risk of losing a job or at risk of contracting a communicable disease; even a nation can be at risk (National Commission on Excellence in Education, 1983). Generally speaking, being *at risk* of something means that a person or thing possesses certain characteristics that interact with a particular environment which, in turn, predisposes them to becoming the victim of a negative outcome if adequate support is not provided to prevent it from taking place. In this chapter, the negative outcome for at-risk students is academic failure.

Characteristics of Persons Who Are At Risk

When a person's characteristics are different in significant ways from the predominant characteristics of the social group in power, the person whose characteristics differ from the majority is likely to find little correspondence between the supports provided by the group in power and her or his needs (Gordon & Yowell, 1994). This lack of correspondence is a function of the operation of a principle of social economy whereby resources are allocated in accordance with the needs, wishes, desires, and valued characteristics of the dominant group. Thus, Gordon and Yowell (1994) define at risk as "a category of persons whose characteristics, conditions in life and circumstances, make it likely that their development and/or education will be less than optimal" (p. 36).

The idea of dominance in any form is incompatible with the principle of equity, which, according to Armour-Thomas and Gopaul-McNicol (1998), is a central tenet of American democracy. Furthermore, they suggest that the problem of access to an adequate education that is responsive to the needs of some learners has led many educators and researchers to question whether the principle of equitable educational opportunity operates in the same way for all children. Thus, when educational equity does not exist for some students, they are *placed* at risk when they experience a significant mismatch between their circumstances and needs and the willingness or capacity of the school or educational system to accept, respond to, or accommodate them in a manner that supports and enables their normal social, emotional, and intellectual growth and development. Consequently, for a population of students, the condition of being at risk or placed at risk is always situational and relative. In other words, it depends.

For example, a hearing student would almost certainly be at risk of academic failure in a classroom where only American Sign Language (ASL) was used and if he or she did not understand or could not communicate in ASL. Similarly, a monolingual student of English would be at risk of academic failure in a classroom in which the teacher and all other students spoke only Spanish. In each of these cases, the students who are at risk of failure in the situations described above would not be, under normal circumstances, at risk. More often, it is the deaf children or the English language learner who is at risk of academic failure in normal situations.

As the preceding examples illustrate, being at risk refers not simply to the characteristics of persons, but to the interactions between the characteristics and the contexts in which the interactions occur. Furthermore, being at risk of failure may be conceptualized as a condition or circumstance brought on by the failure of the environment to support the particular needs of the person, or as the inability of the person to use internal or external resources to alter their circumstances or the environment in order to produce a positive outcome. It takes only one of these conditions to exist to be at risk. Consequently, being at risk of academic failure may be conceptualized as a condition in which learning environments, in particular, are insensitive to the needs of individuals whose personal characteristics are at variance with the valued goals toward which academic learning is directed. Being at risk is not a ubiquitous condition for individuals. Not every person who is at risk of academic failure is universally at risk of all things. For example, not everyone who is an English language learner or an African American or who is deaf is at risk of underachieving. In fact, some persons so characterized achieve extraordinary things and have exemplary lives. In these cases, the evidence shows that such persons develop in environments that are supportive and where obstacles to a positive or successful outcome are circumvented or eliminated (Boykin, 2000; Obiakor & Ford, 2002).

At-risk status for students, then, is a function of the lack of environments to support the needs of those students. Thus, a focus on the characteristics of learning environments and how these may be adjusted is more productive than is a focus on the characteristics of students.

THE INFLUENCE OF CULTURE AND DIVERSITY ON LEARNING AND ACHIEVEMENT

All of the characteristics that make one learner different from another have the potential to place one of them at risk of academic failure; and yet, these differences represent dimensions of a diverse human mosaic. Human learners are more than cognitive beings—they are also cultural beings. They have attitudes, values, beliefs, and interests that shape their worldview and influence their learning (Gordon, DeStefano, & Shipman, 1999). Thus, to the extent that educators are sensitive to and respectful of the diversity in learners' cognition and culture, they will be able to design and manage learning environments that maximize learning and achievement for all learners.

Culture provides the reference points that allow individuals to view themselves not just in terms of their race/ethnicity, social class, or gender, but also in terms of how they are different from and similar to other people. It is the complex sense of self which an individual brings to the classroom that must be acknowledged and integrated into the dynamic culture of the learning environment. Schools are not neutral learning zones (Bourdieu, 1973, 1974); rather, schools embody a particular brand of cultural capital that they use and expect all students to use in some manner. The cultural capital of schools shapes the definitions of success (e.g., going to and graduating from college), the kinds of knowledge schools hold in high esteem (e.g., the classics and mathematics), the nature of the teaching processes most often practiced in them (e.g., group instruction), the forms of assessment they value (e.g., standardized and summative assessments), and the ways in which assessment results are used (e.g., to rank, classify, and sort students) (Olssen, 2004).

In a society where cultural diversity abounds among its citizenry and cultural hegemony defines its educational system, Gordon and Yowell (1994) suggest that what is learned and expected in personal interactions among one's cultural peers may differ significantly from what is expected in educational settings. These differences between cultural expectations and worldviews often lead to cultural dissonance; that is, to perceived conflicts, real or imagined, between a set of rules from one culture and the rules of another. In academic or school settings, culturally based differences in how teachers and students communicate orally or in written form, or how they differentially view and use numbers and time as estimations rather than precise calculations can have a profound effect on student learning and achievement.

The challenge for educational systems is to bridge conflicting cultural gaps so that schools and other learning environments become risk-reducing havens for students. As Gordon and Yowell (1994) note, "Cultural dissonance places students at risk of educational failure" (p. 51), whereas, culturally sensitive formative assessment strategies used by teachers in supportive learning environments hold out the hope of placing students at promise for educational success.

FORMATIVE ASSESSMENT PRACTICES AND AT-RISK STUDENTS

There are a number of definitions of formative assessment in the assessment literature and not all of them agree. In fact, there are some notable differences among them. Often the vocabulary we use as educators starts out with one meaning, but eventually "morphs over time into something entirely different" (Chappuis, 2005, p. 38). Early proponents of formative assessment understood it to be a means for gathering information about student learning in order to inform instruction and improve learning (Bloom, 1968, 1971; Bloom, Hastings, & Madaus, 1971). However, because of the ubiquitous use of assessments for accountability purposes, formative assessment is now at risk of being (mis)understood merely as testing that is done frequently; that originates from sources external to the classroom; and that creates grades or data to be analyzed and used to track student progress toward summative assessments (Chappuis, 2005).

The definition of formative assessment that will serve as the basis for identifying practices that benefit at-risk students was developed by a group of educators, researchers, and scholars under the auspices of the Council of Chief School State Officers (CCSSO), a nonprofit group of public officials who head departments of elementary and secondary education throughout the United States and its jurisdictions. The group considered the definitions of formative assessment proffered by a diverse group of colleagues, including those from other nations where interest in various aspects of formative assessment has existed for years (Black & Wiliam, 1998a; Sadler, 1989; Stiggins, Arter, Chappuis, & Chappuis, 2005). After much deliberation, the members of the group agreed on the following definition: "Formative assessment is a process used by teachers and students during instruction that provides feedback to adjust ongoing teaching and learning to improve students' achievement of intended instructional outcomes" (Council of Chief School State Officers, 2008, p. 3).

It is clear from the above definition that formative assessment is not just a test: It is a process that may employ tests or various other types of formal and informal tools or strategies such as oral questioning, observations, class assignments, homework, quizzes, reflection papers, projects, investigations, or tasks to gauge student learning (Angelo & Cross, 1993; Fennell, 2006). The information generated from these tools and strategies is used to produce feedback to teachers and students in order to ultimately improve learning.

Role of Feedback

Feedback plays a key role in the formative assessment process. From a systems perspective, feedback is "information about the gap between the actual level and the reference level of a system parameter which is used to alter the gap in some way" (Ramaprasad, 1983, p. 4). From a formative assessment perspective, feedback is information about the gap in student learning. The effectiveness of the formative assessment process is dependent on at least two things: the quality of the feedback and the utility of the feedback for making adjustments to teaching and learning. Implicit in the definition of formative assessment, is the assumption that there are two levels of student learning: the current level and the desired level. Information in the feedback should have the effect of reducing, and ultimately eliminating, the gap between the two levels. Furthermore, for maximum effect, the feedback provided by the formative assessment process should be used to make adjustments by both teachers and students.

Teachers may have to adjust a teaching strategy, an example, or an explanation. In making these adjustments, teachers demonstrate a recognition and appreciation that previous attempts at teaching simply were not effective. Furthermore, making adjustments in teaching with the aim of reaching all students, and especially less successful students, leads to improved learning for all students (see Guskey, this volume).

Students also may have to make adjustments. They may have to revisit how they learn, particularly how they use corrective feedback. Successful students typically know how to use corrective feedback to improve their learning. They see the value in learning from their mistakes. Students who are at risk of failure rarely view errors as opportunities to learn. On the contrary, after receiving their scores on an assessment, they may throw their assessments in the nearest wastebasket or ignore any feedback provided by the teacher (Guskey, 2003). In order to maximize the effect of the formative assessment process on their learning, it may be necessary for students who are at risk of academic failure to make adjustments in how they view, process, and use corrective feedback.

In addition to gathering information about what students know and can do, the formative assessment process can be used to provide information about students' affect. Affect, in this context, relates to students' personal perceptions and predispositions about the teaching/learning process or the learning environment. Indeed, teachers may want to determine how students' affect influences or is influenced by the formative assessment strategies designed to enhance their learning. Two affective variables of significant interest are academic efficacy and eagerness to learn. Academic efficacy refers to a student's perceived sense of ability to succeed on academic-related tasks. If students experience success on their academic-related tasks, incrementally and ultimately, then the level of students' academic efficacy should remain high or increase over time.

Eagerness to learn refers to students' engagement in or excitement about the teaching/learning process or the learning environment. If formative assessment strategies are effective, students' eagerness to learn, like their academic efficacy, will remain high or increase over time. Students who are at risk are likely to lack high eagerness to learn because of past academic failures. Periodic assessment of students' affect can provide valuable information about students' dispositions toward learning. The results can be used formatively to make adjustments in students' beliefs about their ability to succeed and their desire to learn.

Formative assessment strategies minimize the effects of the cultural dissonance between the learning environment and the student, and maximize student learning. In order for formative assessment practices to be effective among students who are "at risk," they must accomplish at least two goals: (1) improving student achievement relative to intended instructional outcomes, and (2) thereby reducing or eliminating the at-risk status of students. Student learning can improve but still miss the intended instructional outcomes or goals. Thus, improved learning is a necessary, though not a sufficient, condition to eliminate the status of being at risk. In order for formative assessment strategies to be maximally effective for at-risk students, information gathered from assessments must help students demonstrate that they are successfully progressing toward or have met the intended outcomes. Successful progress toward intended outcomes means keeping pace with increasing demands and expectations across higher levels of training and education. When students are unable to keep up with demands and expectations, even though some improvement is taking place, they soon view their efforts as diminishing returns and most may eventually stop trying.

In his seminal article on formative assessment, Sadler (1989) identified three conditions that are necessary for students, in particular, to benefit from feedback on academic tasks. Students who are at risk of academic failure would be the greatest beneficiaries of the kind of feedback that Sadler described. He argued that a student must: (1) possess a concept of the standard or goal or reference level being aimed for (i.e., know what desired performance looks like); (2) compare the actual or current level of performance with the standard (i.e., know qualitatively the difference between current performance and desired performance); and (3) take appropriate action which leads to some closure of the gap (i.e., know what to do, and do it in order to reduce and ultimately close the gap between current and desired performance).

For most students who are at risk of failure, teachers play a major role in evaluating the extent to which students have engaged in each of the foregoing necessary conditions. However, in order to transition from a state of being at risk to one of not being at risk of academic failure, it is important for students to develop some of the same evaluative skills as their teachers (Sadler, 1989). The evaluative and corrective feedback that teachers provide, coupled with the independently generated feedback that students provide themselves through self-monitoring, can help students make significant progress in their learning.

The ability to assess and evaluate one's own learning through self-monitoring serves both cognitive as well as affective aims. From a cognitive perspective, self-monitoring may help uncover a student's (mis)understanding of a concept, possibly unknown to others, but may help explain qualitatively the difference between current performance and desired performance. From an affective perspective, self-monitoring has the potential to build academic self-efficacy in the learner, especially if the use of the information results in a positive outcome. Clearly, students who are at risk of academic failure can benefit from developing self-evaluative and self-monitoring skills.

Ten Principles of Formative Assessment that Maximize Students' Learning and Reduce the Likelihood Students Will Remain At Risk

The literature on formative assessment practices that benefit all students—particularly students who have been placed at risk of academic failure—builds upon principles that were developed by Nicol and MacFarlane-Dick (2006). Because the locus of formative assessment activity is in the classroom, the 10 principles of good formative assessment are specifically directed at teachers. Teachers are encouraged to compare their current knowledge, skills, and dispositions to those explicated in these 10 principles and use the results formatively to make adjustments in their classrooms and professional practice (Sadler, 1989).

Principle 1: Believe that All Students Can Learn   The belief that all students can learn is a simple proposition. If, however, it is not a core disposition, then it will simply be rhetorical jargon. The belief that all students can learn does not mean that they learn the same things, at the same time, in the same way. Students, like teachers, are individuals, and they come to the teaching/learning process with different likes, dislikes, propensities, talents, and challenges. The belief that all students can learn means believing that, with the proper human and material resources, students can achieve academic goals. The research on teacher effectiveness and teacher expectations, which spans decades, provides evidence of the relationship between teacher beliefs and student learning and achievement (Cruickshank, 1985; Ferguson, 2003; Hawley, Rosenholtz, Goodstien, & Hasselbring, 1984; Irvine, 1991; Johnson and Prom-Jackson, 1986; Ladson-Billings, 1994; Rosenthal and Jacobson, 1968). Irvine (1991) has stated that:

> Effective teachers of minority children [and others who may be at risk] have high expectations for their students. These teachers do not prejudge or categorize students based on standardized test scores, social class, or behavior. When their pupils do not initially master the materials, these effective teachers do not ascribe blame to external factors…nor do they impute negative characteristics to the child. They restructure the learning activities, assuming that the child has not yet mastered the materials, not that the child is incapable or unwilling to learn. (p. 94)

Teachers need to believe that all students can learn to use information about student performance to restructure learning activities. Teachers should ask themselves: "Do I believe that all students can learn?" "How often do I reteach or restructure learning activities when students do not master material the first time it is taught?"

Principle 2: Get to Know Students and Their Communities   Delpit (1995) wrote about the necessity to learn *from* and *about* the people that educators are supposed to teach. Learning about their culture includes learning about their values, customs, beliefs, and the lenses through which they view the world. Delpit provides a good example of why it is important to understand other people's culture. In the following excerpt from *Other People's Children: Cultural Conflict in the Classroom*, she describes the different views that Anglo teachers and Native Alaskan parents have about parenting children. According to Delpit:

> I often heard Anglo teachers in the villages complain that parents don't care about their children. Nothing could have been further from the truth, yet these teachers could not see how care was manifested. They complained that parents didn't make their children come to school, yet the parents believed so strongly in the necessity of respecting children's thinking that they would say that if the child did not want to come to school, then the school must not be a place that welcomed the child. The teachers said that parents didn't make the children do homework, but the parents believed that if the teacher could not present the work so that the child understood its value, then the work must have had no value. In the parents' view, children were not to be coerced with authority, but were to be treated with the respect that provided them with rationales, stated or unstated, to guide them to make decisions based on their own good sense. (pp. 100–101)

In addition, Irvine (1991) noted that cultural misunderstandings between teachers and students often result in conflict and distrust, and place students at risk of school failure. Studies that focus on the cognitive processes among children of different backgrounds have revealed that there are culturally based differences in preferred ways of processing and organizing information. Shade (1982), for example, found that African Americans tend to prefer a field-dependent rather than a field-independent cognitive style. When teachers recognize or appreciate students' preferred ways of learning or demonstrating what they have learned on an assessment task, students' risk of academic failure decreases. By observing or interviewing students, a lot can be learned about who they are culturally, emotionally, socially, and academically. Teachers should ask themselves: "Have I observed that certain groups of students have systematic, preferred ways of approaching or responding to assessment items or tasks?" "Have I attempted to understand their responses in terms of their cultures?"

Principle 3: Learn about Assessment Best Practices and Use Them with At-Risk Students According to Heritage (2007), in the current climate of top-down accountability, too many teachers believe that assessment is synonymous with high-stakes objective testing; that assessment is something done to students after teaching, rather than an activity in which teachers engage with students while they are teaching. Assessment strategies that give students a second chance to demonstrate what they know and can do work well with students who are at risk. Growth portfolio assessment allows students and teachers to document improvements in students' competencies over time. Performance assessment also offers an alternative to forced-choice response assessment; it allows students to demonstrate learning in different modalities, such as writing an essay, singing a song, or building a model. Almost all types of assessment strategies can be used formatively. Using different types of assessment offers students alternative opportunities to provide evidence of achievement if they are disadvantaged by one type or another (Gipps, 1999). Using formative assessment practices regularly can transform both teaching and learning in very positive ways (Stiggins, 2002). An important question for teachers to ask themselves is "How much do I know about how to use formative assessment in your classroom?"

Principle 4: Be Sure Students Understand What the Goal Is and What Desired Performance Looks Like Goals and objectives are usually prescribed at the classroom, school, or system level and are rarely developed in consultation with students. Consequently, teachers and students do not always have the same understanding about the expectations embodied in a goal. Students are better equipped to achieve a learning goal if they understand what the goal is, assume some ownership of it, and can self-assess progress toward it (Doig, 2001; Nicol & MacFarlene-Dick, 2006). Understanding the goal means that there is significant agreement between the goal set by the teacher and the students' conceptions of the goal.

Hounsell (1997) reported that performances on essays in history and psychology among undergraduate students were positively correlated with the degree of the match between students' conceptions of the task and those of their tutors. He concluded that, if students share the same conception of the task or the criteria for assessing and evaluating the task as the teacher or tutor, then the feedback that they receive is likely to be meaningful or used. If the feedback is used, then students are better equipped to demonstrate that they have learned from their errors. Therefore, explicitly stating the goal orally or having students communicate their conceptions of the goal will decrease the probability of misunderstandings about the goal and help improve student performance.

Another way to clarify requirements of the goal is to provide students with written statements of intended outcomes. Statements of expected learning outcomes are generally insufficient to convey the richness of the meaning intended (Yorke, 2003). Hence, another approach that has proven effective in clarifying goals has been to provide students with exemplars of performance. Exemplars are effective for clarifying goals because they provide a standard against which students can compare their work. In addition, an exemplar, particularly one done by another student, provides valuable feedback about what desired performance looks like (Orsmond, Merry, & Reiling, 2002). When students bring completed homework to class, they can use exemplars to compare their work with a sample of work that has been judged to be proficient or above. Students make revisions on their work where necessary and apply what they have learned on a similar homework or classroom assignment. Using an exemplar for criteria generation and a rubric for self-assessment have been shown to have a positive effect, for example, on elementary school students' writing (Andrade, Du, & Wang, 2008).

Clearly, a variety of modalities may be used to clarify goals. Students who are at risk probably would benefit most from the use of exemplars and descriptive rubrics. They provide concrete examples or detailed descriptions of what the desired performance should look like. Teachers who effectively use formative assessment practices to clarify what the goal is and what desired performance looks like work to ensure that they: (a) provide developmentally appropriate explanations of the goal and requirements for the task; (b) provide students with exemplars for homework and in-class assignments or tasks; (c) have students explain their conceptions of the task; (d) allow students to practice the task using the assessment criteria on actual work or through simulated exercises; and (e) help students devise their own assessment criteria for a particular task.

Principle 5: Give High Quality Feedback to Students about Their Learning   High quality feedback helps students improve their learning and performance (Nicol & MacFarlane-Dick, 2006; Sadler, 1989). But as Hattie and Timperley (2007) note, information in the feedback needs to be relevant to the task and fit the needs of the student. Since students come to the classroom with different learning needs, feedback must address those needs so that students do not become or remain at risk of academic failure.

Task-related feedback informs the student about how well a task is being accomplished. First, it lets students know if they understand the goal of the task. Feedback also distinguishes correct from incorrect responses and helps students develop error detection strategies for future use. Over time, students learn to be more effective in applying correct strategies, choosing different strategies, or seeking assistance. In addition, scaffolding strategies which decompose tasks into minitasks help students manage tasks that may otherwise appear to be overwhelming. In essence, when used in concert, these strategies help students become more self-regulated in their learning.

Feedback about learning often comes to students in the form of grades, but grades can have a negative effect on the self-esteem of low achieving students who, by definition, are at risk of academic failure (Craven, Marsh & Debus, 1991). Additionally, it has been demonstrated (Butler 1987, 1988) that assigning grades to student performance has less of an effect on student performance than feedback comments for improving learning. The reason for this is because students often compare their performance against that of others rather than making efforts to correct misunderstandings they may have about a task and thus improve their learning. As Black and Wiliam (1998b) note, any information that draws attention away from the task and toward self-esteem can have a negative effect on attitudes and subsequent performance.

Praise is also a form of feedback. It is important, however, to distinguish between praise that directs attention to the student as self ("Good girl!") and praise directed to the effort, engagement, or completion of the task ("You've done a great job!"). This latter type of praise has a greater effect on achievement because it can assist in enhancing self-efficacy, and thus have an impact on the successful completion of the task (Kluger & DeNisi, 1996). Clearly, students who are at risk of academic failure can benefit from both types of praise. More research on praise as a form of feedback with less successful students may reveal whether there are different patterns of the impact of praise on learning among this population of students.

The quality of the feedback about student learning may also be a function of its delivery mode, timeliness, or tone. Feedback about student learning can be delivered or received both in individual or group settings. While individual settings are preferred, teachers sometimes give feedback to a group of students about group performance. In these instances, quality and usefulness of the feedback about performance may be confounded by the perception that the information pertains to other members of the group and not to oneself. Hence, the effectiveness of the feedback about the task may, according to Nadler (1979), depend on students' commitment and involvement in the task and their notion of whether the feedback relates to their performance. The risk in providing group feedback is that the information needed to progress toward self-regulation may be ignored or missed. Without feedback on an individual level, students who are at risk of academic failure may be put at further risk.

Timeliness and tone are also parameters of the quality of feedback about student learning. Immediate corrective feedback about the processes in carrying out a task is beneficial. This type of feedback allows students to make adjustments or corrections while still completing the task before a summative evaluation of performance is rendered. Summative evaluations of performance are also examples of feedback; however, this type of feedback should be delayed until students have had an opportunity to apply corrective feedback to their work (Kulik & Kulik, 1988).

Both positive and negative feedback can have beneficial effects on student learning. For low self-efficacious students who are at risk of academic failure, positive feedback about initial success may lead to a variety of behaviors. On the one hand, students may become further engaged in the task to remedy any remaining deficiencies and further close the gap between their current performance and the desired performance. Alternatively, they may avoid involving themselves in the task because the positive feedback signals that they have already reached an adequate level of performance and further actions by them may run the risk of disconfirming the favorable feedback, which has already been acquired and will perhaps be difficult to reattain (Kluger & DeNisi, 1996).

To ensure that high quality feedback about student learning helps improve learning, teachers should: (a) make sure that the information provided relates to the task and the criteria for completing the task successfully; (b) provide information that helps students correct their mistakes or errors; (c) avoid giving only grades during the formative stages of completing the task; (d) provide feedback soon after students submit their work; (e) use scaffolding strategies to divide tasks into minitasks; (f) give individual and group feedback, when appropriate; and (g) know when to use positive feedback and how students will respond to it.

Principle 6: Use Results from Formative Assessment Practices to Differentiate Teaching The definition of formative assessment makes clear that information generated in the assessment process is used by teachers to adjust teaching. Employing the science and art of teaching ensures that formative assessment practices will be used in teaching to fully engage students in the teaching and learning process.

The science of good teaching requires teachers to know their content, be able to explain it several ways if necessary, and be able to systematically collect information about student learning in order to discern patterns of understanding as well as misunderstanding. The purpose of teaching is for students to learn. To help a student who is having trouble understanding a concept, teachers must know where and why misunderstandings are occurring. Second, teachers must know how to explain or demonstrate the concept using a variety of modalities, if necessary, in order to facilitate understanding. Third, teachers must be able to collect information about student learning through appropriate assessment techniques in order to inform teaching and help the student close the gap of understanding.

The art of good teaching is illustrated by deferring to the research and writings of some of the most celebrated scholars in the field of culturally relevant teaching. Culturally relevant teaching is mentioned here because it can maximize learning for students who are culturally, ethnically, racially, and linguistically diverse. In the book, *The Dream Keepers: Successful Teachers of African-American Children* (1994, chapter 2, "Does Culture Matter?"), Ladson-Billings describes some of the behaviors of teachers who practice culturally relevant teaching:

> Teachers who practice culturally relevant methods can be identified by the way they see themselves and others. They see their teaching as an *art* rather than a technical skill. They believe that all of their students can succeed rather than that failure is inevitable for some.... They help students make connections between their local, national, racial, cultural, and global identities.... They demonstrate a connectedness with all of their students and encourage the same connectedness between students. They encourage a community of learners; they encourage their students to learn collaboratively. Finally, such teachers are identified by their notions of knowledge: They believe that knowledge is continuously re-created, recycled, and shared by teachers and students alike.... Rather than expecting students to demonstrate prior knowledge and skills, they help students develop that knowledge by building bridges and scaffolding for learning. (p. 25)

Teaching and assessment are interactive and sociocultural activities. Both require the interchange of information between two or more agents for an intended purpose. An agent can be a teacher, a peer, a book, or an assessment. The information is communicated, translated, or received through cultural lenses. Because teaching and assessment are inextricably linked, paying attention to how one teaches provides evidence of how one is likely to assess. Teachers who use culturally relevant teaching strategies in order to engage students from multicultural backgrounds are most likely to embrace culturally sensitive assessment strategies in a formative way so that all students, regardless of their cultural background, will have opportunities to demonstrate what they know and can do. Another poignant example of how culturally based values can manifest themselves in teaching and ultimately in assessing student learning is found in Delpit's (1995) *Other People's Children: Cultural Conflict in the Classroom*. In the following excerpt, Delpit illustrates how knowledge of students' background is used to inform a technique for teaching reading. It also begs the question: Which assessment strategy likely would yield more information about the Native children's reading comprehension—one which involved a group activity or one that required individual recitation? Delpit wrote:

> The Native Alaska teachers usually adopted strategies their progressive administrators thought were outdated: they continued to have children read texts aloud as a group. Since my role as literacy instructor was to update teaching techniques…I tr[ied] to get the Native teachers to change their instructional practices. Having learned…the necessity of learning from the people I was supposed to teach, I presented my "suggestions" by initiating discussion. The comments of the Native teachers were enlightening. They let me know that in order to engage their Native students and to ensure understanding of what was often a text about foreign concepts, they found it vital to read as a group. They believed that students could eventually be led to reading on their own, but that first they needed to introduce them to the new skill and the new concepts in contexts they already found familiar, namely, interactions with people rather than with books. Connectedness was an issue once again…. We risk failure in our educational reforms by ignoring the significance of human [or student] connectedness in many communities of color. (pp. 94–95)

The alignment of culturally relevant teaching and culturally sensitive assessment cannot be understated or overestimated. In fact, the notions of culturally based education can be expanded to include culturally responsive schooling. Castagno and Brayboy (2008) provide a comprehensive review of the literature on culturally responsive schooling for Indigenous youth. In defining culturally responsive schooling, they note that the dynamic nature of the word responsiveness suggests the ability to acknowledge the unique needs of diverse students, take action to address those needs, and be flexible when identifying strategies to meet those needs as demographics change over time. Furthermore, in harmony with Ladson-Billings (1994), Pewewardy and Hammer (2003) describe culturally responsive schooling as "that which builds a bridge between a child's home culture and the school to effect *improved learning and school achievement*" [emphasis added] (p. 1).

All teaching has a cultural basis and is relevant to some students. The question is whether teaching and the associated assessment meet the needs of all students for which they are intended and do students learn as a result of participating in these socio-cultural activities? If only we would look below the surface, we would find that there is an abundance of research on the effects of using culturally relevant information about students and their performance to inform, guide, and shape teaching. In order to use the results of formative assessment activities to shape teaching, teachers should: (a) learn about students and their communities and use the information to inform classroom teaching and assessment; (b) employ culturally relevant teaching and assessment in the classroom; and (c) use a variety of assessment strategies such as portfolios and performance tasks to gather information about student learning and to provide an opportunity for students who may be disadvantaged by one assessment method to demonstrate competency using another method.

Principle 7: Engage Students in the Assessment Process   Whereas most teaching and assessment is, in reality, teacher-centered, research shows that students benefit most when they develop the capacity to assess their own learning and evaluate the feedback they receive from other external sources (Butler & Winne, 1995). This focus on student-centered assessment in the classroom represents a shift in the teaching-assessment relationship between teachers and students. Traditionally, the relationship between teacher and student is top-down: Teaching and assessing are what teachers do to students, not with them. Teachers articulate the goals, create the tasks, define the criteria for assessment and evaluation, and set the assessment timetable. An important component and consequence of formative assessment, however, is the involvement of students in the process at a level where they begin to monitor and reflect on their own performance in order to become self-monitoring and self-regulating (see Andrade, this volume; Topping, this volume). Developing these nontraditional teacher–student relationships around assessment is not straightforward or easy. In the classroom culture, power is imputed to teachers, and they and their students must learn how to share power for the sake of good assessment.

Peer involvement in students' formative assessment is also beneficial in a variety of ways (Topping, this volume). First, peers who have just learned something are often better able than teachers to explain it to their classmates in a language and manner that is clearer because they have similar frames of reference. Second, peers expose students to different perspectives, strategies, and understandings that allow students to alter or revise their original (mis)understandings and construct new knowledge and meanings. Third, through peer-to-peer interaction, students develop evaluative skills that they will use on their own or other's work. Fourth, peer feedback and discussions allow students to expose their weaknesses without the fear of ridicule, criticism, or shame before a significant-other adult such as the teacher. Lastly, peer group feedback about performance is akin to cooperative learning arrangements which have been shown to be very successful in improving achievement among traditionally low-performing students (Slavin, 1980).

Engaging students in the assessment process may not be easy, but will reap many benefits for students if teachers make classroom formative assessment student-centered and use the power of peers to help students develop evaluative skills that promote self-monitoring and self-regulation.

Principle 8: Provide Students with Multiple Opportunities to Demonstrate the Desired Performance   Feedback about their performance allows a student's performance to converge, in an iterative way, to the desired performance. If feedback is not turned into action soon after it is produced, then there is a good chance there will be a missed opportunity for learning. As Boud (2000) notes:

> The only way to tell if learning results from feedback is for students to make some kind of response to complete the feedback loop (Sadler, 1989). This is one of the most often forgotten aspects of formative assessment. Unless students are able to use the feedback to produce improved work, through, for example, re-doing the same assignment, neither they nor those giving the feedback will know that it has been effective. (p. 158)

If students are allowed to use feedback to redo the same assignment before going on to the next it is time-consuming; and redoing the same assignment while going on to the next may overwhelm students who already are struggling. Therefore, providing students with opportunities to close the gap between current and desired performance may mean reducing the amount of content that is to be covered. In doing so, the mantra "less is more" will prevail. Having less material to cover provides more opportunities for students to demonstrate the desired performance and close the gap. Therefore, teachers should remember to: (a) provide multiple opportunities for resubmission of work; (b) focus feedback on the criteria for completing the task at a desired performance; and (c) divide the task into subtasks and provide feedback on each subtask.

Principle 9: Help Students Build Academic Self-Efficacy   Self-efficacy is the belief in one's own capability to perform a particular task or manage a particular situation. Academic self-efficacy is the belief that one can succeed at academic tasks. It is a student's "Yes, I can" or "No, I can't" belief. A distinction is drawn between self-efficacy and academic self-efficacy because self-efficacy is task-specific or situational. Many students have low academic self-efficacy because of persistent past academic failures. Consequently, they may resist attending to academic tasks while, on the other hand, fully engaging in nonacademic activities in which they have experienced success (e.g., sports, extra-curricular activities). In general, self-efficacy influences: (a) the activities in which students engage; (b) how much effort they exert; (c) how persistent they are when obstacles arise; and (d) the level of performance to which they will aspire (Bandura & Schunk, 1981; Lent, Brown, & Larkin, 1984). Students who have low academic self-efficacy do not expect to do well in school. Too often, these students have the ability to achieve academically; they just do not believe that they do.

Interestingly, students who may be at risk of academic failure may not necessarily exhibit low academic self-efficacy. The reason: Students who have low academic self-efficacy do not believe that they have the capability to succeed at a particular academic task; whereas, students who are at risk of academic failure may believe that they have the capability to succeed at a particular academic task, but find themselves in an environment that does not provide the support they need in order to be successful. According to Pajares (1996), Graham's (1994) summary of the literature on expectancy beliefs indicated that African-American students "maintain undaunted optimism and positive self-regard even in the face of achievement failure" (p.103). Lay and Wakstein (1985) reported similar findings for a sample of Hispanic-American students. Thus, it is important for teachers to build on this positive sense of self that students bring to the classroom, in spite of their past experiences, in order to improve their learning and achievement.

Assessment should be a positive learning experience for students; however, for students who are chronically low-achievers, assessment is a constant reminder that they are not up to par. Studies have shown that, contrary to expectations, frequent high-stakes assessment can lower the motivation to learn (Harlen & Crick, 2003). Teachers, however, can use formative assessment strategies to change students' perceptions of the goals and purposes of assessment and the uses of assessment results. Teachers can help build students' academic self-efficacy when they: (a) believe that their student can be academically successful; (b) help students set realistic goals; (c) provide support through instruction, assessment, and feedback about how students can demonstrate the desired performance; (d) give students multiple chances to demonstrate the desired performance; (e) provide verbal, "Yes, you can!" expressions, where appropriate; and (f) identify academic role models that students can emulate—including peers and self (Schunk & Hanson, 1985, 1988).

Principle 10: Help Students Become Self-Regulated Learners There has been an increasing interest in implementing strategies in the classroom that encourage students to take a more active role in the management of their own learning (Butler & Winne, 1995; Nicol, 1997). Black and Wiliam (1998a) argue that a student who blindly follows the prescription of a teacher without understanding its purpose will not learn. Sadler (1989) states that instructional systems are deficient that do not clearly provide for students to acquire evaluative expertise like that of their teachers. The research of these scholars as well as others shows that direct involvement by students in assessing, monitoring, and reflecting on their own work is highly effective in enhancing learning and achievement (Andrade, this volume; McDonald & Boud, 2003).

All students try to self-regulate their academic learning; however, some students are more skillful self-regulators than others. Zimmerman (1998) describes self-regulated learners as individuals whose "view of academic learning as something they do for themselves rather than as something that is done to or for them" (p. 1). Less skillful self-regulators, however, are more inclined to depend on external factors such as the teacher for goal setting, strategic planning, and feedback (Hattie & Timperley, 2007). Students who are at risk of academic failure are more likely to be what Zimmerman (1998) refers to as naïve self-regulators. Naïve self-regulators tend to have low levels of academic self-efficacy, short attention spans or low interest in school tasks. They are not effective in monitoring their own progress and are less likely to engage in self-evaluation. Moreover, when they engage in self-evaluation, naïve self-regulators tend to be negative. Finally, naïve self-regulators tend to attribute their performance to ability-related factors, whereas, skillful self-regulators are more likely to attribute their performance to strategy selection and effort.

The development of self-regulated learning does not happen by chance. In order for students to progress toward self-regulation, teachers must create formal and structured opportunities for the development of self-regulating and evaluative skills. Students who are characterized as being at risk can learn to be lifelong learners without the label of being at risk if these skills are developed progressively over time (Boud, 2000). To that end, teachers who want to help students develop self-regulation skills are encouraged to: (1) select tasks that are of interest to students and that are connected with their communities—it engages them; (2) have students participate in developing assessment criteria—it makes the goal clear; (3) have students identify the strengths and weaknesses of their peers' work—it shows that they know how to apply assessment criteria; (4) have students identify the strengths and weaknesses of their own work—it shows that they know how to apply assessment criteria objectively; (5) provide exemplars or rubrics so that students can compare their work to models or standards—it gives them concrete examples of what the desired performance looks like so that they can make revisions to their own work, if necessary; (6) allow multiple opportunities for students to demonstrate the desired performance on academic tasks with each opportunity representing a successful step toward "closing the gap"—it builds academic self-efficacy; and (7) make the development of self-regulated learners part of the classroom teaching and assessment culture—it will create lifelong learners.

These 10 principles of formative assessment are not intended to be mutually exclusive or exhaustive. There are other principles that can be added to the list. All of the principles are supported by research; therefore, teachers, in particular, are encouraged to conduct their own research in their own classrooms and schools, collaborate with colleagues in the same school building or with teachers in other schools, apply what works, and aim to use formative assessment practices to place students "at promise" for educational success, and not at risk of educational failure.

DIRECTIONS FOR FUTURE RESEARCH AND DEVELOPMENT

Even though interest in and research on formative assessment are growing, the basic premises of formative assessment are not new. They are grounded in the research literature on mastery learning that emerged more than 5 decades ago (see Guskey, this volume). At the risk of oversimplifying the processes, the premises of mastery learning and formative assessment are basically these: set goals; teach students; assess students' learning; compare students' performance to goals; measure the gap; reteach, if necessary; then, reassess and repeat the process until all desired goals are reached. It seems simple enough, but if these steps were all that were necessary to understand how to use formative assessment effectively, there would not be the constant concern about the gap in student performance between those who are at risk and those who are not. Effective use of formative assessment practices can level the academic playing field for all students. Implementation studies can help identify the procedures, infrastructures, and resources that are necessary for effective use of formative assessment practices in classrooms and schools that serve at risk students (Popham, 2006; Wiliam, 2007).

Teaching, Learning, Assessment, and Student Characteristics

Studies that examine the relationships among teaching, learning, assessment, and student characteristics can help researchers discern patterns of effectiveness for critical components of formative assessment such as feedback. For example, Hattie and Timperley (2007) noted that personal feedback such as praise rarely translates into more engagement on the task, commitment to learning goals, or enhanced self-efficacy. Furthermore, Wilkinson's (1981) meta-analysis on teacher praise concluded that it contributes little, if anything, to student achievement. This may be true for students, in general, but what about students who are at risk academically? Do they benefit from praise (as a form of encouragement) when they successfully complete a task? What effect, if any, does personal praise from a beloved teacher have on a student's motivation to complete a task? More research is needed to investigate the relationships between self-efficacy, academic self-efficacy, motivation, and self-regulation of culturally, linguistically, ethnically, and racially diverse students and teachers' attitudes and behaviors toward them, especially as teachers attempt to implement formative assessment practices in a climate of high-stakes testing and accountability. As populations of these students continue to grow in American schools, it will become ever more important to have a body of research findings that can be used to inform educational practice.

Toward a Theory of Effective Formative Assessment

Within the sociological and anthropological education literatures, there are several theories that attempt to explain the academic failure experienced by students who are characterized as being at risk. Cultural deprivation theory assumes that certain students fail in school because they are deficient in the cultural capital that supports and promotes school success (Bourdieu, 1973, 1974). Cultural conflict theory asserts that certain students possess values, beliefs, skills, ways of knowing, and worldviews that are not recognized or appreciated by schools for instructional and assessment purposes (Delpit, 1995). Cultural hegemony theory purports that middle class values dominate throughout society and schools are the primary progenitor of those values to the detriment of students from the lower social classes, in particular (Gordon & Yowell, 1994). There is also the theory that the existence of a castelike structure in society influences certain students' perceptions of schooling and subsequently has an effect on their performance (Ogbu, 1978). In each of these cases, there are winners and losers. The losers in every case are students who have been placed at risk because of their circumstances or personal characteristics.

What is needed is a theory about teaching, learning, and assessment that acknowledges and values individual differences and uses an equity-based approach to education and schooling that results in the elimination of learning and performance gaps that are explained, in part, by students' personal (not academic) characteristics. A theory of effective formative assessment should take into consideration issues related to measurement, curriculum development, professional development, student motivation, and self-regulation (Schunk & Zimmerman, 1998; Shepard, 2000; Zimmerman & Schunk, 2001).

Teachers' Attitudes and Behaviors Toward Academically At Risk Students and the Effectiveness of Formative Assessment Practices

When formative assessment is practiced as intended, it is highly interactive. Teachers and students constantly exchange information about student progress toward the desired goal using various modalities. Implicit in this exchange is an understanding that excellence, through incremental improvement, is desired and expected. Research, however, has consistently documented that teachers often form negative attitudes about at risk students and these attitudes are reflected in their classroom behaviors and expectations. Winfield (1986) reported on the different ways teachers interact with high- and low-expectation students. Low-expectation students are criticized more often for failure and praised less frequently for success; they are provided with less accurate feedback and are called on less often to respond to oral questions; they do not receive as much attention as high-expectation students and teachers interact with them less frequently and demand less work and effort.

Thus, a promising area of research is in examining teachers' attitudes and classroom behaviors toward students who are at risk of academic failure and whether those attitudes and behaviors are complicit in retarding student learning or helpful in maximizing it. Sullivan (2004) noted that students who are educationally traumatized are highly skilled at upsetting teachers who want to teach them. These students are experts in creating chaos, disruption, and undermining behavior. They are masters at noncompliance, noncooperation, and antisocial behaviors. These students are perfect candidates to be ignored or left behind. Sullivan (2004) suggests that, if a teacher encounters a student with these characteristics, she should approach the student in a new way. There should be a willingness on the teacher's part to keep such students at the "forefront of their educational endeavors and not cast them out" (p. 398) or be judgmental or reactionary. Teachers need to be able to make learning attractive to students who have turned their backs on it, and to engage students' interest sufficiently to change a lifetime of negative attitudes on the part of the students who are at risk.

Drunte (2002) examined the extent to which sociocultural factors influenced teachers' perceptions of classroom behavior among students with learning disabilities. The study concluded that teachers' perceptions of students affected teachers' instructional patterns and interactions with their students. When formative assessment is implemented properly, it is very interactive. Students who are at risk of failure because of learning disabilities may be placed further at risk if teachers tend to have less interaction with them because of their disabilities.

Sometimes teachers' attitudes toward students are racially or ethnically based. Cooper, Baturo, Warren, and Doig (2004) reported on teachers' perceptions of mathematics learning among Aboriginal and non-Aboriginal students. The results of this study revealed that White teachers' perceptions of their Black Aboriginal students and their families originated from a deficit model. The two main deficits identified by the teachers were school readiness and attendance. Teachers believed that Aboriginal students were not able to adapt to the culture of school because of a lack of interest in learning in the home environment. There is evidence that teachers' unfounded negative beliefs about students who are racially and ethnically different from themselves crosses national and cultural boundaries. Woolman (2002) investigated this phenomenon in four countries —India, Nigeria, the United Kingdom, and the United States. The results of this study revealed that teachers' negative perceptions about minority children can be reversed and can have the effect of keeping at risk students from dropping out of school and experiencing educational failure. Research on how best to expose and reverse teachers' negative perceptions that adversely affect student learning and achievement should be a top priority for educational systems that are interested in developing all of their human capital.

Gordon (1996) has stated: "The most fundamental issues concerning human diversity, equity and educational assessment have to do with the effectiveness and sufficiency of teaching and learning" (p. 1). Formative assessment is fundamental to effective teaching and sufficient for guaranteeing that all students, regardless of their demographic backgrounds, can learn and demonstrate what they know and can do.

REFERENCES

Andrade, H., Du, Y., & Wang, X. (2008). Putting rubrics to the test: The effect of a model, criteria generation, and rubric-referenced self-assessment on elementary school students' writing. *Educational Measurement: Issues and Practice, 27*(2), 3–13.

Angelo, T. A., & Cross, K. P. (1993). *Classroom assessment techniques: A handbook for college teachers* (2nd ed.). San Francisco: Jossey-Bass.

Armour-Thomas, E., & Gopaul-McNicol, S. (1998). *Assessing intelligence: Applying a biocultural model.* Thousand Oaks, CA: Sage.

Bandura, A., & Schunk, D. H. (1981). Cultivating competence, self-efficacy, and intrinsic interest through proximal self-motivation. *Journal of Personality and Social Psychology, 41,* 586–598.

Black, P., & Wiliam, D. (1998a). Assessment and classroom learning. *Assessment in Education, 5*(1), 7–71.

Black, P., & Wiliam, D. (1998b). Inside the black box: Raising standards through classroom assessment. *Phi Delta Kappan, 80*(2), 139–148.

Bloom, B. S. (1968). Learning for mastery. *Evaluation Comment, 1*(2), 1–12.

Bloom, B. S. (1971). Mastery learning. In J. H. Block (Ed.), *Mastery learning: Theory and practice* (pp. 47–63). New York: Holt, Rinehart & Winston.

Bloom, B. S., Hastings, J. T., & Madaus, G. F. (1971). *Handbook on formative and summative evaluation of student learning.* New York: McGraw-Hill.

Boud, D. (2000). Sustainable assessment: Rethinking assessment for the learning society. *Studies in Continuing Education, 22*(2), 151–167.

Bourdieu, P. (1973). Cultural reproduction and social reproduction. In R. Brown (Ed.), *Knowledge, education and social change* (pp. 71–112). London: Tavistock.

Bourdieu, P. (1974). The school as a conservative force. In J. Eggleston (Ed.), *Contemporary research in the sociology of education* (pp. 32–46). London: Methuen.

Boykin, A. W. (2000). The talent development model of schooling: Placing students at promise for academic success. *Journal of Education for Students Placed at Risk, 5*(1–2), 3–25.

Butler, R. (1987). Task-involving and ego-involving properties of evaluation: Effects of different feedback conditions on motivational perceptions, interest and performance. *Journal of Educational Psychology, 78*(4), 210–216.

Butler, R. (1988). Enhancing and undermining intrinsic motivation: The effects of task-involving and ego-involving on interest and involvement. *British Journal of Educational Psychology, 58,* 1–14.

Butler, D. L., & Winne, P. H. (1995). Feedback and self-regulated learning: A theoretical synthesis. *Review of Educational Research, 65*(3), 245–281.

Castagno, A., & Brayboy, B. (2008). Culturally responsive schooling for Indigenous youth: A review of the literature. *Review of Educational Research, 78*(4), 941–993.

Chappuis, S. (2005, August 10). Is formative assessment losing its meaning? *Education Week, 24*(44), 38.

Cooper, T. J., Baturo, A. R., Warren, E., & Doig, S. M. (2004). Young white teachers' perceptions of mathematics learning of Aboriginal and non-Aboriginal students in remote communities. In J. Mari & A. Fuglestad

(Eds.), *Proceedings 28th Annual Conference of the International Group for the Psychology of Mathematics Education, 2,* 239–246.

Council of Chief State School Officers. (2008). *Attributes of effective formative assessment.* Washington, DC: Author.

Craven, R. G., Marsh, H. W., & Debus, R. L. (1991). Effects of internally focused feedback and attributional feedback on enhancement of academic self-concept. *Journal of Educational Psychology, 83,* 17–27.

Cruickshank, D. R. (1986). Profile of an effective teacher. *Educational Horizon, 64*(2), 80–86.

Delpit, L. (1995). *Other people's children: Cultural conflict in the classroom.* New York: New Press.

Doig, S. M. (2001). Developing an understanding of the role of feedback in education. *Teaching and Education News, 9*(2). Retrieved December 31, 2007, from http://www.tedi.uq.edu.au/TEN/TEN_previous/TEN2_99/ ten2_doig.html

Drunte, E. (2002). Socio-cultural context effects on teachers' readiness to refer for learning disabilities. *Exceptional Children, 69*(1), 41–53.

Fennell, F. (2006, December). Go ahead, teach to the test! *NCTM News Bulletin.*

Ferguson, R. F. (2003). Teachers' perceptions and expectations and the black-white test score gap. *Urban Education, 38*(4), 460–507.

Gipps, C. (1999). Socio-cultural aspects of assessment. *Review of Research in Education, 24,* 355–392.

Gordon, E. W. (1996). Towards an equitable system of educational assessment. *Journal of Negro Education, 64*(3), 1–13.

Gordon, E., DeStefano, L., & Shipman, S. (1999). Characteristics of learning persons and the adaptation of learning environments. In E.W. Gordon (Ed.), *Education and justice: A view from the back of the bus* (pp. 89–103). New York: Teachers College Press.

Gordon, E., & Yowell, C. (1994). Cultural dissonance as a risk factor in the development of students. In R. J. Rossi (Ed.), *Schools and students at risk* (pp. 51–69). New York: Teachers College Press.

Graham, S. (1994). Motivation in African Americans. *Review of Educational Research, 64,* 55–118.

Guskey, T. (2003). How classroom assessments improve learning. *Educational Leadership, 60*(5), 6–11.

Harlen, W., & Crick, R. D. (2003). Testing and motivation for learning. *Assessment in Education, 10*(2), 169–207.

Hattie, J. A., & Timperley, H. (2007). The power of feedback. *Review of Educational Research, 77*(1), 81–112.

Hawley, W. D., Rosenholtz, S. J., Goodstien, H., & Hasselbring, T. (1984). Effective teaching. *Peabody Journal of Education, 61*(4), 15–52.

Heritage, M. (2007). Formative assessment: What do teachers need to know and do? *Phi Delta Kappan, 89*(2), 7–10.

Hounsell, D. (1997). Contrasting conceptions of essay-writing. In F. Marton, D. Hounsell, & N. Entwistle (Eds.), *The experience of learning: Implications for teaching and studying in higher education* (2nd ed., pp. 106–125). Edinburgh, Scotland: Scottish Academic Press.

Irvine, J. J. (1991). *Black students and school failure: Policies, practices, and prescriptions.* New York: Greenwood.

Johnson, S., & Prom-Jackson, S. (1986). The memorable teacher: Implications for teacher selection. *Journal of Negro Education, 55*(3), 272–283.

Kluger, A. N., & DeNisi, A. (1996). The effects of feedback interventions on performance: A historical review, a meta-analysis, and a preliminary feedback intervention theory. *Psychological Bulletin, 119,* 254–284.

Kluger, A. N., & DeNisi, A. (1998). Feedback interventions: Towards the understanding of a double-edged sword. *Current Directions in Psychological Science, 7,* 67–72.

Kulik, J. A., & Kulik, C-L. C. (1988). Timing of feedback and verbal learning. *Review of Educational Research, 58,* 79–97.

Ladson-Billings, G. (1994). *The dreamkeepers: Successful teachers of African American children.* San Francisco, CA: Jossey-Bass.

Ladson-Billings, G. (1995). But that's just good teaching! The case for culturally relevant pedagogy. *Theory Into Practice, 34*(3), 159–165.

Lay, R., & Wakstein, J. (1985). Race, academic achievement, and self-concept of ability. *Research in Higher Education, 22,* 43–64.

Lent, R. W., Brown, S. D., & Larkin, K. C. (1984). Relation of self-efficacy expectations to academic achievement and persistence. *Journal of Counseling Psychology, 31,* 356–362.

McDonald, B., & Boud, D. (2003). The impact of self-assessment on achievement: The effects of self-assessment training on performance in external examinations. *Assessment in Education, 19*(2), 209–220.

Nadler, D. (1979). The effects of feedback on task group behavior: A review of the experimental research. *Organizational Behavior and Human Performance, 23,* 309–338.

National Commission on Excellence in Education. (1983). *A nation at risk: The imperative for educational reform.* Washington, DC: U.S. Government Printing Office.

Nicol, D. J. (1997). *Research on learning and higher education teaching* (UCoSDSA Briefing Paper No. 45). Sheffield, England: Universities and Colleges Staff Development Agency.

Nicol, D. J., & MacFarlane-Dick, M. (2006). Formative assessment and self-regulated learning: A model and seven principles of good feedback practice. *Studies in Higher Education, 31*(2), 199–218.

Obiakor, F., & Ford, B. A. (Eds.). (2002). *Creating successful environments for African American learners with exceptionalities.* Thousand Oaks, CA: Corwin.

Ogbu, J. U. (1978). *Minority education and caste: The American system in cross-cultural perspective.* New York: Academic.

Olssen, M. (2004). Introduction. In M. Olssen (Ed.), *Culture and learning: Access and opportunity in the classroom* (pp. 1–27). Greenwich, CT: Information Age.

Orsmond, P., Merry, S., & Reiling, K. (2002). The use of formative feedback when using student-derived marking criteria in peer and self-assessment. *Assessment & Evaluation in Higher Education, 27*(4), 309–323.

Pajares, F. (1996). Self-efficacy beliefs in academic settings. *Review of Educational Research, 66*(4), 543–578.

Pewewardy, C., & Hammer, P. (2003). *Culturally responsive teaching for American Indian students.* Charleston, WV: ERIC Clearinghouse on Rural Education and Small Schools.

Popham, W. J. (2006). Phony formative assessments: Buyer beware! *Educational Leadership, 64*(3), 86–87.

Ramaprasad, A. (1983). On the definition of feedback. *Behavioral Science, 28*, 4–13.

Rosenthal, R., & Jacobson, L. (1968). *Pygmalion in the classroom.* New York: Holt, Rinehart and Winston.

Sadler, D. R. (1989). Formative assessment and the design of instructional systems. *Instructional Science, 18*, 119–144.

Schunk, D. H., & Hanson, A. R. (1985). Peer model: Influence on children's self-efficacy and achievement. *Journal of Educational Psychology, 77*, 313–322.

Schunk, D. H., & Hanson, A. R. (1988). Influence of peer-model attributes on children's beliefs and learning. *Journal of Educational Psychology, 81*, 431–434.

Schunk, D. H., & Zimmerman, B. J. (Eds.). (1998). *Self-regulated learning: From teaching to self-reflective practice.* New York: Guilford.

Shade, B. J. (1982). Afro-American cognitive style: A variable in school success? *Review of Educational Research, 52*, 219-244.

Shepard, L. A. (2000). The role of assessment in a learning culture. *Educational Researcher, 29*(7), 4–14.

Slavin, R. E. (1980). Cooperative learning. *Review of Educational Research, 50*, 315–342.

Stiggins, R. J. (2002). Assessment crisis: The absence of assessment FOR learning. *Phi Delta Kappan, 83*(10), 758–765.

Stiggins, R. J., Arter, J., Chappuis, J., & Chappuis, S. (2005). *Classroom assessment for student learning: Doing it right—using it well.* Princeton, NJ: Educational Testing Service.

Sullivan, K. (2004). Educational trauma and "at-risk" students. In M. Olssen (Ed.), *Cultural and learning: Access and opportunity in the classroom* (pp. 387–399). Greenwich, CT: Information Age.

Wiliam, D. (2007). Changing classroom practice. *Educational Leadership, 65*(4), 36–42.

Wilkinson, S. S. (1981). The relationship of teacher praise and student achievement: A meta-analysis of selected research. *Dissertation Abstracts International, 41*(9-A), 3998.

Winfield, L. F. (1986). Teacher beliefs toward academically at risk students in inner urban schools. *The Urban Review, 18*(4), 253–267.

Woolman, D. C. (2002, March). *Lost educational opportunity: Can the first and third worlds inform each other and transfer solutions?* Paper presented at the annual meeting of the Comparative and International Education Society, Orlando, FL.

Yorke, M. (2003). Formative assessment in higher education: Moves toward theory and the enhancement of pedagogic practice. *Higher Education, 45*, 477–501.

Zimmerman, B. J. (1998). Developing self-fulfilling cycles of academic regulation: An analysis of exemplary instructional models. In D. H. Schunk & B. F. Zimmerman (Eds.), *Self-regulated learning: From teaching to self-reflective practice* (pp. 1–19). New York: Guilford.

Zimmerman, B. J. (2001). Theories of self-regulated learning and academic achievement: An overview and analysis. In B. Zimmerman & D. H. Schunk (Eds.), *Self-regulated learning and academic achievement: Theoretical perspectives* (2nd ed., pp. 1–38). Mahwah, NJ: Erlbaum.

Zimmerman, B. J., & Schunk, D. H. (2001). *Self-regulated learning and academic achievement: Theoretical perspectives* (2nd ed.). Mahwah, NJ: Erlbaum.

14

ESSENTIAL FORMATIVE ASSESSMENT COMPETENCIES FOR TEACHERS AND SCHOOL LEADERS

RICK STIGGINS

The typical teacher will spend one quarter to one third of her or his available professional time involved in assessment-related activities (Dorre-Bremme & Herman, 1986; Stiggins & Conklin, 1992). Overwhelming evidence cited in earlier chapters in this volume reveals that students' achievement is strongly related to their teachers' ability to develop or select high-quality classroom assessments and to use them productively to support learning—not merely grade it. This requires that teachers develop appropriate levels of assessment literacy.

In this same sense, demands for accountability and expectations of increasing test scores require that principals serve as instructional leaders, not merely building managers. Instructional leadership must include leadership in assessment. Consequently, assessment literacy also underpins success as a principal.

However, the vast majority of currently practicing teachers and administrators graduated from preservice preparation programs almost completely devoid of the relevant, helpful assessment training needed to fulfill their rapidly evolving responsibilities (Black & Wiliam, 1998; Crooks, 1988; Stiggins & Conklin, 1992). As a result, few prospective educators have the opportunity to develop the essential assessment competencies needed to launch their careers. Further, because in-service professional development opportunities in assessment also remain infrequent, assessment illiteracy abounds. It has been so for decades.

Given the great potential of assessment to improve learning, this state of assessment affairs must change. This chapter defines the assessment competencies teachers and school leaders must develop to fulfill their responsibilities. In another chapter in this *Handbook* (see Schneider & Randel, this volume) details are provided regarding the attributes of productive professional development needed to assure that literacy.

As just mentioned, for teachers, competence in classroom assessment centers on the ability to build quality assessments that yield accurate information about student achievement and the ability to use the classroom assessment process and its results, not merely to monitor learning, but to enhance it. This chapter explores a commonsense quality control framework that can guide teachers as they design and implement their day-to-day assessments. In addition, we will consider several principles of assessment *for* learning that permit teachers to collaborate with their students to tap the potential of classroom assessment as a powerful teaching and learning tool. Both the framework and principles delineate essential classroom assessment competencies for teachers.

For school leaders, assessment competence includes mastery of the same principles of sound classroom assessment that teachers must master so that they are able to support their teachers as they face the challenges of day-to-day classroom assessment. In addition, school leaders must be able to use assessment results for productive program evaluation and improvement, as well as for public accountability purposes. This chapter will detail those leadership competencies also.

SETTING THE STAGE FOR PRODUCTIVE ASSESSMENT

Assessments can serve a variety of valuable educational purposes. Some assessments support learning (that is, they are used in a formative manner) while others verify it (they serve summative purposes). To do either well, assessments must be of high quality. Regardless of the context of their use, to serve well, each individual assessment must be designed specifically to serve a preestablished purpose, reflect a clearly articulated and appropriate purpose, yield dependable evidence, and rely on effective communication strategies for delivering results to the intended user. The focus in this *Handbook* is on formative applications; thus, the balance of this chapter considers the keys to quality assessment as they vary across formative contexts (Stiggins, 2006).

First, consider the classroom level of assessment. Here, teachers and their students rely on assessments to tell them where students are now in their preestablished learning progressions, so they can decide what comes next in that learning. In this context, teachers must be able to select or create assessments that accurately reflect student achievement, and they must be able to communicate results effectively. They must understand how to use classroom assessment results to inform instructional decisions, and they must understand how to use them to keep students believing that learning success is within reach if they keep trying. In other words, they need to be capable of using assessment both to motivate and to support learning.

In this same spirit, students interpret their own classroom assessment results and make key instructional decisions that can either assist or inhibit their learning. With thoughtful guidance from their teachers, they can assume considerable responsibility for their own self-assessment, record keeping, and communication about their own journey to success.

At this classroom level, if principals are to provide effective supervision in formative assessment, they too must master the same formative assessment competencies as teachers; that is, they too must know how to assure the accuracy and effective day-to-day use of assessment to support learning.

Next, consider the interim/benchmark level of assessment use, where teacher teams, principals, and curriculum personnel can rely on formative assessments to tell them which achievement standards students are (and are not) mastering across classrooms.

This requires that comparable evidence be gathered across classrooms using interim, benchmark, or common assessments, so the results can be aggregated. By identifying the standards that students are struggling to master, these assessments help the faculty focus their school improvement efforts. Once again at this level, the requirement exists of sufficient assessment literacy to assure quality formative assessments, whether developed locally or selected from test publishers.

Finally, consider the large-scale level of assessment use as in statewide testing programs. In this case, it is most common to center on the summative question to be answered, which is: "Are enough students meeting standards?" State, district, and school leaders are accountable for the answer to that question. However, under the right assessment conditions, this context can also afford leaders opportunities to improve instruction in a formative sense. For annual tests to serve formative purposes, the results must indicate how each student did in mastering each standard. Such results can be aggregated over students to reveal which standards students are struggling to master—once again, providing focal points for instructional improvement. To fulfill their responsibilities here, school leaders must possess sufficient assessment literacy to assure appropriate assessment and the effective communication and use of test results.

Even more importantly and in a larger sense, those in leadership positions must understand both the importance of and differences among these three levels of assessment use. They must know that all three serve important purposes, but the formative purposes are different. At the classroom level, the assessors ask: "How goes the journey to competence for students, and what can we do to help?" The interim/benchmark level asks: "Which standards are our students struggling with, and how can we do a better job of helping them?" And regarding large-scale, annual testing: "For which standards can we improve our instructional programs long term?" School leaders at district and building levels must take primary responsibility for achieving a synergy among these levels of assessment concern and for building balanced assessment systems that meet the formative information needs of all important users across these various contexts.

FORMATIVE SUCCESS REQUIRES QUALITY ASSESSMENTS, PRODUCTIVELY USED

Formative assessment occurs for two reasons: (1) to inform instructional decisions with good data, and (2) to motivate students to try to learn. Quality assessments provide a high-fidelity representation of the learning target in question. Productive assessments also fit comfortably into the role of supporting the learning process by orienting students for success. Both require assessment know-how.

Competence in Quality Assessment

As one example of professional development programs focusing on competence in assessment, the Assessment Training Institute provides teachers with the opportunity to learn to apply a five-part quality control framework to their own assessments. Three keys to quality center on maximizing the dependability of assessment results, while two others

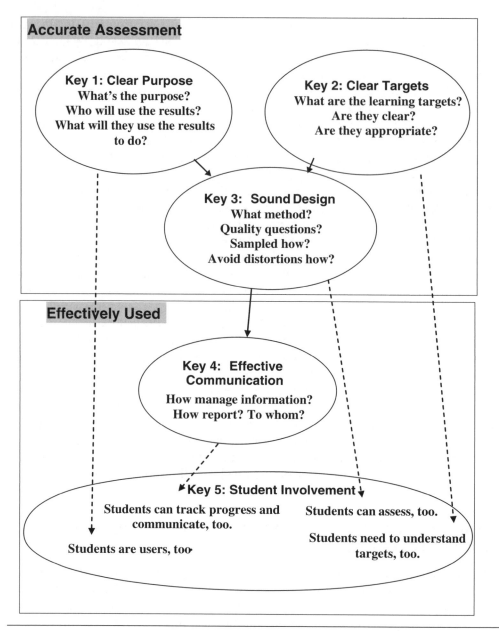

Figure 14.1 Five keys to quality classroom assessment. Adapted from Stiggins, Arter, Chappuis, & Chappuis (2006). *Classroom assessment FOR student learning: Doing it right—using it well.* Portland OR: ETS Assessment Training Institute. Used with permission.

focus on how the assessment process and its results can be used productively to promote student success. Figure 14.1 provides a graphic representation of this framework.

The first key to assessment quality is *clear purpose*. It is important for teachers and educational leaders to grasp that the starting place for the creation of a quality assessment is defining the context within which it will be used. The context includes two important factors that will directly influence the assessment design. The assessor must articulate in advance who will use the assessment results and what specific achievement targets are to be assessed.

With regard to the former, competent classroom assessors (i.e., teachers) know that one starts assessment development with a clear answer to the question, "Why am I assessing?" If this assessment is to inform instructional decisions, then another set of questions must be asked: "What decisions?", "Who is making them?" and, "What information do they need?" As has already been established, assessments can inform a variety of different users and uses. The information needs of users in different contexts vary profoundly. So if an educator doesn't start with a clear sense of who he or she is trying to help and what they need, how can an educator build an assessment to fit that context? Clearly, entire assessment enterprise hinges on a clear sense of purpose.

The second key is specifying *clear targets*. In this case, teachers must understand the importance of starting assessment development with a clear answer to the question: "What is it by way of student achievement that is to be assessed?" Educators cannot dependably assess that which they have not clearly and completely delimited and defined. At present, the starting place for determining local learning targets is state-level academic achievement standards. In a summative accountability sense, the assessment question is: "Are enough students meeting standards?" But in a formative sense, the assessment questions must go much deeper than that. During the learning process, classroom assessments must help us keep track of where the student is now in the progression of standards that are unfolding over time within and across grade levels. Only then can teachers and students answer the question: "What come next in the learning?"

Further, it is virtually never the case that, at first, students are unable to meet standards then all of a sudden they can. Rather, over time in their classrooms during their learning, students ascend through progressive levels of proficiency to a place where they are ready to demonstrate mastery of a standard. During this time, they master the foundations of knowledge, patterns of reasoning, performance skills, and product development capabilities that lead up the scaffolding to competence in terms of the standard. It is these rungs of the scaffolding that teachers need to be able to articulate and assess during the learning.

Finally, with respect to learning targets as a foundation for productive formative assessment, one of the most important lessons for teachers is that students can hit any target that they can see and that holds still for them. Thus, it is essential to transform the scaffolded learning targets into student- and family-friendly versions to be shared with the learner from the very beginning of the learning. This important process will be addressed in a subsequent portion of this chapter focusing on effective use of classroom assessment.

The third key is *sound assessment design*. Once the context is defined—that is, one knows who is to be informed by the assessment results about student mastery of what learning target(s)—then and only then can assessment design begin. To create a quality assessment, teachers need to competently manage four universal and nonnegotiable design features. Assessors must meet all four, or they place students directly in harm's way due to their mismeasurement of their students' achievement.

First, teachers need to know how to select proper assessment methods given the learning target in question. Methodological options abound: selected-response, written response, performance assessment, and direct personal interaction with the student. Teachers must understand that these methods are not interchangeable. Each is capable of reflecting certain kinds of achievement but not others. The first task for the formative assessment developer is to know what method to use and when to use it. Some contexts permit multiple-choice testing, while others demand performance assessment. Assessment-literate teachers understand the difference.

Task two is to devise a sampling plan for the assessment. Every assessment includes a subset of all the questions or tasks that the teacher could have posed if the assessment could be very complex and cover the entire broad domain of learning. Obviously, including all possible questions or tasks on an assessment is impractical. So, samples are taken from the domain to permit inferences based on the student's performance regarding how much of the broad domain the student has mastered. Assessment literate teachers must know the rules of evidence to apply in determining how many items or tasks of what kind to include in any particular assessment. They know how to gather enough evidence while not wasting time gathering too much.

Task three is to build the assessment out of high-quality ingredients: good multiple-choice items, sound performance assessment tasks, high-quality scoring rubrics, and so on. Competent classroom teachers know how to create quality ingredients for their assessments.

Finally, task four requires that the formative assessment developer understands, anticipates, and removes all relevant sources that can distort results and lead to incorrect inferences about student learning. In this case, assessment literate teachers know that, even if they select a proper method, devise a sound sampling plan, and construct sound ingredients, there remains a short list of things that can go wrong in conjunction with the assessment that can distort results, such as distractions, emotional upsets, scoring anomalies, difficulties with the English language, and others. Assessment literate teachers should know what these sources of distortion are and how to prevent them.

In summary, key classroom assessment competencies related to assessment quality include selecting the right method for the context, sampling achievement appropriately, authoring high-quality exercises and scoring schemes, and minimizing bias.

Competence in Productive Assessment Use

On the effective use side of the quality control framework (as shown in the bottom portion of Figure 14.1) there are two active ingredients. Effective communication of assessment results is the first key: the most valid and reliable assessment is wasted if its results are miscommunicated. The second key to effective use is student involvement in the formative assessment process. Research evidence suggests that, when students become partners in the formative assessment, record keeping, and communication process during their learning, their confidence, motivation, and achievement skyrocket.

Accordingly, the fourth key is *effective communication*. In summative assessment contexts, results typically are communicated in brief and focused forms: a report card grade, a state test score, or a standards mastery score. However, effective communication in a formative assessment context requires greater detail, because the mission is to support and not merely judge learning.

Hattie and Timperley (2007) provide a compelling synthesis of research evidence that reveals the positive impact productive communication of formative results can have on student learning. According to these findings, teachers need to learn how to weave attributes such as the following into their communication of formative results. First, communication supports learning when it focuses on attributes of the student's work and not on attributes of the student. Second, productive feedback informs the learner how to do better the next time (and, therefore, feeds into a classroom environment where there will be a next time). Third, feedback works best when it fits into a familiar framework of learning expectations so that the learner understands what it means. And, fourth, feedback works most effectively when it arrives in amounts the student can process versus in amounts so large as to overwhelm.

Also, in summative contexts, the flow of information comes from the teacher (or some other external adult source) to the learner. However, in formative contexts, the flow of useful information can originate with the learner and flow to the teacher, classmates, or parents—as in keeping others informed about changes in their own academic capabilities. Teachers must also be given the opportunity to learn to facilitate these forms of communication. This leads, then, to the final key to quality assessment.

The fifth key is *student involvement.* Black and Wiliam (1998) have synthesized the research on what happens to student learning when students become involved in the formative assessment process while they are learning. The authors urge that teachers be provided with professional learning opportunities that prepare them to increase the quality of their classroom assessments, provide students with continuous access to descriptive feedback, and involve students in self-assessment. These form the basis for what has come to be called "assessment *for* learning" (Stiggins, 2006, p. 3). Teachers must become competent in using assessment to support learning in this sense.

Sadler (1989) provides a conceptual framework for helping teachers understand how to link formative assessment to learning in the student's mind. Educators can help students to understand what good work looks like ("I know where I'm going"), learn to compare their work to that standard of excellence such that the differences become clear to them ("I know where I am now"), and then help them learn to close the gap between them ("I know where and how to improve").

J. Chappuis (2009) has blended these ideas into a series of seven specific assessment/instructional strategies that provide a useful framework for thinking about teachers' formative classroom assessment competence. These strategies are listed in Table 14.1.

Teachers must understand how to use these seven strategies shown in the table as an ordered sequence. The foundation of the sequence is the student's understanding of the target. Without a clear sense of what is expected from the outset, descriptive feedback will be meaningless to the learners—it has no way to help move them forward in their learning. Further, understanding the target, along with practice in using feedback to improve their work, blend to provide students with the conceptual foundation needed to begin to self-assess and generate their own feedback. This, in turn, sets them up to become partners in determining what comes next in their learning so as to close the gap.

Implicit in the seven strategies listed in Table 14.1 is an understanding of how crucial the student's role is in productive formative assessment, a role that has been almost

Table 14.1 Seven Assessment/Instructional Strategies for Formative Classroom Assessment

Teachers must be provided with the opportunity to learn how to help learners answer the following questions:

Where Am I Going?

Strategy 1: Provide a clear, understandable, student-friendly version of the learning target to the student from the beginning of the learning

Strategy 2: Accompany the student-friendly target with examples and models of strong and weak work so students can see the continuum along which they will travel

Where Am I Now?

Strategy 3: Provide students with continuous access to descriptive feedback while they are learning

Strategy 4: Teach students to self-assess and set goals

How Can I Close the Gap?

Strategy 5: Design lessons to help students develop the quality of their work one aspect of quality at a time

Strategy 6: Teach students focused revision—how to make changes in their work to enhance its quality

Strategy 7: Engage students in self-reflection and let them keep track of and share their learning

completely overlooked (but see Andrade, this volume). Two facets of it deserve careful attention: (1) the student's role as an assessment user and decision maker, and (2) the emotional dynamics of the assessment experience from the student's point of view.

At the classroom level of formative assessment, the evidence gathered is used both by teachers and their students to make key instructional decisions. The teachers' role is obvious. They rely on the data to make decisions about content priorities, pacing, grouping, instructional strategies, and so on. This is why formative assessment has traditionally been seen as something *adults do to students*. However, recent analyses have shifted the spotlight to formative assessment as something *students can do for themselves* (Black & Wiliam, 1998; Sadler, 1989).

Upon seeing their assessment results, students go first in the data-based instructional decision making process, as they answer questions like:

"Can I learn this material, or is it just beyond me?"

"Is the learning worth the energy I have to expend to attain it?"

"Is trying to learn this worth the risk that I might fail…again…in public?"

If students answer these questions in a productive way by saying "Yes," then the adult decision makers get to play their role and make their contribution to student success. Students respond productively to assessment results when, upon seeing them, their reaction unfolds as follows: "I understand"; "I know what to do next" ;"I can learn this"; "I will keep trying." But if learners come down on the wrong side of these questions, saying they can't learn this or it's not worth the effort or risk, then the adult decision makers are taken out of action and the learning stops. They respond in a counterproductive way, when their reaction is any of the following: "I don't understand these results"; "I have no idea what to do about them"; "I'm too dumb to learn this stuff anyway";"I quit."

The crucial question teachers need to understand how to address is: "What can I do to help my students respond productively to every assessment?" The answer is to always gather dependable evidence and consistently apply the principles of assessment *for learning* as outlined previously; that is, to help them see where they are headed, where they are now, how to close the gap, and to help them feel in control of the probability of their own success. These requirements frame very important classroom assessment competencies for teachers.

The Emotional Dynamics of the Assessment Experience

It should be obvious from the presentation so far that productive formative classroom assessment requires more than merely quality assessment and instructional decision making that promotes learning. It also requires careful management of the emotional (i.e., affective or dispositional) aspects of the assessment experience from the student's point of view. In an assessment for learning environment, the path to productive student decision making passes through their emotional reactions to assessment and what those emotions cause learners to do in response. Teachers need to understand how students' previous learning/assessment experiences impact their view of themselves as learners, the implications of those experiences for the learner, and how to deal with those emotions in ways that benefit the student. For the successful learner, these issues tend to resolve themselves automatically and comfortably. But for the struggling learner, this typically is not the case. Teachers must understand this and know what to do about it.

In the past, when a primary focus of assessment was ranking students (instead of also assuring that all students meet preestablished standards as is the case today), the amount of time available to learn was fixed: one year per grade. The amount learned by the end of that time was free to vary: some students learned a great deal, some very little. Able learners built on past success to grow rapidly. However, students who failed to master the early prerequisites within the allotted time also failed to learn much of that which followed. After 13 years of cumulative treatment in this manner, students were in effect spread along an achievement continuum that labeled each student's rank in class upon graduation.

The emotional dynamics of this process are clear. From the very earliest grades, some students rode winning streaks to the top. Right from the start, they scored high on assessments and were assigned high grades. The emotional effect of this was that they came to see themselves as capable learners—they became increasingly confident in school. That gave them the emotional strength to risk striving for more success because in their minds success was within reach if they tried. Note that the trigger for the decisions they made about their own learning was their interpretation of their own assessments results.

But other students scored very low on tests and so they were assigned failing grades. This caused them to begin to doubt their own capabilities as learners from the outset. The loss of confidence deprived them of the emotional reserves to continue to risk trying. Chronic failure was hard to hide and became embarrassing. As their motivation waned, of course, their achievement suffered. Notice again how the learners' own interpretation of assessment results influenced their confidence and willingness to strive on.

Overall, if some students worked hard and learned a great deal, that was a positive result, as they would finish high in the rank order. And, if some students gave up in the face of what they believed to be inevitable failure, that was an acceptable result for the institution too, because they would occupy places very low in the rank order. The greater the spread of achievement from top to bottom, the more dependable would be the rank order.

The important lesson we must learn is that the student's emotional reactions to any set of assessment results, whether high, midrange, or low, influences what the student thinks, feels, and does in response to those results. When students who give up in hopelessness also are those who have yet to meet standards, and if educators are to be held accountable by society for all students meeting standards, the teacher has a serious problem. Some students will stop trying and will neither master essential foundational reading, writing, and math problem solving proficiencies nor become lifelong learners. If society wants all students to meet standards, then all students must believe they can meet those standards; they all must be confident enough to be willing to take the risk of trying. Any other emotional state for any student is unacceptable.

In other words, teachers must understand that assessment practices which permitted—even encouraged—some students in a predominantly sort-and-select schooling system to give up on learning must be replaced by those that engender hope and sustained effort for all students in the service of mastering standards. If all students are to meet standards, the emotional environment surrounding the experience of being evaluated must change for all, but especially for struggling learners. The driving emotional forces of fear and intimidation triggered by the prospect of being held accountable now must be replaced by the driving emotions of optimism, engagement, and persistence triggered by the belief that, "I am going to get this if I keep trying." If all students are to succeed, they must have continuous access to credible evidence of their own academic *success* at mastering prescribed achievement standards.

To accomplish this, teachers must help students develop a strong sense of control over their own academic success. Bandura (1994) refers to this sense as self-efficacy:

A strong sense of efficacy enhances human accomplishment and personal well-being in many ways. People with high assurance in their capabilities approach difficult tasks as challenges to be mastered rather than as threats to be avoided. Such an efficacious outlook fosters intrinsic interest and deep engrossment in activities. They set themselves challenging goals and maintain strong commitment to them. They heighten and sustain their efforts in the face of failure. They quickly recover their sense of efficacy after failures or setbacks. They attribute failure to insufficient effort or deficient knowledge and skills which are acquirable. They approach threatening situations with assurance that they can exercise control over them. Such an efficacious outlook produces personal accomplishments, reduces stress and lowers vulnerability....

In contrast, people who doubt their capabilities shy away from difficult tasks which they view as personal threats. They have low aspirations and weak commitment to the goals they choose to pursue. When faced with difficult tasks, they dwell on their personal deficiencies, on the obstacles they will encounter, and all kinds of adverse outcomes rather than concentrate on how to perform successfully. They slacken their efforts and give up quickly in the face of difficulties. They are slow to recover their sense of efficacy following failure or setbacks. Because they view insufficient performance as deficient aptitude, it does not require much failure for them to lose faith in their capabilities. (p. 71)

In terms of classroom assessment competence, teachers must understand how to help students build a strong sense of academic self-efficacy by helping them understand what success looks like and then showing them how to use each assessment to attain ever closer approximations. In these classrooms, assessments become far more than merely one-time events tacked onto the end of the teaching. They become part of the learning process by keeping students posted on their progress and confident enough to continue striving.

Summary of Keys to Quality

Figure 14.2 provides a brief elaboration of the five keys to quality just described by posing a series of questions teachers can ask of their own assessments. Generally, teachers have not been trained to ask or answer these questions. The professional development challenge at hand is to provide them with that opportunity. Again, the chapter by Schneider and Randel (this volume) will address keys to assuring the effectiveness of those adult learning experiences.

ASSESSMENT COMPETENCIES FOR SCHOOL LEADERS

Productive formative assessment requires effective assessment leadership too, but the specific role of the school leader depends on context. At the district level, both the foundation and framework must be put in place for institutional support of formative assessment. At the building level, the principal's role is to provide direct classroom support to teachers. But both carry within them an expectation of assessment literacy for school leaders. Their professional responsibilities are considered next, along with the assessment competencies they suggest.

District-Level Leadership

For formative assessment to play out productively within a school district, there are six institutional conditions that must be satisfied (Chappuis, Commodore, & Stiggins, in press). Each centers on a set of circumstances that must be in place for formative applications to find a comfortable home there. As a matter of assessment competence, it is incumbent on school district leadership to be qualified to conduct a district-wide self-analysis to evaluate the current state of assessment affairs. The ingredients in this analysis relate directly to the above keys to quality, but are viewed from the perspective of institutional support for formative assessment. The six institutional conditions include: (1) the district's achievement standards house must be in order; (2) the district's assessment system must be in balance; (3) the current quality of assessments and the assessment literacy of the faculty must be evaluated; (4) the current communication systems must be checked for effectiveness; (5) the faculty must be capable of involving students deeply in the assessment process and be predisposed to do so; and (6) the district policies must be reviewed to see if they guide sound practice.

Again, these ingredients are essential—if any of them are wanting, then productive assessment will remain beyond reach and the power of formative assessment will suffer. District leaders must bring to the table a sufficiently well-developed foundation of

1. Why Assess? Assessment Processes and Results Serve Clear and Appropriate Purposes	a. Teacher understands who classroom assessment users are and their information needs. b. Teacher understands the assessment and student motivation and can use assessment experiences to maximize motivation. c. Teacher can use classroom assessment processes and results formatively to support learning (assessment *for* learning). d. Teacher uses classroom assessment results in a summative manner to verify learning (assessment *of* learning) at a particular point in time. e. Teacher has a plan for balancing assessment *for* and *of* learning.
2. Assess What? Assessments Reflect Clear and Valued Student Learning Targets	a. Teacher has clear classroom learning targets for students anchored to standards. b. Teacher understands the differences among the various types of learning targets. c. Learning targets focused on the most important things students need to know and be able to do. d. Teacher has plan for assessing learning targets over time.
3. Assess How? Learning Targets Are Translated into Assessments That Yield Accurate Results	a. Teacher understands the various assessment methods. b. Teacher can choose assessment methods that match intended learning targets. c. Teacher designs assessments that fit the purpose/target context. d. Teacher samples learning appropriately in their assessments. e. Teacher creates sound exercises and scoring schemes of all types well. f. Teacher avoids bias that distorts results.
4. Communicate How? Assessment Results Are Managed Well and Communicated Effectively	a. Teacher records and summarizes assessment information so as to accurately reflect student learning. b. Teacher selects the best reporting option (grades, narratives, portfolios, conferences) for each context (learning targets and users). c. Teacher interprets and uses test results correctly. d. Teacher effectively communicates assessment results to students. e. Teacher effectively communicates assessment results to a variety of audiences outside the classroom, including parents, colleagues, and other stakeholders.
5. Involve Students How? Students Are Involved in Their Own Assessment	a. Teacher makes learning targets clear to students. b. Teacher involves students in practice assessment development and use as appropriate. c. Teacher involves students in assessing, tracking, and setting goals for their own learning. d. Teacher involves students in communicating about their own learning.

Figure 14.2 Indicators of sound classroom assessment practice. Adapted from Stiggins, Arter, Chappuis, & Chappuis (2006). *Classroom assessment FOR student learning: Doing it right—using it well.* Portland OR: ETS Assessment Training Institute. Used with permission.

understanding to conduct a self-evaluation of the listed elements and then to respond to the results. The following sections further describe each of the six essential ingredients.

Condition 1: The Status of Achievement Expectations If teachers and their students are to use formative assessment to help them continuously track whether the learner is currently in order to know what comes next in the learning, there needs to be a curricular frame of reference upon which to map student progress within and across grade levels over time. This requires quality curriculum maps as a foundation for productive assessment that includes several components. The self-evaluation questions include the following:

- Are academic achievement standards of high quality? Are they clearly defined, reflecting the best current thinking of the field, and appropriate in number given the resources available to teach them?
- Are those standards arrayed in learning progressions so as to unfold over time in a manner consistent with the way learning actually happens—so it is clear at any point what is prerequisite and what naturally follows?
- Has each standard been deconstructed into the scaffolding students will climb on in the course of their journey to academic success?
- Has each scaffolding target been transformed into student- and family-friendly language to be shared with all stake holders from the beginning of the learning?
- Are we sure that each teacher in each classroom is a confident, competent master of the standards their students are expected to master?

Answering these questions requires district-level work to be completed by district leaders rather than work that should be done on at the school or classroom level, as the institution must present a uniform front on the meaning of academic success. Once the curriculum picture is painted, then all involved can use it to underpin productive assessment and instruction.

Condition 2: The Current State of Balance in the Assessment System   District leaders need to be prepared to verify that assessments are functioning effectively at all levels of use. If they are not, then it will become clear what work needs to be done to be sure they are. This requires self-analysis around the following questions:

- Are we clear about who needs access to the results of accountability test scores and how they will use them? Are they receiving the information they need?
- Are we clear about who needs access to interim assessment results for program improvement and how they use them? Are they being informed appropriately?
- Who needs access to day-to-day classroom assessment evidence of learning and why do they need it? Are they receiving the evidence they need in a timely and understandable form?

Condition 3: The Quality of Assessments   District leaders need to be qualified to ask about both the quality of assessments being used at any of the above levels and about the assessment literacy of those who develop and use them. If either is found wanting, then leaders need to be prepared to respond appropriately. This requires that the self-evaluation ask the following questions:

- Do our faculty and staff possess a sufficient level of assessment literacy to gather dependable evidence of student learning?

- Are we, in fact, gathering dependable information about student achievement in all relevant contexts?
- Are we using the evidence gathered productively to support student learning wherever possible?

Condition 4: The Effectiveness of Communications   Guidelines for communicating about student achievement are issued at the district level in terms of interim reporting procedures, grading policy, ways of sharing test scores, and the like. The self-analysis question in this case is, are the messages about the status of student learning getting through effectively and being heard? District leaders need to be ready and able to ask in all communication contexts, whether communication is via report cards, test score reports, conferences, or whatever mode. The conditions necessary for effective communication include requirements that:

- The message sender and receiver must agree on the definition of the learning target about which they are to communicate.
- The evidence being shared must be accurate.
- The symbols used to share information must carry the same (and an appropriate) meaning for message sender and receiver.
- The communication process must remain sensitive to differences in the message delivered via descriptive and judgmental feedback contexts.
- The message receiver must be open to hearing and acting on the message.

District leaders must be willing and able to check to see if these conditions are satisfied in their operations. They must be willing and able to act on the results to improve practice.

Condition 5: Capacity for Student Involvement   Given that currently practicing teachers and school leaders have rarely been given the opportunity to learn to use assessment to support student learning, leadership in this case demands that they be given that opportunity. As has been argued previously in this chapter, student and teacher success hinges, in large part, on the quality of formative classroom assessment practices. So one facet of district self-study is to find out if faculty can and are predisposed to do the following:

- turn the learners into the assessors during their learning in order to maximize confidence, motivation, engagement, and achievement;
- engage students as partners in the recordkeeping process so as to reveal to them changes in their own capabilities; and
- help students learn how to communicate with others about their achievement status and changes in their academic capabilities.

Condition 6: The Status of Assessment Policies   If policy guides practice, then the self-study question in this case is: Do our policies guide sound assessment practice? Given the keys to quality assessment and the necessary conditions framed in the foregoing discussion, several dimensions of district policy may require reevaluation and revision depending on their current status. Indeed, some essential facets of sound policy may be missing and so need to be added to district directives. Key facets of policy to be investigated include, but are not limited to, the following:

- **assessment policy**, especially as it relates to expectations of quality and matters of balance (meeting the information needs of all users);
- **curriculum policy**, considering the quality and local relevance of standards, learning progressions, deconstructing to scaffolding, and transformation to student-friendly versions;
- **communication policy** as it speaks to delivering achievement messages and making sure those messages get through, are understood, and are acted on; and
- **personnel policy**, particularly centering on the hiring and ongoing supervision criteria for both teachers and administrators to ensure that they foster and promote appropriate levels of assessment literacy.

Summary of Essential Conditions

In considering key assessment competencies for school district leaders, we must consider the kinds of support school leaders and teachers need to fulfill their formative assessment responsibilities. It is at those levels of schooling where formative assessment impacts student success. That support must take the form of making sure the district's achievement expectations are in order, the information needs of all key assessment users are understood, supports are in place for quality assessment, overarching communication processes align with formative uses, and policy guides sound formative assessment practice.

To assure that these conditions are satisfied, assessment literacy for district leaders centers on the development of sufficient curricular awareness to understand that standards, while essential, do not represent a sufficient definition of achievement expectations to promote the development of effective schools. In addition, they must be in proper progressions and task-analyzed for integration into the classroom. In addition, leaders at this level must be sufficiently assessment literate to understand and embrace the concept of balanced assessment systems, acknowledging the importance of instructional decisions made at classroom, program, and institutional levels. They must be given the opportunity to understand the basic keys to assessment quality and effective communication in order to be able to see when and where professional development in assessment literacy is needed. And they must understand how essential that literacy is to student well-being. Only then will they be willing to make sound assessment practice a high priority in organizational development.

ASSESSMENT COMPETENCIES FOR PRINCIPALS

At the school building level, formative assessment leadership centers predominately, although not exclusively, on the classroom and on supporting teachers as they fulfill their assessment responsibilities. Chappuis et al. (in press) identify a series of specific competencies required for effective building-level leadership. The reader will notice that these expectations connect in obvious ways to all matters discussed above about effective formative assessment and teacher competence in classroom assessment, and that there is a great deal of overlap between these competencies and those identified in the previous section for district leaders.

Well-prepared school building principals can provide leadership in formative assessment when they can do the following:

- understand the attributes of a sound assessment system that balances assessment *of* and *for* learning as they play out in the classroom and throughout the building;
- understand specific principles and practices of assessment *for* (that is, used in support of) learning and works with staff to integrate them into classroom instruction;
- understand the necessity of clear academic achievement targets, aligned classroom-level achievement targets, and their relationship to the development of accurate assessments;
- understand how to evaluate the teachers' classroom assessment competencies and help teachers learn and grow over time as needed to assess accurately and use the results productively;
- plan, present, or secure professional development activities for staff and faculty that contribute to the use of sound assessment practices
- accurately analyze student assessment information, use the information to improve curriculum and instruction, and assist teachers in doing the same;
- be able to contribute to the development and implementation of sound assessment-related policies;
- create the conditions necessary for the appropriate use and reporting of student achievement information and communicate effectively with all members of the school community about student assessment results and their relationship to improving curriculum and instruction;
- understand standards of assessment quality and how to encourage and verify their use in their school/district assessments; and
- understand the issues related to the unethical and inappropriate use of student assessment and protect students and staff from such misuse.

ASSESSMENT PAST AND FUTURE

By way of summary, because assessment is so much a part of effective instruction, teachers must be able to apply principles of sound assessment practice within the classroom and administrators must be able to apply them across classrooms. Both must be able to anticipate the information needs of various assessment users, transform achievement expectations into quality assessments, and deliver the results into the hands of those users in a timely and understandable manner.

If all of this is so obviously true, then why is it that neither teachers nor administrators have been given the opportunity to understand principles of sound assessment or how to apply them? I believe it is, at least in part, because U.S. society in general and

American school culture have operated on a set of incorrect beliefs about what role assessment ought to play—and that this error has prevented us from tapping the full potential of assessment as an improvement tool and rendered true assessment literacy irrelevant to the detriment of school quality. A list of those mistaken beliefs is offered below, along with the adjustments needed in our thinking if we are to tap the full potential of assessment for the benefit of learners.

Mistaken Belief 1: Standards are Sufficient

Standards are essential, but they are not sufficient. They must be of high quality, arrayed in learning progressions, each deconstructed in the scaffolding learners climb to master them, and transformed into student-friendly terms to guide teacher teaching and student learning. School leaders must see to these refinements.

Mistaken Belief 2: Standardized Tests Are Sufficient

Clearly, standardized tests are not sufficient. By themselves, whether conducted at district, state, national, international, or interplanetary levels over decades and at a cost of billions, they have not proven their worth in terms of promoting effective schools. But when coupled with program and classroom levels—when balanced with other uses—they can make a contribution. School leaders must see to the achievement of balanced assessment.

Mistaken Belief 3: Classroom Assessment Quality Doesn't Matter

If we had really cared about the quality of classroom assessments over the decades, we would have made sure that each and every teacher and principal was assessment literate from the time she or he entered the classroom. We have not done that. But quality is always essential: Practitioners need to know how to assess well.

Mistaken Belief 4: Assessment Is Something Adults Do to Students

Assessment is indeed something that adults do to students, but students assess themselves too. This phrasing is purposeful: It does not say, students "can assess," it says they do. And they make critically important data-based instructional decisions based on their interpretation of their own assessment results. Teachers need to know how to help them make productive decisions that support their learning.

Mistaken Belief 5: Intimidation Motivates Learning

For some students, intimidation does motivate learning, but this is not true of all students—especially not struggling learners. Intimidation only works to motivate learning for those who have the hope of learning success. For those who have given up in hopelessness, increased anxiety only drives them deeper into despair. Teachers must understand this as well as how to use the classroom assessment process to promote hope for all students.

Mistaken Belief 6: Assessment Is Something that Attaches to the End of Teaching

Our tradition is to think of assessment as the index of the effect of what we do to promote learning. In the future, teachers must come to think of it as part of the cause of the effect—something we do during the learning to help students confidently learn more.

In other words, we know what teachers and school leaders need to know and be able to assess well and use the results productively to promote greater student learning success: All that is missing is the opportunity for them to learn.

REFERENCES

Black, P., & Wiliam, D. (1998). Assessment and classroom learning. *Educational Assessment: Principles, Policy and Practice, 5*(1), 7–74.

Bandura, A. (1994). Self-efficacy. In V. S. Ramachaudran (Ed.), *Encyclopedia of human behavior* (Vol. 4, pp. 71–81). New York: Academic.

Chappuis, J. (2009). *The seven strategies of assessment FOR learning.* Portland, OR: ETS Assessment Training Institute.

Chappuis, S., Commodore, C., & Stiggins, R. (in press). *Assessment balance and quality: An action guide for school leaders.* Portland, OR: ETS Assessment Training Institute.

Chappuis, S., Stiggins, R., Arter, J., & Chappuis, J. (2006). *Assessment FOR learning: An action guide for school leaders.* Portland OR: ETS Assessment Training Institute.

Crooks, T. J. (1988). The impact of classroom evaluations of students. *Review of Educational Research, 58*(4), 48–81.

Dorre-Bremme, D. W., & Herman, J. L. (1986). *Assessing student achievement: A profile of classroom practices.* Los Angeles CA: Center for the Study of Evaluation, University of California, Los Angeles.

Hattie, J., & Timperley, H. (2007). The power of feedback. *Review of Educational Research, 77*(1), 81–112.

Sadler, D. R. (1989). Formative assessment and the design of instructional systems. *Instructional Science, 18,* 119–144.

Stiggins, R. J. (2006). Assessment FOR learning: A key to student motivation and achievement. *Phi Delta Kappan EDGE, 2*(2), 3–19.

Stiggins, R. J., Arter, J., Chappuis, J., & Chappuis, S. (2006). *Classroom assessment FOR student learning: Doing it right—Using it well.* Portland, OR: ETS Assessment Training Institute.

Stiggins, R. J., & Conklin, N. (1992). *In teachers' hands: Investigating the practice of classroom assessment.* Albany, NY: SUNY Press.

15

RESEARCH ON CHARACTERISTICS OF EFFECTIVE PROFESSIONAL DEVELOPMENT PROGRAMS FOR ENHANCING EDUCATORS' SKILLS IN FORMATIVE ASSESSMENT

M. CHRISTINA SCHNEIDER AND BRUCE RANDEL

Teachers engage in formative classroom assessment practices when they use a systematic process of collecting and analyzing diverse types of evidence regarding individual student learning, and use that information to shape and adjust instruction and provide feedback to students (Brookhart, Moss, & Long, 2008). Formative classroom assessment occurs only when the evidence is used to make a needed change. Persons who deliver professional development in formative classroom assessment, therefore, are charged with augmenting teachers' abilities to (1) collect accurate evidence about student learning from well-developed formal and informal classroom assessment practices; (2) analyze that evidence to determine how best to change instruction to address student misconceptions about content, if such a change is needed; and (3) provide specific feedback that helps students understand what they need to do to improve their own learning. Optimally, formative classroom assessment helps students better understand the gaps in their learning and allows them to become engaged and proactive in their mastery of the learning targets set by the teacher and the state.

Proficiency in assessment is considered an area of importance for highly skilled teachers (e.g., the National Board for Professional Teaching Standards document, *Adolescence and Young Adulthood English Language Arts Standards*, 2003). However, Tienken and Wilson (2001) found that 35 states do not require that teachers take a course or demonstrate competency in the area of assessment prior to obtaining teacher certification. Stiggins and Herrick (2007) found that, although competence in assessment is oftentimes addressed in teacher standards adopted by a state, states do not typically require that teachers be formally trained in this area. Most states do not require a dedicated assessment course in order to become certified. In 39 states, assessment is specified as a topic integrated into the general teacher education coursework.

Not surprisingly, researchers have found teachers lack expertise in sound assessment practices (Brookhart, 2001; Haydel, Oescher, & Banbury, 1995; Marso & Pigge, 1993; Plake & Impara, 1997) with only one-quarter to one-third of middle school teachers having coherent assessments (Aschbacher, 1999). Aschbacher defined coherent assessments as assignments aligned with learning goals and criteria. Incoherent assessment practices likely signify an issue larger than a lack of understanding of best practices for measuring student learning. Incoherent assessment practices may also indicate a teacher has not crisply defined the learning targets for students.

Brookhart (2005) wrote that student learning may move in an undesirable direction if a teacher's understanding of a learning target is not sufficiently precise. When teachers have not had adequate training in formative classroom assessment practices, they may measure low-level skills in their content area, or focus on other criteria, such as effort (Schneider, Meyer, Miller, & Lottridge, 2007). This has been documented by Aschbacher (1999) and by Oescher and Kirby (1990), who found many recall items on teacher assessments. Oescher and Kirby also found that teachers could not accurately classify the cognitive complexity of items. Sobolewski (2002) found that 82% of the informal questions teachers posed to students during the daily instructional and assessment cycle were at low cognitive levels.

Yap and her colleagues (2007) found that, out of 131 middle school teachers, 34% could not accurately interpret a state standard of their own choosing. If teachers do not understand the learning targets specified in state standards, they may inappropriately focus instruction or assess at cognitive levels that are not aligned to the standards. Instructional decisions as well as the feedback to the students may be erroneous when teachers use formative classroom assessments at low cognitive levels to gauge students' understanding of a state standard at a higher cognitive level. The mismatch of the cognitive levels and content of classroom instruction and the state content standards results in students who are inadequately prepared to excel on high-stakes achievement tests (Corallo & McDonald, 2001). Students who do not excel on such tests may not be prepared to enter the workforce with the skills stakeholders envisioned as essential when standards were developed.

Teachers have a purpose for formative classroom assessment and they, their students, and parents make decisions based on the informal and formal evidence of student learning that teachers collect and share with students. Formative assessment is often the basis for determining the degree to which a student is achieving the intended learning targets outlined by the state academic standards and enacted by the teacher. Whether formal or informal formative classroom assessment is used, teachers and their students need to make instructional and learning decisions based upon valid and reliable information (Airasian & Jones, 1993). It is for this reason that professional development programs in formative classroom assessment have begun to be implemented.

Researchers investigating effective professional development processes to improve teacher assessment skills are just beginning to use experimental designs (Brookhart, 2005), and a few experimental or quasi-experimental studies exist. In this chapter, quasi-experimental, experimental, and other types of research on professional development in formative classroom assessment are examined, and the common characteristics of effective professional development are identified. Studies with positive findings related to formative classroom assessment best practices (e.g., Andrade, Du, & Wang, 2008;

Newmann, Bryk, & Nagaoka, 2001; Ross, Hogaboam-Gray, & Rolheiser, 2002) but not based in the implementation of comprehensive professional development programs are not reviewed. The chapter concludes by describing the significant challenges of conducting experimental research in this area and highlighting areas where more research is warranted.

QUASI-EXPERIMENTAL STUDIES IN FORMATIVE CLASSROOM ASSESSMENT

Five quasi-experimental studies of professional development in formative classroom assessment are reviewed below. Each study included student achievement as an outcome. These five studies investigated promising approaches to professional development in formative classroom assessment and were conducted in a variety of settings. The studies are described in detail and critiqued in terms of the rigor of their design and data analysis. Common critiques include problems related to nesting of student-level observations and the resultant possibility of biased effect sizes.

Work Sampling System

The Work Sampling System (WSS) is a curriculum-embedded assessment system that allows teachers to systematically document children's skills, knowledge, behavior, and academic accomplishments in a variety of areas. The purpose of the system is to allow teachers to monitor student learning and change instruction as needed. Meisels, Atkins-Burnett, Xue, Nicholson, Bickel, and Son (2003) investigated the efficacy of the WSS in a large school district. The independent variable was implementation of the WSS, and the dependent variables were reading and mathematics change scores from grade 3 to grade 4 on the *Iowa Tests of Basic Skills* (University of Iowa and Riverside Publishing Co., 1994).

For inclusion in the WSS study, schools had to have implemented the WSS for 3 years, and, at the classroom level, teachers had to have implemented the WSS for at least 2 years. In this way, the researchers ensured a full implementation of the WSS intervention was investigated. Researchers compared full implementation WSS classrooms to two different sets of schools: (1) all schools in the district that did not implement the WSS and (2) a subset of classrooms from non-WSS schools matched to WSS classrooms. There were 96 grade 3 students in the WSS schools, 2,922 grade 3 students enrolled in all other schools in the district, and 116 grade 3 students in the matched schools.

Using hierarchical regression analyses, the researchers found significant differences in the change scores for the WSS student group when compared to students in all other schools in the district and the matched schools. The effect sizes were much larger in reading ($d = .68$ when compared to students in all other schools and $d = 1.60$ when compared with matched students) than in mathematics ($d = .20$ when compared to students in all other schools and $d = .76$ when compared with matched students).

The researchers also investigated whether a differential effect existed for high and low achieving students. Above and below average students exposed to the WSS made significantly greater gains than their counterparts in all other schools and the matched schools, except for low achieving students in mathematics. Again, effect sizes were greater in reading than in mathematics. Effect sizes in reading were $d = .83$ and $.55$ for high and low achieving students, respectively, when compared to students in all other schools and $d = 1.77$ and 1.02 for high and low achieving students, respectively, when compared with matched students only. Mathematics effect sizes were $d = .29$ for low achieving students when compared to students in all other schools and $d = .24$ and $.32$ for high and low achieving students, respectively, when compared with matched students only.

The analysis, however, did not account for the nesting of students, which has implications for the interpretation of the reported effect sizes. Just as type I error may be inflated when not accounting for the nesting of data, the same issue is present when calculating effect sizes when the correlation between the two variables is unaccounted for (Dunlap, Cortina, Vaslow, & Burke, 1996; Olejnik & Algina, 2000).

King's Medway Oxford Formative Assessment Project

Wiliam, Lee, Harrison, and Black (2004) guided teachers in a variety of content areas in the use of formative classroom assessment practices (e.g., teacher questioning, comment only feedback, sharing grading criteria, and student self- and peer feedback), and investigated the achievement of those teachers' students with and without those practices using a modified treatment and control group design. During the first 6 months of the intervention, teachers experimented with the formative assessment practices first overviewed by presenters in 6½ one-day in-service sessions. The one-day sessions were approximately 6 hours in length. Later, teachers were observed and supported while they developed their skills in formative classroom assessment. As a component of the process, teachers developed an action plan stipulating which of the formative assessment practices they would like to explore, then they implemented the techniques in a class of their choosing.

On average, the participating teachers chose four different formative assessment strategies to investigate. The actual activities they used to accomplish these strategies often differed. For example, if a teacher wanted to explore questioning, he or she may have used one of the following activities to meet that goal: teacher questioning, students writing questions, giving pretests, and students asking questions. Just as the teacher practices differed in terms of the strategies they chose to implement and the activities they used, the dependent variable also varied.

The researchers used scores on the typical assessments administered by each school as the dependent variable for the study. Scores for national tests for 14-year-olds or the grades on the national school-leaving examination were the most commonly administered outcomes. However, scores from some school-based assessments were also used.

The matching of the control group also differed by teacher. In most cases a teacher had a treatment class in which formative assessment practices were used and control class in which those practices were not used. In other cases the control class was another teacher's class within the same school and year or the same teacher's class in a previous year.

Because of differences in data, content area, and formative assessment strategies, data from each set of intact classes were analyzed individually, and the findings based on each classroom set were aggregated. The researchers found that, when teachers used formative classroom assessment practices with their students, those students scored an average effect size of .32 higher on the achievement measure than their control-group peers; however, as with the Meisels et al. (2003) study, the effect sizes are likely biased to some degree. One reason the effect sizes may be biased is that the study was implemented with intact classrooms and it is not clear if the pooled variance was used. Second, in the case where the treatment and control group were taught by the same teacher within the same year, it is possible that teachers did not restrict the formative assessment techniques to the treatment group only. Should treatment diffusion have occurred, the treatment effects would likely be underestimated.

Keeping Learning on Track

Bell, Steinberg, Wiliam, and Wylie (2008) investigated the Keeping Learning on Track (KLT) professional development program on student reading and mathematics scale scores from the statewide assessment in a large school district using a replication study across grades. Fourteen schools that implemented the KLT program were compared with 73 schools in the district that did not. The KLT professional development program focuses on five research-based formative assessment strategies (Leahy et al., 2005): (1) implementing effective classroom discussions via student questions and learning tasks that elicit evidence of student learning; (2) clarifying and sharing learning targets and criteria for success; (3) providing feedback that moves learners forward; (4) activating students as the owners of their own learning; and (5) using students as instructional resources for one another. Teachers were introduced to techniques to implement these five formative assessment strategies in an introductory workshop with 2-hour monthly follow-up meetings.

For inclusion in the KLT study, students had to be enrolled in the school district in Fall 2006, have test scores on file from the previous year and the intervention year, and have been promoted by one grade from the previous year to the intervention year. Thus, using the intervention year as the reference, students in grades 4 through 8 were included in the study, with 11,916 students in the reading analysis and 11,913 students in the mathematics analysis—approximately 2,383 students per grade level. This is likely the largest study of formative classroom assessment to date.

Bell et al. (2008) used a two-level hierarchical linear model (HLM) with the previous year's test score as a covariate. The researchers did not report the intraclass correlations for the reading and mathematics scores for the unconditional model. The researchers found no significant differences between the KLT schools and the non-KLT schools in the district. The researchers noted that, because many of the alpha levels for the analyses were above 0.5, it was likely that the intervention effects were too small to be detected. Because the 73 non-KLT schools were not matched to the KLT schools, the researchers investigated treatment effects using a subset of non-KLT schools matched to the KLT schools in post hoc exploratory analyses. No statistically significant differences between the KLT schools and their matched counterparts were found, although in these matched-group analyses equaling a total school sample size of 28, the school sample size was still too small to have adequate statistical power (i.e., < .80) to detect differences. There were, however, observable differences, and some significance levels at or below $p = .10$, in reading.

Assessment for Learning

Brookhart, Moss, and Long (2007, 2008) coimplemented an Assessment for Learning professional development program in a district that used a structured, scripted reading curriculum. In the year prior to the program, the district engaged teachers in professional development to strengthen their knowledge of reading development. The Assessment for Learning program engaged six Title I early literacy teachers in formative assessment in reading; two teachers taught extended kindergarten and four teachers taught remedial reading. These teachers were selected by the Title I supervisor, one of the coauthors of the study.

The professional development comprised six face-to-face meetings, online resources, and chat rooms. In general, teachers investigated formative classroom assessment in an inquiry-based approach by (1) identifying their current practice; (2) reflecting on their current practice; (3) seeking information about their areas of concern; and (4) experimenting with ways to improve their own practice in their classrooms. The authors reported that the kindergarten teachers focused on students who were not successfully identifying letters of the alphabet. Two remedial reading teachers focused on the decoding of words with first-grade students, while the two other teachers investigated classroom teachers' use of formative classroom assessment.

To identify a control group, the researchers used the scores on the *Dynamic Indicators of Basic Early Literacy Skills* (DIBELS) of other Title I students enrolled in either extended kindergarten or first grade. Kindergarten student scores on the DIBELS Letter Naming Fluency measure and first grade student scores on the DIBELS Phoneme Segmentation Fluency were used as the dependent variables. It is not known how the comparison group reflected the characteristics of the treatment group, with the exception that pretest scores for each group at each grade were not significantly different from one another.

All kindergarten students in the study improved in their ability to accurately identify letters during the year ($p < .01$ for pretest–posttest difference), but there were no significant differences between the two groups ($p = .80$). All grade 1 students improved their scores over the year on the DIBELS Phoneme Segmentation Fluency ($p < .01$), and there was a significant interaction ($p = .02$) favoring the formative classroom assessment group (effect size $d = .63$). The effect of treatment group and the interaction accounted for 9% of the variance in student scores.

Brookhart et al. (2008) replicated their Assessment for Learning professional development program in the same district with 18 teachers the following year. The authors noted that, because the number of teachers participating in the professional development increased, the face-to-face meetings changed in format from a seminar to a presentation and discussion format for the seven meetings. In the replication, teachers investigated formative classroom assessment using an inquiry-based approach by (1) reflecting on how they made learning goals clear to students; (2) providing feedback on progress toward those goals; and (3) reflecting on how they and the students used that information for improvement.

To identify a control group, the researchers used DIBELS scores of other Title I students enrolled in extended kindergarten. The kindergarten student scores on the DIBELS Letter Naming Fluency measure were used as the dependent variable. In the second year, all Title I students had teachers participating in the formative classroom assessment professional development. To develop the control group, researchers used scores from two sets of students. For the first control group, researchers used non-Title I first grade students from the same year. For the second control group, researchers used the two comparison groups from the previous study: Title I students with and without teachers in the formative assessment professional development. First grade student scores on the DIBELS Phoneme Segmentation Fluency measure were the dependent variable.

As in the first study, all kindergarten students in the second study significantly improved in their ability to accurately identify letters during the year ($p < .01$), but there were no significant differences between the two groups ($p = .26$). Grade 1 students improved their scores over the year on the DIBELS Phoneme Segmentation Fluency ($p < .01$), but there was a statistically significant difference ($p < .01$) favoring the non-Title I students. Group affiliation accounted for 3% of the observed variance in student scores. The authors noted that, because of the larger observable gains for the Title I group, their average score almost matched the average score of the non-Title I students.

In the second set of comparisons for grade 1 students, students in the treatment group in the second study were compared to the treatment and control groups from the first study. Students in the second study scored significantly higher on the DIBELS than did the students in the first study ($p = .02$). Group affiliation accounted for 4% of the observed variance in student scores. Post hoc comparisons showed that the treatment group means for the first and second studies were similar, and both treatment groups scored higher than the control group for the first study.

These findings, however, did not account for the nesting of the student data, which can increase type 1 error, and the effect size was based upon the observed variation in scores. It is probable that the effect size would be slightly smaller when generalized to the population of Title I students, which may call into question whether the professional development is meaningfully changing student achievement in terms of practical significance.

Taken together, the five studies reviewed above suggest that a full implementation of a professional development curriculum in formative classroom assessment is needed in order to improve student achievement, and the professional development program needs to be sustained across time. In addition, the professional development may need to be flexible so that teachers may choose which formative classroom assessment strategies they work to implement in their own classrooms. Allowing teachers to have ownership of their own learning may enhance the depth of implementation of the professional development and may encourage teachers to transfer new strategies into their daily teaching lives in the classroom. However, these findings must be considered tentative because the statistical differences observed in some of these studies did not account for nested student observations, which inflate type 1 error rates.

EXPERIMENTAL STUDIES IN FORMATIVE CLASSROOM ASSESSMENT

Six experimental studies and two qualitative studies of the South Carolina Department of Education's professional development program, entitled *Assessing Standards in the*

Classroom, are reviewed in this section. Four experimental studies investigated student achievement outcomes, and two investigated teacher outcomes. The experimental studies are described in detail and critiqued in terms of the rigor of design and data analysis, with the qualitative findings used to help interpret the empirical findings. Although the student achievement analyses accounted for nesting of student-level observations, control groups were not always present in the studies and in some cases data were missing, making it a challenge to interpret the findings.

South Carolina Department of Education

The South Carolina Department of Education developed a formative classroom assessment professional development program that was evaluated for effectiveness in a series of studies with low performing middle school teachers and their students. The professional development was comprised of 12 modules that had three broad phases. First, teachers viewed a video presentation of material that focused on a specific aspect of classroom assessment (Johnson, Schneider, & Siskind, 2004). Second, an assessment coach at a school led teachers through a collaborative assessment development task so that teachers discussed and practiced the presented guidelines. In many modules, teachers also analyzed and critiqued exemplars presented in a companion document to the video presentations (Schneider & Johnson, 2006). Exemplars comprised both positive and negative attributes in terms of classroom assessment construction guidelines and interpretations of standards identified by the state as confusing to teachers.

Teachers developed a variety of classroom assessments (e.g., performance tasks, checklists, rubrics, multiple choice items) using best practices that included focusing on the cognitive level of the state standard, analyzing student misconceptions of content, and establishing valid grading procedures. Teachers were trained to use classroom assessments formatively and summatively, and learned to interpret standardized test scores. The professional development was designed to consist of approximately 30 contact hours and 24 homework hours.

Efficacy Studies of Year One   Three empirical studies were conducted to examine the impact of the first year of the professional development. Each year 1 study was based upon data from a multisite, cluster randomized trial where randomization occurred at the school level. Schools were randomly assigned to either the treatment group, which received the professional development with support from a trained assessment coach, or a control group, which did not receive professional development.

In the first study of year 1, Schneider, Meyer, Miller, and Lottridge (2007) investigated whether teachers who received professional development in classroom assessment with support from a trained assessment coach more accurately applied measurement principles, cognitive levels, and state standards than teachers who did not receive such professional development or support. This study used a selected response test to measure teachers' skill in applied measurement principles, cognitive levels, and state standards as the outcome variable. One hundred and fifty-one grade 6 teachers in 29 low performing schools completed the professional development program. The teachers in both groups had comparable demographics and pretest scores. Each teacher participating in the study took a selected response pretest and posttest. The parallel forms of the tests were administered 4 months apart and had 60% of the items in common.

A split-plot ANOVA was used to compare experimental and control group results from pretest to posttest. There was a statistically significant interaction ($p < .001$) favoring the teachers in the treatment group across time. Generalized to the population, the interaction between group affiliation and time accounted for 11% of the variance in teacher scores.

In the second study of the year 1 efficacy evaluation of the South Carolina Department of Education professional development program in formative assessment, Schneider, Meyer, Miller, and Kaliski (2007) compared grade 6 English language arts and mathematics achievement between students of the teachers who participated in the professional development program and students of the control group teachers who did not participate in the program. A total of 2,066 students for English language arts (71% of the original sample due to data merging issues) and 2,457 students for mathematics (78% of the original sample) were included in the analysis. Students in each group had similar demographics, and teachers in each group had somewhat similar demographics. For the English language arts analysis, no effect was found for the treatment group. The treatment increased adjusted mathematics scores by 2.07 to 2.55 points, with 95% confidence.

Mazzie (2008) conducted the third study of year 1, investigating whether grade 6 students whose teachers received the professional development had higher science achievement than students of teachers who did not receive such professional development. No effect was found for the treatment.

Yap, Whittaker, Liao, and D'Amico (2006) also investigated the fidelity of the year 1 implementation of the South Carolina professional development program. They found sessions were interrupted or shortened due to field trips, holiday parties, and faculty meetings, or teachers arriving late and leaving sessions early. Teachers were, at times, pulled from the sessions for issues unrelated to the professional development. Teachers reported that they were often tired; other constraints, such as submitting lesson plans, made it hard to focus on the professional development.

Yap and her colleagues also found that coaches implemented 55 to 76% of the activities that comprised the professional development curriculum. Coaches sometimes eliminated some of the recommended collaborative group work and skipped to having teachers create their classroom assessments. This reduced the contact time from the recommended 54 hours to 30 to 41 hours. Yap and her colleagues (2007) found similar issues in the second year fidelity of implementation study.

Efficacy Studies of Year Two   In year 2, the evaluation shifted from comparing a treatment group (professional development with assessment coaches) to a control group (no professional development) to comparing two levels of treatment: professional development with a trained assessment coach versus professional development with an untrained facilitator. Schools in the year 1 study that were randomly assigned to the professional development (now the treatment I group) maintained their trained assessment coach and the previous control group schools became the treatment II group, which received the professional development with a relatively untrained facilitator. The main difference between the two levels of treatment was the level of support provided to the assessment coaches and facilitators. Assessment coaches received assessment training and were trained in evaluating the teacher-generated assessments. The untrained facilitators did not receive assessment training and were not trained in evaluating the teacher-generated assessments.

In year 1 of the study, grade 6 teachers had participated in the professional development, whereas in year 2, grade 7 teachers participated. The components and phases of the formative classroom assessment professional development remained the same as in year 1. The grade 7 teachers in both treatment groups received the same professional development curriculum, sequence, and activities as teachers in year 1. Three studies were conducted to estimate the impact of the formative assessment professional development in year 2.

Schneider, Cid, Ragland, and Kaliski (2007) investigated whether grade 7 teachers who received professional development in classroom assessment with support from a trained assessment coach more accurately applied measurement principles, cognitive levels, and state standards than teachers who received the same professional development from an untrained facilitator. The outcome for this study was a selected-response test that measured teachers' knowledge in creating high-quality classroom assessments aligned to state standards. One hundred and forty grade 7 teachers completed the second year of the professional development implementation. Each grade 7 teacher participating in the study took the selected response pretest and posttest. In this study, the tests were administered 6 months apart. A split-plot ANOVA was used to compare treatment I and treatment II group results from pretest to posttest. There were no differences between groups, however, both treatment groups made significant gains from the pretest to the posttest with testing occasion—prior to the professional development and after the professional development—accounting for 60% of the variance in teacher scores.

Ragland, Schneider, Yap, and Kaliski (2008) investigated whether grade 7 students whose teachers received the professional development had higher English language arts and mathematics achievement than students of teachers who received the professional development with an untrained facilitator. Teacher pretest and posttest self-reported attitudes and beliefs about classroom assessment, self-reported classroom assessment practices, and teachers' self-reported grading practices were collected, in addition to student outcomes. A total of 1,767 students of English language arts and 1,890 students of mathematics were used in the analysis. The percentage of the original sample used for analysis was not reported for English language arts or mathematics. Students and teachers in each group had similar demographics.

The students' ELA scores did not differ significantly depending upon whether their teacher received the professional development with an assessment coach or an untrained facilitator. Unfortunately, missing data resulted in the loss of about half of the teachers (classrooms) during the HLM analysis, which affects the trustworthiness of the analysis.

For the mathematics analysis, the level 2 model resulted in a statistically significant interaction between teacher beliefs about assessment and group affiliation (controlling for the other level 2 covariates), indicating that when a teacher's belief about assessment and learning strengthened in the assessment coach group, so too did adjusted mathematics scores. This finding is dampened, however, by two issues. First, the level 1 model was the best fitting model, which shows the overall variation in student mathematical scores based upon this finding was not practically meaningful. Second, this study did not have a control group, so the overall finding of no difference between the two groups for each subject area lacks an overall interpretation as to whether both treatment groups were equally effective or ineffective.

Mazzie (2008) investigated whether grade 7 students whose teachers received the professional development with an assessment coach had higher science achievement than students of teachers who received the professional development with an untrained facilitator. No difference was found between the coach and facilitator group. As with the previous study, this study did not have a control group, so the overall finding of no difference between the two groups leaves us without an overall interpretation as to whether both treatment groups were equally effective or ineffective.

The studies of the South Carolina professional development initiative show that a partial implementation of a professional development program in formative classroom assessment produces changes in teacher assessment knowledge but these changes were not sufficient to increase student achievement. This finding corroborates the results from the quasi-experimental studies reviewed in the previous section, in which a full implementation of the professional development was needed to see differences in student achievement.

OTHER STUDIES RELATED TO PROFESSIONAL DEVELOPMENT IN FORMATIVE ASSESSMENT

Three quasi-experimental studies investigating alternate methods of professional development relating to formative classroom assessment are reviewed in this section of the chapter. These three studies demonstrate that professional development in formative assessment may also occur in the context of larger efforts to improve student performance or change teacher practice. Each study is briefly described and critiqued in terms of the rigor of its design and data analysis. Common critiques include problems related to small sample sizes.

Quint, Sepanik, and Smith (2008) used an interrupted time series design to investigate the effect of administering a series of short assessments aligned with the content and item types of a state assessment to grade 3 and grade 4 students, as well as the corresponding professional development provided to teachers in schools that volunteered to participate in the program. The professional development for teachers was provided by an instructional coach who taught teachers how to analyze the data from assessments and how to utilize the results of those analyses to inform instruction. Most of the teachers in the study spent 1 to 5 hours in professional development. Comparison schools were located within the same district, and generally received similar amounts of professional development, though not with the particular program under investigation. The researchers found that differences in the grade 3 and grade 4 students' reading scores on the statewide test were generally positive but not statistically significant when compared to the control group.

Sato, Wei, and Darling-Hammond (2008) used a 3-year comparison group design to evaluate the impact of the National Board certification process on teachers' classroom assessment practices. The nine teachers undergoing the certification process showed statistically significant improvement in six dimensions of classroom assessment practice over the comparison group of seven teachers. Teachers were not randomly assigned to groups. The authors of this study suggest that the National Board certification process offers professional development activities that can change teachers' practice in formative classroom assessment, particularly in promoting the use of a variety of assessment methods and how results are used to inform instruction.

Yin et al. (2008) conducted a small experimental study of 12 teachers randomly assigned to either receive training and implement embedded formative instruction as part of a science curriculum, or simply deliver the science curriculum without the embedded formative assessment. Although the design of this study was rigorous, the study was underpowered and no significant differences were found in the achievement of students from the two groups.

Two of the three studies reviewed above support previous findings in the literature. First, professional development must be sustained over time in order to make changes in teacher knowledge and practice. Second, professional development that is not sustained is unlikely to influence student achievement.

CHARACTERISTICS OF EFFECTIVE FORMATIVE CLASSROOM ASSESSMENT PROFESSIONAL DEVELOPMENT PROGRAMS

Rigorous causal evidence linking improved student achievement to professional development in formative classroom assessment is not available but the research reviewed above has pointed to characteristics of professional development that are linked to improvements in teacher practice. In this section, research findings derived from the professional development literature across a variety of content areas are reviewed and linked to the previously reviewed studies investigating professional development in formative classroom assessment. The seven general characteristics of professional development programs in the ensuing discussion are likely to be important when designing future programs in formative classroom assessment, including administrative support, individualization of teachers' learning goals, content knowledge, time, collaboration, coherence, and active learning.

Administrative Support

The WSS study included schools that had fully implemented the program for 3 years (Meisels et al., 2003). Brookhart et al. (2007) worked with a group of teachers selected by the district's Title I supervisor. This suggests that, when teachers participate in a formative assessment professional development program that is endorsed and strongly supported by school and district level administrators, the professional development is likely to have a higher fidelity of implementation. Higher fidelity of implementation is more likely to have an outcome of higher student achievement. Therefore, strong support of a professional development program by administrators may be one of the most important factors in ensuring the professional development is effective.

Individualization of Teacher's Professional Development Learning Goals

Most of the reviewed studies investigated professional development programs that centered in professional learning communities and active learning strategies for participants. A subtle, yet likely important element of a successful formative classroom assessment professional development program may be the use of teacher inquiry of professional development learning goals. Teachers may be more active participants in their own learning when professional development learning goals are not standardized across the study participants but rather personalized by the teachers themselves. The formative classroom assessment professional development programs investigated by Wiliam et al. (2004) and Brookhart et al. (2007, 2008) allowed teachers to develop formative classroom assessment techniques of their own choosing.

The characteristics of effective professional development have been examined in detail and described by Garet and colleagues (Birman, Desimone, Porter, & Garet, 2000; Garet, Porter, Desimone, Birman, & Yoon 2001; Yoon, Duncan, Lee, Scarloss, & Shapley, 2007). The following section describes five of these evidence-based professional development characteristics that are most relevant to professional development in formative classroom assessment, and their relationship to the studies reviewed above: (1) content knowledge, (2) time, (3) collaboration, (4) coherence, and (4) active learning.

Content Knowledge   Increasing teachers' content knowledge is one of the most frequently listed characteristics of effective professional development (Guskey, 2003; Stiggins, this volume). This characteristic includes (1) increasing teachers' knowledge of the content they teach; (2) increasing teachers' knowledge of how to teach a specific content area (i.e., pedagogical content knowledge); and (3) increasing teachers' understanding of the ways in which students learn the content. A focus on content knowledge and pedagogical content knowledge is thought to benefit teachers by providing them with a deep and thorough understanding of the subject matter and an understanding of how students learn that subject matter.

Kennedy (1998) concluded that the successful professional development programs focused specifically on improving teachers' knowledge of how students learn subject matter rather than simply increasing the teachers' knowledge of the subject. One caveat to the existing research on the importance of content knowledge is that most of the research supporting the importance of content knowledge has focused on the effects of professional development for increasing student achievement in mathematics and science (Guskey, 2003).

Professional development focused on general teaching skills or general teaching strategies generic to specific content without emphasizing content that has been found to be less effective (Birman et al., 2000; Kennedy, 1998). These findings suggest that, in effective professional development in formative classroom assessment, teachers are often learning best practices for eliciting valid and reliable information from students in order to change instruction as needed. Strategies and methods for developing sound assessments, collecting accurate information about students' abilities, and communicating that information back to students are applicable to many different content areas and different grade levels. Increasing teachers' knowledge and improving their practice in formative classroom assessment, however, does nothing to directly increase teachers' knowledge of their content area or their knowledge of how students learn in the content area. It is possible that teachers may only internalize this information and apply it to their own content area when all instruction and examples are framed within their own content area.

Although formative classroom assessment professional development may have a pedagogical element to it, the professional development oftentimes occurs with teachers across multiple content areas. With the exception of the Brookhart et al. (2007, 2008) studies, the professional development programs in formative classroom assessment reviewed in this chapter were implemented with teachers in multiple content areas simultaneously. When professional development in formative classroom assessment is delivered to teachers in multiple content areas at once, the assumption is that teachers have the content and pedagogy skills necessary to successfully implement what they have learned: This may not be the case. Future research in professional development for formative classroom assessment may need to differentiate the effectiveness of professional development delivered by content area or across content areas. It may be helpful to have a measure of teacher content knowledge to estimate how this influences formative classroom assessment outcomes and student achievement.

Time   Time, as it relates to professional development, has two main components: contact hours and duration. Contact hours includes all the time teachers spend in the professional development activities, including activities such as workshops or lectures, self-study, meeting with colleagues, and applying the practices and techniques under study. Contact hours can range from only a few hours for a workshop to 50 or more hours for a more comprehensive program. Duration refers to the span of time over which the contact hours are spent. This may involve days, weeks, or months.

Research findings regarding the impact of contact hours and duration, however, are inconsistent. In some studies, contact hours have not been associated with changes in instructional practices (e.g., Desimone Porter, Garet, Yoon, & Birman, 2002; Kennedy, 1998; Wenglinsky, 2002). In other studies, duration has been associated with increases in active learning and collaboration, suggesting an indirect effect on outcomes of knowledge and practice (Ingvarson, Meiers, & Beavis, 2005). These inconsistent findings underscore the importance of how time is used. Time spent during the professional development must be well organized, carefully structured, and purposefully directed (Guskey, 1999).

Teachers need time to first develop their knowledge of the practices and principals underlying sound formative classroom assessment, such as the purposes of assessment, the importance of feedback, and matching assessment target to assessment method. This is often the purpose of contact hours. Teachers also need supported durational time in a professional development program in formative classroom assessment to practice and fully integrate new skills into their daily lives as teachers. Developing formative assessment skills requires trial and error, permission to make mistakes, application of learned principles to their own classroom, and the support of colleagues and administration.

The majority of the studies reviewed in this chapter seem to have been sensitive to implementing the professional development from a duration perspective, but the number of contact hours was not always clearly stated. In the future, consistent collection and reporting of data regarding contact hours and duration will be helpful to better understand how the number of contact hours and the implementation length effect changes in teacher practice and student achievement.

Collaboration   Collaboration is thought to assist teachers in integrating professional development concepts into their daily practice by providing teachers with a supportive environment for reflecting on and exchanging new information and ideas for improving practice, discussing and sharing ideas, experimenting with new practices in the classroom, observing each other, and sharing what works and what does not with colleagues. Professional development programs that include collaboration have been associated with increased active learning and increased coherence with other professional activities and duties (Birman et al., 2000). For collaboration to be effective, it needs to be designed to be purposeful and must be structured so that it supports the goals of improving teaching and learning (Guskey, 2003).

Collaborative professional development is exemplified by professional learning communities (DuFour, 2004, 2005). Professional learning communities can create a school culture that helps teachers work together to improve instructional practice and raise student achievement (DuFour, 2004). Stiggins and colleagues recommend forming learning teams for professional development in formative classroom assessment (Arter, 2001; Stiggins, 1999). Each of the professional development programs in the formative classroom assessment studies reviewed in this chapter implemented professional learning communities in some capacity. For example, the Keeping Learning on Track program referred to learning teams as teacher learning communities (Bell et al., 2008), and the Assessment for Learning studies (Brookhart et al., 2007, 2008) show that a professional learning community may be accomplished successfully online.

Coherence   Schools are under pressure to increase student achievement and may try many different means to achieve this goal. Often there are competing initiatives being implemented simultaneously within schools. For professional development to be effective in this context, it must be part of a coherent effort of reform and teacher training. A coherent professional development program is one that builds upon what already exists in the school in terms of previous professional development, teachers' strengths and weaknesses, and the implemented curriculum. Coherent professional development also dovetails with what is happening at the district level in terms of initiatives, goals, and policies. Coherence can also include alignment with state content and performance standards. Coherence has been found to have a positive, indirect effect on teacher practice through changes in teachers' knowledge and skill, and a direct effect on changes in teacher practice (Garet et al., 2001).

The Assessment for Learning (Brookhart et al., 2007, 2008) professional development program was coherent with previous professional development in the district because it supplemented previous professional development in how children developed reading skills and worked within the prescribed reading curriculum enacted by the district. The South Carolina studies also worked to be coherent by focusing on helping teachers understand how to align classroom assessments to state standards. As noted by Brookhart (2005), formative classroom assessment can suffer when teachers' understanding of the learning targets is incomplete. This suggests that, for professional development in formative classroom assessment to benefit from coherence, it should be aimed at increasing teachers' content knowledge, pedagogical content knowledge, and understanding of content standards.

Active Learning   Professional development that provides teachers with the opportunity to be actively involved in the learning process is associated with positive outcomes (Desimone et al., 2002). Active learning was most strongly related to changes in practice after controlling for the effects of focusing on content knowledge (Ingvarson et al., 2005). Active learning refers to opportunities for teachers to engage in the content and subject matter through various mechanisms such as discussion and interactions with colleagues, hands-on practice, and working with students. These types of learning activities are thought to increase teachers' engagement with the content and help them process the material and subject matter at a deeper level than if they were just passive recipients of information.

Active learning is likely to be a critical component of professional development in formative classroom assessment, and each of the reviewed studies used active learning as a professional development mechanism. To develop skills in formative classroom assessment and to improve the implementation of formative classroom assessment, teachers need to have hands-on experiences rather than just an increased knowledge of the formative classroom assessment principals. Providing teachers with multiple opportunities to develop and administer different types of assessments both formally and informally may be a vital component to improving formative classroom assessment practice.

One of the hallmarks of formative assessment is the interaction and communication between teacher and student regarding the student's progress toward acquiring the knowledge and skills defined by the learning objectives. Formative assessment cannot be effective without this interaction. One important aspect of active learning in professional development is the opportunity to review student work (Garet et al., 2001). It stands to reason, therefore, that effective professional development in formative classroom assessment must train and encourage teachers to actively review student work and to have students review their own work and the work of their peers.

The research on characteristics of effective professional development has found that contextual factors can strongly influence which characteristics contribute to a professional development program's effectiveness (Guskey, 2003). Research also has found that many professional development programs lack the features thought to make them effective (Garet et al., 2001). This finding suggests that professional development programs can be improved by reflecting the seven characteristics discussed above: Administrative support, individualization of teachers' learning goals, content knowledge, time, collaboration, coherence, and active learning.

CHALLENGES FOR THE DESIGN AND STUDY OF EFFECTIVE FORMATIVE CLASSROOM ASSESSMENT PROFESSIONAL DEVELOPMENT PROGRAMS

In addition to shedding light on characteristics of effective professional development programs in formative classroom assessment, the studies reviewed in this chapter also depict how difficult it is to implement a study from which strong causal conclusions can be drawn. There are challenges not only in designing an effective formative classroom assessment professional development program but also substantial challenges in designing research studies that measure the efficacy of the professional development program. Ideally, research in this area would meet the standards of evidence articulated by the What Works Clearinghouse.

What Works Clearinghouse Evidence Standards

In 2002, the U.S. Department of Education's Institute of Educational Sciences established the What Works Clearinghouse (WWC) as a central repository of educational research on specific key topics of interest. The purpose of the WWC is to independently evaluate and publish rigorous reviews of interventions that purport to improve student achievement in a key topic area. While formative classroom assessment is not a key topic, student achievement outcomes used in studies of formative classroom assessment— such as beginning reading and elementary and middle school mathematics—fall under current WWC topics.

The WWC provides criteria for categorizing studies as follows: *Meets Evidence Standards*, *Meets Evidence Standards with Reservations*, and *Does Not Meet Evidence Screens*. Only randomized-controlled trials with sufficient rigor are likely to be given the designation *Meets Evidence Standards*. Quasi-experimental designs with sufficient rigor of only the following three types may be given the designation *Meets Evidence Standards with Reservations*: quasi-experiment with equating, regression discontinuity designs, or single-case designs. As researchers design studies regarding professional development in formative classroom assessment in the future, a review of the *Evidence Standards for Reviewing Studies* may be warranted. Currently, no study of professional development in formative classroom assessment performed to date would have the *Meets Evidence Standards* designation. In fact, few studies investigating the impact of any professional development program on student achievement in general would be considered rigorous. Yoon and colleagues found that only 9 out of 1300 studies met the WWC *Meets Evidence Standards* (Yoon et al., 2007).

Given the paucity of rigorous research, it is difficult to say with any certainty what effective professional development in formative classroom assessment looks like. But in areas outside of formative classroom assessment, rigorous research has linked professional development with gains in student achievement. Yoon et al. (2007) found the average effect of professional development programs was .53 standard deviations or 21 percentile points in terms of student achievement in the nine studies that met the WWC evidence standards. These studies investigated a variety of professional development programs ranging from those that addressed teaching behaviors applicable to any content area to professional development that provided guidance regarding pedagogy for specific curriculum or content area. Two of the nine studies were related to formative classroom assessment.

Research that provides precise estimates of the impact of professional development in formative classroom assessment on student outcomes or teacher outcomes is just beginning. This type of research is essential to determine if professional development in formative classroom assessment is effective in raising student achievement and changing teacher practice. This type of research is also needed to better understand for whom professional development in formative classroom assessment is effective and under what conditions.

Conducting experimental studies to provide unbiased estimates of intervention effects is challenging. School and district administrators often do not understand the role of random assignment and recruiting sites is difficult given the many demands on teachers' and schools' time and resources. The practical realities of day-to-day education often interfere with the constraints of rigorous research. The issues and challenges of conducting randomized trails are many and have been documented elsewhere (e.g., Bloom, 2005; Orr, 1999; Shadish, Cook, & Campbell, 2002). In the following sections of this chapter, issues, challenges, and recommendations for conducting rigorous research on professional development in formative classroom assessment are discussed.

Experimental Designs and Intact Classrooms

Professional development research suggests that collaboration is important to effective professional development in formative classroom assessment. Groups of teachers, rather than individual teachers, will need to be randomly assigned to the intervention or control group when conducting a study to estimate the effectiveness of the professional development. Working together, however, means that teacher observations become dependent upon one another, and researchers should design studies that account for the nesting of teachers when possible. Conducting multilevel analyses to estimate program impacts is technically more challenging than analyzing the data at the individual level, but rigorous analytical procedures that account for the nested structure of the data are widely available (e.g., Raudenbush & Bryk, 2002).

Randomly assigning groups of teachers to treatments, rather than individual teachers, reduces statistical power (Bloom, Bos, & Lee, 1999). When statistical power may be a concern because the units of analysis are too few, a dual analysis approach may be considered. For example, Schneider, Meyer, Miller, and Lottridge (2007) used a split-plot ANOVA to measure the teacher outcomes of 151 teachers in 29 schools. This design likely inflated the type I error, so the authors ran a second split-plot analysis that used the 29 school-level means as the unit of analysis. While there was insufficient evidence to reject the null hypothesis ($p = .065$), the researchers found an effect size comparable to their initial findings. Future studies with clustered sample sizes that do not support a multilevel model may use a dual analysis ANOVA approach on teacher or student data to provide more confidence that the effect sizes found are stable and not being influenced by the nesting of observations.

Outcome Measures

Measurement of outcomes is a nontrivial aspect of any research study. Decisions regarding the measurement of outcomes are associated with at least as much variance in observed effects as other design features (Wilson & Lipsey, 2001). The alignment of outcome measures can have a dramatic effect on the size of the effect of the intervention and the sample size needed to detect that effect.

Improving student achievement is often the ultimate goal of professional development, so some measure of student achievement is often the outcome variable in impact studies of professional development in formative classroom assessment. However, the choice of student achievement measures can have large effects on the results. Student outcomes such as motivation are also likely to be important in impact studies because student motivation may be a mediator between improved classroom assessment practice and student achievement. Although numerous measures of student motivation are available, student motivation variables were not incorporated into the design of the studies reviewed in this chapter.

A full understanding of the impact of professional development in formative assessment cannot be realized without measuring and understanding the impact on teachers. Unfortunately, few instruments are available that measure teacher outcomes related to formative classroom assessment. Some instruments very broadly measure teachers' knowledge of assessment (Mertler & Campbell, 2005; Plake, Impara, & Fager, 1993), teachers' perceptions of competence in formative classroom assessment (Zhang, 1996; Zhang & Burry-Stock, 1995), or teachers' ability to apply best practices for developing performance assessments and multiple choice assessments (Schneider, Meyer, Miller, & Lottridge, 2007). Instruments were not found that measure teachers' conceptual knowledge of the basic principles in formative classroom assessment, such as its purposes, the differences between formative and summative assessment, or the alignment of particular learning targets with the most appropriate assessment methods. There are also no existing instruments that measure teachers' practice of formative classroom assessment, including the quality of the assessments they use in the classroom, their interactions with or involvement of students, or the ways they use and communicate information to students.

Although student achievement is the ultimate outcome, teacher outcomes represent an important proximal outcome for professional development in formative classroom assessment. Research on professional development in formative classroom assessment should include proximal teacher outcomes to help understand the processes or mechanisms that are responsible for producing any potential effects. The proximal outcomes should be chosen based on the "theory of change" of the intervention. For example, professional development in formative assessment may be hypothesized to work through student involvement in assessment, or through improved feedback, or through better communication of learning targets. Some measure of these proximal outcomes is necessary to begin to understand their relations with the ultimate outcome of student achievement. Researchers attempting to study professional development in formative assessment should be warned, however, that they will likely have to develop and validate their own instruments if they plan to measure teacher outcomes.

Sample Size

In general, the effects of educational interventions are often small and difficult to detect, thus requiring large samples for adequate statistical power. According to Bloom (2007), mean effect sizes for educational interventions may range from as small as .07 where the outcome measure is a standardized test, to .23 where the outcome is a standardized test with content aligned with the intervention, to as large as .44 where the outcome measure is a specialized test that targets the focus of the intervention. A study attempting to detect an effect of .23 would require a sample of 69 clusters. Parameters for this power analysis were: $\alpha = .05$, $n = 60$, $\rho = .20$, and $R^2 = .50$. If the intervention is delivered at the school level such that schools are randomly assigned to treatment groups, 69 schools is a large sample to acquire.

Power analyses are useful to help estimate the sample size needed to have a reasonable chance of detecting an effect. Free and easy to use software is available (e.g., Optimal Design, see Liu, Spybrook, Congdon, Martinez, & Raudenbush, 2006). Conducting a power analysis is highly recommended to avoid the situation where the available sample size would provide little or no chance of detecting a statistically significant effect. It should be noted, however, that power analyses require the input of numerous parameters and the results of the power analysis are highly dependent on the assumptions about these parameter estimates.

Black and Wiliam (1998) conducted a review of quantitative studies in the area of classroom assessment and learning, and reported effect sizes ranging from .20 to .70. These differences in effect sizes reflect very different sample sizes needed to achieve adequate statistical power. It is important to note these effect sizes were outcomes of studies of various designs and rigor. In addition, it may be wise to review the effect sizes to determine if they are comparable across studies (Olejnik & Algina, 2000, 2003).

It is unlikely that an effect size of a professional development under investigation will be known a priori. Researchers conducting power analyses will need to carefully estimate the anticipated effect size in order for the results of the power analysis to be accurate. The effect size estimate must be based on a number of factors: (1) the outcome measure being used; (2) any previous research on the professional development program; (3) previous research on programs that are similar to or share components with the program under investigation; (4) the duration of the professional development and the lag between completing the it and measuring the outcome; and (5) a healthy dose of skepticism regarding the size of the effect that actually can be produced.

As noted earlier, power analyses also require assumptions regarding the degree of association between and the amount of variance accounted for by covariates. Recently published research provides help regarding choosing values for these parameters, particularly in terms of student achievement (Hedges & Hedberg, 2007a, 2007b; Schochet, 2005). But little is known about characteristics of data and constructs related to teacher outcomes, particularly those relevant to professional development in formative classroom assessment. The intraclass correlations found in our review of the literature on professional development in formative classroom assessment ranged from .13 to .28 for student achievement. Researchers should attempt to glean what they can from any relevant previous research and use conservative parameter estimates to avoid an underpowered study.

Fidelity of Implementation

An intervention may not be effective if it is not implemented with fidelity to its original design. Researchers are encouraged to strongly consider researching and building measures of fidelity of implementation. Such variables can provide important empirical information useful for interpreting the outcomes of a study. Various sources provide more information regarding this aspect of conducting a large scale-impact trial (e.g., Cordray & Pion, 2006; Lipsey & Cordray, 2000).

Beyond the general benefits of assessing fidelity for any study, the field of research on professional development in formative assessment needs more empirical data on the degree to which teachers are able to implement professional development programs with fidelity, and which elements or aspects of the programs are feasible or not. The Work Sampling System study found large gains for students in the program in schools that had implemented the program for 3 years (Meisels et al., 2003). This suggests that teachers had a great degree of support from their building-level administrators. Conversely, the low performing schools in the South Carolina studies (Yap et al., 2006, 2007) and Keeping Learning on Track study (Bell, Steinberg, Wiliam, & Wylie, 2008) may have difficulty maintaining the momentum and fidelity of implementation for professional development in formative assessment when school-level administrators did not learn about the professional development or actively work to support it. It appears that when administrators do not preserve the sanctity of the professional development time, this affects the fidelity of the professional development implementation.

The professional development implemented by Brookhart et al. (2007, 2008) for the Assessment for Learning program may have proved more successful in this regard because much of their professional development time comprised discussion and reflections online. In this way, the professional development time did not actively compete with the time that school-based administrators wanted to use for meetings and other purposes. Implementation fidelity data can inform many decisions regarding the development and design of professional development programs. Fidelity of implementation may be related to the degree of support the learning communities have from their administration; this warrants investigation in the future. Future researchers will want to collect information on fidelity of implementation and the degree of school and district level support prior to and when conducting experimental and quasi-experimental designs to understand the capacity of similar schools to implement the professional development program as well as to inform the empirical findings of studies.

Study Length

Professional development that is of comparatively longer duration is likely to be more effective than professional development of shorter duration. This may be particularly true of professional development in formative classroom assessment, given the changes in knowledge, skills, and practice necessary to transform teacher practices in formative assessment. Studying a professional development program that requires a long duration poses special challenges. First, the study must examine the training phase of the professional development program. This phase could last as long as one school year. If the training phase lasts one school year, additional time is required to allow the intervention to affect student achievement because the training year likely only represents partial exposure of students to the formative assessment targeted by the professional development. A study of professional development in formative assessment, therefore, is likely to require at least 2 years, if not more, to show effects on student learning.

The longer the study, the longer the participants have to be tracked and the longer they need to stay engaged. As time progresses, changes in teaching staff occur, students move in and out of classrooms and schools, and other initiatives take attention away from the program under study. Teacher transitions and student mobility can reduce power by decreasing the number of participants, but these losses can be planned for when conducting power analyses and recruiting schools. Tracking students over time can pose a greater challenge to the validity of the study, depending on its design, but this challenge is aided by the fact that more states are moving to track students across time using unique student IDs.

There is no question that conducting experimental research in educational settings is a significant challenge. In future studies, researchers need to clearly document the number of contact hours and duration of professional development programs under study. Studies should also be designed to collect multiple data sources to more fully understand what changes as a result of formative classroom assessment professional development. Such data sources include outcomes for teacher achievement, teacher motivation, student achievement, student motivation, fidelity of implementation, and implementation support. Because the needed measures may not currently exist, it is likely that some have to be developed.

With regard to the reporting of study results, researchers may not always provide other researchers with sufficient information to inform the designs of future studies. Increased standards of rigor for research requires more complete information in reporting of results so researchers can synthesize findings across studies, future researchers are able to conduct precise power analyses, and professional development curriculum authors can refine their interventions. For example, if complete tables of variance sources based upon the study design are not included in the reporting of results or the specific calculations shown for determination of effect sizes, other researchers may not be able to parse out information to assist them in the design of future studies or determine accurate estimates of effects in meta analyses. Explicitness in the reporting of results provides the foundation for learning what aspects of professional development in formative assessment are essential for changing student achievement.

CONCLUSION

The findings presented in this chapter suggest that professional development in formative classroom assessment should be of sustained duration with sufficient contact hours to present the formative classroom assessment concepts, and provide substantial support which allows teachers to practice applying new skills. The optimal length of the professional development program has yet to be determined. Supovitz and Turner (2000) found that teachers need between 40 and 79 hours of professional development to change their practices beyond that of the average teacher. The series of efficacy studies from South Carolina show that teachers in low performing schools can change their formative classroom assessment knowledge base in 30 to 41 hours; however, the number of hours needed to change teacher knowledge is not necessarily the number of hours needed to increase student achievement.

Professional development programs in formative classroom assessment are optimally implemented in environments that facilitate full implementation of the program, incorporate professional learning communities, active learning, and teacher ownership of learning goals. Future research, however, is needed to determine if professional development in formative classroom assessment needs to be content specific. Most important, many rigorous investigations need to occur to determine if formative classroom assessment professional development programs do indeed improve student achievement.

REFERENCES

Airasian, P. W., & Jones, A. M. (1993). The teachers as applied measurer: Realities of classroom measurement and assessment. *Applied Measurement in Education, 6*(3), 241–254.

Andrade, H. L., Du, Y., Wang, X. (2008). Putting rubrics to the test: The effect of model, criteria generation, and rubric-referenced self-assessment on elementary school students' writing. *Educational Measurement: Issues and Practice, 27*(2), 3–13.

Arter, J. (2001). Learning teams for classroom assessment literacy. *NASSP Bulletin, 85*(621), 53–65.

Aschbacher, P. R. (1999). *Developing indicators of classroom practice to monitor and support school reform* (CRESST Technical Report No. 513). University of California, Los Angeles: Center for Research on Educational Standards and Student Testing. Retrieved January 30, 2009, from http://research.cse.ucla.edu/Reports/TECH513.pdf

Bell, C., Steinberg, J., Wiliam, D., & Wylie, C. (2008, March). *Formative assessment and teacher achievement: Two years of implementation of the Keeping Learning on Track Program.* Paper presented at the annual meeting of the National Council on Measurement in Education, New York.

Birman, B. F., Desimone, L., Porter, A. C., & Garet, M. S. (2000). Designing professional development that works. *Educational Leadership, 61*, 28–33.

Black, P., & Wiliam, D. (1998). Assessment and classroom learning. *Assessment in Education: Principles, Policy & Practice, 5*(1), 7–74.

Bloom, H. S. (Ed.). (2005). *Learning more from social experiments.* New York: Russell Sage Foundation.

Bloom, H. S. (2007, June). *Sample design for group-randomized trials.* Paper presented at the IES Research Training Institute on Cluster Randomized Trails, Vanderbilt University, Nashville, TN.

Bloom, H. S., Bos, J. M., & Lee, S. W. (1999) Using cluster random assignment to measure program impacts: Statistical implications for the evaluation of educational programs. *Evaluation Review, 23*(4), 445–469.

Brookhart, S. M. (2001, March). *The Standards and classroom assessment research.* Paper presented at the annual meeting of the American Association of Colleges for Teacher Education, Dallas, TX.

Brookhart, S. M. (2005, April). *Research on formative classroom assessment.* Paper presented at the annual meeting of the American Educational Research Association, Montreal, Canada.

Brookhart, S. M., Moss, C. M., & Long, B. A. (2007). *A cross-case analysis of teacher inquiry into formative assessment practices in six Title I reading classrooms.* CASTL Technical Report Series No. 1-07. Retrieved August 18, 2008, from http://www.castl.duq.edu/Castl_TechReports.htm

Brookhart, S. M., Moss, C. M., Long, B. A. (2008, March). *Professional development in formative assessment: Effects on teacher and student learning.* Paper presented at the annual meeting of the National Council on Measurement in Education, New York.

Corallo, C., & McDonald D. (2001). *What works with low-performing schools: A review of research literature on low-performing schools.* Charleston, WV: Appalachian Education Laboratory. (ERIC Document Reproduction Number ED 462 737)

Cordray, D. S., & Pion, G. M. (2006). Treatment strength and integrity: Models and methods. In R. R. Bootzin & P. E. McKnight (Eds.), *Strengthening research methodology: Psychological measurement and evaluation* (pp. 103–124). Washington, DC: American Psychological Association Press.

Desimone, L. M., Porter, A. C., Garet, M. S., Yoon, K. S., & Birman, B. F. (2002). Effects of professional development on teachers' instruction: Results from a three-year longitudinal study. *Educational Evaluation and Policy Analysis, 24*(2), 81–112.

DuFour, R. (2004). What is a "Professional Learning Community"? *Educational Leadership, 61*(8), 6–11.
DuFour, R. (2005). What is a professional learning community? In R. DuFour, R. Eaker, & R. DuFour (Eds.), *On common ground: The power of professional learning communities* (pp. 31–44). Bloomington, IN: National Educational Service.
Dunlap, W. P., Cortina, J. M., Vaslow, J. B., & Burke, M. J. (1996). Meta-analysis of experiments with matched groups or repeated measures designs. *Psychological Methods, 1,* 170–177.
Garet, M. S., Porter, A. C., Desimone, L., Birman, B. F., & Yoon, K. S. (2001). What makes professional development effective? Results from a national sample of teachers. *American Educational Research Journal, 38*(4), 915–945.
Guskey, T. R., (1999). Apply time with wisdom. *Journal of Staff Development, 20*(2), 10–15.
Guskey, T. R. (2003). Analyzing lists of the characteristics of effective professional development to promote visionary leadership. *NASSP Bulletin, 87*(637), 4–20.
Haydel, J. B., Oescher, J., & Banbury, M. (1995, April). *Assessing classroom teachers' performance assessments.* Paper presented at the annual meeting of the American Educational Research Association, San Francisco.
Hedges, L. V., & Hedberg, E. C. (2007a). Intraclass correlations for planning group randomized experiments in rural education. *Journal of Research in Rural Education, 22*(10), 1–15.
Hedges, L. V., & Hedberg, E. C. (2007b). Intraclass correlations for planning group-randomized trials in education. *Educational Evaluation and Policy Analysis, 29*(1), 60–87.
Ingvarson, L., Meiers, M., & Beavis, A. (2005). Factors affecting the impact of professional development programs on teachers' knowledge, practice, student outcomes and efficacy. *Education Policy Analysis Archives, 13*(10). Retrieved July 28, 2008, from http://epaa.asu.edu/epaa/v13n10/
Johnson, R., Schneider, M. C., & Siskind, T. (2004). *Assessing standards in the classroom* [Video series]. Columbia, SC: SCETV.
Kennedy, M. (1998). *Form and substance of inservice teacher education* (Research Monograph No. 13). Madison, WI: National Institute for Science Education, University of Wisconsin-Madison.
Leahy, S., Lyon, C., Thompson, M., & Wiliam, D. (2005). Classroom assessment: Minute by minute, day by day. *Educational Leadership, 63*(3), 18–24.
Lipsey, M. W., & Cordray, D. S. (2000). Evaluation methods for social intervention. *Annual Review of Psychology, 51,* 345–375.
Liu, X., Spybrook, J., Congdon, R., Martinez, A., & Raudenbush, S. (2006). Optimal design for multi-level and longitudinal research (version 1.77) [Software]. Chicago: HLM Software.
Marso, R. N., & Pigge, F. L. (1993). Teachers' testing knowledge, skills, and practices. In S. L. Wise (Ed.), *Teacher training in measurement and assessment skills* (pp. 129–185). Lincoln, NE: Buros Institute of Mental Measurements, University of Nebraska-Lincoln.
Mazzie. D. D. (2008). *The effects of professional development related to classroom assessment on student achievement in science.* Unpublished doctoral dissertation, University of South Carolina, Columbia.
Meisels, S., Atkins-Burnett, S., Xue, Y., Nicholson, J., Bickel, D. D., & Son, S. (2003). Creating a system of accountability: The impact of instructional assessment on elementary children's achievement scores. *Educational Policy Analysis Archives, 11*(9). Retrieved March 23, 2007, from http://epaa.asu.edu/epaa/v11n9/
Mertler, C. A., & Campbell, C. (2005, April). *Measuring teachers' knowledge and application of classroom assessment concepts: Development of the Assessment Literacy Inventory.* Paper presented at the annual meeting of the American Education Research Association, Montreal, Québec.
National Board for Professional Teaching Standards. (2003). *Adolescence and young adulthood English language arts standards.* Retrieved March 30, 2007, from http://www.nbpts.org/the_standards/standards_by_cert?ID=2&x=49&y=4
Newmann, F., Bryk, A. S., & Nagaoka, J. K. (2001). *Authentic intellectual work and standardized tests: Conflict or coexistence?* Retrieved June 27, 2007, from http://ccsr.uchicago.edu/publications/p0a02.pdf
Oescher, J., & Kirby, P. C. (1990, April). *Assessing teacher-made tests in secondary math and science classrooms.* Paper presented at the annual meeting of the National Council on Measurement in Education, Boston. (ERIC Document Reproduction Number ED 322 169).
Olejnik, S., & Algina, J. (2000). Measures of effect size for comparative studies: Applications, interpretations and limitations. *Contemporary Educational Psychology, 25,* 241–286.
Olejnik, S., & Algina, J. (2003). Generalized eta and omega squared statistics: Measures of effect size for some common research designs. *Psychological Methods, 8*(4), 434–447.
Orr, L. L. (1999). *Learning from social experiments.* Thousand Oaks, CA: Sage.
Plake, B. S., & Impara, J. C. (1997). *Teacher assessment literacy: What do teachers know about assessment?* In

G.D. Phye (Ed.), *Handbook of classroom assessment: Learning, adjustment, and achievement* (pp. 55–68). San Diego, CA: Academic.

Plake, B. S., Impara, J. C., & Fager, J. J. (1993). Assessment competencies of teachers: A national survey. *Educational Measurement: Issues and Practice, 12*(4), 10–12, 39.

Quint, J., Sepanik, S., & Smith, J. K. (2008). *Using student data to improve teaching and learning: Findings from an evaluation of the Formative Assessments of Student Thinking in Reading (FAST-R) program in Boston elementary schools.* New York: MDRC.

Ragland, S., Schneider, M. C., Yap, C. C., & Kaliski, P. K. (2008, April). *The effect of classroom assessment professional development on English language arts and mathematics student achievement: Year 2 results.* Paper presented at the annual meeting of the National Council on Measurement in Education, New York.

Raudenbush, S. W., & Bryk, A. S. (2002). *Hierarchical linear models: Applications and data analysis methods* (2nd ed.). Thousand Oaks, CA: Sage.

Ross, J. A., Hogaboam-Gray, A., & Rolheiser, C. (2002). Student self-evaluation in grade 5–6 mathematics effects on problem solving achievement. *Educational Assessment, 8*(1), 43–59.

Sato, M., Wei, R. C., & Darling-Hammond, L. (2008). Improving teachers' assessment practices through professional development: The case of National Board certification. *American Education Research Journal, 45,* 669–700.

Schneider, M. C., Cid, J., Ragland, S., & Kaliski, P. (2007). *Comparing delivery approaches of a professional development program in classroom assessment.* Unpublished manuscript.

Schneider, M. C., & Johnson, R. L. (2006). *Assessing standards in the classroom: Companion document for the video-based professional development series.* Columbia, SC: South Carolina Department of Education. Retrieved June 27, 2007, from http://www.ed.sc.gov/agency/offices/assessment/resources/documents/Latest2I-VIDEOCOMPANION.pdf

Schneider, M. C., Meyer, J. P., Miller, B. J., & Kaliski, P. K. (2007, April). *The effect of classroom assessment professional development on English language arts and mathematics achievement.* Paper presented at the annual meeting of the National Council on Measurement in Education, Chicago, IL.

Schneider, M. C., Meyer, J. P., Miller, B. J., & Lottridge, S. (2007, April). *The effect of a professional development program in classroom assessment on teacher assessment skill.* Paper presented at the annual meeting of the American Educational Research Association, Chicago.

Schochet, P. Z. (2005). Statistical power for randomized assignment evaluations of educational programs. *Journal of Educational and Behavioral Statistics, 33*(1), 62–87.

Shadish, W. R., Cook, T. D., & Campbell, D. T. (2002). *Experimental and quasi-experimental designs for general causal inference.* Boston: Houghton-Mifflin.

Sobolewski, K. B. (2002). *Gender equity in classroom questioning.* Unpublished doctoral dissertation, South Carolina State University, Orangeburg.

Stiggins, R. J. (1999). Teams. *Journal of Staff Development, 20*(3), 17–21.

Stiggins, R. J., & Herrick M. (2007). *A status report on teacher preparation in classroom assessment.* Unpublished research report. Portland, OR: Classroom Assessment Foundation.

Supovitz, J. A., & Turner, H. M. (2000). The effects of professional development on science teaching practices and classroom culture. *Journal of Research in Science Teaching, 33*(9), 963–980.

Tienken, C., & Wilson, M. (2001). Using state standards and tests to improve instruction. *Practical Assessment, Research & Evaluation, 7*(13). Retrieved March 23, 2007, from http://pareonline.net/getvn.asp?v=7&n=13

University of Iowa and Riverside Publishing Co. (1994). *Riverside 2000 Integrated Assessment Program: Technical Summary I.* Chicago: Riverside Publishing.

Wenglinsky, H. (2002). How schools matter: The link between teacher classroom practices and student academic performance. *Education Policy Analysis Archives, 10*(12). Retrieved July 17, 2008, from http://epaa.asu.edu/epaa/v10n12/

Wiliam, D., Lee, C., Harrison, C. & Black, P. (2004). Teachers developing assessment for learning: Impact on student achievement. *Assessment in Education, 11*(1), 49–65.

Wilson, D. B., & Lipsey, M. W. (2001). The role of method in treatment effectiveness research: Evidence from meta-analysis. *Psychological Methods, 6,* 413–429.

Yap, C. C., Pearsall, T., Morgan, G., Wu, M., Maganda, F., Gilmore, J., et al. (2007). *Evaluation of a professional development program in classroom assessment: 2006–07.* Columbia, SC: University of South Carolina.

Yap, C. C., Whittaker, L., Liao, C., & D'Amico, L. (2006). *Evaluation of a professional development program in classroom assessment: 2005–06.* Columbia, SC: University of South Carolina.

Yin, Y., Shavelson, R. J., Ayala, C. C., Ruiz-Primo, M. A., Brandon, P. R., Furtak, E. M., et al. (2008). On the impact of formative assessment on student motivation, achievement, and conceptual change. *Applied Measurement in Education, 21*, 235–359.

Yoon, K. S., Duncan, T., Lee, S., W.-Y., Scarloss, B., & Shapley, K (2007). *Reviewing the evidence on how teacher professional development affects student achievement* (Issues & Answers Report, REL 2007-No. 033). Washington, DC: U.S. Department of Education, Institute of Education Sciences, National Center for Educational Evaluation and Regional Assistance, Regional Educational Laboratory Southwest. Retrieved November 6, 2008, from http://ies.ed.gov/ncee/edlabs

Zhang, Z. (1996, April). *Teacher assessment competency: A Rasch model analysis.* Paper presented at the annual meeting of the American Educational Research Association, New York.

Zhang, Z., & Burry-Stock, J. (1995). *A multivariate analysis of teacher's perceived assessment competency as a function of training and years of teaching.* Paper presented at the annual meeting of the Mid-South Educational Research Association, Biloxi, MI.

III

Challenges and Future Directions for Formative Assessment

16

MIXING IT UP

Combining Sources of Classroom Achievement Information for Formative and Summative Purposes

SUSAN M. BROOKHART

In classroom practice, formative assessment and summative assessment are not neatly divided and discrete activities. Classrooms brew more fusion reactions than fission. This chapter is about understanding the mix.

CAN FORMATIVE AND SUMMATIVE ASSESSMENT MIX?

The terms formative and summative refer to purposes for using assessment results, not to assessment procedures or instruments. Assessment is formative when the information is used to further student learning (it's not formative unless something is formed). Assessment is summative when the information is used for summary judgments about what has been learned. The question of mixing really refers, then, to whether evidence collected for one purpose can be used for the other. Contrasting points of view exist regarding whether the same evidence can be used for both formative and summative purposes.

The Case for No Mixing

The argument that formative and summative assessment cannot (or, at least, should not) commingle rests on claims that evaluation (grades and evaluative comments) can short-circuit learning and motivation and that when presented with both a grade and formative feedback, students tend to pay attention to the evaluation and ignore the formative feedback. This argument gets support from several sources. Reviews of research about the effects of evaluation practices on students have identified serious effects on learning and motivation that, by extension, one would not like to see coming from "practice" work (Crooks, 1988). Historically, research focusing on the effects of "grades versus comments" (Butler & Nisan, 1986; Page, 1958; Stewart & White, 1976) has produced mixed results but ended with the general conclusion that comments are better for learning.

More recently, motivation theorists have suggested that feedback can be perceived as descriptive or evaluative. Evaluative feedback is judgment: "excellent, good, fair, poor," and the like. Descriptive feedback explains or depicts the quality of the work without judging: "This essay says a lot about the global impact of climate change. Can you say more about the local impact?" Descriptive feedback is better for learning, and summative assessment is by definition evaluative. Exactly how much description is involved will vary by situation, but the feedback should describe student work in terms of the learning target that is the object of the student's endeavors (Hattie & Timperley, 2007).

Discussions of the effects of classroom evaluation practices on students (Covington, 1992; Crooks, 1988) have stressed the impact of grades on student motivation and learning. Crooks specifically addressed the question "Are feedback and summative evaluation compatible?" He summarized the arguments in the literature prior to 1988 as having made the case for "no," with one exception being the mastery learning literature that used frequent testing, followed by feedback and correctives, as part of its strategy (see Guskey, this volume). Crooks wrote:

> A final issue to be addressed here is whether the feedback and summative purposes of student evaluation are best separated. Strong arguments for such separation have been presented by McPartland (1987), Miller (1976), Sadler (1983), and Slavin (1978), among others. They argue that where evaluations count significantly toward the student's final grade, the student tends to pay less attention to the feedback, and thus to learn less from it. This effect should be reduced if students are given multiple opportunities to test and prove their achievement, with only the final evaluation counting toward their grade, as is generally the case in mastery learning procedures. (p. 457)

Today, the tests used in mastery learning that don't count toward a grade would be viewed as formative anyway, which removes Crooks's one exception and leaves this an argument for "no"—that formative and summative assessment information should not mix.

The mixed results from the research on "grades versus comments" are instructive here, as well. Over the past 50 years, researchers have investigated the effects of grades, as compared with teacher comments, on student performance. In the classic study that initiated this research agenda, Page (1958) wrote:

> Each year teachers spend millions of hours marking and writing comments upon papers being returned to students, apparently in the belief that their words will produce some result, in student performance, superior to that obtained without such words. Yet on this point solid experimental evidence, obtained under genuine classroom conditions, has been conspicuously absent. Consequently each teacher is free to do as he likes; one will comment copiously, another not at all. And each believes himself to be right. (p. 173)

As an aside, it is comforting to know that at least some things do change in schools!

This paragraph certainly does not describe the state of knowledge of teacher feedback today.

Page (1958) studied 74 different secondary teachers' classrooms, in three school districts, with 2,139 students. He found that student achievement was higher for a group receiving prespecified comments instead of letter grades, and higher still for students receiving free comments written by the teacher. The grades or comments were provided on classroom objective tests, and the criterion was performance on the next objective test in the same class. Presumably the free comments were targeted to the student's work more carefully than the prespecified comments, which were as follows:

A: Excellent! Keep it up.
B: Good work. Keep at it.
C: Perhaps try to do still better?
D: Let's bring this up.
F: Let's raise this grade! (p. 174)

Page concluded that writing comments was more effective for learning than grades. Other researchers replicated Page's study many times over the years, with an interesting result: Sometimes these results replicated and sometimes they didn't (Stewart & White, 1976). More recent research has identified the problem: In these early studies about comments, the feedback was evaluative or judgmental, not descriptive. In fact, the comments from Page (1958) just cited were quoted in part above so that readers of this chapter can hear their evaluative tone. Page himself described those prespecified comments as words that were "thought to be generally 'encouraging'" (p. 180). The nature of "comment studies" changed as the motivation literature began to point to the importance of the functional significance of feedback: How does the student experience the comment, as information or as judgment (Ryan, Connell, & Deci, 2000; Tunstall & Gipps, 1996)?

This insight that function (description or evaluation) is a key distinction for feedback is the final part of the case for not mixing. Good formative feedback is descriptive, and grades are evaluative. As educational psychology became more cognitive, comments were no longer investigated as stimuli to which students would respond, as in a behaviorist paradigm. Questions about why students responded as they did, and what sense they made of the information contained in comments, became more salient. More and more focused descriptions of how students' perceptions about the source and meaning of classroom information were important for student self-regulation decisions—those decisions about what they could and would do in their learning—were advanced by a succession of theoretical work in cognitive psychology: attribution theory Weiner (1979), cognitive evaluation theory (Ryan, Connell, & Deci, 1985), and self-determination theory (Ryan & Deci, 2000). Description that empowers students to do something about their work fosters student beliefs that improvement is under their own control.

These ideas about description versus evaluation helped solve the mystery of why some comments were motivational and others were not. Self-determination theory (Ryan & Deci, 2000) posits that internal motivation is best prompted by circumstances that support students' feelings of autonomy, competence, and relatedness. Descriptive comments that give students information they can use to improve will, in most cases, support feelings of competence. Evaluative comments that judge students' work are less likely to do that.

Butler and Nisan (1986) investigated the effects of grades (evaluative), comments (descriptive), or no feedback on both learning and motivation. The study was conducted by the researchers in nine classes, in three schools, with 261 sixth-graders. To insure that comments were descriptive, Butler and Nisan (1986) used a template for their task-related comments. Comments consisted of one sentence related specifically to the student's performance, with one phrase describing an aspect of the task the child accomplished well and one phrase describing an aspect of the task the child did less well. Comments were related to, and did not go beyond the criteria for performance given as part of the task's directions. Butler and Nisan (1986) used two different tasks, one quantitative task and one divergent-thinking task, administered three times, with comments, grades, or no feedback (depending on group) on the first two.

Students who received descriptive comments as feedback on their first session's work performed better on both tasks in the final session, and reported more motivation for the tasks, as measured by a questionnaire asking about interest, attribution of effort, and attribution of success. Students who received evaluative grades as feedback on their first session's work performed well on the quantitative task in the final session, but poorly on the divergent thinking task, and were less motivated. The no-feedback group performed poorly on both tasks in the final session and also was less motivated.

In brief, then, the case for no mixing rests on theory and research suggesting that descriptive feedback facilitates learning, that evaluative grades preempt descriptive feedback if both are presented together, and that evaluative feedback does not help students see learning as a process over which they have control. However, there are some reasons to believe that formative and summative assessment information can be used together if handled carefully, and we turn to those arguments now.

The Case for Mixing

Some assessment scholars have argued that formative and summative assessment can commingle (Biggs, 1998; Gipps, 1994; Harlen, 2005a, 2005b). Their arguments stem from the fact that formative and summative assessment do, in fact, commingle, although in many classrooms "the giving of marks and the grading function are overemphasized, while the giving of useful advice and the learning function are underemphasized" (Black & Wiliam, 1998b, p. 142). Later in the same article, Black and Wiliam point out that tests, exercises, and homework can be vehicles for feedback and learning if they are frequent and clearly related to the learning aims.

After this common starting point, the arguments diverge a bit. Biggs (1998) articulates the strongest position that these two sources of assessment information should mix. Gipps (1994) and Harlen (2005a, 2005b), respectively and in different ways, each make the case that formative and summative assessment information can mix. Gipps and Harlen both seem somewhat less enthusiastic than Biggs about the fit between the two, but both acknowledge the two do mix and that understanding the mix and handling it appropriately is therefore important.

Biggs (1998) wrote a response to a review by Black and Wiliam (1998a) in which he praised their comprehensive work and noted that in his view, their review considered studies of both formative and summative assessment. While Black and Wiliam's interpretation focused on formative assessment, especially feedback, some of the literature on classroom evaluation that was reviewed involved studies of classroom summative evaluation. Therefore, he reasoned, their conclusions were not strictly based on evidence about formative assessment. Biggs (1998) offered the view that the importance of good formative assessment does not preclude the importance of good summative assessment. He emphasized that the important connection was that both should be based on the same learning goals, noting that: "Sensible educational models make effective use of both FA [formative assessment] and SA [summative assessment]" (p. 105); the key is that they are both based on the curriculum and learning goals and are "deeply criterion-referenced" (p. 107).

Biggs (1998) pointed out that in many studies of the effects of testing, tests were found to contribute to learning. Depending on the timing of testing in the scheme of classroom lessons, however, the feedback available from test results (which Biggs called "backwash" to distinguish it from "feedback" from formative assessments) can come too late for students to use it formatively. Biggs surmised that it was that timing aspect and students' not being able to use the information that led to research findings about the negative, surface, or ego-related effects of testing, rather than a necessary consequence of summative assessment per se. Students' approaches to learning mediate the effects of both formative and summative assessment, and the effects of both can be positive if students use assessment results as opportunities for reflection. (Examples of how students have been found to do this are in the "Student Mixing Practices" section of this chapter.) Biggs summed up his comments with a delightful metaphor:

> I hope my comments can be seen as deriving from a similar starting point as Black and Wiliam, but instead of seeing FA and SA up close as two different trees, I would zoom to a wider angle conceptually. Then, in the broad picture of the whole teaching context—incorporating curriculum, teaching itself (an excellent feature of their review), and summative assessment—instead of two tree trunks, the backside of an elephant appears. (p. 108)

Gipps (1994) pointed out that to the extent that grades function to direct student attention away from the criteria they may be counterproductive for formative purposes, and noted that Sadler (1989) did not count grades as feedback. This focusing of attention is an important point, since one of the main mechanisms by which feedback works is by focusing attention (Kluger & DeNisi, 1996). Gipps (1994) agreed that for some summative purposes formative assessment may be accumulated. Her example was the UK Records of Achievement which consist of a profile of evidence with student self-assessment on various key achievement targets. This use of formative information in a more summative way is especially suited to times when rich information is required for the summative purpose rather than a composite final grade, as with the Records of Achievement, portfolios, and parent conferences. Thus, Gipps was more sanguine about the possibility of using formative assessment also for summative purposes than about using summative assessment also for formative purposes.

Harlen (2005a, 2005b) considered the relationships among formative assessment, summative classroom assessment, and external summative (large-scale) testing. Her position on the question of whether formative and summative assessment can mix is a qualified "yes." She distinguished between two kinds of mixing: using summative assessment results in formative ways, and using assessment information gathered for formative purposes for summative reporting.

Regarding using summative results in formative ways, Harlen (2005b) cautioned that while successful examples prove this can be done, there are limitations of timing, degree of detail, and the potential pressure of "teaching to the test" rather than giving true formative feedback. Where these limitations can be overcome, the results of summative assessment can be used to inform learning. Using existing summative test results as opportunities for review, for example, was one of the action plans used by some of the teachers in the Kings-Medway-Oxfordshire Formative Assessment Project (Wiliam, Lee, Harrison, & Black, 2004).

In regard to the use of assessment information gathered for formative purposes for summative reporting, Harlen (2005b) thought that this required a reinterpretation of evidence. Assessment evidence, she thought, could be reinterpreted from specifying students' achievement on progressive criteria for the skill or understanding as taught in a particular lesson to specifying students' achievement on broader criteria that are the same for all students. In the U.S. context today, one might call the latter "standards."

For an example of such respecification, Harlen (2005b) suggested considering a teacher who needed summative information about student achievement with respect to a standard like "plans scientific investigations." Formative assessment information would most likely have been about smaller-grain indicators; for example, how well a student can pose a relevant question, identify variables that should be manipulated, and so on. As it stands, the teacher might have achievement evidence on these indicators, but not on the broader standard, and so the teacher must reinterpret that evidence. How much achievement with respect to "plans scientific investigations" can be inferred if one has evidence that a student can pose questions and identify variables?

This kind of reinterpretation is more crucial for using teacher assessments for external reporting than for grading, where the current practice is to aggregate, not reinterpret, classroom based evidence to arrive at a report card grade. As U.S. report cards become more standards-based, some teachers hope that classroom summative results might indicate correspondence to external summative results. So far, this hope has not materialized (D'Agostino & Welsh, 2007).

Finally, the argument for mixing is gaining ground as the interest in formative assessment meets the daily realities of teaching. Harlen (2005b) in fact explored the possibility that rather than being a dichotomy, formative and summative assessment might be two ends of a dimension of assessment purposes and practices. She concluded that an argument could indeed be made for such a concept, and she illustrated it with examples that show the boundaries are often blurred in practice. Some formative assessment is very informal, done as a normal part of classroom instruction, and results in immediate feedback that informs the next steps in learning (immediate student thinking during a lesson). Other formative assessment is more formal, introduced at checkpoint opportunities in lesson sequences, and informs the next steps in teaching (future lesson plans). These formal formative assessments are very close to informal summative assessments such as classroom quizzes. Finally, the most formal summative assessment is done primarily for the purpose of reporting.

In the course of making this argument, Harlan succeeded in nicely laying out a description of how the blurring of lines between formative and summative happens in the classroom, no matter what terms analysts use to describe it. Harlan described what she called "asymmetry in dual use" (2005b, p. 116)—that while almost all detailed formative assessment information can be reinterpreted and aggregated for summative use, much summative assessment information is not detailed enough to rely on for formative purposes. She concluded that it would be wise to continue to distinguish formative and summative assessment, while at the same time exploring their relationships.

Conclusion: Can Formative and Summative Assessment Mix?

This author is persuaded by the argument that formative and summative assessment can be mixed. They can mix if teachers give careful attention to some characteristics of the mixing. The research reviewed in this chapter, as well the author's review of research (Brookhart, 2004), suggests that formative assessment and summative assessment work together best when: (1) all aspects of the formative and summative assessments (tasks, scoring, interpretation, and feedback) are firmly criterion-referenced; (2) the timing of all aspects of the formative and summative assessments works logically and purposefully into the students' learning trajectories; and (3) teachers mix formative and summative assessment with other classroom functions, as well, including planning, instruction, classroom management, and understanding students.

Classroom management and understanding students have been added to the usual triad that needs to be integrated (goals, instruction, assessment) because Brookhart (2004) found the assessment literature acknowledged these factors as important, but as yet their relationship with assessment has not been well studied. If teachers are going to use formative assessments without grades, they will need management routines to take the place of the controlling function of grading, and they will need understanding of their students' cognitive and emotional needs in order to fashion appropriate feedback and follow-up activities for formative assessments.

WAYS IN WHICH MIXING HAPPENS FOR STUDENTS IN CLASSROOMS

Many formative assessment techniques occur within the context of instruction. Their results are not recorded or are recorded as teacher notes, and their outcomes are not used in a summative fashion. Working with exemplars, students developing their own rubrics, and self- and peer assessment are examples of this kind of technique. So are working problems on whiteboards, showing letter cards to answer a teacher's multiple choice questions, displaying traffic signals (red/yellow/green) to indicate understanding, or any other indicator system students use to answer formative assessment questions in class. For these strategies, the question of mixing formative and summative assessment is more or less moot. They are more or less "pure" formative assessment.

It is on formal assignments that mixing usually happens in classrooms. Sometimes, assignments that should be mostly formative in nature (for example, practice exercises done in class or for homework) are graded as a part of a classroom routine. This author recommends that formative assessments not be graded; this point merely acknowledges the common practice that in some classrooms almost all formal work is graded. Other times, assignments that should be mostly summative in nature (for example unit tests or final projects) receive a grade but also written feedback that is intended partly as feedback for learning and partly as an explanation of the grade. Realistically, both of these practices need to be co-opted and brought into the formative assessment fold. Teachers need to design ways to extract formative information from all assignments. It is not likely that a "just say no" approach that rigidly requires assessments to be formative-only or summative-only will have a lasting effect on classroom practice.

Teachers' Mixing Practices

The following section uses real-life classroom assessment examples from teachers who are intentionally working on formative assessment. They come from a research project that is still in progress (see Brookhart, Moss, & Long, 2008, for a summary of the project to date). The examples are ones that, from the teachers' own observations, have had positive effects on their students. While these teachers provided formative feedback that was intentionally descriptive, related to the learning target, and useful for student improvement, they did this in ways that fit with their usual instruction. These examples, then, may contain more principled formative feedback than might be typical of all teachers, but they do not represent departures from ordinary classroom practices. After the examples, suggestions are provided for pushing the envelope on these practices to engender even more reform and improvement.

Mostly Formative Practice Work That Also Receives a Grade   It is a common practice to put grades or points on student work, especially on paper assignments, whether they are intended as practice assignments or not. Figure 16.1 shows an example of an in-class assignment in an eighth grade American cultures class. The teacher described his learning target as "to describe early problems American generals had in leading the Continental Army." The problems were summarized in a chapter in the textbook students were using, so the assignment also functioned as a comprehension activity, checking for student understanding of the information in the text. This teacher often used this kind of classroom exercise, so his feedback on this assignment was useful for his students' future work.

As can be seen in the figure, the teacher created an activity that asked students to report the information in the form of a letter. They were to pretend to be an American general and write "to your wife"; female students pretended to be generals and wrote to their husbands. The criteria for the assignment were provided for the students in the form of a checklist, and the teacher scored the assignment as the number of criteria, out of five, that were checked. The teacher said he intended the feedback to be formative, and indeed it was descriptive, but as the assignment was structured the students would have had to use the formative feedback on the next assignment; there was no opportunity to revise this one.

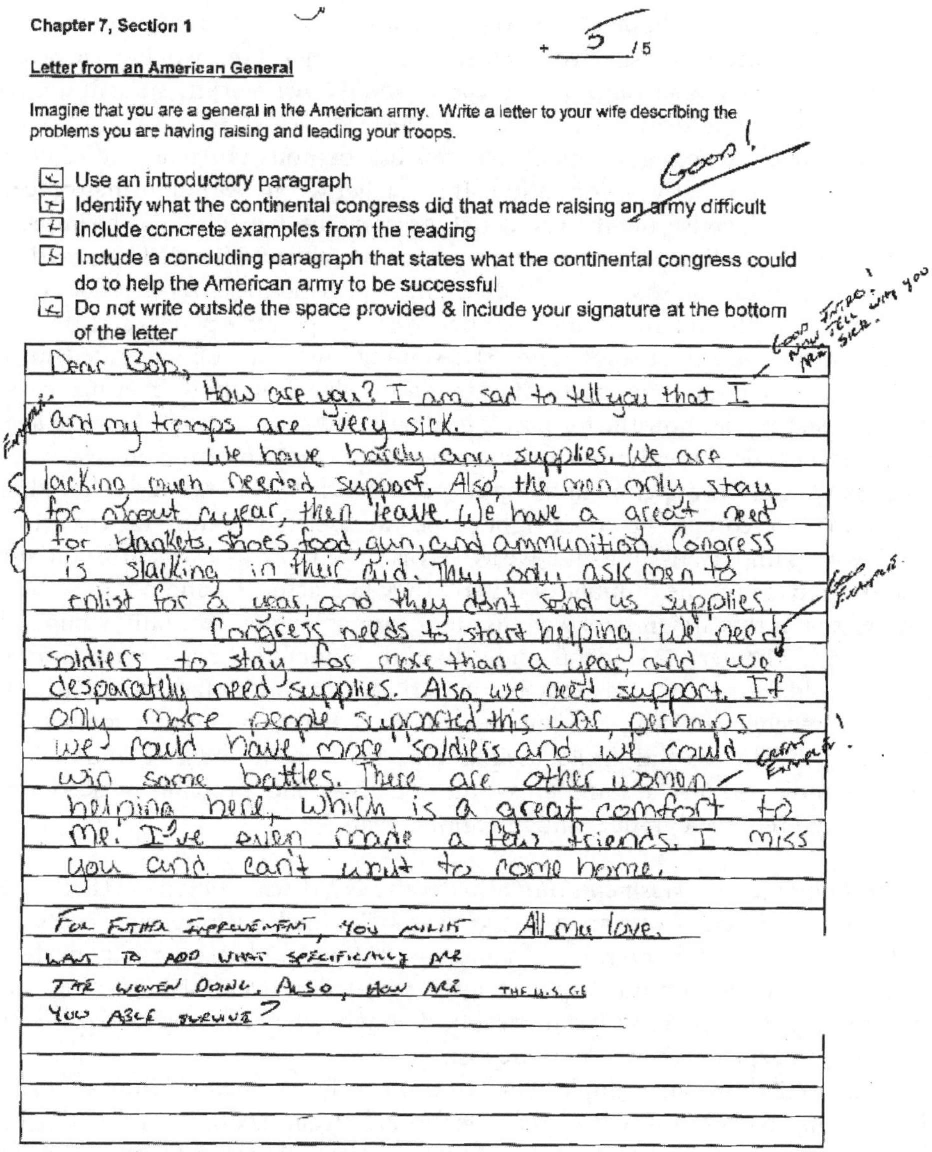

Chapter 7, Section 1

Letter from an American General

Imagine that you are a general in the American army. Write a letter to your wife describing the problems you are having raising and leading your troops.

+ _5_ / 5

Good!

☑ Use an introductory paragraph
☑ Identify what the continental congress did that made raising an army difficult
☑ Include concrete examples from the reading
☑ Include a concluding paragraph that states what the continental congress could do to help the American army to be successful
☑ Do not write outside the space provided & include your signature at the bottom of the letter

Good Intro! Now tell why you were sick.

Dear Bob,

How are you? I am sad to tell you that I and my troops are very sick.

We have hardly any supplies, We are lacking much needed support. Also the men only stay for about a year, then leave. We have a great need for blankets, shoes, food, guns, and ammunition. Congress is slacking in their aid. They only ask men to enlist for a year, and they don't send us supplies.

Good Example!

Congress needs to start helping. We need soldiers to stay for more than a year and we desparately need supplies. Also we need support. If only more people supported this war, perhaps we could have more soldiers and we could win some battles. There are other women helping here, which is a great comfort to me. I've even made a few friends. I miss you and can't wait to come home.

Great Example!

For Futher Improvement, you might want to add what specifically did the women doing. Also, how are the U.S.G you able survive?

All my love.

Figure 16.1 Example of a formative assessment that also receives a grade.

Figure 16.1 shows how this teacher put formative feedback on one student's work. This student got all the points available for the assignment. Just telling the student that all was well, however, would not really provide information for improvement. The teacher still was able to provide descriptive feedback on the reasons why the work met criteria; for example, identifying three places where he felt the student had used good examples from the reading. The teacher also made several suggestions for improvement, each of which amounted to calls for more details. Instead of writing the overly general and not particularly helpful comment, "Add more details," the teacher gave the student some things to think about: "Why were you sick?" "What were the women doing?" and "How are you able to survive?" Addressing these questions would have helped the student expand the letter, and probably also would have sent the student back to the text for additional information.

Formative classroom assessments like this one demonstrate one kind of mixing of formative and summative information. This teacher wrote helpful formative feedback on a classroom exercise, but then graded it. Assessments like this could be improved by (1) not putting grading points on assignments that really are intended for practice only; (2) teaching students the value of feedback in improving the work that does count for a grade, so that they realize doing their best work on practice papers gets them something more valuable than points; and (3) designing a sequence of nongraded, formative assignments followed by opportunities to "show what you know" that make sense to students, so they see how the formative feedback and practice contributes to learning. Many teachers do these things already, some are working toward them.

In the case of the assignment in Figure 16.1, the checklist of criteria should remain even if the 5/5 score in the upper right corner was deleted. Identifying the criteria for good work is important for formative as well as summative assessment. Some students would surely count the number of criteria they had achieved and note the ones they had missed. If this assignment were used for formative purposes only, summative assessment of whether the students understood the difficulties faced by the Continental Army would be measured at some point, perhaps with a unit test. In order for this to work, the teacher would have to convince students there was a connection between the work they did on this and similar assignments, the feedback he gave, and the learning that was indicated on the summative unit test. This could probably be accomplished, but it would require a gradual and intentional plan.

Mostly Summative Assessments that also Receive Feedback   Often in U.S. classrooms, it happens as a matter of course that graded assignments also receive feedback. Students simply expect that written assignments will be graded, especially in the upper grades. That is, the summing-up function is planned in from the beginning. Students are expected to receive and use the feedback, often given as a way to explain a grade, especially to explain where points are lost.

Figure 16.2 shows an example of one common way this is done, using a rubric sheet. This example comes from a third grade health and physical education class that had just finished a unit on disease and disease prevention. As a culminating activity, the teacher asked students to create and perform a play. They wrote their own dialogue, which had to include three vocabulary terms from the unit. They were required to have (and state) a theme, list their characters, and use at least three props. The teacher provided a check sheet for students to use to make sure they had done these things. The final play was graded with the rubric in Figure 16.2.

The annotations on the rubric provide an example of giving formative feedback, at least some of which should be useful for students' future work on a final, graded project. The rubric helped with some of the description. The teacher did not have to write, for example, that three vocabulary words were used properly; he just circled the appropriate text on the rubric. This frees up time for the teacher to write more specific comments

93% ⟳

Rubric: Disease Prevention Play

Group Members: Topic: Missy and her Chickinpox
1. Becky   2. Destiny   3. Madison
4. Veronica-*Not here!* 5. _____

	10	7	4	0
Accuracy/Vocabulary words *Great Job! the class really learned a lot from your play!*	All information was accurate. All three vocabulary words were used. ⟲10	Most information was accurate. Two vocabulary words were used.	Some information was accurate. Only one vocabulary word was used.	Very little to no information was accurate. No vocabulary words were used.
Creativeness *Great props & mask*	The play was very creative. 10	The play was creative.	The play was somewhat creative.	The play lacked creativity.
Acting *Great Job acting! medicine Make sure everyone knows their parts!*	The play was well acted and everyone took part.	The play was well acted and most group members took part. 8	The play was somewhat well acted and some group members took part.	The play was poorly acted and very few group members took part.
Organization and information/Group work *The flow was a little slow*	The play was very well organized and very informational.	The play was well organized and informational.	The play was hard to follow with little information.	The play was poorly organized with very little information.

Total Score: 36/40
+R +1 bonus
37/40

Great Job! You used all the vocab words and your script was very easy to follow along. The flow of the play was too slow sometimes.
What do you think you did well?
What would you change?

Figure 16.2 Example of formative feedback on a summative assessment.

geared toward the particular students' work. It also allows the teacher to use feedback in places where the performance did not earn full points, the description serving to identify what else would be necessary to attain full points.

In Figure 16.2, the teacher's feedback contained some general affirmations ("Great job!" was perhaps repeated too often, but that fit with this teacher's personality) but also several specifics. The group receiving this annotated rubric knows the teacher saw three props: tissues, medicine, and a doctor's mask. They know the teacher heard their vocabulary words in the play, and that he thinks the class learned a lot from watching Missy and Her Chickenpox. In addition to these positives, the teacher identifies some places for improvement. "Make sure everyone knows their parts" suggests that at least one of the students did not. Also, the flow of the play was slow; presumably the message there was something like "keep it moving."

Summative classroom assessments returned with comments, like this one, demonstrate a second kind of mixing of formative and summative information. Such assessments can be improved by: (1) adding positive and strategic feedback, not just descriptions of where points are lost; (2) teaching students explicitly to pay attention to the feedback, and how to do that; (3) following the feedback with an opportunity to revise this assignment; and (4) following grade and feedback events with opportunities to really use the feedback in another event, not just have it go into the general memory bank. Importantly, the formative value of this summative assessment would be improved by having the criteria more accurately embody the learning target. As it stands, the weight of the group work and the play overwhelm the content.

In the case of the example presented here, the teacher could have provided a bit more in the way of strategies for improvement, as the previous teacher did so nicely. For example, he could have suggested ways to work on the flow of the play during presentation. Perhaps he did do some of that orally. In this teacher's class, there are a lot of culminating projects that involve group presentations, and his students did have opportunities in the presentations for subsequent units to benefit from what they learned in this one. He did not report whether he made a point of having students look over feedback on their previous presentations as they were preparing for subsequent ones; it would have been good to activate students' memories so they could build on their past performances.

Effective Mixing: A Prototype   A recent research study (Andrade, Du, & Wang, 2008) illustrates how effective coordination of formative and summative assessment might happen in a classroom. Third and fourth graders in seven different classrooms (n = 116) participated. A treatment group read model writing assignments, used those to generate a list of criteria for effective writing, self-assessed their first drafts using rubrics and highlighters, received teacher feedback, and wrote final drafts. A comparison group followed the same procedure except they generated a list of criteria without using a model paper and self-assessed their first drafts without rubrics. The treatment group's final papers, scored with the 6+1 Trait Writing rubrics, were of better quality than the comparison group, with about 15% of the variance accounted for by treatment. Note that this was a case of coordinated formative and summative assessment each having their place, so that the information was able to mix; separate assessment events were used for each function.

This study was done by a research team, but it nicely illustrates how a classroom teacher might effectively coordinate formative and summative assessment for a writing assignment. A classroom teacher might do much the same thing as the study team did. However, if there had not been a need to standardize the rubric across classes for research purposes, the students and teacher could have cocreated a rubric, using a model paper or several of them, and used the cocreated rubric for both formative (assessing drafts) and summative (final grade) purposes. Cocreating the rubric would help students clearly see expectations for their writing. Students could practice applying the rubric to exemplar papers in order to further understand what these qualities of good writing looked like. Then when students produced their first drafts, they could self-assess using the rubric and also get feedback from peers or the teacher that referenced the criteria on the rubric but did not include points or grades. Using that feedback and continuing to use the same rubrics, students would then revise their writing and turn it in for a final grade, arrived at using the same rubrics. The author looks forward to a day when such a scenario is more than a prototype, but rather the way most classroom work is structured.

Additional Ways in Which Mixing Happens in Teacher Planning

In this chapter, and especially in the previous section on teachers' "mixing" practices, I have concentrated on the commingling of information, especially when ostensibly formative information has been interpreted summatively as well, and vice versa. There are some other ways in which mixing it up happens, ways in which formative assessment and summative assessment commingle in teacher planning. These may not qualify as truly combining sources or mixing sources of evidence and purposes; however, there are two ways that mixing happens in teacher planning that are common enough that they deserve a mention in this chapter: instructional evaluation and planning for differentiated instruction.

Since long before formative assessment was known by that name, teachers have been using the results of prior summative, graded evaluations to inform their own instructional evaluation where a teacher asks questions such as: "Were my teaching strategies and methods effective?" and "What would I change next time I teach this, typically next year?" Strictly speaking, this is formative evaluation as opposed to formative assessment because the students who benefit are often not the students whose information led to the changes in plans.

Differentiated instruction benefits the same students as the assessment information. Differentiated instruction relies heavily on formative assessments as teachers select materials, instructional strategies, and group configurations for students at various places on a learning progression toward instructional goals. But summative assessments (for example, results of state or other standardized tests, or results of classroom graded work) can provide information for differentiating instruction, as well. Sometimes teachers can reinterpret summative assessments for formative purposes to aid future learning. So there can be a bit of mixing as teachers use ostensibly summative assessment results to help plan and implement differentiated instruction in their classrooms.

The converse can occur, as well: ostensibly formative information can end up providing information for grading, a summative purpose. Grading in the differentiated classroom is likely to be grading on assignments and learning goals that vary from student to student, and are intended to provide information about individual growth on learning trajectories that have been tailored to meet their needs. Summative grades after differentiated instruction will not be comparable from student to student but will reflect progress on the appropriate learning goals selected for each student (Tomlinson, 2001).

Student Mixing Practices

Students can (and often do) use formative and summative assessment information simultaneously in a variety of explicit and implicit ways. An example of an implicit use of feedback comes from research on feedback and self-regulated learning (Butler & Winne, 1995), which suggests that feedback is a catalyst for internal regulation. More effective learners develop cognitive routines for creating internal feedback while they are working. According to Butler and Winne, for some effective learners, outcome feedback or knowledge of results is enough information to fuel these cognitive routines, at least in certain familiar domains of learning. For most students, cognitive feedback or feedback that explicitly links characteristics of their achievement to aspects of their work (for example, "You have more details in your paragraph this week; I see you have been thinking about how to pick words that describe") helps develop, sustain, and enrich these cognitive routines. Giving such feedback is a way to scaffold for all (or almost all) learners the kind of internal regulation that effective learners develop.

This author has been interested in how students process assessment expectations and information in order to aid self-regulation. As part of a larger research agenda, Brookhart (2001) interviewed 50 high school students in a midsized suburban school district. The students were in 10th grade English, 11th grade honors English, and 12th grade anatomy, an elective mostly taken by students who wanted to go into medicine as their profession. Almost all of these students would, by any definition, be classified as effective learners. Their interviews afforded a look into some of their cognitive routines, and it was found that students who do take charge of their own learning do not make neat distinctions between formative and summative information. They evaluate all school information as having potential use—for what it can do for them. This is because most of them believed that education is important, either in its own right or because of its instrumental value for future success, or both, and they believed that it was their job to make their education as successful as possible.

Students were asked questions about their understanding of a specific assignment and their teacher's expectations for their work, whether they were interested, whether they felt the work was important, how hard they tried, how well they thought they did, and whether they cared how others did or how others thought they did. These were all graded assignments, and were all major assignments designed to help students learn as well as evaluate their learning.

Students' reasoning about and reported use of assessment information could be grouped into four general categories: (1) formative aspects of studying for summative tests; (2) transfer of learning: formative with a hint of summative; (3) learning to become self-monitoring: summative with a hint of formative; and (4) summative judgments of understanding. The last category was the smallest (10 comments, from 10 students), with all but one of the comments made after anatomy tests, which were in-class examinations. For all of the project work (English research papers, poetry writing, anatomy lab practicals), and for the anatomy tests as well, students made comments in one of the other three categories, all of which mix the formative and summative functions. Below are more details and examples from these three categories.

Formative Aspects of Studying   Students spoke most (43 comments from 31 different students) about the formative nature of completing the assessment—studying for a test, reading resources and preparing papers, and the like. They considered participating in these processes (i.e., doing the assignment) to be learning experiences. In effect, knowing the expectations for an upcoming assessment helped students with self-regulation. For example, a female student said in regard to the skeleton lab practical in her 12th grade anatomy class:

> He expects us of course to pay attention in class, he expects us to study on our own. I guess it's good he gave us quizzes because that forces you to study specif-

ics. And he also expects us to come in and work with the bones, and he gave us class time as well, because you can't learn 3D bones all from a chart. (Brookhart, 2001, p. 162)

The insight from this category is not that studying is good for students. Most teachers would say that. The point here is that the students perceived this, believed this, and acted accordingly. They articulated this point of view when asked what they were expected to do and why it was important. Evidence that this student was not just telling an adult interviewer what she thought the adult would want to hear comes from the same interview:

I think it's really important to get that feeling of mastering something for once. In terms of study skills it's also good preparation for college, where there tend to be big finals and midterms. (Brookhart, 2001, p. 162)

If effective students are convinced that summative assessments can trigger formative work, studying and learning, then it is worth scaffolding this connection with all learners. This sort of mixing of the formative and summative fits into even the most traditional of almost any philosophies of teaching and learning.

Transfer of Learning: Formative with a Hint of Summative   Many of the students, in both English and anatomy classes, were able to articulate the argument that work on assignments now would transfer to future study, for example in college, job performance, or general life skills. Of course these successful students had probably been raised hearing such arguments, but they had clearly appropriated these thoughts as their own. This is a sort of formative use, with the formation projected farther into the future than in the usual definition of formative assessment. In the words of one student: "I think that'll be important because I think it will carry over to college" (Brookhart, 2001, p. 164). Or, it could be argued that using information from present assignments to think about the future is summative but temporary, as, for example, in the logic expressed by one student in response to a question about why doing well on the skeleton lab practical is important: "Because I want to be a doctor…on the other hand, if you're going to be an accountant your time would probably be better spent doing something else unless you just really enjoy bones" (Brookhart, 2001, p. 163). Either of these arguments shows students clearly using assessment expectations and assessment results as part of self-regulation of learning which they intend to enhance their future. Successful students do this kind of thinking regularly, and in so doing mix the formative and summative purposes of assessment.

Learning to Become Self-Monitoring: Summative with a Hint of Formative   As students considered the question "How well do you think you did?"—a summative judgment—they often put their comments into a context that can be interpreted as expressing that they are learning to become self-monitoring. For example, commenting on a poetry assignment, one student said: "I think I'll do pretty well. Like I said, I've learned to pretty much express myself pretty easily, and I think it's becoming easier with each exercise" (Brookhart, 2001, p. 165). While this student, and others who made similar comments, express summative judgments about the quality of their work, they also expressed reasons that indicated these judgments helped support self-monitoring and self-regulation over time. This, too, is a mix of the formative and summative purposes of assessment.

Understanding how these students mix formative and summative assessment results gives us a best case scenario. It is proof of concept (that it can be done); it is evidence of effectiveness (these were excellent students); and it suggests that helping less effective students learn to do this might be something to strive for. In the end, it is more important that students become effective users of whatever information is available to them than that they sort information according to the teacher's intended purpose.

Conditions Required For Students to Use Information Formatively   Tanner and Jones (2003) reviewed the literature, including this author's study of successful students, and noted that there are three conditions under which students will spontaneously use summative information to support their own learning in mathematics, the content area of their study: (1) students' self-efficacy must be high; (2) they must have metacognitive knowledge of their own mathematical abilities; and (3) they must be aware of, and be inclined to use effective strategies for reviewing and revising their work and analyzing their successes and failures.

These conditions, arguably, are the conditions under which students can use any information, whether intended as formative or summative, to support their own learning. And they are a nice statement about what made students judged to be successful in the Brookhart (2001) study actually successful, besides their privileged backgrounds and education.

These conditions also give us strategies for helping less effective students learn how to do what the highly effective students did spontaneously. Unfortunately, these strategies represent a tall order. Teachers must teach for success, differentiating instruction appropriately, and meeting students' real and perceived needs. They must do this enough that students' self-efficacy for learning grows. They must help students accurately judge their own abilities and give students effective strategies for reviewing and revising their work, along the lines of the prototype described in the previous section.

Research suggests both that this can be done (Andrade, Du, & Wang, 2008) and that it will be difficult. Tanner and Jones (2003) found that in a sample of 303 year 9 (age 13–14) students in comprehensive schools in Wales, these conditions were not often met. Over 90% thought it was worthwhile to try hard in mathematics and to revise their work in preparation for examinations. However, only 57% reported knowing what kind of mistakes they were likely to make, and 47% reported they often got a question wrong and didn't understand why. After testing, most students reported that they made sure to understand their mistakes (69%) and figured out how to do better next time (65%), yet 55% said they only looked at their mark when tests were returned, without analyzing mistakes with an intent to learn and improve. This apparent contradiction calls into question the validity of some students' judgments on these matters. Tanner and Jones concluded that a significant majority of students do not have the skills they need to use the results of summative assessment to further their learning.

SUGGESTIONS FOR FUTURE RESEARCH

Except for the articles cited previously in this chapter—most of which are theoretical papers rather than empirical studies—specific studies of students or teachers mixing formative and summative assessment information are nearly nonexistent. In fact, using both "formative assessment" and "summative assessment" as ERIC search terms located one article that pitted these two against each other as two different treatments (Ross, 2005). It would be a huge understatement to say that further research is needed to illustrate and inform the way that formative and summative assessments mix in current classrooms.

What might be the focus of such further research? Based on the discussion and examples in this chapter, it seems that the question is not so much whether formative and summative assessment mix in practice, but how that happens. Descriptive studies about how teachers mix formative and summative classroom achievement information would be first on a list of suggestions for future research. Two descriptive studies about how students mix assessment information were found (Brookhart, 2001; Tanner & Jones, 2003); more will be helpful. Once the landscape is mapped—once practices are labeled and categorized—the next step would be to test the effects of the various practices on student achievement, motivation, and beliefs about learning. Because of the contextual nature of the topic, well documented action research in real classrooms would be especially instructive.

Another important research agenda would be to study the ways teachers can coach students in the use of formative and summative assessment information in such a way as to scaffold for all students the self-efficacy, metacognitive skills, and strategy repertoires that make successful students good consumers of assessment information. This agenda might begin by exploring ways in which teachers can help students experience real success with their lessons, for this is the source of genuine self-efficacy (Bandura, 1997), and develop strategies for using information in that process. If it is true that assessment is not formative if nothing is formed, then in fact this second area might be the most important learning research agenda for the immediate future.

Conceptually, the two agendas will merge at some point. Documenting teacher practices mixing formative and summative information successfully should end up documenting how teachers can coach students and support their self-efficacy, metacognition, and strategy use. Both should end up enhancing student learning.

REFERENCES

Andrade, H. L., Du, Y., & Wang, X. (2008). Putting rubrics to the test: The effect of a model, criteria generation, and rubric-referenced self-assessment on elementary students' writing. *Educational Measurement: Issues and Practice, 27*(2), 3–13.

Bandura, A. (1997). *Self-efficacy: The exercise of control.* New York: Freeman.

Biggs, J. (1998). Assessment and classroom learning: A role for summative assessment? *Assessment in Education, 5,* 103–110.

Black, P., & Wiliam, D. (1998a). Assessment and classroom learning. *Assessment in Education, 5,* 7–74.

Black, P., & Wiliam, D. (1998b). Inside the black box: Raising standards through classroom assessment. *Phi Delta Kappan, 80,* 139–144.

Brookhart, S. M. (2001). Successful students' formative and summative uses of assessment information. *Assessment in Education, 8,* 153–169.

Brookhart, S. M. (2004). Classroom assessment: Tensions and intersections in theory and practice. *Teachers College Record, 106,* 429–458.

Brookhart, S. M., Moss, C. M., & Long, B. A. (2008, April). *Professional development in formative assessment: Effects on teacher and student learning.* Paper presented at the annual meeting of the National Council on Measurement in Education, New York.

Butler, R., & Nisan, M. (1986). Effects of no feedback, task-related comments, and grades on intrinsic motivation and performance. *Journal of Educational Psychology, 78,* 210–216.

Butler, D. L., & Winne, P. H. (1995). Feedback and self-regulated learning: A theoretical synthesis. *Review of Educational Research, 65,* 245–281.

Covington, M. V. (1992). *Making the grade: A self-worth perspective on motivation and school reform.* Cambridge, UK: Cambridge University Press.

Crooks, T. J. (1988). The impact of classroom evaluation practices on students. *Review of Educational Research, 58,* 438–481.

D'Agostino, J., & Welsh, M. (2007, April). *Standards-based progress reports and standards-based assessment score convergence.* Paper presented at the annual meeting of the American Educational Research Association, Chicago.

Gipps, C. V. (1994). *Beyond testing: Towards a theory of educational assessment.* London: Falmer.

Harlen, W. (2005a). Teachers' summative practices and assessment for learning: Tensions and synergies. *Curriculum Journal, 16*(2), 207–223.

Harlen, W. (2005b). On the relationship between assessment for formative and summative purposes. In J. Gardner (Ed.), *Assessment and learning* (pp. 103–117). Thousand Oaks, CA: Sage.

Hattie, J., & Timperley, H. (2007). The power of feedback. *Review of Educational Research, 77,* 81–112.

Kluger, A. N., & DeNisi, A. (1996). The effects of feedback interventions on performance: A historical review, a meta-analysis, and a preliminary feedback intervention theory. *Psychological Bulletin, 119,* 254–284.

McPartland, J. M. (1987, April). *Changing tests and grading practices to improve student motivation and teacher-student relationships: Designs for research to evaluate new ideas for departmental exams and progress grades.* Paper presented at the annual meeting of the American Educational Research Association, Washington, DC.

Miller, G. E. (1976). Continuous assessment. *Medical Education, 10,* 81–86.

Page, E. B. (1958). Teacher comments and student performance: A seventy-four classroom experiment in school motivation. *Journal of Educational Psychology, 49,* 173–181.

Ross, S. J. (2005). The impact of assessment method on foreign language proficiency growth. *Applied Linguistics, 26*(3), 317–342.

Ryan, R. M., Connell, J. P., & Deci, E. L. (1985). A motivational analysis of self-determination and self-regulation in the classroom. In C. Ames & R. Ames (Eds.), *Research on motivation in education: Vol. 2. The classroom milieu* (pp. 13–51). Orlando, FL: Academic.

Ryan, R. M., & Deci, E. L. (2000). Self-determination theory and the facilitation of intrinsic motivation, social development, and well-being. *American Psychologist, 55*(1), 68–78.

Sadler, D. R. (1983). Evaluation and the improvement of academic learning. *Journal of Higher Education, 54,* 60–79.

Sadler, D. R. (1989). Formative assessment and the design of instructional systems. *Instructional Science, 18,* 119–144.

Slavin, R. E. (1978). Separating incentives, feedback, and evaluation: Toward a more effective classroom system. *Educational Psychologist, 13,* 97–100.

Stewart, L. G., & White, M. A. (1976). Teacher comments, letter grades, and student performance: What do we really know? *Journal of Educational Psychology, 68,* 488–500.

Tanner, H., & Jones, S. (2003, July). *Self-efficacy in mathematics and students' use of self-regulated learning strategies during assessment events.* Paper presented at the 27th International Group for the Psychology of Mathematics Education Conference Held Jointly with the 25th PME-NA Conference, Honolulu. (ERIC Document No. ED501134)

Tomlinson, C. A. (2001). Grading for success. *Educational Leadership, 58*(6), 12–15.

Tunstall, P., & Gipps, C. (1996). Teacher feedback to young children in formative assessment: a typology. *British Educational Research Journal, 22,* 389–404.

Weiner, B. (1979). A theory of motivation for some classroom experiences. *Journal of Educational Psychology, 71,* 3–25.

Wiliam, D., Lee, C., Harrison, C., & Black, P. (2004). Teachers developing assessment for learning: Impact on student achievement. *Assessment in Education, 11,* 49–65.

17

PSYCHOMETRIC CHALLENGES AND OPPORTUNITIES IN IMPLEMENTING FORMATIVE ASSESSMENT

WALTER D. WAY, ROBERT P. DOLAN, AND PAUL NICHOLS

In considering psychometrics in the context of formative assessment, we begin with the assumption that reference to an assessment as formative is shorthand for the *formative use* of assessment information—whether coming from a standardized test or teachers' observations—with the explicit goal of informing focused intervention that will close the gap between students' current state of achievement and a targeted state of achievement. We refer to such gaps as "achievement gaps," which are not to be confused with the more common use of the term to describe differences in the achievement levels of different subgroups. The phrase *formative assessment* is therefore an implied claim that assessment information can be used as part of a system to identify achievement gaps, provide guidance in interpreting those gaps, and suggest, in association with an instructional model, practices for closing those gaps (Black & Wiliam, 1998; Wiliam & Black, 1996; Wiliam, 2006).

The chapters in this volume attest to the rich and varied practices of formative assessment. Traditional psychometric notions, by contrast, are much narrower in focus. For the most part, the psychometrics applied to tests used for formative purposes have been largely limited to the same psychometrics applied to summative tests. Test instruments developed for formative purposes often have additional characteristics to directly support instructional decision making, such as immediate scoring, diagnostic information, predictive properties (e.g., of performance on a state summative test), and flexibility in the selection of content. However, the development and evaluation of tests used for either summative or formative purposes are, for the most part, steeped in the psychometric traditions that have held court for the past 60 years and thus only partially address considerations unique to formative assessment. Therefore, the primary psychometric challenges and opportunities in implementing formative assessment are in moving beyond a focus on administering and reporting scores from a single test to one that considers the assessment data that is part of coordinated assessment and instruction targeted to closing achievement gaps.

The definitive guide to the development and use of tests in the United States is the *Standards for Educational and Psychological Testing* (American Educational Research Association, American Psychological Association, and the National Council on Measurement in Education, 1999; hereafter, *Standards*). The *Standards* pay little direct attention to formative assessment. However, the principles and issues discussed in the *Standards* are clearly relevant to formative assessment, and can be extrapolated to the instruments and procedures that may be used in formative assessment practice. These may include off-the-shelf assessments, teacher-made quizzes, or computer-based systems that provide both instruction and assessment.

There are additional reasons to think differently about the psychometrics supporting formative assessment at this time. One is the increased momentum favoring formative assessment of learning in recent years as generated by accumulated research evidence supporting formative approaches to classroom assessment (Black & Wiliam, 1998; Stiggins, Arter, Chappuis, & Chappuis, 2006; Hattie & Timperley, 2007; Wiliam, 2007). Another is the advent of technology-based tools and systems that combine instruction with assessment in more direct ways than ever before.

Russell (this volume) provides an overview of new developments and applications in technology-aided assessment of formative learning. We extend this topic by considering the potential for an extended model of psychometrics in improving several existing systems that combine elements of instruction and assessment. We are optimistic that these and similar online tools and systems will have positive—even revolutionary—impacts on instructional practices, and that psychometric techniques will evolve within these systems that will support formative assessment in new and exciting ways. That we focus on these technology-based systems is not to say that formative assessment practices in other contexts are not equally valuable. Rather, it is to acknowledge that the psychometric challenges and opportunities as they relate to formative assessment systems are the greatest in this context, and as such provide the greatest opportunity for shaping new definitions of psychometrics.

The purpose of this chapter is to identify and discuss several psychometric challenges and opportunities related to formative assessment now and in the future. We begin by sharing examples of technology-based systems that combine instruction and assessment in ways that promote formative uses of test data. We then relate these examples to the *Standards* and ask the questions, "How does one assess the technical quality of assessments used for formative purposes?" and "Which new psychometric techniques will help improve the technical quality of assessments to be used for formative purposes?" In addressing these questions, we rely primarily on the fundamental concepts of reliability and validity, which provide ample stimulation for considering the role of psychometrics within a formative assessment system.

COMBINING INSTRUCTION WITH ASSESSMENT THROUGH FORMATIVE ASSESSMENT SYSTEMS

In a paper commissioned by the National Center on Education and the Economy for the New Commission on the Skills of the American Workforce, Pellegrino (2006) provides a compelling vision of how technology may impact the future of instruction and assessment:

While it is always risky to predict the future, it appears clear that advances in technology will continue to impact the world of education in powerful and provocative ways. Many technology-driven advances in the design of learning environments, which include the integration of assessment with instruction, will continue to emerge, and will reshape the terrain of what is both possible and desirable in education. Advances in curriculum, instruction, assessment and technology are likely to continue to move educational practice toward a more individualized and mastery-oriented approach to learning. This evolution will occur across the K-16+ spectrum. (p. 11)

Pellegrino's predictions about the future of education, shared by others such as Bennett (2002), are beginning to be realized through countless technology-based systems that are available to educators today. Most of these systems involve assessment results that are used formatively by both teachers and learners. These systems typically share three characteristics: (1) explicit alignment of curriculum with learning standards or theories of pedagogy; (2) immediate feedback on student results for students and teachers; and (3) individualization of instruction as a function of ongoing evaluation of student interaction and performance. While the last characteristic is generally understood to be necessary and sufficient for formative assessment, we believe that the former two characteristics are also necessary if formative assessments are to be used successfully in closing achievement gaps.

Examples of Formative Assessment Systems

This section presents examples of technology-based learning systems in mathematics and reading that support the formative use of student data. Particular emphasis is placed on how student interactions with the systems provide data that facilitate formative assessment practice. While many such systems are being used in schools, these simple examples provide a foundation for understanding the importance of the technical quality of assessments used formatively.

Blending Assessment with Instruction Program   The Blending Assessment with Instruction Program (BAIP), developed at the University of Kansas, aligns Kansas state mathematic curriculum standards with instruction that supports teaching and learning (Poggio & Meyen, 2008). The program provides three sets of Web-based resources for students and teachers in grades 3 through high school: (1) self-contained lengthy lessons for use by teachers; (2) independent online study tutorials for students; and (3) a data reporting system designed to provide teachers with immediate feedback on student performance to facilitate instructional decision making. Figure 17.1 illustrates the teacher interface within the BAIP system that provides lessons for the teacher's use and tutorials that can be assigned to individual students. These resources are structured; that is, they are closely aligned to the same content standards and benchmarks that are used with the standards-based Kansas Assessment program and the state's summative assessment program. The focus of the lesson illustrated in the figure is on fourth grade mathematics, with a specific focus on Standard 1 (Number and Computation), Benchmark 2, and Indicator K1, which requires the student to

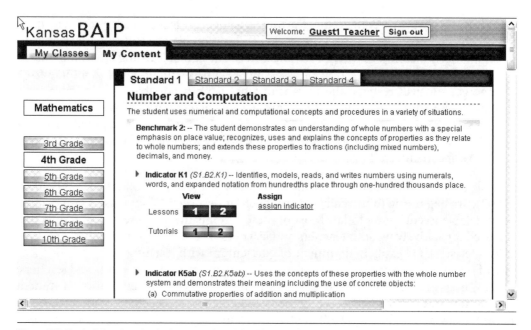

Figure 17.1 Teacher's interface showing lessons and tutorials within the BAIP system. Copyright 2007, The University of Kansas. Used with permission.

identify, model, and write using numerals, words, and expanded notation that falls within a certain range of values.

Two lessons and two tutorials are shown to be available for this content. The lessons are designed to achieve two purposes: first, to assist and support teachers' delivery of diverse content examples to students, and second, to provide content knowledge to teachers whose mastery of the topic is itself deficient or would benefit from additional information. The tutorials are designed to provide independent learning experiences to assist students in learning the associated skills and concepts. They combine lessons with multiple-choice questions which provide immediate feedback to students as they are completed, as shown in Figure 17.2. In this figure, the tutorial question, the incorrect option selected, and the correct option are shown with associated explanations.

The BAIP system also provides teachers with detailed feedback about how students in their classes performed on questions within the tutorials, as shown in Figure 17.3. In this figure, the left side of the screen provides the teacher with details in both tabular and graphical format about how each student in the class responded to each question in the tutorial and identifies incorrect responses chosen by students.

MyReadingWeb   MyReadingWeb is another technology-based tool embedding assessment within instructional activities. This application leverages the widely adopted Lexile Framework for Reading (n.d.) to provide developing readers with text targeted to their abilities and topics being taught in the classroom. One of the most important features of this application is that an estimate of each student's reading ability is continuously updated through responses to embedded sentence cloze items. These cloze items are created by the application in real time. Since item generation is theory-driven, items

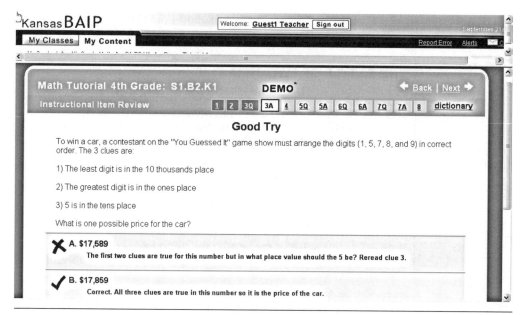

Figure 17.2 Example of tutorial student feedback within the BAIP system. Copyright 2007, The University of Kansas. Used with permission.

do not require field testing. Figure 17.4 illustrates the student interface through which the student reads the assigned material and fills in responses to cloze items.

According to the product developers, each student receives immediate feedback about his or her selection of an answer for each cloze item and an indication of overall performance. The count correct is used to update the student's Lexile reader measure

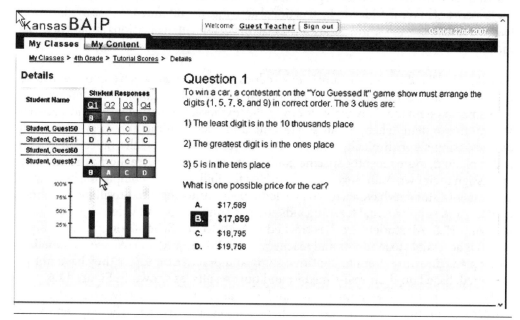

Figure 17.3 Teacher feedback on student tutorial performance within the BAIP system. Copyright 2007, The University of Kansas. Used with permission.

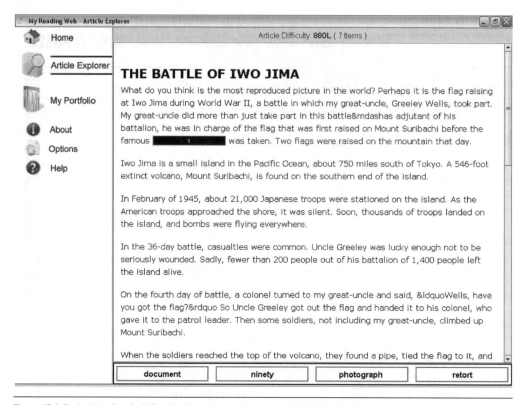

My Reading Web - Article Explorer

Home

Article Explorer

My Portfolio

About

Options

Help

Article Difficulty **880L** (7 Items)

THE BATTLE OF IWO JIMA

What do you think is the most reproduced picture in the world? Perhaps it is the flag raising at Iwo Jima during World War II, a battle in which my great-uncle, Greeley Wells, took part. My great-uncle did more than just take part in this battle&mdashas adjutant of his battalion, he was in charge of the flag that was first raised on Mount Suribachi before the famous ▮▮▮▮▮ was taken. Two flags were raised on the mountain that day.

Iwo Jima is a small island in the Pacific Ocean, about 750 miles south of Tokyo. A 546-foot extinct volcano, Mount Suribachi, is found on the southern end of the island.

In February of 1945, about 21,000 Japanese troops were stationed on the island. As the American troops approached the shore, it was silent. Soon, thousands of troops landed on the island, and bombs were flying everywhere.

In the 36-day battle, casualties were common. Uncle Greeley was lucky enough not to be seriously wounded. Sadly, fewer than 200 people out of his battalion of 1,400 people left the island alive.

On the fourth day of battle, a colonel turned to my great-uncle and said, &ldquoWells, have you got the flag?&rdquo So Uncle Greeley got out the flag and handed it to his colonel, who gave it to the patrol leader. Then some soldiers, not including my great-uncle, climbed up Mount Suribachi.

When the soldiers reached the top of the volcano, they found a pipe, tied the flag to it, and

| document | ninety | photograph | retort |

Figure 17.4 Student interface for MyReadingWeb with cloze item. Copyright 2008, Metametrics, Inc. Used with permission.

which is used to build individual growth trajectories for each student. The results from these assessments embedded in instructional activities are intended for use by classroom teachers, administrators, and policy makers to make informed decisions about curricula, instructional strategies, and the individual student's progress in reading.

MathXL for School   A final example of an educational product which combines instruction and assessment is MathXL for School (n.d.) an online homework, tutorial, and assessment system that is available for over 250 textbooks in mathematics and statistics. Within this system, teachers can create, edit, and assign online homework, tests, and quizzes using algorithmically generated exercises correlated at the objective level to textbooks and, more recently, specific math learning standards. Teachers can also create and assign their own online exercises for added flexibility. While completing homework assignments, students have access to problem-specific tutoring, links to aligned textbook content, and supplemental learning aids such as animations and video clips, as shown in Figure 17.5. All student work is tracked in MathXL for School's online grade book, which is accessible to students and teachers. In addition, students receive personalized study plans directing them to continue study and practice on topics they have not yet mastered, based on their real-time test and quiz results, as shown in Figure 17.6.

The preceding three examples of technology-based systems are drawn from the many similar systems that are available to teachers, schools, and districts. These systems share a number of common features, most notably the ability to collect continuous assessment

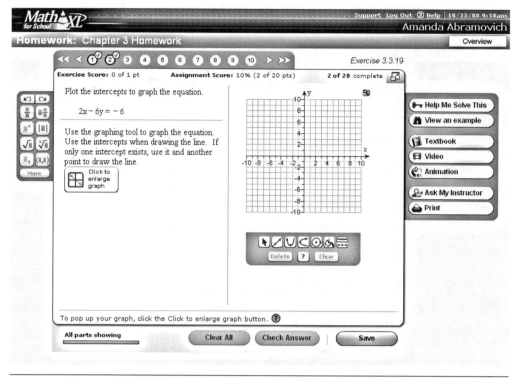

Figure 17.5 Example of homework problem in MathXL for School. Copyright 2008 Pearson Education. Used with permission.

data and auxiliary data about student interactions with the systems. This is precisely where the psychometric challenges and opportunities in implementing formative assessment lie. To return again to Pellegrino's (2006) vision of the future:

> When powerful technology-based systems are implemented in classrooms, rich sources of information about student learning will be continuously available across wide segments of the curriculum and for individual learners over extended periods of time. This is exactly the kind of information we now lack, making it difficult to use assessment to truly support learning. The major issue is not whether this type of data collection and information analysis is feasible in the future. Rather, the issue is how the world of education anticipates and embraces this possibility, and how it will explore the resulting options for effectively using assessment information to meet the multiple purposes served by current assessment and, most important, to enhance student learning. (pp. 12–13)

The quality of the student data produced by these systems and upon which instructional decision making is supported is critically important. If estimates of student knowledge, skills, abilities, and learning progress are off, they cannot serve as sound foundations for informing subsequent instruction. Furthermore, if the processes by which instructional interventions are prescribed or suggested are not reasonable, the ability of these systems to help close achievement gaps will be compromised. To evaluate the technical quality of assessment systems used for formative purposes—and to suggest

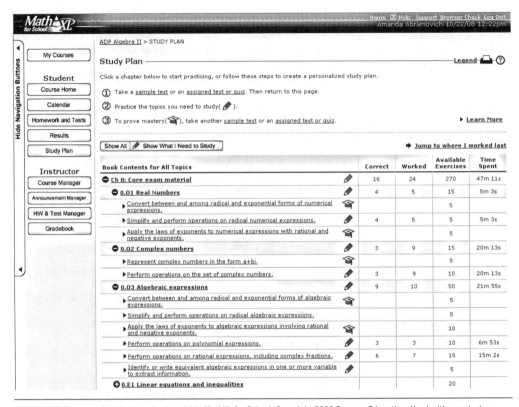

Figure 17.6 Example of student study plan within MathXL for School. Copyright 2008 Pearson Education. Used with permission.

improvements—we must recognize that the information contained in these systems goes beyond test scores and that the goal of assessment goes beyond simple reporting. The evaluation must therefore extend to other assessment information collected within these systems, to the inferences that are made from this assessment information that inform instructional interventions, and to the accumulated evidence that the assessment system is supporting student learning.

TECHNICAL QUALITY AND FORMATIVE ASSESSMENT SYSTEMS

The assessment world has long understood that the educational value of an assessment depends on its technical quality as represented by particular, measurable properties. These properties, such as validity and reliability, help assure that interpretations and decisions derived from the assessment results are reasonable. These properties are not, however, inherent to test instruments themselves but rather emerge from the way assessments are administered and their results are interpreted and used. Validity, for example, is not a property of a test but rather an indication of the degree to which test score interpretation is justifiable for a particular purpose and as supported by evidence and theory (AERA, APA, & NCME, 1999; Messick, 1989). For example, a reading test might have the capacity to support a valid interpretation that a student is deficient in reading comprehension, but only if the student was wearing her eyeglasses at the time

Table 17.1 Comparison of Processes Involved in Summative versus Formative Assessment

	Test Design	Admin-istration	Scoring, scaling, equating, standard setting	Reporting	Interpre-tation	Pre-scription	Imple-mentation	Close achievement gaps
Summative Assessment	X	X	X	X	X			
Formative Assessment	X	X	X	X	X	X	X	X

of testing, and only for particular types of content (e.g., expository versus narrative passages). Designing and evaluating assessments for technical quality is a necessary and complex process involving multiple factors and considerations.

To date, the field of psychometrics, which provides the theory and techniques for designing and evaluating the technical quality of assessments, has largely focused on summative assessments in education. As such, consideration of properties including validity and reliability has typically gone no further than score interpretation. Formative assessment, as discussed earlier, involves additional processes beyond score interpretation that directly address instruction, namely the prescription of instructional interventions, the implementation of these interventions, and reductions in achievement gaps resulting from implementation of these interventions (see Table 17.1). As a result, extant psychometric procedures largely do not directly support the development and evaluation of formative assessment systems.

Judgments about technical quality involve factors that are numerous and complex. The overall judgments can often be controversial, even without considering formative assessment. For the purposes of this chapter we will focus on two factors, reliability and validity. These factors are arguably the most important, and from them many other factors, such as fairness, can, in principle, be derived (i.e., a test that results in valid, repeatable interpretations is inherently fair).

Reliability of Formative Assessment Systems

Central to an understanding of reliability in both classical test theory and generalizability theory is the notion of replications (Brennan, 2001). Reliability, broadly conceived, involves quantifying the consistencies or inconsistencies in outcomes on a test; that is, test scores, across replications. Reliability, like validity, is a characteristic of scores, not of tests or forms of a test. To get direct information about reliability, at least two instances are required. These replications may be somewhat contrived (e.g., all possible split halves), but replications in some form are essential to estimate reliability.

The conceptualization of reliability of a formative assessment system borrows from conventional reliability theory as applied to test scores. As with the reliability for test scores, the notion of replications is central to an understanding of reliability for a system of assessment and instruction. Reliability theory for formative purposes focuses on the aggregate consistency of components that constitute the coordinated system of assessment and instruction.

The field of engineering offers analytic approaches to estimating the reliability of a system by quantifying the consistencies and inconsistencies in system performance. A tool in estimating system reliability is the reliability block diagram (RBD; Leemis, 1995). An RBD is a graphical representation of the components of a system and how they are reliability-wise related. While components may be related in other ways, such as physically, these are not captured in an RBD.

An RBD is constructed out of blocks. The blocks may represent the component, subsystem, or some other element at the chosen "black box" level. The blocks are connected with direction lines that represent the reliability relationship between the blocks. Blocks in an RBD may be decomposed into a more detailed RBD, depending on the level of detail in question. The level of granularity for an RBD should be based on the availability of data and the lowest actionable level.

A system may be represented at a number of different levels, such as component, subsystem, or entire system. The selection of the level of representation determines the detail of the reliability analysis that can be accomplished. There are a number of reasons to represent a formative assessment system at the component level. First, the reliability of components may be easier and less expensive to estimate than the reliability of the entire formative assessment system. Second, the reliability of some components may be easier to manipulate than the reliability of other components.

We can use the BAIP system described earlier as an example of how this approach can be applied to estimate reliability. The first step is to model student tutorials with an RBD. The BAIP tutorials are delivered in eight steps. In four of these steps, students must correctly answer a multiple-choice item before they can proceed to the next step. An incorrect answer cues feedback tailored to the response option selected. The other four steps deliver instruction that is independent of student performance on the multiple-choice items. Only the steps that involve answering a multiple-choice item will be considered as constituting the system of coordinated assessment and instruction because the other steps make no use of the assessment information to deliver instruction.

Figure 17.7 presents an example of an RBD for the student tutorials in the BAIP system, in which the diamond shapes represent actions within the system of coordinated assessment and instruction. These constitute the components that are reliability-wise related, with connecting lines representing the relationships. The components for this system's RBD must all succeed to produce a formative outcome; that is, the formative use of assessment information to improve student achievement. A sequence of actions is required to move from initial student behavior to student learning, such as interpretations of students' scores and implementations of instructional plans. Each of these actions introduces a potential source of inconsistency over replications.

In this example, the RBD for the multiple-choice items that constitute the system of coordinated assessment and instruction includes five actions. The first action, student behavior on the multiple-choice items, is a conventional source of inconsistency in educational testing that captures momentary distractions, illnesses, and other temporary states of the student. Reliability of student behavior on the multiple-choice items may be estimated using test–retest designs or measures of internal consistency.

The second action, interpretation of students' selection of a response option in terms of their mathematical knowledge and skills, is ignored in conventional educational

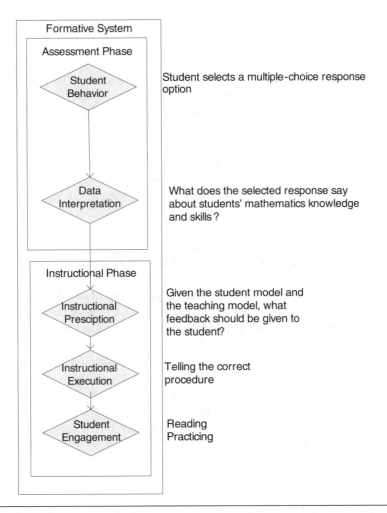

Figure 17.7 Reliability block diagram (RBD) for student tutorials in the BAIP system.

testing but may be a source of inconsistency within a system of assessment and instruction. Teachers, parents, and students themselves may be inconsistent in interpreting student performance. For the student tutorials, the interpretation of students' selection of a response option in terms of their mathematical knowledge and skills is perfectly consistent because the interpretation is represented as a rule in the software. This rule is implicit in the feedback provided to students but might be stated explicitly as, "Selection of this incorrect response option results from this misunderstanding or procedural error." This type of consistency has been termed "mechanical objectivity."

The third action, prescription of feedback to student given the student's selection of a response option, is a source of inconsistency unique to a system of assessment and instruction. Like the interpretation of students' selection of a response option, the prescription of feedback within the student tutorials generally is perfectly consistent and is an instance of mechanical objectivity, as most software provides the same feedback whenever a given response option is selected. Of course, this needn't be the case in more sophisticated systems in which variation is provided to maintain student engagement.

The fourth action, instructional execution, is another source of inconsistency unique to a system of assessment and instruction. Teachers, parents, or peers may be inconsistent in the quality with which they execute the planned instruction. For example, teachers may be tired or distracted on one day but not another day. For the student tutorials, instructional execution is likely to be perfectly consistent, though sources of inconsistency in instructional execution might include hardware malfunctions or environmental conditions such as poor lighting.

The last action, student engagement in response to feedback, is a source of inconsistency within a system of assessment and instruction. The causes of this inconsistency would be the same as the causes of inconsistency in student behavior on the multiple-choice items (e.g., momentary distractions, illnesses, and other temporary states of the student). Much research has underscored the dependence of learning and performance on student engagement (e.g., Bandura, 1997; Cassady & Gridley, 2005; Dweck, 1986; Guthrie & Wigfield, 2000).

This example underscores that evaluating the reliability of a system used for formative assessment purposes requires evaluation of the reliability of each component and how the components are combined in producing information about student learning. Some components (such as those that consist of assessment items) can be evaluated using traditional psychometric techniques (e.g., coefficient alpha, which may be defined as the mean of all possible split-half correlations). However, other components depend upon teacher or student interactions with the system or decision rules that are followed for actions and interventions based on accumulated data. This is likely to be a topic of increased research as the field of education seeks to understand and represent the reliability of formative assessment systems.

Validity of Formative Assessment Systems

A second technical quality of assessments is validity. A comprehensive definition of validity is provided by the Standards (AERA, APA, & NCME, 1999):

> Validity refers to the degree to which evidence and theory support the interpretations of test scores entailed by proposed uses of tests. Validity is, therefore, the most fundamental consideration in developing and evaluating tests. The process of validation involves accumulating evidence to provide a sound scientific basis for the proposed score interpretations. It is the interpretations of test scores required by proposed uses that are evaluated, not the test itself. When test scores are used or interpreted in more than one way, each intended interpretation must be validated. (p. 9)

There are two general types of threats to validity. Both are framed in terms of the constructs—knowledge, skills, and abilities—that a test is designed to measure. The first overarching threat to validity is referred to as *construct underrepresentation* and occurs when the knowledge, skills, or abilities that a test should measure are excluded from the test or its results. The second overarching threat to validity is referred to as *construct-*

irrelevant variance and occurs when superfluous knowledge, skills, and abilities—ones that a test shouldn't measure—influence test scores. In either of these cases, test results provide a skewed representation of a student's knowledge, skills, and abilities and hence cannot support valid interpretation.

As an example, consider a test of general reading comprehension. Including reading passages of only a single genre (e.g., expository versus narrative versus poetic) would introduce construct underrepresentation since the estimate of reading ability would not be based on a comprehensive set of reading tasks. On the other hand, providing only a single, fixed reading passage for all students may introduce construct-irrelevant variance, since students' background knowledge and engagement with the particular content—factors not under consideration—would likely impact their comprehension.

Formative Assessment Validity Framework   The process of demonstrating validity for a formative assessment system involves the construction of a validity framework, a set of explicit assumptions about the assessment's role and capacity. We submit that the following validity framework is appropriate for a formative assessment system:

1.   The instructional goal is for a student to possess a minimum of knowledge, skills, and abilities in a particular domain.
2.   Assessment instruments can be developed, administered, and scored that possess a content domain consistent with these construct-relevant knowledge, skills, and abilities and with minimal interference from construct-irrelevant knowledge, skills, and abilities.
3.   Results of assessments can be interpreted in such a way as to identify the achievement gaps of students.
4.   Assessment results can be interpreted in such a way as to recommend instructional interventions that reduce achievement gaps.
5.   Instructional interventions recommended through the interpretation of assessment results are realizable in the education setting.
6.   Instructional interventions recommended through the interpretation of assessment results, if implemented, will reduce achievement gaps.

Where the validity framework for formative assessment departs from that of summative assessment is in arguments 4 through 6. Specifically, a formative claim for an assessment use requires empirical and theoretical evidence for the efficacy of instructional interventions prescribed by or delivered within the formative assessment system.

Validity Frameworks for Technology-Based Formative Assessment Systems   The technology-based systems described earlier can now be connected to these arguments of the validity framework. For example, the first two arguments of the framework concern instructional goals and the development of instruments that provide construct-relevant measurement of these goals. The BAIP system addresses these elements through its relationship to the Kansas mathematics curriculum standards. These standards provide the content domain and the instructional goals within the domain. The MathXL system, by comparison, relies on alignment with specific textbooks, since it is typically sold as a companion to mathematics textbooks for which its content is customized. The My Reading Web system is tied to the Lexile Framework for Reading, and student performance on the computer-generated embedded sentence cloze items provides one basis for validating theory-based predictions.

For example, Figure 17.8 presents a comparison of predicted and observed student performance (percent correct on all cloze items presented). These data are based on one year of data collection with the product on 1,632 students in grades 2 through 12. The predicted and observed performance is based on nearly 1.5 million cloze items embedded in over 120,000 articles read by these students. As can be seen in Figure 17.8, the predicted percent correct values are very close to the observed percent correct values in grades two through four and eight through 12. This correspondence provides evidence of good model-data fit for these grades; that is, the theoretical model is accurately accounting for the way students respond to the cloze items. However, in grades 5, 6, and 7, the observed percent correct values exceed the predicted percent correct values by about 3 to 5 percentage points. These interesting findings invite further and more detailed analyses, and are no doubt being investigated by the My Reading Web developers.

It is easy to see how data collected from these technology-based systems can be used to identify student achievement gaps, as they include detailed summaries of problems worked on by the students. Nonetheless, consideration of the three elements of validity that separate formative and summative assessment raises additional questions: Can assessment results from technology-based systems be interpreted in such a way as to recommend instructional interventions that reduce achievement gaps? That is, are the intended inferences to be made from students' performances strongly supported? Are instructional interventions recommended through the interpretation of assessment results from technology-based systems realizable? Can instructional interventions recommended from technology-based systems reduce achievement gaps? We believe the

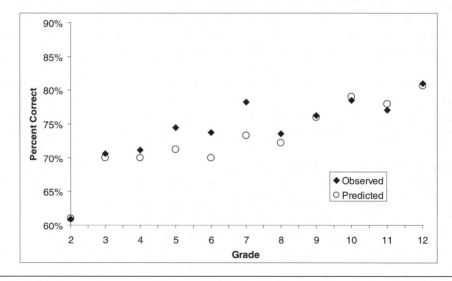

Figure 17.8 Observed and predicted cloze item performance across grade levels in MyReadingWeb.

answer to these questions is yes. Once these systems become part of everyday instruction and learning, their validation will become part of their use. The following section begins to address some of the ways data from technology-based formative assessment systems can be used to accomplish this validation.

Internal versus External Validity Evidence of Technology-based Formative Assessment Systems Both internal and external data can be used to support the validity argument that technology-based formative assessment systems reduce achievement gaps. Internal evidence results from analysis of data provided by the system itself, while external evidence results from correlations of observations with data collected from other systems or measures. Examples of internal evidence gathered from the data collected by the systems over time might include performance on tutorial and homework exercises, time spent on different instructional/assessment modules, documentation of supports accessed in the course of interacting with the system (e.g., hints, targeted instructional feedback, hyperlinked textbook pages accessed, etc.), numbers of times particular instructional/assessment modules are accessed, numbers of articles read, words read per minute, and model-based summaries of incorrect responses provided on homework and tutorial exercises.

While these data might differ across different instructional/assessment systems and content domains, the central concept is that each student compiles an electronic portfolio of activity through their interactions with the system. If the struggling student persists with the areas that he or she has difficulty with, the data in the well-constructed technology-based system will reflect the effort and will provide the data to determine whether or not the student is improving. As we become skilled in summarizing and drawing inferences from these data, internal validity evidence for the formative assessment system will be routinely documented.

Such internal evidence is necessary but not sufficient to support the validation of technology-based formative assessment systems. In addition, external studies are needed to demonstrate the efficacy of the systems. These may take the form of experimental designs involving pretest and posttest instruments, random designs introducing the systems as treatments, or quasi-experimental designs. In such studies, the research questions may not only ask if a particular system is effective at closing achievement gaps and demonstrating student learning, but also whether gains in learning are greater than alternate interventions.

APPLICABILITY OF THE AERA/APA/NCME STANDARDS TO FORMATIVE ASSESSMENT

The *Standards for Educational and Psychological Testing* (AERA, APA, & NCME, 1999) is the primary guide to the development, evaluation, and use of assessments. The approach of the *Standards* is largely that of considering the technical quality of assessments. While factors relevant to formative assessment are touched upon in the *Standards*, techniques for assuring the technical quality of formative assessments are not explicitly addressed. Nonetheless, there are two general ways in which the *Standards* are applicable to formative assessment systems. The first is by extrapolating the reliability and validity frameworks put forth by the *Standards* to include the additional concerns of prescription of instructional interventions, implementation of these interventions, and reductions in achievement gaps resulting from implementation of these interventions. This is what we have done in the previous sections. The second is to extract general recommendations from the *Standards* to the extent that they touch upon formative assessment. These recommendations help guide the development of formative assessment systems that are technically sound and thus most likely to be effective in improving student learning. This section presents these recommendations, along with the individual Standards from which they derive.

As discussed above, it is not a test that is validated, but specific intended interpretations and uses of test scores (Standards 1.1 and 13.2), with the onus lying on the test developer to communicate this and indicate for which population of students it is intended (Standards 1.2, 6.3, and 12.16). These are critically important points, especially to the extent that instruments originally designed for summative assessment may be used to support formative assessment. The *Standards* recommend that test developers explicitly caution against using test scores in ways that have not been validated (Standards 1.3 and 13.9) or that are based on isolated item responses (Standard 1.10). In the case of either assessments or technology-based systems used for formative purposes, both theory for and evidence of the appropriateness and effectiveness of prescribed and implemented interventions must support the validity argument (Standards 1.19, 1.22, and 13.9).

While most summative assessment instruments are designed to provide only single measures, many formative assessment systems rely on tests' ability to provide information on multiple factors of student learning and to prescribe and implement multiple instructional remediations. This is particularly the case with technology-based systems that are focused on connecting the delivery of instruction to assessment performance. It is critical, therefore, that assessment used for these formative purposes be designed to support such uses, with specific consideration of the value of individual sets of exercises or accumulated scores on sets of exercises (Standards 1.11, 1.12, and 2.7).

If test interpretation is to support fine-grained diagnostic decisions, it is critical that any assumptions about specific cognitive operations made by the test developer be explicit, appropriate, and technically defensible (Standard 1.8), especially to the extent that they are based on individual or low numbers of items (Standard 1.10) or on change or gain scores (Standard 13.17). It is also important to consider whether results generalize from assessment to instructional situations (Standard 1.13), especially when the interpretation is computer-based and may exclude relevant contextual data (Standards 5.11 and 11.21). Some technology-based systems used for formative assessment purposes are based on sophisticated cognitive models of student learning. For example Carnegie Learning has developed a mathematics tutoring system based on John Anderson's ACT-R theory of human cognition (Anderson, 1990, 1993; Anderson & Lebiere, 1998; see http://www.carnegielearning.com). In this case, the supporting validity evidence includes not only efficacy studies but also a substantial body of theoretical research.

The *Standards* advocate for test users—teachers, in the case of formative assessments—to not use test instruments blindly, but to understand the intent of the test (Standard 11.1). They further caution about using the test or its results in ways not supported by the test developer (Standards 11.2 and 11.5), unless they or their administrative body plan to validate such uses themselves (Standard 1.4). Furthermore, teachers must be trained in the use of the test (Standard 11.3) and be clear about the rationale for using the test and how results will inform instructional decision making (Standard 11.4). Other stakeholders, including the student, parents, and other teachers need to be considered in this process as well (Standard 11.5).

Additional sources of evidence beyond test results should be considered both by test developers and by teachers when making instructional decisions and in evaluating the effectiveness of prescribed and implemented instructional remediations. Factors such as motivation, familiarity with assessment systems, and the presence of diagnosed or undiagnosed disabilities may provide data that needs to be taken into account in real-life instructional settings (Standards 1.14 and 11.20). Furthermore, close attention must be paid to any instructional and/or testing accommodations students are typically provided, such as through their Individualized Education Program (IEP) or Section 504 plans. Ideally, such supports should be considered simultaneously across instruction and assessment and across in-school and out-of-school student environments (Standard 11.23).

Communication with stakeholders, including students, teachers, and parents, is critically important for programs involving formative assessment systems, especially score interpretation and the prescription, implementation, and effectiveness of interventions. Such communications must be presented in timely and appropriate ways for the audience, and provide perspective on the process (Standards 5.10 and 11.6).

From these recommendations, six overarching recommendations for the development and use of formative assessments have been synthesized from the *Standards*. First, the technical quality of a formative assessment system must address not only the soundness of results interpretation but the appropriateness and effectiveness of interventions prescribed as a result of this interpretation. Second, tests not designed to support instructional decision making should be used to do so only with extreme caution. Third, the limitations of results in supporting instructional decision making should be acknowledged and communicated to stakeholders. Fourth, the importance of additional sources of data during interpretation and instructional decision making—either internal or external to the assessment system—should be considered. Fifth, the rationale behind instructional decision making is important and should be communicated to students, teachers, and parents. And finally, tight coupling of testing and instruction, both in design and implementation, is important for valid instructional decision making.

LOOKING TOWARD THE FUTURE

This chapter has addressed the psychometric challenges and opportunities in implementing formative assessment. We have approached this topic by first illustrating the opportunities that exist for utilizing technology-based formative assessment systems. In our view, these systems are a breeding ground for not only traditional assessment data that can be used for formative purposes (e.g., performance on test items and instruments) but also for data that might otherwise not be considered assessment data at all (time spent on tasks within the system, number of times particular instructional or assessment modules are accessed, documentation of supports accessed during the course of student engagement, etc.). We predict that the refinement and utilization of these latter data sources will become the subject of increased research as these systems continue to develop in the future.

Our discussion in this chapter has also touched upon the existing testing standards and in particular, the traditional concepts of reliability and validity as measures of technical quality. We have shown how the concept of reliability within a formative assessment system depends upon the reliability of different components that are combined to produce information about student learning. Similarly, validity evidence within a formative assessment system involves not only inferences about assessment results but also the efficacy of instructional interventions prescribed by the assessment results to promote student learning and close identified achievement gaps.

Our assertion of the importance of reliability and validity in formative assessment agrees with those recently made by Cizek (2009) in considering classroom-based assessments. These conceptions point to broadening the role of assessment information from test scores to indicators of learning to prescriptions of intervention. This is an important psychometric evolution that will continue to invite changes to the instruments, procedures, and theoretical approaches to measurement.

This evolution also has at least two implications for the testing *Standards*, which at the time of publication of this *Handbook* are being revised and updated. The existing *Standards* (1999) are not intended to directly apply to tests used in classroom settings. For example, the introduction to chapter 13, "Educational Testing and Assessment," includes the following caveat: "This chapter does not explicitly address issues related to tests constructed and administered by teachers in their own classroom use or provided by publishers of instructional materials" (p. 137). We believe that the *Standards* should apply to technology-based formative assessment systems, despite the fact that they are often developed by publishers of instructional materials and used in classroom settings.

A second implication for the *Standards* is that the assessment data collected and summarized by technology-based systems goes beyond traditional notions of test scores. It seems reasonable to formally acknowledge that decisions and uses of information from technology-based formative assessment systems should be subject to the same considerations of reliability and validity that have been traditionally applied to test instruments used for summative assessment.

As technology-based formative assessment systems continue to evolve, it is likely that they will become increasingly based on theories of learning and cognition. A committee supported by the National Science Foundation has been convened to review and synthesize advances in the cognitive sciences and measurement and to explore their implications for improving educational assessment (Pellegrino, Glaser, & Chudowsky, 2001). Their report emphasized that three foundational elements underlie all assessments, referred to in the report as the "assessment triangle": a model of how students represent knowledge and develop competence in the subject domain, the tasks or situations that allow one to observe students' performance, and an interpretation method for drawing inferences from the performance evidence thus obtained. In looking to the future, we note that the psychometric challenges and opportunities in implementing formative assessment, especially within technology-based systems, will be largely focused on these foundational elements.

REFERENCES

American Educational Research Association (AERA), American Psychological Association (APA), & the National Council on Measurement in Education (NCME). (1999). *Standards for educational and psychological testing*. Washington, DC: AERA.

Anderson, J. R. (1990). *The adaptive character of thought*. Hillsdale, NJ: Erlbaum.

Anderson, J. R. (1993). *Rules of the mind*. Hillsdale, NJ: Erlbaum.

Anderson, J. R., & Lebière, C. (1998). *The atomic components of thought*. Mahwah, NJ: Erlbaum.

Bandura, A. (1997). *Self-efficacy: The exercise of control*. New York: Freeman.

Bennett, R. E. (2002). Inexorable and inevitable: The continuing story of technology and assessment [Electronic version]. *Journal of Technology, Learning, and Assessment, 1*(1), 1–23.

Black, P., & Wiliam, D. (1998). Assessment and classroom learning. *Educational Assessment: Principles, Policy and Practice, 5*(1), 7–74.

Brennan, R. L. (2001). *Generalizability theory*. New York: Springer-Verlag.

Cassady, J. C., & Gridley, B. E. (2005). The effects of online formative and summative assessment on test anxiety and performance. *Journal of Technology, Learning, and Assessment, 4*(1), 1–30. http://www.jtla.org

Cizek, G. J. (2009). Reliability and validity of information about student achievement: Comparing large-scale and classroom testing contexts. *Theory into Practice, 48*(1), 63–71.

Dweck, C. S. (1986). Motivational processes affecting learning. *American Psychologist, 41,* 1040–1048.

Guthrie, J. T., & Wigfield, A. (2000). Engagement and motivation in reading. In M. L. Kamil, P. B. Mosenthal, P. D. Pearson, & R. Barr (Eds.), *Reading research handbook* (Vol. 3, pp. 403–424). Mahwah, NJ: Erlbaum.

Hattie, J., & Timperley, H. (2007). The power of feedback. *Review of Educational Research, 7*(1), 81–112.

Leemis, L. M. (1995). *Reliability: Probabilistic models and statistical methods*. Englewood Cliffs, NJ: Prentice Hall.

Lexile Framework for Reading. (n.d.). http://www.lexile.com

MathXL. (n.d.). http://www.mathxlforschool.com/support/school/product_info.html

Messick, S. (1989). Validity. In R. L. Linn (Ed.), *Educational measurement* (3rd ed., pp. 13–103.). Washington, DC: American Council on Education.

Pellegrino, J. W. (2006). *Rethinking and redesigning curriculum, instruction and assessment: What contemporary research and theory suggest*. Retrieved September 24, 2008, from ttp://www.skillscommission.org/pdf/commissioned_papers/Rethinking%20and%20Redesigning.pdf

Pellegrino, J., Glaser, R., & Chudowsky, N. (Eds.). (2001). *Knowing what students know: The science and design of educational assessments*. Washington, DC: National Academy Press.

Poggio, J., & Meyen, E. (2008). *Blending assessment with instruction program*. Retrieved November 12, 2008, from http://www.elearndesign.org/baip_demo/index_home.htm

Stiggins, R. J., Arter, J., Chappuis, J., & Chappuis, S. (2006). *Classroom assessment for student learning: Doing it right—using it well*. Portland, OR: ETS Assessment Training Institute.

Wiliam, D. (2006). Formative assessment: Getting the focus right. *Educational Assessment, 11*(3–4), 283–289.

Wiliam, D. (2007). Changing classroom practice. *Educational Leadership, 65*(4), 36–42.

Wiliam, D., & Black, P. (1996) Meaning and consequences: A basis for distinguishing formative and summative functions of assessment? *British Educational Research Journal, 22*(5), 537–548.

18

STRATEGIES AND POLICIES FOR INCORPORATING FORMATIVE ASSESSMENT INTO COMPREHENSIVE AND BALANCED STATE ASSESSMENT SYSTEMS

DOUGLAS A. RINDONE AND DUNCAN MACQUARRIE

The purposes of this chapter are to review state efforts in the area of formative assessment and define an appropriate state role. Three recent state efforts will be described, each of which is sponsored or cosponsored by the Council of Chief State School Officers: The Formative Assessment for Students and Teachers state collaborative, the Technical Issues in Large Scale Assessment state collaborative, and the Delaware Enhanced Assessment Grant.

FORMATIVE ASSESSMENT DEFINED

Scriven (1967) is generally credited with coining the educational terms *formative* and *summative* to differentiate between two major roles of curriculum evaluation. He used the term *formative* when evaluations were used to modify a project while it was still in development, and *summative* when an evaluation was to be used for making final or conclusive decisions on the effectiveness of a program.

Bloom, Hastings, and Madaus (1971) later used the term *formative* when referring to classroom tests used for formative purposes, that is, to modify instruction and check on learning. Since the publication of the Bloom et al. text, a host of other educators have referred to tests as having formative value if they serve to inform instruction or learning. Black and Wiliam (1998) coauthored an article entitled "Inside the Black Box," which reviewed a large number of studies and concluded that classroom formative assessment has a positive association with classroom learning and achievement in large scale accountability assessments. Black and Wiliam also argued that formative assessment is an integral part of the instructional process.

The Council of Chief State School Officers (CCSSO) is involved in assessment-related efforts. Among the Council's many endeavors is a set of projects collectively known as the State Collaborative on Assessment and Student Standards (SCASS). The

Table 18.1 CCSSO Formative Assessment Advisory Group, 2006

Annette Bohling, Sr. Vice President of Accreditation, AdvancED, Arizona State University

William Bushaw, Executive Director, Phi Delta Kappa, Bloomington, IN

Doug Christensen, Commissioner of Education, Nebraska Department of Education

Angela Faherty, Deputy Associate Superintendent, Standards and Assessment Section, Maine Department of Education

Gerunda Hughes, Associate Professor, Curriculum and Instruction Program Coordinator, Secondary Education, Howard University

Henry Johnson, Assistant Secretary for Elementary and Secondary Education, U.S. Department of Education

Stuart Kahl, President and CEO, Measured Progress, Dover, NH

Ken Kay, President, Partnership for 21st Century Skills, Tucson, AZ

Sarah McManus, Section Chief, Testing Policy and Operations, North Carolina Department of Public Instruction

Bob Nielsen, Superintendent, Bloomington, Illinois Public Schools

Scott Norton, Director, Student Standards & Assessments, Louisiana Department of Education

W. James Popham, Emeritus Professor, University of California at Los Angeles

Doris Redfield, President/CEO, Edvantia, Charleston, WV

Wendy Roberts, Assessment Director, Delaware Department of Education

Lorrie Shepard, Dean, School of Education, Professor of Education, University of Colorado at Boulder

Rick Stiggins, CEO, Assessment Training Institute (ATI), ETS, Princeton, NJ

Martha Thurlow, Professor, National Center on Education Outcomes, University of Minnesota

Dylan Wiliam, Director, Learning and Teaching Research Center, ETS, Princeton, NJ

Valerie Woodruff, Secretary of Education, Delaware Department of Education

SCASS projects provide opportunities for states to join together to identify and address common assessment issues and opportunities. In 2006, the Council initiated work on formative assessment by convening an advisory committee of distinguished educators and scholars representing a broad spectrum of educational institutions. The membership of that group, known as Formative Assessment for Students and Teachers (FAST), is shown in Table 18.1. Table 18.2 identifies the 18 states that were members of the FAST SCASS during the 2007–2008 program year.

The focus of the FAST project for 2007–2008 was to adopt and disseminate a definition of formative assessment and to develop companion documents that would help articulate the essential characteristics of this key component of a comprehensive and balanced state assessment program. The FAST committee reviewed various definitions of formative assessment and crafted a working draft of a definition to help American educators understand what formative assessment is. At the first FAST meeting held in Austin, Texas in October 2006, the members refined and adopted a definition of formative assessment: "Formative assessment is a process used by teachers and students during instruction that provides feedback to adjust ongoing teaching and learning to improve students' achievement of intended instructional outcomes" (McManus, 2008, p. 3).

Table 18.2 FAST SCASS State Members, 2007–2008

Alaska	Hawaii	Maine	South Dakota
Arizona	Indiana	Michigan	West Virginia
Arkansas	Iowa	North Carolina	Wisconsin
Connecticut	Kentucky	Nebraska	
Delaware	Louisiana	South Carolina	

There are two salient aspects of this definition. First, formative assessment is a process, not a product. The process can be as simple as a teacher questioning students before moving on, or creating and using rubrics that help students monitor and revise their own work. In other words, formative assessment is generally not a product, such as a test that can be purchased from a vendor.

The second salient feature of the FAST definition of formative assessment is that it is more about good teaching than about creating assessments. Said differently, formative assessment is a matter of using assessment techniques and processes to guide instruction and stimulate learning; not just measuring what has been learned. Furthermore, formative assessment is not something that is done to students. Rather, students should be full partners who are actively involved in the formative assessment process in order to monitor and improve their own learning.

Because formative assessment seemed to encompass so many aspects of teaching, the FAST SCASS committee articulated five key attributes that have been identified in the literature as critical features of the formative assessment process. These five key attributes are: (1) *Learning progressions,* which should clearly articulate the subgoals of the ultimate learning goal; (2) *Learning goals and criteria for success*, which should be clearly identified and communicated to students; (3) *Descriptive feedback* provided to students, which should be evidence-based, linked to the intended instructional outcomes, and include criteria for success; (4) *Self- and peer assessment*, which are important for providing students with an opportunity to think metacognitively about their learning; and (5) *Collaboration*, which refers to a classroom culture in which teachers and students are partners in learning (McManus, 2008).

In addition to articulating and disseminating a clear definition of formative assessment, the FAST committee produced several papers designed to support states' efforts to promote formative assessment at the local level. One of these, by McManus (2008), describes the five key attributes of formative assessment. Companion papers include one by Heritage (2008), in which she calls for greater articulation of the likely progress of learning in any particular domain. Such "learning progressions," she argues, can provide a clearer view of what is to be learned and act as a touchstone for formative assessment.

A paper by Wylie (2008) provides examples and nonexamples of formative assessment practice, along with more extended examples intended to illustrate the attributes of effective formative assessment and their interconnectedness. The extended examples have been collected from observations of teacher's formative assessment practices in a variety of schools across the United States.

A final paper, by Brockman (2008), introduces the fundamental concepts of formative assessment for use by practitioners at the school and classroom level. It was written for those who work directly with students in schools and classrooms, which is where policy and theory with respect to formative assessment should either begin or be aimed. It is intended to serve as a foundational document to describe key formative assessment concepts and ideas which policymakers at district, state, and national levels should support. The paper synthesizes key ideas that can transform classroom practices and change the way we think about teaching and learning.

Distinctions between Formative and Interim Assessment

Due to the accountability demands of No Child Left Behind (2002), there is a definite trend for more frequent testing by schools and districts in order to better understand the needs of students and to inform curriculum. "These tests are called by several names, including diagnostic, periodic, predictive, interim, benchmark, and sometimes even formative assessments. The assessments are often sold as commercial products, marketed to school districts by publishers of tests and other educational materials" (Crane, 2008, p. 1). Therefore, it is vital for state and school personnel to understand the important differences between formative assessment and interim assessments. To address this need, a second SCASS project, "Technical Issues in Large Scale Assessment" (TILSA) sponsored a study of interim assessment practices that included an attempt to differentiate formative and interim assessment activities (Crane, 2008).

The term *interim assessment* may have first been defined by Perie, Marion, Gong, and Wurtzel in 2007:

Assessments administered during instruction to evaluate students' knowledge and skills relative to a specific set of academic goals in order to inform policymaker or educator decisions at the classroom, school, or district level. The specific interim assessment designs are driven by the purpose and intended uses, but the results of any interim assessment must be reported in a manner allowing aggregation across students, occasions, or concepts. (p. 5)

Members of TILSA agreed with much of this definition, but took exception to one concept and felt that two additional features need to be added for any definition of interim assessment to be complete. The TILSA committee felt that it is not necessarily true that interim assessment occurs during instruction. Interim assessments are events that are more likely to happen on a scheduled and intermittent basis. The members felt that the frequency of interim assessments should be an important distinguishing characteristic. In addition, they believed the availability of student level information to be an important feature of interim assessments. Thus, TILSA has expanded on and modified the Perie et al. (2007) definition:

Assessments administered multiple times during a school year, usually outside of instruction, to evaluate students' knowledge and skills relative to a specific set of academic goals in order to inform policymaker or educator decisions at the student, classroom, school, or district level. The specific interim assessment designs are driven by the purposes and intended uses, but the results of any interim assessment must be reported in a manner allowing aggregation across students, occasions, or concepts. (Crane, 2008, p. 2)

Interim assessments fall between formative assessments, which are seamless with instruction, and large scale summative assessments, which clearly focus on assessing what has been learned in larger chunks of instruction. Interim assessments are a hybrid and offer some formative information, usually at the curricular or programmatic level. Perhaps immediacy of information to affect instruction and learning is the key criterion that distinguishes formative from interim assessment.

THE STATE ROLE IN FORMATIVE ASSESSMENT

Numerous states are beginning to rethink the role of state assessment as a vehicle for student learning. In response to the No Child Left Behind (NCLB) legislation of 2002, many states rushed to beef up their state testing programs by adding content areas and testing additional grade levels. However, as more and more schools and districts are classified as "in need of improvement," many states and districts are looking at other assessment tools and procedures to influence teaching, learning, and achievement. States are beginning to realize that a purely summative approach to state assessment may not help schools and districts meet the goals of NCLB.

Some states are examining more comprehensive and balanced approaches to their state assessment program. In fact, a state assessment system does not necessarily have to include only components that are state controlled. The system can be broader, more comprehensive, and can include procedures and instruments that are under the logical control of the district or even teachers and students.

A balanced assessment system starts by looking at the information needs of all users, and builds assessment and evaluation tools that will satisfy those needs. In a comprehensive and balanced assessment system (CBAS) not all components have to be of equal weight but there must be a component for each information user. To be comprehensive and balanced, all components of the assessment system must also be aligned to the same set of learning standards. By doing this, the system will have more breadth and depth than a simple state summative assessment (Redfield, Roeber, Stiggins, & Phillip, 2008; Stiggins, 2008).

With respect to formative assessment, the primary information users are classroom teachers and students. Since formative assessment has been shown to be effective in improving student achievement (Black & Wiliam, 1998), states are looking to foster it at the school and district levels, often by integrating formative assessment into the state assessment system through professional development.

Foci of the Formative Assessment for Students and Teachers SCASS

Identifying state policies and practices that will promote and support formative assessment was a major focus of the FAST SCASS in 2009. First, FAST sought to optimize communications and outreach strategies to promote the overall formative assessment literacy of policymakers, stakeholders, and the public through understanding of the direct connection between classroom formative assessment and learning. Second, FAST continued to build and extend a policy and implementation framework that can make formative assessments more effective as a component of a balanced and comprehensive learning and assessment system.

Third, FAST clarified and strengthened the appropriate systems connections between assessment and curriculum, instruction, teacher quality, preservice and in-service teacher and administrator education programs, school improvement, program evaluation, and accountability. Fourth and finally, FAST continued to provide leadership and professional development opportunities, including the facilitation of an ongoing collaborative community of practice among state members, experts, and partners using the Councils' members-only Web portal.

The Delaware Enhanced Assessment Grant

Another state level activity seeking to promote formative assessment is the Delaware Enhanced Assessment Grant (EAG): These grants are awarded by the U.S. Department of Education through a competitive proposal process, and are intended to enhance the quality of assessment instruments and systems used by states for measuring the achievement of all students. Through a project titled "Implementing and Improving Comprehensive and Balanced Learning and Assessment Systems for Success in High School and Beyond," the Delaware EAG is focused on two broad areas where state action can have an appropriate role and possible impact on school district work in formative assessment: building policy structures that support the use of reform-based local assessments, and creating and fostering professional learning (Marion, 2007). The Delaware EAG is a 10-state collaborative, led by the State of Delaware, in concert with the Council of Chief State School Officers: The other members of the collaborative are Arizona, Connecticut, Iowa, Louisiana, Maine, Michigan, Nebraska, North Carolina, and Virginia.

The Delaware EAG project has two primary goals. One goal is to provide intensive, high-quality professional and leadership development for state department teams to examine the implementation and improvement of a comprehensive and balanced learning and assessment system, which would include a strong emphasis on formative classroom assessment practices. The second goal is to support high school learning teams in implementing a formative assessment process through a collaborative, active learning approach to professional development. In these study teams, teachers meet to discuss formative assessment and collectively implement strategies in their classrooms. Typically, these groups last the school year, with teachers sharing best practices and providing feedback to each other on how strategies have worked and what can be done better.

Nine of the 10 Delaware EAG states are also members of the FAST SCASS. Each of the Delaware EAG states adopted the FAST definition of formative assessment as they worked to build capacity to support high schools in providing high-quality professional and leadership development in balanced assessment systems, as well as specific practices of formative classroom assessment. The project has promoted the two goals identified above over a 2-year period by providing: (1) online professional development for state leadership teams with respect to learning team facilitation; (2) a 2-day professional development opportunity where state teams learned about classroom formative assessment techniques; (3) customized training for state leaders, who then worked with local high school teams in formative classroom assessment techniques; and (4) online training and Web-ex presentations and discussions for state and local teams (Weinbaum, in press).

Each of the Delaware EAG states have developed action plans for the delivery of technical assistance regarding formative classroom assessment to high school learning teams within the state. Arizona has utilized the Web for distance learning and providing extensive professional development each month to two high school learning teams. The classroom assessment training material developed by the Assessment Training Institute (n.d.) has been placed on the state's Web site and training has been paced each month for the last year. The Arizona state department has been directive and hands on in its attempt to roll out this type of professional development.

Maine has drafted a Strategic Professional Learning state plan that requires school districts to submit an annual professional learning plan that incorporates formative assessment practices. An annual performance report on this professional learning plan will also be required.

Iowa awards continuing education credits to the members of the high school learning teams as they complete their professional development plans. In addition, the Iowa legislature has mandated that each K-12 educator embed the essential concepts and skill sets in rigorous and relevant instruction informed by ongoing formative assessment. Since formative assessment is a process, it will be interesting to follow the Iowa state department's attempt to monitor and evaluate this legislation.

North Carolina has brought many stakeholders together, including the State Board of Education and the state Superintendent, to create a vision of a balanced assessment system which includes formative assessment. This system will be aligned with graduation standards, include authentic assessment tasks, provide diagnostic information to teachers, and include professional development for teachers in formative assessment techniques. A brochure has been created to share this vision with the educational community. North Carolina is also developing a number of online modules to explain and demonstrate this system, especially key elements of formative assessment.

Nebraska has been working in the area of classroom testing for several years (see Gallagher, this volume) and, until recently, based its NCLB accountability on locally based classroom test results. Almost all of Nebraska's recent efforts in the area of assessment have been based on the belief that true instructional change will only occur if the teacher is at the center of the change effort (Christensen, 2006).

Delaware has been working on building the assessment literacy of its teachers since 2003. Since 2004, professional development efforts have included learning teams with lots of professional discussion, reflection and modeling. Teachers that complete 90 hours of approved professional development work receive a 2% salary increase for 5 years. This stipulation included teachers working in formative assessment learning teams in the Delaware EAG.

Connecticut has not been very directive or hands on during the school year but has provided intensive professional development summer workshops for high school learning teams. Formative assessment concepts, such as student-friendly targets, assessments of and for learning, and improving student and teacher communication, have been the focus of the workshops.

The Delaware EAG project contracted with the University of Pennsylvania's Consortium for Policy Research in Education (CPRE) to provide a quantitative and qualitative evaluation of the success of this project. The evaluation will provide guidance to states and districts in implementing and improving the practices of standards-based balanced assessment systems (Weinbaum, in press).

FAST Survey of State Efforts to Promote Formative Assessment

An additional source of information about state formative assessment practices and plans is a survey of state efforts to promote formative assessment that was conducted by the authors of this chapter. The survey responses were collected during the spring of 2008, when a link to an online survey tool was sent to state assessment directors. The directors were invited to respond to questions regarding their state agency's role in promoting and supporting local efforts to implement formative assessment practices. Among the research questions addressed by the survey were the extent to which state departments of education had a formal or informal role in promoting formative assessment, whether or not some portion of a staff member's time was given to that issue, and what kinds of state level activities were promoted and/or supported.

Twenty-five usable replies to this survey were provided by 24 states and one territory. Table 18.3 provides a list of respondents to the survey. Of the 25 jurisdictions, 14 described their role with regard to promoting and/or supporting formative assessment as defined by FAST as formal. Nine other jurisdictions indicated that, while they did not have a formal role in promoting formative assessment, they did have an informal role. Among the 14 states who described their role as more formal, 11 indicated they had a staff member who had some responsibility for formative assessment. Five of these states indicated this assignment represented three-quarter time or more (see Table 18.4). The kinds of activities these states engage in to promote and/or support the implementation of formative assessment processes at the local level are diverse, as shown in Table 18.5.

Of the remaining 11 states responding to the survey, ten indicated that, while not having a formal role in promoting formative assessment practices in their state, they did have an informal role. As might be expected, these states did not assign the same level of staff support to this role as did the states with a more formal approach. Table 18.6 shows this pattern.

The directors that indicated they had an informal role in promoting formative assessment in their state were also asked to identify the kinds of activities they engaged in to

Table 18.3 States/Territories Completing FAST Survey

Alaska*	Hawaii*	Maryland	Montana	South Dakota*
American Samoa	Iowa*	Michigan	Nevada	Utah
Arizona*	Kansas	Minnesota	New Jersey	Vermont
Connecticut*	Kentucky*	Missouri	New Mexico	West Virginia*
Delaware*	Louisiana	Mississippi	Oregon	Wisconsin

*These states were among those belonging to the FAST SCASS in 2007-2008

Table 18.4 Staff Assigned by States with Formal Role in Promotion of Formative Assessment

Proportion of Time	Number of States
No staff assigned	3
Less than quarter-time	3
Quarter-time or more but less than half-time	3
Three-quarter time or more but less than full-time	2
Full-time	3

Table 18.5 Activities Engaged in by States with Formal Role in Promotion of Formative Assessment

Activity	Number of States
Share information at regional meetings/workshops	11
Support travel of SEA staff to attend professional meetings and/or training sessions on formative assessment	10
Share information on SEA web page	9
Send information bulletins to district superintendents/curriculum directors/assessment directors	8
Sponsor or otherwise support one or more meetings each year focused on formative assessment	8
Present or sponsor regional training sessions	7
Fund district efforts to promote/foster quality formative assessment	7
Support and/or facilitate consortia of districts to work on formative assessment issues	6
Disseminate non-binding guidance or criteria to school districts	6
Seek legislative funding to foster and/or support formative assessment	5
Seek grants to help foster and/or support formative assessment	4
Support travel for district staff to attend professional meetings and/or training sessions on formative assessment	3
Work directly with higher education programs to integrate formative assessment techniques into teacher training	3
Support a web-based formative assessment system	1

informally promote and/or support formative assessment practices. The pattern for these states was similar to those states having a more formal role, as shown in Table 18.7.

Interpretations of the findings from the survey need to be made with caution because only half the states responded with usable data. That said, it is unlikely that the pattern of staffing and activities supporting formative assessment in the nonresponding state education agencies would depart dramatically from that found in this study. The most significant difference between states identifying their role in promoting formative assessment as formal compared to informal is in the staffing levels. This should not be surprising. Almost all of the states have committed to providing staff development opportunities related to formative assessment for state education agency staff, but only 6 of the 25 agencies reported support for the same opportunities for local district staff.

The FAST members have noted the importance of integrating formative assessment techniques into preservice teacher training, but only six of the states responding to the survey indicated working directly with the higher education community to support this effort. The results of the survey also show that sharing information is a widely used

Table 18.6 Staff Assigned by States with Informal Role in Promotion of Formative Assessment

Proportion of Time	Number of States
No staff assigned	6
Less than quarter-time	1
Quarter-time or more, but less than half-time	3

Table 18.7 Activities Engaged in by States with Informal Role in Promotion of Formative Assessment

Activity	Number of States
Share information at regional meetings/workshops	8
Support travel of SEA staff to attend professional meetings and/or training sessions on formative assessment	7
Disseminate non-binding guidance or criteria related to formative assessment to districts	5
Facilitate consortia of districts to work on formative assessment issues	3
Seek grants to help foster and/or support formative assessment	3
Work indirectly with higher education to integrate formative assessment techniques into teacher training	3
Share information on our SEA web page	2
Support travel for district staff to attend professional meetings and/or training sessions on formative assessment	2

activity, and should be helpful in making local district staff aware of the importance of formative assessment. However, sustained training and direct support of local efforts sponsored by state education agencies does not appear to be widely available. Given the current economic situations of most states, it does not seem that this situation will change soon. And, given the continued commitment to large scale accountability programs, it is unlikely that the federal government will make available a large amount of funding for formative assessment.

CONCLUSIONS AND RECOMMENDATIONS

Classroom formative assessment is associated with substantial learning gains and improved scores on tests (Black & Wiliam, 1998; Wiliam, this volume). Yet there continue to be serious obstacles to the implementation of formative assessment practices in everyday instruction. To some extent this is due to confusion over what formative assessment is but the greater obstacle is the age old problem of depth versus breadth. Teachers and college professors cover too much content with little or no depth, no practice time, and no formative assessment.

Let us remember that the Black and Wiliam meta-analysis (1998) looked at research studies where teachers were performing only one or two formative techniques, and they still seemed to make a big difference in terms of student learning. The typical American response to most innovations is to overdo it. Rather than teaching a few simple concepts to help teachers get a better handle on student understanding, we want to radically change everything, including grading, standards of learning, and implementing learning progressions, before anything else can be done. The risk, of course, is that formative assessment is seen as too all encompassing and becomes almost impossible to implement in the classroom.

Two approaches should be simultaneously promoted by state education departments to begin strengthening formative assessment practices in the classroom: Professional development for in-service educators (see Schneider & Randel, this volume; Stiggins, this volume), and training for preservice educators. With a commitment to these two approaches, state agencies can make a significant impact on achieving the goal of supporting all children's learning by high quality formative assessment classroom practices.

First, with regard to in-service teachers and principals, it is important for state agencies to support and promote professional development programs that teach a few basic formative assessment strategies, perhaps those already identified by the FAST SCASS. Principals should be involved so that there is commitment and support for teachers trying different techniques. Professional development should be implemented through collaborative learning teams, since research indicates that one-shot issues workshops may not be as effective as collaborative, content focused models (Cohen & Hill, 2000).

Second, state agencies typically have considerable influence on preservice teacher education programs. State agencies should take advantage of this position to make sure that students in these programs receive a more in-depth training program in formative assessment. It is with these future teachers that the largest impact can be made. They are not yet in the classroom. They are not yet under the institutional restrictions of the school systems. Higher education needs to understand the implications of formative assessment for teaching and student learning, and make a serious commitment to making it a core component of teacher preparation programs. To date this is happening only sporadically; state departments of education can make it happen more widely. Many state departments of education have approval authority over the higher education teacher training programs in their state; they need to take the necessary steps to see that the principles and practices of formative assessment are integrated in those programs.

REFERENCES

Assessment Training Institute. (n.d.). http://www.ets.org/ati

Black, P., & Wiliam, D. (1998). Inside the black box: Raising standards through classroom assessment. *Phi Delta Kappan, 80*(2), 139–148.

Bloom, B. S., Hastings, J. T., & Madaus, G. F (Eds.). (1971). *Handbook on formative and summative evaluation of student learning.* New York: McGraw-Hill.

Brockman, F. (2008). Formative assessment: Concepts and key ideas for practitioners. Retrieved January 8, 2009, from http://www.ccsso.org/content/PDFs/FAST%Formative%Assessment%.pdf

Christensen, D. (2006). *School-based teacher-led assessment and reporting system: A summary.* Lincoln: Nebraska Department of Education.

Cohen, D., & Hill, H. (2000). Instructional policy and classroom performance: The mathematics reform in California. *Teachers' College Record, 102*(2), 294–343.

Crane, E. (2008). Interim assessment practices and avenues for state involvement. Retrieved January 8, 2009, from http://www.ccsso.org/publications/details.cfm?PublicationID=372

Heritage, M. (2008). Learning progressions. Retrieved January 8, 2009, from http://www.ccsso.org/content/PDFs/FAST%20Learning%20Progressions.pdf

Marion, S. (2007, June). *The state role in supporting formative assessment systems: Policy considerations and decisions.* Paper presented at the 37th Annual National Conference on Large-Scale Assessment, Nashville, TN.

McManus, S. (2008). Attributes of effective formative assessment. Retrieved January 8, 2009, from http://www.ccsso.org/publications/details.cfm?PublicationID=362

No Child Left Behind Act, 20 U.S.C. 6301. (2002).

Perie, M., Marion, S., Gong, B., & Wurtzel, J. (2007). *The role of interim assessment in a comprehensive assessment system: A policy brief.* Queenstown, MD: Aspen Institute.

Redfield, D., Roeber, E., Stiggins, R., & Phillip, F. (2008, June). *Building balanced assessment systems to guide educational improvement.* A background paper for the keynote presentation at the National Conference on Student Assessment, Orlando, FL.

Scriven, M. S. (1967). The methodology of evaluation. In R. W. Tyler, R. M. Gagne, & M. Scriven (Eds.), *Perspectives of curriculum evaluation* (AERA Monograph Series on Curriculum Evaluation, Vol. 1, pp. 39–83). Chicago: Rand McNally.

Stiggins, R. J. (2008). *A call for the development of balanced assessment systems.* Portland, OR: Educational Testing Service.

Weinbaum, E. (in press). Learning about assessment: An evaluation of a ten-state effort to build assessment capacity in high schools. Philadelphia, PA: Consortium for Policy Research in Education, University of Pennsylvania.

Wylie, E. C. (2008). Formative assessment: Examples of practice. Retrieved January 8, 2009, from http://www.ccsso.org/publications/details.cfm?PublicationID=363

19

KEEPING THE FOCUS, EXPANDING THE VISION, MAINTAINING THE BALANCE

Preserving and Enhancing Formative Assessment in Nebraska

CHRIS W. GALLAGHER

Policymakers, it seems, are coming to embrace what educators have long known and researchers have recently confirmed: formative assessments promote as well as measure student learning and increase student achievement (Black & Wiliam, 1998a), with the greatest gains evident among students who are low achieving and have special needs (Black & Wiliam, 1998b). At present, several states and national initiatives such as the Council of Chief State School Officers' Formative Assessment for Students and Teachers (CCSSO FAST; see Rindone and MacQuarrie, this volume) are exploring policies and practices that promote the use of formative assessment in "comprehensive, balanced, and coherent" assessment and education systems (CCSSO, 2008, p. 1).

Begun in 2006, FAST's mission is to establish definitions, standards, and guidance to states regarding the use of formative assessment, which CCSSO defines as "a process used by teachers and students during instruction that provides feedback to adjust ongoing teaching and learning to improve students' achievement of intended instructional outcomes" (CCSSO, 2008, p. 1). Currently, FAST is identifying effective professional development models, promoting outreach and communication strategies, developing a policy and implementation framework, facilitating a national community of practice, and more.

Though proponents of formative assessment should applaud such developments, policymakers have yet to confront a key challenge to the effective practice of formative assessment and the implementation of comprehensive, balanced, and coherent systems—namely, the way in which summative assessment has set the terms for the technical and policy conversations in most states and nationally. Put simply, if reforms begin with systems designed around summative assessments, it will be difficult, if not impossible, to realize the potential of formative assessment. Rather, formative assessment will be placed in the service of summative assessment, as too often happens with so-called benchmark, midcycle, and interim assessments, which often are touted as formative assessments but really function as minisummative assessments in preparation for larger, less frequent summative tests.

Most states are beginning with systems built around—and sometimes entirely constituted by—summative assessments (i.e., state-mandated student achievement tests). If state test scores are what count in assessment and education systems, and if, as a result, formative assessments are used only to help gauge how well students will perform on summative assessments, then the potential of formative assessment will not be realized. Worse yet, "students' achievement of intended *instructional* outcomes" (to borrow CCSSO's language) may be co-opted by the makers of state tests. (One might wish that CCSSO had used the word *learning* in place of "achievement.")

A related challenge is that traditional conceptions of validity and reliability were designed for large-scale summative tests, not for formative assessment. Appropriate and convincing psychometrics for classroom assessments in particular is in its infancy (see Brookhart, 2003; Cizek, 2009). If formative assessments, including those conducted in classrooms, are to count beyond simply preparing students for summative tests, then it will be necessary to validate those assessments in ways that do justice to their unique nature and function. If not, educators will be justified in responding to new initiatives for formative assessment with skepticism and perhaps resentment.

Nebraska, the state that is the focus of the case study reported in chapter, has laid the groundwork for validating and documenting the assessment quality of formative assessment, including formative classroom assessment, with its School-based, Teacher-led Assessment and Reporting System (STARS), a statewide system of local assessments, rather than a set of state tests. It encouraged schools and districts to develop and document both formative and summative assessments. Because its assessment system did not subordinate formative assessment to summative assessment, Nebraska stood alone among the states in realizing the distinct potential of formative assessment within a state system. At the same time, the state did not go far enough in developing, using, and convincing others (particularly state politicians) of the legitimacy of distinct metrics for formative and especially classroom assessments. As a result, the system was viewed by some, including state senators who pushed for and enacted a new state law phasing out STARS, as arbitrary, chaotic, or—in a phrase often heard in the state over the last couple of years—comparing apples to oranges.

In the wake of the state's new testing law that requires testing in grades 3 through 8 plus one high school grade, the Nebraska Department of Education (NDE) is seeking to help districts integrate the new tests into what are already, for the most part, comprehensive, balanced, and coherent local assessment and education systems. At this writing, the NDE is developing a new policy framework that requires the implementation (or, more accurately, the continuation) and documentation of formative assessment as part of the required continuous improvement process for each Nebraska school and district in the state under accreditation guidelines. Perhaps more importantly, the NDE is crafting a conceptual framework dubbed "keeping the focus, expanding the vision, maintaining the balance" (Roschewski, 2008). The chief message of this approach is that schools and districts can integrate the new state tests into their existing systems (which, again, already include both formative and summative assessment), rather than seeking to integrate their local work into the state tests, as so often happens in other states. It is too early to tell if this approach will gain traction, although Nebraska educators appear generally to have received it warmly so far. It is also unclear if the state will continue to explore alternative metrics appropriate to formative assessment, especially of the classroom variety. In any event, both Nebraska's STARS and its new conceptual model hold important lessons for those of us interested in preserving and perhaps enhancing the unique potentialities of formative assessment.

NEBRASKA'S STARS

In the year 2000, Nebraska policymakers, led by Commissioner of Education Doug Christensen, decided to develop a homegrown assessment and accountability system that included no state tests in core content areas. At that time, many states had adopted standardized tests to measure student learning on standards. Nebraskans recognized that these high-stakes testing programs often produced unintended negative consequences, including the narrowing and rationing of curricula, emphasis on rote memorization rather than higher-order skills, misuse and misreporting of data, cheating scandals, and more (Gallagher, 2007; Nichols & Berliner, 2007). It was clear, too, that each of these negative consequences disproportionately affected the most vulnerable students, who received the most test preparation, the worst curricula, and the least qualified teachers (Darling-Hammond, 1997; Kohn, 1999; Kozol, 2005; McNeil, 2000; Wood, 2004).

Christensen led the state's resistance to state tests. His campaign to develop an alternative model—despite interest among some state senators in following the dominant state-testing approach—was buttressed by the state's longstanding populist aversion to big business and state control, a strong tradition of community schools and place-based education, and a track record of high student achievement (Gallagher, 2007). In blunt terms, Nebraskans resisted taking control of education out of the hands of educators and communities and reassigning it to testing companies and state officials.

The STARS legislation (LB812) called for one state test: a writing assessment administered annually at three grade levels and scored by trained Nebraska educators. All other assessments reported to the state—in reading, math, social studies, and science, again at three grade levels—were left to local discretion. With technical support from the NDE, regional Educational Service Units, and the state's primary technical partner, the Buros Center for Testing (now the Buros Institute for Assessment Consultation and Outreach), each Nebraska district developed its own assessment process; many did so in collaboration with other districts. The districts measured student learning on state or approved local standards in various ways. Some developed district-wide standards-referenced assessments. Others relied heavily, or even exclusively, on classroom assessments. Most devised a combination of these. In any case, districts developed assessments that suited their particular curricular and instructional goals. The NDE provided a number of resources to help districts design and implement their local assessment processes and in particular classroom assessments (e.g., Leadership Conference for Assessment, n.d.; Nebraska Department of Education, n.d.a). A key premise of STARS was that assessment quality could be ensured—and indeed was likely to be higher—if districts designed their own assessments and then submitted them for review and feedback rather than requiring all districts to use the same instrument at the same time. To this end, the NDE developed a set of guidelines and criteria for assessment quality review and conducted annual audits. These guidelines and criteria were applied to documentation of each district's assessment process, and those processes included both formative and summative assessments. (Note that the CCSSO definition conceptualizes formative assessment as a process.) First, districts documented and reviewed their assessment process locally via panels of educators and experts, examining their assessments for six quality criteria: alignment to standards, opportunity to learn, freedom from bias, developmental appropriateness, consistency in scoring, and appropriate mastery levels. Then Nebraska and national assessment experts reviewed this process during an annual on-site review. Districts received formative feedback and public ratings for student performance and assessment quality.

Under STARS, Nebraska left decisions about how to assess student achievement vis-à-vis content standards to local discretion—as long as districts documented the assessment process they used to arrive at their judgments and submitted that documentation for evaluation. The genius of the system lay in its conceptualization of the relationship between formative and summative assessment. It did not rely on the simplistic, conventional notion that formative and summative name different *kinds* of assessments. Rather, STARS recognized that the distinction really hinges on what is done with the data generated from assessments, not necessarily the *format* of the assessment.

Of course, there is a rich assessment literature that frames the distinction between formative and summative assessment in terms of their distinct purposes and uses (see Black, Harrison, Lee, Marshall, & Wiliam, 2003; McMillan, 2007; Scriven, 2003; Stiggins, 2007; Wiggins, 1998; see also Black, this volume; Cizek, this volume). Nonetheless, it remains the case that discussions of formative and summative assessment often turn quickly to *forms* of assessment. For example, it is not uncommon to see teachers and researchers refer to quick-write response papers and learning logs as formative and projects and performances as summative; in fact, the status of any of these activities depends upon what teachers and students *do* with them. For instance, teachers may grade the quick-writes (a summative use) or use student projects as an ungraded activity to assess how much students know, with the sole purpose of adjusting instruction (a formative use).

What made STARS unique was that it allowed, even encouraged, districts to implement assessment processes in which teachers designed and conducted formative assessments, using the data to improve their instruction, and then used the same assessments to arrive at summative judgments. These latter data—along with documentation of the assessment process itself and the assessment quality of that process—were reported to the state, allowing for further summative judgments about the assessment process itself. Thus, STARS encouraged balanced, comprehensive, and coherent assessment systems that incorporated both formative and summative assessments at the local level.

Districts were afforded flexibility in how they designed these systems, however. Some districts used only classroom assessments as part of STARS (i.e., for reporting student achievement on standards). In these cases, one set of assessments was used for formative and summative purposes. Other districts used a mix of classroom assessments, district standards-referenced assessments, and norm-referenced tests; here, classroom and district-level criterion-referenced assessments were used for both purposes and norm-referenced tests were used primarily for summative purposes. Overall, STARS was a policy framework that honored both formative and summative assessment purposes without sacrificing the former on the altar of the latter.

The STARS initiative can be thought of as a fusion model. In the chemical reaction of fusion, distinct elements are brought together with sufficient pressure and energy to create a single new entity that is distinct from the previously separate elements. Analogously, STARS allowed educators to combine formative and summative assessment into a single, distinctly new entity—sometimes quite literally, in the form of a single assessment that met both assessment purposes. These new assessments—and by extension the teaching and learning experiences they sponsored—were different in important respects from what they would have been had they been developed for only one purpose.

In the book *Reclaiming Assessment* (Gallagher, 2007), for example, a student/teacher assessment guide (i.e., rubric) is featured that was designed by Nebraska teacher Suzanne Ratzlaff and her fourth-grade students (see Figure 19.1).

This rubric shown in Figure 19.1 bears the unique stamp of Ms. Ratzlaff and her students and is clearly intended to be used by them for formative purposes. It includes images of stick figures giving and listening to an oral presentation (complete with thought bubbles); it is written in student-friendly language (e.g., "My sensors have two statements of factual information"); the highest score point is on the left, rather than the right, as convention dictates; and there is an "above and beyond" box that is not attached to any score point. Ms. Ratzlaff explains that her students insisted on these last two; regarding the sequencing of the score point, they asked, "Why would you want us to see the worst first?" (Gallagher, 2007, p. 71). At the same time, this rubric directly reproduces the relevant fourth-grade state reading standard and could easily be used for scoring students' presentations against that standard—as indeed it was. In fact, a version of this rubric was used by Ms. Ratzlaff and a colleague for double-scoring.

What is not evident on the page itself but is nonetheless true is that this assessment instrument was evaluated according to Nebraska's six quality criteria. It was included in Ms. Ratzlaff's district's assessment portfolio and used to render summative judgments about both her students' achievement and the quality of the assessment teachers used to classify those achievement levels.

This brief example shows how assessment purposes commingled within this single assessment. To be sure, Ms. Ratzlaff and her students used the rubric to obtain and provide feedback during instruction. Indeed, in this case, building the rubric together in the classroom was itself a learning experience for students and teacher alike. But the rubric was used subsequently for summative purposes—first by Ms. Ratzlaff for grading, then by the teacher and her colleagues for reporting, and finally by state-sanctioned auditors for evaluation of the quality of the assessment instrument. Had the rubric been only a formative instrument, Ms. Ratzlaff may not have been as attentive to the six assessment quality criteria, and she may not have included score points, either. On the other hand, had it been only a summative instrument, there would be no need to make it student-friendly. But it is both formative and summative—a unique product of fusion.

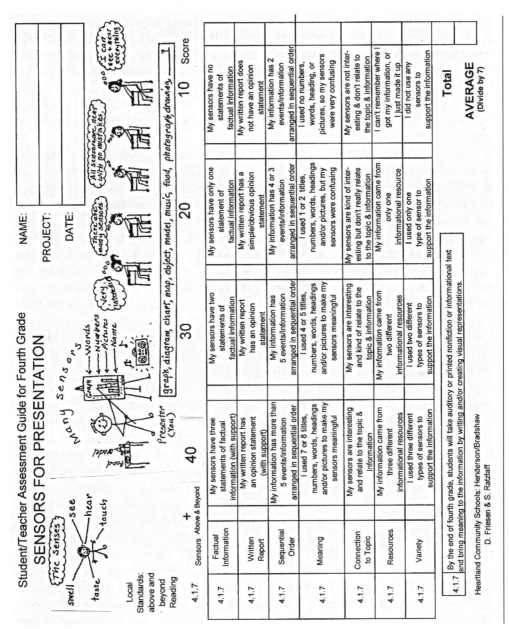

Figure 19.1 Student/teacher rubric designed by Nebraska teacher and fourth-grade students. Reprinted with permission.

STARS was premised on the notion that if formative assessments could subsequently be used for summative purposes there would be no need to place a layer of summative assessments—state tests—on top of those local assessments. However, the 2008 Nebraska legislature broke with this logic when it passed LB1157, which mandates annual state tests in reading, math, social studies, and science in grades 3 through 8 and one high school grade. The reasons most often cited by senators for the new testing legislation were that STARS was too cumbersome and time-consuming, that it "compared apples to oranges," and that state tests were more amenable to NCLB compliance. Some observers of the public hearings on the bills and many who corresponded with the senators came away from the experience believing that what actually had taken place was a political power struggle and an unwillingness among some politicians to trust, or even listen to, educators.

In fact, STARS enjoyed strong support from many national education leaders and assessment experts. During its eight-year run, STARS garnered a great deal of national attention, including a special issue of *Educational Measurement: Issues and Practice*, articles in several major education journals, acclaim from organizations such as the Forum for Education and Democracy and FairTest, and criticism from others, including the Fordham Foundation and *Education Week*. The Nebraska state senators were also presented with documentation of the success of the system, passionate testimony in support of STARS by many Nebraska educators, and strong opposition to state tests from both the NDE—at the time, still under the leadership of Doug Christensen who would resign shortly before passage of the bill—and (initially, at least) from the State Board of Education.

It would not be useful to rehearse the internecine political arguments here, but it is worth noting the voluminous documentation of the effectiveness of STARS. Indeed, one of the curiosities of the move to standardized testing in Nebraska is that no one— including the state senators who voted for the new law—denied that STARS was having positive effects on schools and student learning. In the following sections of this chapter, a bare outline of the quantitative and qualitative results of STARS generated by the various available data sources is presented. Readers interested in learning more should consult the Nebraska Department of Education's annual Report Cards (n.d.b), the annual reports of the university-based, independent Comprehensive Evaluation Project (CEP; n.d.), and the book, *Reclaiming Assessment* (Gallagher, 2007).

Overall, student performance on reading and mathematics improved steadily and significantly under STARS, as the annual reports cards and the reports produced by the CEP showed. The quality of the assessments that districts used to classify student proficiencies improved steadily as well, according to the trained assessment experts who rated district assessment portfolios. In terms of standardized measures, Nebraska students' scores on the statewide writing assessment rose sharply and their tradition-ally high performance on nationally normed tests remained stable, although the state's rapidly changing demographics over the past decade might lead us to predict slip-page in this performance. Like other states, Nebraska continued to struggle to close achievement gaps, but most demographic subgroups showed improved performance, graduation rates were up, and dropout rates were down during the period in which STARS was in effect.

Qualitative results were positive as well. Since it began in 2001, the CEP, housed at the University of Nebraska-Lincoln, has conducted hundreds of interviews and observations in well over 100 Nebraska districts and administered thousands of educator surveys. Excerpts from the interviews, including many quoted below, can be found in Gallagher (2007). Among the statewide trends identified by the CEP between 2001 and 2008 were the following:

A Move toward Individualized, Learning-Focused, Data-Informed Instruction

Local assessments embedded in curriculum and instruction allowed teachers to respond to their students immediately and with detailed information. As one teacher noted,

> Instead of focusing on just what your objectives are [classroom assessment], focuses on what your objectives are *for each student*. In essence, then, I think that each student almost has an individual education plan.

A teacher in another district elaborated this point:

> [Classroom assessment] makes it much clearer what I need to teach and how I need to teach and whether I taught it correctly or whether I taught it and it got through to the kids. It's given me a measurement so that I know that what I'm doing is successful. And if it isn't successful, then it's very clear that I need to go back and re-teach.

Widespread Assessment Literacy among Educators

Early CEP research revealed considerable unease among Nebraska educators at the prospect of having to become assessment experts. But, over time, as teachers and school administrators learned about assessment through a variety of professional development opportunities offered by the NDE, educational service units, and individual districts, they become more confident, and indeed more expert. Many teachers offered comments such as:

> It's gotten easier and we've gotten better at looking at what needs to be changed and revised [in our curriculum, instruction, and assessment]…I've learned about… good question techniques, watching for biases, and just knowing what a good assessment looks like.

A regional staff developer agreed:

> If the teachers could hear themselves today compared to five years ago, they would not even know they were the same teachers. Their vocabulary, their literacy in the assessment world, their ability to figure out how to get it all together, their reporting, their knowing about how to make things reliable, they just had no idea they could stretch like that.

It is important to note that in Nebraska, assessment literacy does not entail detailed technical knowledge and course work in statistics. Rather, it entails knowing the different purposes and uses of various kinds of assessment, choosing or developing appropriate assessments that meet quality criteria, and using the information generated by those assessments to inform instruction. In addition, many Nebraska teachers were focused on helping students use assessment information. According to one teacher:

> If you're looking at a one-time-only test, the kids don't learn much from that assessment. When you're doing the ongoing assessments, where the kids look at the feedback, they turn around before the next time and they think, "Ok, what can we work on to improve for next time?

Overall, the CEP found a strong trend toward student self-assessment in Nebraska schools under STARS.

Increasing Teacher Ownership of STARS and Local Assessment Processes

Again, in the early years, the CEP encountered considerable skepticism about STARS among teachers. But over time, as teachers came to appreciate how STARS supported their teaching and their students' learning, the majority bought in to the approach. In particular, teachers evinced strong support for teacher-designed, classroom assessments. As one teacher observed:

> These tests were created by teachers and [what] I like about that is, it's really down to earth and again, it's related to what we teach, to our curriculum…because it is aligned. And I like that.

This sense of ownership among teachers often came as a surprise, as a school principal indicated in relating a story about a presentation two of his teachers made to their local school board:

> Our board was just amazed to see how impassioned our teachers are. They were like, "Man, if I wasn't sitting here, I would have never believed that those two teachers, specifically, could get that excited about curriculum and assessment."…I mean, you just don't mess with our teachers when it comes to this right now.

Sometimes, teachers even surprised themselves with their support for STARS:

> I would have said, six years ago—I did say six years ago when I moved here [from Texas]—"Why do we have to do all this? Why don't we just give a state test?"… Now, six years later, I've taken a change because I've seen what kind of information you can gain from tests that are written to your curricula, that you have written, and that the teachers have said [are] important to them…. If you can take this information that we're getting based on our test, on our kids, and use it wisely, that is the way to go. And I wouldn't want to be in any other state right now, even though it's a lot of work.

Nebraska educators expressed similar sentiments at the public hearing on the testing bill. Several teachers and school administrators indicated that they would continue with their local assessment process no matter the outcome of the legislature's vote.

Increasing Teacher Leadership

Teachers' sense of ownership led to their exerting considerable leadership in their school improvement processes; indeed, emerging teacher leadership has been one of the strongest trends identified by the CEP. Sometimes this leadership was exercised by virtue of a formal position such as assessment coordinator, school improvement chair, or learning community facilitator. Other times the leadership was more informal and ongoing, as is evident in the comments of one teacher who said:

> Within my building, I've been a leader as far as helping other teachers understand the assessment process. When they have a question as to…a certain assessment, they would come to me and we would discuss how you go about doing that so that there is reliability and validity.…

In any case, school administrators routinely told CEP researchers that teachers knew more about the school improvement process than they did because under STARS, curriculum, instruction, and assessment were tied together under the school improvement umbrella. A principal explained:

> Rather than everything coming down from the administration that this is how we need to do that, [the school improvement process] is coming from the other direction, where teachers get together and talk about areas that need improve[ment].

In addition, several administrators described setting school and district goals based on teacher judgment.

Growth of Collaborative Learning Cultures in Schools

The majority of CEP study schools were moving away from what some Nebraska educators call the *teacher-in-private-practice* model to a more open, collaborative working environment in which everyone—students, teachers, and administrators—is a learner. Professional development in most schools relied heavily on teachers teaching teachers; the CEP found decreasing reliance on traditional in-service activities and conferences. This description, from a teacher who also serves as the school assessment coordinator, is typical:

> You see teachers having more conversations about curriculum and instruction and assessment than ever before …I have been a teacher for a number of years. [Before,] everybody did their own little thing—you know, you went in your room and you did it any way you chose as long as you covered basic things. And now teachers are working together, which to me is more equitable for kids.

Districts were finding time and resources to embed professional development in teachers' school day, often using collaborative models such as professional learning communities, action research projects, inquiry groups, or learning teams. This teacher's description typifies the resulting climate:

> We work together, we converse, we talk about problems. It's a good climate, it's a good rapport that we have together, and very cooperative. I think we get along very

well and we have our students' best interests at heart and whatever it takes to do what we need to do for those kids, for those assessments, and beyond, we do.

In learning cultures such as this, continuous change is expected. The following testimony from a superintendent describes the kind of learning culture that a number of CEP study schools had achieved and the vast majority was at least moving toward:

It doesn't matter what system they throw at us. The process that we have in place is a good process and we'll be able to make it adapt and work for whatever the case is because it's child centered. And as long as it remains child-centered, we're going to be OK. It's not perfect. It's going to change. We know that. We expect that. We expect to improve every year. I mean…you know, that's the expectation that we have for our kids; that's the expectation that we have for ourselves.

Admittedly, only positive trends have been described in this chapter. This is not to suggest that STARS was perfect or that Nebraska had designed the ideal comprehensive, balanced, and coherent system. The state standards on which STARS was based—which are now revised—were too numerous, too specific, and not challenging enough. The sheer amount of time required to develop and document district assessment systems was a challenge for educators, despite attempts by the state and many districts to streamline the process. Too few community members and parents understood the unconventional data generated by STARS. And, particularly important for our purposes, Nebraska still has a lot of work to do to develop appropriate metrics for evaluating the quality of classroom assessments—a point that will be reprised in the concluding section of this chapter.

Still, warts and all, it is clear that STARS was having profoundly positive consequences for students, educators, and schools. Certainly the evidence is strong enough to earn STARS the attention of those who are interested in how to protect and enhance formative assessment within comprehensive, balanced, and coherent assessment systems.

A NEW LAW, AN EMERGING APPROACH

Equally important to consideration of formative assessment is Nebraska's emerging approach to sustaining and enhancing the robust local assessment systems that districts designed under STARS. As of this writing, STARS is being phased out under a new state testing law. In 2009–2010, each core subject transitions from the current STARS model to state tests—which means that for the purposes of this law, all local assessment reporting will cease in 2011–2012.

However, the NDE and Nebraska school districts, while fully intending to comply with the law, are unwilling to allow their assessment and accountability efforts to be constrained to a single annual test, especially after coming to understand the value of developing balanced, comprehensive, and coherent local assessment systems. Although it is true that some Nebraska educators breathed a sigh of relief at the news that the state was moving to a "simple" state test, the Comprehensive Evaluation Project found that the majority of educators in most districts preferred STARS to state tests. This sentiment was expressed a number of times, in no uncertain terms, by educators at the public hearings on the testing bill. This is why NDE is working with districts to incorporate the new state tests into existing local systems rather than attempting to reverse-engineer those systems around the new state tests, which by design will be limited in size and scope.

Implementation will not be easy, of course. Teaching to the test is rampant in many existing state testing programs, and there is no reason to think that it will not be so in Nebraska. The numbers generated by the new state tests will be published, and those numbers are likely to attain a halo in the eyes of many in the media, policy circles, and the general public. Moreover, those numbers will become a proxy for school quality and may be used for all kinds of purposes, no matter how inappropriate: to rank schools, to claim bragging rights, to publicly shame, to advertise good neighborhoods to prospective homebuyers, to evaluate teachers, to make high-stakes decisions (promotion, graduation) about students, and so on. No school administrator or teacher can afford to ignore this political reality.

However, even if it can safely predicted that there will be teaching to the (state) test in Nebraska, this does not mean that Nebraska educators are ready to scrap the local assessment processes they so painstakingly developed over the past decade. As was illustrated here, many Nebraska teachers and school administrators are committed to—and sometimes fiercely protective of—their local assessment processes. So while Nebraska's new testing system looks quite familiar, and while we cannot deny the power of state tests, the role of these state tests in the local assessment processes of Nebraska districts is at best an open question. Because summative assessment has not been the only assessment that counts in Nebraska, and because Nebraskans have realized the potential of formative assessments under STARS, it is possible that the new state tests will be integrated into local assessment systems without diluting or supplanting the existing formative assessments.

This is the hope of the NDE. The Nebraska Coordinator of Statewide Assessment, Pat Roschewski (2008), is touting an approach that she calls "keeping the focus, expanding the vision, maintaining the balance." In her work with districts and other stakeholders, Roschewski insists that Nebraska's focus remains on student learning, not test scores. That will be the case, she maintains, if districts "remember the CIA: curriculum, instruction, and assessment." According to Roschewski—and she is confirmed by the findings of the CEP—Nebraska educators used STARS as an opportunity to ensure the connections among curriculum, instruction, and assessment under the umbrella of continuous school improvement. And even with the advent of new state tests, the three fundamental tasks at the local level as outlined by Roschewski remain the same.

The first fundamental task is K-12 curriculum alignment. All teachers (every grade, every subject) should have a sequenced, agreed-upon, written curriculum guide; all teachers should examine the curriculum in light of state and/or local standards and school/instructional goals.

The second task is learning-focused instruction. This means that all teachers should have regular opportunities to collaborate with colleagues in structured small K-12 groups to discuss, develop, and share instruction; all teachers should understand their school's data and participate in the development of instruction that is data-informed; all teachers should assure that instruction serves all students and supports intended goals.

The third fundamental task is implementing informative assessment. All teachers should use assessment as a learning tool in the classroom; all teachers should understand the difference between assessment and accountability as well as the different types and purposes of assessment; all teachers should know how to use assessment results to inform instruction. These three tasks, Roschewski claims, have been and should continue to be the focus of districts' efforts.

In terms of expanding the vision, Roschewski (2008) emphasizes that the new state tests will add another piece of information, another lens through which to view students' learning. Roschewski is not naïve about the limitations—even the potential distortions—inherent in the lens provided by a single annual state test. But she notes that while we cannot see much or clearly through this lens alone, the same is true of any type of assessment. The key is to combine these views so that we develop a more complex, multidimensional vision of our students. We need the best possible lenses, of course, but we also need multiple lenses, which together are likely to provide a more complete and accurate picture of what students know and can do than any single assessment—of whatever sort—could provide.

Mindful of skeptics' warning that formative classroom assessments may be sacrificed in favor of summative assessments on the altar of accountability, Roschewski (2008) encourages Nebraska educators to maintain the balance. She reminds them that under STARS, they (ideally, at least) already balanced formative and summative purposes for assessment. The challenge now, she continues, is to add the new state tests without allowing them to tip the scales in favor of summative assessment (Roschewski, 2008). This explains why the NDE is working with the Nebraska State Board of Education to develop a policy framework that supports the continuation and documentation of formative assessment under the continuous improvement provision of the state's accreditation process.

PROSPECTS AND CHALLENGES

Can Nebraskans succeed in enacting Roschewski's (2008) approach? Can state tests be incorporated into comprehensive, balanced, and coherent local assessment systems without diluting or corrupting formative and summative local assessments? Can formative classroom assessment in particular hold its own in such a scenario?

Two competing realities make prediction an uncertain proposition. On the one hand, Nebraska enters this effort with a strong foundation: STARS was in operation for 8 years—a decent run, in school reform terms. As the Comprehensive Evaluation Project has revealed, the majority of Nebraska districts were at least in the late stages of developing rich, sustainable local assessment systems by the time the legislature passed the new state testing law. As discussed previously in this chapter, the CEP also identified evidence of assessment literacy among educators, strong teacher leadership, ownership of the local curriculum-instruction-assessment process, and collaborative learning cultures in schools. In short, capacity for school improvement is at an unprecedented high in Nebraska. It is difficult to imagine teachers such as Ms. Ratzlaff—a vocal opponent of the testing legislation, incidentally—scrapping her hard-won, teacher-designed, student-friendly assessments in order to accommodate a single state test. Moreover, it is difficult to imagine that she and her colleagues will not continue to bring her assessment knowledge to bear on their classroom assessment work. Surely they will not forget or ignore what they know about designing their own, ongoing formative and summative assessments that minimize bias and are appropriate to students' learning levels, for instance.

On the other hand, Nebraska educators face a number of serious challenges. As has already been discussed, the political pressure of accountability should not be underestimated. Nebraska lawmakers might have mitigated the emphasis on standardized test scores and aided districts in sustaining their local systems if they had chosen to integrate the new state tests into the existing large-scale system. They chose instead to discontinue local reporting of student performance on standards to the state, thereby effectively decoupling summative and formative assessment on the state level. In doing so, they removed policy support—and therefore, importantly, financial and professional development resources—for local assessment activities. So although Nebraska educators have a wealth of experience and expertise, the new law provides them with little incentive to draw on it. Instead, because the summative state tests are the only assessments that count under the new law, the incentives redound to those tests.

Although Nebraska's experience is unique, and although its lawmakers did not ultimately choose to include formative assessment in its large-scale system, this case study offers important lessons to those interested in combining formative and summative assessment in large-scale systems. First, and chiefly, STARS offers a fusion approach in which formative and summative assessment are combined, sometimes in a single assessment instrument. And STARS encourages us to consider carefully the distinction between these kinds of assessment and to exploit the idea that the distinction hinges not upon the format of the assessment, but in the purposes, uses, and timing of assessment data. Though STARS was discontinued in Nebraska as a *policy*, it may yet inform our thinking about models of assessment that fully realize the potentialities of both summative and formative assessment.

Nebraska's emerging approach points to the importance of giving formative assessment its due in comprehensive, balanced, and coherent systems; rather than allow it to reside in the shadow of summative assessment. Roschewski and her colleagues are right to worry that without a revised, expanded policy framework, the new state law will shrink-wrap assessment around accountability: scores on state tests, rather than rich, ongoing learning will become the end of assessment work. There is hope that assessment-literate Nebraska educators, with the new policy support, will be able to preserve and enhance their existing local systems. But the lesson for states with existing large-scale systems that rely heavily or exclusively on state tests may be that additional resources or training for formative assessment may not be enough; instead, new, overarching assessment policy frameworks are needed to keep (or switch) the focus to student learning, expand the vision by including multiple assessments, and maintain the balance between formative and summative assessment.

Beyond this visioning work, this case study of Nebraska suggests the need to educate various stakeholders—certainly including lawmakers—about the uses, purposes, values, and quality of formative assessment (and especially classroom assessment) in balanced, and coherent assessment systems. One important next step for proponents of formative assessment is to develop communication strategies—and perhaps a comprehensive public engagement campaign—to disseminate to multiple audiences the research and expertise about formative assessment captured in this *Handbook*.

Another next step is to develop more sophisticated and appropriate psychometrics for formative, and especially classroom, assessments (see Way, Dolan, & Nichols, this volume). The research is clear that formative assessment supports student learning and achievement, but there remains a need to develop sensitive instruments to evaluate the assessment quality of formative assessments: STARS provides an important place to begin. Nebraska's six quality criteria are somewhat amenable to formative assessments, including classroom assessments, though they were derived primarily from traditional psychometrics for summative assessments. Technical advisors to STARS—including the Buros Institute—helped lay the groundwork for evaluating the assessment quality of formative and classroom assessments, but Brookhart (2003) is correct that the emerging field of what she has called *classroometrics* requires further research and development.

By way of conclusion, it is important to again emphasize that it is far from clear what the future holds for Nebraska. Perhaps one of the most important tasks for those of us interested in exploring the nature, uses, and potentialities of formative assessment is to document various approaches to this work so that states can learn from each other how to keep the focus, expand the vision, and maintain the balance.

REFERENCES

Black, P., Harrison, C., Lee, C., Marshall, B., & Wiliam, D. (2003). *Assessment for learning*. Maidenhead, UK: Open University Press.

Black, P., & Wiliam, D. (1998a). Inside the black box: Raising standards through classroom assessment. *Phi Delta Kappan, 80*(2), 139–148.

Black, P., & Wiliam, D. (1998b). Assessment and classroom learning. *Assessment in Education, 5*(1), 7–74.

Brookhart, S. M. (2003). Developing measurement theory for classroom assessment: Purposes and uses. *Educational measurement: Issues and Practice, 22*(4), 5–12.

Cizek, G. J. (2009). Reliability and validity of information about student achievement: Comparing the contexts of large-scale and classroom testing. *Theory into Practice, 48*, 63–71.

Comprehensive Evaluation Project (CEP). (n.d.). http://www.nde.state.ne.us/stars/STARSTechnicalReports.htm

Council of Chief State School Officers. (2008). Mission and history of the Formative Assessment for Students and Teachers SCASS. Retrieved December 28, 2009, from http://www.ccsso.org/content/PDFs/FAST%20history%20and%20mission%2008-09.pdf

Darling-Hammond, L. (1997). *The right to learn*. San Francisco: Jossey-Bass.

Gallagher, C. W. (2007). *Reclaiming assessment*. Portsmouth, NH: Heinemann.

Kohn, A. (1999). *The schools our children deserve*. New York: Houghton-Mifflin.

Kozol, J. (2005). *The shame of the nation: The restoration of apartheid schooling in America*. New York: Crown.

Leadership Conference for Assessment. (n.d.). http://www.lcaconference.com

McMillan, J. H. (2007). *Formative classroom assessment: Theory into practice*. New York: Teachers College Press.

McNeil, L. (2000). *Contradictions of reform: The educational costs of standardized testing*. New York: Routledge.

Nebraska Department of Education. (n.d.a). http://www.nde.state.ne.us/cba

Nebraska Department of Education. (n.d.b). Annual Report Cards. http://reportcard.nde.state.ne.us/Main/Home.aspx

Nichols, S. L., & Berliner, D. C. (2007). *Collateral damage*. Cambridge, MA: Harvard University Press.

Roschewski, P. (2008, June). *Keeping the focus, expanding the vision, maintaining the balance*. Presentation, Nebraska Assessment Cohort, University of Nebraska-Lincoln.

Scriven, M. (2003). Evaluation theory and metatheory. In T. Kellaghan & D. Stufflebeam (Eds.), *International handbook of educational evaluation* (pp. 15–30). Boston: Kluwer.

Wiggins, G. (1998). *Educative assessment: Designing assessments to inform and improve student performance.* San Francisco: Jossey-Bass.

Wood, G. (2004). A view from the field: NCLB's effects on classrooms and schools. In D. Meier & G. Wood (Eds.), *Many children left behind: How the No Child Left Behind Act is damaging our children and our schools* (pp. 33–50). Boston: Beacon Press.

20

SUMMING UP AND MOVING FORWARD
Key Challenges and Future Directions for Research and Development in Formative Assessment

HEIDI L. ANDRADE

This *Handbook of Formative Assessment* encompasses diverse aspects of formative assessment, including classroom assessment, large-scale applications, technological advances, case studies, K-12 contexts, psychometric considerations, applications for students with special needs, and a variety of formats. This concluding chapter highlights several themes that cut across the chapters herein, with a focus on significant advancements as well as lingering challenges and the opportunities they present. The themes discussed include a definition of formative assessment that emphasizes effectively responding to feedback about student learning; the active role of students in assessment; pre- and in-service teacher and administrator education; and the technical quality of formative assessment tools. The chapter concludes with an acknowledgment of other important areas of research and development such as technology and students with special needs.

A DEFINITION AND ARCHITECTURE OF FORMATIVE ASSESSMENT

A central achievement of this book is the affirmation of a relatively common definition and architecture of formative assessment. It is now clear that formative assessment is not a particular assessment tool but rather a matter of the uses to which assessment data are put. As many authors indicate in their chapters in this volume, formative assessment refers to the purposes of assessment information, not to particular assessment procedures or instruments. Therefore, any definition of formative assessment must be grounded in its purposes, which include: (1) providing information about students' learning to teachers and administrators in order to guide them in designing instruction; and (2) providing feedback to students about their progress in order to help them determine how to close any gaps between their performance and the targeted learning goals. The essence of formative assessment is *informed action*.

Informed Action

The emphasis on informed action is intended to indicate the relative importance of feedback and an effective response to that feedback by teachers and students. As Wiliam (this volume) notes in his definition of formative assessment, an assessment is formative only to the extent to which its use improves student outcomes. The obvious implication of this assertion is that teachers must not only know how to create and implement formative assessments but also—and crucially—they must know how to respond to the information provided by those assessments by adjusting instruction, if necessary, according to students' needs. Similarly, students must be armed with the strategies and motivation needed to improve their work and deepen their learning after getting feedback. Both teachers and students must know how to close the gap between current and desired performance levels (Sadler, 1989), and have opportunities to do so.

Although several areas of theory and research related to closing the gap are available, they have not yet been sufficiently integrated into current conceptions of formative assessment. Advances in formative assessment will be made to the extent that linkages are forged with existing research in areas of inquiry such as revision (e.g., Graham & MacArthur, 1988, 1995; MacArthur, 1994), instructional adaptations (e.g., Graham, Harris, Fink-Chorzempa, & MacArthur, 2003), correctives (e.g., Guskey, 1997, 2008, this volume), and strategies related to studying and self-regulated learning (e.g., Pape, Zimmerman, & Pajares, 2002). By drawing on these bodies of research, new ideas can be incorporated into existing conceptions of formative assessment, and useful tactics for responding to the feedback provided by formative assessments can be developed.

A particularly promising development related to responding to information about student learning (or the lack thereof) provided by formative assessment is research on learning progressions. Learning progressions are models of how learning typically progresses within a domain, as well as common variations from the usual patterns of learning (Shepard, 2006; Wilson & Black, 2007). According to Heritage (2008), when teachers understand the continuum of learning in a subject and have information about a student's performance relative to the learning goals, they will be better able to make decisions about what the next steps in learning should be. Relatively well mapped learning progressions exist for writing (Masters & Forster, 1997), as well as for learning about counting, functions, buoyancy, genetics, matter, history, listening, and speaking (see Heritage, 2008 for sample progressions). Models of typical and atypical learning progressions of other topics and in other domains, including the arts and physical education, are needed.

Clarity about Assessment Purposes

Although methods for responding to formative assessments may be lacking, an abundance of methods exists for collecting formative data: Numerous research-based approaches to collecting formative information about student learning are discussed in this *Handbook*. It is clear that, given the broad goals of formative assessment, the forms it can take are quite diverse. As detailed in Guskey's chapter (this volume) on mastery learning, even the traditional, summative test can be repurposed as a formative assessment with great success. Formative assessments also take the shape of informal conversations, dress rehearsals of formal exhibitions, and nearly everything in between—as long as the information about student learning they provide is used to improve teaching and learning.

The variety in the types of assessment tools that can be used formatively, however, should not mask the differences between traditional testing and performance assessment. Although multiple-choice tests can be used formatively, they will never have some of the key qualities of good performance assessment, such as the use of authentic contexts and skills. Traditional multiple-choice tests also tend not to lend themselves to meaningful self- or peer feedback, or to the assessment of high level thinking skills (Shepard, 2000). On the other hand, performance assessments cannot do what tests do best: sample a wide range of content and quickly produce reliable total scores and subscores (Haladyna, Downing, & Rodriguez, 2002). Importantly, the notion of formative assessment does not make all assessment instruments equal: Those who use tests must continue to carefully select assessments in terms of their intended purposes.

THE ROLE OF THE STUDENT IN FORMATIVE ASSESSMENT

The notion of student-involved assessment (Stiggins, 2005) is supported by convincing research and has near unanimous support from the educational community. Yet it appears that many educators continue to think of assessment as something done for and by the teacher. Although no arguments have been proffered for purely teacher-centered assessment, much of the current rhetoric surrounding assessment reform reveals such an orientation. For example, a commonly cited purpose of formative assessment is to provide information about student learning that guides teachers in adjusting instruction. That is certainly one important purpose of formative assessment but it is not the whole story.

Neglecting or deemphasizing the equally important function of providing information that guides students in revising their own ideas, products, and approaches to both risks overlooking opportunities for learners to exercise and develop valuable skills of self-regulation, including setting goals, selecting strategies for meeting them, monitoring their progress, and adjusting both their goals and the strategies they employ, as needed (Pintrich, 2000; Zimmerman, 2000). The ability to self-regulate is arguably among the most important qualities of healthy and successful learners, workers, and citizens (Boekaerts, Pintrich, & Zeidner, 2000). If it is true that "you get what you assess" (Resnick & Resnick, 1990, p. 60), then neglecting self-regulated learning in assessment theory and practice is likely to have serious consequences for students.

A student-centered approach to formative assessment could also have a positive effect on students beyond increasing achievement. According to Stiggins and Popham (2007), a strongly student-focused approach to classroom assessment is "almost certain to have an impact on students' affect" (p. 1), including their academic efficacy, motivation, and eagerness to learn. Carefully attending to theory, research, and practice related to a student-centered approach to formative assessment will yield better understandings of the associations between formative assessment, academic motivation, and self-regulated learning.

THE COEXISTENCE OF SUMMATIVE AND FORMATIVE ASSESSMENT

Another accomplishment of this book is that it has lain to rest the debate about whether or not it is possible for formative and summative assessment to peacefully coexist. Coexistence is possible, as evidenced by the chapters by Brookhart, Davidson, Gallagher, and Wiliam in this volume—but peaceful coexistence is unlikely without Herculean efforts on the part of policy makers, administrators, teachers, and community members. Such efforts must begin by understanding and honoring the very different purposes served by formative classroom assessments and summative standardized tests. Even given clear distinctions and uses, however, the relationship is likely to remain contentious and unstable in the short term.

The optimistic view is that the generativity in the tension between summative and formative assessment can propel advances in assessment theory and practice. The tension represents both a challenge and an opportunity to explore fruitful relationships between formative assessment and summative evaluation. Given recent advancements in the field, rigorous research can now be focused on pressing questions such as: Is formative assessment any more or less effective when summative evaluations are not used? Do the negative associations between academic motivation and grades change at all when students and their teachers understand the purposes of formative and summative assessment and faithfully engage in practices associated with each? Do the new products being offered by testing companies represent truly formative assessments when put into practice in schools, or is formative assessment being mislabeled and distorted? If the latter, what are the consequences of the misuse? What are the most effective ways to educate parents and the general public about the important distinctions between types of assessment?

TEACHING EDUCATORS

Another theme of this book is the need for educational practitioners—the teachers, staff, and administrators who have the most direct influence on daily classroom activities— to understand and implement effective formative assessments. In-service professional development has been underway for some years, as noted by Stiggins (this volume) and by Schneider and Randel (this volume). The preservice education of teachers and administrators also deserves attention.

Preservice Education

Many preservice teacher and administrator education programs do not adequately prepare new teachers in terms of assessment, particularly the formative kind (Popham, 2009). The most self-evident implication is that preservice education must include instruction in and experience with formative assessment. Stand-alone assessment courses in undergraduate and graduate programs would represent a good start but most states do not currently require assessment training in preservice teacher and administrator preparation programs (Schneider & Randel, this volume). Shepard's (2000) recommendation to provide methods courses that embed assessment concerns within curriculum and instruction issues is also worthy of further consideration.

Teaching preservice teachers to keep the purposes of each type of assessment in mind is fundamental to helping them learn to judge the appropriateness of one over the other. In addition to knowing how to make careful distinctions between summative and formative assessment, a skill in need of special emphasis in coursework and practica is interpreting the results of formative assessments and deciding on next steps (Harlen, 2005a, 2005b)—the *action* component of *informed action*. As models of learning progressions develop, they should be incorporated into preservice coursework in order to prepare teachers to adjust their instruction and collaborate with students on determining what they need to do to improve their work and understanding. A discipline-based understanding of learning progressions—for example, the Berkley Evaluation and Assessment Research (BEAR) System being developed by Wilson and his colleagues (Wilson & Black, 2007)—can be helpful in figuring out what students are likely to need next.

Perhaps most importantly, given the human tendency to do what was done to us, is the need to assess preservice teachers in ways that reflect current knowledge about formative assessment. Alverno College in Wisconsin, for example, views assessment as an integral process to the learning experience of all students, including education majors. Other teacher education programs can similarly immerse their students in progressive assessment practices. If the assessments students are exposed to in postsecondary education are transparent, formative, collaborative, and constructive, students will gain first-hand experience with effective assessment tools that they can then employ in their own teaching.

Programmatic change in higher education does not happen just because of good intentions and ideas, of course. If teacher education programs are refocused to emphasize formative assessment, teacher certification organizations such as the Teacher Education Accreditation Council and the National Council for Accreditation of Teacher Education must also be engaged. Teacher educators are not immune to the pressures of external evaluation, so accrediting bodies should be encouraged to include specific requirements related to formative assessment in their criteria for teacher education programs.

Similarly, dialogue about assessment reforms should also include policymakers. Shepard (2000) noted that researchers in the United States "have engaged policymakers and the public on the topic of testing but have focused almost exclusively on the features of state and district accountability testing programs" (p. 10). It is time to enlighten politicians and policymakers about the other, formative side of the assessment coin. Rindone and MacQuarrie (this volume) describe early efforts to do so.

In-Service Professional Development

Stiggins, a leader in assessment-related professional development and the author of a chapter on the subject in this volume, has asserted that "The only important formative assessment priority is to help practitioners learn how to do it productively" (personal communication, January 8, 2009). Researchers could quibble, of course, noting the need to push ahead on theoretical and experimental as well as practical fronts, but Stiggins's assertion accurately reflects the magnitude of the professional development challenges ahead.

Several of the challenges to implementing formative assessment in classrooms identified by Cizek (this volume), including issues of purpose, preparation, validity, and resources, must be addressed through high quality professional development for teachers. A solid understanding of the purposes of formative assessment will help teachers preserve it, rather than inadvertently blurring the distinctions between formative and summative. Similarly, an understanding of the value and processes of checking the validity of their assessments will enable teachers to create, find, or adapt effective assessments rather than making use of ineffective or even harmful assessments. All this will require the commitment of adequate resources, of course, including time and money.

TECHNICAL QUALITY OF FORMATIVE ASSESSMENTS

Concerns about the reliability, validity, and fairness of the uses of formative assessments are widespread in this *Handbook* (see Abedi; Cizek; Stiggins; Way, Dolan, & Nichols; Wiliam, this volume) and well grounded, given the documented lack of technical backgrounds possessed by those who are in a position to create and carry out formative assessments—teachers. Although there is evidence from Nebraska's recent experiment (see Gallagher, this volume) that it is possible for classroom-based assessments to meet rigorous standards of quality, teaching teachers about traditional conceptions of validity and reliability will not suffice. Sophisticated processes for ensuring the technical quality of large-scale, summative assessments cannot be transferred wholesale to classroom-based formative assessments (Cizek, 2009), although of course we should draw on the measurement literature as appropriate.

Cizek (2009) provides illustrative examples of how modern conceptualizations of reliability do and do not apply to classroom assessment, including the formative kind. He notes that reliability estimates such as coefficients of equivalence or internal consistency are unlikely to be useful to teachers, but that many teachers implement informal test-retest procedures when they repeatedly assign similar tasks such as speeches, lab reports, or essays. The repetition of tasks provides an opportunity for a teacher to assess the reliability of the conclusions drawn from student performance. Teachers can also check inter- and intrarater reliability by consistently applying the criteria contained in a scoring guide to each student's work, and by asking a colleague to apply the same scoring guide to a subset of student work, comparing the scores, and revising the scoring guide as needed.

These procedures are rarely done by classroom teachers but could, in theory, become common practice if teachers and administrators are provided with feasible methods with which to ensure the technical quality of assessments and convinced of the value of using them. The need for a new theory of validity and reliability for formative assessment represents an opportunity in the field with both theoretical and practical significance. Without a solid theoretical base and practicable procedures for ensuring the accuracy of inferences, the promise of formative assessment may not be fully realized.

ADDITIONAL OPPORTUNITIES FOR RESEARCH AND DEVELOPMENT

Several issues related to the success of formative assessment in improving teaching and learning did not have enough of a presence in this book to qualify as themes but merit mention. They include the need for standards of formative assessment (Cizek, this volume), the value of distinguishing between various kinds of formative assessment with an eye for which kinds are most likely to improve student learning (Wiliam, this volume), and the potential of technological innovations to transform how and how often teachers and students receive feedback on teaching and learning (Russell, this volume; Way, Dolan, & Nichols, this volume). Although very different, as they represent developments in policy, research, and technology, respectively, each of these areas seem poised to play an essential role in the rapidly developing field of formative assessment. In addition, recent scholarship (Dunn & Mulvenon, 2009) suggests that more basic research should be conducted to gain an accurate, complete understanding of the effect sizes that can be anticipated when formative assessments are implemented in various educational contexts.

Finally, much more work is needed in order to understand the role of formative assessment in the education of certain subgroups of students, including those with special needs (Elliott, Kettler, Beddow, & Kurz, this volume), English language learners (Abedi, this volume; Meskill, this volume), and students identified as at risk of academic failure (Hughes, this volume). Scholars tout the potential for formative assessments to be especially helpful to these students, while also acknowledging the lack of research that closely focuses on their particular contexts and needs. As "the next best hope for stimulating gains in student achievement" (Cizek, this volume, p. 3), formative assessment must be used with precision, including and especially with those most in need of our support.

REFERENCES

Boekaerts, M., Pintrich, P., & Zeidner, M. (Eds.). (2000). *Handbook of self-regulation*. San Diego, CA: Academic.

Cizek, G. J. (2009). Reliability and validity of information about student achievement: Comparing the contexts of large-scale and classroom testing. *Theory into Practice, 48*(1), 63–71.

Dunn, K. E., & Mulvenon, S. W. (2009). A critical review of research on formative assessments: The limited scientific evidence of the impact of formative assessments in education. *Practical Research & Education 14*(7). Available online: http://pareonline.net/getvn.asp?v=14&n=7

Graham, S., Harris, K., Fink-Chorzempa, B., & MacArthur, C. (2003). Primary grade teachers' instructional adaptations for struggling writers: A national survey. *Journal of Educational Psychology, 95*(2), 249–293.

Graham, S., & MacArthur, C. (1988). Improving learning disabled students' skills at revising essays produced on a word processor: Self-instructional strategy training. *Journal of Special Education, 22*(2), 133–152.

Graham, S., & MacArthur, C. (1995). Effects of goal setting and procedural facilitation on the revising behavior and writing performance of students with writing and learning problems. *Journal of Educational Psychology, 87*(2), 230–240.

Guskey, T. (1997). *Implementing mastery learning* (2nd ed.). Belmont, CA: Wadsworth.

Guskey, T. (2008). The rest of the story. *Educational Leadership, 65*(4), 28–35.

Haladyna, T., Downing, S., & Rodriguez, M. (2002). A review of multiple-choice item-writing guidelines for classroom assessment. *Applied Measurement in Education, 15*(3), 309–334.

Harlen, W. (2005a). Teachers' summative practice and assessment for learning: Tensions and synergies. *The Curriculum Journal, 16*(2), 207–223.

Harlen, W. (2005b). On the relationship between assessment for formative and summative purposes. In J. Gardner (Ed.), *Assessment and learning* (pp. 103–118). Thousand Oaks, CA: Sage.

Heritage, M. (2008). Learning progressions. Retrieved February 11, 2009, from http://www.ccsso.org/content/ PDFs/FAST%20Learning%20Progressions.pdf

MacArthur, C. (1994). Peers + word processing + strategies = A powerful combination for revising student writing. *Teaching Exceptional Children, 27*(1), 24–29.

Masters, G., & Forster, M. (1997). *Mapping literacy achievement: Results of the 1996 National School English Literacy Survey.* Canberra, Australia: Department of Employment, Education, Training and Youth Affairs.

Pape, S. J., Zimmerman, B. J., & Pajares, F. (Eds.) (2002). [Special issue] *Theory into Practice, 41*(2).

Pintrich, P. (2000). The role of goal orientation in self-regulated learning. In M. Boekaerts, P. Pintrich, & M. Zeidner (Eds.), *Handbook of self-regulation* (pp. 452–502). San Diego, CA: Academic.

Popham, W. J. (2009). Assessment literacy for teachers: Faddish or fundamental? *Theory into Practice, 48*(1), 4–11.

Resnick, L., & Resnick, D. (1990). Tests as standards of achievement in schools. In J. Pfleiderer (Ed.), *The uses of standardized tests in American education: Proceedings of the 1989 ETS Invitational Conference* (pp. 63–80). Princeton, NJ: Educational Testing Service.

Sadler, D. R. (1989). Formative assessment and the design of instructional systems. *Instructional Science, 18,* 119–144.

Shepard, L. A. (2000). The role of assessment in a learning culture. *Educational Researcher, 29*(7), 4–14.

Shepard, L. A. (2006). Classroom assessment. In R. Brennan (Ed.), *Educational measurement* (4th ed., pp. 624–646). Westport, CT: Praeger.

Stiggins, R. J. (2005). *Student-involved assessment for learning.* Upper Saddle River, NJ: Prentice-Hall.

Stiggins, R. J., & Popham, W. J. (2007). *Assessing students' affect related to assessment for learning.* Washington, DC: Council of Chief State School Officers.

Wilson, M., & Black, P. (2007, April). *Assessing understanding through the use of learning progressions.* Paper presented at the meeting of the American Educational Research Association, Chicago, IL.

Zimmerman, B. (2000). Attaining self-regulation: A social cognitive perspective. In M. Boekaerts, P. Pintrich, & M. Zeidner (Eds.), *Handbook of self-regulation* (pp. 13–41). New York: Academic.

CONTRIBUTORS

Jamal Abedi is a Professor at the School of Education of the University of California, Davis and a research partner at the National Center for Research on Evaluation, Standards, and Student Testing (CRESST). His research interests include studies in the area of psychometrics and test and scale developments. His recent works include studies on the validity of assessments, accommodations and classification for English language learners (ELLs) and students with disabilities, opportunity to learn for ELLs, and measurement of creativity. Abedi is the recipient of the 2003 award by the American Educational Research Association for "Outstanding Contribution Relating Research to Practice." He is also the recipient of the 2008 "Lifetime Achievement Award" by the California Educational Research Association. He holds a Master's and a PhD degree in psychometrics from Vanderbilt University.

Heidi L. Andrade is an Assistant Professor of Educational Psychology and Methodology at the University at Albany, State University of New York. She teaches courses on classroom assessment, educational psychology, and self-regulated learning. Her research focuses on the relationships between thinking, learning, and assessment, with an emphasis on student self-assessment. Prior to taking a position at the University at Albany, she spent 3 years on the faculty at Ohio University and 11 years at Harvard University, where she earned her master's and doctoral degrees. While at Harvard she worked on a variety of teaching, research, and development initiatives at Harvard Project Zero, including educational initiatives in South Africa and Cyprus. She has designed thinking-centered instruction and assessments for classrooms, after-school programs, children's television shows, and CD-ROMs. She has written two books, as well as numerous articles, book chapters, and conference presentations, and regularly consults with K-12 schools on assessment-related issues.

Carlos Ayala is Associate Professor of Education at California State University, Sonoma. In addition, he teaches secondary science methods and quantitative research methods at the University of California at Davis. His current research focuses on understanding student science learning, formative assessment, and computer science simulations for learning and assessment. Ayala is developing simulations to tap into middle school students' notions of forces and motion as well as developing high school chemistry formative assessments using Minstrell's DIAGNOSER program. He currently serves as an advisor to multiple NSF formative assessment projects as well as serves on the NAEP Technology Literacy Planning Committee. In his published work, he has proposed "Assessment Pedagogies" as a model of formative assessment. Ayala started his professional career as a fuel alcohol chemist; he then taught science and math in California public schools for 10 years and served as a school principal of a bilingual whole language elementary school. He completed his graduate work at Stanford University in 2002.

Peter A. Beddow is currently completing his doctorate in special education at Peabody College of Vanderbilt University where he has worked for the past 4 years on federally funded grant projects examining issues related to assessments and interventions for students with a broad range of abilities and needs. After earning his teaching license at Middlebury College in Vermont in 1998, Peter taught middle school English and Drama for 2 years in an urban school district in Los Angeles County in California.

For 5 years prior to coming to Vanderbilt, Beddow was a teacher at Five Acres (Altadena, CA), a residential school and treatment center where he developed a passion for helping children who have emotional, behavioral, social, and academic difficulties. Peter has authored multiple peer-reviewed publications and has worked with state departments of education in several states, providing expertise with alternate assessment validity and developing accessible tests. He also facilitates behavior management workshops for teachers and parents at Christ Church in Nashville, Tennessee.

Susan M. Brookhart is an independent educational consultant based in Helena, Montana. She is a former Professor and Chair of the Department of Educational Foundations and Leadership at Duquesne University, where she currently serves as Senior Research Associate in the Center for Advancing the Study of Teaching and Learning. She serves on state assessment technical advisory committees in two states. Prior to her higher education experience, she taught in both elementary and middle school. Her research interests include the role of formative and summative classroom assessment in student motivation and achievement, the connection between classroom assessment and large-scale assessment, and grading.

Professor Brookhart has served as editor of the journal *Educational Measurement: Issues and Practice* and as the education columnist for *National Forum*, the journal of Phi Kappa Phi. She is a past president of the American Educational Research Association's Special Interest Group on Classroom Assessment. She has been the education columnist for *National Forum*, the journal of Phi Kappa Phi. She is the author or coauthor of six books and over 40 articles on classroom assessment, educational measurement, program evaluation, and professional development. Her research has appeared in journals such as *Applied Measurement in Education, Assessment in Education, Educational Measurement: Issues and Practice, Journal of Educational Measurement, Journal of Educational Research, Review of Educational Research, Teachers College Record* and elsewhere. She serves on the editorial boards of *Teachers College Record* and *Applied Measurement in Education*.

Gregory J. Cizek is Professor of Educational Measurement and Evaluation at the University of North Carolina at Chapel Hill, where he teaches courses in applied testing, statistics, and research methods. His scholarly interests include standard setting, classroom assessment, testing policy, and test security. He is the author of over 250 journal articles, book chapters, conference papers, and other publications. His work has been published in journals such as *Educational Researcher, Educational Assessment, Review of Educational Research, Journal of Educational Measurement, Educational Measurement: Issues and Practice, Educational Policy, Phi Delta Kappan, Education Week* and elsewhere. He is a contributor to the *Handbook of Classroom Assessment* (1998); editor and contributor to the *Handbook of Educational Policy* (1999) and *Setting Performance Standards: Concepts, Methods, and Perspectives* (2001); and author of *Filling in the Blanks* (1999), *Cheating on Tests: How to Do It, Detect It, and Prevent It* (1999), *Detecting and Preventing Classroom Cheating: Promoting Integrity in Educational Assessment* (2003), *Addressing Test Anxiety in a High Stakes Environment* (with S. Burg, 2005) and *Standard Setting: A Guide to Establishing and Evaluating Performance Standards on Tests* (with M. Bunch, 2007). He provides expert consultation at the state and national level on testing programs and policy, including service as a member of the U.S. Department of Education's National Technical Advisory Council and as a member of the National Assessment Governing Board that oversees the National Assessment of Educational Progress (NAEP).

Dr. Cizek received his doctorate in measurement, evaluation, and research design from Michigan State University. He has managed national licensure and certification testing programs for American College Testing (ACT) in Iowa City, Iowa and served as a test development specialist for the Michigan Educational Assessment Program (MEAP). Previously, he was an elementary school teacher for 5 years in Michigan, and professor of educational research and measurement at the University of Toledo (OH). From 1997 to 1999, he was elected to and served as vice president of a local board of education in Ohio.

Jill Davidson has been the editor of *Horace*, the quarterly journal of the Coalition of Essential Schools (CES), since 2001. As the Director of Publications at CES, Davidson directs all of the organization's publications and editorial projects. She has published work that describes and documents CES practices in national journals and publications, and she is a coauthor of *Small Schools, Big Ideas: The Essential Guide to Successful School Transformation* (Jossey-Bass, 2009). Previously, Davidson was an online community Web site producer, university learning center director, and high school humanities teacher. Davidson earned a bachelor's degree from Brown University and a master's from the Harvard Graduate School of Education. She lives with her family in Providence, Rhode Island, where she is a local community leader and activist for excellent public schools for students.

Robert P. Dolan is a senior research scientist in Assessment and Information at Pearson. His work focuses on technology-based summative and formative assessment with emphases on cognition, accessibility, and usability. Prior to joining Pearson in 2007, Dr. Dolan was a senior research scientist at the Center for Applied Special Technology (CAST), where his research focused on designing, implementing, and evaluating advanced technology-based learning environments that support diverse learners. He currently serves on the Formative Assessment for Students and Teachers (FAST) State Collaborative on Assessment and Student Standards (SCASS), on the advisory boards for several federally supported research projects in technology-based assessment and instruction, and on the editorial board of the *Journal of Technology, Learning and Assessment*. Dr. Dolan has served as principal investigator on research projects funded by the National Institutes of Health, the National Science Foundation, the U.S. Department of Education, and private foundations. Over the past 25 years, Dr. Dolan has pursued parallel tracks in research and development in systems and cognitive neuroscience, and the development and engineering of technology-based tools for educational, scientific, and medical research. He received his doctorate in brain and cognitive sciences from MIT in 1992.

Stephen N. Elliott is a Professor of special education and the Dunn Family Chair of Educational and Psychological Assessment in Peabody College at Vanderbilt University where he teaches courses on measurement and assessment of academic and social behavior. Elliott currently codirects three USDE research grants concerning the assessment of learning-focused school leadership and the validity of testing modifications and alternate assessments for students with disabilities. He also directs Peabody College's Interdisciplinary Program in Educational Psychology and serves as the Director of the Learning Sciences Institute, a transinstitutional center for externally funded research. Elliott has authored more than 130 journal articles, 22 books, 40 chapters, and five widely used behavior-rating scales. His research focuses on scale development, the assessment of children's social skills and academic competence, and the use of testing accommodations and alternate assessment methods for evaluating the academic performance of students with disabilities for purposes of educational accountability. Along with several colleagues, he has recently designed and validated a new measure of learning-focused leadership that is being used to evaluate the performance of principals and school leadership teams. Elliott received his doctorate from Arizona State University in 1980.

Jay Feldman is the Director of Research at the Coalition of Essential Schools (CES) where his work has included leading the development of the CES School Benchmarks and Essential Analysis and conducting research on the Small Schools Network. Prior to joining CES, he worked at the Center for Collaborative Education, a CES affiliate center in Boston, where he conducted research on the practices and efficacy of the Boston Pilot Schools and External Coaching models. Feldman has also conducted research in child development, whole school change, forms of democratic and equitable schooling, and alternative education. His interests include the educative functions of play and age-mixing, children's moral development, and understandings of race and diversity. He is the author of *Choosing Small: The Essential Guide to Successful High School Conversion* (Jossey-Bass, 2005).

Erin Marie Furtak is Assistant Professor of Education specializing in science education at the University of Colorado at Boulder. As a former public school teacher, Furtak's research interests involve issues pertaining to the training and retention of secondary science teachers, and the improvement of student learning through reform-based science teaching. In 2006, she received a Chancellor Scholarship from the Humboldt Foundation to perform research at the Max Planck Institute for Human Development in Berlin and the Leibniz Institute for Science Education in Kiel, Germany. She is a research fellow of the Knowles Science Teaching Foundation. Her current research centers around building teachers' knowledge for science teaching through formative assessment techniques, and linking teachers' practices to student learning, an experimental study of the role of autonomy supportive teaching in improving student learning and motivation, as well as an analysis of formative assessment as a scaffold for students' evidence-based argumentation. She has two forthcoming books: *Formative Assessment for Secondary Science Teachers* (Corwin) and *The Dilemma of Guidance: An Exploration of Scientific Inquiry Teaching* (VDM Publishing).

Chris W. Gallagher is Professor and Director of Writing Programs at Northeastern University, where he teaches courses in writing, rhetoric, literacy, and teaching. His is author of three books: *Radical Departures: Composition and Progressive Pedagogy* (NCTE, 2002), *Reclaiming Assessment: A Better Alternative to the Accountability Agenda* (Heinemann, 2007), and *Teaching Writing That Matters* (with A. Lee, Scholastic, 2008). He has also published numerous articles and reviews in education and rhetoric/composition journals, including *Phi Delta Kappan, Educational Leadership, English Journal, Composition Studies,* and *jac: Journal of Advanced Composition*. From 2001 to 2004, Gallagher was Coordinator and Principal Investigator of the Comprehensive Evaluation of Nebraska's K-12 assessment and accountability system. He also has led a variety of committees and task forces, including serving as cochair of Nebraska's P-16 Language Arts Initiative and facilitator of the Commissioner of Education's Advisory Committee.

Thomas R. Guskey is Professor Emeritus, University of Kentucky. A graduate of the University of Chicago's renowned Measurement, Evaluation, and Statistical Analysis (MESA) program, he served as director of research and development for the Chicago Public Schools and was the first director of the Center for the Improvement of Teaching and Learning, a national research center. The author of numerous award-winning books and over 200 articles and papers, his work has been published in prominent research journals such as *American Educational Research Journal, Educational Researcher,* and *Educational Measurement: Issues and Practice,* as well as *Educational Leadership, Kappan,* and *School Administrator*. Guskey served on the Policy Research Team of the National Commission on Teaching & America's Future, on the task force to develop the National Standards for Staff Development, and was recently named a Fellow in the American Educational Research Association.

Guskey is coeditor of the "Experts in Assessment" series (Corwin Press) and has been featured on the National Public Radio programs "Talk of the Nation" and "Morning Edition." He is a contributor to *Psychology of Classroom Learning: An Encyclopedia* (2009), *21st Century Education: A Reference Handbook* (2009), and the *International Handbook on the Continuing Professional Development of Teachers* (2004). His most recent books include *Practical Solutions for Serious Problems in Standards-Based Grading* (2009), *Benjamin S. Bloom: Portraits of an Educator* (2006), *How's My Kid Doing? A Parents' Guide to Grades, Marks, and Report Cards* (2002), *Developing Grading and*

Reporting Systems for Student Learning (with J. Bailey, 2001), and *Evaluating Professional Development* (2000). He is a consultant to schools throughout the United States and around the world on many complex educational problems.

Gerunda B. Hughes is Director of the Office of Institutional Assessment and Evaluation at Howard University and an Associate Professor in the Department of Curriculum and Instruction in the School of Education, Washington, DC. As Director, she has oversight for the development and implementation of institution-wide outcomes assessment efforts which support and facilitate university strategic planning and decision making. Prior to assuming the position of Director, she taught courses in classroom assessment, research methods, and mathematics methods in the School of Education. Her research interests focus on topics in the fields of assessment and measurement including differential item functioning, classroom assessment, assessment literacy, and curriculum alignment. She has served a principal investigator or coprincipal investigator of several projects related to professional development and assessment literacy for elementary and middle school mathematics and science teachers. She has written about these experiences and presented her findings at local and national conferences. Hughes has served as a coeditor-in-chief of the *Journal of Negro Education*, as associate editor of *Review of Educational Research* and as a member of several editorial boards, including the *American Educational Research Journal*. She regularly consults with local, state, and national assessment boards and panels on testing programs and policy. Her academic background includes bachelor's and master's degrees in mathematics and a doctorate in educational psychology.

Ryan J. Kettler is the Coordinator of Data Services for the Learning Sciences Institute and a research assistant professor in special education at Peabody College of Vanderbilt University. He received his doctorate in educational psychology, with a specialization in school psychology, from the University of Wisconsin-Madison in 2005. Kettler has worked on multiple federally funded grants examining the effectiveness of alternate assessments, academic and behavioral screening systems, and testing accommodations. He is the author of peer-reviewed publications and presentations within the broader area of data-driven assessment for intervention, representing specific interests in academic and behavioral screening, test development, reliability and validity issues, and intervention evaluation. He currently serves as a consultant to several state departments of education, as well as to College Board, providing expertise in the area of alternate assessment.

Alexander Kurz is a doctoral student in special education and the Interdisciplinary Program in Educational Psychology at Peabody College of Vanderbilt University. Alex has studied special education in Germany and the United States, earning degrees in special education and philosophy. He is a licensed special education teacher and board-certified behavior analyst. He has taught special education classes in Tennessee and California, designed and implemented curricula for reading intervention classes, and participated in school reform activities through the Bill and Melinda Gates Foundation. Prior to beginning his doctoral studies, Alex worked as behavior analyst for children with autism and as an educational consultant to Discovery Education Assessment. During his graduate work at Vanderbilt, he collaborated with the Wisconsin Center for

Education Research and Discovery Education Assessment leading research efforts to examine curricular alignment and its relation to student achievement for students with and without disabilities. Kurz has coauthored several peer-reviewed publications on alignment and alternate assessment as well as multiple research reports and a technical manual for Discovery Education Assessment.

Duncan MacQuarrie currently works as a consultant to the Council of Chief State School Officers (CCSSO) where he coordinates state collaborative projects. He is currently the Assistant Coordinator of the Technical Issues in Large Scale Assessment (TILSA) Collaborative. Dr. MacQuarrie has also served as the Co-Coordinator for the Formative Assessment for Students and Teachers (FAST) Collaborative and the Coordinator of the English Language Development Assessment (ELDA) Collaborative for 2 years.

From 2003 through 2007, MacQuarrie was employed by Harcourt Assessment, Inc. as a Senior State Measurement Consultant, where he provided assessment expertise and support to state clients. From 2000 to 2003, MacQuarrie served as the Manager of Assessment for the Tacoma (WA) Public Schools (TPS) where he directed the administration and reporting for state assessment and district-developed assessments. Before joining the TPS, MacQuarrie worked for 15 years for the Washington Office of Superintendent of Public Instruction (OSPI) as a supervisor of assessment and evaluation and, for his final 5 years with that agency, as director of assessment and curriculum. Before beginning his work for the OSPI he managed a regional service center's cooperative providing assessment services and consultations for over 20 school districts. From 1970 to 1983 Duncan was a member of the psychology faculty at Central Washington University where he taught courses in educational psychology, program evaluation, statistics, and research methodology. He also did consultative work in program evaluation and assessment and he has served on the board of directors of the National Council on Measurement in Education. Recently, he coauthored a CCSSO policy paper entitled "Developing Student Achievement Tests Under No Child Left Behind (NCLB): A Policy Maker's Primer."

James H. McMillan is Professor and Chair of the Department of Foundations of Education in the School of Education at Virginia Commonwealth University. He has been a faculty member in higher education since 1976, and has taught at Virginia Commonwealth University for 30 years. He is also Director of the Metropolitan Educational Research Consortium, a 15-year partnership between his university and seven Richmond area school districts to conduct collaborative applied research in areas of study identified by the districts. Dr. McMillan teaches research methods, assessment, and evaluation, and coordinates the research and evaluation track of the doctorate in education program. He obtained his doctorate from Northwestern University and master's degree from Michigan State University.

McMillan has published in over 40 journals, including articles in *Educational Measurement: Issues and Practice, Educational Psychologist, Journal of Social Psychology, Contemporary Educational Psychology, American Journal of Educational Research, Journal of Higher Education*, and the *Journal of Educational Psychology*. He has made more than 60 professional presentations, primarily at the annual meetings of the American Educational Research Association. Dr. McMillan has published several books, including recent editions of *Research in Education: Evidence-Based Inquiry, Educational Research: Fundamentals for the Consumer, Understanding and Evaluating Educational Research, Assessment Essentials for Standards-Based Education,* and *Classroom Assessment: Principles and Practice for Effective Standards-based Instruction.* His current research interests include the relationships between classroom assessment and grading and student motivation, formative assessment, and the effectiveness of benchmark testing. His most recent study is a qualitative investigation of the use of benchmark testing for formative assessment.

Carla Meskill is Professor, Department of Educational Theory and Practice at the University at Albany, State University of New York. Her research and teaching explore new forms of technology use in language education as well as the influences of new technologies on developing language and literacy practices. In tandem, her work explores the nature of electronic literacy and its centrality in teacher professional development. On these and related topics she has published widely. Meskill is the former director of the federally funded Technology Assisted Language Learning project, Training all Teachers project, the Language Advocacy project and coeditor of Multimedia Educational Resources for Learning and Online Teaching (MERLOT), a searchable collection of peer-reviewed higher education online learning materials. She currently serves as associate editor of *Language Learning Technology.*

Paul Nichols is Vice President for Research in Assessment and Information at Pearson. His research focuses on applying the theories and methods from cognitive science to educational measurement. His research has addressed standard setting, scoring, test development, reliability, and validity. Prior to serving as vice president for research, Dr. Nichols served as Director of Psychometric Services for Pearson, taught at the University of Wisconsin-Milwaukee, and worked as a research scientist at ACT.

Bruce Randel is a principal researcher at Mid-Continent Research for Education and Learning (McREL) in Denver, Colorado, where he leads numerous applied research projects. His key responsibilities include research design, instrument development, data analysis, and communication of results. Randel is currently working on a 3-year cluster randomized trial of a professional development program in formative assessment. His research interests focus on methods for cluster randomized trials in education, educational assessment and psychometrics, high school dropout and graduation rates, and power analyses. He also provides consultation to internal and external clients regarding research design, statistical analysis, educational measurement and assessment. Prior to joining McREL, Randel served as a Senior Research Scientist at CTB/McGraw-Hill, where he worked on large custom state assessment programs, national achievement and aptitude tests, and early childhood diagnostic assessments. He received a master's in developmental psychology from San Francisco State University and a doctorate in developmental psychology from the University of Michigan.

Douglas A. Rindone currently works for the Council of Chief State School Officers (CCSSO) as a consultant and coordinator for state collaborative projects. He is currently the Coordinator of the Technical Issues in Large Scale Assessment (TILSA) Collaborative, as well as the CCSSO liaison for two state collaborative projects working on federal enhanced assessment grants. Rindone was also the Coordinator of the Formative Assessment for Students and Teachers (FAST) Collaborative for 3 years. From 2003 through 2006, Rindone was employed by Harcourt Assessment, Inc. where he worked with state clients to provide assessment expertise related to a state's educational policies, curricula, politics, and psychometrics. Prior to his work at Harcourt, he served as the Chief of the Bureau of Research, Evaluation and Student Assessment within the Connecticut State Department of Education where he directed the development and administration of all statewide student assessment programs, large-scale statewide evaluations, the design and production of report cards of all schools and districts, and the collection and reporting of all demographic and programmatic student data.

Rindone was recently commissioned to coauthor a CCSSO manuscript titled "Developing Student Achievement Tests Under No Child Left Behind (NCLB) Accountability Requirements: A Policy Maker's Primer." He has also authored several papers presented at the meetings of the American Educational Research Association and the National Council on Measurement in Education.

Maria Araceli Ruiz-Primo is Associate Professor of Educational Psychology at the School of Education and Human Development, University of Colorado Denver. She is the Director of the Research Center and Director of the Laboratory for Educational Assessment, Research, and Innovation (LEARN). She specializes in educational assessment. Her research work focuses on the development and technical evaluation of innovative science learning assessment tools—including performance tasks, concept maps, and student science products—and on the development of a conceptual framework of academic achievement. She has conducted research on the instructional sensitivity of assessments and their proximity to the enacted curriculum and worked on the evaluation of curriculum implementation and assessment practices in the classroom. She has also participated in the development of the science teacher certification assessment of the National Board for Professional Teaching Standards and in the development and evaluation of teacher enhancement programs for elementary science teachers. In 1993, Ruiz-Primo received the American Educational Research Association program evaluation fellowship. During the year 2001-2002, she was Program Officer at National Science Foundation, at the Research, Evaluation, and Communication (REC), and at the Elementary, Secondary, and Informal Education (ESIE) divisions. She is the first author of the Student Guide, *Statistical Reasoning for the Behavioral Sciences* and chapters and articles published in major peer-reviewed educational research journals.

Michael K. Russell is an Associate Professor in Boston College's Lynch School of Education Department of Education Research, Measurement and Evaluation. He also directs the Technology and Assessment Study Collaborative, which conducts research on emerging applications of technology to assessment and the effects of educational technology on teaching and learning in K-12 schools. His current research interests focus on the use of computer-based technologies to advance formative assessment and to make assessment content more accessible for students with disabilities and special needs. He has received several grants from the Institute of Education Sciences to develop computer-based diagnostic assessment systems and to create a universally designed computer-based test delivery system. Most recently, he has formed a 12-state consortium to explore the effects of universally designed computer-based testing on test validity and on the total cost of testing. He has authored numerous articles and three books on student assessment, computer-based testing and educational technology.

M. Christina Schneider is a research scientist with CTB/McGraw-Hill where her duties include psychometric work on large custom state assessment programs and the design and implementation of standard settings nationwide. Dr. Schneider is the principal investigator of a federally funded 4-year grant that investigates the efficacy of a professional development program on teacher assessment skill and student achievement, and she is the coauthor of the professional development series *Assessing Standards in the Classroom*. Previously, she managed the psychometric and data analysis unit within the Office of Assessment at the South Carolina Department of Education and she was a middle school band director in South Carolina for 7 years. Schneider's research interests include formative assessment, standard setting, and the use of accommodations. She received her degrees from the University of South Carolina.

Richard J. Shavelson is the Margaret Jacks Professor of Education, Professor of Psychology (courtesy), former I. James Quillen Dean of the School of Education at Stanford University, and Senior Fellow in the Woods Institute for the Environment at Stanford. He has served as president of the American Educational Research Association; he is a fellow of the American Association for the Advancement of Science, the American Educational research Association, the American Psychological Association, and the American Psychological Society; and a Humboldt Fellow (Germany). His current work includes the assessment of science achievement, the study of formative assessment in inquiry-based science teaching and its impact on students' knowledge and performance, the enhancement of women's and minorities' performance in organic chemistry, and the role of mental models of climate change on sustainability decisions and behavior. Other work includes studies of computer cognitive training on working memory, fluid intelligence and science achievement, assessment of undergraduates' learning, accountability in higher education, the scientific basis of education research, and new standards for measuring students' science achievement in the National Assessment of Educational Progress (*The Nation's Report Card*). His publications include *Statistical Reasoning for the Behavioral Sciences, Generalizability Theory: A Primer* (with Noreen Webb); *Scientific Research in Education* (edited with Lisa Towne); and *Measuring College Learning Responsibility: Accountability in a New Era* (in press).

Rick Stiggins created the Assessment Training Institute (ATI) in Portland, Oregon in 1992 to provide the professional development teachers and school leaders need to fulfill rapidly evolving assessment responsibilities. ATI joined the ETS family in 2006. Rick has developed print, interactive video, and online learning experiences to help school leaders create balanced assessment systems and to help teachers learn how to use high-quality classroom assessment to both support and verify learning. The foundation of these programs is his textbook, *Classroom Assessment FOR Student Learning: Doing It Right—Using It Well*. He has worked with government agencies and local school districts across North America and around the world to help them implement productive professional development in this arena.

Rick received his doctorate in educational measurement from Michigan State University. He has served on the faculties of the University of Minnesota and Lewis and Clark College. He directed test development at ACT in Iowa City, chaired research and development programs in performance assessment and classroom assessment at the Northwest Regional Educational Laboratory, and has been a visiting scholar at Stanford University and at the University of Southern Maine.

Keith J. Topping is Professor of Educational and Social Research and Director of the Centre for Paired Learning at the University of Dundee, Scotland, where he is also Associate Dean for Research and Director of the Doctor in Educational Psychology program. He has degrees from the universities of Sussex, Nottingham, and Sheffield, and is a Fellow of the British Psychological Society and the Royal Society of Arts. His research interests are in the development and evaluation of methods for nonprofessionals (e.g., peers, parents) to tutor others in fundamental skills and higher order learning. He also has interests in electronic literacy, computer-aided assessment, behavior management, and social competence in schools. He has extensive previous experience working in schools with teachers, children and parents in Britain, the United States, and many other countries. He presents, trains, and consults around the world.

His publications include 19 books, 44 chapters, and 137 peer reviewed journal papers, in addition to numerous multimedia in-service training and distance learning packs and professional publications. His books include *Peer-Assisted Learning* (1998, with S. Ehly), *Thinking Reading Writing: A Practical Guide to Paired Learning with Peers, Parents & Volunteers* (2001), *Inclusive Education* (2005, with S. Maloney) and *Intervening with Disruptive Adolescents: Using the Evidence* (with Flynn & Hershfield, 2009).

Walter D. Way is Senior Vice President of Psychometric and Research Services at Pearson. Dr. Way has over 20 years of assessment experience in a variety of settings. He is a nationally known expert on computer-based testing and has worked on testing programs in higher education, licensure and certification, and K-12 assessment. Dr. Way received his doctorate in Educational Measurement and Statistics from the University of Iowa. Prior to working at Pearson, he spent 16 years with Educational Testing Service in Princeton, New Jersey.

Dylan Wiliam is Deputy Director (Provost) of the Institute of Education, University of London. In a varied career, he has taught in urban public schools, directed a large-scale testing program, served a number of roles in university administration, including dean of a school of education, and pursued a research program focused on supporting teachers to develop their use of assessment in support of learning. From 2003 to 2006 he was Senior Research Director at the Educational Testing Service in Princeton, New Jersey.

Yue Yin is an Assistant Professor of Educational Psychology at the University of Illinois, Chicago (UIC). Her scholarly interests include classroom assessment, science education, and applied measurement. She has conducted research on performance assessment, concept mapping assessment, and formative assessment. Her work has been published in journals including *Journal of Research in Science Teaching, Applied Measurement in Education, Educational Assessment*, and *Science Scope*. In her research, she used learning theory as a foundation, measurement and statistics as tools, to examine ways of using assessments to improve students' learning. She teaches educational measurement and applied statistics. Yin received her bachelor of science degree in chemistry at Peking University, her master's in psychology and doctorate in science education at Stanford University. Prior to taking a position at the UIC, she worked at the University of Hawaii at Manoa for 3 years as an assistant professor in educational psychology.

AUTHOR INDEX

SUBJECT INDEX

Page numbers in italics refer to figures or tables.

eBooks – at www.eBookstore.tandf.co.uk

A library at your fingertips!

eBooks are electronic versions of printed books. You can store them on your PC/laptop or browse them online.

They have advantages for anyone needing rapid access to a wide variety of published, copyright information.

eBooks can help your research by enabling you to bookmark chapters, annotate text and use instant searches to find specific words or phrases. Several eBook files would fit on even a small laptop or PDA.

NEW: Save money by eSubscribing: cheap, online access to any eBook for as long as you need it.

Annual subscription packages

We now offer special low-cost bulk subscriptions to packages of eBooks in certain subject areas. These are available to libraries or to individuals.

For more information please contact webmaster.ebooks@tandf.co.uk

We're continually developing the eBook concept, so keep up to date by visiting the website.

www.eBookstore.tandf.co.uk